PRACTICAL GUIDE TO U.S. TAXATION OF INTERNATIONAL TRANSACTIONS

TENTH EDITION

ROBERT J. MISEY, JR.
MICHAEL S. SCHADEWALD

Wolters Kluwer

Editorial Staff

Production . . . . Jennifer Schencker, Vijayalakshmi Suresh and Prabhu Meenakshi

ISBN 978-0-8080-4084-2

© 2015 CCH Incorporated. All Rights Reserved.
4025 W. Peterson Ave.
Chicago, IL 60646-6085
800 248 3248
CCHGroup.com

Printed in the United States of America

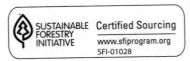

To Monica.

To my sons, Doug and Tom.

Robert J. Misey, Jr.

Michael S. Schadewald

Preface

This book provides the reader with a practical command of the tax issues raised by international transactions and how those issues are resolved by U.S. tax laws. The book emphasizes those areas generally accepted to be essential to tax practice. The book is written primarily as a desk reference for tax practitioners and is organized into four parts. Part I provides an overview of the U.S. system for taxing international transactions and also discusses the U.S. jurisdictional rules and source-of-income rules. Part II explains how the United States taxes the foreign activities of U.S. persons and includes chapters on the foreign tax credit, anti-deferral provisions, foreign currency translation and transactions, export tax benefits, and planning for foreign operations. Part III describes how the United States taxes the U.S. activities of foreign persons, including the taxation of U.S.-source investment income and U.S. trade or business activities, as well as planning for foreign-owned U.S. operations. Finally, Part IV covers issues common to both outbound and inbound activities, including transfer pricing, tax treaties, cross-border mergers and acquisitions, state taxation of international operations, and international tax practice and procedure.

Robert J. Misey, Jr.
Michael S. Schadewald

July 2015

About the Authors

Robert J. Misey, Jr., J.D., M.B.A., LL.M., is a shareholder with the U.S. law firm of Reinhart Boerner Van Deuren s.c. and chair of the firm's International Department. Mr. Misey concentrates his practice in the areas of international taxation, transfer pricing, and tax controversies. He previously worked as an attorney with the IRS Chief Counsel (International) in Washington, D.C. and as a large-case attorney in the Western and Southeast Regions. He has led a region of Deloitte's International Tax Services Group and has tried 23 cases before the U.S. Tax Court.

Mr. Misey received his Master of Laws degree, with high distinction, from Georgetown University, where he was the Graduate Student Editor of *The Tax Lawyer,* and received his Juris Doctor and Master of Business Administration degrees from Vanderbilt University. He also studied international law at Emmanuel College in Cambridge, England. He is a member of the Tax Section of the District of Columbia, Wisconsin, Kentucky, and California bar associations.

Mr. Misey has authored the book *Federal Taxation: Practice and Procedure* and spoken on international taxation, transfer pricing, and tax controversies at continuing education programs in many states and countries. He is also an adjunct faculty member of the law schools at the University of Wisconsin and the University of Alabama.

Michael S. Schadewald, Ph.D., CPA, is on the faculty of the University of Wisconsin-Milwaukee, where he teaches courses in business taxation. A graduate of the University of Minnesota, Professor Schadewald also co-authors the *Multistate Corporate Tax Guide* and writes a column for the *Journal of State Taxation*, both of which are published by Wolters Kluwer, CCH. He has published numerous articles in academic and professional journals, including *The Accounting Review, Journal of Accounting Research, Contemporary Accounting Research, Journal of the American Taxation Association, Journal of Taxation*, and *The Tax Adviser*. Professor Schadewald has served on the editorial boards of *Journal of the American Taxation Association, International Tax Journal, International Journal of Accounting, Journal of State Taxation, Advances in Accounting Education, Issues in Accounting Education*, and *Journal of Accounting Education*. Prior to entering academics, he worked in the Milwaukee office of Arthur Young (now Ernst & Young).

Acknowledgments

I would like to acknowledge the assistance of my father and mentor, Robert J. Misey, Sr., Esq., who provided organizational and, as always, motivational input with respect to various aspects of this work. I would also like to acknowledge the support of my fellow shareholders at Reinhart Boerner Van Deuren s.c.

Robert J. Misey, Jr.

I would like to acknowledge the support and encouragement of my colleagues, past and present, at the University of Minnesota, the University of Texas, and the University of Wisconsin-Milwaukee.

Michael S. Schadewald

Table of Contents

Chapter 5: Anti-Deferral Provisions

Chapter 6: Foreign Currency Translation and Transactions

Chapter 7: Export Benefits

Chapter 15: State Taxation of International Operations

List of Appendices

IRS PUBLICATIONS

MODEL TREATY

REVENUE PROCEDURE

Chapter 1
Overview of U.S. Taxation of International Transactions

¶ 101   **Basic Principles**
¶ 102   **Taxation of U.S. Person's Foreign Activities**
¶ 103   **Taxation of Foreign Person's U.S. Activities**
¶ 104   **Issues Common to Outbound and Inbound Activities**
¶ 105   **Organization of International Provisions in Internal Revenue Code**

¶ 101 BASIC PRINCIPLES

.01 Tax Jurisdiction

In designing a system to tax international transactions, a government must determine which "persons" to tax as well as what "income" to tax. One basis upon which countries assert tax jurisdiction is a personal relationship between the taxpayer and the country. For example, a country may wish to tax any individual who is either a citizen or a resident of the country, or a corporation that is created or organized in the country. A second basis upon which countries assert tax jurisdiction is an economic relationship between the taxpayer and the country. An economic relationship exists whenever a person derives income from property or activities that are located within a country's borders.

A double taxation problem may arise when a taxpayer who has a personal relationship with one country (the home country) derives income from sources within another country (the host country). The host country usually asserts jurisdiction on the basis of its economic relationship with the taxpayer. The home country also may assert jurisdiction over the income on the basis of its personal relationship with the taxpayer. Traditionally, it has been up to the home country to solve the double taxation problem of its citizens and residents, either by allowing them to exclude foreign-source income from taxation, or by taxing foreign-source income but allowing a credit for any foreign taxes paid on that income.

The United States employs a credit system. Therefore, the United States taxes U.S. persons on their worldwide income.[1] U.S. persons include U.S. citizens, resident alien individuals, and domestic corporations (i.e., corporations organized under U.S. law). An alien is considered a U.S. resident if he or she meets either the green card test (i.e., lawful permanent immigrant status) or the substantial presence test.[2] To mitigate double taxation, a U.S. person can claim a credit for the

---

[1] Code Sec. 61.   [2] Code Sec. 7701(b).

foreign income taxes imposed on foreign-source income.[3] A key feature of the U.S. credit system is the foreign tax credit limitation, which restricts the credit to the portion of the pre-credit U.S. tax that is attributable to foreign-source income.[4]

One major exception to the U.S. credit system is the deferral privilege, whereby the United States does not tax foreign-source income earned by a U.S. person through a foreign corporation until those profits are repatriated by the domestic shareholder through a dividend distribution. The policy rationale for deferral is that it allows U.S. companies to compete in foreign markets on a tax parity with their foreign competitors. A second major exception to the U.S. credit system is the foreign earned income exclusion, under which a U.S. citizen or resident alien who lives and works abroad for extended periods of time may exclude from U.S. taxation a limited amount of foreign earned income plus a housing cost amount.[5]

U.S. tax law contains a two-pronged system for taxing the U.S.-source income of foreign persons, including nonresident aliens and foreign corporations (i.e., corporations organized under the laws of a foreign country). The United States taxes foreign persons at graduated rates on the net amount of income effectively connected with the conduct of a trade or business within the United States.[6] The United States also taxes the gross amount of a foreign person's U.S.-source investment-type income at a flat rate of 30%.[7] The U.S. person controlling the payment of U.S.-source investment income must withhold the 30% tax.[8] Income tax treaties usually reduce the withholding tax rate on interest, dividend, and royalty income to 15% or less.[9] In addition, the United States provides a broad statutory exemption for portfolio interest income.[10] Capital gains from sales of stocks, bonds and other securities also are generally exempt from U.S. taxation.[11] Special rules apply to gains from the sale of U.S. real property, which are taxed in the same manner as income effectively connected with the conduct of a U.S. trade or business.[12]

.02 Source of Income Rules

The source of income rules play an important role in the computation of a U.S. person's foreign tax credit limitation, which equals the portion of a taxpayer's pre-credit U.S. tax attributable to foreign-source income.[13] Foreign taxes in excess of the foreign tax credit limitation are referred to as "excess credits." One strategy for eliminating excess credits is to increase the foreign tax credit limitation by increasing the percentage of the taxpayer's total taxable income that is classified as foreign-source for U.S. tax purposes. The source rules play a more prominent role in the taxation of foreign persons, since the United States generally taxes foreign persons only on their U.S.-source income.

---

[3] Code Sec. 901.

[4] Code Sec. 904.

[5] Code Sec. 911.

[6] Code Secs. 871(b) and 882.

[7] Code Secs. 871(a) and 881.

[8] Code Secs. 1441 and 1442.

[9] Articles 10, 11 and 12 of the United States Model Income Tax Convention of November 16, 2006 ("U.S. Model Treaty").

[10] Code Secs. 871(h) and 881(c).

[11] Reg. § 1.1441-2(b)(2).

[12] Code Sec. 897.

[13] Code Sec. 904.

The source rules for gross income are organized by categories of income. Under the general rules, interest income is U.S.-source if the payer is a domestic corporation or a U.S. resident, and foreign-source if the payer is a foreign corporation or nonresident. Dividend income is U.S.-source if the payer is a domestic corporation and foreign-source if the payer is a foreign corporation. Personal services income is U.S.-source if the services are performed in the United States, and foreign-source if the services are performed abroad. Rental and royalty income is U.S.-source if the property is used in the United States and foreign-source if the property is used abroad. A gain on the sale of a U.S. real property interest is U.S.-source income, whereas a gain on the sale of real property located abroad is foreign-source income.[14]

As a general rule, gains on the sale of personal property are U.S.-source income if the taxpayer is a U.S. resident and foreign-source income if the taxpayer is a nonresident. There are exceptions, however, for inventories, depreciable property, intangibles, and stock of a foreign affiliate. As a consequence, the residence-of-seller source rule applies primarily to sales of stocks, bonds and other securities.[15]

Gross income from the sale of inventory that the taxpayer purchased for resale is sourced based on where the sale occurs.[16] The place of sale is determined solely by where title to the goods passes from the seller to the buyer.[17] Therefore, such income is U.S.-source income if title passes in the United States, and foreign-source income if title passes abroad. On the other hand, income from the sale of inventory produced by the taxpayer generally is allocated between U.S.-source and foreign-source income using the 50-50 method. Under the 50-50 method, a U.S. manufacturer apportions 50% of the gross profit from export sales based on the percentage of export sales for which title passes abroad, and the other 50% based on the percentage of production assets located abroad.[18]

If the operative tax attribute is the net amount of U.S.-source or foreign-source income, the taxpayer allocates and apportions its deductions between U.S.-source and foreign-source gross income. Deductions are allocated to a related class of gross income, and are then apportioned between U.S.-source and foreign-source gross income using an apportionment base that reflects the factual relationship between the deduction and the gross income.[19]

Special source of income rules apply to currency exchange gains and losses, insurance underwriting income, international communications income, space and ocean activities income, and transportation income. In addition, special allocation and apportionment rules apply to interest expense and research and experimentation expenditures.

---

[14] Code Secs. 861 and 862.
[15] Code Sec. 865.
[16] Code Secs. 861(a)(6) and 862(a)(6).

[17] Reg. § 1.861-7(c).
[18] Reg. § 1.863-3.
[19] Reg. § 1.861-8.

¶ 102 TAXATION OF U.S. PERSON'S FOREIGN ACTIVITIES

.01 Foreign Tax Credit

A U.S. citizen, resident alien, or domestic corporation may claim a credit for foreign income taxes paid or incurred.[20] The credit is limited, however, to the portion of the taxpayer's pre-credit U.S. tax that is attributable to foreign-source income.[21] This limitation prevents U.S. persons operating in high-tax foreign countries from offsetting those higher foreign taxes against the U.S. tax on U.S.-source income, and thereby confines the effects of the foreign tax credit to mitigating double taxation of foreign-source income. Foreign income taxes that exceed the limitation can be carried back one year and forward up to ten years and taken as a credit in a year that the limitation exceeds the amount of creditable foreign taxes.[22]

The relation of U.S. and foreign tax rates is a major determinant of whether a taxpayer is in an excess limitation or an excess credit position. In general, taxpayers will be in an excess limitation position when the foreign tax rate is lower than the U.S. rate and in an excess credit position when the foreign tax rate is higher than the U.S. rate. When a taxpayer is in an excess credit position, the non-creditable foreign income taxes increase the total tax burden on foreign-source income beyond what it would have been if only the United States had taxed the income.

One strategy for eliminating excess credits is to increase the limitation by increasing the percentage of the taxpayer's total taxable income that is classified as foreign-source for U.S. tax purposes. For example, the title-passage rule for sourcing income from inventory sales provides U.S. companies with a significant opportunity to increase foreign-source income. By arranging for the passage of title in the importing country rather than the United States, export sales will generate foreign-source income.

Another strategy for eliminating excess credits is cross-crediting. If a taxpayer can blend low-tax and high-tax foreign-source income within a single foreign tax credit limitation, then the excess limitation on the low-tax income will soak up the excess credits on the high-tax income. This averaging process produces an excess credit only when the average foreign tax rate on all of the items of foreign-source income within a single limitation is higher than the U.S. rate.

The current foreign tax credit limitation system is found in Code Sec. 904(d), which applies separate limitations to passive category income and general category income. The separate limitations are designed to prevent cross-crediting between lightly taxed passive foreign investment income and more heavily taxed active foreign business profits. Cross-crediting is still allowed, however, with respect to active business profits derived from different foreign countries or passive investment income derived from different foreign countries.

Passive category income primarily includes dividends, interest, rents, and royalties, and net gains from dispositions of property that produces such income.

---

[20] Code Sec. 901.
[21] Code Sec. 904(a).

[22] Code Sec. 904(c).

General category income includes all income other than passive category income, and generally includes most income from active foreign business operations, such as manufacturing, distribution, and service activities. Special look-through rules apply to dividends, interest, rents, and royalties received by a U.S. shareholder from a controlled foreign corporation (CFC), as well as dividends received by a domestic corporation from a non-controlled Code Sec. 902 corporation. For example, a dividend received from a CFC that earns only manufacturing income is treated as general category income, not passive category income.[23]

.02 Deemed Paid Foreign Tax Credit

A domestic corporation generally cannot claim a dividends-received deduction for a dividend from a foreign corporation. As a result, dividends from foreign subsidiaries are included in a domestic parent corporation's U.S. taxable income. However, the domestic parent may claim a foreign tax credit for any foreign withholding taxes paid on the dividend, as well as a deemed paid foreign tax credit for the foreign income taxes paid by a 10%-or-more-owned foreign corporation.[24] Congress enacted the deemed paid credit to protect domestic corporations with foreign subsidiaries against double taxation, as well as to better equate the tax treatment of U.S. companies with foreign subsidiaries to those with foreign branches.

A domestic corporation that receives a dividend from a 10%-or-more-owned foreign corporation is deemed to have paid an amount of foreign income taxes equal to the foreign corporation's post-1986 foreign income taxes multiplied by the ratio of the dividend to the foreign corporation's post-1986 undistributed earnings. Post-1986 undistributed earnings equal the cumulative amount of the foreign corporation's undistributed earnings and profits, reduced by actual and deemed dividend distributions in prior years. Post-1986 foreign income taxes equal the cumulative amount of the foreign corporation's foreign income taxes, reduced by the amount of foreign income taxes related to prior-year actual or deemed dividend distributions. A domestic corporation that operates abroad through multiple tiers of foreign corporations may also be eligible to claim deemed paid credits for taxes paid by second-tier through sixth-tier foreign corporations.[25] Only a domestic corporation may claim a deemed paid foreign tax credit. U.S. citizens and resident aliens are not eligible, nor are S corporations.[26]

Because the amount of dividend income recognized by a domestic parent corporation is net of any foreign income taxes paid by a foreign subsidiary, the domestic corporation is implicitly allowed a deduction for those foreign taxes. To prevent a double tax benefit, the domestic corporation must gross up its dividend income by the amount of the deemed paid foreign taxes, which offsets the implicit deduction.[27]

---

[23] Code Sec. 904(d). In addition to separate limitations for passive category income and general category income, a separate limitation also applies to income that would be treated as U.S.-source income under the Internal Revenue Code, but is treated as foreign-source income under an income tax treaty.

[24] Code Sec. 902.
[25] Code Sec. 902.
[26] Reg. § 1.902-1(a)(1).
[27] Code Sec. 78.

The U.S. tax consequences of dividend repatriations depend on whether the foreign corporation is operating in a low-tax or high-tax foreign jurisdiction. No U.S. tax is due on a dividend from a foreign corporation operating in a high-tax foreign jurisdiction because the available deemed paid foreign tax credits exceed the pre-credit U.S. tax, whereas a dividend from a foreign corporation operating in a low-tax foreign jurisdiction results in a residual U.S. tax. Through cross-crediting, the excess credits on dividends from high-tax foreign subsidiaries can be used to offset the residual U.S. tax due on dividends from low-tax foreign subsidiaries. The CFC look-through rule makes cross-crediting possible with respect to dividends from CFCs located in low-tax and high-tax foreign jurisdictions, as long as the underlying earnings of both types of CFCs are assigned to the limitation for general category income.[28]

Foreign withholding taxes can exacerbate the excess credit problems associated with dividends from high-tax foreign subsidiaries. However, income tax treaties usually reduce the statutory withholding tax rate on dividends to 15% or less. Therefore, a domestic parent corporation may be able to use tax treaties to reduce foreign withholding taxes by, for example, owning foreign operating subsidiaries through a foreign holding company located in a country with a favorable treaty network that contains lenient limitation of benefits articles.

Finally, it may be advantageous for a domestic parent corporation to repatriate the earnings of a foreign subsidiary through interest and royalty payments rather than dividend distributions. A foreign corporation usually can claim a foreign tax deduction for interest and royalties paid to its U.S. parent, whereas dividend distributions typically are not deductible. On the other hand, only a dividend distribution can provide the domestic parent corporation with a deemed paid credit. If the foreign corporation is operating in a high-tax foreign jurisdiction, the benefits of a deduction at the foreign subsidiary level may exceed the cost of losing the deemed paid credit at the domestic parent level.

.03 Anti-Deferral Provisions

The United States generally does not tax a U.S. multinational corporation's foreign-source income earned through a foreign subsidiary corporation until the subsidiary repatriates those earnings through a dividend. This policy, known as "deferral," potentially creates an opportunity to avoid U.S. taxes on portable income which is easily shifted to a foreign corporation located in a tax haven country. Congress closed this loophole by enacting Subpart F (Code Secs. 951–965), which denies deferral to certain types of tainted income earned through a foreign corporation.

Subpart F requires a U.S. shareholder of a "controlled foreign corporation" (CFC) to include in income a deemed dividend equal to a pro rata share of the CFC's Subpart F income.[29] A foreign corporation is a CFC if U.S. shareholders own more than 50% of the stock of the foreign corporation, by vote or value. A "U.S. shareholder" is any U.S. person who owns at least 10% of the voting stock of the foreign corporation. Examples of Subpart F income include foreign personal hold-

---

[28] Code Sec. 904(d)(3).   [29] Code Sec. 951.

¶102.03

ing company income, and foreign base company sales income. Foreign personal holding company income includes dividends, interest, rents, and royalties, whereas foreign base company sales income includes income from the sale of goods which the CFC buys from or sells to a related person, and are neither manufactured nor sold for use in the CFC's country of incorporation.[30] Subpart F also requires a U.S. shareholder of a CFC to recognize a deemed dividend equal to its pro rata share of the CFC's earnings invested in U.S. property. This rule reflects the reality that a CFC's investment in U.S. property often is substantially equivalent to distributing a dividend to its U.S. shareholders.[31]

Consistent with the notion that a Subpart F inclusion represents a deemed dividend, a domestic corporation which directly owns 10% or more of a CFC's voting stock can claim a deemed paid foreign tax credit for the CFC's foreign income taxes attributable to a deemed dividend.[32] In addition, to prevent a second layer of U.S. tax on the CFC's earnings, a U.S. shareholder can exclude from income the receipt of an actual distribution of a CFC's earnings that were taxed to the U.S. shareholder in a prior tax year by reason of a Subpart F inclusion.[33] Finally, to prevent the conversion of ordinary income into capital gains, a U.S. shareholder must treat the gain on the sale of the stock of a CFC as a dividend to the extent of the shareholder's pro rata share of the CFC's (non-Subpart F) earnings and profits.[34]

Congress enacted the passive foreign investment company (PFIC) regime to expand the reach of U.S. taxing authority with respect to passive investment income earned by U.S. persons through a foreign corporation. Congress enacted the PFIC provisions to deal with perceived abuses by U.S. investors in foreign mutual funds, but the regime applies to any foreign corporation which qualifies as a PFIC. A foreign corporation is a PFIC if either 75% or more of the corporation's gross income is passive income, or 50% or more of the corporation's assets (by value) are passive assets.[35]

A PFIC's undistributed earnings are subject to U.S. taxation under one of three methods, each of which eliminates the benefits of deferral. Under the qualified electing fund (QEF) method, U.S. investors who can obtain the necessary information can elect to be taxed currently on their pro rata share of the PFIC's earnings and profits.[36] A U.S. investor who does not make a QEF election is not taxed on the PFIC's earnings until the U.S. person receives an excess distribution, which includes a gain realized on the sale of PFIC stock. An excess distribution is taxed as if it had been realized pro rata over the holding period for the PFIC's stock. Thus, the tax due on an excess distribution is the sum of the deferred yearly tax amounts, increased by interest charges.[37] Finally, a U.S. investor in a PFIC may make a mark-to-market election with respect to the stock of the PFIC if such stock is marketable.[38]

---

[30] Code Sec. 954.
[31] Code Secs. 951 and 956.
[32] Code Sec. 960.
[33] Code Sec. 959.
[34] Code Sec. 1248.

[35] Code Sec. 1297.
[36] Code Sec. 1293.
[37] Code Sec. 1291.
[38] Code Sec. 1296.

.04 Foreign Currency Translation and Transactions

The foreign branches and subsidiaries of domestic corporations often conduct business and maintain their books and records in the currency of the host country. This creates a currency translation problem for the U.S. parent, which must translate into U.S. dollars the income and earnings remittances of a foreign branch, as well as actual and deemed distributions from a foreign subsidiary. In addition, a domestic corporation may realize currency exchange gains and losses when it engages in transactions denominated in a foreign currency, or when a foreign branch or subsidiary repatriates earnings that were previously taxed to the U.S. parent. Finally, foreign income taxes are paid in the local currency, and must be translated in U.S. dollars.

A domestic corporation must make all of its U.S. tax determinations in its functional currency, which is the U.S. dollar. However, a separate qualified business unit (QBU) of the domestic corporation may have a non-dollar functional currency if that QBU conducts a significant part of its activities in an economic environment in which a foreign currency is used and maintains its books and records in that foreign currency. A foreign subsidiary corporation is automatically a QBU, and a foreign branch qualifies as a QBU if it is a separate and clearly identified unit of a trade or business of the corporation for which separate books and records are maintained.[39]

If a foreign branch qualifies as a QBU and has a functional currency other than the U.S. dollar, the taxable income of the branch is computed in its functional currency and then translated into dollars using the average exchange rate for the branch's tax year. Any foreign income taxes paid on branch income generally are translated into U.S. dollars at the average exchange rate for the tax year to which the taxes relate.[40] In addition, the domestic corporation recognizes a foreign currency gain or loss if the branch remits foreign currency or other property to the domestic corporation, and the U.S. dollar value of the distribution differs from the domestic corporation's basis in the branch's accumulated earnings, as determined by prior year income inclusions.[41]

If a foreign subsidiary corporation pays a dividend in a foreign currency, the domestic parent corporation translates the dividend into U.S. dollars using the spot rate. A deemed dividend of Subpart F income is translated into dollars using the average exchange rate for the tax year, and a deemed dividend for a CFC's investment in U.S. property is translated into dollars using the spot rate on the last day of the CFC's tax year. If a domestic parent corporation receives a distribution of previously taxed income, it recognizes a currency exchange gain or loss equal to the difference between the dollar value of the distribution (determined using the spot rate) and the taxpayer's basis in the distribution (determined by the dollar amount at which the earnings were previously included in U.S. taxable income). For purposes of computing the deemed paid foreign income taxes attributable to an

---

[39] Code Secs. 985 and 989.
[40] Code Secs. 987 and 989.

[41] Code Sec. 987(3). Under proposed regulations, the exchange gain or loss is computed using the foreign exchange exposure pool method (Prop. Reg. §§ 1.987-5 and -6, Sept. 7, 2006).

¶102.04

actual or deemed dividend distribution, the foreign corporation's pool of post-1986 foreign income taxes are translated into dollars using the average exchange rate for the year, whereas the dividend distribution and post-1986 undistributed earnings are maintained in the foreign corporation's functional currency.[42]

Finally, Code Sec. 988 provides rules for determining the amount, timing, character, and source of foreign currency gains and losses associated with the following transactions: (i) dispositions of a nonfunctional currency, (ii) acquisition or issuance of a debt obligation denominated in a nonfunctional currency, (iii) accruing an item of income or expense denominated in a nonfunctional currency, and (iv) acquiring or entering into a forward contract, futures contract, option, or similar instrument involving a nonfunctional currency.

¶ 103 TAXATION OF FOREIGN PERSON'S U.S. ACTIVITIES

.01 Foreign Persons Investing in the United States

U.S. tax law contains a two-pronged system for taxing the U.S.-source income of foreign persons, including nonresident aliens and foreign corporations. The United States taxes foreign persons at graduated rates on the net amount of income effectively connected with the conduct of a trade or business within the United States.[43] The United States also taxes the gross amount of a foreign person's U.S.-source investment-type income at a flat rate of 30%.[44] The U.S. person controlling the payment of the U.S.-source investment income must withhold the 30% tax.[45] Income tax treaties usually reduce the withholding tax rate on interest, dividend, and royalty income to 15% or less.[46] In addition, the United States provides a broad statutory exemption for portfolio interest income.[47] Capital gains from sales of stocks, bonds and other securities also are generally exempt from U.S. taxation.[48]

Withholding is required because it is the only sure way to collect taxes from passive offshore investors. Once the appropriate amount of U.S. tax is withheld, the foreign recipient of U.S. source investment-type income generally has no further U.S. tax obligations. The withholding tax agent is any person having control, receipt, custody, disposal, or payment of an item of U.S.-source investment-type income to a foreign person.[49] Examples include corporations distributing dividends, borrowers paying interest, and licensees paying royalties. A withholding agent who fails to withhold is liable for the uncollected tax.[50]

Special rules apply to gains from the sale of U.S. real property. Under Code Sec. 897, gains or losses realized by foreign persons from dispositions of a U.S. real property interest are taxed in the same manner as income effectively connected with the conduct of a U.S. trade or business. A U.S. real property interest includes stock of a domestic corporation which is a U.S. real property holding corporation. A domestic corporation is a U.S. real property holding corporation if the market value of its U.S. real property interests equals 50% or more of the net fair market value of

---

[42] Code Secs. 986 and 989.
[43] Code Secs. 871(b) and 882.
[44] Code Sec. 871(a) and 881.
[45] Code Secs. 1441 and 1442.
[46] Articles 10, 11 and 12 of the U.S. Model Treaty.

[47] Code Secs. 871(h) and 881(c).
[48] Reg. §1.1441-2(b)(2).
[49] Code Secs. 1441 and 1442.
[50] Code Sec. 1461.

the sum of its total real property interests (U.S. and foreign) and its trade or business assets. To ensure collection, any purchaser of a U.S. real property interest must withhold a tax equal to 10% of the amount realized by the foreign person on the sale.[51]

.02 Foreign Persons Doing Business in the United States

A foreign person that is engaged in a U.S. trade or business is subject to U.S. tax on the income effectively connected with the conduct of that U.S. trade or business.[52] Case law suggests that a foreign person's activities within the United States must be considerable, continuous, and regular to constitute a U.S. trade or business. An example of a U.S. trade or business is a foreign corporation that operates an unincorporated sales branch located in the United States. If the foreign person is a resident of a country that has entered into an income tax treaty with the United States, then the foreign person's business profits are exempt from U.S. taxation unless those profits are attributable to a "permanent establishment" (i.e., a fixed place of business) located within the United States.[53]

Effectively connected income includes all of the foreign person's U.S.-source income, except for U.S. source investment-type income that is subject to U.S. withholding tax.[54] In computing its effectively connected income, a foreign person may deduct expenses related to the effectively connected gross income.

The progressive rate schedules applicable to domestic corporations and U.S. citizens also apply to the effectively connected income of foreign corporations and nonresident aliens, which means the tax rates range from 10% to 39.6% in the case of nonresident aliens and 15% to 35% in the case of foreign corporations. Effectively connected income is also subject to the alternative minimum tax.[55]

A foreign corporation engaged a U.S. trade or business is also subject to the Code Sec. 884 branch profits tax, the purpose of which is to better equate the tax treatment of a foreign corporation's U.S. branch and subsidiary operations. The branch profits tax equals 30% (subject to treaty reductions) of a foreign corporation's dividend equivalent amount, which is an estimate of the amount of effectively connected earnings and profits that a U.S. branch remits to its foreign home office during the year. A foreign corporation's U.S. branch operation may also be subject to the tax on excess interest.

Congress enacted the Code Sec. 163(j) anti-earnings stripping provisions to prevent foreign corporations from avoiding U.S. tax by "stripping" out the earnings of a U.S. subsidiary through deductible intercompany interest payments, rather than repatriating the U.S. subsidiary's earnings through nondeductible dividend distributions. If certain requirements are met, Code Sec. 163(j) denies a domestic corporation a deduction for interest that is paid to a related person and is exempt from U.S. tax, as well as any interest paid to an unrelated person on a loan that is guaranteed by a related foreign person and the interest income is not subject to U.S. withholding tax. Interest deductions are disallowed only if the domestic

---

[51] Code Sec. 1445.
[52] Code Secs. 871(b) and 882.
[53] Articles 5 and 7 of the U.S. Model Treaty.

[54] Code Sec. 864.
[55] Code Secs. 871(b) and 882.

corporation's debt-to-equity ratio exceeds 1.5 to 1 and it has excess interest expense. The amount of disallowed interest deductions may not exceed the corporation's excess interest expense, and any disallowed deductions may be carried forward.

¶ 104 ISSUES COMMON TO OUTBOUND AND INBOUND ACTIVITIES

.01 Transfer Pricing

The operating units of a multinational corporation usually engage in a variety of intercompany transactions. For example, a U.S. manufacturer may market its products abroad through foreign marketing subsidiaries. A domestic parent corporation also may provide managerial, technical, and administrative services for its foreign subsidiaries, and may license its manufacturing and marketing intangibles to its foreign subsidiaries for commercial exploitation abroad. A "transfer price" must be computed for each of these controlled transactions. Although a transfer price does not affect the combined income of commonly controlled corporations, it does affect how that income is allocated among the group members. Therefore, when tax rates vary across countries, transfer pricing can have a significant effect on a multinational corporation's total tax costs.

Congress enacted Code Sec. 482 to ensure that related corporations report and pay tax on their actual share of income arising from controlled transactions. The Regulations under Code Sec. 482 adopt an arm's length standard for evaluating the appropriateness of a transfer price. Under this standard, a taxpayer must recognize the same amount of income from a controlled transaction as an uncontrolled party would have recognized from a similar transaction under similar circumstances.

To arrive at an arm's length result, the taxpayer must select and apply the method that provides the most reliable estimate of an arm's length price. The reliability of a pricing method is primarily a function of the degree of comparability between the controlled and uncontrolled transactions. As a practical matter, however, comparable transactions often are not readily available. For example, inventory sales between affiliated companies often involve component parts and semi-finished goods that are unique and are not sold in public markets. As a consequence, the appropriate arm's length price is often ambiguous.

The regulations under Code Sec. 482 provide specific methods for determining an arm's length transfer price for various types of transactions, including transfers of tangible property, transfers of intangible property, loans, and services. For example, the regulations provide five specified methods for estimating an arm's length charge for transfers of tangible property, including the comparable uncontrolled price method, the resale price method, the cost plus method, the comparable profits method, and the profit split method.

To promote compliance with the arm's length standard, Congress enacted the Code Sec. 6662(e) transactional and net adjustment penalties. Both penalties equal 20% of the tax underpayment related to an IRS transfer pricing adjustment. The transactional penalty applies if the transfer price used by the taxpayer is 200% or more (or 50% or less) of the amount determined under Code Sec. 482 to be correct. The net adjustment penalty applies if the net increase in taxable income for a year as a result of Code Sec. 482 adjustments exceeds the lesser of $5 million or 10% of the taxpayer's gross receipts. The penalties may be waived if the taxpayer can demonstrate that it had reasonable cause and acted in good faith. In the case of the net adjustment penalty, the reasonable cause and good faith requirements can be met only if the taxpayer also satisfies contemporaneous documentation requirements.

.02 Income Tax Treaties

The primary purpose of an income tax treaty is to mitigate international double taxation through tax reductions and exemptions for certain types of income derived by residents of one treaty country from sources within the other treaty country. Because tax treaties often substantially modify U.S. and foreign tax consequences, a taxpayer must consider the impact of the applicable treaty on the tax consequences of any outbound or inbound transaction. In addition to treaties governing income taxes, the United States has also entered into bilateral tax treaties governing social security taxes, estate and gift taxes, and international shipping and aviation. The United States currently has income tax treaties with about 60 countries, including most of its major trading partners.

The income tax treaties to which the United States is a party are generally similar to the United States Model Income Tax Convention of November 15, 2006 (hereinafter, the "U.S. Model Treaty"), which reflects the baseline negotiating position of the United States in establishing income tax treaties with other countries.

Treaty tax reductions and exemptions are generally available only to a resident of one of the treaty countries. Under the U.S. Model Treaty, a resident is any person who, under a country's internal laws, is subject to taxation by reason of domicile, residence, citizenship, place of management, place of incorporation, or other criterion of a similar nature.[56]

Most income tax treaties contain a permanent establishment provision, under which the business profits of a resident of one treaty country are exempt from taxation by the other treaty country, unless those business profits are attributable to a "permanent establishment" (i.e., a fixed place of business) located within the host country.[57]

Income tax treaties also usually limit the withholding tax rates imposed on dividend, interest, and royalty income derived from sources within the treaty country to 15% or less.[58] In many cases, treaties exempt such income from host country taxation. Treaties also generally exempt from host country taxation any gains from the disposition of property, such as capital gains on the sale of stocks, bonds and other securities. This exemption does not apply to gains from disposi-

---

[56] Article 4 of the U.S. Model Treaty.
[57] Articles 5 and 7 of the U.S. Model Treaty.
[58] Articles 10, 11 and 12 of the U.S. Model Treaty.

¶104.02

tions of real property, or gains from dispositions of personal property that are attributable to a permanent establishment.[59]

Because income tax treaties provide lower withholding tax rates on dividend, interest, and royalty income, a multinational corporation may be able to reduce its foreign withholding taxes by owning its operating subsidiaries through strategically located holding companies, a practice known as "treaty shopping." To restrict the ability of taxpayers to engage in treaty shopping, many treaties contain anti-treaty shopping rules, which are formally known as limitation on benefits provisions. The basic thrust of these provisions is to deny treaty benefits to a corporation that is organized in a treaty country by a resident of a non-treaty country merely to obtain the benefits of that country's income tax treaty.[60]

¶ 105 ORGANIZATION OF INTERNATIONAL PROVISIONS IN INTERNAL REVENUE CODE

Most of the provisions governing how the United States taxes income derived from international transactions are found in Subtitle A, Chapter 1, Subchapter N of the Internal Revenue Code. Subchapter N is titled "Tax Based on Income from Sources Within or Without the United States" and includes Code Sections 861 to 999. Subchapter N is organized into the following five parts:

- Part I, Source Rules and Other General Rules Relating to Foreign Income (Code Secs. 861-865)

- Part II, Nonresident Aliens and Foreign Corporations (Code Secs. 871-898)

- Part III, Income from Sources Without the United States (Code Secs. 901-989)

- Part IV, Domestic International Sales Corporations (Code Secs. 991-997)

- Part V, International Boycott Determinations (Code Sec. 999)

Part II contains the primary provisions governing inbound transactions, including the taxation of both nonresident alien individuals and foreign corporations. The source of income rules found in Part I also play a central role in the taxation of foreign persons, because foreign persons are generally taxed only on their U.S.-source income.

Part III contains the primary provisions governing outbound transactions, including the taxation of foreign-source income derived by U.S. citizens, resident aliens, and domestic corporations. The two most important subparts of Part III are Subpart A, Foreign Tax Credit (Code Secs. 901 to 909), and Subpart F, Controlled Foreign Corporations (Secs. 951 to 965). Two other subparts that practitioners commonly encounter are the foreign earned income exclusion provisions found in Subpart B (Code Secs. 911 and 912), and the foreign currency transactions provisions found in Subpart J (Code Secs. 985 to 989). As with inbound transactions, the source of income rules found in Part I play an important role in the taxation of outbound transactions.

---

[59] Article 13 of the U.S. Model Treaty. [60] Article 22 of the U.S. Model Treaty.

Parts IV and V deal with relatively minor issues. Part IV creates a special purpose entity called a "domestic international sales corporation" or DISC. Congress enacted the DISC provisions in 1971 in an attempt to stimulate U.S. exports. In 1984, Congress enacted the foreign sales corporation provisions (since repealed) as a replacement for the DISC regime. However, a vestige of the DISC regime, known as interest-charge DISCs, remains in the law.

Part V contains a single Code section enacted in 1976 to deny certain tax benefits to a company doing business in a country that may require participation in or cooperation with an international boycott. These countries currently include Iraq, Kuwait, Lebanon, Libya, Qatar, Saudi Arabia, Syria, United Arab Emirates, and Yemen.[61]

Subchapter N does not include all of the relevant Code Sections governing international transactions, and other provisions are sprinkled throughout other portions of the Internal Revenue Code. Examples include the provisions governing the transfer of property by a U.S. person to a foreign corporation (Code Sec. 367), transfer pricing (Code Sec. 482), passive foreign investment companies (Code Secs. 1291 to 1298), and withholding taxes on U.S.-source income derived by foreign persons (Code Secs. 1441 to 1474).

---

[61] 80 F.R. 17152.

¶105

Chapter 2
Tax Jurisdiction

¶ 201 JURISDICTIONAL ISSUES

.01 Bases for Asserting Jurisdiction

A government must answer two basic questions in determining how to tax international transactions: Which "persons" should be taxed? and What "income" is subject to tax? One basis on which countries assert tax jurisdiction is a personal relationship between the taxpayer and the country. For example, a country may wish to tax any individual who is either a citizen or a resident of the country. The concept of a personal relationship also applies to corporations and other types of entities. A country may treat a corporation as a resident of the country of incorporation. However, another country may treat a corporation as a resident of the country where its management activities occur or its principal place of business operates.

A second basis on which countries assert tax jurisdiction is an economic relationship between the taxpayer and the country. An economic relationship exists whenever a person derives income from property or activities that are located within a country's borders. The set of persons deriving income from sources within a country includes not only citizens and residents (those persons who already have a personal relationship with the country), but also foreign persons who are neither citizens nor residents of the taxing country.

Under the current U.S. system, personal relationships are the basis for taxing U.S. citizens, resident aliens, and domestic corporations, whereas the source of income is the basis for taxing nonresident aliens and foreign corporations.

.02 Territorial versus Credit Systems

A double taxation problem usually arises when a taxpayer who has a personal relationship with one country (the home country) derives income from sources within another country (the host country). The host country will usually assert jurisdiction on the basis of its economic relationship with the taxpayer. The home country may also assert jurisdiction over the income on the basis of its personal relationship with the taxpayer. In these situations, the countries involved must decide whether and how to adjust their tax systems so as to avoid international double taxation. Traditionally, the home country tries to resolve the double taxation problems of its citizens and residents. The home country can accomplish this only by forfeiting part or all of its jurisdictional claim over the foreign-source income of its citizens and residents, either through a territorial system or a credit system.

Under a territorial system, the home country taxes citizens and residents on income derived from sources within the home country, but allows them to exclude from taxation all income derived from foreign sources. For example, the home country would tax a citizen's wages that were earned domestically, but would exempt from tax any wages earned abroad. This leaves only the host country to tax the citizen's wages earned abroad. Therefore, under a territorial system, the foreign income of a citizen or resident is taxed only one time at the host country's rate.

Under a credit system, the home country taxes both the home country-source income and the foreign-source income of its citizens and residents, but allows a credit for any taxes paid on that foreign-source income to the host country. In effect, the home country asserts secondary jurisdiction over the foreign-source income of its citizens and residents. The claim is secondary in the sense that taxpayers are allowed to claim a foreign tax credit to the extent the host country taxes their foreign-source income. The net result is that foreign-source income incurs tax only one time at the higher of the host country's rate or the home country's rate.

> **Example 2.1:** ABC Corporation earns taxable income of $100, that it derives entirely from foreign sources. Assume the home country tax rate is 30% and the host country tax rate is 20%.

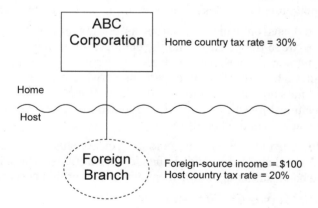

Case 1—No mechanism for mitigating double taxation: If the home country does not provide a mechanism for mitigating international double taxation, the total tax on ABC's $100 of foreign-source income is $50 [$30 home country tax + $20 host country tax], computed as follows:

¶201.02

Home country tax return	
Taxable income	$100
Tax rate	× .30
Tax	$ 30

Host country tax return	
Taxable income	$100
Tax rate	× .20
Tax	$ 20

Case 2—Territorial system: Under a territorial system, the total tax on ABC's foreign-source income is $20 [$0 home country tax + $20 host country tax], computed as follows:

Home country tax return	
Taxable income	$0
Tax rate	× .30
Tax	$ 0

Host country tax return	
Taxable income	$100
Tax rate	× .20
Tax	$ 20

Case 3—Credit system: Under a credit system, the total tax on ABC's foreign-source income is $30 [$10 home country tax + $20 host country tax], computed as follows:

Home country tax return	
Taxable income	$100
Tax rate	× .30
Pre-credit tax	$30
Foreign tax credit	− 20
Tax	$10

Host country tax return	
Taxable income	$100
Tax rate	× .20
Tax	$ 20

Both a credit system and a territorial system resolve ABC's double taxation problem, but they do so in fundamentally different ways. A territorial system eliminates the $30 home country tax on ABC's foreign-source income, resulting in taxation once at the lower host country rate. In contrast, from ABC's perspective a credit system effectively eliminates the $20 host country tax on ABC's foreign-source income, resulting in taxation once at the higher home country rate.

As Example 2.1 illustrates, territorial and credit systems produce different results when the host country tax rate is lower than the home country rate. Under a territorial system, the taxpayer pays only the lower host country tax. Under a credit system, the taxpayer pays not only the host country tax, but also any home country tax in excess of the lower host country tax.

In contrast, when the host country tax rate is higher than the home country rate, territorial and credit systems produce equivalent results. Under a territorial system, foreign-source income is taxed once at the higher host country rate. A credit system also results in taxation once at the higher host country rate, since the foreign tax credit completely offsets the pre-credit home country tax on the foreign-source income. Therefore, no home country tax is collected on the high-tax foreign-source income under either system.

Example 2.2: The facts are the same as in Example 2.1, except now assume that the host country tax rate is 40%, rather than 20%.

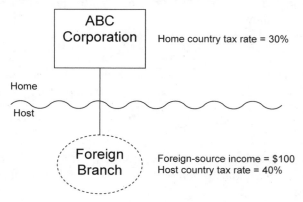

Case 1—Territorial system: Under a territorial system, the total tax on ABC's foreign-source income is $40 [$0 home country tax + $40 host country tax], computed as follows:

Home country tax return		Host country tax return	
Taxable income	$0	Taxable income	$100
Tax rate	× .30	Tax rate	× .40
Tax	$ 0	Tax	$ 40

Case 2—Credit system: Under a credit system, the total tax on ABC's foreign-source income also is $40 [$0 home country tax + $40 host country tax], computed as follows:

Home country tax return	
Taxable income	$100
Tax rate	× .30
Pre-credit tax	$ 30
Foreign tax credit	– 30
Tax	$ 0

Host country tax return	
Taxable income	$100
Tax rate	× .40
Tax	$ 40

.03 Tax Treaties

Territorial and credit systems represent unilateral solutions to the international double taxation problem because they are created by the internal laws of countries. Tax treaties, on the other hand, represent bilateral solutions to the international double taxation problem since they are created by and apply to both of the countries that are parties to the agreement. In general, tax treaties mitigate double taxation through reciprocal tax exemptions and lower tax rates for income derived by residents of one treaty country from sources within the other treaty country. For example, under the income tax treaty between the United States and the United Kingdom, the United Kingdom agrees not to tax U.S. residents on any interest derived from sources within the United Kingdom. In exchange, the United States agrees not to tax U.K. residents on any interest derived from sources within the United States.[1] As a result, tax treaties often shift the claim of primary tax jurisdiction from the host country to the home country, thereby saving a larger share of the tax on international transactions for the home country. The increase in the home country's tax revenues comes at the host country's expense, however, which explains why tax treaty provisions are always reciprocal in nature. Tax treaties are discussed in more detail in Chapter 13 (¶ 1301).

¶ 202 OVERVIEW OF U.S. JURISDICTIONAL SYSTEM

.01 Foreign Activities of U.S. Persons

The United States taxes U.S. persons on their worldwide income.[2] U.S. persons include the following:[3]

(i) *U.S. citizens.*[4]

(ii) *Resident alien individuals*—Citizens of foreign countries who meet either the green card test or the substantial presence test.[5]

---

[1] Article 11 of the U.S.-U.K. Income Tax Treaty.
[2] Code Sec. 61(a).
[3] Code Sec. 7701(a)(30).

[4] *Cook v. Tait*, SCt, 1 USTC ¶ 92, 265 US 47, 44 SCt 444.
[5] Code Sec. 7701(b)(1)(A).

   (iii) *U.S. corporations*—Corporations incorporated under the laws of one of the 50 states or the District of Columbia.[6] The location of a corporation's headquarters office or seat of management is irrelevant for purposes of determining whether a corporation is domestic or foreign under U.S. tax principles.

   (iv) *U.S. partnerships*—Partnerships created or organized under the laws of one of the 50 states or the District of Columbia.[7]

   (v) Any *estate* other than a foreign estate. An estate is foreign if its foreign-source income, other than any income effectively connected with a U.S. trade or business does not incur U.S. taxation.[8]

   (vi) Any *trust* if a U.S. court is able to exercise primary supervision over the administration of the trust and one or more U.S. persons have the authority to control all substantial decisions of the trust.[9]

The United States uses a credit system to mitigate international double taxation. Therefore, a U.S. person can claim a credit for the foreign income taxes imposed on foreign-source income.[10] Under this credit system, foreign-source income is taxed one time at the higher of the U.S. tax rate or the foreign rate. In other words, the United States collects any residual U.S. tax due on foreign-source income that the host country taxes at a rate lower than the U.S. rate. On the other hand, if the foreign tax rate exceeds the U.S. rate, the United States does not collect any tax on that foreign-source income because the available foreign tax credits sufficiently offset the pre-credit U.S. tax on that income.

A key feature of the U.S. credit system is the foreign tax credit limitation, which restricts the credit to the portion of the pre-credit U.S. tax that is attributable to foreign-source income.[11] The limitation confines the effect of the credit to mitigating double taxation of foreign-source income by preventing U.S. persons operating in high-tax foreign countries from offsetting those higher foreign taxes against the U.S. taxes on U.S.-source income.

   Example 2.3: USAco, a domestic corporation, has $200 of U.S.-source taxable income and $100 of foreign-source taxable income. Assume that the foreign tax rate is 45% and the U.S. rate is 35%.

---

[6] Code Sec. 7701(a)(4) and (a)(9). A corporation organized or created under the laws of a U.S. possession is considered a foreign corporation.

[7] Code Sec. 7701(a)(4) and (a)(9).

[8] Code Sec. 7701(a)(30)(D) and (a)(31)(A).

[9] Code Sec. 7701(a)(30)(E).

[10] Code Sec. 901(a).

[11] Code Sec. 904(a).

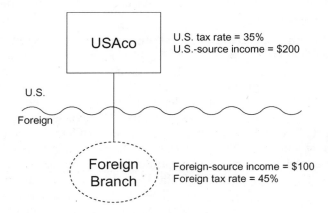

Case 1—Credit is limited: If the foreign tax credit is limited to the U.S. tax on foreign-source income (i.e., 35% × $100 = $35), the total tax on USAco's $300 of worldwide income is $115 [$70 U.S. tax + $45 foreign tax], computed as follows:

U.S. tax return		Foreign tax return	
Taxable income	$300	Taxable income	$100
U.S. tax rate	× .35	Foreign tax rate	× .45
Pre-credit tax	$105	Foreign tax	$ 45
Foreign tax credit	– 35		
U.S. tax	$ 70		

Case 2—No limitation: If there were no limitation on the foreign tax credit, the total tax on USAco's $300 of worldwide income would drop from $115 to $105 [$60 U.S. tax + $45 foreign tax], computed as follows:

U.S. tax return		Foreign tax return	
Taxable income	$300	Taxable income	$100
U.S. tax rate	× .35	Foreign tax rate	× .45
Pre-credit tax	$105	Foreign tax	$ 45
Foreign tax credit	– 45		
U.S. tax	$ 60		

Without the limitation, the net U.S. tax on the $100 of foreign-source income is negative $10 [$35 pre-credit U.S. tax – $45 credit], which reduces the effective U.S. tax rate on USAco's U.S.-source income to only 30% ($60/$200). Therefore, <u>without the limitation, the U.S. Treasury does not collect the full 35% U.S. tax on U.S.-source income.</u>

Deferral from U.S. taxation of income earned by foreign corporations. One major exception to the U.S. taxing jurisdiction is the deferral privilege, whereby the United States does not tax foreign-source income earned by a U.S. person through a foreign corporation until those profits are repatriated by the domestic shareholder through a dividend distribution. The deferral privilege results from <u>several features of U.S. tax law. First, U.S. consolidated reporting rules take a "domestic" consolidation approach, whereby affiliates organized in foreign countries cannot join their U.S. counterparts in filing a federal consolidated income tax return.[12] Second, the earnings of a corporation are not taxed to its shareholders until distributed as a dividend. Third, the United States does not tax the foreign-source income of foreign corporations</u>. Therefore, as long as a foreign subsidiary derives only foreign-source income, those earnings will not enter the U.S. tax base until the foreign subsidiary distributes a dividend to the U.S. parent corporation.

> **Example 2.4:** USco earns $5 million from its U.S. operations and has two foreign operations. The first foreign operation, in country F1, is an unincorporated branch that earns $1 million. The second foreign operation, in country F2, is incorporated as a foreign subsidiary that earns $2 million. USco's worldwide income is $6 million comprised of $5 million earned in the United States and $1 million earned in country F1. The $2 million earned in country F2 is deferred until repatriated as a dividend.

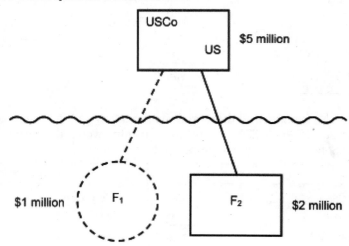

> **Example 2.5:** USAco, a domestic corporation, owns 100% of FORco, a foreign corporation. FORco operates a factory in a country that has granted FORco a 10-year tax holiday. In its first year of operations, FORco has $10 million of foreign-source income and repatriates $4 million of those earnings to

---

[12] Code Sec. 1504. In contrast, U.S. accounting principles require a "worldwide" consolidation, whereby all majority-owned subsidiaries, domestic and foreign alike, must be consolidated with the U.S. parent corporation for financial reporting purposes. ASC-810.

USAco through a dividend distribution. Because FORco is a foreign corporation, the United States does not tax FORco on its $10 million of foreign-source income. However, the United States does tax USAco on the $4 million dividend that it receives from FORco. The dividend is included in USAco's gross income and there is not an offsetting dividends-received deduction. If USAco does not receive a dividend during the year, USAco would not have taxable income from FORco that year, regardless of how profitable FORco may be.

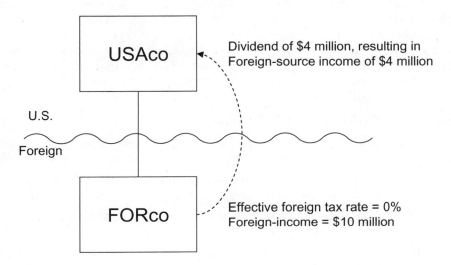

The policy behind deferral is to allow U.S. companies to compete in foreign markets on a tax parity with their foreign competitors. However, deferral also opens the door to tax avoidance, particularly with respect to passive investment income, the source of which U.S. persons can easily shift to a foreign country. Congress enacted the Subpart F and Passive Foreign Investment Company regimes to prevent taxpayers from using deferral as a device to avoid U.S. tax. Under these two anti-deferral regimes (which are discussed in Chapter 5 (¶ 501)), certain types of unrepatriated earnings of a foreign corporation, such as passive investment income, are subject to immediate U.S. taxation.

The foreign earned income exclusion. Another major exception to the U.S. credit system is the foreign earned income exclusion. Under the general rules, the United States taxes U.S. citizens and resident aliens on their worldwide income, even when they live and work abroad for extended periods of time. To provide some relief, a U.S. expatriate who meets certain requirements can exclude from U.S. taxation a limited amount of foreign earned income plus a housing cost amount.[13] The foreign earned income exclusion is discussed later in this chapter.

The jurisdictional scheme for domestic corporations impacts tax planning for foreign operations. Because the foreign earnings of U.S. companies are subject to

---

[13] Code Sec. 911.

both U.S. and foreign income taxes, <u>a commonly used metric for evaluating these tax costs is the total effective tax rate on foreign earnings</u>. When evaluating a U.S. corporation's effective tax rate, the de facto benchmark is the top U.S. statutory rate of 35 percent.[14] However, it is quite common for the total tax rate on foreign earnings to be greater than or less than 35 percent. The total tax rate can exceed 35 percent when the foreign jurisdiction taxes corporate income at a rate in excess of 35 percent (as, for example, in Japan) and the foreign tax credit limitation prevents U.S. companies from claiming a credit for those "excess" foreign taxes. In contrast, the total tax rate on foreign earnings can fall below 35 percent when the foreign jurisdiction taxes corporate income at a rate less than 35 percent (as, for example, in Hong Kong, Ireland, or Switzerland) and the U.S. company takes advantage of its ability to defer the residual U.S. tax on low-tax foreign earnings until repatriated as a dividend distribution. Tax planning for foreign operations is discussed in detail in Chapter 8 (¶ 801).

.02 U.S. Activities of Foreign Persons

U.S. tax law contains a two-pronged territorial system for taxing the U.S.-source income of foreign persons. Foreign persons include the following:

(i) *Nonresident alien individuals*—Individuals who are neither citizens nor residents of the United States.[15]

(ii) *Foreign corporations*—Corporations created or organized under the laws of a foreign country or a U.S. possession.[16]

(iii) *Foreign partnerships*—Partnerships created or organized under the laws of a foreign country or a U.S. possession.[17]

(iv) *Foreign estate*—Any estate that is not subject to U.S. taxation on its foreign-source income that is not effectively connected with a U.S. trade or business.[18]

(v) *Foreign trust*—A trust is foreign if either no U.S. court is able to exercise primary supervision over the administration of the trust or no U.S. person has the authority to control all substantial decisions of the trust.[19]

The United States taxes foreign persons at graduated rates on the net amount of effectively connected income to the conduct of a trade or business within the United States.[20] In addition, the United States taxes the gross amount of a foreign person's U.S.-source investment-type income at a flat rate of 30%.[21] The U.S. person controlling the payment of U.S.-source investment-type income to a foreign person must deduct and withhold the 30% U.S. tax.[22] Withholding is required because it is the only sure way to collect taxes from passive offshore investors. In order to withhold, the withholding agent must be able to readily ascertain both the tax base and the applicable rate. This explains both the gross basis taxation and the use of a

---

[14] Code Sec. 11.
[15] Code Sec. 7701(b)(1)(B).
[16] Code Sec. 7701(a)(5).
[17] Code Sec. 7701(a)(5).
[18] Code Sec. 7701(a)(31)(A).

[19] Code Sec. 7701(a)(31)(B) and (a)(30)(E).
[20] Code Secs. 871(b) and 882(a).
[21] Code Secs. 871(a) and 881(a).
[22] Code Secs. 1441 and 1442.

flat tax rate because the U.S. withholding agent may not have any way to determine a foreign person's allocable expenses and appropriate tax bracket.

There are several major exceptions to the general rules for taxing foreign persons. For example, income tax treaties usually reduce the withholding tax rate on interest, dividend, and royalty income from the statutory rate of 30% to 15% or less. In addition, portfolio interest income is exempt from U.S. tax.[23] Capital gains are also exempt from U.S. tax,[24] except for gains from the sale of U.S. real property, which are taxed in the same manner as income effectively connected with the conduct of a U.S. trade or business.[25] Table 2.1 summarizes the general rules regarding U.S. taxation of international transactions.

TABLE 2.1. U.S. TAXATION OF INTERNATIONAL TRANSACTIONS—GENERAL RULES

Type of person	Type of income	U.S. taxation
U.S. person	Foreign-source income	U.S. collects the excess of the pre-credit U.S. tax over the related foreign tax credit
Foreign person	Income effectively connected with a U.S. trade or business	U.S. taxes the net amount of income at marginal rates
	U.S.-source investment-type income	U.S. taxes the gross amount of income at 30%

¶ 203 DEFINITION OF RESIDENT ALIEN

The United States taxes resident aliens on their worldwide income, but taxes nonresident aliens only on their U.S.-source income. As a consequence, the taxation of foreign nationals depends critically on whether the alien is considered a U.S. resident. An alien is considered a U.S. resident in any calendar year that he meets either the green card test or the substantial presence test.[26]

.01 Green Card Test (Lawful Permanent Residence)

Under the so-called green card test, an alien individual is a U.S. resident for a calendar year if, at any time during that calendar year, the alien is a lawful permanent resident of the United States.[27] An alien qualifies as a lawful permanent resident of the United States if he has been lawfully accorded, and has not revoked or abandoned, the privilege of residing permanently in the United States as an immigrant.[28] These "green card" holders are U.S. residents for tax purposes, regardless of whether they are actually physically present in the United States during the year.[29]

This rule forces aliens who have obtained a green card and occasionally come to the United States, but have not yet moved to the United States on a permanent basis, to pay U.S. taxes on their worldwide income. These individuals are expected to pay taxes on the same basis as U.S. citizens because, as with U.S. citizens, they have the right to exit and reenter the United States at will.

---

[23] Code Secs. 871(h) and 881(c).
[24] Reg. § 1.1441-2(b)(2).
[25] Code Sec. 897(a)(1).
[26] Code Sec. 7701(b)(1)(A).

[27] Code Sec. 7701(b)(1)(A)(i).
[28] Code Sec. 7701(b)(6).
[29] Code Sec. 7701(b)(2)(a)(ii).

.02 Substantial Presence Test

An alien who does not hold a green card is a U.S. resident for a calendar year if she is <u>physically present in the United States for 183 or more days during that year</u>.[30] The policy behind the substantial presence test is that spending more than half of a year in the United States establishes a stronger connection with the United States than with any other country for that year.

> **Example 2.6:** T is not a U.S. citizen and does not hold a green card. However, T is physically present in the United States from January 1 through September 30 of the current year. T is a U.S. resident for that year because T is physically present in the United States for 183 or more days.

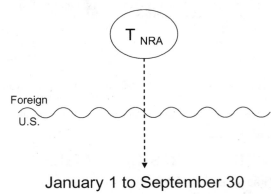

January 1 to September 30

A day is counted as a day of U.S. presence if the alien is physically present in the United States at any time during that day.[31] Therefore, presence for part of a day, such as the day of arrival to or the day of departure from the United States, counts as a full day. However, <u>certain types of U.S. presence are disregarded</u>, including commuters from Mexico or Canada,[32] travelers between two foreign points,[33] individuals with medical conditions,[34] and certain exempt individuals.[35] Exempt individuals primarily include <u>qualifying students</u>, teachers, trainees, and foreign-government-related individuals.[36]

The substantial presence test includes carryover days, which extends U.S. residence to aliens whose stay in the United States is prolonged, but is less than 183 days in any given calendar year. For example, under the general rule, an alien could be physically present in the United States for the last 182 days of one year and the first 182 days of the succeeding year (for a total of 364 consecutive days in the United States) without establishing U.S. residency. <u>Including carryover days accounts for days spent in the United States during the two preceding calendar years</u>. Accordingly, an individual applies the 183-day standard by counting a day of presence during the current year as a full day, a day of presence last year as one-

---

[30] Code Sec. 7701(b)(3)(A).
[31] Code Sec. 7701(b)(7)(A).
[32] Code Sec. 7701(b)(7)(B).
[33] Code Sec. 7701(b)(7)(C).

[34] Code Sec. 7701(b)(3)(D)(ii).
[35] Code Sec. 7701(b)(3)(D)(i).
[36] Code Sec. 7701(b)(5).

third of a day, and a day of presence two years ago as one-sixth of a day.[37] In all cases, an individual must be physically present in the United States at least 31 days during the current calendar year to be considered a resident for that year.[38]

Example 2.7: T is not a U.S. citizen and does not hold a green card. However, T is physically present in the United States for 90 days during year 1, 150 days during year 2, and 120 days during year 3. T is not physically present in the United States for 183 days in any of the three years. However, she satisfies the substantial presence test for residence for the first time in year 3 due to the carryover days [120 days + (1/3 of 150 days) + (1/6 of 90 days) = 185 days].

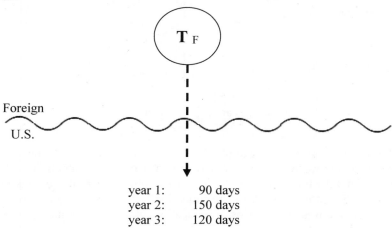

By counting carryover days, an individual who consistently spends just one-third of the year in the United States (122 days to be exact) is treated as a U.S. resident.[39] This potentially unfair result is mitigated by an exception for an alien who satisfies the following requirements:

 (i) the alien is present in the United States for less than 183 days during the current year,

 (ii) the alien's tax home (i.e., principal or regular place of business) for the current year is in a foreign country, and

 (iii) the alien has a closer connection to that foreign country than to the United States (a very subjective test).[40]

Example 2.8: T is not a citizen and does not hold a green card. However, T is physically present the first five months (150 days) for each of two consecutive years. Although T is not physically present for 183 days in either of the two years, she satisfies the substantial presence test for residence in year 2 due to the carryover days from year 1 [150 days + (1/3 of 150 days) =

---

[37] Code Sec. 7701(b)(3)(A)(ii).
[38] Code Sec. 7701(b)(3)(A)(i).

[39] 122 days + (1/3 of 122 days) + (1/6 of 122 days) = 183 days.
[40] Code Sec. 7701(b)(3)(B).

190 days]. However, because she is not physically present in the United States for 183 days during year 2, if she has a tax home (i.e., employment) in a foreign country and has a closer connection to a foreign country, she is not a U.S. resident during year 2.

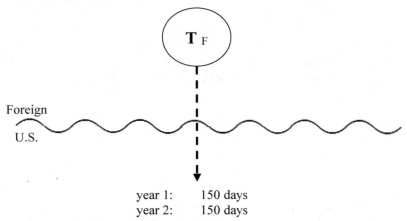

year 1:	150 days
year 2:	150 days

This exception does not apply, however, if the alien has applied for a green card.[41] Determining whether a taxpayer has a closer connection with a foreign country than with the United States requires considering all the facts and circumstances, such as the location of the individual's family, permanent residence, and personal belongings, as well as the location of the individual's social, political, cultural, and religious relationships.[42]

.03 First Year of Residency

If an alien establishes U.S. residency after January 1, that alien is generally treated as a nonresident alien for the portion of the calendar year preceding the residency starting date and as a resident alien for the remainder of the year.[43] The U.S. residency starting date depends on whether the alien establishes residency under the green card test or the substantial presence test. If the alien establishes residency under the substantial presence test, the residency starting date is the first day the alien is physically present in the United States.[44] For this purpose, visits to the United States of 10 days or less, such as for a house-hunting trip, are ignored if at the time of the visit the alien had a closer connection to a foreign country than to the United States.[45]

Example 2.9: T is not a U.S. citizen and does not hold a green card. However, T is physically present in the United States from June 1 through December 31 of the current year. T is a U.S. resident for the year because she is physically present in the United States for 183 or more days, with the date of residency beginning on June 1. Therefore, T's tax year is split and T is a

---

[41] Code Sec. 7701(b)(3)(C).
[42] Reg. § 301.7701(b)-2(d).
[43] Code Sec. 7701(b)(2)(A)(i).

[44] Code Sec. 7701(b)(2)(A)(iii).
[45] Code Sec. 7701(b)(2)(C).

nonresident alien from January 1 through May 31 and a resident alien from June 1 through December 31.

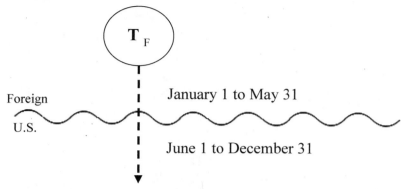

If the alien establishes residency under the green card test, the residency starting date is the first day the alien is physically present in the United States with a green card.[46] If the alien satisfies <u>both residency tests</u> in the first year of residency, the residency starting date is the <u>earlier of the two starting dates.</u>[47] Finally, to prevent a gap in residency when an alien is a resident in two consecutive calendar years, the residency starting date for an alien who was a U.S. resident in the preceding year is January 1, regardless of when a test is satisfied.[48]

Example **2.10:** T is not a citizen and does not hold a green card. However, T is physically present in the United States in year 1 the entire 365 days and, therefore, is a U.S. resident for year 1 pursuant to the substantial presence test. T returns to foreign country F for the beginning of year 2, but is physically present in the United States from April 1 through December 31. For year 2, T only passes the substantial presence test at the end of June. However, because T was a U.S. resident for year 1, T is a U.S. resident the entire year 2.

---

[46] Code Sec. 7701(b)(2)(A)(ii). If the green card holder is not in the United States during the year, residency does not begin until the following year. Reg. § 301.7701(b)-4(e)(3).

[47] Reg. § 301.7701(b)-4(a).
[48] Reg. § 301.7701(b)-4(e)(1).

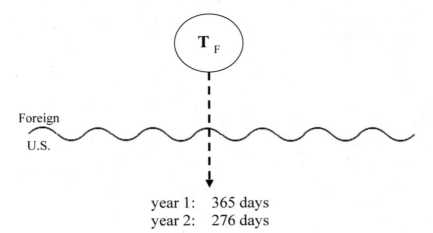

year 1:   365 days
year 2:   276 days

A special first-year residency election is available to certain qualifying aliens. Under this provision, in the first year that an alien satisfies either the green card test or the substantial presence test, she can elect to be taxed as a U.S. resident for a portion of the preceding year, if any, in which she was present in the United States.[49] This election allows the alien to itemize her deductions and claim a foreign tax credit, beginning with the entry date into the United States. However, the election also exposes all of the alien's income to U.S. taxation, including her foreign-source income.

.04 Last Year of Residency

An alien's U.S. residency termination date is the last day of the year on which the individual was physically present in the United States under the substantial presence test or the last day she had a green card, provided the taxpayer establishes that for the remainder of the year she had a closer connection to, and a tax home in, a foreign country.[50] Accordingly, the alien is taxed as a U.S. resident from January 1 to the residency termination date and as a nonresident alien for the remainder of the year.

> **Example 2.11:** T is not a U.S. citizen, but has been a resident of the United States for several years pursuant to the substantial presence test. On July 31, T leaves the United States and returns to her country of citizenship where she has taken a job and purchases a house. Because T has established a closer connection to her country of citizenship and has a tax home there, T's residency in the United States ends on July 31. T is a nonresident alien from August 1 through December 31.

---

[49] Code Sec. 7701(b)(4).   [50] Code Sec.7701(b)(2)(B).

¶203.04

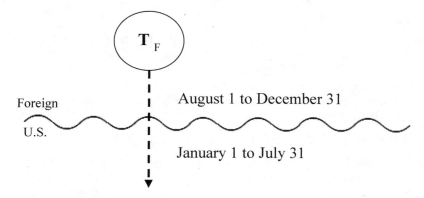

If an alien qualifies as a resident during the current year under <u>both</u> the green card and the substantial presence tests, the <u>residency termination date is the later of the termination dates under either of the two residency tests.</u>[51]

Example 2.12: T, a citizen of country F, has a green card and is physically present in the United States from January 1 through September 30, thereby satisfying both alternatives for residence. T relinquishes his green card on September 15. However, because T was also a U.S. resident under the substantial presence test and did not leave the United States until September 30, his residency terminates on September 30.

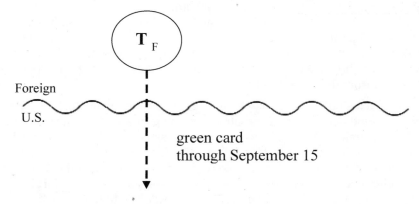

January 1 to September 30

To prevent a gap in residency when an alien is a resident in two consecutive calendar years, the normal residency termination date rules do not apply if the alien is a U.S. resident in the succeeding year. In such cases, the alien is a resident through December 31, regardless of when the green card test or the substantial presence test was last met for the year.[52]

---

[51] Reg. § 301.7701(b)-4(b)(2).   [52] Reg. § 301.7701(b)-4(e)(2).

¶**203.04**

.05 Filing a Joint Return

A married couple generally is not eligible to file a joint return for a given taxable year if, at any time during that year, one or both spouses was a nonresident alien.[53] However, if a U.S. person's nonresident alien spouse becomes a U.S. resident during the year, the couple may elect to treat that spouse as a U.S. resident for the entire taxable year.[54] A similar election is also available when the spouse is a nonresident alien for the entire year.[55]

¶ 204 FOREIGN EARNED INCOME EXCLUSION

The United States ordinarily taxes U.S. citizens and resident aliens on their worldwide income, even when they live and work abroad for an extended period of time. To provide some relief, a U.S. citizen or resident who meets certain requirements can elect to exclude from U.S. taxation a limited amount of foreign earned income plus a housing cost amount.[56] However, the Code does not allow a double tax benefit so a taxpayer cannot claim a credit for foreign income taxes related to excluded foreign earned income.[57]

.01 Exclusion versus Credit

Because an expatriate must elect the foreign earned income exclusion, an expatriate must decide whether to elect the exclusion or to rely on the foreign tax credit.[58] A key factor in deciding which option is more advantageous is the relative amounts of U.S. and foreign taxes imposed on the foreign earned income before the exclusion or credit. The exclusion completely eliminates the U.S. income tax on the qualifying amount of foreign earned income. As a result, the exclusion allows expatriates who work in low-tax foreign countries or who qualify for special tax exemptions in those countries to benefit from the lower foreign tax rates. In contrast, under the foreign tax credit option, the United States collects any residual U.S. tax on lightly-taxed foreign-source income and the expatriate does not derive any benefit from the lower foreign rates.

The exclusion also eliminates the U.S. tax on the qualifying amount of foreign earned income derived by an expatriate working in a high-tax foreign jurisdiction. The credit option also achieves this result, since the higher foreign taxes are sufficient to fully offset the U.S. tax on the foreign earned income. In addition, under the credit option, the expatriate receives a potential added benefit in the form of a foreign tax credit carryover. Foreign taxes in excess of the foreign tax credit limitation can be carried back one year and forward up to ten years.[59] Therefore, an expatriate can use these excess credits in a carryover year in which he has foreign-source income that attracts little or no foreign tax.[60] For example, expatriates who

---

[53] Code Sec. 6013(a)(1).

[54] Code Sec. 6013(h) and Reg. § 1.6013-7.

[55] Code Sec. 6013(g) and Reg. § 1.6013-6.

[56] Code Sec. 911.

[57] Code Sec. 911(d)(6) and Reg. § 1.911-6(c). The foreign earned income exclusion does not apply to FICA taxes. A U.S. citizen or resident alien employed abroad by an "American employer" (as defined in Code Sec. 3121(h)) is subject to FICA taxes on his wages, unless

there is a social security totalization agreement (a type of tax treaty) between the United States and the host foreign country. Code Sec. 3121(b).

[58] It also is possible to deduct foreign income taxes. Code Sec. 164(a). Typically, however, a credit or exclusion is more advantageous.

[59] Code Sec. 904(c).

[60] Under the separate-category-of-income foreign tax credit limitations, excess foreign tax credits related to foreign earned income ordinarily are assigned to the

return to the United States may be able to use their foreign tax credit carryforwards to the extent their future compensation is attributable to foreign business trips.[61]

.02 Qualified Individuals

The foreign earned income exclusion is available only to U.S. citizens or resident aliens who meet the following two requirements:

(i) the individual is physically present in a foreign country (or foreign countries) for at least 330 full days[62] during any 12-month period or (in the case of a U.S. citizen) is a bona fide resident of a foreign country for an uninterrupted period that includes an entire taxable year, and

(ii) the individual's tax home is in a foreign country.[63]

In applying the 330-day physical presence test, the expatriate counts every full day in a foreign country.[64] Therefore, a taxpayer can add a series of foreign stays, including foreign vacations, to meet the 330-day test.

> **Example 2.13:** Oscar, a U.S. citizen, takes a job with a European basketball team in foreign Country F to play and to promote the team in the offseason, residing there from January 1, 20X2 to March 31, 20X3. During 20X2, Oscar earns $90,000 in Foreign Country F, which does not impose an income tax. Although Oscar qualifies for the foreign earned income exclusion under both the bona fide residence test and the physical presence test, he should use the physical presence test to complete the Form 2555.

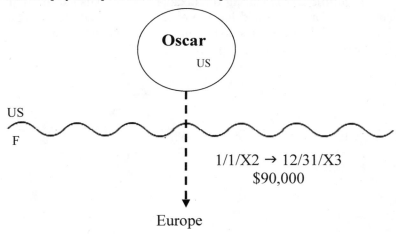

U.S. citizens who are unable to meet the objective 330-day physical presence test must satisfy the bona fide foreign resident test, a subjective test. Whether an individual is a bona fide foreign resident is determined by his intentions with regard

---

(Footnote Continued)

general limitation basket and can only offset an excess limitation from that basket. Code Sec. 904(d).

[61] Compensation is treated as foreign-source income to the extent the related services are performed abroad. Code Sec. 862(a)(3).

[62] Partial days do not count.

[63] Code Sec. 911(d)(1).

[64] Reg. §1.911-2(d)(2) For this purpose, U.S. possessions are not considered foreign countries. Reg. §1.911-2(g).

to the length and nature of the stay.[65] Factors which suggest that an expatriate is a bona fide foreign resident include the presence of family, the acquisition of a foreign home or long-term lease, and involvement in the social life of the foreign country.[66]

The individual must have a foreign tax home.[67] An individual's tax home is his principal or regular place of business, provided that an individual is not treated as having a tax home in a foreign country during any period in which the taxpayer's abode is in the United States.[68] An individual's abode is in the United States if that is where his economic, social, and personal ties are closest.[69]

When both spouses work abroad, they separately determine if they qualify for the foreign earned income exclusion and each spouse individually elects the exclusion.[70] Therefore, it is possible for one qualifying spouse to elect the exclusion, while the other qualifying spouse chooses not to elect the exclusion.

.03 Computing the Exclusion

The maximum amount of foreign earned income that is eligible for the exclusion is both adjusted annually for inflation and prorated for the number of qualifying days in a taxable year.[71] The maximum exclusion amount is $99,200 for 2014[72] and $100,800 for 2015.[73] A qualifying day is any day within the period during which the individual meets the foreign tax requirement and either the bona fide resident requirement or the 330-day physical presence requirement.[74]

> **Example 2.14:** During the taxable year, T satisfied the requirement for claiming a foreign earned income exclusion and had 292 qualifying days for the year. Therefore, T's maximum earned income exclusion is $79,360 [$99,200 × (292 days ÷ 365 days)].

---

[65] Reg. §§ 1.911-2(c) and 1.871-2(b). An individual with earned income from sources within a foreign country is not a bona fide resident of that country if the individual claims to be a nonresident of that country for local tax purposes. Reg. § 1.911-2(c).

[66] For example, *see G.H. Jones,* CA-5, 91-1 USTC ¶ 50,174, 927 F2d 849. Rev'g and rem'g 58 TCM 689, Dec. 46,157 (M), TC Memo. 1989-616.

[67] Code Sec. 911(d)(1).

[68] Code Sec. 911(d)(3) and Reg. § 1.911-2(b).

[69] For example, *see J.T. Lemay,* CA-5, 88-1 USTC ¶ 9182, 837 F2d 681 (5th Cir. 1988). Aff'g 53 TCM 862, Dec. 43,931(M), TC Memo. 1987-256; *and D.P. Lansdown,* 68 TCM 680, Dec. 50,114(M), TC Memo. 1994-452. Aff'd, 73 F3d 373 (10th Cir. 1995).

[70] Reg. § 1.911-5.

[71] Code Sec. 911(b)(2)(D)(i).

[72] Rev. Proc. 2013-35, IRB 2013-47.

[73] Rev. Proc. 2014-61, IRB 2014-47.

[74] Reg. § 1.911-3(d)(3).

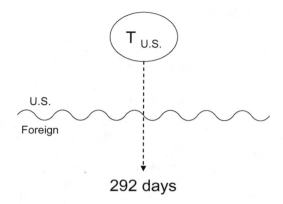

292 days

The exclusion is available only for foreign-source income earned during the period in which the taxpayer meets the foreign tax home requirement, while meeting either the bona fide foreign resident test or the 330-day physical presence test.[75] Therefore, when identifying compensation that qualifies for the exclusion, the taxpayer must determine whether a paycheck or taxable reimbursement is attributable to services performed during the qualifying period, not whether the expatriate actually received the compensation during that period.[76] A deferred payment, such as a bonus, qualifies for the exclusion only if it is received before the close of the taxable year following the year in which it was earned.[77] Pension income does not qualify for the exclusion.[78]

Employment-related allowances, such as foreign housing and automobile allowances, also qualify for the exclusion if the allowance represents compensation for services performed abroad during the qualifying period. In this regard, any taxable reimbursements received for expenses incurred in moving from the United States to a foreign country ordinarily are treated as compensation for services performed abroad. However, any taxable reimbursements received for expenses incurred in moving back to the United States ordinarily are treated as U.S.-source income.[79]

It would be inequitable to allow deductions related to excluded income. As a result, the Code disallows any deductions allocable to excluded foreign earned income, such as unreimbursed employee business expenses.[80] The taxpayer may deduct in full certain expenses considered unrelated to any specific item of gross income. These include medical expenses, charitable contributions, alimony payments, IRA contributions, real estate taxes and mortgage interest on a personal residence, and personal exemptions.[81]

---

[75] Code Sec. 911(b)(1)(A). For this purpose, U.S. possessions are considered part of the United States. Reg. § 1.911-2(g).

[76] Reg. § 1.911-3(e)(1).

[77] Code Sec. 911(b)(1)(B)(iv).

[78] Code Sec. 911(b)(1)(B)(i).

[79] Reg. § 1.911-3(e)(5)(i). An exception applies if, prior to moving abroad, there was a written agreement that the

expatriate would be reimbursed for the expense of moving back to the United States, even if he were to leave the employer upon returning to the United States. In such cases, the reimbursement is treated as foreign-source income.

[80] Code Sec. 911(d)(6).

[81] Reg. § 1.911-6(a).

.04 Housing Cost Amount

An expatriate that qualifies for the foreign earned income exclusion also can claim an exclusion for the housing cost amount.[82] The housing cost amount equals the excess of eligible expenses incurred for the expatriate's foreign housing over a stipulated base amount ($15,872 in 2014 and $16,128 in 2015) that is pro-rated for the number of qualifying days in the year.[83]

Eligible housing expenses normally include rent, utilities (other than telephone charges), real and personal property insurance, certain occupancy taxes, nonrefundable security deposits, rental of furniture and accessories, household repairs, and residential parking. Housing expenses do not include the costs of purchasing or making improvements to a house, mortgage interest and real estate taxes related to a house that the taxpayer owns, purchased furniture, pay television subscriptions, or domestic help.[84]

> **Example 2.15:** During 2014, T satisfies the requirements for claiming a foreign earned income exclusion and has 300 qualifying days for the year. Therefore, T's base amount for 2014 is $13,045 [$15,872 base amount for 2014 × (300 days ÷ 365 days)]. T's eligible housing expenses of $23,500 include $15,000 of apartment rentals, $2,000 of utility expenses (not including telephone charges), $5,000 of rental expenses for furniture and accessories, and $1,500 of residential parking expenses. Therefore, T's housing cost amount for 2014 is $10,455 [($15,000 + $2,000 + $5,000 + $1,500) – $13,045].

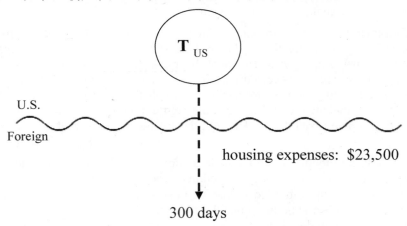

.05 Electing the Exclusion

The taxpayer elects the foreign earned income exclusion and housing cost amount by filing Form 2555, Foreign Earned Income Exclusion, and remains in effect until revoked by the taxpayer.[85] A taxpayer can revoke an exclusion election,

---

[82] Code Sec. 911(a)(2).

[83] Code Sec. 911(c)(1); Notice 2014-29, IRB 2014-18; Notice 2015-33, IRB 2015-18.

[84] Reg. § 1.911-4(b). Special rules apply to the computation of a married couple's housing cost amount. Reg. § 1.911-5(a)(3).

[85] Reg. § 1.911-7(a)(1).

but must then wait five years to reinstate the exclusion.[86] If significant uncertainties exist regarding whether to elect the exclusion, a taxpayer can file an original return without making the election, and then file an amended return at a later date electing the exclusion.[87] (Form 2555 is reproduced in the appendix to this chapter.)

¶ 205 MARK-TO-MARKET EXIT TAX FOR EXPATRIATES

U.S. persons (i.e., U.S. corporations, U.S. citizens, and U.S. resident aliens) are subject to U.S. tax on their worldwide income, whereas foreign persons (i.e., foreign corporations and nonresident aliens) are subject to U.S. tax only on certain types of U.S.-source income. Consequently, this differing treatment could lead U.S. persons to strategically forfeit their U.S. citizenship.

> *Example 2.16:* Benedict Arnold, a U.S. citizen, is a man of leisure who enjoys clipping coupons. Benedict owns securities with an adjusted basis of $10 million and a fair market value of $30 million. During the last 5 years, his annual net income tax obligation to the United States has averaged $400,000. Aware that foreign persons would not be subject to tax on gain on the sale of securities, Benedict forfeits his citizenship and takes residence in a tropical tax haven.

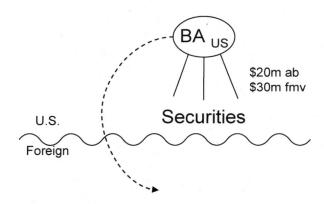

To combat such tax-motivated expatriations, Congress deems a citizen as having sold all his assets for fair market value on the day before the expatriation occurs; if the expatriate (a) has an average annual net income tax obligation to the United States for the 5 years preceding the expatriation that exceeds an inflation-adjusted base amount of tax ($160,000 in 2015), (b) has a net worth greater than or equal to $2 million as of the date of the expatriation or (c) fails to certify to the IRS that he complied with U.S. federal tax obligations for the 5 years preceding the expatriation (or to provide the IRS with evidence of such compliance).[88] Finally, a taxpayer may exclude an inflation-adjusted base amount of mark-to-market gain ($690,000 in 2015).[89]

---

[86] Reg. § 1.911-7(b).

[87] Reg. § 1.911-7(a)(2)(i)(B).

[88] Code Sec. 877A(a), and Rev. Proc. 2014-61, IRB 2014-47.

[89] Rev. Proc. 2012-41, IRB 2012-45.

Example 2.17: Assume the same facts as in the previous Example. Despite his expatriation, the $20 million of gain ($30 million fair market value of the securities less the $10 million basis), less the $690,000 exclusion, will result in $19,310,000 of gain subject to U.S. income tax.

This regime similarly applies to long term residents, which are defined as aliens who are residents due to the Green Card test in 8 of the prior 15 taxable years.

Example 2.18: Kato, a foreign national, has been a U.S. resident since acquiring his Green Card in 1967. Kato owns shares in Black Beauty, Inc. with an adjusted basis of $10 million and a fair market value of $30 million. During the last 5 years, his annual net income tax obligation to the United States has averaged $400,000. Aware that foreign persons would not be subject to tax on gain on the sale of securities, Kato forfeits his Green Card and becomes a resident of a tropical tax haven.

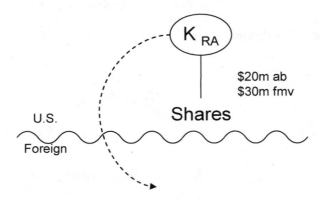

Because Kato has been a long term resident, the $20 million of gain ($30 million fair market value of the shares less the $10 million basis), less the $690,000 exclusion, will result in $19,310,000 of gain subject to U.S. income tax.

¶ 206 REPORTING OF FOREIGN FINANCIAL ASSETS

Congress has become greatly concerned with U.S. persons not reporting and paying tax on income produced by foreign financial assets. As a result, Congress continually enacts new provisions to require taxpayers to report them.

U.S. persons with foreign financial accounts must file a Form FinCEN 114, Report of Foreign Bank and Financial Accounts (or FBAR).[90] A U.S. person must file a FBAR if it has a financial interest in or signature authority over any financial account in a foreign country and the aggregate value of these accounts exceeds $10,000 at any time during the calendar year. The U.S. person does not attach the FBAR to his U.S. income tax return, but instead electronically files it separately with the Treasury Department by June 30 of the following year (see ¶ 1610).

---

[90] Bank Secrecy Act of 1970.

Despite the FBAR reporting requirement, Congress believed that many wealthy U.S. citizens continued to evade U.S. tax through the use of unreported foreign financial assets and that this tax evasion resulted in a significant loss of tax revenues. As a consequence, Congress enacted new reporting requirements with respect to foreign financial assets held by individuals, as well as new reporting and withholding requirements with respect to foreign financial institutions that potentially hold assets of U.S. persons, which is known as the Foreign Account Tax Compliance Act (FATCA).

Under Code Secs. 1471 to 1474 for FATCA, new information reporting and the threat of withholding requirements are imposed on foreign financial institutions that potentially hold assets of U.S. persons. Generally, a withholding agent must deduct and withhold a 30% tax on any U.S.-source withholdable payments to a foreign financial institution. Withholding is not required, however, if the foreign financial institution satisfies certain reporting requirements. Similar rules also apply to non-financial foreign entities (see ¶ 903).

Under new Code Sec. 6038D, individuals who hold an interest in specified foreign financial assets during the tax year must attach to their annual income tax returns certain information with respect to each asset if the aggregate value of all the assets exceeds $50,000. Specified foreign financial assets generally include foreign financial accounts, stock, securities, instruments and other interests in foreign entities. A taxpayer must disclose the maximum value of the foreign financial assets during the tax year and other information specific to each type of asset.

¶ 207 A POLICY NOTE REGARDING THE CURRENT U.S. SYSTEM

The current U.S. jurisdictional system reflects a variety of tax policy objectives, including fairness, the need to collect tax revenues, economic neutrality, and enforcement constraints.

The concept of fairness encompasses both horizontal equity and vertical equity. Horizontal equity requires similar treatment of taxpayers in similar economic situations, whereas vertical equity requires more taxes paid by higher income taxpayers.

The U.S. government's use of a credit system to mitigate international double taxation generally enhances vertical equity. Under a territorial system, U.S. persons could split their total income between domestic and foreign sources. Under a credit system, however, U.S. persons must aggregate their worldwide income and the United States taxes the total amount at marginal rates.

Whether the taxation of a U.S. person's worldwide income enhances or diminishes horizontal equity depends on how one interprets the concept of similarly situated. For example, one could argue that U.S. citizens residing abroad should benefit less from U.S. government expenditures and, therefore, should pay less U.S. tax than citizens residing at home. The Supreme Court addressed this issue in

1924 in the case of *G.W. Cook v. G.L. Tait*.[91] The Court ruled that the U.S. government could tax the Mexican-source income of a U.S. citizen who was a permanent resident of Mexico on the grounds that government expenditures benefit U.S. citizens regardless of their residence or the source of their income. In other words, the basic rights and protections accorded all U.S. citizens, including the right to exit and re-enter the United States at will (and thereby control the enjoyment of these benefits) are the primary determinants of whether individuals are similarly situated.

The collection of tax revenues to fund public services is another tax policy objective. The United States mitigates international double taxation by allowing U.S. persons to claim a credit for foreign income taxes imposed on their foreign-source income. The appeal of the credit system, as compared to a territorial system, is that the United States can mitigate international double taxation without completely forgoing jurisdiction over the foreign-source income of U.S. persons. The United States avoids double taxation by allowing the host country to claim primary jurisdiction over a U.S. person's foreign-source income. However, the United States does assert secondary jurisdiction and, therefore, collects any residual U.S. tax on lightly-taxed foreign-source income. Asserting secondary jurisdiction over foreign-source income increases U.S. tax collections and promotes fairness. Under a territorial system, U.S. persons could avoid U.S. taxes simply by shifting their income-producing assets to tax-haven countries that impose little or no income taxes.

Another tax policy objective is economic neutrality, or the effect of taxation on business and investment decisions. In terms of international trade, neutrality is an issue with respect to both the location of production facilities and investment assets (capital export neutrality) and competition between domestic and foreign companies within the same country or market (capital import neutrality). Capital export neutrality exists if the decision to invest capital at home or abroad is unaffected by taxes. Therefore, capital export neutrality does not exist if tax rates are lower abroad, in which case there is a tax incentive to export capital. U.S. labor groups, in particular, seek tax laws that do not give U.S. companies an incentive to move their manufacturing plants and other facilities overseas. Capital import neutrality exists if domestic and foreign companies competing within the same country or market all face the same total tax rate. U.S. companies attempting to compete in foreign markets seek tax laws that promote capital import neturality.

The U.S. system exhibits elements of both capital export and capital import neutrality. For example, subjecting a U.S. company's worldwide income to taxation enhances capital export neutrality. On the other hand, U.S. companies that operate abroad through lightly-taxed foreign subsidiaries can defer payment of most residual U.S. taxes, which enhances capital import neutrality. During the 1950s and 1960s, capital export neutrality was the major U.S. tax policy goal, as U.S. multinational corporations dominated foreign competitors at home and abroad. However,

---

[91] SCt, 1 USTC ¶ 92, 265 US 47, 44 SCt 444.

¶207

as global competition has intensified in recent decades, the U.S. policy goal of capital import neutrality has increased.

The tensions created by the trade-offs between these two types of tax neutrality have created an on-going political debate. On one side are those U.S. lawmakers and constituency groups (e.g., organized labor organizations) that wish to emphasize capital export neutrality. These groups are concerned that too many high-paying U.S. manufacturing jobs are migrating offshore due, in part, to the tax savings offered by a number of low-tax foreign jurisdictions. These interests have resulted in recurring proposals to eliminate deferral. On the other side are those U.S. lawmakers and constituency groups (e.g., trade associations representing U.S. multinational corporations) that wish to emphasize capital import neutrality. These groups are concerned that U.S. businesses are at a competitive disadvantage in foreign markets, due to what they perceive to be the unusually harsh approach that U.S. laws take in taxing foreign earnings.

Another major policy issue is enforcement constraints. The United States can enforce a tax on a foreign person only if it can verify the correctness of the resulting tax liability and collect the tax if the taxpayer does not voluntarily pay it. This is possible only when either the taxpayer or the taxable income is located within U.S. borders. The U.S. system for taxing foreign persons reflects these constraints under the international sovereignty principle that one country will not enforce the revenue laws of another.[92] For example, because withholding is the only sure way to collect taxes from passive offshore investors, the United States taxes the gross amount of a foreign person's U.S.-source investment income through flat rate withholding.

In sum, the current system for taxing international transactions, like the U.S. tax system generally, represents a compromise between the competing policy objectives of fairness, tax collections, economic neutrality, and enforcement constraints.

---

[92] This international legal principle is known as "Lord Mansfield's Rule." *Hollman v. Johnson*, 98 Eng. Rep. 1120, 1121 (K.B. 1775).

¶ 208 APPENDIX

Mr. Brewster, a U.S. citizen, is employed by the OK Oil Company and he accepts a foreign assignment with the OK Oil Company Foreign Affiliate in foreign country F beginning in 2014. During 2014, Mr. Brewster earned $100,000 in foreign country F, which does not impose an income tax, and incurred $20,000 of qualifying housing cost expenses. Mr. Brewster takes both the foreign earned income exclusion and the foreign housing exclusion. Although Mr. Brewster qualifies for the foreign earned income exclusion under either the bona fide residence test or the physical presence test, he completes the attached Form 2555 using the physical presence test.

Form 2555

Department of the Treasury
Internal Revenue Service

Foreign Earned Income

▶ Attach to Form 1040.
▶ Information about Form 2555 and its separate instructions is at *www.irs.gov/form2555*.

OMB No. 1545-0074

2014

Attachment
Sequence No. **34**

For Use by U.S. Citizens and Resident Aliens Only

Name shown on Form 1040

Mr. Brewster

Your social security number

345-67-8912

Part I   **General Information**

1 Your foreign address (including country)

1234 Naffier Way, Foreign Country F

2 Your occupation

Petroleum Man

3 Employer's name ▶   OK Oil Company Foreign Affiliate

4a Employer's U.S. address ▶

  b Employer's foreign address ▶

5 Employer is (check any that apply):   **a** ☐ A foreign entity   **b** ☐ A U.S. company   **c** ☐ Self
                                  d ☑ A foreign affiliate of a U.S. company   **e** ☐ Other (specify) ▶

6a If you previously filed Form 2555 or Form 2555-EZ, enter the last year you filed the form. ▶

  b If you did not previously file Form 2555 or 2555-EZ to claim either of the exclusions, check here ▶ ☐ and go to line 7.

  c Have you ever revoked either of the exclusions? . . . . ☑ Yes ☐ No

  d If you answered "Yes," enter the type of exclusion and the tax year for which the revocation was effective. ▶

7 Of what country are you a citizen/national? ▶   United States

8a Did you maintain a separate foreign residence for your family because of adverse living conditions at your tax home? See **Second foreign household** in the instructions . . . . ☐ Yes ☐ No

  b If "Yes," enter city and country of the separate foreign residence. Also, enter the number of days during your tax year that you maintained a second household at that address. ▶

9 List your tax home(s) during your tax year and date(s) established. ▶   Foreign Country F, established January 1

Next, complete either Part II or Part III. If an item does not apply, enter "NA." If you do not give the information asked for, any exclusion or deduction you claim may be disallowed.

Part II   **Taxpayers Qualifying Under Bona Fide Residence Test** (see instructions)

10 Date bona fide residence began ▶   , and ended ▶

11 Kind of living quarters in foreign country ▶   **a** ☐ Purchased house   **b** ☐ Rented house or apartment   **c** ☐ Rented room
                                   d ☐ Quarters furnished by employer

12a Did any of your family live with you abroad during any part of the tax year? . . . . ☐ Yes ☐ No

  b If "Yes," who and for what period? ▶

13a Have you submitted a statement to the authorities of the foreign country where you claim bona fide residence that you are not a resident of that country? See instructions . . . . ☐ Yes ☐ No

  b Are you required to pay income tax to the country where you claim bona fide residence? See instructions . ☐ Yes ☐ No

     If you answered "Yes" to 13a and "No" to 13b, you do not qualify as a bona fide resident. Do not complete the rest of this part.

14 If you were present in the United States or its possessions during the tax year, complete columns **(a)–(d)** below. **Do not** include the income from column **(d)** in Part IV, but report it on Form 1040.

(a) Date arrived in U.S.	**(b)** Date left U.S.	**(c)** Number of days in U.S. on business	**(d)** Income earned in U.S. on business (attach computation)	**(a)** Date arrived in U.S.	**(b)** Date left U.S.	**(c)** Number of days in U.S. on business	**(d)** Income earned in U.S. on business (attach computation)

15a List any contractual terms or other conditions relating to the length of your employment abroad. ▶

  b Enter the type of visa under which you entered the foreign country. ▶

  c Did your visa limit the length of your stay or employment in a foreign country? If "Yes," attach explanation . ☐ Yes ☐ No

  d Did you maintain a home in the United States while living abroad? . . . . ☐ Yes ☐ No

  e If "Yes," enter address of your home, whether it was rented, the names of the occupants, and their relationship to you. ▶

For Paperwork Reduction Act Notice, see the Form 1040 instructions.   Cat. No. 11900P   Form **2555** (2014)

Form 2555 (2014)   Page **2**

| Part III | Taxpayers Qualifying Under Physical Presence Test (see instructions) |

16 The physical presence test is based on the 12-month period from ▶ ___January 1___ through ▶ ___December 31___

17 Enter your principal country of employment during your tax year. ▶ ___Foreign Country F___

18 If you traveled abroad during the 12-month period entered on line 16, complete columns **(a)–(f)** below. Exclude travel between foreign countries that did not involve travel on or over international waters, or in or over the United States, for 24 hours or more. If you have no travel to report during the period, enter "Physically present in a foreign country or countries for the entire 12-month period." **Do not** include the income from column **(f)** below in Part IV, but report it on Form 1040.

(a) Name of country (including U.S.)	**(b)** Date arrived	**(c)** Date left	**(d)** Full days present in country	**(e)** Number of days in U.S. on business	**(f)** Income earned in U.S. on business (attach computation)

| Part IV | All Taxpayers |

Note: *Enter on lines 19 through 23 all income, including noncash income, you earned and actually or constructively received during your 2014 tax year for services you performed in a foreign country. If any of the foreign earned income received this tax year was earned in a prior tax year, or will be earned in a later tax year (such as a bonus), see the instructions.* **Do not** *include income from line 14, column* **(d)***, or line 18, column* **(f)***. Report amounts in U.S. dollars, using the exchange rates in effect when you actually or constructively received the income.*

If you are a cash basis taxpayer, report on Form 1040 all income you received in 2014, no matter when you performed the service.

2014 Foreign Earned Income		Amount (in U.S. dollars)	
19 Total wages, salaries, bonuses, commissions, etc.	**19**	100,000	00
20 Allowable share of income for personal services performed (see instructions):			
a In a business (including farming) or profession	**20a**		
b In a partnership. List partnership's name and address and type of income. ▶ _____	**20b**		
21 Noncash income (market value of property or facilities furnished by employer—attach statement showing how it was determined):			
a Home (lodging)	**21a**		
b Meals	**21b**		
c Car	**21c**		
d Other property or facilities. List type and amount. ▶ _____	**21d**		
22 Allowances, reimbursements, or expenses paid on your behalf for services you performed:			
a Cost of living and overseas differential	**22a**		
b Family	**22b**		
c Education	**22c**		
d Home leave	**22d**		
e Quarters	**22e**		
f For any other purpose. List type and amount. ▶ _____	**22f**		
g Add lines 22a through 22f	**22g**		
23 Other foreign earned income. List type and amount. ▶ _____	**23**		
24 Add lines 19 through 21d, line 22g, and line 23	**24**	100,000	00
25 Total amount of meals and lodging included on line 24 that is excludable (see instructions) . .	**25**		
26 Subtract line 25 from line 24. Enter the result here and on line 27 on page 3. This is your **2014 foreign earned income** . . . . ▶	**26**	100,000	00

Form **2555** (2014)

Form 2555 (2014) Page **3**

Part V   **All Taxpayers**

27	Enter the amount from line 26	27	100,000	00

Are you claiming the housing exclusion or housing deduction?
☐ **Yes.** Complete Part VI.
☐ **No.** Go to Part VII.

Part VI   **Taxpayers Claiming the Housing Exclusion and/or Deduction**

28	Qualified housing expenses for the tax year (see instructions)	28	20,000	00
29a	Enter location where housing expenses incurred (see instructions) ▶ Foreign Country F			
b	Enter limit on housing expenses (see instructions)	29b	26,280	00
30	Enter the **smaller** of line 28 or line 29b	30	20,000	00
31	Number of days in your qualifying period that fall within your 2014 tax year (see instructions)	31 365 **days**			
32	Multiply $43.48 by the number of days on line 31. If 365 is entered on line 31, enter $15,872.00 here	32	15,216	00
33	Subtract line 32 from line 30. If the result is zero or less, do not complete the rest of this part or any of Part IX	33	4,784	00
34	Enter employer-provided amounts (see instructions)	34			
35	Divide line 34 by line 27. Enter the result as a decimal (rounded to at least three places), but do not enter more than "1.000"	35	× 1 .	00
36	**Housing exclusion.** Multiply line 33 by line 35. Enter the result but do not enter more than the amount on line 34. Also, complete Part VIII . . . . ▶	36	4,784	00

    Note: *The housing deduction is figured in Part IX. If you choose to claim the foreign earned income exclusion, complete Parts VII and VIII before Part IX.*

Part VII   **Taxpayers Claiming the Foreign Earned Income Exclusion**

37	Maximum foreign earned income exclusion	37	$99,200	00
38	• If you completed Part VI, enter the number from line 31.			
	• All others, enter the number of days in your qualifying period that fall within your 2014 tax year (see the instructions for line 31).	38 365 **days**			
39	• If line 38 and the number of days in your 2014 tax year (usually 365) are the same, enter "1.000."			
	• Otherwise, divide line 38 by the number of days in your 2014 tax year and enter the result as a decimal (rounded to at least three places).	39	× 1 .	00
40	Multiply line 37 by line 39	40	97,600	00
41	Subtract line 36 from line 27	41	95,216	00
42	**Foreign earned income exclusion.** Enter the **smaller** of line 40 or line 41. Also, complete Part VIII ▶	42	95,216	00

Part VIII   **Taxpayers Claiming the Housing Exclusion, Foreign Earned Income Exclusion, or Both**

43	Add lines 36 and 42	43	100,000	00
44	Deductions allowed in figuring your adjusted gross income (Form 1040, line 37) that are allocable to the excluded income. See instructions and attach computation	44		
45	Subtract line 44 from line 43. Enter the result here and in parentheses on **Form 1040, line 21.** Next to the amount enter "Form 2555." On Form 1040, subtract this amount from your income to arrive at total income on Form 1040, line 22	45	100,000	00

Part IX   **Taxpayers Claiming the Housing Deduction**—Complete this part only if **(a)** line 33 is more than line 36 and **(b)** line 27 is more than line 43.

46	Subtract line 36 from line 33	46		
47	Subtract line 43 from line 27	47		
48	Enter the **smaller** of line 46 or line 47	48		

    Note: *If line 47 is **more than** line 48 and you could not deduct all of your 2013 housing deduction because of the 2013 limit, use the housing deduction carryover worksheet in the instructions to figure the amount to enter on line 49. Otherwise, go to line 50.*

49	Housing deduction carryover from 2013 (from the housing deduction carryover worksheet in the instructions)	49		
50	**Housing deduction.** Add lines 48 and 49. Enter the total here and on Form 1040 to the left of line 36. Next to the amount on Form 1040, enter "Form 2555." Add it to the total adjustments reported on that line . . . . ▶	50		

Form **2555** (2014)

¶208

Chapter 3
Source-of-Income Rules

¶ 301   **Importance of Source Rules**
¶ 302   **Source Rules for Gross Income**
¶ 303   **Source Rules for Deductions**

¶ 301 IMPORTANCE OF SOURCE RULES

.01 U.S. Persons

The United States taxes U.S. persons on all of their income, from whatever source derived.[1] Therefore, the source of income generally has no effect on the computation of a U.S. person's taxable income. Sourcing can have a significant effect, however, on the computation of a U.S. person's foreign tax credit limitation, which equals the portion of the pre-credit U.S. tax that is attributable to foreign-source income (see Figure 3.1).[2] The limitation establishes a ceiling on the amount of foreign taxes that can offset U.S. taxes and prevents U.S. persons operating in high-tax foreign countries from offsetting those higher foreign taxes against the U.S. tax on U.S.-source income.

Figure 3.1 Foreign Tax Credit Limitation

$$\text{Foreign tax credit limitation} = \text{Pre-credit U.S. tax} \times \frac{\text{Foreign-source taxable income}}{\text{Worldwide taxable income}}$$

The limitation is important to the extent it prevents taxpayers from crediting all of their foreign income taxes. When a U.S. person's creditable foreign taxes are less than the limitation, the cost of paying foreign income taxes is entirely offset by the U.S. tax savings associated with the credit and, therefore, foreign taxes do not represent an out-of-pocket tax cost for the U.S. person. In contrast, when a U.S. person's creditable foreign taxes exceed the limitation, the noncreditable foreign income taxes may increase the U.S. person's total tax burden beyond what it would have been if only the United States had taxed the foreign-source income. Although creditable foreign taxes in excess of the limitation cannot be taken in the current year, they can be carried back one year and carried forward up to ten years, and taken as a credit in a year in which the limitation exceeds the amount of creditable foreign taxes.[3] In sum, the computation of the foreign tax credit limitation determines whether foreign taxes have an incremental effect on a U.S. person's worldwide tax costs.

---

[1] Code Sec. 61(a).
[2] Code Sec. 904(a).

[3] Code Sec. 904(c).

Example **3.1:** USAco, a domestic corporation, has taxable income of $100, all of which is attributable to a foreign branch operation. Assume the U.S. tax rate is 35%.

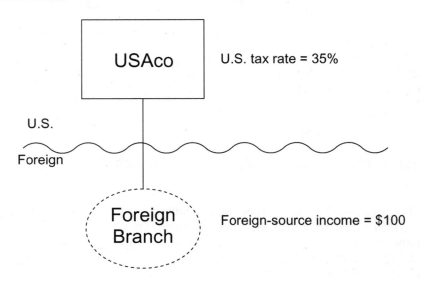

Case 1—Operating in a low-tax foreign country: If USAco's foreign branch is subject to foreign taxation at a 30% rate, USAco can claim a credit for the entire $30 of foreign taxes paid, as follows.

Foreign tax return	
Taxable income	$100
Tax rate	×.30
Foreign tax	$30

U.S. tax return	
Taxable income	$100
Tax rate	×.35
Pre-credit tax	$ 35
Foreign tax credit	– 30
U.S. tax	$ 5

The total tax burden on USAco's foreign profits is $35 [$5 U.S. tax + $30 foreign tax]. Foreign taxes do not represent an incremental tax cost in this case. For example, if USAco were able to reduce its foreign tax from $30 to $29, the foreign tax savings would be completely offset by an increase in U.S. taxes from $5 to $6.

Case 2—Operating in a high-tax foreign country: If USAco's branch is subject to foreign taxation at a 40% rate, the foreign tax credit limitation (which equals the U.S. tax of $35 on USAco's foreign-source income) will prevent USAco from claiming a credit in the current year for $5 of the $40 of foreign taxes paid, as follows.

Foreign tax return	
Taxable income	$100
Tax rate	×.40
Foreign tax	$40

U.S. tax return	
Taxable income	$100
Tax rate	×.35
Pre-credit tax	$ 35
Foreign tax credit	− 35
U.S. tax	$ 0

Foreign taxation now increases the current-year tax burden on USAco's foreign profits from $35 to $40, resulting in a $5 out-of-pocket tax cost.

Foreign taxes in excess of the foreign tax credit limitation are referred to as "excess credits." One strategy for eliminating excess credits is to increase the percentage of total taxable income that is classified as foreign-source for U.S. tax purposes. As a consequence, the rules for sourcing gross income and deductions play an important role in eliminating excess credits. For example, the title passage rule for sourcing income from inventory sales provides U.S. exporters with a significant opportunity for increasing their foreign-source income.[4] By arranging for the passage of title in the importing country, rather than in the United States, export sales will generate foreign-source income and thereby increase the taxpayer's foreign tax credit limitation. Recharacterizing deductions is also an effective strategy for eliminating excess credits. A deduction reduces a taxpayer's pre-credit U.S. tax, regardless of how apportioned. However, deductions allocated to foreign-source income also reduce the foreign tax credit limitation. In contrast, deductions allocated to U.S.-source income do not affect the foreign tax credit limitation and, therefore, provide a full U.S. tax benefit.

A domestic corporation computes its foreign-source taxable income on Schedule A of Form 1118. Separate foreign tax credit limitations are computed for passive category income and general category income.[5] Therefore, separate Form 1118s are filed for each category of foreign-source taxable income. Individual taxpayers compute foreign-source taxable income on Part I of Form 1116, and file separate Form 1116s for passive category income and general category income.

.02 Foreign Persons

The source rules play a more prominent role in the taxation of foreign persons, since they effectively define the boundaries of U.S. taxation. The United States taxes the gross amount of a foreign person's U.S.-source investment-type income at a flat rate of 30%.[6] The United States also taxes foreign persons at graduated rates on the net amount of income effectively connected with the conduct of a U.S. trade or business.[7] As a result, the United States generally taxes the U.S.-source income of foreign persons and exempts their foreign-source income. The source of a foreign person's income also is an important issue for potential U.S. withholding agents since they may be liable for any U.S. taxes that they fail to withhold from

---

[4] Reg. § 1.861-7(c).

[5] Code Sec. 904(d).

[6] Code Secs. 871(a) and 881(a).

[7] Code Secs. 871(b) and 882(a).

payments of U.S.-source investment-type income to a foreign person.[8] U.S. with-holding taxes are discussed in Chapter 9 (¶ 901).

Example 3.2: Norman Ray Allen (NRA), a nonresident alien, owns 100 shares of USAco, a domestic corporation. If USAco pays a dividend of $100 to NRA, the $100 is U.S.-source income, which may be subject to withholding.

Example 3.3: Norman Ray Allen (NRA), a nonresident alien, collects and sells movie memorabilia. NRA visits the United States for three months and derives $100,000 of net income from selling memorabelia from his hotel room in Hollywood, California. Assuming NRA's activities constitute the conduct of a trade or business within the United States, the net amount of income effectively connected with that U.S. trade or business is subject to U.S. tax at the regular graduated rates.

¶ 302 SOURCE RULES FOR GROSS INCOME

.01 Introduction

The source rules for gross income are organized by categories of income, such as interest, dividends, personal services income, rentals, royalties, and gains from

---

[8] Code Sec. 1461.

the disposition of property.[9] Therefore, the first step in the sourcing process is to determine the applicable statutory category. This determination is sometimes ambiguous. For example, the same transaction may exhibit characteristics of both an installment sale and a lease. This distinction is important because a lease generates rental income, which is sourced on the basis of where the property is used, whereas an installment sale results in a gain on the sale of property as well as interest income, both of which are sourced under different rules. Therefore, the same item of income may be allocated between U.S. and foreign sources differently, depending on how it is categorized.

An example of the importance of determining the applicable category of income is a transaction involving computer programs (or software), which must be classified as one of the following:

   (i) a transfer of a copyright right in the computer program,

   (ii) a transfer of a copyrighted article (a copy of the computer program),

   (iii) the provision of services for the development or modification of the computer program, or

   (iv) the provision of know-how relating to computer programming techniques.[10]

For example, transactions involving mass-market software generally are classified as transfers of copyrighted articles.[11] Therefore, the source of income derived from the transfer of a copyrighted article is determined under the rules applicable to a sale of inventory if the underlying transfer provides all substantial rights. However, the copyrighted article is a lease of tangible personal property if the rights to use the copyrighted article are limited.[12] Income derived from transfers classified as inventory sales is sourced under the title passage rule or the 50-50 method (whichever applies),[13] whereas income derived from transfers classified as leases are sourced under a place of use rule.[14]

Another situation in which the proper categorization of an item of gross income may be ambiguous is the distinction between personal services income and royalty income.[15]

    Example 3.4: T is an orchestra conductor. A U.S. company hired T to conduct various songs at a recording session that took place in the United States. T was compensated based on a percentage of the sales of the recording, which is owned by the U.S. company. Ninety percent of the recording sales took place outside the United States. Personal services income is sourced based on where the services are performed, whereas royalty income is sourced based on where the intangible is used. Therefore, T's income is entirely U.S.-source income if it is classified as personal services income, but is mainly foreign-source income if it is classified as royalty income.

---

[9] Code Secs. 861 and 862.

[10] Reg. § 1.861-18(b)(1).

[11] Reg. § 1.861-18(f)(2).

[12] Reg. § 1.861-18(h), Examples 1 and 2.

[13] Reg. § 1.861-7(c) and § 1.863-3.

[14] Code Secs. 861(a)(4) and 862(a)(4).

[15] *See*, for example, *P. Boulez*, 83 TC 584, Dec. 41,557 (1984); *R. Goosen*, 136 TC 547, Dec. 58,655 (2011); and *Sergio Garcia*, 140 TC No. 6, Dec. 59,484 (2013).

Once a taxpayer has determined the appropriate category of income, the next step is to apply the applicable source rule to classify the item of income as either U.S.-source or foreign-source. In general, the rules for sourcing income are based on the location of the underlying income-producing property or activity. The general rules for sourcing gross income, which are described in detail in the following pages, are summarized in Table 3.1.

TABLE 3.1. GENERAL RULES FOR SOURCING GROSS INCOME

Type of income	U.S.-source income if:	Foreign-source income if:
Interest income	Debtor is a U.S. resident or a domestic corporation	Debtor is a foreign resident or a foreign corporation
Dividends	Payer is a domestic corporation	Payer is a foreign corporation
Personal services income	Services are performed in U.S.	Services are performed abroad
Rentals and royalties	Property is used in U.S.	Property is used abroad
Gain on sale of real property	Property is located in U.S.	Property is located abroad
Gain on sale of personal property	Seller is a U.S. resident	Seller is a foreign resident
Income from the sale of inventory purchased for resale	Title passes in U.S.	Title passes abroad
Income from the sale of inventory produced by taxpayer	Allocate using 50-50 method	Allocate using 50-50 method
Gain on sale of depreciable property	Title passes in U.S.[a]	Title passes abroad[a]

| Gain on sale of patents and other intangible property | Seller is a U.S. resident[b] | Seller is a foreign resident[b] |

[a] Different rules apply to the portion of the gain attributable to prior-year depreciation deductions.

[b] Different rules apply if the intangible is sold for a contingent price, or if a portion of the gain is attributable to prior-year amortization deductions.

For purposes of sourcing income, the term "United States" means only the 50 states and the District of Columbia, and does not include U.S. possessions (Puerto Rico, U.S. Virgin Islands, Guam, American Samoa, Northern Mariana Islands, etc.).[16] However, for purposes of sourcing personal services income from mines, oil and gas wells, and other natural deposits, the United States also includes continental shelf areas.[17]

.02 Interest Income

Interest income is U.S.-source income if the payer is a domestic corporation or U.S. resident and foreign-source income if the payer is a foreign corporation or a nonresident.[18] U.S.-source interest also includes interest paid by the United States government or any agency or instrumentality thereof (not including U.S. possessions), one of the 50 states or any political subdivisions thereof, or the District of Columbia.[19] For this purpose, the following taxpayers are considered to be U.S. residents:

    (i) individuals who, at the time the interest is paid, are residents of the United States;

    (ii) domestic corporations;

    (iii) domestic partnerships which at any time during the taxable year were engaged in a U.S. trade or business; and

    (iv) foreign corporations or foreign partnerships, which at any time during the taxable year were engaged in a U.S. trade or business.[20]

Factors other than the residence (or the place of incorporation) of the debtor, such as where the debt was incurred or where the interest is paid are irrelevant. Although this approach is relatively objective, it can produce dubious results.

    Example 3.5: USAco, a domestic corporation, is a retailer of women's apparel. Five years ago, USAco opened a retail store in London, which is structured as a foreign corporation that is treated as a disregarded entity for U.S. tax purposes (i.e., a branch). USAco financed the store through a $10 million loan from a U.K. bank. The loan is being repaid out of the profits of the U.K. branch. Therefore, the acquisition, use, and repayment of funds all occurred abroad. Nevertheless, under the residence-of-debtor source rule, the

---

[16] Code Sec. 7701(a)(9).

[17] Code Sec. 638.

[18] Code Secs. 861(a)(1) and 862(a)(1). For this purpose, interest income includes original issue discount, as well as any imputed interest. Reg. § 1.861-2(a)(4).

[19] Reg. § 1.861-2(a)(1).

[20] Reg. § 1.861-2(a)(2). Note that interest paid by a U.S. citizen residing abroad is treated as foreign-source income.

interest that USAco pays to the U.K. bank is U.S.-source income because USAco is a domestic corporation.

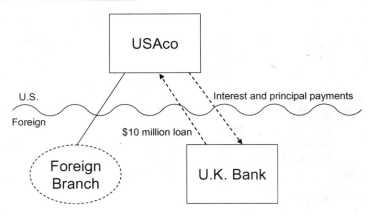

There are several exceptions to the general rules for sourcing interest income, including the following:

(i)   Interest received from deposits made with a foreign branch of a domestic corporation or partnership engaged in the commercial banking business is treated as foreign-source income.[21]

(ii) Interest paid to a 10% or more U.S. shareholder by a foreign corporation that is at least 50% owned by U.S. persons is U.S.-source income to the extent the interest payment is attributable to income that the foreign corporation derived from U.S. sources.[22] This exception applies only for purposes of computing the foreign tax credit limitation and is designed to prevent U.S. shareholders from artificially increasing their foreign tax credit limitation by routing U.S.-source income through a U.S.-owned foreign corporation.

(iii) Interest paid by a U.S. branch of a foreign corporation is treated as if it were paid by a domestic corporation,[23] which generally makes the interest U.S.-source income and potentially subject to U.S. withholding tax. This exception is part of the branch tax regime, which is designed to better equate the tax treatment of the U.S. branch and U.S. subsidiary operations of foreign corporations. The branch taxes are discussed in Chapter 10 (¶ 1002).

.03 Dividend Income

Under the general rules, dividends are U.S.-source income if the payer is a domestic corporation and foreign-source income if the payer is a foreign corporation.[24] There are several exceptions to the general rules, including the following:

---

[21] Code Sec. 861(a)(1)(B)(i).

[22] Code Sec. 904(h)(3). This exception does not apply if less than 10% of the U.S.-owned foreign corporation's earnings and profits are attributable to U.S.-source income. Code Sec. 904(h)(5).

[23] Code Sec. 884(f)(1)(A).

[24] Code Secs. 861(a)(2) and 862(a)(2).

(i) A portion of the dividends paid by a foreign corporation are U.S.-source income if, during the preceding three taxable years, 25% or more of the foreign corporation's gross income was effectively connected with the conduct of a U.S. trade or business. If a foreign corporation meets the 25% test, the U.S. source-portion equals the amount of the dividend times the ratio of the foreign corporation's gross income that was effectively connected with a U.S. trade or business during the three-year testing period to the foreign corporation's total gross income during the testing period.[25] The U.S.-source portion of the dividend is not subject to U.S. withholding tax.[26]

(ii) Dividends paid by a foreign corporation that is at least 50% owned by U.S. persons are U.S.-source income to the extent the dividend is attributable to income that the foreign corporation derived from U.S. sources.[27] This exception applies only for purposes of computing the foreign tax credit limitation and is designed to prevent U.S. persons from artificially increasing their foreign tax credit limitation by routing U.S.-source income through a U.S.-owned foreign corporation.

(iii) A domestic corporation that claims a dividends-received deduction with respect to a portion of a dividend from a foreign corporation must treat that portion of the dividend as U.S.-source income.[28] This exception applies only for purposes of computing the foreign tax credit limitation and prevents a double tax benefit in the form of both a dividends-received deduction and a foreign tax credit with respect to the same dividend income.

Example 3.6: ForCo, a foreign corporation, derived 40% of its gross income for the three preceding taxable years from a U.S. branch operation. Under the 25% look-through rule, 40% of any dividends that ForCo pays are U.S.-source income for purposes of computing the shareholder's foreign tax credit limitation. The remaining 60% is foreign-source income by reason of ForCo's foreign corporation status.

---

[25] Code Sec. 861(a)(2)(B).

[26] Code Secs. 871(i)(2)(D) and 881(d). However, the effectively connected earnings and profits of the foreign corporation's U.S. trade or business are subject to the Code Sec. 884 branch profits tax.

[27] Code Sec. 904(h)(4). This exception does not apply if less than 10% of the U.S.-owned foreign corporation's

earnings and profits are attributable to U.S.-source income. Code Sec. 904(h)(5).

[28] Code Sec. 245(a)(9). Under Code Sec. 245(a)(1), a domestic corporation that owns 10% or more of a foreign corporation may claim a dividends-received deduction for the portion of a dividend attributable to income derived by the foreign corporation from either the conduct of a U.S. trade or business or dividends received from an 80%-or-more-owned domestic corporation.

¶302.03

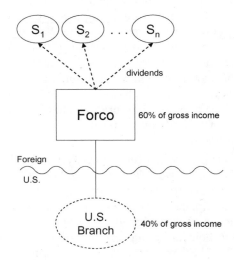

.04 Personal Services Income

Compensation for personal services performed in the United States is U.S.-source income and compensation for personal services performed abroad is foreign-source income.[29] Personal services income includes salaries, wages, fees, and commissions, including any payments that an employer receives as compensation for services performed by employees or other agents.

Under a *de minimis* rule, income of a nonresident alien that is attributable to services performed in the United States is recharacterized as foreign-source income if the following requirements are met:

   (i) the nonresident alien is present in the United States for 90 days or less during the taxable year,

   (ii) the nonresident alien receives no more than $3,000 for his or her U.S. services, and

   (iii) the nonresident alien works as an employee or under contract for either a foreign person who is not engaged in a U.S. trade or business or the foreign office of a U.S. person.[30]

This exception allows nonresident aliens to make short business trips to the United States free of U.S. taxes. Income tax treaties often contain more generous exemptions which allow for longer stays and, more importantly, increase or eliminate the limitation on earnings for business travelers who are residents of treaty countries (see Chapter 13 (¶ 1302.03)).

Another exception applies to the compensation of nonresident aliens engaged in international transportation services. Under this exception, compensation for

---

[29] Code Secs. 861(a)(3) and 862(a)(3).

[30] Code Sec. 861(a)(3). A nonresident alien who meets these requirements also is considered not to be engaged in a U.S. trade or business. Code Sec. 864(b)(1).

services performed by a nonresident alien in connection with the individual's temporary presence in the United States as a regular member of a foreign vessel engaged in transportation between the United States and a foreign country or U.S. possession is generally treated as foreign-source income that is exempt from U.S. tax.[31]

An allocation issue arises when a taxpayer is paid a lump-sum amount, such as an annual salary, for services performed both within and without the United States. In these situations, the lump-sum amount is apportioned between U.S.-source and foreign-source income, typically on the basis of the relative number of days worked in the United States and abroad.[32]

> *Example* **3.7:** T, a U.S. citizen, lived and worked in the United States throughout the current year, except for a five-week foreign business trip. T received an annual salary of $60,000 for a total of 250 working days, including the 25 days spent working abroad. The foreign-source component of T's $60,000 salary is $6,000 [$60,000 × (25 days ÷ 250 days)], and the remaining $54,000 is U.S.-source income.

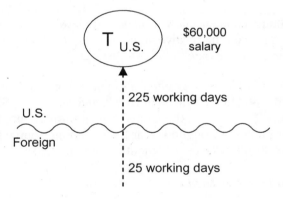

An employee who receives certain fringe benefits is required to source those benefits on a geographical basis, as follows: housing (principal place of work), education (principal place of work), local transportation (principal place of work), hazardous or hardship duty pay (location of zone), tax reimbursement (jurisdiction imposing tax), and moving expense reimbursement fringe benefits (new principal place of work).[33]

The need to allocate compensation between U.S. and foreign sources also can arise with respect to payments from a defined benefit plan. Pension income has two basic components: employer contributions for services performed and interest on those contributions. The compensation component is sourced under the general

---

[31] Code Sec. 861(a)(3). This exception does not apply for purposes of Code Sec. 79 (group-term life insurance), Code Sec. 105 (amounts received under accident and health plans), and Subchapter D (pertaining to deferred compensation, retirement plans, and other employee benefits).

[32] Reg. § 1.861-4(b).

[33] Reg. § 1.861-4(b)(2)(ii)(B).

rules for sourcing personal services income. As a result, the compensation component of pension income received by an individual for services performed both within and without the United States must be allocated between U.S.-source and foreign-source income based on the ratio of employer contributions made while the retiree was working abroad to the total of all employer contributions made for that retiree.[34]

> **Example 3.8:** T receives an annual pension of $15,000 from a domestic trust, $5,000 of which is attributable to the earnings of the pension plan, and the remaining $10,000 to employer contributions. T's former employer contributed a total of $100,000 to the pension plan on T's behalf, $20,000 of which was contributed while T was on foreign assignments. Assuming the $5,000 of interest income is U.S. source, the foreign-source portion of T's annual pension is $2,000 [$10,000 × ($20,000 ÷ $100,000)].

The exercise of nonqualified stock options also gives rise to personal services income. If the taxpayer performed services both within and without the United States during the period beginning on the grant date and ending on the exercise date, the resulting compensation is allocated between U.S.-source and foreign-source income based on the relative number of months worked in the United States and abroad from the grant date to the exercise date.[35]

> **Example 3.9:** T is granted a stock option on January 1 of year 1. T exercises the option on June 30 of year 2, and recognizes $30,000 of compensation income. T worked in the United States throughout year 1, but was on a foreign assignment throughout year 2. The foreign-source portion of T's option income is $10,000 [$30,000 × (6 months ÷ 18 months)].

.05 Rental and Royalty Income

Rentals and royalties are U.S.-source income if the property is located or used in the United States and foreign-source income if the property is located or used abroad.[36] All other factors, such as where the property was produced or where the contract was negotiated, are ignored.

> **Example 3.10:** A California production company produces a motion picture at its Hollywood studio. The movie is licensed for use in, among other places, the United Kingdom. Royalties received for the presentation of the movie in U.K. theaters are foreign-source income, even though the movie was produced entirely in the United States.

---

[34] Rev. Rul. 79-388, 1979-2 CB 270, and Rev. Rul. 79-389, 1979-2 CB 281. The interest component of pension income is sourced based on the residence of the payer. Code Secs. 861(a)(1) and 862(a)(2). *See* Rev. Proc. 2004-37, IRB 2004-26, for a method of determining the source of income for defined-benefit pension plan payments made to nonresident aliens where the trust is organized in the United States.

[35] Reg. § 1.861-4(b)(2)(ii)(F) and (G), Example 6.

[36] Code Secs. 861(a)(4) and 862(a)(4).

The characterization of income as a royalty, rather than gains from a sale, depends not only on where the intangible is actually used, but also on whether the licensee is legally entitled to use, and legally protected in using, the intangible in that country.[37] For this purpose, an intangible includes any patent, copyright, secret process or formula, goodwill, trademark, trade brand, franchise, or other like property.[38]

The place of use of personal property may be both within and without the United States, in which case the taxpayer must apportion the rental income between U.S. and foreign sources. This apportionment may be done on the basis of time, mileage, or some other appropriate base.

> **Example 3.11:** Acme, a dometic corporation, leases environmental testing equipment to a manufacturer for $50,000 per year. The lessee uses the equipment at manufacturing plants located both in the United States and abroad. Therefore, the lessor must apportion its rental income between U.S. and foreign sources, probably on the basis of the relative amount of time the lessee uses the equipment at its U.S. and foreign plants.

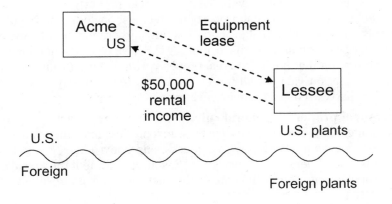

---

[37] For example, *see* Rev. Rul. 84-78, 1984-1 CB 173. [38] Code Sec. 861(a)(4).

.06 Income from the Disposition of Property

Real property. A gain on the sale or exchange of a U.S. real property interest is U.S.-source income, whereas a gain on the sale or exchange of real property located abroad is foreign-source income.[39] All other factors, including where the selling activities took place, are ignored. For example, a gain on the sale of a U.S. office building to foreign investors is U.S.-source income, even if all of the related sale activities take place abroad.

> **Example 3.12:** Norman Ray Allen (NRA) is a nonresident alien who owns Blackacre Estate, which is located in Music City, USA. Several years later, NRA sells Blackacre for a gain. Because Blackacre is located in the United States, the gain on NRA's sale is U.S.-source income.

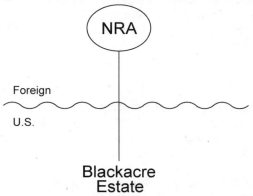

For this purpose, the term "United States real property interest" means a wide array of real property interests located within the United States or the U.S. Virgin Islands, including: (i) land and unsevered natural products of the land, including growing crops, timber, mines, wells, and other natural deposits; (ii) improvements on land, including buildings and other inherently permanent structures; and (iii) personal property associated with the use of real property, such as mining and farming equipment. A U.S. real property interest also includes shares of a corporation that is, or was, a U.S. real property holding corporation at any time during the five-year period preceding the disposition. A U.S. real property holding corporation is any corporation that holds U.S. real property with a market value equal to 50% or more of the market value of all the corporation's real property (U.S. and foreign) plus any property used in a trade or business.[40]

Personal property—general rule. Personal property includes a wide variety of assets, including stocks and securities, inventories, machinery and equipment, and intangibles such as patents, trademarks, and copyrights. As a general rule, a gain on the sale of personal property is U.S.-source income if the taxpayer is a U.S. resident and foreign-source income if the taxpayer is a nonresident.[41] However,

---

[39] Code Secs. 861(a)(5) and 862(a)(5).

[40] Code Sec. 897(c) and Reg. §1.897-1(b). The definition of U.S. real property interests is discussed in more detail in Chapter 9 (¶ 905.02).

[41] Code Sec. 865(a). For this purpose, the term "sale" includes an exchange or any other disposition. Code Sec. 865(i)(2).

¶302.06

there are numerous exceptions to this residence-of-seller rule, including special source rules for depreciable property, intangibles, inventories, and stock of a foreign affiliate. As a consequence, the residence-of-seller source rule applies primarily to security sales.

> **Example 3.13:** T, a citizen and resident of Ireland, sells at a gain 100 shares of USAco, a domestic corporation whose shares are traded on the New York Stock Exchange. Even though USAco is a domestic corporation that conducts business operations only within the United States, T's gain is nevertheless treated as foreign-source income because T is a nonresident.

For purposes of this source rule, the following taxpayers are considered to be U.S. residents:

(i) a domestic corporation,

(ii) a U.S. citizen or resident alien who does not have a tax home in a foreign country,

(iii) a nonresident alien who has a tax home in the United States, and

(iv) a trust or estate whose situs is in the United States.[42]

A nonresident is any person other than a U.S. resident.[43] An individual's tax home is his or her principal or regular place of business, provided that the individual is not treated as having a tax home in a foreign country during any period in which his or her abode is in the United States.[44]

Special rule for U.S. citizens and resident aliens who have a foreign tax home. One consequence of sourcing gains based on the residency of the taxpayer is that a gain realized by a U.S. citizen or resident alien who has a tax home in a

---

[42] Code Sec. 865(g)(1)(A). In the case of a sale of property by a partnership, the determination of residency generally is made at the partner level. Code Sec. 865(i)(5).

[43] Code Sec. 865(g)(1)(B).

[44] Code Secs. 865(g)(1)(A) and 911(d)(3), and Reg. § 1.911-2(b). An individual's abode is in the United States

if that is where his or her economic, social, and personal ties are closest. For example, *see J.T. Lemay,* CA-5, 88-1 USTC ¶ 9182, 837 F2d 681 (5th Cir. 1988). Aff'g 53 TCM 862, Dec. 43,931(M), TC Memo. 1987-256; *and D.P. Lansdown,* 68 TCM 680, Dec. 50,114(M), TC Memo. 1994-452. Aff'd, 73 F3d 373 (10th Cir. 1995).

foreign country is treated as foreign-source income, which has the beneficial side effect of increasing the taxpayer's foreign tax credit limitation. Code Sec. 865(g)(2) closes this potential loophole by providing that, despite the taxpayer's foreign tax home, such gains are treated as U.S.-source income, unless the gain is subject to foreign tax at a rate of at least 10%.

Special rule for sales by U.S. residents through a foreign office. Another special rule applies to sales of personal property by a U.S. resident who maintains an office or other fixed place of business in a foreign country. If a sale is attributable to that foreign office and the gain on the sale is subject to foreign tax at a rate of 10% or more, then the gain is treated as foreign-source income, despite the taxpayer's U.S. residency. This exception does not apply to sales of intangibles for a contingent price, inventory, depreciable personal property, goodwill, or stock of certain foreign affiliates.[45] For purposes of this exception, income is attributable to a foreign office if the office is a material factor in making the sale and the office regularly engages in these types of sales activities.[46]

> *Example 3.14:* Ann, a U.S. citizen, maintains an office in Paris, France, where she buys and sells securities. Ann realizes a $100,000 gain from the sale of stock. If the foreign tax on the gain is at least $10,000 (a 10% or greater tax rate), the gain is foreign-source income. On the other hand, if the foreign tax on the gain is less than $10,000 (a less than 10% rate), the gain is U.S.-source income.

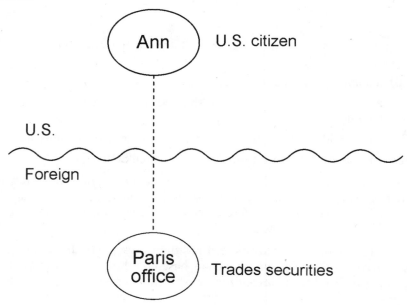

Sales of inventory—overview. For purposes of the source-of-income rules, inventory includes personal property (and not real property) that is held by the

---

[45] Code Sec. 865(e)(1).

[46] Code Secs. 865(e)(3) and 864(c)(5)(b).

taxpayer primarily for sale to customers in the ordinary course of business.[47] Developing an accurate, yet simple, source rule for income from the sale of inventories is a difficult task, given the complex nature of the underlying income-producing activities. For example, income from the sale of inventory by a wholesaler or retailer may be attributable to a number of geographically dispersed economic activities, such as purchasing, marketing, and distribution. The problem of tracing inventory profits to the underlying income-producing activities is more severe for manufacturers. In addition to the functions outlined above for retailers and wholesalers, manufacturers also engage in research and development, production, and post-sale warranty activities. One way in which U.S. lawmakers have sought to address these complexities is to promulgate separate source rules for inventory purchased for resale, as opposed to inventory produced by the taxpayer.

Inventory purchased for resale. Gross income from the sale of inventory that the taxpayer purchased for resale is sourced on the basis of where the sale occurs.[48] Therefore, such income is U.S.-source income if the sale occurs within the United States and foreign-source income if the sale occurs abroad. Other functions performed by a wholesaler or retailer, such as purchasing and distribution, are ignored. The place of sale is generally determined by where title to the goods passes from the seller to the buyer.[49]

> ***Example* 3.15:** USAco, a domestic corporation, is an independent broker that purchases used commercial aircraft from U.S. airlines for resale abroad. During the current year, USAco purchased 20 planes from a regional airline based in Texas and then resold the planes to a Spanish airline. The Spanish airline first learned about USAco's services at a trade show held in Las Vegas, Nevada. The sales agreement between USAco and the Spanish airline was negotiated and signed in Miami, Florida. Title to the airplanes passed in Spain upon delivery at the Madrid airport. Even though all of the selling activities, including solicitation, negotiation, and closing, took place within the United States, the entire profit from the sale of the airplanes is foreign-source income because title passed abroad.

---

[47] Code Secs. 865(i)(1) and 1221(1). *See also* Code Secs. 861(a)(6) and 863(b)(2).

[48] Code Secs. 861(a)(6) and 862(a)(6).

[49] Reg. § 1.861-7(c).

Passing title at the destination point rather than at the shipping point generally is not of great economic consequence to a U.S. exporter, since it is a common business practice to insure shipments and obtain letters of credit from offshore customers. Therefore, the title passage rule provides U.S. exporters with a significant opportunity for increasing their foreign tax credit limitation. Foreign title passage has some potential disadvantages, however, such as the burden of satisfying local customs requirements and the possibility of creating a taxable presence in countries with which the United States does not have an income tax treaty.

An exception to the title passage rule prevents nonresidents from avoiding U.S. tax by passing title abroad on sales to U.S. customers. This exception applies if a foreign resident maintains an office or other fixed base in the United States and the U.S. office is a material factor in making the sale and regularly engages in these types of sales activities. Income from such sales is treated as U.S.-source income, unless the inventory is sold for use, disposition, or consumption outside the United States and a foreign office of the taxpayer materially participates in the sale.[50]

Inventory produced by taxpayer. In contrast to the all-or-nothing approach of the title passage rule used to source gross income from the sale of inventory purchased for resale, income from the sale of inventory that the taxpayer produced (in whole or in part) in the United States and sells abroad is apportioned between U.S. and foreign-source income using one of three methods: the 50-50 method, the independent factory price method, or the taxpayer's own books and records.[51] Taxpayers are generally required to use the 50-50 method.[52] For this purpose, production activity means an activity that creates, fabricates, manufactures, extracts, processes, cures, or ages inventory.[53]

---

[50] Code Sec. 865(e)(2) and (3). Another exception applies to income from the sale of unprocessed timber which is softwood and which was cut from an area within the United States. Such income is treated as U.S.-source income, regardless of where title passes. Code Sec. 865(b).

[51] Code Sec. 863(b), and Reg. §1.863-3(a)(1) and (b). Special rules apply to the sale of goods produced in the United States and sold in a U.S. possession (or vice versa). Reg. §§1.863-3(f) and 1.863-3A(c).

[52] Reg. §1.863-3(b)(1).

[53] Reg. §1.863-3(c)(1)(i)(A).

The 50-50 method is analogous to the apportionment formulas used to source a corporation's income for state income tax purposes. Under the 50-50 method, a U.S. manufacturer apportions 50% of the gross income from export sales based on a sales activity factor and the other 50% based on a production activity factor.[54] The sales activity factor equals the ratio of the gross amount of export sales that are classified as foreign (using the title passage rule) to the gross amount of all export sales.[55] The production activity factor equals the ratio of the average adjusted basis of the taxpayer's production assets located abroad to the average adjusted basis of the taxpayer's production assets everywhere. The average adjusted basis is computed by averaging the adjusted basis of production assets at the beginning and end of the taxable year. Production assets include tangible and intangible assets owned by the taxpayer and directly used to produce inventory sold abroad (e.g., a factory building, machinery and equipment, and patents). Production assets do not include accounts receivables, intangibles not related to the production of inventory (e.g., marketing intangibles, including trademarks and customer lists), transportation assets, warehouses, the inventory itself, raw materials, or work-in-process. In addition, production assets do not include cash or other liquid assets (including working capital), investment assets, prepaid expenses, or stock of a subsidiary.[56]

If a U.S. manufacturer's foreign production assets are insignificant or nonexistent and the taxpayer passes title abroad on all foreign sales, the 50-50 method will allocate roughly 50% of the taxpayer's gross income from export sales to foreign-source income.[57]

> **Example 3.16:** USAco, a domestic corporation, manufactures computers at its U.S. plant at a cost of $1,200 per unit. USAco markets its computers in Mexico through a branch sales office located in Mexico City with title passing in Mexico on these Mexican sales. During the year, USAco sold 1,000 computers through its Mexican branch at a price of $2,000 per unit. Therefore, USAco realized gross income of $800,000 [1,000 units × ($2,000 sales price – $1,200 cost of goods sold)] from its Mexican sales. USAco has no production assets located abroad, whereas the average value of its U.S. production assets is $5 million. As a result, the sales activity factor apportions $400,000 of income to foreign sources [50% × $800,000 × ($2 million of foreign export sales ÷ $2 million of total export sales)], and the production activity factor apportions no income to foreign sources [50% × $800,000 × ($0 of foreign production assets ÷ $5 million of production assets worldwide)]. In sum, the foreign-source portion of USAco's export gross income is $400,000 and the remaining $400,000 is U.S.-source income.

---

[54] Reg. § 1.863-3(b)(1) and (c).

[55] Reg. § 1.863-3(c)(2).

[56] Reg. § 1.863-3(c)(1). Production assets used to produce inventory sold both domestically and abroad are included in the formula based on the ratio of export sales of the related inventory to sales everywhere of that inventory.

[57] The regulations are generally less favorable for exporters of natural resources, which must apply a special export terminal rule. Reg. § 1.863-1(b). This rule applies to sales outside the United States of products derived from the ownership or operation of any farm, mine, oil or gas well, other natural deposit, or timber within the United States. Reg. § 1.863-1(b)(1). However, any income from the sale of unprocessed timber which is softwood and was cut from an area within the United States is always treated as U.S.-source income. Code Sec. 865(b).

After a taxpayer has apportioned the gross income from export sales based on the sales activity and production activity factors, the taxpayer then apportions any related deductions between U.S. and foreign source income on a pro rata basis.[58]

If the taxpayer regularly sells part of its output to independent distributors such that an independent factory price can be fairly established, the taxpayer may elect to use the independent factory price method.[59] Under the independent factory price method, any gross profit on export sales beyond that earned on sales to independent distributors is foreign-source income, assuming title passes abroad on export sales. The 50-50 method generally will classify more of a U.S. manufacturer's export profits as foreign-source income than will the independent factory price method. Therefore, it is generally not advantageous for purposes of the U.S. foreign tax credit to elect the independent factory price method. A taxpayer may also elect to use the books and records method, but only if the taxpayer receives advance permission from the IRS.[60]

Special rule for sales by nonresidents through a U.S. office. Notwithstanding any other source of income provision, if a nonresident (i.e., a foreign corporation) maintains an office or other fixed place of business in the United States, income from any sale of personal property (including inventory) attributable to that U.S. office is treated as U.S.-source income. This special rule does not apply, however, to inventory that is sold for use, disposition, or consumption outside the United States and an office or other fixed place of business of the taxpayer in a foreign country materially participates in the sale.[61]

Example **3.17:** ForCo, a foreign corporation that manufactures and sells widgets, has a U.S. branch that performs sales and warehousing functions with

---

[58] Reg. § 1.863-3(d). An exception applies to research and experimental expenditures.

[59] Reg. § 1.863-3(b)(2).

[60] Reg. § 1.863-3(b)(3).

[61] Code Sec. 865(e)(2).

¶302.06

respect to sales in North America. A Canadian customer purchases a widget that the U.S. branch office ships from its warehouse. If ForCo has a foreign office that materially participates in the sale, the sale is foreign-source income. If a foreign office of ForCo does not materially participate in the sale (e.g., the sales personnel in the U.S. branch perform all of the sales functions), the income is U.S.-source income.

Depreciable personal property. Depreciation deductions reduce a taxpayer's basis in the depreciable property and thereby increase the gain computed on the disposition of that property. The portion of the gain on the disposition of depreciable personal property that is attributable to prior depreciation deductions is treated as having the same source as the related deductions.[62] For example, if the prior depreciation deductions offset both U.S.-source and foreign-source income in prior years, the depreciation recapture portion of the gain is generally allocated between U.S.-source and foreign-source income in the same proportion as the prior deductions. A rule of administrative ease applies to property "used predominantly" in the United States (or outside the United States), under which all of the depreciation deductions related to such property are deemed to have been allocated to U.S.-source income (or foreign-source income).[63]

When the total gain exceeds the prior depreciation deductions (i.e., the property has appreciated in value since its acquisition), that appreciation is sourced using the rules applicable to inventories.[64] This generally means the gain is sourced based upon where title to the property passes from seller to buyer.[65]

Example 3.18: During the current year, USAco (a domestic corporation) sold a machine to a Canadian company for $230,000, with title passing to the buyer upon delivery in Canada. USAco purchased the machine several years ago for $200,000 and took $120,000 of depreciation deductions on the machine. USAco used the machine exclusively at its plant in the United States; therefore, the entire $120,000 of depreciation deductions are treated as having been

---

[62] Code Sec. 865(c)(1).

[63] Code Sec. 865(c)(3)(B). This exception does not apply to certain property used outside the United States, such as transportation and communication equipment.

[64] Code Sec. 865(c)(2).

[65] Code Sec. 865(b) and Reg. § 1.861-7(c).

¶302.06

allocated to U.S.-source income. USAco's adjusted basis in the machine is $80,000 [$200,000 original cost − $120,000 of accumulated depreciation], and the total gain on the sale of the machine is $150,000 [$230,000 sales price − $80,000 adjusted basis]. The $120,000 depreciation recapture portion of the gain is U.S.-source income, whereas the $30,000 of appreciation is foreign-source income.

Intangibles. For purposes of the source-of-income rules, an intangible is any patent, copyright, secret process or formula, goodwill, trademark, trade brand, franchise, or other like property.[66] As with depreciable personal property, a gain on the disposition of an intangible may be attributable in whole or in part to prior amortization deductions. The portion of the gain that is attributable to prior amortization deductions is treated as having the same source as the related deductions, determined using the same tracing rules applicable to depreciation on tangible personal property.[67] Unlike tangible personal property, however, the inventory source rules do not apply to any gain in excess of the depreciation recapture income.[68] Instead, any gain attributable to appreciation in the value of the intangible is sourced using the residence-of-seller rule, assuming the intangible is sold for a price that is not contingent on its productivity, use, or disposition.[69] If the intangible is sold for a price that is contingent on its productivity, use, or disposition, then the appreciation portion of the gain is sourced as if it were a royalty payment.[70] As discussed above, royalties are sourced based on the location of the actual use of, or the right to use, the underlying intangible.[71] A special rule also applies to a gain on the disposition of goodwill, which is treated as arising from sources within the country in which the goodwill was generated.[72]

Sale of stock of a foreign affiliate. Under the general rule, a domestic corporation treats a gain on the sale of stock as U.S.-source income.[73] However, if certain requirements are met, a domestic corporation can treat a gain on the sale of the stock of a foreign affiliate as foreign-source income, which has the beneficial side effect of increasing the taxpayer's foreign tax credit limitation (albeit in the passive category income basket). This exception applies if the following requirements are met:

  (i) the domestic corporation sells stock in an 80%-or-more-owned affiliate that is a foreign corporation,

  (ii) the sale occurs in a foreign country in which the affiliate is engaged in the active conduct of a trade or business, and

  (iii) the affiliate derived more than 50% of its gross income during the preceding three taxable years from the active conduct of a trade or business in such foreign country.[74]

---

[66] Code Sec. 865(d)(2).
[67] Code Sec. 865(d)(4)(A).
[68] Code Sec. 865(d)(4)(B).
[69] Code Sec. 865(d)(1)(A).
[70] Code Sec. 865(d)(1)(B).
[71] Code Secs. 861(a)(4) and 862(a)(4).
[72] Code Sec. 865(d)(3).

[73] Code Sec. 865(a).

[74] Code Sec. 865(f). For this purpose, an affiliate is a member of the same affiliated group as defined in Code Sec. 1504(a), but without regard to the domestic corporation requirement of Code Sec. 1504(b). Code Sec. 865(i)(4). In addition, for purposes of satisfying requirements (ii) and (iii), the domestic corporation can elect to treat the affiliate and all the corporations which are

Example **3.19:** USAco, a domestic corporation, owns all the stock of ForCo, a foreign corporation. During the past three years, ForCo has earned approximately 60% of its gross income from the active conduct of a trade or business in foreign country F. USAco personnel travel to foreign country F where they offer to sell all the shares of ForCo to a foreign purchaser. The deal is negotiated and closed in foreign country F. As a result, the gain on the sale of the ForCo shares is foreign-source income.

.07 Other Types of Income

Foreign currency gains and losses. Special source-of-income rules apply to a defined group of transactions referred to as "Section 988 transactions." Section 988 transactions include the following:

  (i) dispositions of a nonfunctional currency, and

  (ii) debt instruments, receivables and payables, and currency forward, futures, and option contracts, where the amount the taxpayer is entitled to receive, or required to pay, is denominated in (or determined by reference to) a nonfunctional currency.[75]

An example of a Section 988 transaction is a domestic corporation that makes a sale on account to a European customer where the sales price is denominated in the euros rather than the U.S. dollar.

Foreign currency gains and losses attributable to a Section 988 transaction are sourced by reference to the residence of the taxpayer or the qualified business unit of the taxpayer (e.g., a foreign branch) on whose books the underlying asset, liability, or item of income or expense is properly reflected.[76] For purposes of this source rule, a U.S. resident is any corporation, partnership, trust, or estate that is a U.S. person, as well as any individual who has a tax home in the United States.[77] An individual's tax home is his or her principal or regular place of business, provided that an individual is not treated as having a tax home in a foreign country during any period in which the taxpayer's abode is in the United States.[78] A foreign resident is any corporation, partnership, trust, or estate that is a foreign person, as well as any individual who has a tax home in a foreign country.[79] The residence of a qualified business unit of the taxpayer is the country in which the qualified business unit's principal place of business is located.[80]

A different source rule applies if the foreign currency gain or loss arises as a result of a branch remittance. If a foreign branch that has a functional currency

---

(Footnote Continued)

wholly owned, directly or indirectly, by the affiliate as one corporation.

[75] Code Sec. 988(c)(1).

[76] Code Sec. 988(a)(3)(A). However, any foreign currency gain or loss realized by a foreign person from the conduct of a U.S. trade or business is treated as U.S.-source income. Reg. § 1.988-4(c).

[77] Code Sec. 988(a)(3)(B)(i)(I) and (II).

[78] Code Secs. 988(a)(3)(B)(i)(I) and 911(d)(3), and Reg. § 1.911-2(b). An individual's abode is in the United States if that is where his or her economic, social, and

personal ties are closest. For example, *see J.T. Lemay,* CA-5, 88-1 USTC ¶ 9182, 837 F2d 681 (5th Cir. 1988). Aff'g 53 TCM 862, Dec. 43,931(M), TC Memo. 1987-256; *and D.P. Lansdown,* 68 TCM 680, Dec. 50,114(M), TC Memo. 1994-452. Aff'd, 73 F3d 373 (10th Cir. 1995)). An individual who does not have a tax home is treated as a U.S. resident if the individual is a U.S. citizen or resident alien, and a foreign resident if the individual is not a U.S. citizen or resident alien. Code Sec. 988(a)(3)(B)(i).

[79] Code Sec. 988(a)(3)(B)(i)(I) and (III).

[80] Code Sec. 988(a)(3)(B)(ii).

other than the U.S. dollar remits its earnings to the U.S. home office, then the U.S. parent must recognize a foreign currency gain or loss equal to the difference between the U.S. dollar value of the remittance and the U.S. parent's basis in the branch's accumulated earnings, as determined by prior year income inclusions.[81] The resulting gain or loss is sourced by reference to the source of income giving rise to the branch's accumulated earnings.[82] In a similar vein, if a U.S. shareholder receives a distribution from a foreign corporation of earnings previously taxed as either a Subpart F inclusion or a qualified electing fund inclusion, the U.S. shareholder must recognize a foreign currency gain or loss equal to the difference between the U.S. dollar value of the distribution and the U.S. shareholder's basis in the distributed earnings, as determined by the prior year income inclusions.[83] Such gains have the same source as the associated Subpart F or qualified electing fund inclusion.[84]

See Chapter 6 (¶ 603) for a more detailed discussion of foreign currency gains and losses.

Insurance underwriting income. Insurance income generally is sourced on the basis of where the insured risk is located. Therefore, premiums from issuing or reinsuring any insurance or annuity contract in connection with property located in the United States, a liability arising out of an activity located in the United States or in connection with the lives or health of residents of the United States, is treated as U.S.-source income.[85] Under an anti-abuse rule, U.S.-source insurance income also includes income from insuring risks located outside the United States if, as a result of an arrangement, another corporation receives a substantially equal amount of premiums for insuring risks located within the United States.[86] Any other type of underwriting income is treated as foreign-source income.[87]

International communications income. International communications income includes income derived from the transmission of communications or data from the United States to a foreign country or from a foreign country to the United States.[88] Examples include transmitting telephone calls or other data, images, or sounds by satellite or underwater cable. The source rule for international communications income varies depending on whether the taxpayer is a U.S. person or a foreign person. In the case of a U.S. person, 50% of international communications income is treated as U.S.-source income and the other 50% is treated as foreign-source income.[89] In contrast, a foreign person generally treats all international communications income as foreign-source income, unless that person maintains an office or other fixed place of business within the United States, in which case any income attributable to that fixed place of business is treated as U.S.-source income.[90]

Scholarships and fellowships. Scholarships and fellowships received by someone who is not required to perform services for the payer are sourced based

---

[81] Code Sec. 987(3) and Prop. Reg. § 1.987-5.

[82] Code Sec. 987(3)(B).

[83] Code Sec. 986(c)(1) and Notice 1988-71.

[84] Code Sec. 986(c)(1).

[85] Code Sec. 861(a)(7)(A).

[86] Code Sec. 861(a)(7)(B).

[87] Code Sec. 862(a)(7).

[88] Code Sec. 863(e)(2).

[89] Code Sec. 863(e)(1)(A).

[90] Code Sec. 863(e)(1)(B).

¶302.07

on the residence of the payer. Therefore, an award is treated as U.S.- source income if it is made by a U.S. citizen or resident, a domestic corporation, the United States (or any instrumentality or agency thereof), one of the 50 states (or any political subdivision thereof), or the District of Columbia. On the other hand, awards made by a nonresident alien, a foreign corporation, a foreign government (or any instrumentality, agency, or political subdivision thereof), or an international agency, are treated as foreign-source income.[91]

Social security benefits. U.S. social security benefits are considered U.S.-source income,[92] regardless of whether the recipient spent his or her employment years working in the United States or abroad.

Space and ocean activities. Space and ocean activities include any activity conducted in space, any activity conducted on or under water not within the jurisdiction of a foreign country or the United States and any activity conducted in Antarctica.[93] Examples include fishing and mining activities undertaken on the high seas. Space and ocean activities are unique in the sense that they do not take place within the territory of any country. As a result, income from space and ocean activities is treated as U.S.-source income if derived by a U.S. person and as foreign-source income if derived by a foreign person.[94] Space and ocean activities do not include any activity that gives rise to transportation income or international communications income, or any activity connected with a mine, oil and gas well, or other natural deposit in a continental shelf area.[95]

Transportation income. Transportation income includes income derived from the use or lease of a vessel or aircraft (including any container used in connection with a vessel or aircraft) or from the performance of services directly related to the use of a vessel or aircraft.[96] Transportation income does not include income derived from transporting passengers or property between the United States and a foreign country by truck, rail, or bus, which is sourced under different rules.[97]

Income from transportation that both begins and ends within the United States is treated as U.S.-source income.[98] If the transportation begins in the United States and ends abroad or begins abroad and ends in the United States, then 50% of the resulting income is treated as U.S.-source income and the other 50% is treated as foreign-source income.[99] This rule generally does not apply to transportation income derived from personal services performed by the taxpayer.[100] Therefore, flight and ship personnel source their compensation using the source rule for personal services income.

---

[91] Reg. § 1.863-1(d). An exception applies if a nonresident alien receives an award for study or research activities to be conducted outside the United States. Such grants are treated as foreign-source income, irrespective of the residence of the payer.

[92] Code Sec. 861(a)(8).

[93] Code Sec. 863(d)(2)(A).

[94] Code Sec. 863(d)(1).

[95] Code Sec. 863(d)(2)(B).

[96] Code Sec. 863(c)(3).

[97] *See* Reg. § 1.863-4.

[98] Code Sec. 863(c)(1). Round trip travel from the United States to a foreign country is not transportation that begins and ends in the United States.

[99] Code Sec. 863(c)(2)(A). The source of transportation income may be of little or no consequence to a foreign person since both the Code and numerous tax treaties provide exemptions for income from the international operation of a vessel or aircraft. For example, *see* Code Secs. 872(b) and 883(a).

[100] Code Sec. 863(c)(2)(B).

.08 Distributive Share of Income from a Pass-Through Entity

In the case of partnerships and S corporations, the source of income usually is determined at the entity level and that source characterization carries over to the partners or shareholders in their distributive shares of income.[101] For example, a partner's distributive share of a partnership's foreign-source dividend income is foreign-source income to the partner. The same principle applies to trusts. As a result, income of a trust has the same character in the hands of the beneficiary as in the hands of the trust.[102]

> **Example 3.20:** SCorp is a domestic S corporation that is owned by Larry (25%), Curly (25%) and Moe (50%). SCorp earns $100,000 of income, $20,000 of which is U.S.-source and $80,000 of which is foreign-source. As 25% shareholders, Larry and Curly each have $5,000 of U.S.-source income and $20,000 of foreign-source income. As a 50% shareholder, Moe has $10,000 of U.S.-source income and $40,000 of foreign-source income.

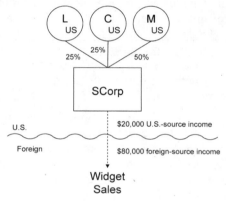

An exception applies to the sale of personal property by a partnership, in which case the applicable source rule is applied at the partner level rather than the partnership level.[103]

¶ 303 SOURCE RULES FOR DEDUCTIONS

.01 Introduction

Sourcing a taxpayer's gross income will be sufficient in some situations. For example, there is no need to source the deductions of a foreign person whose only connection to the United States is as a passive investor deriving U.S.-source investment-type income, since such income is taxed on a gross basis through a flat rate withholding tax.[104] In other cases, however, the operative tax attribute is net taxable income, which necessitates the sourcing of items of both gross income and deduction. For example, a foreign corporation with a branch office in the United States is taxed on the net amount of income effectively connected with the conduct

---

[101] Code Secs. 702(b) and 1366(b).
[102] Code Secs. 652(b) and 662(b).

[103] Code Sec. 865(i)(5).
[104] Code Secs. 871(a) and 881(a).

of that U.S. trade or business.[105] Similarly, a U.S. person's foreign tax credit limitation is based on the ratio of net taxable income from foreign sources to net taxable income from all sources.[106]

In computing taxable income from sources within (or without) the United States, the taxpayer is allowed deductions for expenses and losses directly related to either U.S.- or foreign-source gross income, as well as a ratable portion of expenses and losses that are not definitely related to any specific item of gross income.[107] The taxpayer makes these determinations through a two-step process commonly referred to as "allocation and apportionment."

.02 Allocation

The first step in sourcing a deduction is to allocate it to a related income-producing activity or class of gross income.[108] Examples of potential classes of gross income include compensation for services (including fees and commissions), gross income derived from business, gains derived from dealings in property, interest, rents, royalties, and dividends (see Figure 3.2).[109] A deduction is related, and therefore allocable, to a class of gross income if it is incurred as a result of, or incident to, the activity or property from which the gross income is derived. Therefore, the allocation rules emphasize the factual relationship between a deduction and a class of gross income. The classes of gross income are not predetermined, but instead, are determined on the basis of the deductions to be allocated. Although most deductions are definitely related to a specific class of gross income, some deductions are related to all gross income.[110] Examples include overhead, general and administrative, and supervisory expenses. These deductions ordinarily are allocated to a class consisting of all of the taxpayer's gross income.[111]

> **Example 3.21:** USAco, a domestic corporation, derives $800,000 of gross income from sales of services and $200,000 of gross income from product sales. USAco's expenses include $500,000 of salaries paid to service technicians, $130,000 of salaries paid to product salespersons, and $100,000 of rent paid on its headquarters offices. Because the rent expense is related to all of USAco's gross income, USAco allocates 80% of the rent expense to sales of services and 20% to product sales.

If the taxpayer incurring the expenses is a corporation that is a member of an affiliated group, the expense is allocated and apportioned as if all members of the group were a single corporation.[112]

---

[105] Code Sec. 882(a).

[106] Code Sec. 904(a).

[107] Code Secs. 861(b) and 862(b).

[108] Reg. § 1.861-8(a)(2).

[109] Reg. § 1.861-8(a)(3).

[110] Reg. § 1.861-8(b)(1) and (b)(2).

[111] Temp. Reg. § 1.861-8T(b)(3).

[112] Code Sec. 864(e)(6) and Temp. Reg. § 1.861-14T.

Figure 3.2 Allocation and apportionment of deductions

Step 1: Allocate deductions to a class of gross income	**Step 2:** Apportion deductions between U.S. and foreign sources
• Compensation for services	• Gross income
• Gross income from business	• Gross sales
• Gains from dealings in property	• Units sold
• Interest	• Cost of goods sold
• Rents	• Profit contributions
• Royalties	• Expenses incurred
• Dividends	• Assets used
	• Salaries paid
	• Space utilized
	• Time spent

.03 Apportionment

The second step in sourcing a deduction is to apportion the deduction between U.S.-source and foreign-source gross income.[113] This is accomplished by using an apportionment base that reflects, to a reasonably close extent, the factual relationship between the deduction and the gross income. Examples of potential apportionment bases include gross income, gross receipts or sales, units sold, cost of goods sold, profit contributions, expenses incurred, assets used, salaries paid, space utilized, and time spent (see Figure 3.2). The effect of the resulting apportionment on the tax liability and the related record-keeping burden are both considered when determining whether or not the apportionment is sufficiently precise.[114]

The relationship between deductions and U.S. and foreign operations is often ambiguous. For example, in theory, a U.S. exporter should apportion its marketing expenses between U.S. and foreign sources based upon the relative amounts of marketing resources expended to generate U.S., as opposed to foreign, sales. However, often it is unclear which, if any, of the conventional apportionment bases, such as unit sales, gross sales, or gross margin, accurately reflects this relation. Moreover, if the mix of products sold in the United States differs from the mix of products sold abroad, the use of different apportionment bases will lead to different results.

> **Example 3.22:** USAco is a domestic corporation that sells its products both in the United States and abroad. During the current year, USAco had $10 million of sales and a gross profit of $5 million, and incurred $1 million of selling, general, and administrative (SG&A) expenses. USAco's $10 million of sales included $6 million of foreign sales and $4 million of domestic sales. On

---

[113] Reg. § 1.861-8(a)(2).   [114] Temp. Reg. § 1.861-8T(c)(1).

¶303.03

the other hand, because USAco's domestic sales generally involved <u>higher margin products</u> than its foreign sales, USAco's gross profit of $5 million was split 50-50 between U.S. and foreign sources. So, <u>if USAco uses gross profit as an apportionment base, it would apportion $500,000 of SG&A expenses to foreign-source income</u> [50% × $1 million of SG&A expenses], <u>as opposed to $600,000 if gross sales is used as an apportionment base</u> [($6 million of foreign sales ÷ $10 million of total sales) × $1 million of SG&A expenses].

500 eP

600 GS

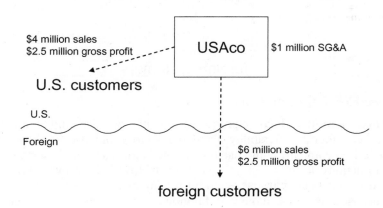

The selection of an apportionment base also is impacted by the type of records that the taxpayer maintains.

Example 3.23: The facts are the same as in Example 3.22, except now assume that USAco's SG&A expenses of $1 million consist of the president's salary of $250,000, the sales manager's salary of $100,000, and other SG&A expenses of $650,000. Also assume that USAco's president and sales manager maintain time records which indicate that the president devoted 30% of her time to foreign operations and 70% to domestic operations, while the sales manager devoted 40% of her time to foreign operations and 60% to domestic operations. USAco should now apportion the <u>salaries of the president and sales manager on the basis of time spent</u> and apportion the other SG&A expenses on the basis of gross profit. Therefore, USAco apportions to foreign-source income $75,000 of the president's salary [30% × $250,000], $40,000 of the sales manager's salary [40% × $100,000], and $325,000 of the remaining SG&A expenses [50% × $650,000], for a total of <u>$440,000 of SG&A expenses</u> apportioned to foreign-source income.[115]

440 T

---

[115] Compare Reg. § 1.861-8(g), Examples (19) and (20).

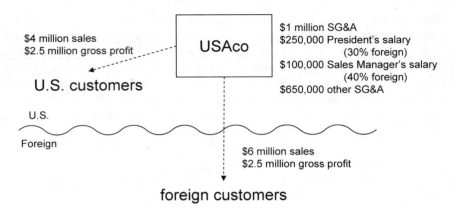

U.S. customers

$4 million sales
$2.5 million gross profit

USAco

$1 million SG&A
$250,000 President's salary
(30% foreign)
$100,000 Sales Manager's salary
(40% foreign)
$650,000 other SG&A

U.S.

Foreign

$6 million sales
$2.5 million gross profit

foreign customers

.04 Specialized Apportionment Rules

Interest expense. Income-producing activities require funding and a taxpayer often has considerable flexibility as to the source and use of those funds. For example, a U.S. company could use the proceeds from a second mortgage on a U.S. factory to acquire an office building located in Brazil. Moreover, when money is borrowed for a specific purpose, such borrowing generally will free other funds for other purposes. Because money is fungible, interest expense is assumed to be related to all of the taxpayer's activities and property, regardless of the specific purpose of the borrowing. Therefore, interest expense is allocated to all of the taxpayer's gross income.[116] Moreover, members of an affiliated group of U.S. corporations must allocate and apportion interest expense as if all the members of the affiliated group were a single corporation.[117]

Interest expense is apportioned between U.S.- and foreign-source income using assets as an apportionment base.[118] For example, if 20% of a taxpayer's assets are foreign in nature, then that taxpayer must apportion 20% of its interest expense to foreign-source income. For this purpose, an asset is characterized as U.S. or foreign based upon whether the asset produces U.S.-or foreign-source income.[119] For example, inventory is characterized as a foreign asset to the extent that inventory sales give rise to foreign-source income.[120] The physical location of the asset is not relevant. Normally, the asset figures for a taxable year are the averages of the adjusted basis amounts at the beginning and the end of the year.[121] In computing asset values, a taxpayer's basis in the stock of any nonaffiliated, 10%-or-more-owned corporation (e.g., a U.S. parent's basis in the stock of a controlled foreign corporation) is adjusted for changes in that investee's earnings and profits over time.[122]

In lieu of using adjusted basis amounts, a taxpayer may elect to apportion interest expense on the basis of the fair market value of its assets, which may be

---

[116] Temp. Reg. § 1.861-9T(a).
[117] Code Sec. 864(e)(1).
[118] Code Sec. 864(e)(2).
[119] Temp. Reg. § 1.861-9T(g)(3).

[120] Temp. Reg. § 1.861-12T(b).
[121] Temp. Reg. § 1.861-9T(g).
[122] Code Sec. 864(e)(4). Tax-exempt assets are not taken into account when computing a taxpayer's U.S. versus foreign assets. Code Sec. 864(e)(3).

advantageous if the adjusted basis of the taxpayer's U.S. assets is lower than their market value or if the adjusted basis of the taxpayer's foreign assets is higher than their market value.[123] Taxpayers may also elect to use the alternative tax book value method, which allows the taxpayer to depreciate its U.S. assets using the same alternative depreciation system (ADS) that applies to foreign assets.[124] The use of ADS depreciation for U.S. assets applies only for purposes of apportioning interest expense, and may increase the taxpayer's basis in its U.S. assets.

Under the CFC netting rule, a U.S. parent corporation may be required to specifically allocate a portion of its third-party interest expense against the interest income received from a controlled foreign corporation.[125] Congress enacted this provision to prevent a U.S. parent from borrowing money from third-party lenders and re-loaning the funds to its foreign subsidiaries (i.e., back-to-back loans) merely as a device to artificially increase the portion of worldwide income classified as foreign-source income. Absent the netting rule, back-to-back lending would create net foreign-source income for the U.S. parent because the entire amount of interest income would be foreign-source, whereas only a portion of the interest expense would be apportioned against foreign-source income.

Post-2020 election to apportion interest expense on a worldwide affiliated group basis. As discussed above, the interest expense of an affiliated group filing a U.S. consolidated return is apportioned between U.S.-source and foreign-source income. On the other hand, contrary to the fungibility assumption, the interest expense of a foreign subsidiary, which is not includible in the U.S. consolidated return, is effectively allocated 100% to foreign-source income.

> *Example 3.24:* USP, a domestic corporation, owns all the stock of FSub, a foreign corporation. USP has a basis of $1,000 in its U.S. operating assets and a basis of $500 in its shares of FSub. FSub has foreign operating assets with a basis of $600 as well as $200 of debt, on which FSub pays $20 of interest expense. Under current law, the full amount of FSub's $20 of interest expense is effectively allocated against USP's foreign-source income because it reduces FSub's earnings and profits and ultimately any dividends it pays to USP by $20.

---

[123] Reg. § 1.861-9T (g) (1) (ii).
[124] Reg. § 1.861-9 (i).

[125] Reg. § 1.861-10 (e).

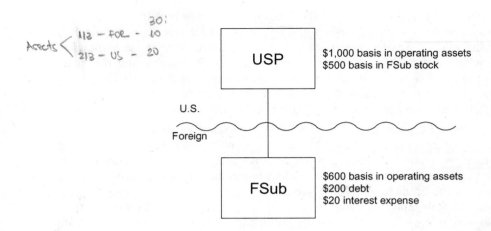

Assets $\Big\langle$ 113 — FOR — 10
213 — US — 20

30:

Example 3.25: The facts are the same as in Example 3.24, except that USP now has $300 of debt, on which it pays $30 of interest expense. Under current law, USP apportions $20 of interest expense to U.S.-source income ([$1,000 U.S. operating assets / $1,500 total assets] × $30 interest expense), and $10 of interest expense to foreign-source income ([$500 basis in FSub shares / $1,500 total assets] × $30 interest expense). Thus, any foreign-source dividend income derived by USP from FSub is reduced by the full amount of FSub's $20 in interest expense, as well as $10 (or one-third) of USP's interest expense. In sum, USP's foreign-source taxable income is arguably understated due to the asymmetric treatment of the interest expense incurred by USP and FSub.

CURRENT

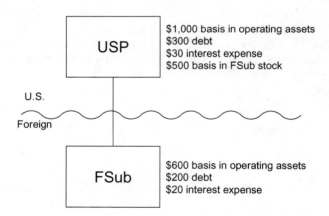

To address this issue, in 2004 Congress enacted Code Sec. 864(f), which permits a domestic corporation to elect to apportion interest expense on the basis of the taxpayer's worldwide affiliated group, which includes all 80% or more owned U.S. and foreign affiliates (other than certain financial institutions). Code Sec. 864(f) was originally scheduled to take effect for taxable years beginning after 2008.

¶303.04

Due to budgetary constraints, however, Congress has delayed the effective date until taxable years beginning after December 31, 2020.

Research and experimental expenditures. The rules for allocating and apportioning research and experimental (R&E) expenditures are found in Code Sec. 864(g) and Reg. § 1.861-17. These rules provide that a taxpayer must generally apportion the entire amount of the deduction for R&E expenditures incurred solely to meet legal requirements imposed by a government (i.e., legally mandated R&E) to that jurisdiction (U.S. or foreign). In contrast, deductions for non-legally mandated R&E expenditures are apportioned between U.S. and foreign sources using the sales method, unless the taxpayer elects to use the gross income method. This election applies to all R&E expenditures and is binding for five years.

Under the sales method, if more than 50% of R&E activities are performed in a single geographic source (U.S. or foreign), 50% of the deductions for non-legally mandated R&E are exclusively apportioned to that source. The remaining R&E deductions are apportioned based on proportion of U.S. and foreign sales of the related products. Under the gross income method, only 25% of the deductions for non-legally mandated R&E are exclusively apportioned to the geographic source where more than 50% of R&E activities are performed, and the remaining R&E deductions are apportioned based on proportion of U.S. and foreign source gross income (sales, royalties, etc.) derived from the related products. The amount of deductions apportioned to foreign-source income under the gross income method must be at least 50% of the amount apportioned to foreign-source income under the sales method, and the amount apportioned to U.S.-source income under the gross income method must be at least 50% of the amount apportioned to U.S.-source income under the sales method.

Members of an affiliated group of U.S. corporations must allocate and apportion R&E deductions as if all the members of the affiliated group were a single corporation.

Losses from disposition of stock and other personal property. Losses from the sale or other disposition of stock and other personal property are generally sourced under the same rules that apply to gains from such property, that is, based on the residence of the seller.[126] For example, a loss from the sale of stocks and bonds issued by U.S. corporations are classified as foreign-source income if the seller resides outside the United States. However, as with the source rules governing gains from personal property, numerous exceptions apply. Exceptions governing stock sales include a recapture rule with respect to dividends received within 24 months of the stock sale,[127] stock attributable to a foreign office,[128] stock of an S corporation[129] and stock of a real property holding company.[130] Exceptions governing sales of personal property other than stock include inventory sales,[131]

---

[126] Reg. § 1.865-2 (stock) and Reg. § 1.865-1 (personal property).

[127] A de minimis exception applies when the dividend is less than 10% of the recognized loss. Reg. § 1.865-2(b)(1).

[128] Reg. § 1.865-2(a)(2).

[129] Reg. § 1.865-2(b)(3).

[130] Reg. § 1.865-2(a)(4).

[131] Reg. § 1.865-1(c)(2).

depreciable property,[132] foreign currency and certain financial instruments,[133] losses attributable to a foreign office[134] and trade receivables and certain interest equivalents.[135]

Other specialized rules. Code Sec. 861 and the regulations thereunder provide additional guidance regarding the following types of deductions:

(i) *Legal and accounting expenses*—Legal and accounting expenses incurred with respect to a specific property or activity (for example, to obtain a patent) are allocated to the gross income produced by that property or activity (for example, royalties from the patent). On the other hand, the cost of general legal and accounting functions is allocated to all gross income and apportioned on the basis of gross income.[136]

(ii) *State income taxes*—State income taxes are allocated to the gross income on which the taxes were imposed and apportioned on the basis of gross income.[137]

(iii) *Net operating losses*—A net operating loss deduction allowed under Code Sec. 172 is allocated and apportioned in the same manner as the deductions giving rise to the net operating loss deduction.[138]

(iv) *Stewardship expenses attributable to dividends*—Expenses associated with stewardship activities (e.g., activities undertaken by a parent corporation as an investor in a subsidiary) are allocated to the class of gross income that includes the dividends received from the subsidiary.[139]

(v) *Standard deduction*—The standard deduction is allocated to all of the individual taxpayer's gross income and apportioned on the basis of gross income.[140]

(vi) *Certain personal expenses*—An individual taxpayer's deductions for real estate taxes on a personal residence, medical expenses, and alimony payments are allocated to all of the taxpayer's gross income and apportioned on the basis of gross income.[141]

(vii) *Personal exemption*—Personal exemption deductions are not taken into account for purposes of allocating and apportioning deductions.[142]

(viii) *Charitable contributions*—Charitable contributions are allocated to all of the taxpayer's gross income and apportioned on the basis of gross income.[143]

---

[132] Reg. § 1.865-1(b)(1).
[133] Reg. § 1.865-1(c)(1).
[134] Reg. § 1.865-1(a)(2).
[135] Reg. § 1.865-1(c)(3).
[136] Reg. § 1.861-8(e)(5).
[137] Reg. § 1.861-8(e)(6).

[138] Reg. § 1.861-8(e)(8).
[139] Reg. § 1.861-8(e)(4).
[140] Code Secs. 861(b) and 862(b).
[141] Reg. § 1.861-8(e)(9).
[142] Reg. § 1.861-8(e)(11).
[143] Temp. Reg. § 1.861-8(e)(12).

Chapter 4
Foreign Tax Credit

¶ 401 INTRODUCTION

The United States mitigates international double taxation by allowing U.S. persons a credit for any foreign income taxes paid on their foreign-source income. Chapter 4 explains how to compute the direct foreign tax credit, the deemed paid foreign tax credit, and the foreign tax credit limitation. Chapter 4 also discusses some planning strategies for maximizing the credit.

Example **4.1:** USAco operates an Asian branch that generates $10 million of foreign-source taxable income, on which USAco pays $2 million of foreign income taxes. Under Code Sec. 901, USAco may claim a credit for the $2 million of foreign income taxes. Assuming a U.S. tax rate of 35%, USAco must pay only $1.5 million of U.S. tax ([35% U.S. tax rate × $10 million taxable income] – $2 foreign tax credit) on the $10 million of foreign-source taxable income.

.01 Computing the Foreign Tax Credit

The United States taxes U.S. persons on all income, regardless of its source.[1] This creates a double taxation problem with respect to a U.S. person's foreign-source income, since foreign countries usually tax all the income earned within their borders, including income derived by U.S. persons. If the United States did nothing to mitigate international double taxation, U.S. persons would be at a competitive disadvantage in overseas markets, since their total tax rate would exceed that of their foreign competitors by the amount of the U.S. tax burden on foreign-source income. The centerpiece of the U.S. system for mitigating international double taxation is the foreign tax credit.[2]

The computation of the foreign tax credit is a three-step process, as follows:

Step 1—Compute creditable foreign income taxes. To be creditable, a foreign levy must be a tax, the predominant character of which is an income tax in the U.S. sense.[3]

Step 2—Compute the foreign tax credit limitation. A key feature of the U.S. credit system is the foreign tax credit limitation, which restricts the credit to the portion of the pre-credit U.S. tax on total taxable income that is attributable to foreign-source taxable income.[4] The purpose of the limitation is to confine the effects of the credit to mitigating double taxation of foreign-source income. The limitation accomplishes this by preventing U.S. persons operating in high-tax foreign countries from offsetting those higher foreign taxes against the U.S. taxes on U.S.-source income. As discussed below in the section entitled Separate Category of Income Limitations (¶ 405), separate limitations apply to foreign income taxes imposed on passive category income and general category income.

---

[1] Code Sec. 61(a).
[2] Code Sec. 901(a).

[3] Reg. § 1.901-2(a)(1).
[4] Code Sec. 904(a).

Step 3—Determine the lesser of creditable foreign income taxes (step 1) or the foreign tax credit limitation (step 2). Creditable foreign taxes in excess of the limitation cannot be claimed as a credit in the current year. However, these excess credits can be carried back one year and carried forward up to ten years and taken as a credit in a year that the limitation exceeds foreign income taxes.[5]

Example 4.2: USAco has $10 million of taxable income, including $3 million of foreign-source taxable income, on which USAco paid $1.5 million in foreign income taxes. Assume that the U.S. tax rate is 35%.

Step 1: Compute the foreign income taxes	$1.5 million
Step 2: Compute the foreign tax credit limitation	
(A) Total taxable income	$10 million
(B) Pre-credit U.S. tax [35% × $10 million] . .	$3.5 million
(C) Foreign-source taxable income	$3 million
Limitation = [line B × (C ÷ A)]	
= [$3.5 million × ($3 million ÷ $10 million)] .	$1,050,000
Step 3: Credit equals the lesser of creditable taxes ($1.5 million)	
or the limitation ($1,050,000)	$1,050,000

USAco can carry its excess credits of $450,000 [$1,500,000 − $1,050,000] back one year and forward ten years.

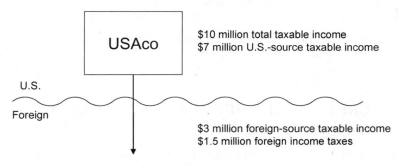

Foreign Operations

.02 Credit versus Deduction

Taxpayers have the option of deducting foreign income taxes in lieu of taking a credit.[6] A double tax benefit is not allowed, however, and a taxpayer cannot both deduct and claim a credit for the same foreign income taxes.[7] Generally, <u>a credit is more advantageous than a deduction</u> because a credit reduces a person's tax dollar for dollar as opposed to a reduction in taxable income. For example, if a domestic

---

[5] Code Sec. 904(c).
[6] Code Sec. 164(a).

[7] Code Sec. 275(a)(4).

corporation is subject to U.S. tax at a 35% rate, deducting $1 of foreign income taxes saves only $0.35 in taxes, compared to $1 in tax savings from a credit.

The choice between a deduction and a credit applies to all foreign income taxes paid or accrued during the year.[8] In other words, a taxpayer cannot claim a credit for a portion of the foreign income taxes incurred in a taxable year and claim a deduction for the remaining foreign income taxes. However, taxpayers can change their election from year to year. In addition, taxpayers can change their election any time before the expiration of the applicable statute of limitations, which is 10 years in the case of a refund claim based on the foreign tax credit.[9] A taxpayer makes the annual election to claim a credit by attaching Form 1118 (for domestic corporations) or Form 1116 (for individuals) to its annual tax return.[10] In the case of a partnership or S corporation, the election to claim a credit in lieu of a deduction for the foreign income taxes paid or accrued by the partnership or S corporation is made at the partner or shareholder level.[11]

.03 Who Can Claim a Credit

The purpose of the foreign tax credit is to mitigate double taxation of foreign-source income. Therefore, the credit is available to U.S. citizens, resident aliens, and domestic corporations, all of which are subject to U.S. taxation on a worldwide basis.[12] An affiliated group of U.S. corporations that files a consolidated return computes its foreign tax credit on a consolidated basis.[13] A U.S. citizen, resident alien or domestic corporation that is a partner in a partnership or a beneficiary of an estate or trust may also claim a credit for a proportionate share of the creditable foreign taxes incurred by the partnership, estate, or trust.[14] The rules applicable to partners in a partnership also apply to shareholders in an S corporation.[15]

In certain limited situations, nonresident alien individuals and foreign corporations can claim a foreign tax credit against the U.S. tax on their income effectively connected to the conduct of a U.S. trade or business.[16] See the discussion in Chapter 10 (¶ 1001).

¶ 402 CREDITABLE FOREIGN INCOME TAXES

.01 Qualifying Foreign Levies

The foreign tax credit is intended to mitigate international double taxation of a U.S. person's foreign-source income. Therefore, the United States restricts the credit to foreign income taxes that duplicate the U.S. income tax against which the credit is taken. Specifically, to be creditable under Code Sec. 901, a foreign levy must satisfy the following two requirements:

---

[8] Reg. § 1.901-1(c).
[9] Reg. § 1.901-1(d) and Code Sec. 6511(d)(3)(A).
[10] Reg. § 1.905-2(a).
[11] Code Secs. 703(b)(3) and 1363(c)(2)(B).
[12] Code Sec. 901(b)(1)–(3).

[13] Reg. § 1.1502-4(c).
[14] Code Sec. 901(b)(5).
[15] Code Sec. 1373(a).
[16] Code Secs. 901(b)(4) and 906.

   (i) the levy must be a tax paid to a foreign country, a political subdivision of a foreign country, or a U.S. possession (i.e., Puerto Rico, the Virgin Islands, Guam, the Northern Mariana Islands, and American Samoa), and

   (ii) the predominant character of the tax must be that of an income tax in the U.S. sense.[17]

If a foreign levy satisfies the first requirement but not the second, the foreign tax may still be creditable under Code Sec. 903 as a tax imposed "in lieu of" an income tax.[18] Foreign taxes other than income taxes, such as sales and property taxes, are not creditable but generally are deductible.[19]

Tax requirement. A foreign levy is a tax if it requires a compulsory payment pursuant to the authority of a foreign country to levy taxes. Penalties, fines, interest and custom duties do not qualify. A payment of a foreign levy is not considered compulsory if it exceeds the amount of the liability under foreign tax law. In other words, a U.S. taxpayer is obligated to determine its foreign income taxes in such a way as to reduce, over time, its reasonably expected tax liability, and exhaust all effective and practical administrative remedies to reduce its liability for foreign taxes.[20] The policy underlying this requirement is that the United States does not want to cede primary taxing jurisdiction with respect to credits for foreign taxes that did not have to be paid. As a practical matter, the taxpayer may wish to obtain an opinion from foreign counsel stating that only the proper amount of foreign taxes has been paid and that it would be unreasonable, ineffective and unpractical to try to lower the amount of foreign taxes through further administrative procedures.[21]

Example 4.3: USCo, a domestic corporation, owns UKCo, a United Kingdom corporation, which in turn owns DutchCo, a Dutch corporation that is treated as a disregarded entity for U.S. tax purposes. Due to a transfer pricing dispute regarding product sales by UKCo to DutchCo, DutchCo pays an assessment for additional Dutch taxes. DutchCo procures Dutch counsel, which opines that it would be impossible to reduce the Dutch tax further by appealing the assessment, which would include pursuing competent authority procedures. As a result, the payment of the foreign tax assessment would be considered compulsory, and DutchCo would have additional creditable foreign income taxes.

---

[17] Code Sec. 901(b) and Reg. § 1.901-2(a)(1).
[18] Code Sec. 903.
[19] Code Sec. 164(a).

[20] Reg. § 1.901-2(e)(5)(i).
[21] *Procter & Gamble v. Comm'r*, 2010-2 USTC ¶ 50,593 (S.D. Oh).

A foreign levy also does not qualify as a tax if the payer receives a specific economic benefit in exchange for the levy.[22] Historically, the problem of distinguishing taxes from payments for specific economic benefits has been most difficult in the oil and gas industry. In countries where the government owns the oil and gas resources, the local treasury is in a position to both collect taxes on a U.S. oil and gas company's profits and receive royalties from those same companies. Therefore, the foreign government might designate as a tax what is actually a royalty, without affecting its total revenues. If the characterization of the payment as a tax is accepted for U.S. tax purposes, a U.S. company could claim a credit for what should be only a deductible royalty expense.

To prevent this result, a foreign levy is not considered a tax to the extent the taxpayer receives a specific economic benefit in exchange for the levy. A person who is both a taxpayer and the recipient of a specific economic benefit is referred to as a dual-capacity taxpayer. Dual-capacity taxpayers have the burden of establishing what portion of a levy is a tax[23] and can use either a facts and circumstances approach or an elective safe-harbor method to satisfy their burden of proof.[24]

Income tax requirement. It generally is fairly obvious whether a particular levy is a tax on income, as opposed to a tax on some other base. However, governments occasionally impose hybrid taxes that are difficult to classify, such as a tax on the value of minerals extracted from mining, a tax on the receipts from banking, or a tax on windfall profits.[25] Such taxes are creditable only if their predominant character is that of an income tax in the U.S. sense.[26] In this regard, three aspects of U.S. income taxation are considered fundamental, and the foreign

---

[22] Reg. § 1.901-2(a)(2)(i).

[23] Reg. § 1.901-2(a)(2)(i).

[24] Reg. § 1.901-2A(c) and (d).

[25] *See*, for example, *Entergy Corporation*, CA-5, 2012-1 USTC ¶ 50,386, *aff'g* 100 TCM 202, CCH Dec. 58,326(M); and *PPL Corporation*, SCt, 2013-1 USTC ¶ 50,335, *rev'g* CA-3, 2012-1 USTC ¶ 50,115.

[26] Reg. § 1.901-2(a)(1).

levy must exhibit each of these characteristics in order to be considered an income tax.[27]

(i) *Realization test*—The tax must be imposed on income resulting from an exchange transaction or other event that would trigger a realization of income under U.S. principles.[28]

(ii) *Gross receipts test*—The tax must be imposed either upon actual gross receipts or according to a formulary method that is not likely to produce an amount that is greater than fair market value.[29]

(iii) *Net income test*—The tax base must permit the recovery of significant costs and expenses attributable to the taxpayer's gross income.[30]

Even if a tax satisfies all three requirements, the tax will still be denied income tax status if it is a soak-up tax.[31] A soak-up tax is a levy that a host country imposes only if the taxpayer can claim the tax as a credit on its home country tax return.[32] Soak-up taxes allow a country to collect taxes on inbound investments with the cost borne solely by the foreign investors' home country. Denying a credit for a soak-up tax does not result in double taxation because a soak-up tax is not imposed if a credit is not available. Income tax status also is denied to any foreign levy that a foreign country uses to provide some type of subsidy to the taxpayer, a related person, or any party to a transaction to which the taxpayer is a party.[33]

Foreign withholding taxes. Creditable taxes also include any foreign taxes imposed "in lieu of" an income tax.[34] The most common type of in-lieu-of tax are the flat rate withholding taxes that most countries impose on the gross amount of interest, dividends, rents, and royalties derived by passive offshore investors. Withholding is required because it is the only sure way to collect taxes from passive offshore investors. In order to withhold, the withholding agent must be able to readily ascertain both the tax base and the applicable rate. This explains both the gross basis taxation and the use of a flat tax rate since it would be difficult for the withholding agent to determine the offshore investor's allocable expenses and appropriate tax bracket based on total taxable income. A withholding tax generally does not qualify as an income tax because no deductions are allowed in computing the tax base, which results in failing the net income test (test iii, above).[35] A withholding tax is creditable, however, if it is imposed in lieu of the foreign country's general income tax, which is generally the case.[36]

Taxpayers cannot claim a credit for foreign withholding taxes imposed on dividends unless the taxpayer holds the stock of the foreign corporation for at least 16 days during the 31-day period beginning 15 days before the ex-dividend date. In the case of dividends on preferred stock, the requisite holding period increases to 46 days during a 91-day period. The holding period requirement does not apply to

---

[27] Reg. § 1.901-2(a)(3)(i) and (b)(1).
[28] Reg. § 1.901-2(b)(2).
[29] Reg. § 1.901-2(b)(3).
[30] Reg. § 1.901-2(b)(4).
[31] Reg. § 1.901-2(a)(3)(ii).

[32] Reg. § 1.901-2(c)(1).
[33] Code Sec. 901(i) and Reg. § 1.901-2(e)(3).
[34] Code Sec. 903.
[35] Reg. § 1.901-2(b)(4).
[36] Reg. § 1.903-1(b)(3), Example 2.

security dealers.[37] These minimum holding period requirements also apply to foreign withholding taxes imposed on interest, rent and royalty income.[38] Congress enacted these provisions to curtail tax-avoidance transactions designed to transfer foreign tax credits from persons unable to realize a benefit from the credit to persons that can use the credit.[39]

Denial of credit for taxes paid to sanctioned countries. In an attempt to further U.S. foreign policy objectives, a credit is denied to any foreign income taxes paid to a country whose government the United States does not recognize, does not conduct diplomatic relations with, or has designated as a government that repeatedly supports acts of international terrorism.[40] This provision currently applies to Cuba, Iran, North Korea, Sudan, and Syria.[41]

In addition, any taxpayer who participates in or cooperates with an international boycott must reduce its creditable foreign taxes by an international boycott factor.[42] Countries that may require participation in or cooperation with an international boycott include Iraq, Kuwait, Lebanon, Libya, Qatar, Saudi Arabia, Syria, United Arab Emirates, and Yemen.[43]

.02 Accounting Method

Accrual-basis taxpayers compute the foreign tax credit on an accrual basis.[44] Under the accrual method, creditable foreign income taxes equal the taxpayer's foreign tax liability for the current year, regardless of when those taxes are actually paid. Normal accrual-basis accounting principles apply when determining the liability for the year. Therefore, a foreign tax liability cannot be accrued unless all the events have occurred that determine the fact of the liability and the amount of the liability can be determined with reasonable accuracy.[45]

Cash-basis taxpayers generally compute the credit on a cash basis.[46] Under the cash method, creditable foreign taxes equal the amount of foreign income taxes paid during the year, regardless of whether the payment relates to the current year or some other year. A tax payment is not creditable, however, to the extent that it is reasonably certain that the amount will be refunded in the future.[47]

Cash-basis taxpayers can elect to compute the credit on an accrual basis. Once made, this election applies for all subsequent years.[48] Allowing cash-basis taxpayers to account for foreign income taxes on an accrual basis may provide a better matching of foreign income taxes to the associated foreign-source income. Matching is important because the foreign tax credit limitation for a given year is based on the amount of foreign-source income recognized in that year.

---

[37] Code Sec. 901(k).

[38] Code Sec. 901(l).

[39] See Notice 2004-19, IRB 2004-11.

[40] Code Sec. 901(j).

[41] Rev. Rul. 2005-3, IRB 2005-3. Cuba is under review.

[42] Code Sec. 908.

[43] 80 F.R. 17152.

[44] Reg. § 1.905-1(a).

[45] Reg. § 1.446-1(c)(1)(ii). The economic performance requirement does not apply to an accrual for foreign taxes. Reg. § 1.461-4(g)(6)(iii)(B).

[46] Reg. § 1.905-1(a).

[47] Reg. § 1.901-2(e)(2)(i).

[48] Code Sec. 905(a).

.03 Currency Translation

Income taxes are paid in the currency of the country imposing the tax. Consequently, in order to compute its foreign tax credit, a U.S. taxpayer must translate its foreign income taxes into U.S. dollars. Accrual-basis taxpayers generally translate foreign income taxes into U.S. dollars using the average exchange rate for the tax year to which the taxes relate.[49] On the other hand, cash-basis taxpayers translate foreign income taxes into U.S. dollars using the spot rate (i.e., the exchange rate on the date of payment).[50] See Chapter 6 (¶ 602) for more details.

¶ 403 EXCESS CREDIT VERSUS EXCESS LIMITATION POSITIONS

.01 Purpose of Limitation

After a taxpayer has computed the amount of creditable foreign income taxes, the next step is to compute the foreign tax credit limitation. The limitation equals the portion of the pre-credit U.S. tax that is attributable to foreign-source income.[51] The purpose of the limitation is to confine the effects of the credit to mitigating double taxation of foreign-source taxable income. The limitation accomplishes this by preventing U.S. persons operating in high-tax foreign countries from offsetting those higher foreign taxes against the U.S. tax on U.S.-source taxable income.

> **Example 4.4:** During the current year, USAco has $200 of U.S.-source taxable income and $100 of foreign-source taxable income that is subject to foreign income taxation. Assume that the foreign tax rate is 45% and the U.S. tax rate is 35%.

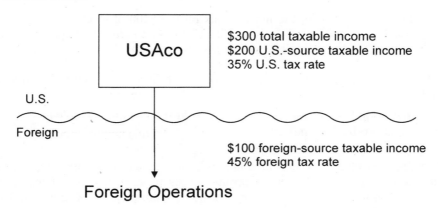

> *Case 1—Credit is limited:* If the foreign tax credit is limited to the U.S. tax on foreign-source income (i.e., 35% × $100 = $35), the total tax on USAco's $300 of total income is $115, computed as follows:

---

[49] Code Sec. 986(a)(1).
[50] Code Sec. 986(a)(2)(A).

[51] Code Sec. 904(a).

Foreign tax return		U.S. tax return	
Taxable income	$100	Taxable income	$300
Foreign tax rate	× .45	U.S. tax rate	× .35
Foreign tax	$ 45	Pre-credit tax	$105
		Foreign tax credit	– 35
		U.S. tax	$ 70

Case 2—No limitation: If there were no limitation on the foreign tax credit, the total tax on USAco's total income would drop from $115 to $105, computed as follows:

Foreign tax return		U.S. tax return	
Taxable income	$100	Taxable income	$300
Foreign tax rate	× .45	U.S. tax rate	× .35
Foreign tax	$ 45	Pre-credit tax	$105
		Foreign tax credit	– 45
		U.S. tax	$ 60

Without the limitation, the net U.S. tax on the $100 of foreign-source taxable income is negative $10 [$35 pre-credit U.S. tax – $45 credit], which reduces the U.S. tax on USAco's domestic profits from $70 to $60.

Taxpayers compute their foreign tax credit limitation using the following formula.[52]

$$\text{Pre-credit U.S. tax on Total taxable income} \quad \times \quad \frac{\text{Foreign-source taxable income}}{\text{Total taxable income}}$$

With a single foreign tax credit limitation, all foreign-source income, regardless of its character (e.g., active business profits versus passive investment income) or country of origin (e.g., low-tax country versus high-tax country), is commingled to arrive at a single limitation. It also is possible to make more precise comparisons of the U.S. and foreign tax burdens on foreign-source income, including separate category of income limitations and separate country limitations. As discussed later in this chapter, taxpayers currently must compute separate limitations for two different categories of income.[53]

---

[52] Code Sec. 904(a).   [53] Code Sec. 904(d).

¶403.01

.02 Exemption for Individuals with *De Minimis* Foreign Tax Credits

An individual with $300 or less of creditable foreign income taxes may elect to be exempt from the foreign tax credit limitation, provided he or she has no foreign-source income other than passive investment income. The $300 amount is increased to $600 in the case of married persons filing a joint return. Congress enacted this provision to relieve individuals of the need to file Form 1116 in situations where the amount of the foreign tax credit is small. If the election is made, the creditable foreign taxes are limited to the amount reported on a payee statement furnished to the taxpayer.[54]

.03 Importance of Relative Tax Rates

The relation of U.S. and foreign tax rates is a major determinant of whether a taxpayer is in an excess limitation or an excess credit position. Taxpayers will be in an excess limitation position when the foreign tax rate on a taxpayer's foreign-source taxable income is lower than the U.S. rate, and in an excess credit position when the foreign tax rate is higher than the U.S. rate. Other factors that impact the effective foreign tax rate, such as the use of different accounting methods or local country tax incentives, will also affect whether a taxpayer is in an excess limitation or an excess credit position.

Example 4.5: USAco has foreign-source taxable income of $100 and no U.S.-source taxable income. Assume the U.S. tax rate is 35%.

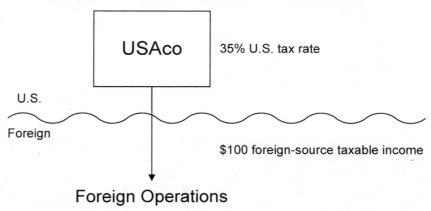

Case 1—Foreign tax rate is 30%: If USAco's foreign-source taxable income is subject to foreign income tax at a rate of 30%, USAco can claim a credit for the entire $30 of foreign income taxes paid, as follows:

---

[54] Code Sec. 904(k). The election is not available to estates or trusts.

U.S. tax return		Foreign tax return	
Taxable income	$100	Taxable income	$100
U.S. tax rate	× .35	Foreign tax rate	× .30
Pre-credit tax	$ 35	Foreign tax	$ 30
Foreign tax credit	– 30		
U.S. tax	$ 5		

Case 2—Foreign tax rate is 40%: If the foreign income tax rate is 40% rather than 30%, the foreign tax credit limitation (which equals the U.S. tax of $35 on USAco's $100 of foreign-source income) will prevent USAco from claiming a credit for $5 of the $40 of foreign income taxes paid, as follows:

U.S. tax return		Foreign tax return	
Taxable income	$100	Taxable income	$100
U.S. tax rate	× .35	Foreign tax rate	× .40
Pre-credit tax	$ 35	Foreign tax	$ 40
Foreign tax credit	– 35		
U.S. tax	$ 0		

.04 Planning Implications

The foreign tax credit limitation determines whether foreign taxes have an incremental effect on a U.S. person's total tax costs. When a taxpayer is in an excess limitation position (i.e., the taxpayer's creditable foreign taxes are less than the limitation), foreign taxes do not represent an out-of-pocket tax cost since the cost of paying those taxes is entirely offset by the U.S. tax savings associated with the credit. Therefore, tax planning focuses on reducing the residual U.S. tax due on foreign-source income. In contrast, when a taxpayer is in an excess credit position (i.e., creditable foreign taxes exceed the limitation), no U.S. tax is collected on foreign-source income because the credit fully offsets the pre-credit U.S. tax on that income. In addition, the noncreditable foreign income taxes increase the total tax burden on foreign-source income beyond what it would have been if only the United States had taxed that income.[55] Therefore, planning focuses on reducing those excess credits.

---

[55] Although creditable foreign taxes in excess of the limitation cannot be taken in the current year, they can be carried back one year and carried forward up to ten years and taken as a credit in a year in which the limitation exceeds the amount of creditable foreign taxes. Code Sec. 904(c).

¶ 404 STRATEGIES FOR ELIMINATING EXCESS CREDITS

Strategies for eliminating excess credits include foreign tax reduction planning, increasing the limitation, and cross-crediting.

.01 Foreign Tax Reduction Planning

When a taxpayer is in an excess limitation position, any decrease in foreign tax costs is accompanied by an offsetting increase in the residual U.S. tax on foreign income. As a result, foreign tax reduction planning has no effect on the taxpayer's total tax costs.[56] The circumstances are quite different, however, for U.S. persons in excess credit positions. Foreign taxes increase the total tax costs of such taxpayers by the amount of the excess credits. As a consequence, every dollar of foreign income taxes saved reduces the taxpayer's total tax costs by a dollar, up to the amount of excess credits.

The techniques that a U.S. person can use to reduce foreign income taxes often are the same as those used to reduce income taxes in a purely domestic context. Examples include taking advantage of any special exemptions, deductions, or credits provided by local law, realizing income in a form that is taxed at a lower rate (such as a preferential rate for capital gains), deferring the recognition of gross income, and accelerating the recognition of deductions. Other foreign tax reduction planning strategies, including the use of debt financing, transfer pricing, and tax treaties, are discussed in Chapter 8 (¶ 805).

> **Example 4.6:** USCo plans to build a new plant in country F, which offers low production costs. Unfortunately, country F has a 40% corporate tax rate, which is problematic because USCo is in an excess credit position. To address this issue, USCo negotiates a tax holiday with the government of country F, which is eager to attract foreign investment. Under the agreement, USCo will pay tax at only a 25% rate for ten years.

.02 Increasing the Limitation

A second basic strategy for reducing excess credits is to increase the foreign tax credit limitation by increasing the proportion of total taxable income that is classified as foreign-source income for U.S. tax purposes. As a consequence, the U.S. rules for sourcing gross income and deductions can play an important role in eliminating excess credits. For example, the title-passage rule for sourcing the income from inventory sales provides U.S. companies with a significant opportunity to increase foreign-source income. By arranging for the passage of title in the foreign country rather than the United States, export sales will generate foreign-source income.

Recharacterizing deductions also is an effective strategy for eliminating excess credits. Deductions reduce a taxpayer's pre-credit U.S. tax, regardless of how they are sourced. However, if the deduction is allocated to foreign-source income, the deduction also reduces the foreign tax credit limitation. As a result, a taxpayer in an

---

[56] However, foreign tax reduction planning does affect the allocation of tax revenues between the United States and other countries. Reducing foreign taxes reduces the foreign tax credit and, in turn, increases U.S. tax revenues.

excess credit position derives no net U.S. tax benefit from deductions allocated to foreign-source income. In contrast, deductions allocated to U.S.-source income do not affect the foreign tax credit limitation and, therefore, provide a full U.S. tax benefit. An example of how a taxpayer can recharacterize deductions is the use of alternative apportionment bases for sourcing selling, general, and administrative expenses that reduce the amount of these deductions allocated to foreign-source income (see ¶ 303).

As with any international tax planning strategy, reducing excess credits by resourcing gross income and deductions requires a careful analysis of both U.S. and foreign tax consequences. In particular, if a taxpayer takes an action that increases foreign-source income for both U.S. and foreign tax purposes, the resourced income may increase the taxpayer's foreign tax costs more than it increases the taxpayer's foreign tax credit limitation. If this happens, the net effect of the action may be an increase, rather than the desired decrease, in the taxpayer's excess credits. Therefore, the effectiveness of resourcing income as a strategy for eliminating excess credits depends on the existence of differences between the source-of-income rules used by the United States and other countries.

> **Example 4.7:** USAco has $2 million of U.S.-source taxable income and $4 million of foreign-source taxable income that is subject to foreign income tax. Further assume that the foreign income tax rate is 50% and the U.S. rate is 35%.

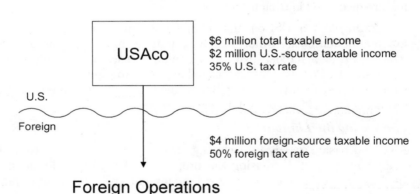

Foreign Operations

USAco has $600,000 of excess credits, computed as follows:

Foreign income taxes [$4 million × 50%] . . . . $2 million

Foreign tax credit limitation:

(A) Total taxable income	$ 6 million
(B) Pre-credit U.S. tax [$6 million × 35%] . . .	$2.1 million
(C) Foreign-source taxable income	$ 4 million
Limitation = [line B × (C ÷ A)]	
= [$2.1 million × ($4 million ÷ $6 million)] . .	– $1.4 million

Excess foreign tax credits $600,000

Now assume that USAco can recharacterize $1 million of its U.S.-source income as foreign-source income, but only for U.S. tax purposes so that there is now $5 million of foreign-source taxable income (under the U.S. sourcing rules) even though only $4 million is subject to income tax in the foreign country. Every dollar of resourced income increases USAco's limitation and has no effect on USAco's foreign taxes. The net effect is a reduction in USAco's excess credits from $600,000 to $250,000, computed as follows:

Foreign income taxes [$4 million × 50%] .... $2 million

Foreign tax credit limitation:

      (A) Total taxable income .... $ 6 million

      (B) Pre-credit U.S. tax [$6 million × 35%] ... $2.1 million

      (C) Foreign-source taxable income........ $ 5 million

  Limitation = [line B × (C ÷ A)]

        = [$2.1 million × ($5 million ÷ $6 million)] .. – $1.75 million

Excess foreign tax credits $250,000

On the other hand, if the resourcing of USAco's income for U.S. tax purposes was to also increase USAco's taxable income for foreign tax purposes, the $1 million of resourced income would increase USAco's foreign income taxes at a faster rate than it will increase its limitation. The net effect will be an increase in USAco's excess credits from $600,000 to $750,000, computed as follows.

Foreign income taxes [$5 million × 50%] .... $2.5 million

Foreign tax credit limitation:

      (A) Total taxable income .... $ 6 million

      (B) Pre-credit U.S. tax [$6 million × 35%] ... $2.1 million

      (C) Foreign-source taxable income........ $ 5 million

  Limitation = [line B × (C ÷ A)]

        = [$2.1 million × ($5 million ÷ $6 million)] .. – $1.75 million

Excess foreign tax credits $750,000

.03 Cross-Crediting

A third basic strategy for eliminating excess credits is cross-crediting. This strategy is based on the fact that different items of foreign-source income have distinctly different effects on a taxpayer in an excess credit position. Foreign income that bears foreign income taxes at a rate higher than the U.S. tax rate increases a taxpayer's excess credits, whereas foreign income that bears a low rate of foreign income tax can reduce a taxpayer's excess credits. Within a single foreign tax credit limitation, the excess credits on high-tax foreign income are credited against the excess limitation on low-tax foreign income. Through this process, known as "cross-crediting," the effects of individual items of high and low

¶404.03

tax foreign-source income are averaged. This averaging process produces an excess credit only when the average foreign tax rate on all of the items of foreign-source income within a single limitation is higher than the U.S. rate.

Example **4.8:** USAco has $1 million of country X source income and no U.S.-source income. Assume the U.S. tax rate is 35% and the country X rate of 40% applies to the $1 million of X income.

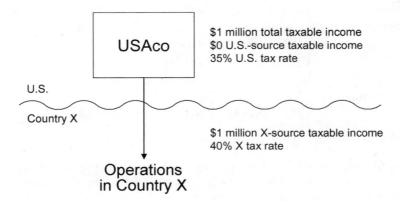

USAco

$1 million total taxable income
$0 U.S.-source taxable income
35% U.S. tax rate

U.S.

Country X

$1 million X-source taxable income
40% X tax rate

Operations
in Country X

USAco has $50,000 of excess credits, computed as follows:

Foreign income taxes [$1 million × 40%]	$400,000
Foreign tax credit limitation:	
(A) Total taxable income	$ 1 million
(B) Pre-credit U.S. tax [$6 million × 35%]	$350,000
(C) Foreign-source taxable income...........	$ 1 million
Limitation = [line B × (C ÷ A)]	
= [$350,000 million × ($1 million ÷ $1 million)]..	$350,000
Excess foreign tax credits	$50,000

Now assume that in addition to the $1 million of country X income, USAco also has $1 million of country Y income, which is subject to foreign tax at a 30% rate. Further assume that the Country Y income is assigned to the same limitation as the Country X income.

¶404.03

$1 million X-source taxable income
40% X tax rate

$1 million Y-source taxable income
30% Y tax rate

Cross-crediting will eliminate the $50,000 of excess credits as follows:

Foreign income taxes [($1 million × 40%) + ($1 million × 30%)] ... $700,000

Foreign tax credit limitation:

        (A) Total taxable income
           [$1 million + $1 million] .... $ 2 million

        (B) Pre-credit U.S. tax [$2 million × 35%] $700,000

        (C) Foreign-source taxable income .... $ 2 million

  Limitation = [line B × (C ÷ A)]

          = [$700,000 × ($2 million ÷ $2 million)] $700,000

Excess foreign tax credits .... None

USAco no longer has any excess credits because the average rate of foreign income tax is now 35% (foreign taxes of $700,000 ÷ $2 million of foreign income), which is the same as the U.S. rate.

The third strategy for eliminating excess credits exploits the cross-crediting phenomenon. If a taxpayer can blend low-tax and high-tax foreign-source income within a single limitation, then the excess limitation on the low-tax income will soak up the excess credits on the high-tax income.

¶ 405 SEPARATE CATEGORY OF INCOME LIMITATIONS

.01 History

Cross-crediting is possible only to the extent the operative foreign tax credit limitation encompasses both low-tax and high-tax foreign-source income. Foreign income tax rates vary not only across countries, but also across different types of income within the same country. For example, whereas a U.S. person's foreign business profits often attract a high rate of foreign tax, a U.S. person's foreign-source passive investment income often bears little or no foreign tax. Therefore, restrictions on cross-crediting can be implemented by imposing either separate country or separate category of income limitations on the foreign tax credit.

Under a separate country limitation approach, a separate limitation would be computed for each foreign country. Separate country limitations prevent cross-crediting on income derived from different countries, but still allow cross-crediting on low-tax and high-tax income derived from the same foreign country. Under a separate category of income limitation approach, a separate limitation is applied to each category of income designated by lawmakers. Cross-crediting is allowed between countries but not between the different categories of income. For example, a separate limitation may be required for interest income. Interest income is a prime target for lawmakers wishing to restrict cross-crediting because interest income often bears little or no foreign taxes and because it is easy to shift investment funds from domestic securities to foreign securities.

Over the years, U.S. lawmakers have employed both separate country and separate category of income limitations (see Table 4.1).

TABLE 4.1. U.S. RESTRICTIONS ON CROSS-CREDITING

Time period	Type of foreign tax credit limitation	Prohibited form of cross-crediting
1918 to 1921	No limitation	n.a.
1922 to 1931	Overall limitation	None
1932 to 1975	Various types of separate country limitations	Between countries
1976 to 1986	Limited number of separate income limitations	Between categories of income
1987 to 2002	Nine separate income limitation categories	Between categories of income
2003 to 2006	Eight separate income limitation categories	Between categories of income
Post-2006	Two separate income limitation categories	Between categories of income

.02 Separate Category of Income Limitations

The primary purpose of the current separate category of income limitation system is to prevent cross-crediting between low-tax passive foreign investment income and high-tax active foreign business profits. Cross-crediting is still allowed, however, with respect to active business profits derived from different foreign countries or passive investment income derived from different foreign countries. Congress enacted the current system because it believed that little residual U.S. tax was being collected on foreign-source investment income, even though this income often bears little or no foreign tax. Congress attributed these negligible tax collections to the ability of U.S. companies to credit the excess foreign taxes on their foreign business profits against the residual U.S. tax on foreign-source investment income. Congress also believed that cross-crediting provided an undesirable tax incentive for U.S. companies to shift investment funds overseas merely as a device to increase the foreign tax credit limitation.[57]

Taxpayers must compute separate limitations for "general category income" and "passive category income."[58]

---

[57] S. Rep. No. 445 (100th Cong., 2d Sess. 217 (1988)).

[58] Code Sec. 904(d)(1). A separate limitation also applies to income that would be treated as U.S.-source income under the Internal Revenue Code, but is treated as foreign-source income under an income tax treaty. Code Sec. 904(d)(6).

¶405.02

The formula for computing the separate category of income limitations is the same as that for computing the overall limitation, except that the numerator of the fraction is now separate category foreign-source taxable income, as follows:

$$\text{Pre-credit U.S. tax on total taxable income} \times \frac{\text{Separate category foreign-source taxable income}}{\text{Total taxable income}}$$

The credit allowed with respect to each category of income is the lesser of that category's limitation or the foreign income taxes related to that category. A taxpayer's total credit for the year is the sum of the credits for each of the individual limitation categories.

Example **4.9:** USAco has $12 million of U.S.-source taxable income, $8 million of foreign-source general limitation income (on which USAco paid $3 million in foreign income taxes) and $2 million of foreign-source passive income (on which USAco paid $400,000 in foreign income taxes). Assume that the U.S. tax rate is 35%.

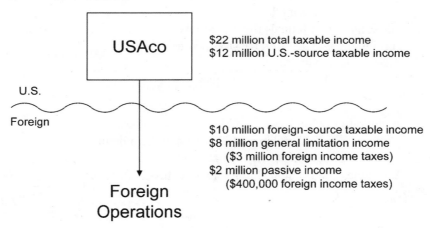

USAco

$22 million total taxable income
$12 million U.S.-source taxable income

U.S.

Foreign

$10 million foreign-source taxable income
$8 million general limitation income
($3 million foreign income taxes)
$2 million passive income
($400,000 foreign income taxes)

Foreign
Operations

Under a single overall limitation, all of USAco's foreign taxes are creditable, as follows:

Foreign income taxes [$3 million + $400,000] . . . . $3.4 million
Foreign tax credit limitation:
        (A) Total taxable income
           [$12 million + $8 million + $2 million] . . . . $ 22 million
        (B) Pre-credit U.S. tax [$22 million × 35%] . . $7.7 million
        (C) Foreign-source taxable income
           [$8 million + $2 million] . . . . $ 10 million
Overall
limitation   = [line B × (C ÷ A)]
            = [$7.7 million × ($10 million ÷ $22 million)]
. . . . $3.5 million
Foreign tax credit (equals creditable foreign taxes) . . . . $3.4 million

¶405.02

In contrast, under the separate income limitations, USAco has $200,000 of excess credits within the general income limitation and $300,000 of excess limitation in the passive income limitation, computed as follows:

Pre-credit U.S. tax:

(A) Total taxable income	$ 22 million
(B) Pre-credit U.S. tax [$22 million × 35%] . .	$7.7 million

Foreign tax credit:

Foreign income taxes on general
limitation income $ 3 million

General income limitation:

(C) Foreign-source general limitation income $ 8 million

General
income
limitation   = [line B × (C ÷ A)]
               = [$7.7 million × ($8 million ÷ $22 million)]
               = $2.8 million

Allowable credit [equals the limitation] . . . . $2.8 million

Foreign income taxes on passive income $ 400,000

Passive income limitation:

(D) Foreign-source passive income . . . . $ 2 million

Passive
income
limitation   = [line B × (D ÷ A)]
               = [$7.7 million × ($2 million ÷ $22 million)]
               = $700,000

Allowable credit [equals foreign income taxes] . . . . $ 400,000

Total foreign tax credit . . . . $3.2 million

Although the Internal Revenue Code contains both an overall income limitation and the separate income limitations, as a practical matter, the IRS has only implemented the separate income limitations.[59]

General category income. General category income includes all "income other than passive category income."[60] Consequently, this category includes most of the foreign-source active business profits of domestic corporations and their foreign subsidiaries.

---

[59] *See* Forms 1116 and 1118 in the Appendix.   [60] Code Sec. 904(d)(2)(A)(ii).

Passive category income. Passive category income includes "passive income" and "specified passive category income."[61] The term "passive income" means:

    (i) foreign personal holding company income (as defined in Code Sec. 954(c)), which generally includes:

        (a) dividends, interest, royalties, rents, and annuities,

        (b) net gains from the disposition of property that produces dividend, interest, rent, and royalty income (except for net gains from certain dealer sales and inventory sales), and

        (c) net gains from commodity and foreign currency transactions (except for net gains from certain active business transaction or qualified hedging transactions); and

    (ii) income of a passive foreign investment company that has made a qualified electing fund election.[62]

The term "specified passive category income" means certain income received from a domestic international sales corporation (DISC) or foreign sales corporation (FSC).[63] In 1971, Congress enacted the DISC provisions in an attempt to stimulate U.S. exports. In 1984, Congress enacted the FSC provisions as a replacement for the DISC regime, but later repealed the FSC regime in 2000. However, a vestige of the DISC regime, known as interest-charge DISCs, remains in the law.

There are numerous exceptions to the general rules for determining passive income, including the following items of income, which are treated as general category income:

    (i) *Highly-taxed income*—Passive income does not include any "high-taxed income."[64] Income is high-taxed if the creditable foreign taxes related to the income exceed the product of the amount of that income multiplied by 35% (in the case of a corporation) or 39.6% (in the case of an individual).[65] This exception limits cross-crediting of low-tax and high-tax passive income by removing any investment-type income that gives rise to excess credits from the passive income limitation.

    (ii) *Controlled foreign corporation and 10/50 company look-through rules*—A U.S. shareholder allocates payments received from a controlled foreign corporation, including dividends, interest, rents, royalties and Subpart F inclusions, to the separate categories of income limitations based on the character of the controlled foreign corporation's earnings.[66] A look-through rule also applies to dividends received from a noncontrolled Code Sec. 902 corporation (10/50 company).[67] These look-through rules are discussed in detail in the next section.

---

[61] Code Sec. 904(d)(2)(A)(i).
[62] Code Sec. 904(d)(2)(B).
[63] Code Sec. 904(d)(2)(B)(v).
[64] Code Sec. 904(d)(2)(B)(iii)(II).

[65] Code Sec. 904(d)(2)(F) and Reg. § 1.904-4(c)(1).
[66] Code Sec. 904(d)(3).
[67] Code Sec. 904(d)(4).

(iii) *Active rents and royalties*—Passive income does not include rents and royalties that are derived in the active conduct of a trade or business, such as royalties derived from intangible property of the type that the taxpayer regularly produces.[68]

(iv) *Export financing interest*—Passive income does not include any "export financing interest."[69] Export financing interest is any interest (other than related-person factoring income) that is derived from financing the sale or other disposition of property for use or consumption outside the United States, if the property is manufactured, produced, grown, or extracted in the United States by the taxpayer or a related person, and if not more than 50% of the fair market value of the property is attributable to products imported into the United States.[70]

(v) *Financial services income.* Passive income does not include financial services income. Instead, such income is specifically included in general limitation income. The term "financial services income" means income derived in the active conduct of a banking, insurance, financing or similar business by a person predominantly engaged in the active conduct of such a business.[71] This provision allows financial services companies to engage in cross-crediting in the general limitation with respect to all of their financial services income, including both low-tax investment-type income and high-tax services income, such as income derived from investment advisory, brokerage, fiduciary, investment banking, and trust services.

.03 Look-Through Rules

Look-through rules apply to income received from a controlled foreign corporation, including dividends, interest, rents, royalties and Subpart F inclusions. A separate look-through rule applies to dividends received from 10/50 companies.

Controlled foreign corporations. Under the general rules, the separate income limitations would yield significantly different results for domestic corporations operating abroad through foreign subsidiaries as opposed to foreign branches. For example, if a domestic corporation structures a foreign manufacturing operation as a branch, the related income is general limitation income. In contrast, if the domestic corporation were to structure the same manufacturing operation as a subsidiary, the dividend distributions from that manufacturing subsidiary would be passive income. To better equate the treatment of branches and subsidiaries, a U.S. shareholder allocates income derived from a controlled foreign corporation (or CFC), including dividends, interest, rents, royalties and Subpart F inclusions, to the separate income categories based on the character of the controlled foreign corporation's underlying earnings.

A foreign corporation is a controlled foreign corporation if, on any day during the foreign corporation's taxable year, U.S. shareholders own more than 50% of the combined voting power of all classes of stock or 50% of the total value of the stock,

---

[68] Reg. § 1.904-4(b)(2).
[69] Code Sec. 904(d)(2)(B)(iii)(I).
[70] Code Sec. 904(d)(2)(G).
[71] Code Sec. 904(d)(2)(C) and (D).

of the foreign corporation.[72] A U.S. shareholder is any U.S. person owning at least 10% of the total combined voting power of all classes of voting stock of the foreign corporation.[73]

The specific look-through rule varies with the type of income derived from the CFC, as follows:

(i) *Dividends*—Dividends paid by a CFC to a taxpayer who is a U.S. shareholder of that CFC are allocated between passive income and general limitation income based on the ratio of the CFC's earnings and profits within each category of income to the CFC's total earnings and profits.[74] For example, if a CFC has $1 million of earnings and profits, $900,000 of which is attributable to general limitation income and the other $100,000 to passive income, then 90% of a dividend distribution from the CFC is general limitation income and the other 10% is passive income.

(ii) *Rents and royalties*—Rents and royalties paid by a CFC to a U.S. shareholder of that CFC are allocated between passive income and general limitation income based on the extent to which the related deduction (at the CFC level) is properly allocable to the CFC's income in that category of income.[75] For example, if the entire amount of a CFC's current-year taxable income is general limitation income, then any royalty paid to a U.S. shareholder is general limitation income.

(iii) *Interest*— Interest paid by a CFC to a U.S. shareholder of that CFC is treated as passive income to the extent of the CFC's foreign personal holding company income.[76] This interest netting rule is designed to maintain the integrity of the separate category of income limitations by preventing a U.S. shareholder from artificially increasing its general limitation income by making a loan to a CFC, rather than purchasing foreign securities, merely as a device to use the look-through rule to recharacterize interest income as general limitation income.[77] Interest paid by a CFC to a U.S. shareholder of that CFC in excess of the CFC's foreign personal holding company income is allocated between passive income and general limitation income based on the expense allocation principles of Reg. § 1.861-9T.[78]

(iv) *Subpart F inclusion*—A Subpart F inclusion for an increase in a CFC's earnings invested in U.S. property is allocated between passive income and general limitation income using the same rule that applies to actual dividend distributions made by a CFC (see discussion above).[79] In contrast, a Subpart F inclusion for Subpart F income is allocated between the separate categories of income based on the nature of the CFC's

---

[72] Code Sec. 957(a).

[73] Code Sec. 951(b). All forms of ownership, including direct, indirect (i.e., beneficial ownership through intervening foreign entities), and constructive (i.e., attribution of ownership by one related party to another), are considered in applying both the 10% shareholder and the 50% aggregate ownership tests. Code Sec. 958.

[74] Code Sec. 904(d)(3)(D) and Reg. § 1.904-5(c)(4)(i).

[75] Code Sec. 904(d)(3)(C) and Reg. § 1.904-5(c)(3).

[76] Code Sec. 954(b)(5). *See* Chapter 5 (¶ 501) for a definition of foreign personal holding company income.

[77] Code Sec. 904(d)(3)(C).

[78] Reg. § 1.904-5(c)(2)(ii).

[79] Code Sec. 904(d)(3)(G) and Reg. § 1.904-5(c)(4)(i).

taxable income that gave rise to the Subpart F inclusion.[80] For example, if a CFC has $1 million of Subpart F income, including $850,000 of foreign base company sales income and $150,000 of foreign personal holding company income, $850,000 of the Subpart F inclusion is general limitation income and the other $150,000 is passive income.[81]

    (v) *Passive foreign investment company inclusion*—If the taxpayer is a U.S. shareholder of a CFC that also is a passive foreign investment company that has made a qualified electing fund (or QEF) election, then the look-through rule that applies to Subpart F inclusions also applies to a QEF inclusion from that CFC.[82] If the QEF is neither a CFC nor a 10/50 company, the QEF inclusion is passive income.[83]

    Example 4.10: USAco has owned 100% of FORco, a foreign corporation, since its formation. FORco has earnings and profits of $1 million, of which $800,000 is general limitation income and $200,000 is passive income. FORco distributes a $100,000 dividend to USAco.

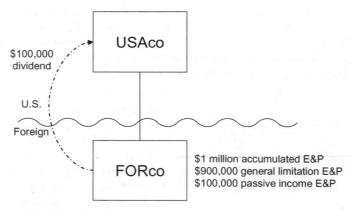

    Pursuant to the CFC look-through rule for dividends, because 80% of FORco's earnings and profits is general limitation income and 20% is passive income, USAco allocates $80,000 of the dividend to the general income limitation and $20,000 to the passive income limitation.

    10/50 companies. A look-through rule also applies to dividends received by a domestic corporation from a noncontrolled Code Sec. 902 corporation (10/50 company). A foreign corporation is a 10/50 company if a domestic corporation owns between 10% and 50% of the foreign corporation, in which case the domestic corporation satisfies the 10% or more ownership requirement for claiming a Code Sec. 902 deemed paid credit with respect to a dividend from the foreign corporation, but the foreign corporation does not meet the more than 50% U.S. ownership requirement for CFC status.

---

[80] Code Sec. 904(d)(3)(B) and Reg. § 1.904-5(c)(1)(i).
[81] Reg. § 1.904-5(c)(1)(ii), Example (1).
[82] Code Sec. 904(d)(3)(H) and Reg. § 1.904-5(j).
[83] Code Sec. 904(d)(2)(A)(ii).

¶405.03

Under the 10/50 company look-through rule, a dividend is allocated between passive income and general limitation income based on the ratio of the 10/50 company's earnings and profits within each separate category of income to the 10/50 company's total earnings and profits.[84] In contrast to a CFC, however, look-through treatment does not apply to interest, rents, and royalties received from a 10/50 company.

.04 Partnerships

A partner allocates its distributive share of partnership income between passive income and general limitation income based on the character of the income at the partnership level.[85] For example, if a partnership has $800,000 of general limitation income and $200,000 of passive income, 80% of the partner's distributive share of the partnership's income is general limitation income and the other 20% is passive income. This look-through rule also applies to payments of interest, rents, and royalties by a partnership to a 10% or more partner not acting in its capacity as a partner (so-called Code Sec. 707 payments).[86] However, this look-through rule does not apply to a limited partner or corporate general partner that owns less than 10% of the value of the partnership. In such cases, the partner's entire distributive share of partnership income is treated as passive income, unless the partner holds the partnership interest in the ordinary course of the partner's trade or business, in which case the general look-through rule applies.[87] The rules applicable to partners in a partnership also apply to shareholders in an S corporation.[88]

.05 Allocating Foreign Income Taxes

In order to apply the separate category of income limitations, foreign income taxes also must be allocated between the passive and general income limitations. Foreign income taxes are allocated to the category of income that includes the income on which the foreign taxes were imposed.[89] For example, foreign withholding taxes imposed on passive interest income are assigned to the passive income limitation, whereas withholding taxes imposed on active royalty income are assigned to the general income limitation.

If the base upon which a foreign income tax is imposed includes both passive and general limitation income, the taxpayer prorates the foreign taxes among the categories of income using the following formula:[90]

$$\text{Foreign income taxes related to more than one category of income} \times \frac{\text{Net income subject to the foreign tax included in category of income}}{\text{Total net income subject to the foreign tax}}$$

Net income for this purpose is determined under the tax accounting rules of the foreign country to which the tax was paid or accrued, rather than under U.S. law.

---

[84] Code Sec. 904(d)(4).

[85] Reg. § 1.904-5(h)(1).

[86] Reg. § 1.904-5(h)(1).

[87] Reg. § 1.904-5(h)(2). A gain on the sale of a partnership interest also is treated as passive income. Reg. § 1.904-5(h)(3).

[88] Code Sec. 1373(a).

[89] Reg. § 1.904-6(a)(1)(i).

[90] Reg. § 1.904-6(a)(1)(ii).

Example **4.11:** USAco paid $300,000 of foreign income taxes on $1 million of foreign-source taxable income, which includes $800,000 of general limitation income and $200,000 of passive income.

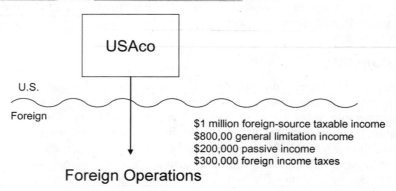

For purposes of applying the separate income limitations, USAco allocates $240,000 of foreign taxes [$300,000 × ($800,000 ÷ $1,000,000)] to the general income limitation and the remaining $60,000 of foreign taxes [$300,000 × ($200,000 ÷ $1,000,000)] to the passive income limitation.

A problem arises when the foreign income tax base includes an item of income that is nontaxable for U.S. purposes. Under the general allocation rules, the income in question is not reflected in the numerators of any separate income limitation and, therefore, the related foreign income tax will not be allocated to any of the separate income limitations. To prevent this result, a taxpayer may elect to treat such taxes as imposed on general limitation income.[91] A similar problem arises when an item of income is subject to taxation in different years for U.S. and foreign tax purposes. For purposes of allocating the related foreign income taxes, such income is deemed to be recognized for U.S. tax purposes in the same year that it is recognized for foreign tax purposes.[92]

¶ 406 OTHER COMPLEXITIES OF THE LIMITATION

.01 *Capital Gains and Losses*

Under general U.S. tax principles, capital gains and losses receive special treatment in the form of the netting of individual capital gains and losses, a preferential tax rate on a noncorporate taxpayer's net long-term capital gain,[93] and limited deductibility of a net capital loss.[94] This special treatment can distort the accuracy of the foreign tax credit limitation as an estimate of the U.S. tax burden on foreign-source income. To prevent these distortions, taxpayers with capital gains and losses must make various special adjustments to the limitation.

One potential distortion arises when a taxpayer nets a foreign-source capital gain against a U.S.-source capital loss in computing the net capital gain or loss for

---

[91] Code Sec. 904(d)(2)(H) and Reg. § 1.904-6(a)(1)(iv).
[92] Reg. § 1.904-6(a)(1)(iv).

[93] Code Sec. 1(h).
[94] Code Sec. 1211.

the year. Because capital losses are generally deductible only against capital gains, one U.S. tax benefit derived from the foreign-source capital gain is to soak up the U.S.-source capital loss. If the taxpayer also includes the foreign-source capital gain in the numerator of the foreign tax credit limitation, a second U.S. tax benefit may be realized in the form of additional foreign tax credits. To prevent this double tax benefit, a foreign-source capital gain is excluded from the numerator of the foreign tax credit limitation to the extent it offsets a U.S.-source capital loss.[95]

A second potential distortion arises when the tax rate applied to a taxpayer's net long-term capital gain is lower than the tax rate applied to the taxpayer's ordinary income. Under current tax law, there is no capital gain rate differential for corporations, but there is a significant rate differential for individuals. When a capital gain rate differential exists, the attribution of the pre-credit U.S. tax to foreign-source taxable income for purposes of computing the foreign tax credit limitation will be based on the "average" rate of U.S. tax on both ordinary income and the net long-term capital gain. This is advantageous when the long-term capital gain is from foreign sources, since the average U.S. rate is greater than the actual U.S. tax burden on the foreign-source capital gain. This result is disadvantageous, however, when the long-term capital gain is from U.S. sources, since the average U.S. rate underestimates the actual U.S. tax burden on foreign-source income, which is all ordinary in nature.

To prevent these distortions, a taxpayer that has a capital gain rate differential must reduce the numerator of the foreign tax credit limitation fraction by a portion of any foreign-source capital gain net income.[96] The taxpayer also must reduce the denominator of the limitation by a portion of the overall capital gain net income.[97] The amount of these reductions is determined by the magnitude of the capital gain rate differential enjoyed by the taxpayer and is computed so as to remove the precise amount of bias in the unadjusted foreign tax credit limitation.

The adjustment for the capital gain rate differential should only impact the foreign tax credit limitation for U.S. individuals receiving foreign-source dividends in unique situations. More specifically, if the only item of foreign-source income is a dividend received from a foreign corporation incorporated in a treaty country, which would typically not incur a withholding tax at a rate greater than 15%, the qualified dividend would incur a pre-credit U.S. tax at the maximum capital gain rate of 20%.[98] These facts would render all of the withholding taxes creditable. However, if there is an effective rate of foreign tax on the dividend that is greater than 20%, due to either the apportionment of expenses to the foreign-source dividend or a high foreign withholding tax rate, the capital gain rate differential adjustment may result in some noncreditable foreign withholding taxes.

A capital gain rate differential also can similarly create a distortion when a taxpayer in a net long-term capital gain position nets a foreign-source capital loss

---

[95] Code Sec. 904(b)(2)(A).

[96] Code Sec. 904(b)(2)(B)(i).

[97] Code Sec. 904(b)(2)(B)(ii).

[98] Code Sec. 1(h)(11)(C). Such dividends are also potentially subject to the 3.8% Medicare contribution tax on net investment income. Code Sec. 1411. A taxpayer may not claim a foreign tax credit against the net investment income tax. Reg. § 1.1411-1(e).

¶406.01

against a U.S.-source long-term capital gain. Under the general rules, the effect of the foreign-source capital loss on the foreign tax credit limitation is based on the average rate of U.S. tax on both ordinary income and the net long-term capital gain. This average rate overstates the U.S. tax benefit of the foreign-source capital loss and, therefore, understates the U.S. tax burden on foreign-source taxable income. To prevent this result, a taxpayer that has a capital gain rate differential can increase the numerator of the foreign tax credit limitation fraction by a portion of the foreign-source capital loss.[99]

.02 Impact of Losses

Under basic U.S. tax principles, a loss from one business activity ordinarily is deductible against income from any other business activity. This principle ignores two important distinctions that must be made when computing the foreign tax credit limitation: the distinction between U.S.- and foreign-source income and the assignment of income to one of the two separate categories of income limitations. As a consequence, for purposes of computing the taxpayer's foreign tax credit limitation, special rules apply when a taxpayer's business activity gives rise to a net loss.

Overall foreign losses. An "overall foreign loss" (or OFL) arises in a tax year in which the deductions properly allocated and apportioned to foreign-source gross income exceed the amount of such income.[100] Potential causes of an OFL include losses on export sales of inventory, the flow-through of foreign branch or partnership losses, and the allocation and apportionment of deductions to foreign-source gross income.

An OFL provides the taxpayer with a current-year U.S. tax benefit to the extent the OFL shelters the taxpayer's U.S.-source taxable income. Moreover, future U.S. tax collections on foreign-source income will not compensate for this initial U.S. tax benefit if, in subsequent tax years, the foreign tax credit completely offsets the pre-credit U.S. tax on foreign-source income. Therefore, an OFL presents the possibility of the best of both worlds: the immediate utilization of foreign losses to shelter U.S.-source income and the potential availability of foreign tax credits in profitable years to shield foreign-source income from U.S. tax.

To prevent this result, a taxpayer that sustains an OFL must, in each succeeding year, recapture as U.S.-source income the lesser of the following two amounts:

   (i) 50% (or a larger percentage if the taxpayer so elects) of its foreign-source taxable income for that succeeding year, or

   (ii) the amount of the OFL that has not yet been recaptured.[101]

This recapture rule prevents a double U.S. tax benefit by reducing the foreign tax credit limitation, and thereby denying the taxpayer foreign tax credits on that foreign-source income.

---

[99] Code Sec. 904(b)(2)(B)(iii).
[100] Code Sec. 904(f)(2).

[101] Code Sec. 904(f)(1). A gain on the disposition of foreign business property or stock of a CFC also results in the recapture of an overall foreign loss. Code Sec. 904(f)(3).

¶406.02

***Example* 4.12:** USAco has operations in both the United States and foreign country F. In year 1, the foreign country F operations produced an OFL of $100,000. In the United States, USAco's operations produced taxable income of $100,000, on which USAco would otherwise pay $35,000 of U.S. tax. However, the OFL reduces USAco's net profit to $0, so USAco does not pay any U.S. income tax. In year 2, USAco again has $100,000 of U.S.-source income. However, the foreign operations turn around and produce a profit of $100,000 for total taxable income of $200,000.

Foreign Operations

In year 2, USAco must recapture as U.S.-source taxable income $50,000, which is the lesser of 50% of foreign-source taxable income in year 2 or the previously unrecaptured OFL of $100,000. As a result, USAco's foreign tax credit limitation for year 2 is computed as follows:

$$\text{Pre-credit U.S. tax on total taxable income} \times \frac{\text{Foreign-source taxable income}}{\text{Total taxable income}}$$

$$35\% \times \$200,000 \times \frac{\$50,000}{\$200,000}$$

$$= \$17,500$$

Consequently, by reducing USAco's foreign-source taxable income, the OFL recapture provisions reduce the amount of foreign tax credits that USAco can claim in year 2.

Separate limitation losses. Separate foreign tax credit limitations are computed for passive income and general limitation income. A "separate limitation loss" (or SLL) arises in a year that the deductions properly allocated and apportioned to the foreign-source gross income within one of the limitations exceed the amount of such income.[102]

A taxpayer must offset a SLL against the foreign-source income in the other limitation before it can offset the SLL against its U.S.-source income.[103] Furthermore, to maintain the integrity of the separate income limitations, in subsequent tax years, any income earned in the limitation from which the SLL arose is recharacterized as income in the other limitation to the extent the SLL was allocated to that

---

[102] Code Sec. 904 (f) (5) (E) (iii).   [103] Code Sec. 904 (f) (5) (A).

other limitation in the prior year.[104] For example, if a loss from general limitation income is used to offset passive income, then any general limitation income earned in succeeding tax years is recharacterized as passive income to the extent of the prior year loss deduction.[105]

> **Example 4.13:** In year 1, USAco has total taxable income of $150,000, including a general limitation loss of $50,000, $100,000 of passive income, and $100,000 of U.S.-source taxable income. After allocating the general limitation loss against the passive income, the numerator of the passive income limitation is only $50,000 ($100,000 – $50,000 allocation of SLL), and the numerator of the general income limitation is $0. In year 2, USAco has total taxable income of $275,000, including $75,000 of general limitation income, $100,000 of passive income, and $100,000 of U.S.-source taxable income. Because USAco reduced its passive income by the $50,000 general limitation loss in year 1, in year 2 USAco must recharacterize $50,000 of its general limitation income as passive income. After the recapture of the SLL, the numerator of the passive income limitation is $150,000 ($100,000 + $50,000 recapture of SLL), and the numerator of the general income limitation is $25,000 ($75,000 – $50,000 recapture of SLL). The following table summarizes the year 1 allocation and year 2 recapture of the SLL.

| | | Foreign-source income | | U.S.-source income |
		General	Passive	
Year 1	Income	($50,000)	$100,000	$100,000
	Allocation	$0	$50,000	$100,000
Year 2	Income	$75,000	$100,000	$100,000
	Recapture	$25,000	$150,000	$100,000

Overall domestic losses. An "overall domestic loss" (or ODL) arises in a taxable year in which the deductions properly allocated and apportioned to a taxpayer's U.S. source gross income exceed the amount of such income and, accordingly, the net U.S.-source loss offsets the taxpayer's foreign-source taxable income.[106] By reducing the taxpayer's foreign-source income, an ODL may deny a taxpayer foreign tax credits. Therefore, in each succeeding taxable year, a taxpayer may recapture and treat as foreign-source income an amount equal to the lesser of 50% of the taxpayer's U.S.-source taxable income in the succeeding taxable year or the amount of the ODL that has not yet been recaptured.[107]

> **Example 4.14:** In year 1, USAco has total taxable income of $0, which includes $100,000 of foreign-source taxable income on which USAco paid $35,000 of foreign income taxes and an ODL of $100,000. Consequently, USAco is in the unenviable position of paying $35,000 of income taxes, despite having

---

[104] Code Sec. 904(f)(5)(C).

[105] A gain from the disposition of foreign business property or stock of a CFC that is related to a separate limitation loss also is subject to recharacterization. Code Sec. 904(f)(5)(F).

[106] Code Sec. 904(f)(5)(D).

[107] Code Sec. 904(g)(1).

no net taxable income. However, these excess foreign tax credits can be carried forward 10 years.

Foreign Operations

In year 2, USAco again has $100,000 of foreign-source taxable income on which it pays $35,000 of foreign income taxes. However, the U.S. operations turn around and produce a profit of $100,000, resulting in a pre-credit U.S. tax of $70,000 [35% × $200,000 total taxable income]. In addition, USAco may recapture as foreign-source income $50,000, which is the lesser of 50% of the U.S.-source taxable income in year 2 or the previously unrecaptured ODL of $100,000. The ODL recapture income increases USAco's foreign tax credit limitation from $35,000 [$70,000 × ($100,000 ÷ $200,000)] to $52,500 [$70,000 × ($150,000 ÷ $200,000)]. Consequently, in year 2 USAco may claim a foreign tax credit for $17,500 of the excess credits from year 1.

.03 Oil and Gas Activities

Special restrictions prevent oil and gas companies from using excess credits on foreign oil and gas income to soak up the residual U.S. tax on other types of income. Specifically, a domestic corporation's creditable foreign oil and gas related income taxes are limited to an amount equal to the maximum U.S. corporate tax rate of 35% multiplied by the sum of the taxpayer's foreign oil-related income (FORI) [108] and its foreign oil and gas extraction income (FOGEI). [109] Foreign taxes that are disallowed because of this restriction can be carried back one year or forward up to ten years and taken as a credit in a year in which the taxpayer has an excess limitation on the combined FOGEI and FORI. [110]

Congress enacted these restrictions because it believed that high rates of foreign tax on oil and gas income may represent disguised royalties for the right to extract oil and gas resources from government-owned land. As discussed earlier in this chapter, another way in which lawmakers address this issue is to deny a credit

---

[108] FORI includes income from refining, processing, transporting, distributing, or selling oil and gas or primary products derived from oil and gas. Code Sec. 907(c)(2). Under a look-through rule, FORI also includes dividends and interest derived from a 10%-or-more-owned foreign corporation to the extent the interest or dividends are attributable to FORI. Code Sec. 907(c)(3).

[109] Code Sec. 907(a). Individual taxpayers are subject to a different limitation.

[110] Code Sec. 907(f).

for a foreign levy if the taxpayer receives a specific economic benefit in exchange for the levy.[111]

.04 Special Source-of-Income Rules

As discussed in Chapter 3 (¶ 302), there are several source-of-income rules which apply solely for purposes of computing the foreign tax credit limitation. For example, certain types of income derived from a foreign corporation that is at least 50% owned by U.S. persons are recharacterized as U.S.-source income to the extent the income is attributable to earnings that the foreign corporation derived from U.S. sources. This rule applies to interest, dividends, Subpart F inclusions, and income derived from a passive foreign investment corporation that has made a qualified electing fund election.[112] Another example is the CFC netting rule, which requires a domestic corporation to specifically allocate certain interest expense deductions against any foreign-source interest income derived from a CFC in computing its foreign tax credit limitation (see ¶ 303.04).[113]

¶ 407 EXCESS CREDIT CARRYOVERS

Foreign taxes that exceed the limitation in a given taxable year can be carried back one year and forward up to ten years and taken as a credit in a year that the limitation exceeds the amount of creditable foreign taxes.[114] This carryover process must take place, however, within the confines of the separate category of income limitations. For example, excess credits on general limitation income can offset only past or future excess limitations on general limitation income.[115] Excess credits that are carried back or forward to another taxable year must be credited and cannot be deducted in the carryback or carryforward year.[116]

This carryover provision prevents U.S. persons from being denied a foreign tax credit solely because of changes in the effective rate of foreign taxation over time. Such fluctuations arise when a country changes its statutory tax rates, when income or expense is recognized at different times for U.S. and foreign tax purposes, or when a country enacts or eliminates tax preference items.

> **Example 4.15:** USAco realizes $20 million of foreign-source gross income in both year 1 and year 2. Assume that the U.S. and foreign tax rates are both 35%. The only deduction allocable against this income is a $20 million expenditure that is deducted over two years for U.S. tax purposes, but just one year for foreign tax purposes. As a consequence, USAco's foreign taxes are $0 in year 1 [35% × $0 foreign taxable income] and $7 million in year 2 [35% × $20 million of foreign taxable income]. In contrast, USAco's foreign-source taxable income for U.S. tax purposes is $10 million [$20 million of gross income − $10 million of deductions] in both year 1 and year 2. Therefore, USAco's foreign tax credit limitation is $3.5 million in each year [$3.5 million × ($10 million ÷ $10 million)]. If there were no excess credit carryover provision, USAco could

---

[111] Reg. § 1.901-2(a)(2)(i).

[112] Code Sec. 904(g)(1). This rule does not apply if less than 10% of the U.S.-owned foreign corporation's earnings are attributable to U.S.-source income. Code Sec. 904(g)(5).

[113] Reg. § 1.861-10.

[114] Code Sec. 904(c).

[115] Code Sec. 904(d)(1).

[116] Code Sec. 904(c).

claim a credit in year 2 for only $3.5 million of the $7 million in foreign taxes paid. With the carryover provisions, USAco can carry the excess credits from year 2 back to year 1 and credit them against the excess limitation of $3.5 million for that year.

¶ 408 COMPUTING THE ALTERNATIVE MINIMUM TAX FOREIGN TAX CREDIT

U.S. persons can use foreign tax credits to offset not only the regular income tax, but also the alternative minimum tax (or AMT). A U.S. person is subject to the AMT if the taxpayer's tentative minimum tax exceeds the regular tax for the year.[117] A corporate taxpayer's tentative minimum tax equals 20% (26% or 28% in the case of noncorporate taxpayers) of the excess of the taxpayer's alternative minimum taxable income over the exemption amount, reduced by the alternative minimum foreign tax credit.[118]

A taxpayer computes the AMT foreign tax credit in the same manner as the credit for regular tax purposes, with one major exception. For regular tax purposes, the limitation equals the pre-credit U.S. tax multiplied by the ratio of foreign-source taxable income to total taxable income, with separate limitations computed for passive category income and general category income. For AMT purposes, the same basic formula and separate income limitations apply, except that the pre-credit U.S. tax amount is now the tentative minimum tax (before any foreign tax credits) and the foreign-source and total income amounts are computed on the basis of alternative minimum taxable income.[119] For example, the AMT limitation for passive income equals the pre-credit tentative minimum tax multiplied by the ratio of foreign-source passive alternative minimum taxable income to total alternative minimum taxable income.

Taxpayers may elect to use a simplified AMT foreign tax credit limitation when calculating their AMT foreign tax credit. The simplified limitation is the ratio of the taxpayer's foreign-source regular taxable income to the entire alternative minimum taxable income (AMTI). Because the simplified limitation uses foreign-source regular taxable income, rather than foreign-source AMTI, the taxpayer is not required to reallocate and reapportion deductions for AMTI purposes based on assets and income that reflect AMT adjustments (including depreciation). Under the simplified method, a domestic corporation would compute its limitation as follows:[120]

$$20\% \times [\text{Entire AMTI - AMT exemption}] \quad \times \quad \frac{\text{Foreign-source regular taxable income}}{\text{Entire AMTI}}$$

The election may be made only in the taxpayer's first tax year for which the taxpayer claims an AMT foreign tax credit. The election applies to all subsequent tax years and can be revoked only with the consent of the IRS.[121]

---

[117] Code Sec. 55(a).

[118] Code Sec. 55(b)(1).

[119] Code Sec. 59(a)(1).

[120] For purposes of the simplified limitation, foreign-source regular taxable income cannot exceed the taxpayer's entire AMTI.

[121] Code Sec. 59(a)(3).

¶ 409 DEEMED PAID FOREIGN TAX CREDIT—OVERVIEW

.01 Dividend Income

A domestic corporation generally includes in its U.S. taxable income the entire amount of a dividend received from a foreign corporation. Such dividends are included in gross income,[122] and the domestic corporation generally cannot claim an offsetting dividends-received deduction, even if the foreign corporation is a wholly-owned subsidiary.[123]

A dividends-received deduction is not allowed because a domestic parent corporation's receipt of a dividend from a foreign corporation is normally the U.S. Treasury's first opportunity to tax the underlying foreign-source earnings. In contrast, a dividends-received deduction is allowed for a dividend received from a domestic corporation, based on the premise that the United States has already taxed the underlying earnings at the subsidiary corporation level and, therefore, those earnings should not be taxed again at the parent corporation level.

Under an exception, a domestic corporation that owns 10% or more of a foreign corporation may claim a dividends-received deduction for the portion of a dividend attributable to income derived by the foreign corporation from either the conduct of a U.S. trade or business or dividends received from an 80%-or-more-owned domestic corporation.[124] The domestic corporation can claim a dividends-received deduction in this situation because the dividends represent a distribution of earnings that have already incurred U.S. tax.

.02 Direct Foreign Tax Credit

Most foreign countries impose flat rate withholding taxes on the gross amount of dividends paid by a locally organized corporation to a U.S. shareholder. Tax treaties usually reduce the statutory withholding tax rate to 15% or less and the treaty withholding rate often is lower for controlling shareholders (e.g., a corporate shareholder owning 10% or more of the payer's stock) than for noncontrolling shareholders. Under Code Sec. 903, a U.S. person can claim a direct foreign tax credit for any foreign withholding taxes it incurs on a dividend from a foreign corporation.[125]

.03 Deemed Paid Foreign Tax Credit

In addition to the direct foreign credit for foreign withholding taxes, under Code Sec. 902 a domestic corporation can also claim a deemed paid foreign tax credit if it owns 10% or more of the voting stock of the foreign corporation from which it receives a dividend distribution.[126] The term "deemed paid" is a reference to how the foreign income taxes paid by a foreign corporation are made available as a credit to the domestic corporation. Specifically, the domestic corporation is

---

[122] Code Sec. 61(a)(7).

[123] Code Sec. 243(a).

[124] Code Sec. 245(a). However, a domestic corporation cannot claim either a direct or deemed paid credit for any foreign taxes related to the portion of the foreign divi-

dend for which the taxpayer claims a dividends-received deduction. Code Sec. 245(a)(8).

[125] Reg. § 1.903-1(b)(3), Example (2).

[126] Code Sec. 902(a).

deemed to have paid the foreign corporation's foreign income taxes upon receipt of a dividend from that subsidiary.

Example 4.16: USAco owns 100% of FORco, a foreign corporation. During its first year of operations, FORco derives $1 million of foreign-source taxable income, pays $250,000 of foreign income taxes, and distributes its $750,000 of after-tax earnings to USAco as a dividend. The $750,000 dividend is subject to foreign withholding taxes at a 5% rate. USAco can claim a direct ① WHT foreign tax credit for the foreign withholding taxes of $37,500 [$750,000 dividend × 5% withholding rate]. In addition, because USAco owns 10% or more of FORco and receives a dividend distribution from FORco during the year, USAco also can claim a deemed paid credit for the $250,000 of foreign income ② E&P taxes related to the earnings distribution. As discussed in the next section, distribution USAco must also recognize $250,000 of Code Sec. 78 gross-up income.

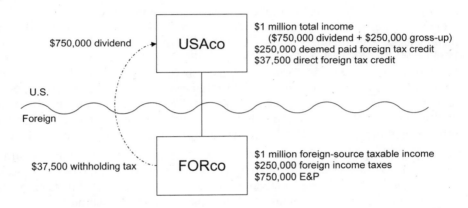

Congress enacted the deemed paid credit to protect domestic corporations with foreign subsidiaries against double taxation, as well as to better equate the tax treatment of U.S. companies with foreign subsidiaries to those with foreign branches. A domestic corporation operating abroad through a branch can claim a direct foreign tax credit for the foreign taxes it pays directly on its foreign earnings.[127] In contrast, a domestic corporation operating abroad through a foreign subsidiary cannot claim a direct credit because the foreign subsidiary, not the domestic parent, is the entity paying the foreign taxes. Allowing domestic corporations to claim a credit for the foreign taxes paid by their foreign subsidiaries enables domestic corporations to structure their foreign operations based on general business considerations rather than U.S. tax consequences. Sometimes the deemed paid foreign tax credit is referred to as the indirect foreign tax credit because, in contrast to the direct foreign tax credit for taxes that are directly paid by the U.S. taxpayer, the indirect foreign tax credit is for taxes that are indirectly paid by the domestic corporation via a foreign subsidiary.

---

[127] Code Sec. 901(a).

SUBSIDIARY → can claim DEEMED PAID FTC (902)

BRANCH → '' DIRECT FTC (903)

Taxpayers cannot claim a credit for foreign withholding taxes imposed on dividends unless the taxpayer holds the stock of the foreign corporation for at least 16 days during the 31-day period beginning 15 days before the ex-dividend date. In the case of dividends on preferred stock, the requisite holding period increases to 46 days during a 91-day period. These holding period requirements do not apply to security dealers.[128] These minimum holding period requirements also apply to foreign withholding taxes imposed on interest, rent and royalty income.[129] Congress enacted these provisions to curtail tax-avoidance transactions designed to transfer foreign tax credits from persons unable to realize a benefit from the credit to persons that can use the credit.[130]

.04 Gross-Up for Deemed Paid Foreign Taxes

Because a dividend represents a distribution from earnings and profits (i.e., after-tax earnings), the amount of income that a domestic corporation recognizes upon receiving a dividend from a foreign corporation is net of all the foreign income taxes paid by that foreign corporation. In effect, the domestic corporation is allowed a deduction for the foreign corporation's income taxes when computing the gross income from a dividend. To prevent a double tax benefit in the form of both an implicit deduction and a deemed paid credit with respect to the same foreign income taxes, a domestic corporation must gross up its dividend income by the amount of the deemed paid credit.[131] In other words, the taxpayer must report an amount of income (dividend plus Code Sec. 78 gross-up) equal to the foreign corporation's pre-tax earnings related to the dividend distribution. This gross-up requirement prevents the double tax benefit by eliminating the implicit deduction.

> **Example 4.17:** USAco owns 100% of ASIAco, a foreign corporation. During its first year of operations, ASIAco derives $10 million of foreign-source taxable income, pays $2 million of foreign income taxes, and distributes its $8 million of after-tax earnings to USAco as a dividend. Assume the dividend is not subject to foreign withholding taxes and that the U.S. tax rate is 35%.

---

[128] Code Sec. 901(k). If the holding period requirement is not satisfied, the taxpayer may still take a deduction for the foreign tax credits disallowed.

[129] Code Sec. 901(l).

[130] *See* Notice 98-5, 1998-1 CB 334, and Notice 2004-19, IRB 2004-11.

[131] Code Sec. 78.

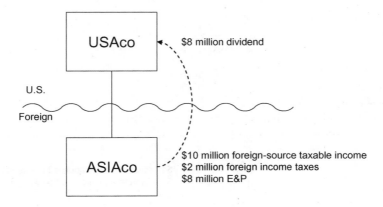

Because USAco owns 10% or more of ASIAco and received a dividend distribution from ASIAco during the year, USAco can claim a deemed paid credit for the $2 million of foreign income taxes related to the $8 million of earnings and profits that were distributed. After the gross-up of $2 million of foreign income taxes, USAco has a pre-credit U.S. tax of $3.5 million [35% × ($8 million dividend + $2 million gross-up)], $2 million of deemed paid credits, and a residual U.S. tax of $1.5 million. Therefore, the total tax on the $10 million of repatriated foreign earnings is $3.5 million [$2 million of foreign taxes + $1.5 million of U.S. taxes], which indicates that ASIAco's earnings are being taxed only once at the higher U.S. rate of 35%. In other words, the deemed paid credit in conjunction with the gross-up achieves its intended effect, which is to prevent both an implicit deduction and a credit for foreign income taxes paid. Absent the gross-up, the residual U.S. tax on ASIAco's repatriated earnings would drop from $1.5 million to $800,000 [(35% U.S. rate × $8 million dividend) – $2 million deemed paid credit]. The $700,000 reduction in the residual U.S. tax reflects the U.S. tax benefit of an implicit deduction for ASIAco's $2 million of foreign income taxes that would arise if USAco included only ASIAco's after-tax earnings in its U.S. taxable income.

The gross-up is also consistent with the policy of equating operating abroad as a foreign subsidiary with operating abroad as a foreign branch. In branch form, the Asian operations would still have $10 million of foreign-source taxable income and $2 million of foreign income taxes. USAco would report the $10 million of foreign-source taxable income, claim a $2 million direct foreign tax credit, and pay a residual U.S. tax of $1.5 million. Again, the total tax on the $10 million of foreign earnings is $3.5 million [$2 million of foreign taxes + $1.5 million of U.S. taxes], which indicates that the Asian earnings are being taxed only once at the higher U.S. rate of 35%. (Compare with Example 4.1 for a comparable result for the direct foreign tax credit when operating abroad as a branch.)

¶409.04

¶ 410 WHO CAN CLAIM A DEEMED PAID CREDIT

Only a domestic C corporation is eligible to claim a deemed paid foreign tax credit. A domestic C corporation can claim a deemed paid foreign tax credit only if it owns 10% or more of the voting stock of a foreign corporation and receives a dividend distribution from that foreign corporation.[132] For this purpose, stock of a foreign corporation that is owned by a partnership is considered to be owned proportionately by its corporate partners.[133] As a result, a domestic C corporation which is a partner in a partnership that owns stock of a foreign corporation is eligible to claim a deemed paid credit with respect to the foreign corporation if the domestic C corporation indirectly owns at least 10% of the voting stock of the foreign corporation and the foreign corporation distributes a dividend. In addition, for purposes of the deemed paid credit, the term "dividend" means a distribution of property out of a foreign corporation's earnings and profits, as well as other transactions that are treated as dividends under the Code, such as a Code Sec. 302(d) stock redemption or a Code Sec. 1248 gain on the sale of stock of a CFC.[134]

U.S. persons other than a domestic C corporation, such as a U.S. citizen or resident alien, are not eligible for the deemed paid credit. This includes an S corporation since, for purposes of the deemed paid credit, an S corporation is treated as a partnership.[135] An S corporation's shareholders, who by statute must be individuals, estates, or trusts, also cannot claim a deemed paid credit. Therefore, an S corporation may wish to structure its foreign operations as an entity that is treated as a branch or a partnership for U.S. tax purposes, in which case the S corporation's shareholders can claim a direct credit for the foreign income taxes incurred by the foreign branch or partnership.[136]

---

[132] Code Sec. 902(a). Members of an affiliated group may not aggregate their ownership interests for purposes of satisfying the 10% ownership requirement. *First Chicago NBD Corp.*, CA-7, 98-1 USTC ¶ 50,169, 135 F3d 457 (7th Cir. 1998). Aff'g 96 TC 421, Dec. 47,218. Rev. Rul. 85-3, 1985-1 CB 222.

[133] Code Sec. 902(c)(7).

[134] Reg. § 1.902-1(a)(11).

[135] Code. Sec. 1373(a), and Reg. § 1.902-1(a)(1).

[136] Code Sec. 901.

Although U.S. citizens and resident aliens cannot claim a deemed paid credit, they can take advantage of the 20% maximum U.S. tax on qualified dividend income, which includes dividends received from foreign corporations that reside in countries that have entered into an income tax treaty with the United States.[137] Such dividends are also potentially subject to the 3.8% Medicare contribution tax on net investment income.[138]

Matching foreign taxes and income. In 2010, Congress enacted the Code Sec. 909 anti-splitting rules to prevent taxpayers from claiming a credit for foreign income taxes before the related foreign income is taken into account for U.S. tax purposes. These rules apply to both direct and deemed paid foreign tax credits. A foreign tax credit splitting event occurs with respect to foreign income taxes if the related income (or earnings and profits) is taken into account by a person who owns or is owned by the person actually paying the foreign tax. Any split taxes are not creditable for U.S. tax purposes before the tax year in which the related income is taken into account by the payer of those taxes.

Example **4.18***:* USP, a domestic corporation, organizes a wholly-owned country A corporation (H), which is treated as a corporation for country A tax purposes, but a disregarded entity for U.S. tax purposes (i.e., a hybrid entity). H organizes a wholly-owned country A entity (RH), which is treated as fiscally transparent for country A tax purposes, but a corporation for U.S. tax purposes (i.e., a reverse hybrid entity). Country A imposes a 30% income tax on H with respect to the income earned by RH.

In year 1, RH earns 200u of income on which H pays 60u of country A tax. For U.S. tax purposes, USP is treated as legally liable for the 60u of foreign taxes paid by H. Nevertheless, under the anti-splitting rules, USP may not claim a credit for these foreign taxes because USP has not yet taken into account the related foreign income of 200u.

In year 2, RH reports no income or loss, and distributes 50% of its earnings and profits from year 1, or 100u, to H. The distribution is treated as a dividend to USP because H is a disregarded entity. Accordingly, 50% of the foreign taxes paid by H in year 1, or 30u, are no longer treated as split taxes, and USP may claim a Sec. 902 deemed paid credit for these taxes.[139]

---

[137] Code Sec. 1(h)(11).

[138] Code Sec. 1411. A taxpayer may not claim a foreign tax credit against the net investment income tax. Reg. § 1.1411-1(e).

[139] Compare Reg. § 1.909-2(b)(1)(v), Example (1), which describes a reverse hybrid splitter arrangement.

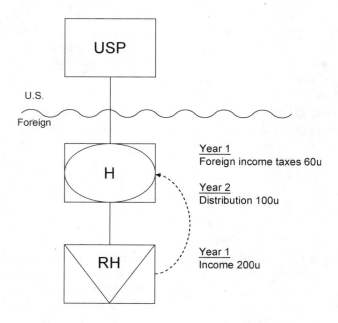

¶ 411 COMPUTING THE DEEMED PAID CREDIT

.01 Tracing Foreign Taxes to Dividend Distributions

Dividends Post-1986 USCORP

Pooling rule. To compute the deemed paid credit, the taxpayer must determine the amount of foreign income taxes that are attributable to a foreign corporation's dividend distribution. In theory, a dividend represents a distribution of corporate earnings from one or more taxable years. Associated with each year's earnings are the foreign income taxes for that year. The practical problem is determining the taxable year(s) from which the earnings distribution emanates. If a foreign corporation distributes all of its after-tax earnings each year, then the tracing problem is relatively easy to solve. The foreign income taxes related to each year's dividend are simply the foreign income taxes paid for that taxable year. However, if a foreign corporation does not distribute all of its earnings and profits each year (a common occurrence), a tracing problem arises.

One possible approach to solving this problem is to assume that dividend distributions pull out a foreign corporation's undistributed earnings and profits and the related foreign income taxes in chronological order (a first-in, first-out rule) or in reverse chronological order (a last-in, first-out rule). Another approach is to pool a foreign corporation's undistributed earnings and profits and foreign income taxes, and then assume that a dividend distribution pulls out deemed paid taxes equal to the pool of foreign income taxes multiplied by the ratio of the dividend to the pool of undistributed earnings and profits. If the effective foreign tax rate varies over time, the amount of deemed paid foreign taxes associated with a dividend will vary with the approach taken.

¶411

RATIO?   FOR taxes × Dividends / FOR E&P

Example **4.19:** USAco owns 100% of EURco, a foreign corporation. EURco's earnings and profits, foreign income taxes, and dividend distributions for its first two years of operations are as follows.

Year	Pre-tax earnings	Foreign income taxes	Effective foreign rate	Earnings & Profits	Dividend distributions
Year 1	$10 million	$2 million	20%	$8 million	$0
Year 2	$10 million	$4 million	40%	$6 million	$3 million

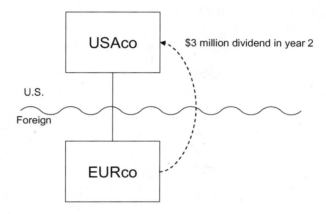

Because the foreign tax rate on EURco's earnings increased from 20% in year 1 to 40% in year 2, the last-in, first-out method would pull out more foreign taxes than the pooling method, as discussed below.

Last-in, first-out method: Under a last-in, first-out tracing rule, the $3 million dividend represents a distribution of 50% of EURco's year 2 earnings and profits of $6 million and, therefore, the dividend pulls out foreign income taxes of $2 million [50% × $4 million of year 2 foreign income taxes].

Pooling method: Prior to the dividend, EURco has undistributed earnings and profits of $14 million [$8 million + $6 million] and foreign income taxes of $6 million [$2 million + $4 million]. Therefore, under a pooling approach, the $3 million dividend pulls out foreign income taxes of roughly $1,285,714 [$6 million of foreign income taxes × ($3 million dividend ÷ $14 million of earnings and profits)].

A pooling approach is required for post-1986 dividends, whereby a domestic corporation that receives a dividend from a 10% or more owned foreign corporation is deemed to have paid the following portion of the foreign corporation's foreign income taxes:[140]

---

[140] Code Sec. 902(a).

$$\text{Foreign corporation's post-1986 foreign income taxes} \times \frac{\text{Dividend}^{141}}{\text{Foreign corporation's post-1986 undistributed earnings}}$$

Example ***4.20:*** USAco owns 100% of AFRIco, a foreign corporation. During its first year of operations, AFRIco derives $10 million of foreign-source taxable income, pays $4 million of foreign income taxes, and distributes a $3 million dividend to USAco. The amount of deemed paid foreign income taxes related to the $3 million dividend is $2 million [$4 million of post-1986 foreign income taxes × ($3 million dividend ÷ $6 million of post-1986 undistributed earnings)].

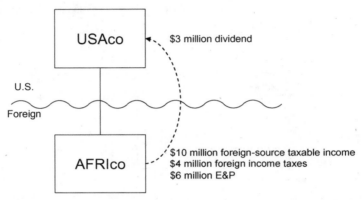

If a dividend exceeds the amount of post-1986 undistributed earnings (i.e., the dividend represents a distribution of pre-1987 earnings), then the tracing rule in effect prior to 1987 is used.[142] Prior to 1987, a last-in, first-out rule was used, whereby pre-1987 annual earnings were layered in chronological order and a dividend pulled out a layer of earnings (and, in turn, a layer of foreign income taxes) in reverse chronological order.[143] The portion of a dividend traced to a pre-1987 year's profits pulls out deemed paid taxes equal to the foreign income taxes for that year multiplied by the ratio of the dividend from that year to the total earnings and profits for that year. The pre-1987 last-in, first-out layering rule also applies to post-1986 earnings and profits derived by a foreign corporation before a domestic corporation first meets the ownership test for claiming a deemed paid credit with respect to the foreign corporation.[144]

Congress enacted the pooling method in 1986, in part, because it believed that U.S. companies were manipulating the preexisting rule to maximize their deemed paid credits. Under a last-in, first-out rule, there is an advantage to bunching a foreign corporation's taxable income and, in turn, its foreign income taxes into particular years before having the foreign corporation distribute its earnings for those high-tax years. This technique causes deemed paid taxes to flow through to

---

[141] The dividend amount in the numerator does not include the Code Sec. 78 gross-up income.
[142] Code Sec. 902(c)(6).

[143] Code Sec. 902(c)(1), before amendment in 1986.
[144] Code Sec. 902(c)(3).

¶411.01

the domestic parent corporation at a higher rate than the long-run average effective rate of foreign taxation. In contrast, under the pooling method, the amount of foreign taxes pulled out by a dividend more accurately reflects the long-run effective rate of foreign taxation.

Post-1986 undistributed earnings. A foreign corporation's "post-1986 undistributed earnings" is computed as of the close of the taxable year in which the foreign corporation distributes the dividend, and equals the cumulative amount of the foreign corporation's undistributed earnings and profits for taxable years beginning after December 31, 1986. Post-1986 undistributed earnings and profits is reduced by actual dividend distributions from prior taxable years, as well as any prior year Subpart F inclusions of the foreign corporation's earnings and profits in a shareholder's income. However, post-1986 undistributed earnings and profits are not reduced by current-year dividend distributions or Subpart F inclusions.[145]

The earnings and profits of a foreign corporation are computed substantially as if it were a domestic corporation.[146] This is accomplished through the following three-step process:

  (i) Prepare a profit and loss statement from the books regularly maintained by the foreign corporation for the purpose of accounting to its shareholder;

  (ii) Make any adjustments necessary to conform the profit and loss statement to U.S. generally accepted accounting principles; and

  (iii) Make any adjustments necessary to conform the profit and loss statement to U.S. tax accounting standards.[147]

An adjustment is not required unless it is material in light of the facts and circumstances.[148]

Post-1986 foreign income taxes. A foreign corporation's "post-1986 foreign income taxes" equal the cumulative amount of a foreign corporation's foreign income taxes for taxable years beginning after December 31, 1986 (including the foreign income taxes for the year of the dividend), reduced by the amount of foreign income taxes related to prior-year dividend distributions and Subpart F inclusions, regardless of whether the shareholders were eligible to claim a deemed paid credit.[149]

The term "foreign income taxes" has the same meaning for purposes of the deemed paid credit as it does for purposes of the direct foreign tax credit.[150] As a result, to be creditable, a levy paid by a foreign corporation must meet two basic requirements. First, the levy must be a tax that is paid to a foreign country or U.S. possession. Second, the predominant character of the tax must be that of an income tax in the U.S. sense.[151] If a foreign levy satisfies the first requirement but not the second, the foreign levy may still be creditable if the tax is imposed in lieu of an

---

[145] Code Sec. 902(c)(1) and Reg. § 1.902-1(a)(9).

[146] Code Sec. 964(a); *Goodyear Tire & Rubber Co.*, SCt, 89-2 USTC ¶ 9658, 493 US 132, 110 SCt 462; *rev'g* and *rem'g* CA-FC, 88-2 USTC ¶ 9491.

[147] Reg. § 1.964-1(a)(1).

[148] Reg. § 1.964-1(a)(2).

[149] Code Sec. 902(c)(2) and Reg. § 1.902-1(a)(8).

[150] Code Sec. 902(c)(4)(A) and Reg. § 1.902-1(a)(7).

[151] Code Sec. 901(b) and Reg. § 1.901-2(a)(1).

income tax.[152] A common example is a foreign withholding tax imposed on dividends, interest or royalties. Foreign income taxes also include any taxes that a foreign corporation is deemed to have paid by reason of receiving a dividend from a lower-tier foreign corporation (see discussion below).[153] If two or more commonly controlled foreign corporations file a consolidated foreign income tax return and the corporations are jointly and severally liable for the foreign income tax, then each corporation is treated as having paid a portion of the foreign income tax equal to its proportionate share of the combined income tax base.[154]

Currency translation. Foreign corporations usually conduct business and keep their books and records in a foreign currency. This creates a currency translation problem for a domestic corporation, which must translate the dividends, Subpart F inclusions, and foreign income taxes of the foreign corporation into U.S. dollars. These currency translation rules are discussed in Chapter 6 (¶ 601).

.02 Credit for Taxes Paid by Lower-Tier Foreign Corporations

A domestic corporation that operates abroad through multiple tiers of foreign corporations can obtain a deemed paid foreign tax credit for taxes paid by lower-tier foreign corporations (down six tiers). This is possible because an upper-tier foreign corporation's post-1986 foreign income taxes include not only the foreign income taxes it pays, but also the foreign income taxes it is deemed to have paid by reason of receiving a dividend from a lower-tier foreign corporation, as long as both the upper-tier and the lower-tier foreign corporations are members of a "qualified group."[155] A qualified group consists of a first-tier foreign corporation for which a domestic corporation may claim a deemed paid foreign tax credit, as well as any other foreign corporation if the domestic corporation owns at least 5% of the voting stock of the foreign corporation indirectly through the chain, the chain of foreign corporations are connected through stock ownership of at least 10% of their voting stock at each tier in the chain, and the lower-tier foreign corporation is not below the sixth tier in the chain. In addition, to be included in the qualified group, any foreign corporation below the third tier must be a CFC in which the domestic corporation is a U.S. shareholder.[156]

Example 4.21: USAco owns 100% of F1, F1 owns 40% of F2, and F2 owns 10% of F3. F1, F2 and F3 are foreign corporations.

---

[152] Code Sec. 903.
[153] Code Sec. 902(c)(4)(B).
[154] Reg. § 1.901-2(f)(3).

[155] Code Secs. 902(b)(1) and (c)(4).
[156] Code Sec. 902(b)(2).

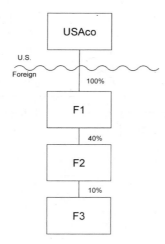

USAco may claim a deemed foreign tax credit for the foreign income taxes paid by F2 because USAco owns at least 10% of F1 (100%), F1 owns at least 10% of F2 (40%), and USAco indirectly owns at least 5% of F2 (100% × 40% = 40%). However, even though F2 owns at least 10% of F3 (10%), because the indirect ownership by USAco of F3 is less than 5% (100% × 40% × 10% = 4%), USAco may not claim a deemed foreign tax credit for foreign income taxes paid by F3.

The foreign income taxes of lower-tier foreign corporations move up the chain of foreign corporations included in the qualified group as dividends are paid up the chain, such that a first-tier foreign corporation's pool of post-1986 foreign income taxes includes not only the foreign income taxes that it pays, but also the foreign income taxes it is deemed to have paid upon receiving dividends from lower-tier corporations. The amount of foreign income taxes associated with a dividend paid by a lower-tier foreign corporation to an upper-tier foreign corporation is computed using the same formula used by a domestic corporation to compute its deemed paid foreign income taxes.[157]

Example 4.22: USAco owns 100% of F1, and F1 owns 100% of F2. F1 and F2 are both foreign corporations. At end of the current year, the post-1986 undistributed earnings and post-1986 foreign income taxes of F1 and F2 are as follows:

	Post-1986 undistributed earnings	Post-1986 foreign income taxes
F1	$18 million	$4 million
F2	$6 million	$3 million

During the current year, F2 distributes a $2 million dividend to F1 and F1 distributes a $2 million dividend to USAco. The $2 million dividend from F2 pulls out $1 million of deemed paid taxes for F1 [$3 million of post-1986 foreign

---

[157] Code Sec. 902(b)(1). One difference is that the first-tier foreign corporation does not recognize any gross-up income for deemed paid taxes, since the Code Sec. 78 gross-up requirement applies only to a domestic corporation that claims a credit against its U.S. taxes.

income taxes × ($2 million dividend ÷ $6 million of post-1986 undistributed earnings)]. After taking into account the $2 million dividend from F2, F1's post-1986 undistributed earnings and profits increase to $20 million [$18 million + $2 million] and (assuming F2's dividend is exempt from local taxation in F1's country) F1's post-1986 foreign income taxes increase to $5 million [$4 million + $1 million]. As a consequence, USAco's receipt of a $2 million dividend from F1 pulls out deemed paid taxes of $500,000 [$5 million of post-1986 foreign income taxes × ($2 million dividend ÷ $20 million of post-1986 undistributed earnings)] and USAco must recognize dividend income of $2.5 million [$2 million dividend + $500,000 gross-up].

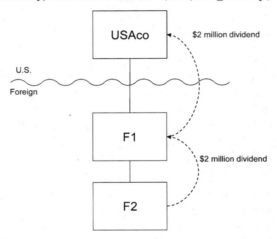

.03 CFC and 10/50 Company Look-through Rules

As discussed in ¶ 405.03 with respect to direct credits, for purposes of computing the separate income foreign tax credit limitations, look-through rules apply to dividends received from either a CFC or a 10/50 company.[158] The look-through rule also applies to deemed paid credits. If it were not for these look-through rules, the separate category of income limitations would yield significantly different results for domestic corporations operating abroad through foreign subsidiaries as opposed to foreign branches. For example, if a domestic corporation structures a foreign manufacturing operation as a branch, the related income and foreign taxes would be assigned to the general income limitation. In contrast, if a domestic corporation were to structure the same foreign manufacturing operation as a subsidiary, absent a look-through rule, dividend distributions from that foreign manufacturing subsidiary would be assigned to the passive income limitation.

To better equate the treatment of foreign branch and foreign subsidiary operations, dividends paid by a foreign corporation to a domestic corporation are allocated between passive income and general limitation income based on the ratio of the foreign corporation's earnings and profits within each category of income to the foreign corporation's total earnings and profits.[159] For example, if a foreign

---

[158] Code Sec. 904(d)(3) and (4).   [159] Code Sec. 904(d)(3)(D) and Reg. § 1.904-5(c)(4)(i).

corporation has $1 million of earnings and profits, $900,000 of which is attributable to general limitation income and the other $100,000 to passive income, then 90% of a dividend distribution from the foreign corporation is general limitation income and the other 10% is passive income. The amount of deemed paid foreign taxes related to each separate category of income is then determined using the following formula:[160]

$$\begin{matrix} \text{Post-1986 foreign} \\ \text{income taxes related to} \\ \text{category of income}^{161} \end{matrix} \times \frac{\text{Portion of dividend allocated to category of income}}{\begin{matrix}\text{Post-1986 undistributed earnings}\\\text{related to category of income}\end{matrix}}$$

To make these computations, a domestic corporation must maintain separate pools of post-1986 undistributed earnings and post-1986 foreign income taxes for passive income and general limitation income with respect to any 10%-or-more-owned foreign corporation.

> **Example 4.23:** USAco owns 100% of FORco, a foreign corporation. At end of the current year, FORco's pools of post-1986 undistributed earnings and post-1986 foreign income taxes are as follows:

	Post-1986 undistributed earnings	Post-1986 foreign income taxes
General limitation income	$8 million	$7 million
Passive income	$4 million	$1 million
	$12 million	$8 million

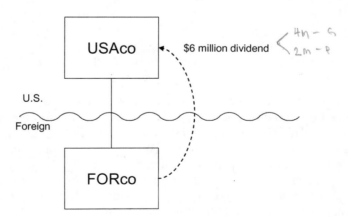

> During the current year, FORco distributed a $6 million dividend to USAco. Under the CFC look-through rule, $4 million of this amount [$6 million × ($8

---

[160] Reg. § 1.902-1 (d) (2) (i).

[161] Foreign income taxes are allocated to the category of income that includes the income upon which the foreign taxes were imposed. Reg. § 1.904-6(a) (1) (i). If the base upon which a foreign income tax is imposed includes income from more than one category, the taxpayer allocates the foreign income taxes between passive income and general limitation income based on the relative amount of foreign taxable income within each category. Reg. § 1.904-6(a) (1) (ii).

million ÷ $12 million)] is general limitation income and the other $2 million [$6 million × ($4 million ÷ $12 million)] is passive income. Therefore, FORco's $6 million dividend pulls out deemed paid taxes of $3.5 million in the general income limitation [$7 million of post-1986 foreign income taxes × ($4 million dividend ÷ $8 million of post-1986 undistributed earnings)] and $500,000 in the passive income limitation [$1 million of post-1986 foreign income taxes × ($2 million dividend ÷ $4 million of post-1986 undistributed earnings)].

.04 Deemed Paid Credits for Subpart F and QEF Inclusions

Subpart F requires a U.S. shareholder of a CFC to recognize a deemed dividend equal to its pro rata share of the CFC's Subpart F income and its pro-rata share of a CFC's investment of earnings in U.S. property.[162] In the case of a domestic corporation that owns 10% or more of the CFC's voting stock, a Subpart F inclusion carries with it a deemed paid foreign tax credit that is computed in the same manner as the deemed paid credit that is allowed with respect to actual dividend distributions.[163] Domestic corporations that own 10% or more of the voting stock of a passive foreign investment company that has made a qualified electing fund election can also claim a deemed paid credit with respect to the qualified electing fund income inclusion.[164] The taxation of Subpart F and qualified electing fund inclusions, including the computation of the related deemed paid foreign tax credit, is discussed in Chapter 5.

¶ 412 COMPLIANCE REQUIREMENTS

A corporation claiming a foreign tax credit must attach Form 1118 to its tax return, whereas an individual claiming a foreign tax credit must attach Form 1116 to his or her tax return (both forms are reproduced in the appendix to this chapter).[165] A domestic corporation claiming a deemed paid foreign tax credit generally must satisfy the same filing and documentation requirements that apply to the direct credit.[166] A separate Form 1118 (or Form 1116) is completed for passive income and general limitation income.

Regardless of whether the foreign tax credits taken are direct credits or deemed paid credits, the IRS may ask for proof of the foreign income taxes paid or incurred. The primary substantiation for foreign income taxes paid by a cash basis taxpayer is a receipt for payment. The primary substantiation for foreign income taxes incurred by an accrual basis taxpayer is the foreign tax return.[167] If the IRS, in its discretion, is satisfied that a taxpayer cannot furnish primary substantiation, a taxpayer may furnish secondary substantiation.[168] In lieu of a receipt for payment of foreign income taxes, a cash basis taxpayer must be able to provide a photocopy of the check, draft or other medium of payment showing the amount and date, with evidence establishing that the tax was paid. In lieu of a foreign tax return showing the foreign income taxes incurred, an accrual basis taxpayer must be able to

---

[162] Code Sec. 951(a)(1).
[163] Code Sec. 960(a)(1).
[164] Code Sec. 1293(f)(1).
[165] Reg. § 1.905-2(a)(1).

[166] Reg. § 1.902-1(e).
[167] Reg. § 1.905-2(a)(2).
[168] Reg. § 1.905-2(b).

provide a certified statement of the accrued amount, with excerpts from its books showing the computation of the accrued amount.

Foreign withholding taxes represent unique problems, since they are not paid directly by the taxpayer. Indirect evidence, such as a letter from the foreign payer stating that the tax was withheld and paid, may not provide sufficient proof of payment to claim a credit. Instead, the taxpayer may be required to produce evidence that the foreign payer actually remitted the foreign withholding taxes to the foreign government.[169] Whenever possible, taxpayers should obtain a government receipt for any foreign withholding taxes that it paid.

Although these substantiation rules apply to both direct and deemed paid credits, record retention can be a challenge for a corporation claiming the deemed paid credit. Considering that the deemed paid credit is based on pools of foreign taxes and earnings and profits that have accumulated since 1987, domestic corporations should ensure that they are keeping primary substantiation and, if they do not have primary substantiation, putting together the appropriate secondary substantiation.

> *Example 4.24:* USAco has owned 100% of FORco, a foreign corporation, since 1990. FORco distributes its first dividend ever to USAco in 2015. When filing its 2015 tax return, USAco claims a deemed paid credit with respect to the dividend received from FORco. In 2017, the IRS audits USAco and requests substantiation of the foreign income taxes paid by FORco. If USAco cannot substantiate the foreign income taxes paid by FORco going back to 1990, the IRS may deny the deemed paid credit.

If an adjustment by a foreign tax authority (i.e., a "redetermination") results in an increase in the amount of foreign taxes paid, the taxpayer has 10 years from the date the U.S. return was originally filed to claim a refund of U.S. taxes for the increase in creditable foreign taxes.[170] On the other hand, if the foreign tax redetermination results in a refund of foreign taxes, the taxpayer must notify the IRS by filing an amended tax return on which the taxpayer recomputes the U.S. tax liability for the year in which the foreign tax credit was originally claimed.[171] In addition, special IRS notification rules apply to taxpayers under the jurisdiction of the Large Business and International Division.[172] A failure to provide notification to the IRS can result in a penalty of up to 25% of the amount of the deficiency associated with the redetermination.[173] In the case of a redetermination of the foreign taxes of a foreign corporation that are deemed paid by a domestic corporation under Code Sec. 902 or 960, adjustments are made to the foreign corporation's pools of post-1986 foreign income taxes and post-1986 undistributed earnings.[174] Special currency translation rules apply to redeterminations.[175]

---

[169] Reg. § 1.905-2(b)(3), *Continental Illinois Corp.*, CA-7, Dec. 47,178(M), 998 F2d 513 (7th Cir. 1993), aff'g, rev'g, and rem'g 61 TCM 1916, Dec. 47,178(M), TC Memo. 1991-66; and *Norwest Corp.*, 70 TCM 779, Dec. 50,906(M), TC Memo. 1995-453.

[170] Code Sec. 6511(d)(3)(A).

[171] Temp. Reg. § 1.905-4T(b)(2). The amended tax return must be filed within 180 days of the redetermination.

[172] Temp. Reg. § 1.905-4T.

[173] Code Sec. 6689.

[174] Code Sec. 905(c).

[175] Temp. Reg. § 1.905-3T.

¶ 413 PLANNING FOR DIVIDEND REPATRIATIONS

The decision to repatriate earnings from a foreign subsidiary may be influenced by a variety of factors, such as the cash needs of the domestic parent corporation, the preferences of foreign managers, financial reporting considerations, local company laws requiring the maintenance of reserves, as well as U.S. and foreign tax consequences. As discussed below, the precepts of U.S. tax planning for dividend repatriations include cross-crediting, minimizing foreign withholding taxes, and considering alternative methods of repatriating earnings.

.01 Cross-Crediting

The U.S. tax consequences of a dividend repatriation depend on whether the foreign corporation is operating in a low- or high-tax foreign jurisdiction. No U.S. tax is due on a dividend from a foreign corporation operating in a high-tax foreign jurisdiction, because the deemed foreign tax credits more than offset the pre-credit U.S. tax. Therefore, planning focuses on reducing these excess credits. In contrast, a dividend from a foreign corporation operating in a low-tax foreign jurisdiction results in a residual U.S. tax. In such situations, planning focuses on reducing that residual U.S. tax. For example, through cross-crediting, the excess credits on dividends from high-tax foreign subsidiaries can be used to soak up the residual U.S. tax due on dividends from low-tax foreign subsidiaries. The look-through rule makes cross-crediting possible with respect to dividends from foreign corporations located in low-tax and high-tax foreign jurisdictions, as long as the underlying earnings of the foreign corporation are assigned to the same separate category of income limitation (e.g., the general limitation income).

> **Example 4.25:** USAco owns 100% of both LOWco and HIGHco, two foreign corporations. At end of the current year, LOWco's and HIGHco's pools of post-1986 undistributed earnings and post-1986 foreign income taxes are as follows:
>
> | | LOWco | HIGHco |
> |---|---|---|
> | Post-1986 undistributed earnings attributable to general limitation income . . . . | $8 million | $6 million |
> | Post-1986 foreign income taxes attributable to general limitation income . . . . | $2 million | $9 million |
>
> Assume the U.S. tax rate is 35%, and that any dividends that LOWco or HIGHco distribute to USAco are not subject to foreign withholding taxes.

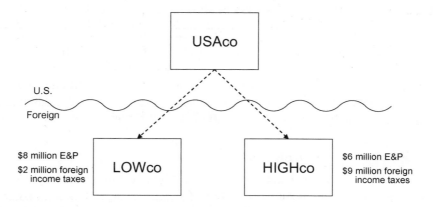

Case 1—Repatriate earnings from low-tax subsidiary: Assume LOWco distributes a $4 million dividend to USAco. The dividend would pull out $1 million of deemed paid taxes [$2 million of post-1986 foreign income taxes × ($4 million dividend ÷ $8 million of post-1986 undistributed earnings)]. With the gross-up of $1 million, USAco would have dividend income of $5 million [$4 million dividend + $1 million gross-up]. Under the CFC look-through rule, the entire amount of this dividend and the related foreign income taxes are assigned to the general income limitation. Therefore, within USAco's general income limitation, there would be a limitation of $1.75 million [35% U.S. rate × $5 million], deemed paid taxes of $1 million, and a residual U.S. tax of $750,000 [$1.75 million – $1 million].

Case 2—Repatriate earnings from both low- and high-tax subsidiaries: Every dollar of dividends from HIGHco increases the deemed paid taxes within USAco's general income limitation by $1.50 [$9 million of post-1986 foreign income taxes × ($1 dividend ÷ $6 million of post-1986 undistributed earnings)], but only increases USAco's general income limitation by $0.875 [35% U.S. tax rate × ($1.00 dividend + $1.50 gross-up)]. The net effect is an excess credit of $0.625 for every dollar of dividends [$1.50 of additional deemed paid taxes – $0.875 of additional limitation]. Therefore, USAco can completely eliminate the $750,000 residual U.S. tax on LOWco's $4 million dividend by having HIGHco distribute a dividend of $1.2 million [$750,000 ÷ $0.625]. A $1.2 million dividend from HIGHco would pull out $1.8 million of deemed paid taxes [$9 million of post-1986 foreign income taxes × ($1.2 million dividend ÷ $6 million of post-1986 undistributed earnings)] and increase USAco's general limitation income by $1,050,000 [35% U.S. tax rate × ($1.2 million dividend + $1.8 million gross-up)]. The net effect is $750,000 of additional foreign tax credits.

.02 Minimizing Foreign Withholding Taxes

Most foreign countries impose flat rate withholding taxes on the gross amount of dividends paid by a locally organized corporation to its U.S. shareholders. Foreign withholding taxes can exacerbate the excess credit problem created by dividends from foreign subsidiaries operating in high-tax foreign jurisdictions as

¶413.02

the creditable foreign taxes include both the deemed paid taxes and the withholding taxes. However, tax treaties usually reduce the statutory withholding rate on dividends to 15% or less. Moreover, the treaty withholding rate often is lower for controlling shareholders (e.g., corporate shareholder owning 10% or more of the payer's stock) than for noncontrolling shareholders. Therefore, a domestic corporation may be able to use tax treaties to reduce foreign withholding taxes by, for example, owning foreign operating subsidiaries through a foreign holding company located in a country with a favorable treaty network that contains lenient limitation of benefits articles.

.03 Alternatives to Dividend Repatriations

It may be advantageous for a domestic parent corporation to repatriate the earnings of a foreign subsidiary through interest, rental, and royalty payments and higher transfer prices, rather than dividend distributions. A foreign subsidiary usually can claim a tax deduction for interest, rents, and royalties paid to its domestic parent as well as for higher transfer prices, whereas dividend distributions typically are not deductible. On the other hand, only a dividend distribution can provide the domestic parent with a deemed paid credit. Nevertheless, if the foreign subsidiary is operating in a high-tax foreign jurisdiction, the benefits of a deduction at the foreign subsidiary level may exceed the costs of losing the deemed paid credit at the domestic parent level.

> **Example 4.26:** USAco owns 100% of ASIAco, a foreign corporation. During its first year of operations, ASIAco's had taxable income of $10 million and made no deductible interest payments to USAco. Assume that the foreign income tax rate is 45%, the U.S. rate is 35%, and no foreign withholding taxes are imposed on any dividend distributions or interest payments that ASIAco makes to USAco.

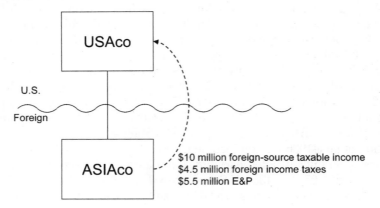

> *Case 1—Repatriate earnings through dividend:* If USAco repatriated all of ASIAco's after-tax earnings through a dividend, the foreign tax on those earnings would be $4.5 million [$10 million of taxable income × 45% foreign tax rate]. USAco would receive a $5.5 million dividend distribution, which would pull out $4.5 million of deemed paid foreign taxes [$4.5 million of post-1986

¶413.03

foreign income taxes × ($5.5 million dividend ÷ $5.5 million of post-1986 undistributed earnings)]. With the gross-up, USAco would have dividend income of $10 million [$5.5 million dividend + $4.5 million gross-up] and its pre-credit U.S. tax would be $3.5 million [$10 million × 35% U.S. tax rate]. There would be no residual U.S. tax due on the dividend income since USAco's deemed paid credits would offset the entire pre-credit U.S. tax. In sum, if USAco repatriates ASIAco's earnings through a dividend distribution, the total tax on those earnings would equal the foreign tax of $4.5 million.

Case 2—Repatriate earnings through interest payments: USAco may be able to reduce the total tax burden on ASIAco's earnings by repatriating those earnings through deductible interest payments, as opposed to dividend distributions. As an extreme example, if USAco financed ASIAco in a way that provided ASIAco with $10 million of deductible interest payments, that interest expense would reduce ASIAco's taxable income to $0. On the other hand, USAco would owe $3.5 million of U.S. tax on the interest payments it received from ASIAco [$10 million of interest income × 35% U.S. rate]. Nevertheless, the total tax on ASIAco's repatriated earnings would equal the U.S. tax of $3.5 million, which is $1 million less than the total tax if ASIAco's earnings are repatriated through a dividend distribution.

The tax implications of using debt financing for a foreign subsidiary are discussed in more detail in Chapter 8 (¶ 805).

¶ 414 APPENDIX

An S corporation is owned by Uncle Sam, a U.S. citizen who pays tax at a 40% U.S. rate. The S corporation earns $300,000 of worldwide gross profits, $150,000 of which is attributable to its U.S. sales. A sales branch office in foreign country F earns $150,000 of gross profits. All of the goods sold abroad (with title passing abroad) are manufactured at the S corporation's manufacturing facility in East Palo Alto, California. The foreign sales branch pays $40,000 of foreign income taxes during the year. The S corporation incurs $100,000 of expenses to be allocated and apportioned, $12,000 of which are itemized. Uncle Sam's pre-credit U.S. tax liability on the worldwide taxable income of $200,000 is $80,000. Under the 50-50 method of sourcing income from the foreign sales of manufactured inventory, $75,000 of the gross profit on foreign sales is gross foreign-source income. After an allocation and apportionment of expenses based on gross profit, Uncle Sam has only $50,000 of net foreign-source income. Therefore, some of the foreign income taxes paid will not be creditable due to the foreign tax credit limitation. On his Form 1116, Uncle Sam will only be able to credit $20,000 of foreign income taxes paid. The remaining $20,000 of foreign income taxes paid constitutes an excess foreign tax credit that may be carried back or carried forward.

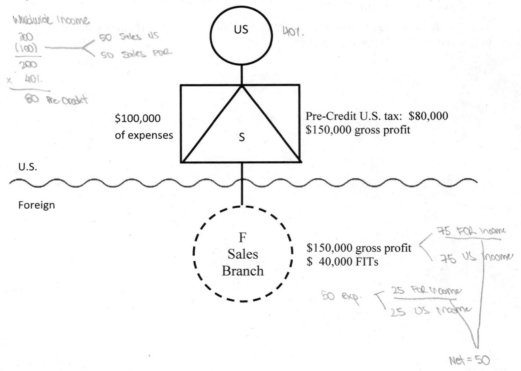

Form **1116**	**Foreign Tax Credit**	OMB No. 1545-0121
Department of the Treasury Internal Revenue Service (99)	(Individual, Estate, or Trust) ▶ Attach to Form 1040, 1040NR, 1041, or 990-T. ▶ Information about Form 1116 and its separate instructions is at *www.irs.gov/form1116*.	20**14** Attachment Sequence No. **19**

Name	Identifying number as shown on page 1 of your tax return
Uncle Sam	123-45-6789

Use a separate Form 1116 for each category of income listed below. See **Categories of Income** in the instructions. Check only one box on each Form 1116. Report all amounts in U.S. dollars except where specified in Part II below.

a ☐ Passive category income   **c** ☐ Section 901(j) income   **e** ☐ Lump-sum distributions

b ☑ General category income   **d** ☐ Certain income re-sourced by treaty

f Resident of (name of country) ▶

Note: *If you paid taxes to only one foreign country or U.S. possession, use column A in Part I and line A in Part II. If you paid taxes to* **more than one** *foreign country or U.S. possession, use a separate column and line for each country or possession.*

Part I   **Taxable Income or Loss From Sources Outside the United States (for Category Checked Above)**

		Foreign Country or U.S. Possession			Total
		A	**B**	**C**	(Add cols. A, B, and C.)
g	Enter the name of the foreign country or U.S. possession . . . . ▶				
1a	Gross income from sources within country shown above and of the type checked above (see instructions): _____ _____	75,000			**1a** 75,000
b	Check if line 1a is compensation for personal services as an employee, your total compensation from all sources is $250,000 or more, and you used an alternative basis to determine its source (see instructions) . . ▶ ☐				
	Deductions and losses (*Caution: See instructions***):**				
2	Expenses **definitely related** to the income on line 1a (attach statement)				
3	Pro rata share of other deductions **not definitely related:**				
a	Certain itemized deductions or standard deduction (see instructions)	12,000			
b	Other deductions (attach statement)	88.000			
c	Add lines 3a and 3b	100,000			
d	Gross foreign source income (see instructions) .	75,000			
e	Gross income from all sources (see instructions) .	300,000			
f	Divide line 3d by line 3e (see instructions) . . .	.25			
g	Multiply line 3c by line 3f	25,000			
4	Pro rata share of interest expense (see instructions):				
a	Home mortgage interest (use the Worksheet for Home Mortgage Interest in the instructions) . .				
b	Other interest expense				
5	Losses from foreign sources				
6	Add lines 2, 3g, 4a, 4b, and 5	25,000			**6** 25,000
7	Subtract line 6 from line 1a. Enter the result here and on line 15, page 2 . . . . ▶				**7** 50,000

Part II   **Foreign Taxes Paid or Accrued** (see instructions)

Country	Credit is claimed for taxes (you must check one) **(h)** ☑ Paid **(i)** ☐ Accrued	Foreign taxes paid or accrued								
		In foreign currency				In U.S. dollars				
		Taxes withheld at source on:			**(n)** Other foreign taxes paid or accrued	Taxes withheld at source on:			**(r)** Other foreign taxes paid or accrued	**(s)** Total foreign taxes paid or accrued (add cols. (o) through (r))
	(j) Date paid or accrued	**(k)** Dividends	**(l)** Rents and royalties	**(m)** Interest		**(o)** Dividends	**(p)** Rents and royalties	**(q)** Interest		
A	12/31/14								40,000	40,000
B										
C										
8	Add lines A through C, column (s). Enter the total here and on line 9, page 2 . . . . ▶ **8**									40,000

For Paperwork Reduction Act Notice, see instructions.   Cat. No. 11440U   Form **1116** (2014)

¶414

Part III **Figuring the Credit**

9	Enter the amount from line 8. These are your total foreign taxes paid or accrued for the category of income checked above Part I . . .	9	40,000
10	Carryback or carryover (attach detailed computation)	10	
11	Add lines 9 and 10	11	40,000
12	Reduction in foreign taxes (see instructions)	12 (	)
13	Taxes reclassified under high tax kickout (see instructions) . .	13	
14	Combine lines 11, 12, and 13. This is the total amount of foreign taxes available for credit . . .	14	40,000
15	Enter the amount from line 7. This is your taxable income or (loss) from sources outside the United States (before adjustments) for the category of income checked above Part I (see instructions)	15	50,000
16	Adjustments to line 15 (see instructions)	16	
17	Combine the amounts on lines 15 and 16. This is your net foreign source taxable income. (If the result is zero or less, you have no foreign tax credit for the category of income you checked above Part I. Skip lines 18 through 22. However, if you are filing more than one Form 1116, you must complete line 20.)	17	50,000
18	**Individuals:** Enter the amount from Form 1040, line 41, or Form 1040NR, line 39. **Estates and trusts:** Enter your taxable income without the deduction for your exemption	18	200,000
	Caution: *If you figured your tax using the lower rates on qualified dividends or capital gains, see instructions.*		
19	Divide line 17 by line 18. If line 17 is more than line 18, enter "1"	19	.25
20	**Individuals:** Enter the amounts from Form 1040, lines 44 and 46. If you are a nonresident alien, enter the amounts from Form 1040NR, lines 42 and 44. **Estates and trusts:** Enter the amount from Form 1041, Schedule G, line 1a, or the total of Form 990-T, lines 36 and 37	20	80,000
	Caution: *If you are completing line 20 for separate category* **e** *(lump-sum distributions), see instructions.*		
21	Multiply line 20 by line 19 (maximum amount of credit)	21	20,000
22	Enter the **smaller** of line 14 or line 21. If this is the only Form 1116 you are filing, skip lines 23 through 27 and enter this amount on line 28. Otherwise, complete the appropriate line in Part IV (see instructions) . . . . ▶	22	20,000

Part IV **Summary of Credits From Separate Parts III** (see instructions)

23	Credit for taxes on passive category income	23	
24	Credit for taxes on general category income	24	20,000
25	Credit for taxes on certain income re-sourced by treaty	25	
26	Credit for taxes on lump-sum distributions	26	
27	Add lines 23 through 26	27	
28	Enter the **smaller** of line 20 or line 27	28	
29	Reduction of credit for international boycott operations. See instructions for line 12	29	20,000
30	Subtract line 29 from line 28. This is your **foreign tax credit.** Enter here and on Form 1040, line 48; Form 1040NR, line 46; Form 1041, Schedule G, line 2a; or Form 990-T, line 40a . . . . . ▶	30	

Form **1116** (2014)

¶414

M&M Enterprises, Inc. (M&M), a U.S. C corporation, earns $150,000 of gross profit from U.S. sources and owns a foreign subsidiary that operates a manufacturing/sales facility. The foreign subsidiary earns $100,000 on which $40,000 of foreign incomes taxes are paid. On December 31, the foreign subsidiary distributes a $30,000 dividend on which Country F imposes a 10% withholding tax of $3,000. M&M incurs $28,000 of expenses, $7,000 of which is apportioned to foreign source income. The remaining $21,000 of expenses is apportioned to the $150,000 of gross income from operations in the United States. M&M will take two types of foreign tax credits—an "in lieu of" foreign tax credit for the withholding taxes and a "deemed paid" foreign tax credit for the foreign income taxes paid by the foreign subsidiary that come with the dividend repatriation. Only half of the $40,000 of accumulated foreign taxes paid by the foreign subsidiary ($20,000) comes with the dividend because only half of the undistributed earnings of $60,000 are repatriated as a $30,000 dividend. As a result, the grossed-up dividend is $50,000. Due to the foreign tax credit limitation, the Form 1118 for M&M Enterprises, Inc. will show a foreign tax credit of $15,229, with an excess foreign tax credit of $7,771 that may be carried back or carried forward.

[handwritten margin notes: Direct / Indirect]

[handwritten note: Form shows only 15,150 (p.139) → where is the #179?]

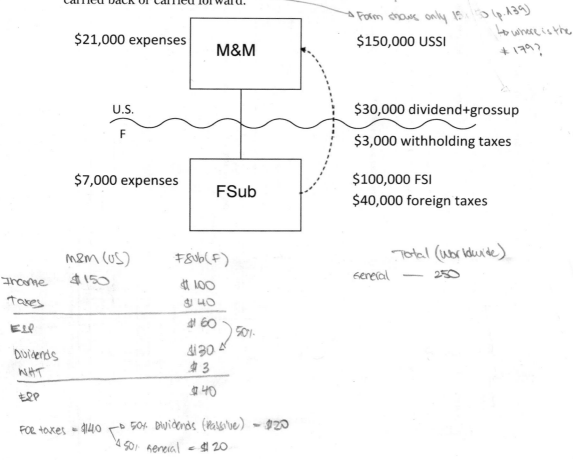

$21,000 expenses — M&M — $150,000 USSI

U.S.
F

$30,000 dividend+grossup
$3,000 withholding taxes

$7,000 expenses — FSub — $100,000 FSI
$40,000 foreign taxes

[handwritten table:]

	M&M (US)	FSub (F)	Total (worldwide)
Income	$150	$100	General — 250
Taxes		$40	
E&P		$60 ⎱ 50%	
Dividends		$130	
NHT		$3	
E&P		$40	

For taxes = $40 ⎡ 50% Dividends (Passive) = $20
              ⎣ 50% General = $20

Income Inclusion = $30 dividend + $20 FTC = $50

Form **1118**
(Rev. December 2014)
Department of the Treasury
Internal Revenue Service

Foreign Tax Credit—Corporations

▶ Information about Form 1118 and its separate instructions is at *www.irs.gov/form1118*.
▶ Attach to the corporation's tax return.

OMB No. 1545-0123

Name of corporation

Employer identification number

M&M Enterprises

For calendar year 20 **14** , or other tax year beginning , 20 , and ending , 20

Use a **separate** Form 1118 for each applicable category of income listed below. See **Categories of Income** in the instructions. Also, see **Specific Instructions.**
Check only one box on each form.

☐ Passive Category Income   ☐ Section 901(j) Income: Name of Sanctioned Country ▶ _____

☑ General Category Income   ☐ Income Re-sourced by Treaty: Name of Country ▶ _____

Schedule A   Income or (Loss) Before Adjustments *(Report all amounts in U.S. dollars. See Specific Instructions.)*

Gross Income or (Loss) From Sources Outside the United States *(INCLUDE Foreign Branch Gross Income here and on Schedule F)*

1. Foreign Country or U.S. Possession (Enter two-letter code; see instructions. Use a separate line for each.) *	2. Deemed Dividends (see instructions)		3. Other Dividends		4. Interest	5. Gross Rents, Royalties, and License Fees	6. Gross Income From Performance of Services	7. Other (attach schedule)	8. Total (add columns 2(a) through 7)
	(a) Exclude gross-up	**(b)** Gross-up (sec. 78)	**(a)** Exclude gross-up	**(b)** Gross-up (sec. 78)					
A		30,000		20,000					50,000
B									
C									
D									
E									
F									
Totals (add lines A through F)									50,000

* For section 863(b) income, NOLs, income from RICs, and high-taxed income, use a single line (see instructions).

Deductions *(INCLUDE Foreign Branch Deductions here and on Schedule F)*

	9. Definitely Allocable Deductions					10. Apportioned Share of Deductions Not Definitely Allocable (enter amount from applicable line of Schedule H, Part II, column (d))	11. Net Operating Loss Deduction	12. Total Deductions (add columns 9(e) through 11)	13. Total Income or (Loss) Before Adjustments (subtract column 12 from column 8)
Rental, Royalty, and Licensing Expenses			**(d)** Other Definitely Allocable Deductions	**(e)** Total Definitely Allocable Deductions (add columns 9(a) through 9(d))					
(a) Depreciation, Depletion, and Amortization	**(b)** Other Expenses	**(c)** Expenses Related to Gross Income From Performance of Services							
A				7,000			7,000	43,000
B								
C								
D								
E								
F								
Totals							7,000	43,000

For Paperwork Reduction Act Notice, see separate instructions.   Cat. No. 10900F   Form **1118** (Rev. 12-2014)

Form 1118 (Rev. 12-2014)   Page **2**

Schedule B   Foreign Tax Credit *(Report all foreign tax amounts in U.S. dollars.)*

Part I—Foreign Taxes Paid, Accrued, and Deemed Paid *(see instructions)*

1. Credit is Claimed for Taxes (check one):		2. Foreign Taxes Paid or Accrued (attach schedule showing amounts in foreign currency and conversion rate(s) used)							3. Tax Deemed Paid (from Schedule C— Part I, column 12, Part II, column 8(b), and Part III, column 8)
☑ Paid ☐ Accrued		Tax Withheld at Source on:		Other Foreign Taxes Paid or Accrued on:				(h) Total Foreign Taxes Paid or Accrued (add columns 2(a) through 2(g))	
Date Paid	Date Accrued	(a) Dividends	(b) Interest	(c) Rents, Royalties, and License Fees	(d) Section 863(b) Income	(e) Foreign Branch Income	(f) Services Income	(g) Other		
A 12/31		3,000							3,000	20,000
B										
C										
D										
E										
F										
Totals (add lines A through F)		3,000							3,000	20,000

Part II—Separate Foreign Tax Credit *(Complete a **separate** Part II for **each** applicable category of income.)*

1a	Total foreign taxes paid or accrued (total from Part I, column 2(h))	3,000
b	Foreign taxes paid or accrued by the corporation during prior tax years that were suspended due to the rules of section 909 and for which the related income is taken into account by the corporation during the current tax year (see instructions)	20,000
2	Total taxes deemed paid (total from Part I, column 3)	
3	Reductions of taxes paid, accrued, or deemed paid (enter total from Schedule G)	( )
4	Taxes reclassified under high-tax kickout	
5	Enter the sum of any carryover of foreign taxes (from Schedule K, line 3, column (xiv) and from Schedule I, Part III, line 3) plus any carrybacks to the current tax year	23,000
6	Total foreign taxes (combine lines 1a through 5)	
7	Enter the amount from the applicable column of Schedule J, Part I, line 11 (see instructions). If Schedule J is **not** required to be completed, enter the result from the "Totals" line of column 13 of the applicable Schedule A	
8a	Total taxable income from all sources (enter taxable income from the corporation's tax return)	43,000
b	Adjustments to line 8a (see instructions)	
c	Subtract line 8b from line 8a	172,000
9	Divide line 7 by line 8c. Enter the resulting fraction as a decimal (see instructions). If line 7 is greater than line 8c, enter 1	.25
10	Total U.S. income tax against which credit is allowed (regular tax liability (see section 26(b)) minus American Samoa economic development credit)	172,000
11	Credit limitation (multiply line 9 by line 10) (see instructions)	60,200
12	**Separate foreign tax credit** (enter the smaller of line 6 or line 11 here and on the appropriate line of Part III)	15,050

Part III—Summary of Separate Credits *(Enter amounts from Part II, line 12 for **each** applicable category of income. **Do not** include taxes paid to sanctioned countries.)*

1	Credit for taxes on passive category income	
2	Credit for taxes on general category income	15,050
3	Credit for taxes on income re-sourced by treaty (combine all such credits on this line)	
4	Total (add lines 1 through 3)	15,050
5	Reduction in credit for international boycott operations (see instructions)	
6	**Total foreign tax credit** (subtract line 5 from line 4). Enter here and on the appropriate line of the corporation's tax return	15,050

Form **1118** (Rev. 12-2014)

¶414

Form 1118 (Rev. 12-2014)   Page **3**

| **Schedule C** | **Tax Deemed Paid by Domestic Corporation Filing Return** |

Use this schedule to figure the tax deemed paid by the corporation with respect to dividends from a first-tier foreign corporation under section 902(a), and deemed inclusions of earnings from a first- or lower-tier foreign corporation under section 960(a). *Report all amounts in U.S. dollars unless otherwise specified.*

Part I—Dividends and Deemed Inclusions From Post-1986 Undistributed Earnings

1a. Name of Foreign Corporation (identify DISCs and former DISCs)	1b. EIN (if any) of the foreign corporation	1c. Reference ID number (see instructions)	2. Tax Year End (Yr-Mo) (see instructions)	3. Country of Incorporation (enter country code - see instructions)	4. Post-1986 Undistributed Earnings (in functional currency —attach schedule)	5. Opening Balance in Post-1986 Foreign Income Taxes	6. Foreign Taxes Paid and Deemed Paid for Tax Year Indicated	
							(a) Taxes Paid	**(b)** Taxes Deemed Paid (see instructions)
Foreign Sub			12/31	F	60,000			40,000

7. Post-1986 Foreign Income Taxes (add columns 5, 6(a), and 6(b))	8. Dividends and Deemed Inclusions		9. Divide column 8(a) by column 4	10. Multiply column 7 by column 9	11. Section 960(c) Limitation	12. Tax Deemed Paid (subtract column 11 from column 10)
	(a) Functional Currency	**(b)** U.S. Dollars				
40,000		30,000	.5	20,000		

Total (Add amounts in column 12. Enter the result here and include on "Totals" line of Schedule B, Part I, column 3.) . . . . ▲ | 20,000

Form **1118** (Rev. 12-2014)

Form 1118 (Rev. 12-2014)

Page **4**

Schedule C | Tax Deemed Paid by Domestic Corporation Filing Return *(Continued)*

Part II—Dividends Paid Out of Pre-1987 Accumulated Profits

1a. Name of Foreign Corporation (identify DISCs and former DISCs)	1b. EIN (if any) of the foreign corporation	1c. Reference ID number (see instructions)	2. Tax Year End (Yr-Mo) (see instructions)	3. Country of Incorporation (enter country code - see instructions)	4. Accumulated Profits for Tax Year Indicated (in functional currency) (attach schedule)	5. Foreign Taxes Paid and Deemed Paid on Earnings and Profits (E&P) for Tax Year Indicated (in functional currency) (see instructions)	6. Dividends Paid		7. Divide column 6(a) by column 4	8. Tax Deemed Paid (see instructions)
							(a) Functional Currency	**(b)** U.S. Dollars		**(b)** U.S. Dollars

Total (Add amounts in column 8b. Enter the result here and include on "Totals" line of Schedule B, Part I, column 3.) . . . . . . ▲

Part III—Deemed Inclusions From Pre-1987 Earnings and Profits

1a. Name of Foreign Corporation (identify DISCs and former DISCs)	1b. EIN (if any) of the foreign corporation	1c. Reference ID number (see instructions)	2. Tax Year End (Yr-Mo) (see instructions)	3. Country of Incorporation (enter country code - see instructions)	4. E&P for Tax Year Indicated (in functional currency translated from U.S. dollars, computed under section 964) (attach schedule)	5. Foreign Taxes Paid and Deemed Paid for Tax Year Indicated (see instructions)	6. Deemed Inclusions		7. Divide column 6(a) by column 4	8. Tax Deemed Paid (multiply column 5 by column 7)
							(a) Functional Currency	**(b)** U.S. Dollars		**(b)** U.S. Dollars

Total (Add amounts in column 8. Enter the result here and include on "Totals" line of Schedule B, Part I, column 3.) . . . . . . ▲

Form **1118** (Rev. 12-2014)

¶414

Form 1118 (Rev. 12-2014)   Page 5

Schedule D Tax Deemed Paid by First- and Second-Tier Foreign Corporations under Section 902(b)

*Use Part I to compute the tax deemed paid by a first-tier foreign corporation with respect to dividends from a second-tier foreign corporation. Use Part II to compute the tax deemed paid by a second-tier foreign corporation with respect to dividends from a third-tier foreign corporation. **Report all amounts in U.S. dollars unless otherwise specified.***

Part I—Tax Deemed Paid by First-Tier Foreign Corporations

Section A—Dividends Paid Out of Post-1986 Undistributed Earnings (Include the column 10 results in Schedule C, Part I, column 6(b).)

1a. Name of Second-Tier Foreign Corporation and Its Related First-Tier Foreign Corporation	1b. EIN (if any) of the second-tier foreign corporation	1c. Reference ID number (see instructions)	2. Tax Year End (Yr-Mo) (see instructions)	3. Country of Incorporation (enter country code - see instructions)	4. Post-1986 Undistributed Earnings (in functional currency—attach schedule)	5. Opening Balance in Post-1986 Foreign Income Taxes

6. Foreign Taxes Paid and Deemed Paid for Tax Year Indicated		7. Post-1986 Foreign Income Taxes (add columns 5, 6(a), and 6(b))	8. Dividends Paid (in functional currency)		9. Divide column 8(a) by column 4	10. Tax Deemed Paid (multiply column 7 by column 9)
(a) Taxes Paid	(b) Taxes Deemed Paid (see instructions)		(a) of Second-tier Corporation	(b) of First-tier Corporation		

Section B—Dividends Paid Out of Pre-1987 Accumulated Profits (Include the column 8(b) results in Schedule C, Part I, column 6(b).)

1a. Name of Second-Tier Foreign Corporation and Its Related First-Tier Foreign Corporation	1b. EIN (if any) of the second-tier foreign corporation	1c. Reference ID number (see instructions)	2. Tax Year End (Yr-Mo) (see instructions)	3. Country of Incorporation (enter country code - see instructions)	4. Accumulated Profits for Tax Year Indicated (in functional currency—attach schedule)	5. Foreign Taxes Paid and Deemed Paid for Tax Year Indicated (in functional currency—see instructions)

6. Dividends Paid (in functional currency)		7. Divide Column 6(a) by Column 4	8. Tax Deemed Paid (see instructions)	
(a) of Second-tier Corporation	(b) of First-tier Corporation		(a) Functional Currency of Second-tier Corporation	(b) U.S. Dollars

Form **1118** (Rev. 12-2014)

¶414

Form 1118 (Rev. 12-2014)

Page 6

Schedule D | Tax Deemed Paid by First- and Second-Tier Foreign Corporations under Section 902(b) *(Continued)*

Part II—Tax Deemed Paid by Second-Tier Foreign Corporations

Section A—Dividends Paid Out of Post-1986 Undistributed Earnings (In general, include the column 10 results in Section A, column 6(b), of Part I. However, see instructions for Schedule C, Part I, column 6(b) for an exception.)

1a. Name of Third-Tier Foreign Corporation and Its Related Second-Tier Foreign Corporation	1b. EIN (if any) of the third-tier foreign corporation	1c. Reference ID number (see instructions)	2. Tax Year End (Yr-Mo) (see instructions)	3. Country of Incorporation (enter country code - see instructions)	4. Post-1986 Undistributed Earnings (in functional currency—attach schedule)	5. Opening Balance in Post-1986 Foreign Income Taxes

6. Foreign Taxes Paid and Deemed Paid for Tax Year Indicated		7. Post-1986 Foreign Income Taxes (add columns 5, 6(a), and 6(b))	8. Dividends Paid (in functional currency)		9. Divide column 8(a) by column 4	10. Tax Deemed Paid (multiply column 7 by column 9)
(a) Taxes Paid	(b) Taxes Deemed Paid (from Schedule E, Part I, column 10)		(a) of Third-tier Corporation	(b) of Second-tier Corporation		

Section B—Dividends Paid Out of Pre-1987 Accumulated Profits (In general, include the column 8(b) results in Section A, column 6(b), of Part I. However, see instructions for Schedule C, Part I, column 6(b) for an exception.)

1a. Name of Third-Tier Foreign Corporation and Its Related Second-Tier Foreign Corporation	1b. EIN (if any) of the third-tier foreign corporation	1c. Reference ID number (see instructions)	2. Tax Year End (Yr-Mo) (see instructions)	3. Country of Incorporation (enter country code - see instructions)	4. Accumulated Profits for Tax Year Indicated (in functional currency—attach schedule)	5. Foreign Taxes Paid and Deemed Paid for Tax Year Indicated (in functional currency—see instructions)	6. Dividends Paid (in functional currency)		7. Divide Column 6(a) by Column 4	8. Tax Deemed Paid (see instructions)	
							(a) of Third-tier Corporation	(b) of Second-tier Corporation		(a) In Functional Currency of Third-tier Corporation	(b) U.S. Dollars

Form **1118** (Rev. 12-2014)

¶414

¶414

Form 1118 (Rev. 12-2014)   Page **7**

Schedule E   **Tax Deemed Paid by Certain Third-, Fourth-, and Fifth-Tier Foreign Corporations Under Section 902(b)**

Use this schedule to report taxes deemed paid with respect to dividends paid from eligible post-1986 undistributed earnings of fourth-, fifth- and sixth-tier controlled foreign corporations. **Report all amounts in U.S. dollars unless otherwise specified.**

Part I—Tax Deemed Paid by Third-Tier Foreign Corporations (In general, include the column 10 results in Schedule D, Part II, Section A, column 6(b). However, see instructions for Schedule C, Part I, column 6(b) for an exception.)

1a. Name of Fourth-Tier Foreign Corporation and Its Related Third-Tier Foreign Corporation	1b. EIN (if any) of the fourth-tier foreign corporation	1c. Reference ID number (see instructions)	2. Tax Year End (Yr-Mo) (see instructions)	3. Country of Incorporation (enter country code– see instructions)	4. Post-1986 Undistributed Earnings (in functional currency—attach schedule)	5. Opening Balance in Post-1986 Foreign Income Taxes

6. Foreign Taxes Paid and Deemed Paid for Tax Year Indicated

(a) Taxes Paid	(b) Taxes Deemed Paid (from Part II, column 10)	7. Post-1986 Foreign Income Taxes (add columns 5, 6(a), and 6(b))	8. Dividends Paid (in functional currency)		9. Divide column 8(a) by column 4	10. Tax Deemed Paid (multiply column 7 by column 9)
			(a) of Fourth-tier CFC	(b) of Third-tier CFC		

Form **1118** (Rev. 12-2014)

Form 1118 (Rev. 12-2014)

Page **8**

Schedule E   **Tax Deemed Paid by Certain Third-, Fourth-, and Fifth-Tier Foreign Corporations Under Section 902(b)** *(Continued)*

Part II—Tax Deemed Paid by Fourth-Tier Foreign Corporations (In general, include the column 10 results in column 6(b) of Part I. However, see instructions for Schedule C, Part I, column 6(b) for an exception.)

1a. Name of Fifth-Tier Foreign Corporation and Its Related Fourth-Tier Foreign Corporation	1b. EIN (if any) of the fifth-tier foreign corporation	1c. Reference ID number (see instructions)	2. Tax Year End (Yr-Mo) (see instructions)	3. Country of Incorporation (enter country code - see instructions)	4. Post-1986 Undistributed Earnings (in functional currency—attach schedule)	5. Opening Balance in Post-1986 Foreign Income Taxes

6. Foreign Taxes Paid and Deemed Paid for Tax Year Indicated

(a) Taxes Paid	(b) Taxes Deemed Paid (from Part III, column 10)	7. Post-1986 Foreign Income Taxes (add columns 5, 6(a), and 6(b))	8. Dividends Paid (in functional currency)		9. Divide column 8(a) by column 4	10. Tax Deemed Paid (multiply column 7 by column 9)
			(a) of Fifth-tier CFC	(b) of Fourth-tier CFC		

Part III—Tax Deemed Paid by Fifth-Tier Foreign Corporations (In general, include the column 10 results in column 6(b) of Part II above. However, see instructions for Schedule C, Part I, column 6(b) for an exception.)

1a. Name of Sixth-Tier Foreign Corporation and Its Related Fifth-Tier Foreign Corporation	1b. EIN (if any) of the sixth-tier foreign corporation	1c. Reference ID number (see instructions)	2. Tax Year End (Yr-Mo) (see instructions)	3. Country of Incorporation (enter country code - see instructions)	4. Post-1986 Undistributed Earnings (in functional currency—attach schedule)	5. Opening Balance in Post-1986 Foreign Income Taxes

6. Foreign Taxes Paid for Tax Year Indicated	7. Post-1986 Foreign Income Taxes (add columns 5 and 6)	8. Dividends Paid (in functional currency)		9. Divide column 8(a) by column 4	10. Tax Deemed Paid (multiply column 7 by column 9)
		(a) of Sixth-tier CFC	(b) of Fifth-tier CFC		

Form **1118** (Rev. 12-2014)

¶414

Form 1118 (Rev. 12-2014)   Page **9**

Schedule F — Gross Income and Definitely Allocable Deductions for Foreign Branches

1. Foreign Country or U.S. Possession (Enter two-letter code from Schedule A, column 1. Use a separate line for each.)	2. Gross Income	3. Definitely Allocable Deductions
A		
B		
C		
D		
E		
F		
Totals (add lines A through F)* ▶		

* **Note:** The Schedule F totals are not carried over to any other Form 1118 Schedule. (These totals were already included in Schedule A.) However, the IRS requires the corporation to complete Schedule F under the authority of section 905(b).

Schedule G — Reductions of Taxes Paid, Accrued, or Deemed Paid

Part I - Reduction Amounts

A	Reduction of Taxes Under Section 901(e)—Attach separate schedule
B	Reduction of Foreign Oil and Gas Taxes—Enter amount from Schedule I, Part II, line 4
C	Reduction of Taxes Due to International Boycott Provisions—Enter appropriate portion of Schedule C (Form 5713), line 2b. **Important:** Enter only "specifically attributable taxes" here.
D	Reduction of Taxes for Section 6038(c) Penalty—Attach separate schedule
E	Taxes suspended under section 909
F	Other Reductions of Taxes—Attach schedule(s)
Total (add lines A through F). Enter here and on Schedule B, Part II, line 3 . . . . ▲	

Part II - Other Information

Check this box if, during the tax year, the corporation paid or accrued any foreign tax that was disqualified for credit under section 901(m) . . . . ☐

Form **1118** (Rev. 12-2014)

Form 1118 (Rev. 12-2014)　　　　　　　　　　　　　　　　　　　　　　　Page 10

Schedule H　Apportionment of Deductions Not Definitely Allocable *(complete only once)*

Part I—Research and Development Deductions

	(a) Sales Method				(b) Gross Income Method – Check method used: ☐ Option 1　☐ Option 2				(c) Total R&D Deductions Not Definitely Allocable (enter the sum of all amounts entered in all applicable "R&D Deductions" columns)
	Product line #1 (SIC Code:)*		Product line #2 (SIC Code:)*		Product line #1 (SIC Code:)*		Product line #2 (SIC Code:)*		
	(i) Gross Sales	(ii) R&D Deductions	(iii) Gross Sales	(iv) R&D Deductions	(v) Gross Income	(vi) R&D Deductions	(vii) Gross Income	(viii) R&D Deductions	
1 Totals (see instructions)									
2 Total to be apportioned									
3 Apportionment among statutory groupings:									
a General category income									
b Passive category income									
c Section 901(j) income*									
d Income re-sourced by treaty*									
4 Total foreign (add lines 3a through 3d)									

* **Important: See *Computer-Generated Schedule H* in instructions.**

Form **1118** (Rev. 12-2014)

Form 1118 (Rev. 12-2014)   Page **11**

Schedule H Apportionment of Deductions Not Definitely Allocable *(continued)*

Part II—Interest Deductions, All Other Deductions, and Total Deductions

(a) Average Value of Assets – Check method used:
☐ Fair market value ☐ Tax book value
☐ Alternative tax book value

	(a) Average Value of Assets		**(b)** Interest Deductions		**(c)** All Other Deductions Not Definitely Allocable	**(d)** Totals (add the corresponding amounts from column (c), Part I; columns (b)(iii) and (b)(iv), Part II; and column (c), Part II). Enter each amount from lines 3a through 3d below in column 10 of the corresponding Schedule A.
	(i) Nonfinancial Corporations	**(ii)** Financial Corporations	**(iii)** Nonfinancial Corporations	**(iv)** Financial Corporations		
1a Totals (see instructions)					28,000	
b Amounts specifically allocable under Temp. Regs. 1.861-10T(e)						
c Other specific allocations under Temp. Regs. 1.861-10T						
d Assets excluded from apportionment formula						
2 Total to be apportioned (subtract the sum of lines 1b, 1c, and 1d from line 1a)						
3 Apportionment among statutory groupings:						
a General category income					7,000	7,000
b Passive category income						
c Section 901(j) income*						
d Income re-sourced by treaty*						
4 Total foreign (add lines 3a through 3d)						7,000

*Important: See *Computer-Generated Schedule H* in instructions.

Form **1118** (Rev. 12-2014)

¶414

Chapter 5
Anti-Deferral Provisions

¶ 501　SUBPART F

.01 Background

The United States generally does not tax foreign business profits earned through a <u>foreign subsidiary</u> until the subsidiary repatriates those earnings as a <u>dividend</u>. This policy, known as "deferral," allows U.S. companies to compete in foreign markets on a tax parity with their foreign competitors. In contrast, the United States taxes the income of a <u>foreign branch</u> <u>contemporaneously as the foreign branch earns the income</u>.

> ***Example* 5.1***:*** USco earns $5 million from its U.S. operations and has two foreign operations. The first foreign operation, in country F1, is an unincorporated branch that earns $1 million. The second foreign operation, in country F2, is incorporated as a foreign subsidiary that earns $2 million. USco's <u>worldwide income is $6 million comprised of $5 million earned in the United States and $1 million earned in country F1</u>. <u>The $2 million earned in country F2 is</u> deferred until repatriated as a dividend.

worldwide income = 6m

USCo — $5 million

U.S.

Foreign

$1 million — F$_1$

branch

F$_2$ — $2 million

subsidiary　*→Deferred !*

In addition to promoting the competitiveness of U.S. companies abroad, <u>deferral creates an opportunity for avoiding U.S. taxes on passive investment income</u>, inventory trading profits and other income that taxpayers can easily shift to a foreign base company. Various foreign countries, such as the Cayman Islands, Hong Kong, Ireland, and Singapore, offer tax holidays or low tax rates to attract foreign investment. A U.S. multinational can shift income to a base company organized in these tax-haven countries by, for example, selling goods to the base company at an artificially low price. The base company can then resell the goods at a higher price to a sales subsidiary located in the same country as the ultimate foreign customers. The spread between the two transfer prices shifts the profit on the export sale from the countries in which manufacturing and marketing actually take place to a tax-haven country.

> ***Example 5.2:*** USAco is a domestic corporation that manufactures electric generators for sale both in the United States and Germany. German sales are made through GERco, a wholly-owned German sales subsidiary. USAco's generators have a cost of goods sold of $600 and sell for $1,000 in Germany. Therefore, the combined income from a German sale is $400 per generator [$1,000 final sales price – $600 cost of goods sold]. USAco also has a wholly-owned Cayman Island subsidiary, CAYco, which performs no significant functions with respect to the manufacture or sale of USAco's generators. Assume that the U.S. tax rate is 35%, the German rate is 30%, and the Cayman Islands does not have a corporate income tax.

Case 1—Do not route sale through base company: If a German sale is not routed through CAYco and the transfer price used for USAco's sale to GERco is, for example, $800, the $400 of gross profits will be allocated as follows:

Transaction	Effect on USAco	Effect on CAYco	Effect on GERco
Manufacture good	COGS = $600		
Intercompany sale	Sales = $800		COGS = $800
Final sale			Sales = $1,000
	Gross profit = $200		Gross profit = $200

Assuming there are not any operating expenses, the total tax on the $400 gross profit equals $130 [($200 × 35% U.S. tax rate) + ($200 × 30% German tax rate)], which results in an <u>overall effective tax rate of 32.5%</u> ($130/$400).

Case 2—Route sale through base company: Now assume that the German sale is routed through CAYco. USAco sells to CAYco at a $700 transfer price and CAYco sells to GERco for a $900 transfer price. CAYco, which is not subject to any tax, has <u>skimmed away $200 of gross profits</u> as the parties now allocate the total $400 of profits as follows:

Transaction	Effect on USAco	Effect on CAYco	Effect on GERco
Manufacture good	COGS = $600		
Intercompany sale	Sales = $700	COGS = $700	
Intercompany sale		Sales = $900	COGS = $900
Final sale			Sales = $1,000
	Gross profit = $100	Gross profit = $200	Gross profit = $100

¶501.01

Again, assuming there are not any operating expenses, the total tax on the $400 gross profit now equals $65 [($100 × 35% U.S. tax rate) + ($200 × 0% Cayman Island tax rate) + ($100 × 30% German tax rate)], which results in an overall effective tax rate of 16.25% ($65/$400). Therefore, ignoring Code Sec. 482 and Subpart F, USAco can reduce the total tax burden on its German sales by routing those sales through a Cayman Island base company.

One tool that the IRS can use against this planning is Code Sec. 482, which gives the IRS the authority to allocate income among domestic and foreign affiliates whenever an allocation is necessary to clearly reflect the income of each party. However, the arm's-length standard of Code Sec. 482 (see Chapter 12) has proven difficult to administer due to a lack of information regarding comparable uncontrolled transactions. As a result, Subpart F automatically denies deferral to certain types of tainted income earned through a foreign corporation.[1]

.02 Subpart F Overview

If a foreign corporation is a controlled foreign corporation (or CFC) for an uninterrupted period of 30 days or more during the taxable year, every person who was a U.S. Shareholder of the CFC at any time during the taxable year and who owns stock in such corporation on the last day of the CFC's taxable year must include in gross income its pro rata share of:

    (i) Subpart F income, and

    (ii) Investment of earnings in U.S. property.[2]

A U.S. Shareholder's pro rata share is the amount that the shareholder would have received if, on the last day of its taxable year, the CFC had actually distributed pro rata to all of its shareholders a dividend equal to the Subpart F inclusion.[3] For

---

[1] The term "Subpart F" refers to the part of the Internal Revenue Code where the applicable statutes, i.e., Code Secs. 951–965, are found.

[2] Code Sec. 951(a)(1). Two other less common types of Subpart F inclusions are (i) previously excluded Subpart F income withdrawn from investments in less developed countries (see Code Sec. 955 as in effect prior to the enactment of the Tax Reduction Act of 1975 (P.L. 94-12)) and (ii) previously excluded Subpart F income withdrawn from foreign base company shipping operations (see Code Sec. 955).

[3] Code Sec. 951(a)(2). The shareholder's pro rata amount may be reduced if the foreign corporation was a

¶501.02

the income inclusion only, both direct ownership of the CFC's stock and indirect ownership through foreign entities (but not constructive ownership) are considered.[4]

    Example 5.3: USAco, a domestic corporation, owns 100% of the stock of FORco, a foreign corporation. During the current year, FORco derives $10 million of Subpart F income in the form of passive interest income, pays $1 million in foreign income taxes (for an effective foreign rate of 10%), and does not distribute any dividends. USAco is not allowed to defer the residual U.S. tax due on FORco's earnings. Instead, USAco must recognize a Subpart F inclusion income equal to FORco's $9 million of net Subpart F income.

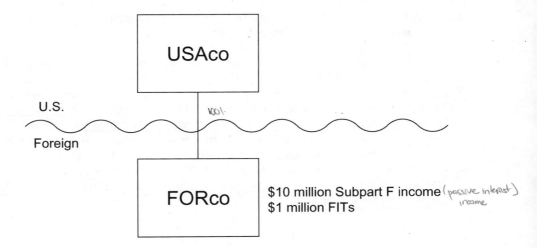

USAco

U.S.

Foreign

100%

FORco $10 million Subpart F income *(passive interest income)*
    $1 million FITs

    Consistent with the notion that a Subpart F inclusion is similar to a dividend, a domestic corporation reports a Subpart F inclusion as "Dividends" on Line 4 of Form 1120 (see Schedule C, Line 14).[5] Although similar to a dividend, Subpart F inclusions do not qualify for the reduced individual rate of tax on qualified dividend income under Code Sec. 1(h).[6] *NO REDUCED TAX RATE!*

.03 Definition of a Controlled Foreign Corporation

    Subpart F applies only to a foreign corporation that qualifies as a controlled foreign corporation (CFC). The determination of whether a business entity is considered a "corporation" is determined under the U.S. entity classification regulations.[7] A corporation is a "foreign corporation" if it is incorporated outside the United States.[8]

(Footnote Continued)

CFC for only part of the year or if the U.S. shareholder acquired the CFC's stock during the year.

  [4] Code Sec. 958(a).

  [5] Subpart F income is also reported on line 1 of Schedule I on Form 5471.

  [6] Notice 2004-70, 2004-2 CB 724.

  [7] Reg. §§301.7701-1 to 3. These are also known as the check-the-box regulations.

  [8] Code Secs. 7701(a)(4) and (a)(5).

A foreign corporation is a CFC if, on any day during the foreign corporation's taxable year, U.S. Shareholders own more than 50% of the combined voting power of all classes of stock or more than 50% of the total value of the foreign corporation.[9] A U.S. Shareholder is defined under Subpart F as any U.S. person owning at least 10% of the total combined voting power of all classes of voting stock of the foreign corporation.[10] Only U.S. Shareholders are considered in applying the 50% test. Unlike ownership for the income inclusion, all forms of ownership, including direct ownership, indirect or beneficial ownership through intervening foreign entities, and constructive ownership[11] (i.e., attribution of ownership from one related party to another), are considered when applying both the 10% ownership test for U.S. Shareholder status and the more than 50% ownership test for CFC status.[12] Obviously, a foreign subsidiary that is 100%-owned by a U.S. parent is a CFC. However, due to all these attribution rules, determining a foreign corporation's CFC status is complex and can produce unexpected results.

Example 5.4: USAco, a domestic corporation, owns 50% of the stock of F1, a foreign corporation. Unrelated foreign persons own the remaining 50% of F1. USAco also owns 10% of the stock of F2, a foreign corporation. F1 owns 51% of F2, and unrelated foreign persons own the remaining 39%. F1 is not a CFC because USAco, F1's only U.S. Shareholder, does not own more than 50% of the stock. USAco also is a U.S. Shareholder of F2 because it owns 10% of F2 directly. Under the constructive ownership rules, F1 constructively owns 100% of F2 because F1 owns more than 50% of F2.[13] Therefore, USAco is treated as owning 60% of F2, 10% directly and 50% through F1 [50% of 100%]. As a consequence, F2 is a CFC.

100%

SEE:
§318
§958 (b)(2)

---

[9] Code Sec. 957(a). The taxable year of a CFC generally must conform to that of its majority U.S. shareholder. Code Sec. 898.

[10] Code Sec. 951(b).

[11] An exception to constructive ownership is that a nonresident alien's shares are not constructively attrib-uted to a family member that is a U.S. person. Code Secs. 318(a)(1) and 958(b)(1).

[12] Code Sec. 958. This is in contrast to the actual income inclusion, which considers the percent of subpart F income based on only direct and indirect ownership (and not constructive) ownership.

[13] Code Secs. 318 and 958(b)(2).

¶501.03

Even if a foreign owner holds the greatest ownership interest of a foreign corporation, the foreign corporation is a CFC if U.S. Shareholders own more than 50% of the vote or value.

Example 5.5: Uncle Sam and George Washington, both U.S. persons, each own 26% of FORco for the entire taxable year. The remaining 48% is owned by Norman Ray Allen, a nonresident alien. Because the two 10% Shareholders, Uncle Same and George Washington, combine to own more than 50% of the value of FORco during the entire taxable year, FORco is a CFC.

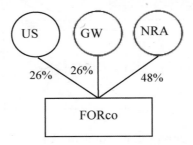

Accordingly, U.S. persons can collectively own over 50% of the vote or value of the foreign corporation, but the foreign corporation is not a CFC if not all the U.S. persons own the requisite 10% to be U.S. Shareholders.

Example 5.6: Uncle Sam owns 50% of FORco and George Washington owns 9% of FORco for the entire taxable year. Norman Ray Allen, a nonresident alien, owns the remaining 41%. Because the only U.S. Shareholder does not own more than 50% of the vote or value of FORco, FORco is not a CFC.

Scenarios can even result where a foreign corporation is entirely owned by U.S. persons, but is not a CFC.

Example 5.7: One hundred unrelated U.S. citizens each own 1% of FORco, a foreign corporation. Although FORco is 100%-owned by U.S. persons, none of them satisfies the 10% ownership test for U.S. Shareholder status. Therefore, FORco is not a CFC.

¶501.03

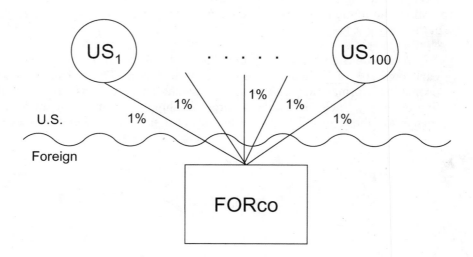

In theory, a foreign corporation can avoid CFC status by spreading ownership of a foreign corporation among 11 U.S. persons, each owning only 9.09% of the company. However, because direct, indirect, and constructive ownership are considered in applying the 10% U.S. Shareholder test,[14] the 11 U.S. persons would have to be unrelated to one another, by both family and business connections to avoid U.S. Shareholder status. In addition, even if the U.S. persons can structure ownership of a foreign corporation to avoid CFC status, the foreign corporation may still be a passive foreign investment company (see ¶ 502). Therefore, planning designed to take advantage of the deferral privilege requires a careful analysis of all of the anti-deferral provisions.

.04 Subpart F Income—Overview

Subpart F income includes the following five categories of income derived by a CFC:[15]

   (i) Insurance income,

   (ii) Foreign base company income,

   (iii) A portion of international boycott income,[16]

   (iv) The sum of any illegal bribes or kickbacks paid by or on behalf of the CFC to a government employee or official, and

   (v) Income derived from certain disfavored foreign countries.[17]

---

[14] Code Sec. 958.

[15] Code Sec. 952(a).

[16] Code Sec. 999 defines international boycott income is determined under Code Sec. 999. Countries which may require participation in or cooperation with an international boycott include Iraq, Kuwait, Lebanon, Libya, Qatar, Saudi Arabia, Syria, United Arab Emirates, and the Republic of Yemen. Boycott Notice, (April 13, 2012).

[17] These include foreign countries whose governments the United States does not recognize, does not conduct diplomatic relations with, or has designated as a government which repeatedly supports acts of international terrorism. Code Sec. 901(j). Countries to which this provision has applied in the past or present include Cuba, Iran, North Korea, Sudan, and Syria. Rev. Rul. 2005-3, IRB 2005-3.

¶501.04

The amount of a CFC's Subpart F income for any taxable year cannot exceed the CFC's current-year earnings and profits before any reductions for current-year dividend distributions.[18] Insurance income and foreign base company income, which are the two most prevalent types of Subpart F income, are discussed in detail below.

.05 Insurance Income

Premiums and other income from insurance activities represent the type of portable income that U.S. persons can easily try to shift to a foreign corporation to avoid U.S. taxation. Prior to the enactment of Subpart F, a U.S. corporation could exploit the portability of insurance income by establishing an offshore insurance company. For example, a U.S. insurance company that had issued policies insuring U.S. risks (e.g., a casualty policy on a U.S. office building) might form a subsidiary in a low-tax jurisdiction and reinsure that U.S. risk with that foreign subsidiary. Assuming there was a bona fide shifting and distribution of risks, the U.S. parent could deduct the premiums paid to the subsidiary against its U.S. taxable income. In addition, assuming the foreign subsidiary had no office or other taxable presence in the United States, the premium income did not incur U.S. taxation. The net effect was the avoidance of U.S. taxes on the premium income routed through the foreign subsidiary.

To negate the tax benefits of such arrangements, Subpart F income includes any income attributable to issuing or reinsuring any insurance or annuity contract in connection with a risk located outside the CFC's country of incorporation. The location of a risk is determined by where the insured property or activity is located or by where the insured individual resides.[19] Income from insuring risks located within the CFC's country of incorporation also qualifies as Subpart F income if, as a result of an arrangement, another corporation receives a substantially equal amount of premiums for insuring risks located outside the CFC's country of incorporation.[20] The taxable amount of insurance income equals the gross amount of such income, less any deductions properly allocable to such income.[21]

> **Example 5.8:** USCo insures itself along with four other U.S. companies by each owning 20% of CaptiveCo, a Bermuda corporation. Each owner pays CaptiveCo a premium to insure risks that each owner incurs in the United States. As a U.S. Shareholder of a CFC, USCO will have to report its share of CaptiveCo's profits, as CaptiveCo earned all its profits for insuring risks located outside of Bermuda.

---

[18] Code Sec. 952(c)(1)(A) and Reg. §1.952-1(c)(1). Under certain conditions, prior-year deficits also can be used to reduce the amount of Subpart F income. Code Sec. 952(c)(1)(B) and (C).

[19] Code Sec. 953(a)(1)(A) and (e)(1)(A).
[20] Code Sec. 953(e)(1)(B).
[21] Code Sec. 953(b)(4).

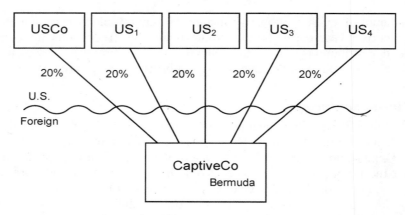

More stringent rules apply to related-person insurance income. Related-person insurance income includes any income attributable to issuing or reinsuring any insurance or annuity contract that directly or indirectly covers a U.S. Shareholder or a person related to a U.S. Shareholder.[22] For insurance income purposes only, a U.S. Shareholder is any U.S. person who owns any stock of the foreign corporation and a CFC is defined as any foreign corporation that is 25% or more owned by such U.S. shareholders.[23] Under this rule, any U.S. Shareholder who owns stock of such a CFC is taxed on his or her pro rata share of related-person insurance income.[24]

.06 Foreign Base Company Income

Subpart F income also includes foreign base company income, which consists of the following four categories of income derived by a CFC:

   (i)   Foreign personal holding company income,

   (ii)   Foreign base company sales income,

   (iii)   Foreign base company services income, and

   (iv)   Foreign base company oil-related income.[25]

The taxable amount of foreign base company income equals the gross amount of such income, less any deductions (including foreign income taxes) properly allocable to such income.[26]

Foreign personal holding company income. Under the general rules, foreign personal holding company income primarily includes:

   (i)   Dividends, interest, royalties, rents, and annuities,

> ***Example 5.9:*** USPharmCo wholly owns BVIPharmCo, a CFC incorporated in the British Virgin Islands. BVIPharmCo's only employee is the British Virgin Islands attorney who incorporated BVIPharmCo. USPharmCo contributed cash to BVIPharmCo that BVIPharmCo used to

---

[22] Code Sec. 953(c)(2).

[23] Code Sec. 953(c)(1).

[24] Code Sec. 953(c)(1)(C). Code Sec. 953(c)(3) provides several exceptions to the related-person insurance rules.

[25] Code Sec. 954(a).

[26] Code Sec. 954(b)(5).

purchase the rights to a drug that calms the nerves of over-zealous suburban soccer parents. BVIPharmCo licenses the drug world-wide for royalties, which are foreign personal holding company income.

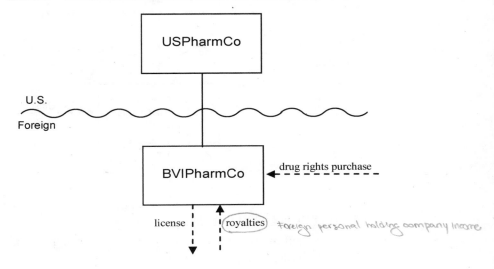

(ii) Net gains from the disposition of property that produces dividend, interest, rent, and royalty income (except for net gains from certain dealer sales and inventory sales), and

(iii) Net gains from commodity and foreign currency transactions (excluding net gains from active business and hedging transactions).[27]

Numerous special rules exclude selected types of dividend, interest, rent and royalty income from foreign personal holding company income, including:

(i) Rents and royalties derived from the active conduct of a trade or business and received from an unrelated person,[28]

   ***Example* 5.10:** As in the previous example, USPharmCo wholly owns BVIPharmCo, a CFC incorporated in the British Virgin Islands. However, BVIPharmCo employs twenty scientists in white lab coats (with pocket protectors) who develop a drug to calm the nerves of over-zealous suburban hockey parents. BVIPharmCo licenses the drug world-wide for royalties, which are not foreign personal holding company income because BVIPharmCo actively conducts a trade or business of developing the drug.

---

[27] Code Sec. 954(c)(1). *See* Reg. § 1.954-2(g)(2) regarding the excludable commodity and foreign currency transactions.

[28] Code Sec. 954(c)(2)(A).

(ii) Export financing interest derived,[29]

(iii) Dividends and interest received from related parties incorporated in the same country as the CFC,[30]

     ***Example* 5.11:** USACo operates UKHoldCo, a holding company in the United Kingdom. UKHoldCo owns three operating companies in the United Kingdom - UK1, UK2, and UK3. Dividends paid by any of the three U.K. operating companies are not foreign personal holding company income because UKHoldCo receives them all from the United Kingdom.

---

[29] Code Sec. 954(c)(2)(B).   [30] Code Sec. 954(c)(3)(A)(i).

(iv) Rents and royalties received from related parties for the use of property in the CFC's country of incorporation,[31]

(v) Income derived from the active conduct of a banking, financing, insurance or similar business (temporarily extended for tax years of a CFC through 2014),[32]

(vi) Dividends, interest, rents, and royalties received from a related CFC, provided the payments are attributable to income of the related CFC which is neither Subpart F income nor income that is effectively connected with a U.S. trade or business (temporarily extended for tax years of a CFC through 2014). Under this exception, cross-border payments between related CFCs do not constitute Subpart F income as long as the payments are attributable to active foreign business income, and[33]

(vii) Personal services income received by a CFC whose U.S. owner performs the services.[34]

> *Example **5.12:*** Chef Raoul, a U.S. citizen and world-renown chef, is hired by The Gourmet Club of Barbados to prepare a world-class dining experience for its members. Not wanting to pay tax at a 39.6% rate in the United States, Chef Raoul forms BarbCo to contract with The Gourmet Club of Barbados, hoping to keep the service income in a low-tax jurisdiction. However, pursuant to Subpart F, Chef Raoul must report the income because The Gourmet Club of Barbados had the right to designate him as the performer and he owns over 25% of BarbCo.

---

[31] Code Sec. 954(c)(3)(A)(ii).
[32] Code Sec. 954(h)(a) and (i).
[33] Code Sec. 954(c)(6).

[34] Code Sec. 954(c)(1)(H). This rule prevents a U.S. provider of foreign services from forming a foreign corporation that provides the services to avoid U.S. tax.

Gourmet Club

Foreign base company sales income. Foreign base company sales income includes any gross profit, commissions, fees, or other income derived from the sale of personal property that meets the following requirements:

    (i)   The property is manufactured, produced, grown, or extracted outside the CFC's country of incorporation by someone other than the CFC;

    (ii)   The property is sold for use, consumption, or disposition outside the CFC's country of incorporation; and

    (iii)   The CFC purchases the property from or sells the property to a related person.[35]

The definition of foreign base company sales income theorizes that if a good is neither manufactured nor sold for use in the CFC's country of incorporation, then the CFC may not be a bona-fide manufacturing or sales subsidiary, but rather a base company organized primarily to avoid tax. The related party aspect helps conclude that the income is mobile and, therefore, tainted.

    Example **5.13:** USAco, a domestic corporation, manufactures consumer goods for sale both in the United States and Norway. Norwegian sales are made through NORco, a wholly-owned Norwegian marketing subsidiary. USAco also has a wholly-owned Belgian subsidiary, BELco, which performs no real functions with respect to the manufacture or sale of USAco's products. The gross profit realized by NORco on the resale of goods to Norwegian customers is not foreign base company sales income because the goods are sold for use in NORco's country of incorporation. In contrast, if a sale to a Norwegian customer is made by BELco, the gross profit realized by BELco is foreign base company sales income because the good was neither manufactured nor sold for use in Belgium.

---

[35] Code Sec. 954(d)(1); Reg. § 1.954-3(a)(4)(i).

The regulations effectively provide four alternative tests for determining whether a CFC manufactured or produced a good, including: (i) a safe-harbor test, (ii) a substantial transformation test, (iii) a generally considered manufacturing test, and (iv) a substantial contribution to manufacturing test. A CFC needs to satisfy only one of these tests to avoid the foreign base company sales income taint. Minor assembly, packaging, repackaging, or labeling does not constitute manufacturing.[36]

Under the safe-harbor test, manufacturing is deemed to occur if the CFC's conversion costs (i.e., direct labor and factory burden) account for 20% or more of the total cost of the goods sold.

Example 5.14: USAco, a domestic corporation, owns 100% of the stock of CANco, a Canadian corporation. CANco sells industrial engines for use outside of its country of incorporation. CANco performs some machining and assembly operations with respect to the engines it sells, but purchases the component parts for these engines from related and unrelated suppliers. On a per engine basis, CANco's direct material costs are $30,000 and its conversion costs (direct labor and factory burden) are $10,000. Although it is unclear whether CANco meets either the substantial transformation test or the generally considered manufacturing test, CANco does meet the safe-harbor test because conversion costs are 25% of the total costs of goods sold [$10,000 ÷ ($10,000 + $30,000)]. As a result, CANco's gross profits from the sale of engines are not foreign base company sales income.[37]

---

[36] Reg. § 1.954-3(b)(4)(iii).　　　　[37] Compare Reg. § 1.954-3(a)(4)(iii), Example (1).

engine sales
to customers
outside of
Canada

A CFC is considered to have manufactured the goods if the CFC substantially transforms the goods. Examples of substantial transformation include converting wood pulp to paper, steel rods to screws and bolts, and fresh fish to canned fish. Whether or not the substantial transformation test is met depends on the facts and circumstances of each case[38] to determine if the finished product looks different than its components.

Manufacturing also occurs if a CFC purchases component parts and its activities in the assembly or conversion of the component parts into the final product are substantial in nature and generally considered to constitute manufacturing, based on the facts and circumstances.[39]

Example 5.15: USCo provides the frames, wings, tinted lenses, and screws to IrishCo, USCo's wholly-owned Irish subsidiary. IrishCo's low-skilled high school dropouts put together the sunglasses for resale on the European continent. If putting together sunglasses constitutes a substantial activity that is generally considered manufacturing in the industry, IrishCo does not have any foreign base company sales income.[40]

---

[38] Reg. § 1.954-3(a)(4)(ii).
[39] Reg. § 1.954-3(a)(4)(iii).

[40] *Bausch & Lomb, Inc.,* TC Memo. 1996-57.

Finally, the substantial contribution test treats a CFC as a manufacturer of goods if, based on the facts and circumstances, the CFC substantially contributed to the manufacturing process, even if the CFC did not physically manufacture the goods. The following non-exclusive list provides various activities conducted by employees of the CFC to determine whether the CFC has substantially contributed to the manufacturing process:[41]

- oversight and direction of manufacturing activities;

- material and vendor selection; control of raw materials;

- management of manufacturing costs or capacities;

- control of manufacturing-related logistics;

- quality control; and

- development of intellectual property.

Example 5.16: CFC purchases parts from its U.S. parent and engages KM, a contract manufacturer in a third country, to manufacture the product for sale to customers outside CFC's country. Because CFC's employees conduct research and development, quality control, and logistical management over the manufacturing process, CFC has substantially contributed to the manufacturing process and there is not any foreign base company sales income.

---

[41] Reg. § 1.954-3(a)(iv)(b).

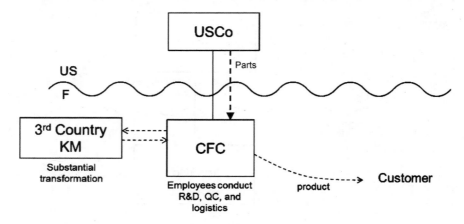

A branch rule attempts to close a potential loophole that arises if a CFC's country of incorporation does not tax income derived from sources outside its borders (i.e., employs a territorial system). In these countries, the foreign base company sales income taint could be avoided by having a CFC sell goods through a sales branch located in a low-tax country, because there would be no related-party sale between the CFC and its sales branch. A similar tax result could be obtained if a CFC manufactures its goods in another foreign country through a low-taxed branch rather than a subsidiary.

The so-called branch rule closes this potential loophole by treating a branch as if it were a subsidiary of the CFC if the activities of the branch have substantially the same effect as a subsidiary.[42] By treating a branch as a subsidiary, the branch/subsidiary and the CFC are related parties that result in satisfying the definition of foreign base company sales income. This rule applies if there is a substantial tax rate disparity between the country in which the branch is located and the CFC's country of incorporation.[43] In the case of a sales branch, this is defined as an effective tax rate that is less than 90% of, and at least 5 percentage points less than, the effective rate of tax in the CFC's country of incorporation.[44]

> **Example 5.17:** Assume the tax rate in the CFC's country of incorporation is 30% and the CFC establishes a sales branch in another foreign country that has a 10% tax rate. The tax rate disparity test is met because both 10% is less than 90% of 30% (27%) and 10% is at least 5 percentage points less than 30%. Therefore, the sales branch is treated as a subsidiary of the CFC and the income from sales made through the branch may qualify as foreign base company sales income because there is now a related party transaction.

---

[42] Code Sec. 954(d)(2).

[43] Reg. §1.954-3(b). The determination of what constitutes a foreign branch is an unsettled issue. In *Ashland Oil, Inc.*, 95 TC 348 (1990), the Tax Court ruled that an unrelated contract manufacturer of a CFC was not a branch.

[44] Reg. §1.954-3(b)(1)(ii)(B).

Foreign base company services income. Foreign base company services income includes any <u>compensation, fees, or other income derived from the per-</u><u>formance of technical, managerial, engineering, architectural, scientific, skilled,</u><u>industrial, commercial, and like services,</u>[45] where the CFC <u>performs the services for</u><u>or on behalf of a related person</u> and the <u>services are performed outside the CFC's</u><u>country of incorporation.</u>[46] This provision denies deferral to a foreign service subsidiary that is separated from its manufacturing and sales affiliates and that is organized in another country.

Example **5.18:** USAco, a domestic corporation, owns 100% of GERco, a German corporation. USAco is in the business of manufacturing drill presses for industrial use. During the year, USAco sells drill presses to both French and German customers. A condition of these sales is that USAco will install and provide maintenance services with respect to the drill presses. GERco <u>performs these services on USAco's behalf in both France and Germany. The</u><u>fees that GERco receives for services performed in Germany are not foreign</u><u>base company services income.</u> In contrast, the fees that GERco receives for <u>services performed in France are foreign base company services income</u><u>because they are performed outside the CFC's country of incorporation on</u><u>behalf of a related party.</u>[47]

---

[45] Services fees do not include purchase or sales commissions, which can be foreign base company sales income.

[46] Code Sec. 954(e)(1). An exception applies to services which are directly related to the sale of property which was manufactured, produced, grown, or extracted by the CFC and the services are performed before the time of the sale. This would except, for example, fees a CFC receives from related parties for advertising in other countries the products that the CFC manufactures. Code Sec. 954(e)(2).

[47] Reg. §1.954-4(b)(1)(ii). *See also*, Reg. §1.954-4(b)(3)(Ex. 2).

Foreign base company oil-related income. Foreign base company oil-related income includes foreign-source income derived from refining, processing, transporting, distributing, or selling oil and gas or primary products derived from oil and gas. However, it does not include oil-related income of a CFC derived from sources within a foreign country in which the oil or gas is either extracted or used. Under a look-through rule, foreign base company oil-related income also includes dividends and interest derived from a 10%-or-more-owned foreign corporation to the extent such dividends or interest are attributable to foreign base company oil-related income.[48]

   Example **5.19:** OilCo, a U.S. corporation, owns two CFCs - ForOil in foreign country 1 and InvoiceCo in foreign country 2. ForOil refines oil for sale to customers in foreign country 1 and for sale to InvoiceCo, which resells the refined oil to customers in foreign country 2. The income earned by ForOil is not foreign base company oil-related income because the oil was refined in foreign country 1. However, the income earned by InvoiceCo is foreign base company oil-related income because the oil was neither refined nor extracted in foreign country 2.

---

[48] Code Secs. 954(g)(1) and 907(c)(2) and (3). An exception applies to foreign corporations which are not "large oil producers," as defined in Code Sec. 954(g)(2).

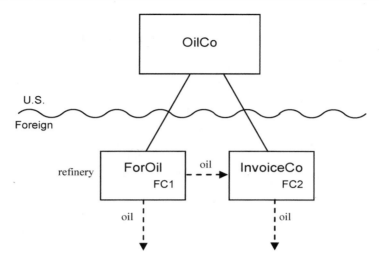

.07 Special Exclusions and Inclusions

There are four exceptions to the general rules for computing Subpart F income. The first two exceptions are rules of administrative simplicity. The first exception is a *de minimis* rule, under which no part of a CFC's income is treated as insurance income or foreign base company income if the sum of the CFC's gross insurance and gross foreign base company income for the taxable year (before taking into account any deductions) is less than both $1 million and 5% of the CFC's total gross income for the year.[49]

> *Example 5.20:* During the current year, ASIAco (a CFC) has gross income of $30 million, including $800,000 of interest income and $29.2 million of gross income from the sale of inventory that ASIAco manufactured at a factory located within its country of incorporation. Under the general rules, the $800,000 of interest income would be treated as foreign base company income because the interest is foreign personal holding company income. Under the *de minimis* rule, however, none of ASIAco's income is foreign base company income because $800,000 is less than both $1 million and 5% of ASIAco's gross income, which is $1.5 million (5% × $30 million).

<table>
<tr><td>

ASIAco

</td><td>

$800,000 of interest income

$29.2 million of gross income
from sales of inventory

</td></tr>
</table>

The second exception is a full-inclusion rule, under which all of a CFC's gross income is treated as Subpart F income if the sum of the CFC's gross insurance

---

[49] Code Sec. 954(b)(3)(A). This exception also does not apply to any U.S.-source portfolio interest derived by a CFC from an unrelated U.S. person. Code Sec. 881(c)(5)(A)(i).

income and gross foreign base company income for the taxable year (before taking into account any deductions) exceeds 70% of the CFC's total gross income for the year.[50]

> *Example* **5.21:** During the current year, AFRIco (a CFC) has gross income of $20 million, including $16 million of interest income and $4 million of gross income from the sale of inventory that AFRIco manufactured at a factory located within its country of incorporation. Foreign base company income ordinarily would include only the $16 million of interest income. Under the full-inclusion rule, however, AFRIco's entire $20 million of gross income is Subpart F income since the $16 million of gross foreign base company income exceeds 70% of AFRIco's total gross income.

AFRIco	$16 million of interest income
	$4 million of gross income from sales of inventory

The third and fourth exceptions are more policy oriented.

The third exception is an elective high-tax rule, under which a U.S. shareholder can elect to exclude from Subpart F income any insurance or foreign base company income that is subject to foreign income tax at an effective rate exceeding 90% of the maximum U.S. corporate rate.[51] The effective rate of foreign tax on an item of foreign income equals the amount of foreign income taxes paid or accrued with respect to that income divided by the net amount of that income, as determined under U.S. tax principles.[52] The high-tax exception reflects the reality that there is little or no residual U.S. tax for the U.S. Treasury to collect after the foreign tax credit when the foreign tax rate exceeds 90% of the U.S. corporate tax rate. At present, this exception is available whenever the effective foreign rate exceeds 31.5% (90% × 35%).

> *Example* **5.22:** USAco, a domestic corporation, owns 100% of the stock of ITALco, an Italian corporation. ITALco purchases goods that USAco manufactures in the United States, and then resells them to foreign customers located outside of Italy. ITALco's taxable income from inventory sales is $9 million, on which ITALco pays $3 million in foreign income taxes. The entire $9 million of taxable income is foreign base company sales income because the goods were neither manufactured nor sold for use within Italy and there is a related-party transaction. However, USAco can elect to exclude the $9 million of taxable income from Subpart F income because the effective rate of foreign income tax on that income of 33% [$3 million of foreign income taxes ÷ $9 million of net

---

[50] Code Sec. 954(b)(3)(B).

[51] Code Sec. 954(b)(4). The high-tax exception does not apply to foreign base company oil-related income.

[52] Reg. § 1.954-1(d)(2).

foreign base company sales income] exceeds 90% of the maximum U.S. corporate rate of 35%.

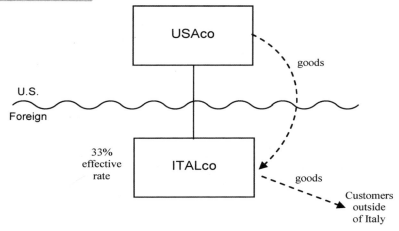

The fourth exception provides that if any part of a CFC's Subpart F income is U.S.-source income that is effectively connected to the conduct of a U.S. trade or business, such income is excluded from Subpart F income. The policy is that there is no reason to tax effectively connected income to the U.S. Shareholder because, as effectively connected income, it already incurs U.S. taxation at marginal rates at the CFC level.[53] This exception does not apply, however, to any effectively connected income that is exempt from U.S. taxation or that is subject to a reduced rate of tax by reason of a tax treaty.[54]

.08 Investment of Earnings in U.S. Property

A CFC's investment of earnings in U.S. property can be substantially equivalent to distributing a dividend to its U.S. Shareholders. For example, a loan made by a CFC to its U.S. parent makes funds available for the U.S. parent's use in the same manner as a dividend distribution. The advantage of disguising a dividend as a loan used to be that, under the general rules, a loan did not trigger a shareholder-level tax on the CFC's earnings. Congress closed this loophole by enacting provisions that automatically recharacterize investments made by a CFC in U.S. property as an income inclusion. Under this provision, a U.S. Shareholder must include in gross income the excess of the U.S. Shareholder's pro rata share of the CFC's current-year investment in U.S. property over investments in U.S. property taxed to the U.S. Shareholder in prior tax years, but only to the extent the CFC has undistributed earnings which have not yet been taxed to U.S. Shareholders.[55]

Example 5.23: USAco wholly owns FORsub, a CFC that has $10 million of undistributed earnings from manufacturing and selling widgets in country F. Wanting cash from FORsub, but not wanting to pay tax on a dividend from

---

[53] Code Sec. 882(a).
[54] Code Sec. 952(b) and Reg. § 1.952-1(b)(2).

[55] Code Secs. 951(a)(1)(B) and 956(a).

FORsub, USAco's CFO would like USAco to borrow $5 million from FORsub. However, the loan results in a Subpart F inclusion for a CFC's earnings invested in U.S. property.

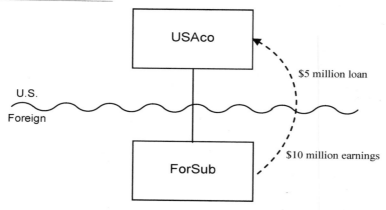

The amount of a CFC's investment in U.S. property is the quarterly average of the adjusted basis of U.S. property held (directly or indirectly) by the CFC, reduced by any liabilities to which the property is subject.[56] To determine the quarterly average, the U.S. Shareholder determines the amount of a CFC's investment in U.S. property at the end of each quarter, totals the quarterly amounts, and divides by four.

Example 5.24: FORco (a CFC) has no investments in U.S. property at the end of either the first or the second quarter, $5 million invested in U.S. property at the end of the third quarter and $11 million invested in U.S. property at the end of the fourth quarter. FORco's average quarterly investment in U.S. property for the year is $4 million [($0 + $0 + $5 million + $11 million) ÷ 4]. If FORco has undistributed earnings of $4 million, its U.S. Shareholder would have an income inclusion of $4 million. However, if FORco has undistributed earnings of $3 million, its U.S. Shareholder would have an income inclusion limited to $3 million.

FORco	Investments in U.S. property
	1st ¼: $0
	2nd ¼: $0
	3rd ¼: $5 million
	4th ¼: $11 million

The definition of "U.S. property" attempts to distinguish U.S. investments that are similar to a dividend distribution from U.S. investments that are part of the CFC's normal business operations. The principal types of U.S. property are as follows:

---

[56] Code Sec. 956(a).

(i) *Debt obligations*—U.S. property includes an obligation of a U.S. person, such as a <u>loan to a U.S. Shareholder</u>,[57] including any pledge or guarantee by a CFC of a U.S. person's obligation.[58] There are exceptions for obligations of unrelated domestic corporations,[59] obligations of the United States and deposits with a U.S. bank,[60] obligations that arise from regular business transactions to the extent such amounts are ordinary and necessary (e.g., purchases of product for resale),[61] certain deposits of cash or securities made or received by a securities or commodities dealer,[62] and obligations to U.S. persons who are neither U.S. Shareholders of the CFC nor entities related to the CFC.[63]

(ii) *Certain receivables*—U.S. property includes trade or service receivables acquired, directly or indirectly, from a <u>related U.S. person</u>, such as a U.S. Shareholder, where the obligor is a U.S. person.[64]

(iii) *Stock*—U.S. property includes stock of a <u>U.S. Shareholder or other related U.S. corporation</u>, but not stock of unrelated U.S. corporations.[65]

(iv) *Tangible property*—U.S. property includes any tangible property located in the United States, such as a U.S. manufacturing facility.[66] There are exceptions for property that is purchased in the United States for export to or use in foreign countries,[67] as well as aircraft, railroad rolling stock, vessels, motor vehicles, and transport containers used predominantly outside the United States.[68]

(v) *Intangibles*—U.S. property includes any right to use in the United States a patent, copyright, invention, model, design, secret formula or process, or any similar property right.[69]

Example 5.25: CANco is a wholly-owned Canadian subsidiary of USAco, a domestic corporation. During the year, USAco obtains a $2 million loan from a U.S. bank. At the bank's request, the loan agreement contains a provision whereby the loan is guaranteed by all of USAco's affiliates, including CANco. <u>CANco's guarantee of USAco's loan from the U.S. bank may inadvertently trigger an investment in U.S. property.</u>

---

[57] Code Sec. 956(c)(1)(C).

[58] Code Sec. 956(d). However, pledges of less than two-thirds of a CFC's shares do not constitute an investment in U.S. property. Reg. § 1.956-2(c).

[59] Code Sec. 956(c)(2)(F).

[60] Code Sec. 956(c)(2)(A).

[61] Code Sec. 956(c)(2)(C).

[62] Code Sec. 956(c)(2)(J).

[63] Code Sec. 956(c)(2)(M).

[64] Code Sec. 956(c)(3).

[65] Code Sec. 956(c)(1)(B) and (2)(F).

[66] Code Sec. 956(c)(1)(A).

[67] Code Sec. 956(c)(2)(B).

[68] Code Sec. 956(c)(2)(D).

[69] Code Sec. 956(c)(1)(D).

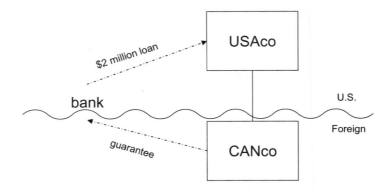

.09 Deemed Paid Foreign Tax Credit

Consistent with the notion that a <u>Subpart F inclusion is similar to a dividend</u>, a U.S. C corporation that directly owns 10% or more of a CFC's voting stock can claim a <u>deemed paid foreign tax credit</u> for the CFC's foreign income taxes in the same year that the <u>U.S. Shareholder is taxed on the CFC's earnings.</u>[70] The deemed paid <u>credit that is allowed with respect to a Subpart F inclusion</u> is similar to the deemed paid credit that is allowed with respect to actual dividend distributions.[71]

> ***Example 5.26:*** USAco, a domestic corporation, owns 100% of the stock of ASIAco, a foreign corporation. During its first year of existence, ASIAco had <u>$20 million of Subpart F income, paid $2 million in foreign income taxes, and did not distribute any dividends.</u> Because ASIAco is a CFC, USAco must include in income its share of ASIAco's net Subpart F income, which is $18 million [$20 million of Subpart F income – $2 million of foreign income taxes]. <u>The inclusion of Subpart F income carries with it a deemed paid foreign tax credit of $2 million</u> [ASIAco's post-1986 foreign income taxes of $2 million × ($18 million Subpart F inclusion ÷ $18 million of post-1986 undistributed earnings)]. <u>With the $2 million gross-up, USAco has $20 million of taxable income and $2 million of deemed paid foreign tax credits.</u>

---

[70] Code Sec. 960(a)(1). A U.S. Shareholder who is an individual can elect to have a Subpart F inclusion taxed as if the taxpayer were a domestic corporation, in which case the individual can claim a deemed paid credit. Code Sec. 962.

[71] Reg. §§ 1.960-1–1.960-7.

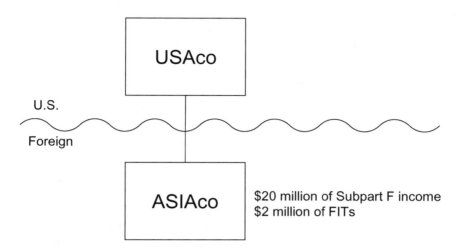

For foreign tax credit limitation purposes, allocate a Subpart F inclusion among the separate categories of income under one of two CFC look-through rules.

First, allocate an increase in a CFC's investment in U.S. property between general category income and passive category income based on the ratio of the CFC's post-1986 undistributed earnings within each separate category of income to the CFC's total post-1986 undistributed earnings.[72]

Example 5.27: USAco, a U.S. corporation, owns 100% of the stock of MEXco, a Mexican corporation. As of the end of the current year, MEXco has $100 million of post-1986 undistributed earnings, including $90 million of earnings attributable to general category income and $10 million attributable to passive category income. During the current year, MEXco made a $1 million loan to USAco, which resulted in a $1 million Subpart F inclusion for an investment in U.S. property. Under the CFC look-through rule, $900,000 of this amount [$1 million × ($90 million ÷ $100 million)] is general category income, and the other $100,000 [$1 million × ($10 million ÷ $100 million)] is passive category income.

---

[72] Code Sec. 904(d)(3)(G).

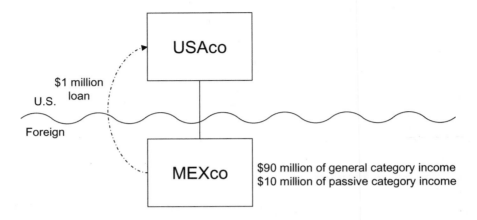

Second, allocate an inclusion of Subpart F income between the general and passive categories of income based on the nature of the CFC's current year taxable income that result in the Subpart F inclusion.[73]

> **Example 5.28:** USAco, a U.S. corporation, owns 100% of the stock of EURco, a foreign corporation. During the current year, EURco earns $1 million of Subpart F income that is taxed to USAco, including $850,000 of foreign base company sales income and $150,000 of foreign personal holding company income. Under the CFC look-through rule, $850,000 of this amount is general category income and the other $150,000 is passive category income.[74]

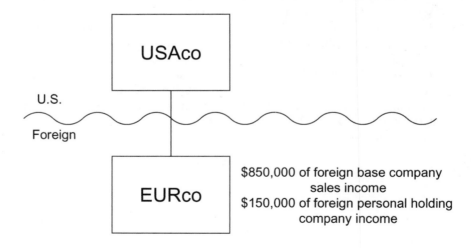

An individual who has an income inclusion under Subpart F must pay tax on the inclusion at ordinary rates as the income inclusion is not a dividend that would incur tax at the lower capital gains rates on qualified dividends.[75]

---

[73] Code Sec. 904(d)(3)(B).

[74] Compare Reg. § 1.904-5(c)(1)(ii), Example (1).

[75] Code Sec. 1(h); Notice 2004-70, 2004-70, 2004-2 CB 724.

¶501.09

.10 Mechanisms to Prevent Double Taxation

To avoid taxing the same earnings twice, the current taxation of a CFC's undistributed earnings to its U.S. shareholders must be coordinated with both the taxation of actual dividend distributions made by the CFC and the taxation of dispositions of the CFC's stock.

Distributions of previously-taxed income. A U.S. shareholder can exclude distributions of a CFC's earnings and profits that were previously-taxed income (PTI) to U.S. Shareholders as a result of a Subpart F income inclusion.[76] For this purpose, distributions made by a CFC are traced first to PTI attributable to a Subpart F inclusion for an investment in U.S. property and then to PTI attributable to a Subpart F inclusion for Subpart F income. The remaining portion of the distribution, if any, is traced to the CFC's other earnings and profits.[77] Only the portion of a distribution traced to these other earnings and profits (i.e., non-Subpart F earnings and profits) represents a taxable dividend to the U.S. Shareholder.

A U.S. Shareholder cannot claim a deemed paid credit with respect to a distribution of PTI to the extent a credit was already taken for those taxes in the year of the Subpart F inclusion.[78] However, the U.S. Shareholder can increase its foreign tax credit limitation by the lesser of (i) the amount of excess limitation, if any, created in the prior year by the Subpart F inclusion or (ii) the amount of foreign withholding taxes imposed on the distribution of PTI.[79] This adjustment is designed to prevent a U.S. Shareholder from being unfairly denied an "in lieu of" credit[80] for any foreign withholding taxes imposed on an actual dividend distribution simply because, for U.S. tax purposes, the dividend income was recognized in a prior year.

> **Example 5.29:** USAco, a domestic corporation, owns 100% of the stock of AFRIco, a foreign corporation that was organized in year 1. During year 1, AFRIco had $10 million of foreign personal holding company income, paid $2 million in foreign income taxes, and did not distribute any dividends. In year 2, AFRIco did not have any earnings and profits, did not pay any foreign income taxes, but distributed an $8 million dividend. The $8 million dividend is subject to $800,000 of foreign withholding taxes. The U.S. tax consequences of AFRIco's activities are as follows.

---

[76] Code Sec. 959(a). In addition, a distribution of previously-taxed income by a lower-tier CFC is not included in the income of a higher-tier CFC. Code Sec. 959(b).

[77] Code Sec. 959(c).

[78] Code Sec. 960(a)(2).

[79] Code Sec. 960(b)(1). A U.S. Shareholder keeps track of these excess limitation amounts by establishing an excess limitation account in the year of the Subpart F inclusion. Code Sec. 960(b)(2).

[80] Code Sec. 903.

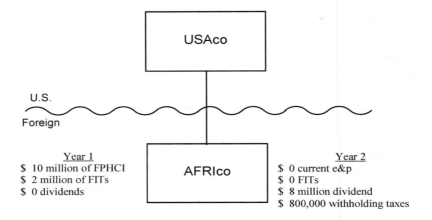

USAco

U.S.

Foreign

Year 1	AFRIco	Year 2
$ 10 million of FPHCI		$ 0 current e&p
$ 2 million of FITs		$ 0 FITs
$ 0 dividends		$ 8 million dividend
		$ 800,000 withholding taxes

Year 1. Because AFRIco is a CFC, USAco must include in gross income its share of AFRIco's net Subpart F income, which is $8 million [$10 million of Subpart F income – $2 million of foreign income taxes]. The inclusion of Subpart F income carries with it a deemed paid credit of $2 million [AFRIco's post-1986 foreign income taxes of $2 million × ($8 million Subpart F inclusion ÷ $8 million of post-1986 undistributed earnings)]. With the gross-up, USAco has $10 million of foreign-source passive limitation income and a pre-credit U.S. tax of $3.5 million (assuming a 35% U.S. rate). Therefore, USAco's residual U.S. tax on the Subpart F income is $1.5 million [$3.5 million pre-credit U.S. tax – $2 million foreign tax credit].

Year 2. USAco can exclude the $8 million dividend from U.S. taxation because it represents a distribution of PTI. In addition, USAco cannot claim a deemed paid credit because it claimed a credit for AFRIco's income taxes in year 1. However, USAco can claim an "in lieu of" credit for the $800,000 of foreign withholding taxes. USAco's foreign tax credit limitation equals the lesser of the excess limitation from year 1 of $1.5 million or the $800,000 of withholding taxes imposed on the distribution of previously-taxed earnings and profits and, therefore, USAco can claim a credit for the full amount of withholding taxes.

CFC stock basis adjustments. A U.S. Shareholder increases its basis in the stock of a CFC by the amount of a Subpart F inclusion.[81] This adjustment prevents double taxation of any proceeds from the sale or exchange of a CFC's stock that are attributable to earnings and profits that were already taxed to the U.S. Shareholder as a Subpart F inclusion. When the CFC distributes the PTI, the U.S. Shareholder treats the distribution as a nontaxable return-of-capital that reduces its basis in the stock of a CFC.[82]

    ***Example* 5.30:** In January of year 1, Tom (a U.S. citizen) organizes FORco, a wholly-owned foreign corporation, and contributes $10 million of cash to FORco in exchange for 100% of its stock. During year 1, FORco derives $2 million of Subpart F income (net of foreign income taxes and other allocable

---

[81] Code Sec. 961(a).   [82] Code Sec. 961(b).

deductions), which is taxed to Tom in year 1 as a Subpart F inclusion. In January of year 2, Tom completely liquidates FORco and receives a $12 million liquidating distribution. If no adjustments are made to Tom's basis in FORco's stock, Tom would recognize a $2 million capital gain on the receipt of the liquidating distribution [$12 million amount realized – $10 million original basis].[83] In effect, FORco's year 1 Subpart F income of $2 million would be subject to U.S. taxation for a second time. However, because Tom is allowed to increase his basis in the FORco stock by the $2 million Subpart F inclusion to $12 million, he does not recognize any gain on the receipt of the liquidating distribution.

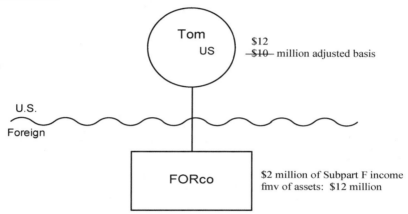

.11 Currency Translation

CFCs usually conduct business and keep their books and records in a foreign currency. This creates currency translation issues for U.S. shareholders, who must report Subpart F inclusions in U.S. dollars. The currency translation rules for Subpart F inclusions are discussed in detail in Chapter 6 (¶ 602). Briefly, to determine the amount of a Subpart F inclusion, Subpart F income is translated into U.S. dollars using the average exchange rate for the taxable year and an investment in U.S. property is translated into U.S. dollars using the spot rate on the last day of the taxable year.[84] If the exchange rate fluctuates between the time of the Subpart F inclusion and the time the CFC distributes the PTI, the U.S. Shareholder recognizes a foreign currency gain or loss.[85]

.12 Earnings and Profits

A CFC's earnings and profits play an important role in determining a U.S. shareholder's Subpart F inclusions. For example, the amount of a U.S. Shareholder's Subpart F inclusion for Subpart F income is limited to the CFC's current earnings and profits.[86] Likewise, the amount of a U.S. Shareholder's Subpart F inclusion for an investment in U.S. property is limited to the sum of the CFC's

---

[83] Code Sec. 331.
[84] Code Secs. 986(b) and 989(b).

[85] Code Sec. 986(c). The procedure for computing the gain is described in Notice 1988-71, 1988-2 CB 374.
[86] Code Sec. 952(c)(1)(A).

current and accumulated earnings and profits.[87] The earnings and profits of a CFC are computed substantially as if the CFC were a domestic corporation, by starting with the CFC's profit and loss statement, and then making any adjustments necessary to conform the profit and loss statement to U.S. GAAP and tax accounting standards.[88]

.13 Information Reporting for CFCs

In order to provide the IRS with the information necessary to ensure compliance with Subpart F, each year a U.S. Shareholder of a CFC must file a Form 5471, Information Return of U.S. Persons With Respect to Certain Foreign Corporations.[89] Other persons who must file a Form 5471 include (i) U.S. persons who acquire a 10% ownership interest, acquire an additional 10% ownership interest or dispose of stock holdings to reduce their ownership in the foreign corporation to less than 10%[90] and (ii) U.S. citizens and residents who are officers or directors of a foreign corporation in which a U.S. person acquires a 10% ownership interest or an additional 10% interest.[91]

In Form 5471, the reporting agent must provide the following information regarding the CFC:[92]

(i)   Stock ownership, including current year acquisitions and dispositions,

(ii) U.S. Shareholders,

(iii) GAAP income statement and balance sheet,

(iv) Foreign income taxes,

(v)   Current and accumulated earnings and profits, including any actual dividend distributions during the year,

(vi) The U.S. shareholder's pro rata share of Subpart F income and any increase in earnings invested in U.S. property, and

(vii) Transactions between the CFC and shareholders or other related persons.

U.S. persons ordinarily file a Form 5471 by attaching it to their regular federal income tax return.[93] Any U.S. person who fails to furnish the required information may be subject to an annual penalty of $10,000, as well as a reduction in their foreign tax credit.[94] A completed Form 5471 is included in the appendix to this chapter.

Reporting requirements also apply to controlled foreign partnerships and foreign disregarded entities. Any U.S. person that is a more-than-50% partner must annually file Form 8865, Return of U.S. Persons With Respect to Certain Foreign Partnerships,[95] and any U.S. person that is a tax owner of a foreign disregarded entity must annually file Form 8858, Information Return of U.S. Persons with Respect to Foreign Disregarded Entities (see ¶ 809). U.S. persons that are required

---

[87] Code Sec. 956(a)(2).

[88] Reg. § 1.964-1(a)(1).

[89] Reg. § 1.6038-2(a) and (b).

[90] Reg. § 1.6046-1(c)(1).

[91] Reg. § 1.6046-1(a)(2)(i) and Code Sec. 6046(a).

[92] Reg. § 1.6038-2(f) and (g).

[93] Reg. § 1.6038-2(i).

[94] Code Sec. 6038(b) and (c).

[95] Reg. § 1.6038-3(a)(1).

to file Form 5471 with respect to a CFC that is a tax owner of a foreign disregarded entity also must file Form 8858.

¶ 502 PASSIVE FOREIGN INVESTMENT COMPANIES

.01 Background

U.S. investors in U.S. mutual funds (i.e., a regulated investment company) are taxed currently on the fund's investment income because a domestic fund must distribute at least 90% of its income each year in order to avoid U.S. taxation at the corporate level.[96] In contrast, U.S. investors in foreign mutual funds were previously able to avoid current U.S. taxation. The foreign mutual fund itself avoided U.S. tax because it was a foreign corporation that derived only foreign-source income. The U.S. investors avoided U.S. tax because the foreign mutual fund typically did not pay any dividends. These funds were able to avoid the CFC taint because its ownership was dispersed among a large number of U.S. and foreign investors, each owning a relatively small percentage of the fund. Another significant tax benefit was that when U.S. investors eventually sold their investment they were able to effectively convert the fund's ordinary income (dividends and interest) into capital gains.

The enactment of the passive foreign investment company (or PFIC) regime significantly expanded the reach of the U.S. taxing authorities with respect to passive investment income earned by U.S. persons through foreign corporations.[97] Congress enacted the PFIC provisions to deal with perceived abuses by U.S. investors in foreign mutual funds. However, the PFIC rules apply to any foreign corporation that meets either the PFIC income test or assets test, regardless of whether U.S. shareholders individually or in the aggregate have a significant ownership stake in the foreign corporation. The lack of a U.S. control requirement represents a major policy shift from Subpart F, which applies only to foreign corporations with controlling U.S. Shareholders.

Under an overlap rule, a foreign corporation that qualifies as both a CFC and a PFIC is not treated as a PFIC by a U.S. Shareholder (i.e., a U.S. person who owns 10% or more of the stock). Therefore, a U.S. Shareholder that is subject to the current inclusion rules of Subpart F is not also subject to the PFIC rules with respect to the same stock.[98] On the other hand, the PFIC provisions do apply to any U.S. persons who own less than 10% of the foreign corporation.

.02 Definition of a PFIC

A foreign corporation is a PFIC if it meets either an income test or an asset test.[99]

Income test. Under the income test, a foreign corporation is a PFIC if 75% or more of the corporation's gross income for the taxable year is passive income.[100] Passive income is generally foreign personal holding company income as defined

---

[96] Code Secs. 851 and 852.

[97] Code Secs. 1291–1298.

[98] Code Sec. 1297(d).

[99] Code Sec. 1297(a). Exceptions to the income test and asset test apply to a foreign corporation's first taxable

year and to a year in which a foreign corporation experiences a change in business. Code Sec. 1298(b)(2) and (3).

[100] Code Sec. 1297(a)(1).

for purposes of Subpart F (See ¶ 9.06), with certain adjustments.[101] The adjustments include exclusions for income derived from the active conduct of a banking, insurance, or securities business, as well as any interest, dividends, rents, and royalties received from a related person to the extent such income is properly allocable to nonpassive income of the related person.[102]

> *Example* **5.31:** Grandma buys 1% of ForFund. ForFund deposits all the money it receives from investors in an interest bearing bank account at the Hong Kong Bank. ForFund is a PFIC because 100% of its income is passive income.

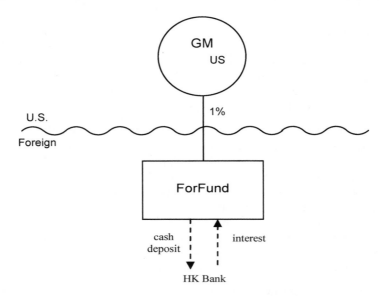

To prevent foreign holding companies of operating subsidiaries from being treated as PFICs, a foreign corporation that owns directly or indirectly at least 25% (by value) of the stock of another corporation is treated as if it earned a proportionate share of that corporation's income.[103]

> *Example* **5.32:** Grandma buys 1% of ForFund, which owns 100% of two companies - ForOps1 and ForOps2 - that earn all their income from distributing widgets and gadgets. All of ForFund's income appears to be passive income as the result of dividends received from ForOps1 and ForOps2. However, by looking through to the 100% of the active income earned by ForOps1 and ForOps2, ForFund fails the 75% passive income test. Therefore, ForFund is not a PFIC.

---

[101] Code Sec. 1297(b)(1) by reference to Code Sec. 954(c).

[102] Code Sec. 1297(b)(2).

[103] Code Sec. 1297(c)(2).

¶502.02

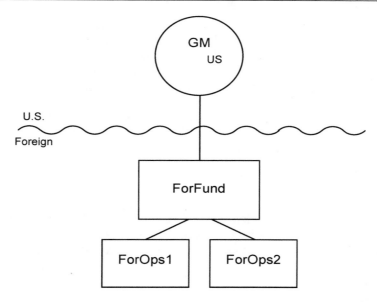

Assets test. Under the assets test, a foreign corporation is a PFIC if the foreign corporation's passive assets are more than 50% of the corporation's total assets. Passive assets are assets that produce passive income (as defined for purposes of the PFIC income test), with certain adjustments.

Example **5.33**: Grandma purchases 1% of the shares of ForFund, a foreign corporation. ForFund takes all the money it receives from investors and buys gold bullion. Although the bullion does not produce any income, ForFund is a PFIC because the gold bullion, which comprise 100% of ForFund's assets, is a passive asset.

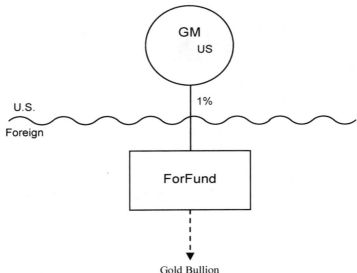

Gold Bullion

As with the income test, a foreign corporation that owns directly or indirectly at least 25% (by value) of the stock of another corporation is treated as if it owned directly a proportionate share of that corporation's assets.[104] Moreover, a CFC can increase its active assets by the amount of research or experimental expenditures incurred by the CFC during the current and preceding two taxable years and by an amount equal to 300% of the payments made by the CFC for certain licensed intangibles used by the CFC in the active conduct of a trade or business.[105] In addition, a foreign corporation is treated as the owner of any tangible personal property that it leases for a term of 12 or more months.[106]

Example 5.34: Grandma purchases 1% of the shares of ForCo, a foreign corporation that has $1 million of cash (a passive asset), machinery that ForCo recently purchased for $900,000, and the license to use an intangible in the manufacturing process for which ForCo pays a royalty of $50,000 this year. By taking 300% of the $50,000 royalty, ForCo adds $150,000 to the $900,000 machinery for $1.05 million of active assets. As a result, ForCo's passive assets (the $1 million of cash) are less than half of ForCo's total assets of $2.05 million.

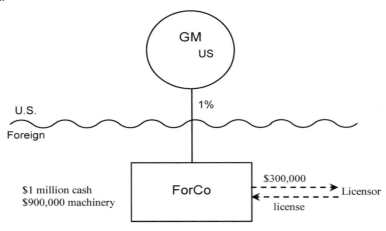

There are different tests to measure the assets of a foreign corporation that depend on whether the foreign corporation is a CFC or is publicly-traded. Taxpayers measure the assets of a publicly traded foreign corporation based on a fair market value computation. Accordingly, a publicly traded foreign corporation is a PFIC if the fair market value of its passive income-producing assets equals or exceeds 50% of the sum of the fair market value of its outstanding shares plus its liabilities.[107] However, taxpayers measure the assets of a non-publicly traded CFC by their adjusted basis.[108] Finally, taxpayers may use either method to measure the assets of a privately-held foreign corporation that is not a CFC.[109]

---

[104] Code Sec. 1297(c)(1).

[105] Code Sec. 1298(e). This provision does not apply if the licenser is a related foreign person.

[106] Code Sec. 1298(d). This provision does not apply if the lessor is a related person.

[107] Code Sec. 1297(e)(1)(A).

[108] Code Sec. 1297(e)(2)(A).

[109] Code Sec. 1297(e)(2)(B).

¶502.02

Many foreign corporations only have cash at the beginning of their existence as they are merely capitalized with cash received from equity or debt before they actively begin operations. Under the policy that it was unfair to make these foreign corporations incur the PFIC taint, the PFIC regime excepts certain foreign corporations during their first year of existence. To qualify for this exception, newly-formed foreign corporations must not be a PFIC in either their second or third year of existence.[110]

.03 Taxation of a PFIC

A PFIC's undistributed earnings are subject to U.S. taxation under one of three methods, each of which is designed to eliminate the benefits of deferral. These include the qualified electing fund method, the mark-to-market method, and the excess distribution method.

Qualified Electing Fund Method. Under the qualified electing fund (QEF) method, shareholders who can obtain the necessary information can elect to be taxed currently on their pro rata share of the PFIC's earnings and profits. The income inclusion is treated as ordinary income to the extent of the taxpayer's pro rata share of the QEF's ordinary income[111] and capital gains to the extent of the taxpayer's pro rata share of the QEF's capital gains.[112] A taxpayer's pro rata share is the amount that the taxpayer would have received if, on each day of the QEF's taxable year, the QEF had actually distributed to each of its shareholders a pro rata share of that day's ratable share of the QEF's ordinary earnings and net capital gains for the year.[113]

> **Example 5.35:** Grandma purchases 1% of the shares of ForFund, a foreign corporation. ForFund deposits all the money it receives from investors in an interest bearing account at the Hong Kong Bank. During 20X1, ForFund earns $500,000 of interest. When filing her 20X1 return, Grandma makes a QEF election and reports $5,000 (1% of $500,000) of income on her return.

---

[110] Code Sec. 1298(b)(2).

[111] The ordinary income component of a QEF inclusion is not a qualified dividend. Notice 2004-70, 2004-2 CB 724.

[112] Code Secs. 1293(a) and 1295(a). When the QEF method and Subpart F apply to the same income, the item is included in the U.S. shareholder's gross income under Subpart F. Code Sec. 951(c).

[113] Code Sec. 1293(b).

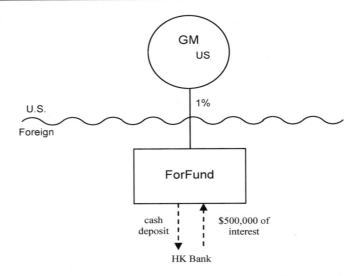

The collateral effects of a QEF inclusion are similar to those of a Subpart F inclusion (See ¶ 501.10). To prevent double taxation of the QEF's earnings, any actual distributions made by a QEF out of its PTI are tax-free to the U.S. investor.[114] In addition, a U.S. investor increases its basis in the QEF's stock for any income inclusions and reduces its basis in the stock when it receives a distribution of previously taxed income.[115] If a taxpayer does not have the cash to pay the tax on the QEF income, the taxpayer can elect to later pay the tax, with interest, on receipt of a distribution.[116] Finally, a 10% corporate shareholder may receive a deemed paid foreign tax credit.[117]

Mark-To-Market Method. The mark-to-market method extends the current income inclusion method to PFIC shareholders who could not obtain the information from the PFIC necessary to make a QEF election and, therefore, were forced to use the complex and burdensome excess distribution method described below. If the stock of a PFIC is marketable, the taxpayer may elect to use the mark-to-market method.[118] If elected, any excess of the fair market value of the PFIC stock at the close of the taxable year over the shareholder's adjusted basis in the stock is included as ordinary income to the shareholder.

Example 5.36: On January 1, 20Y1, Grandma (a U.S. citizen) pays $1 million for 1% of the stock of FM, a foreign mutual fund that constitutes a PFIC. As a minority shareholder, Grandma cannot obtain the necessary information from FM to make a QEF election. However, because the stock of FM is marketable, Grandma makes a mark-to-market election. On December 31, 20Y1, the stock is worth $1.2 million, and Grandma recognizes $200,000 of income.

---

[114] Code Sec. 1293(c).

[115] Code Sec. 1293(d).

[116] Code Sec. 1294.

[117] Code Sec. 1293(f). Even though 10% corporate tax-payers may treat the QEF inclusion as a deemed dividend that is eligible for a deemed paid foreign tax credit, U.S. individuals must pay tax at ordinary rates and are not entitled to the preferential rate of tax on qualified dividends. Code Sec. 1(h)(11)(C)(iii).

[118] Code Sec. 1296.

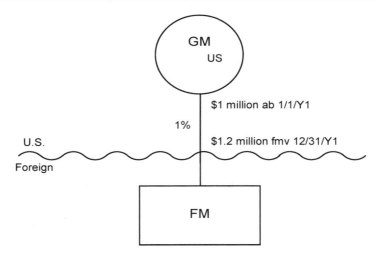

The shareholder may similarly deduct any excess of the adjusted basis of the PFIC stock over its fair market value at the close of the tax year.[119] However, deductions are limited to the net mark-to-market gains on the stock that the shareholder included in income in prior years, or so-called "unreversed inclusions." In addition, a shareholder's adjusted basis of PFIC stock is both increased by the income recognized and decreased by the deductions pursuant to the mark-to-market method.[120]

Excess Distribution Method. Under the excess distribution method, the taxpayer is allowed to defer taxation of the PFIC's undistributed income until the PFIC makes an excess distribution, which is defined as any actual distribution made by the PFIC, but only to the extent the total actual distributions received by the taxpayer for the year exceeds 125% of the average actual distribution received by the taxpayer in the preceding three taxable years (or, if shorter, the taxpayer's holding period before the current taxable year).[121]

The amount of an excess distribution is treated as if it had been realized pro rata over the holding period for the PFIC's stock and the tax due on an excess distribution is the sum of the deferred yearly tax amounts (computed using the highest tax rate in effect in the years the income was accumulated), plus interest.[122] Therefore, the excess distribution method eliminates the benefits of deferral by assessing an interest charge on the deferred yearly tax amounts. Any actual distributions that fall below the 125% threshold are treated as dividends (assuming

---

[119] Codes Sec. 1296(a).

[120] Code Sec. 1296(b).

[121] Code Sec. 1291(b)(1) and (2)(A). Any amounts currently or previously included in the U.S. investor's gross income by reason of Subpart F are not treated as excess distributions. Prop. Reg. § 1.1291-2(b)(2). In addition, it is

not possible to have an excess distribution in the year that the taxpayer first acquires shares in the PFIC. Code Sec. 1291(b)(2)(B).

[122] Code Sec. 1291(a)(1) and (c). The interest is the underpayment rate, which is the AFR short term rate plus 3%. Code Secs. 1291(c)(3) and 6621.

they represent a distribution of earnings and profits), which are currently taxable in the year of receipt and are not subject to the special interest charge.[123]

   Example **5.37**: On January 1, 20Y1, Grandma (a U.S. citizen) purchases 1% of the stock of FM, a foreign mutual fund that is a PFIC. Grandma does not make a QEF or mark-to-market election. FM is highly profitable, but FM does not make a distribution until December 31, 20Y3, when it pays Grandma a dividend of $300,000. Under the excess distribution method, the entire dividend is an excess distribution as the entire $300,000 is greater than the average distribution over the prior three years ($0). Accordingly, the dividend is treated as if it were received ratably ($100,000 per year) over 20Y1, 20Y2 and 20Y3, taxed at the highest rate in effect for 20Y1 and 20Y2, and subject to an interest charge.

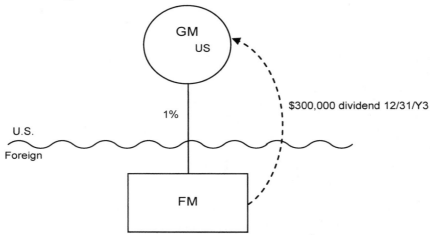

   Had FM distributed $100,000 during 20Y2 and later distributed $300,000 on December 31, 20X3, 125% of the previous years' distributions would be $62,500 (125% of $100,000 divided by 2) and the excess amount of $237,500 ($300,000 less $62,500) would result in an allocation of $79,166 to each of the three years. Similar to the original facts in this example, the $79,166 allocated to 20Y1 and 20Y2 would incur tax at the highest rate in effect for those years and an interest charge.

   Taxpayers can claim a Code Sec. 903 "in lieu of" foreign tax credit with respect to any withholding taxes imposed on a distribution by a PFIC and a U.S. corporation owning 10% or more of the PFIC's voting stock also can claim a deemed paid foreign tax credit.[124] An excess distribution also includes any gain realized on the sale of PFIC stock.[125]

   Example **5.38**: On January 1, 20Y1, Grandma (U.S. citizen) pays $10,000 to purchase the stock of FM, a foreign mutual fund that is a PFIC. Grandma does not elect either the QEF method or the mark-to-market method. FM is

---

[123] Prop. Reg. § 1.1291-2(e)(1).
[124] Code Sec. 1291(g) and Prop. Reg. § 1.1291-5.
[125] Code Sec. 1291(a)(2).

highly profitable, but it does not make a distribution and on December 31, 20Y3, with $30 million of accumulated earnings and profits (Grandma's share is $300,000) Grandma sells her shares for $310,000. Under the excess distribution method, her $300,000 gain is treated as if it were received as ordinary income ratably ($100,000 per year) over 20Y1, 20Y2 and 20Y3, taxed at the highest rate in effect for 20Y1 and 20Y2, and subject to an interest charge.

.04 Information Reporting for PFICs

Code Sec. 1298(f) requires each U.S. person who is a shareholder of a PFIC to file an annual report on Form 8621. A completed Form 8621 is included in the appendix to this chapter.

¶ 503 GAIN FROM THE SALE OR EXCHANGE OF A CFC'S STOCK

A gain on the sale or exchange of stock of a foreign corporation normally is capital in nature.[126] However, an exception applies if, at any time during the five-year period ending on the date of the sale or exchange, the taxpayer was a U.S. Shareholder of the foreign corporation when the foreign corporation qualified as a CFC. In such cases, the U.S. Shareholder must treat the gain on the sale or exchange of the foreign corporation's stock as a dividend to the extent of the U.S. Shareholder's pro rata share of the corporation's earnings and profits that were accumulated while the U.S. Shareholder owned the stock and the corporation was a CFC.[127] Any gain in excess of the deemed dividend is still accorded capital gain treatment. For purposes of this provision, earnings and profits do not include certain amounts already subject to U.S. tax, including prior-year Subpart F inclu-

---

[126] Code Sec. 1221.

[127] Code Sec. 1248(a). In the case of U.S. shareholders who are individuals, the tax attributable to the deemed

dividend cannot exceed the tax that would have been due if the foreign corporation had been a domestic corporation. Code Sec. 1248(b).

¶503

sions, income effectively connected with the conduct of a U.S. trade or business, and an inclusion from a PFIC that has made a QEF election.[128]

Congress enacted section 1248 to ensure that the U.S. Treasury collects the "full U.S. tax" when a U.S. Shareholder repatriates the foreign earnings of a CFC by selling the CFC's shares. Previously, a U.S. Shareholder that operated abroad through a CFC could defer U.S. taxes on the CFC's earnings, before repatriating those earnings through the sale of the CFC's stock (rather than a dividend distribution), in which case the CFC's earnings were subject to U.S. tax at a lower capital gains rate. The policy of treating part or all of the gain on the sale of a CFC's stock as a dividend is to tax the CFC's accumulated earnings as ordinary income.

At present, there is not a capital gains rate differential for corporate taxpayers. Nevertheless, because a dividend carries with it deemed paid foreign tax credits, the re-characterization of a gain as a dividend remains an important feature of the law for U.S. corporations that are U.S. shareholders of a CFC.[129] Therefore, this anti-abuse provision can work to a U.S. corporation's advantage by allowing it to claim deemed paid foreign tax credits that can be used to offset the tax on the disposition of a CFC's stock.

Example 5.39: ASIAco is a wholly-owned manufacturing subsidiary of USAco, a U.S. corporation. USAco has been ASIAco's sole shareholder since ASIAco was organized several years ago. At the end of the current year, USAco sells all of ASIAco's stock to an unrelated foreign buyer for $15 million. At that time, ASIAco had $3 million of post-1986 undistributed earnings and profits and $1 million of post-1986 foreign income taxes. USAco's basis in ASIAco's stock was $10 million immediately prior to the sale. Assume USAco's capital gain on the sale of ASIAco's stock is not subject to foreign taxation and that the U.S. corporate tax rate is 35%.

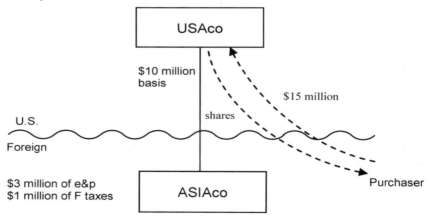

USAco realizes a gain on the sale of ASIAco's stock of $5 million [$15 million amount realized – $10 million basis in ASIAco's stock]. The dividend portion of the gain equals ASIAco's undistributed earnings of $3 million, and the remain-

---

[128] Code Sec. 1248(d).   [129] Reg. § 1.1248-1(d).

ing $2 million is treated as a capital gain. The $3 million dividend carries with it $1 million of deemed paid foreign taxes. With the $1 million gross-up, ASIAco has $4 million of foreign-source dividend income. Further assume that the $2 million capital gain also is foreign-source income.[130] Therefore, the pre-credit U.S. tax on the stock sale is $2.1 million [35% U.S. tax rate × ($4 million dividend + $2 million capital gain)], the credit is $1 million, and USAco has a residual U.S. tax of $1.1 million. In contrast, if the entire $5 million gain had been treated as a capital gain, the U.S. tax would have been $1.75 million [35% U.S. tax rate × $5 million capital gain] without any foreign tax credit.

Although a capital gains rate differential does not exist for U.S. corporations, there is a capital gains rate differential for U.S. individuals, which extends to qualified dividends.[131] Qualified dividends include dividends received from a foreign corporation in a country with which the United States has a tax treaty. Therefore, a deemed-dividend a U.S. individual receives from a CFC under section 1248 is a qualified dividend if the foreign corporation is incorporated in a treaty country.[132]

---

[130] Code Sec. 865(f).
[131] Code Sec. 1(h)(11)(B).

[132] Code Sec. 1(h)(11)(C).

¶ 504 APPENDIX

Mark Twain, a resident of Hannibal, Missouri, owns 51 of the 100 outstanding common shares of BritCo, a United Kingdom corporation headquartered in Cambridge, England. The remaining 49 outstanding common shares are owned by diverse foreign interests. BritCo purchases bowling balls from Mark Twain for resale throughout Europe. Although all of BritCo's purchases and sales are in British pounds, approximately 25% of BritCo's sales are to customers in Finland.

Mark Twain, as President, is the only officer and director of BritCo. The small business tax rate in the United Kingdom is 20%. Both Mark Twain and BritCo are on the calendar year. BritCo does not pay any dividends and neither Mark Twain nor BritCo own an interest in any other foreign entities. During 20X2, the average exchange rate for the pound was $1.50, which was also the spot rate on December 31, 20X2. BritCo keeps all its cash in a non-interest bearing account.

Mark Twain acquired his shares of BritCo, as did all the other foreign shareholders, on January 1, 20X2, based on his capital contribution of £5,100,000 for common shares. Mark Twain files his return with the Kansas City Service Center on April 15 of each year, without ever pursuing an extension.

The chartered accountant in Cambridge provides you with the following account information for the year ended December 31, 20X2:

Sales:	£ 25,000,000
Cost of Good Sold:	£ 15,000,000
Compensation to U.K. employees:	£ 2,000,000
Taxes:	£ 1,600,000
Cash:	£ 16,400,000
Inventory:	£ 15,000,000
Accounts Payable:	£ 15,000,000
Common Stock:	£ 10,000,000
Retained Earnings:	£ 6,400,000

When filing Form 5471, Mark Twain is a Category 2 filer because he is a U.S. citizen who is an officer or director of BritCo and he has acquired at least 10% of his shares during 20X2. He is a Category 3 filer because he is a U.S. shareholder (at least 10% share holdings). He controls a foreign corporation, BritCo, for an uninterrupted period of at least 30 days during 20X2 and, accordingly, is a Category 4 filer. He is a Category 5 filer because he is a U.S. shareholder of BritCo, which was a CFC, on the last day of the 20X2 taxable year.

Mark Twain will report $1,224,000 of Subpart F income, which constitutes foreign base company sales income from BritCo's purchase of bowling balls from Mark and BritCo's resale to customers in Finland. Twenty-five percent of gross income from Finnish sales is £2.5 million. After apportionable expenses of £500,000 (compensation) and taxes of £400,000, net Subpart F income is £1.6 million, of which Mark's 51% share was £816,000. At the exchange rate of $1.50 per pound, the Subpart F income inclusion is $1,224,000.

Form **5471** (Rev. December 2012) Department of the Treasury Internal Revenue Service	**Information Return of U.S. Persons With Respect** **To Certain Foreign Corporations** ▶ For more information about Form 5471, see *www.irs.gov/form5471* Information furnished for the foreign corporation's annual accounting period (tax year required by section 898) (see instructions) beginning Jan 1 , 20 **X2**, and ending Dec 31 , 20 **X2**	OMB No. 1545-0704 Attachment Sequence No. **121**

Name of person filing this return **Mark Twain**	**A** Identifying number 123-45-6789
Number, street, and room or suite no. (or P.O. box number if mail is not delivered to street address) **1234 Main Street**	**B** Category of filer (See instructions. Check applicable box(es)): 1 (repealed) 2 ☑ 3 ☑ 4 ☑ 5 ☑
City or town, state, and ZIP code **Hannibal, MO 63401**	**C** Enter the total percentage of the foreign corporation's voting stock you owned at the end of its annual accounting period %

Filer's tax year beginning **January 1** , 20 **X2** , and ending **December 31** , 20 **X2**

D Person(s) on whose behalf this information return is filed:

(1) Name	(2) Address	(3) Identifying number	(4) Check applicable box(es)		
			Shareholder	Officer	Director

Important: *Fill in all applicable lines and schedules. All information **must** be in English. All amounts **must** be stated in U.S. dollars unless otherwise indicated.*

1a Name and address of foreign corporation **BritCo** **Cambridge, England**	b(1) Employer identification number, if any
	b(2) Reference ID number (see instructions)
	c Country under whose laws incorporated **United Kingdom**

d Date of incorporation **January 1, 20X2**	e Principal place of business **United Kingdom**	f Principal business activity code number **423910**	g Principal business activity **Sporting and Recreational Goods & Supplies**	h Functional currency **British Pound**

2 Provide the following information for the foreign corporation's accounting period stated above.

a Name, address, and identifying number of branch office or agent (if any) in the United States	b If a U.S. income tax return was filed, enter:	
	(i) Taxable income or (loss)	(ii) U.S. income tax paid (after all credits)

c Name and address of foreign corporation's statutory or resident agent in country of incorporation **Controller** **Cambridge, United Kingdom**	d Name and address (including corporate department, if applicable) of person (or persons) with custody of the books and records of the foreign corporation, and the location of such books and records, if different **Controller** **Cambridge, United Kingdom**

Schedule A	Stock of the Foreign Corporation

(a) Description of each class of stock	(b) Number of shares issued and outstanding	
	(i) Beginning of annual accounting period	(ii) End of annual accounting period
Common Stock	0	100

For Paperwork Reduction Act Notice, see instructions.   Cat. No. 49958V   Form **5471** (Rev. 12-2012)

¶504

Form 5471 (Rev. 12-2012) Page **2**

Schedule B U.S. Shareholders of Foreign Corporation (see instructions)

(a) Name, address, and identifying number of shareholder	(b) Description of each class of stock held by shareholder. **Note:** This description should match the corresponding description entered in Schedule A, column (a).	(c) Number of shares held at beginning of annual accounting period	(d) Number of shares held at end of annual accounting period	(e) Pro rata share of subpart F income (enter as a percentage)
Mark Twain 1234 Main Street Hannibal, MO 63401	Common Stock	None	51	
				51%

Schedule C Income Statement (see instructions)

Important: *Report all information in functional currency in accordance with U.S. GAAP. Also, report each amount in U.S. dollars translated from functional currency (using GAAP translation rules). However, if the functional currency is the U.S. dollar, complete only the U.S. Dollars column. See instructions for special rules for DASTM corporations.*

				Functional Currency	U.S. Dollars
Income	1a	Gross receipts or sales	1a	25,000,000	37,500,000
	b	Returns and allowances	1b		
	c	Subtract line 1b from line 1a	1c	25,000,000	37,500,000
	2	Cost of goods sold	2	15,000,000	22,500,000
	3	Gross profit (subtract line 2 from line 1c)	3	10,000,000	15,000,000
	4	Dividends	4		
	5	Interest	5		
	6a	Gross rents	6a		
	b	Gross royalties and license fees	6b		
	7	Net gain or (loss) on sale of capital assets	7		
	8	Other income (attach statement)	8		
	9	Total income (add lines 3 through 8)	9	10,000,000	15,000,000
Deductions	10	Compensation not deducted elsewhere	10	2,000,000	3,000,000
	11a	Rents	11a		
	b	Royalties and license fees	11b		
	12	Interest	12		
	13	Depreciation not deducted elsewhere	13		
	14	Depletion	14		
	15	Taxes (exclude provision for income, war profits, and excess profits taxes)	15		
	16	Other deductions (attach statement—exclude provision for income, war profits, and excess profits taxes)	16		
	17	Total deductions (add lines 10 through 16)	17	2,000,000	3,000,000
Net Income	18	Net income or (loss) before extraordinary items, prior period adjustments, and the provision for income, war profits, and excess profits taxes (subtract line 17 from line 9)	18	8,000,000	12,000,000
	19	Extraordinary items and prior period adjustments (see instructions)	19		
	20	Provision for income, war profits, and excess profits taxes (see instructions)	20	1,600,000	2,400,000
	21	Current year net income or (loss) per books (combine lines 18 through 20)	21	6,400,000	9,600,000

Form **5471** (Rev. 12-2012)

Form 5471 (Rev. 12-2012)   Page **3**

Schedule E	Income, War Profits, and Excess Profits Taxes Paid or Accrued (see instructions)			
		Amount of tax		
	(a) Name of country or U.S. possession	**(b)** In foreign currency	**(c)** Conversion rate	**(d)** In U.S. dollars
1	U.S.			
2	United Kingdom	1,600,000	0.66667	2,400,000
3				
4				
5				
6				
7				
8	Total . . . . ▶			2,400,000

Schedule F	Balance Sheet

Important: *Report all amounts in U.S. dollars prepared and translated in accordance with U.S. GAAP. See instructions for an exception for DASTM corporations.*

	Assets		**(a)** Beginning of annual accounting period	**(b)** End of annual accounting period
1	Cash	**1**		24,600,000
2a	Trade notes and accounts receivable	**2a**		
b	Less allowance for bad debts	**2b**	(	)(	)
3	Inventories	**3**		22,500,000
4	Other current assets (attach statement)	**4**		
5	Loans to shareholders and other related persons	**5**		
6	Investment in subsidiaries (attach statement)	**6**		
7	Other investments (attach statement)	**7**		
8a	Buildings and other depreciable assets	**8a**		
b	Less accumulated depreciation	**8b**	(	)(	)
9a	Depletable assets	**9a**		
b	Less accumulated depletion	**9b**	(	)(	)
10	Land (net of any amortization)	**10**		
11	Intangible assets:			
a	Goodwill	**11a**		
b	Organization costs	**11b**		
c	Patents, trademarks, and other intangible assets	**11c**		
d	Less accumulated amortization for lines 11a, b, and c	**11d**	(	)(	)
12	Other assets (attach statement).	**12**		
13	Total assets	**13**		47,100,000
	Liabilities and Shareholders' Equity			
14	Accounts payable	**14**		22,500,000
15	Other current liabilities (attach statement)	**15**		
16	Loans from shareholders and other related persons	**16**		
17	Other liabilities (attach statement)	**17**		
18	Capital stock:			
a	Preferred stock	**18a**		
b	Common stock	**18b**		15,000,000
19	Paid-in or capital surplus (attach reconciliation)	**19**		
20	Retained earnings	**20**		9,600,000
21	Less cost of treasury stock	**21**	(	)(	)
22	Total liabilities and shareholders' equity	**22**		47,100,000

Form **5471** (Rev. 12-2012)

¶504

Form 5471 (Rev. 12-2012)   Page **4**

Schedule G	Other Information

		Yes	No
1	During the tax year, did the foreign corporation own at least a 10% interest, directly or indirectly, in any foreign partnership?	☐	☑
	If "Yes," see the instructions for required statement.		
2	During the tax year, did the foreign corporation own an interest in any trust?	☐	☑
3	During the tax year, did the foreign corporation own any foreign entities that were disregarded as entities separate from their owners under Regulations sections 301.7701-2 and 301.7701-3 (see instructions)?	☐	☑
	If "Yes," you are generally required to attach Form 8858 for each entity (see instructions).		
4	During the tax year, was the foreign corporation a participant in any cost sharing arrangement?	☐	☑
5	During the course of the tax year, did the foreign corporation become a participant in any cost sharing arrangement?	☐	☑
6	During the tax year, did the foreign corporation participate in any reportable transaction as defined in Regulations section 1.6011-4?	☐	☑
	If "Yes," attach Form(s) 8886 if required by Regulations section 1.6011-4(c)(3)(i)(G).		
7	During the tax year, did the foreign corporation pay or accrue any foreign tax that was disqualified for credit under section 901(m)?	☐	☑
8	During the tax year, did the foreign corporation pay or accrue foreign taxes to which section 909 applies, or treat foreign taxes that were previously suspended under section 909 as no longer suspended?	☐	☑

Schedule H	Current Earnings and Profits (see instructions)

Important: *Enter the amounts on lines 1 through 5c in **functional** currency.*

		Net Additions	Net Subtractions		
1	Current year net income or (loss) per foreign books of account			1	8,000,000
2	Net adjustments made to line 1 to determine current earnings and profits according to U.S. financial and tax accounting standards (see instructions):				
a	Capital gains or losses				
b	Depreciation and amortization				
c	Depletion				
d	Investment or incentive allowance				
e	Charges to statutory reserves				
f	Inventory adjustments				
g	Taxes		1,600,000		
h	Other (attach statement)				
3	Total net additions				
4	Total net subtractions		1,600,000		
5a	Current earnings and profits (line 1 plus line 3 minus line 4)			5a	6,400,000
b	DASTM gain or (loss) for foreign corporations that use DASTM (see instructions)			5b	
c	Combine lines 5a and 5b			5c	6,400,000
d	Current earnings and profits in U.S. dollars (line 5c translated at the appropriate exchange rate as defined in section 989(b) and the related regulations (see instructions))			5d	9,600,000
	Enter exchange rate used for line 5d ▶				

Schedule I	Summary of Shareholder's Income From Foreign Corporation (see instructions)

If item D on page 1 is completed, a separate Schedule I must be filed for each Category 4 or 5 filer for whom reporting is furnished on this Form 5471. This schedule I is being completed for:

Name of U.S. shareholder ▶ Mark Twain   Identifying number ▶   123-45-6789

1	Subpart F income (line 38b, Worksheet A in the instructions)	1	1,224,000
2	Earnings invested in U.S. property (line 17, Worksheet B in the instructions)	2	
3	Previously excluded subpart F income withdrawn from qualified investments (line 6b, Worksheet C in the instructions)	3	
4	Previously excluded export trade income withdrawn from investment in export trade assets (line 7b, Worksheet D in the instructions)	4	
5	Factoring income	5	
6	Total of lines 1 through 5. Enter here and on your income tax return. See instructions	6	1,224,000
7	Dividends received (translated at spot rate on payment date under section 989(b)(1))	7	
8	Exchange gain or (loss) on a distribution of previously taxed income	8	

	Yes	No
• Was any income of the foreign corporation blocked?	☐	☑
• Did any such income become unblocked during the tax year (see section 964(b))?	☐	☑

If the answer to either question is "Yes," attach an explanation.

Form **5471** (Rev. 12-2012)

SCHEDULE J
(Form 5471)
(Rev. December 2012)
Department of the Treasury
Internal Revenue Service

Accumulated Earnings and Profits (E&P) of Controlled Foreign Corporation

▶ Information about Schedule J (Form 5471) and its instructions is at *www.irs.gov/form5471.*
▶ Attach to Form 5471.

OMB No. 1545-0704

Name of person filing Form 5471: **Mark Twain**

Identifying number: **123-45-6789**

Name of foreign corporation: **BritCo**

Reference ID number (see instructions)

EIN (if any)

Important: Enter amounts in functional currency.	(a) Post-1986 Undistributed Earnings (post-86 section 959(c)(3) balance)	(b) Pre-1987 E&P Not Previously Taxed (pre-87 section 959(c)(3) balance)	(c) Previously Taxed E&P (see instructions) (sections 959(c)(1) and (2) balances)			(d) Total Section 964(a) E&P (combine columns (a), (b), and (c))
			(i) Earnings Invested in U.S. Property	(ii) Earnings Invested in Excess Passive Assets	(iii) Subpart F Income	
1 Balance at beginning of year	0					
2a Current year E&P	6,400,000					
b Current year deficit in E&P						
3 Total current and accumulated E&P not previously taxed (line 1 plus line 2a **or** line 1 minus line 2b)	6,400,000					
4 Amounts included under section 951(a) or reclassified under section 959(c) in current year	(1,600,000)					
5a Actual distributions or reclassifications of previously taxed E&P						
b Actual distributions of nonpreviously taxed E&P						
6a Balance of previously taxed E&P at end of year (line 1 plus line 4, minus line 5a)						
b Balance of E&P not previously taxed at end of year (line 3 minus line 4, minus line 5b)	4,800,000					
7 Balance at end of year. (Enter amount from line 6a or line 6b, whichever is applicable.)	4,800,000				0	4,800,000

For Paperwork Reduction Act Notice, see the Instructions for Form 5471.   Cat. No. 21111K   Schedule J (Form 5471) (Rev. 12-2012)

SCHEDULE M
(Form 5471)
(Rev. December 2010)
Department of the Treasury
Internal Revenue Service

Transactions Between Controlled Foreign Corporation and Shareholders or Other Related Persons

OMB No. 1545-0704

▶ Attach to Form 5471. See Instructions for Form 5471.

Name of person filing Form 5471	Identifying number
Mark Twain	123-45-6789

Name of foreign corporation

BritCo

Important: Complete a **separate** Schedule M for each controlled foreign corporation. Enter the totals for each type of transaction that occurred during the annual accounting period between the foreign corporation and the persons listed in columns (b) through (f). All amounts must be stated in U.S. dollars translated from functional currency at the average exchange rate for the foreign corporation's tax year. See instructions.

Enter the relevant functional currency and the exchange rate used throughout this schedule ▶   **British pound at £.66667**

(a) Transactions of foreign corporation	(b) U.S. person filing this return	(c) Any domestic corporation or partnership controlled by U.S. person filing this return	(d) Any other foreign corporation or partnership controlled by U.S. person filing this return	(e) 10% or more U.S. shareholder of controlled foreign corporation (other than the U.S. person filing this return)	(f) 10% or more U.S. shareholder of any corporation controlling the foreign corporation
1 Sales of stock in trade (inventory)					
2 Sales of tangible property other than stock in trade					
3 Sales of property rights (patents, trademarks, etc.)					
4 Platform contribution transaction payments received					
5 Cost sharing transaction payments received					
6 Compensation received for technical, managerial, engineering, construction, or like services					
7 Commissions received					
8 Rents, royalties, and license fees received					
9 Dividends received (exclude deemed distributions under subpart F and distributions of previously taxed income)					
10 Interest received					
11 Premiums received for insurance or reinsurance					
12 Add lines 1 through 11					
13 Purchases of stock in trade (inventory)	22,500,000				
14 Purchases of tangible property other than stock in trade					
15 Purchases of property rights (patents, trademarks, etc.)					
16 Platform contribution transaction payments paid					
17 Cost sharing transaction payments paid					
18 Compensation paid for technical, managerial, engineering, construction, or like services					
19 Commissions paid					
20 Rents, royalties, and license fees paid					
21 Dividends paid					
22 Interest paid					
23 Premiums paid for insurance or reinsurance					
24 Add lines 13 through 23	22,500,000				
25 Amounts borrowed (enter the maximum loan balance during the year) — see instructions					
26 Amounts loaned (enter the maximum loan balance during the year) — see instructions					

For Paperwork Reduction Act Notice, see the Instructions for Form 5471.   Cat. No. 49963O   Schedule M (Form 5471) (Rev. 12-2010)

SCHEDULE O (Form 5471) (Rev. December 2012) Department of the Treasury Internal Revenue Service	**Organization or Reorganization of Foreign Corporation, and Acquisitions and Dispositions of its Stock** Information about Schedule O (Form 5471) and its instructions is at *www.irs.gov/form5471* ▶ Attach to Form 5471.	OMB No. 1545-0704

Name of person filing Form 5471		Identifying number
Mark Twain		123-45-6789
Name of foreign corporation	EIN (if any)	Reference ID number (see instructions)
BritCo		

Important: *Complete a **separate** Schedule O for each foreign corporation for which information must be reported.*

Part I   **To Be Completed by U.S. Officers and Directors**

(a) Name of shareholder for whom acquisition information is reported	(b) Address of shareholder	(c) Identifying number of shareholder	(d) Date of original 10% acquisition	(e) Date of additional 10% acquisition
Mark Twain	1234 Main Street Hannibal, MO 63401	123-45-6789	Jan 1, 20X2	

Part II   **To Be Completed by U.S. Shareholders**

Note: *If this return is required because one or more shareholders became U.S. persons, attach a list showing the names of such persons and the date each became a U.S. person.*

Section A—General Shareholder Information

(a) Name, address, and identifying number of shareholder(s) filing this schedule	(b) For shareholder's latest U.S. income tax return filed, indicate:			(c) Date (if any) shareholder last filed information return under section 6046 for the foreign corporation
	(1) Type of return (enter form number)	(2) Date return filed	(3) Internal Revenue Service Center where filed	
Mark Twain 1234 Main Street Hannibal, MO 63401	1040	April 15, 20X3	Kansas City, MO	

Section B—U.S. Persons Who Are Officers or Directors of the Foreign Corporation

(a) Name of U.S. officer or director	(b) Address	(c) Social security number	(d) Check appropriate box(es)	
			Officer	Director
Mark Twain	1234 Main Street Hannibal MO 63401	123-45-6789	✓	✓

Section C—Acquisition of Stock

(a) Name of shareholder(s) filing this schedule	(b) Class of stock acquired	(c) Date of acquisition	(d) Method of acquisition	(e) Number of shares acquired		
				(1) Directly	(2) Indirectly	(3) Constructively
Mark Twain	Common	Jan 1 20X2	Contribution	51		

For Paperwork Reduction Act Notice, see the Instructions for Form 5471.	Cat. No. 61200O	Schedule O (Form 5471) (Rev. 12-2012)

¶504

Schedule O (Form 5471) (Rev. 12-2012)   Page **2**

(f) Amount paid or value given	(g) Name and address of person from whom shares were acquired

Section D—Disposition of Stock

(a) Name of shareholder disposing of stock	(b) Class of stock	(c) Date of disposition	(d) Method of disposition	(e) Number of shares disposed of		
				(1) Directly	(2) Indirectly	(3) Constructively

(f) Amount received	(g) Name and address of person to whom disposition of stock was made

Section E—Organization or Reorganization of Foreign Corporation

(a) Name and address of transferor	(b) Identifying number (if any)	(c) Date of transfer

(d) Assets transferred to foreign corporation			(e) Description of assets transferred by, or notes or securities issued by, foreign corporation
(1) Description of assets	(2) Fair market value	(3) Adjusted basis (if transferor was U.S. person)	

Section F—Additional Information

(a) If the foreign corporation or a predecessor U.S. corporation filed (or joined with a consolidated group in filing) a U.S. income tax return for any of the last 3 years, attach a statement indicating the year for which a return was filed (and, if applicable, the name of the corporation filing the consolidated return), the taxable income or loss, and the U.S. income tax paid (after all credits).

(b) List the date of any reorganization of the foreign corporation that occurred during the last 4 years while any U.S. person held 10% or more in value or vote (directly or indirectly) of the corporation's stock ▶

(c) If the foreign corporation is a member of a group constituting a chain of ownership, attach a chart, for each unit of which a shareholder owns 10% or more in value or voting power of the outstanding stock. The chart must indicate the corporation's position in the chain of ownership and the percentages of stock ownership (see instructions for an example).

Schedule O **(Form 5471)** (Rev. 12-2012)

¶504

Worksheet A—Foreign Base Company Income and Insurance Income and Summary of U.S. Shareholder's Pro Rata Share of Subpart F Income of a CFC (See instructions beginning on page 6.)
Enter the amounts on lines 1a through 38a in functional currency.

1	**Gross foreign personal holding company income:**		
a	Dividends, interest, royalties, rents, and annuities (section 954(c)(1)(A) (excluding amounts described in sections 954(c)(2), (3), and (6)))	1a	
b	Excess of gains over losses from certain property transactions (section 954(c)(1)(B))	1b	
c	Excess of gains over losses from commodity transactions (section 954(c)(1)(C))	1c	
d	Excess of foreign currency gains over foreign currency losses (section 954(c)(1)(D))	1d	
e	Income equivalent to interest (section 954(c)(1)(E))	1e	
f	Net income from a notional principal contract (section 954(c)(1)(F))	1f	
g	Payments in lieu of dividends (section 954(c)(1)(G))	1g	
h	Certain amounts received for services under personal service contracts (see section 954(c)(1)(H))	1h	
i	Certain amounts from sales of partnership interests to which the look-through rule of section 954(c)(4) applies	1i	
2	Gross foreign personal holding company income. Add lines 1a through 1i	**2**	
3	Gross foreign base company sales income (see section 954(d))	**3**	£2,500,000
4	Gross foreign base company services income (see section 954(e))	**4**	
5	Gross foreign base company oil-related income (see section 954(g)) after application of section 954(b)(6)	**5**	
6	Gross foreign base company income. Add lines 2 through 5	**6**	
7	Gross insurance income (see sections 953 and 954(b)(3)(C) and the instructions for lines 20 and 21)	**7**	
8	Gross foreign base company income and gross insurance income. Add lines 6 and 7	**8**	£2,500,000
9	Enter 5% of total gross income (as computed for income tax purposes)	**9**	£500,000
10	Enter 70% of total gross income (as computed for income tax purposes)	**10**	£7,000,000
11	If line 8 is less than line 9 and less than $1 million, enter -0- on this line and skip lines 12 through 21	**11**	
12	If line 8 is more than line 10, enter total gross income (as computed for income tax purposes)	**12**	
13	**Total adjusted gross foreign base company income and insurance income** (enter the greater of line 8 or line 12)	**13**	£2,500,000
14	**Adjusted net foreign personal holding company income:**		
a	Enter amount from line 2	14a	
b	Expenses directly related to amount on line 2	14b	
c	Subtract line 14b from line 14a	14c	
d	Related person interest expense (see section 954(b)(5))	14d	
e	Other expenses allocated and apportioned to the amount on line 2 under section 954(b)(5)	14e	
f	Net foreign personal holding company income. Subtract the sum of lines 14d and 14e from line 14c	14f	
g	Net foreign personal holding company income excluded under high-tax exception	14g	
h	Subtract line 14g from line 14f		14h
15	**Adjusted net foreign base company sales income:**		
a	Enter amount from line 3	15a	£2,500,000
b	Expenses allocated and apportioned to the amount on line 3 under section 954(b)(5)	15b	£900,000
c	Net foreign base company sales income. Subtract line 15b from line 15a	15c	£1,600,000
d	Net foreign base company sales income excluded under high-tax exception	15d	£1,600,000
e	Subtract line 15d from line 15c		15e £1,600,000
16	**Adjusted net foreign base company services income:**		
a	Enter amount from line 4	16a	
b	Expenses allocated and apportioned to line 4 under section 954(b)(5)	16b	
c	Net foreign base company services income. Subtract line 16b from line 16a	16c	
d	Net foreign base company services income excluded under high-tax exception	16d	
e	Subtract line 16d from line 16c		16e

Instructions for Form 5471

Worksheet A (continued) (See instructions.)

17	**Adjusted net foreign base company oil-related income:**		
a	Enter amount from line 5	**17a**	
b	Expenses allocated and apportioned to line 5 under section 954(b)(5)	**17b**	
c	Subtract line 17b from line 17a	**17c**	0
18	**Adjusted net full inclusion foreign base company income:**		
a	Enter the excess, if any, of line 12 over line 8	**18a** 0	
b	Expenses allocated and apportioned under section 954(b)(5) . . .	**18b** 0	
c	Net full inclusion foreign base company income. Subtract line 18b from line 18a	**18c** 0	
d	Net full inclusion foreign base company income excluded under high-tax exception	**18d** 0	
e	Subtract line 18d from line 18c	**18e**	0
19	**Adjusted net foreign base company income.** Add lines 14h, 15e, 16e, 17c, and 18e	**19**	£1,600,000
20	**Adjusted net insurance income** (other than related person insurance income):		
a	Enter amount from line 7 (other than related person insurance income).	**20a**	
b	Expenses allocated and apportioned to the amount from line 7 under section 953	**20b**	
c	Net insurance income. Subtract line 20b from line 20a	**20c**	
d	Net insurance income excluded under high-tax exception	**20d**	
e	Subtract line 20d from line 20c	**20e**	0
21	**Adjusted net related person insurance income:**		
a	Enter amount from line 7 that is related person insurance income .	**21a**	
b	Expenses allocated and apportioned to related person insurance income under section 953.	**21b**	
c	Net related person insurance income. Subtract line 21b from line 21a	**21c**	
d	Net related person insurance income excluded under high-tax exception	**21d**	
e	Subtract line 21d from line 21c	**21e**	0
22	International boycott income (section 952(a)(3))	**22**	
23	Illegal bribes, kickbacks, and other payments (section 952(a)(4))	**23**	
24	Income described in section 952(a)(5) (see instructions)	**24**	
25	Subpart F income before application of sections 952(b) and (c) and section 959(b). Add lines 19, 20e, 21e, and 22 through 24	**25**	£1,600,000
26	Enter portion of line 25 that is U.S. source income effectively connected with a U.S. trade or business (section 952(b))	**26** 0	
27	Exclusions under section 959(b)	**27** 0	
28	Total subpart F income. Subtract the sum of lines 26 and 27 from line 25	**28**	£1,600,000
29	Current E&P	**29**	£6,400,000
30	Enter the smaller of line 28 or line 29	**30**	£1,600,000
31	Shareholder's pro rata share of line 30	**31** £ 816,000	
32	Shareholder's pro rata share of export trade income	**32**	
33	Subtract line 32 from line 31.	**33** £ 816,000	
34	Divide the number of days in the tax year that the corporation was a CFC by the number of days in the tax year and multiply the result by line 33	**34** £ 816,000	
35	Dividends paid to any other person with respect to your stock during the tax year	**35** 0	
36	Divide the number of days in the tax year you did not own such stock by the number of days in the tax year and multiply the result by line 33	**36** 0	
37	Enter the smaller of line 35 or line 36	**37** 0	
38a	**Shareholder's pro rata share of subpart F income.** Subtract line 37 from line 34	**38a**	£ 816,000
b	Translate the amount on line 38a from functional currency to U.S. dollars at the average exchange rate. See section 989(b). Enter the result here and on line 1, Schedule I	**38b**	$1,224,000

Instructions for Form 5471

¶504

On January 1, 20X1, Aunt Harriet pays $500 for one of the 100 outstanding shares in Hong Kong Equities (HKE), a Hong Kong corporation that invests in Asian entities not incorporated in Hong Kong. In the 28% bracket, Aunt Harriet fails to make a qualified electing fund election when filing her U.S. income tax return for 20X1. HKE earns ordinary income of $100,000 in 20X1, $100,000 in 20X2, and $100,000 in 20X3. On December 31, 20X3, HKE distributes a $3,000 dividend to Aunt Harriet. Aunt Harriet must prepare a Form 8621 reporting 2003's excess distribution. Of the $3,000 dividend $1,000 is attributable to 20X1 and $1,000 is attributable to 20X2. Because Aunt Harriet must pay tax at a 40% rate, which is the highest rate in effect for 20X1 and 20X2, she will pay an additional $400 for each of 20X1 and 20X2. Aunt Harriet will also have to pay interest on the deferred tax from 20X1 and 20X2 on the $400 of tax due each year. Assuming an underpayment rate of 6%,[133] that amount will total $49.44.

---

[133] Code Sec. 6621.

Form **8621**	**Information Return by a Shareholder of a Passive Foreign**	OMB No. 1545-1002
(Rev. December 2014) Department of the Treasury Internal Revenue Service	**Investment Company or Qualified Electing Fund** ► Information about Form 8621 and its separate instructions is at *www.irs.gov/form8621*.	Attachment Sequence No. **69**

Name of shareholder	Identifying number (see instructions)
Aunt Harriet	987-65-4321

Number, street, and room or suite no. (If a P.O. box, see instructions.)

Stately Wayne Manor

Shareholder tax year: calendar year 20 **X3** or other tax year
beginning   , 20   and ending   , 20   .

City or town, state, and ZIP code or country

Gotham City

Check type of shareholder filing the return: ☑ Individual ☐ Corporation ☐ Partnership ☐ S Corporation ☐ Nongrantor Trust ☐ Estate

Name of passive foreign investment company (PFIC) or qualified electing fund (QEF)	Employer identification number (if any)
Hong Kong Equities	

Address (Enter number, street, city or town, and country.)

	Reference ID number (see instructions)
Hong Kong	A1

Tax year of PFIC or QEF: calendar year 20 **X3** or other tax year
beginning   , 20   and
ending   , 20   .

Part I   **Summary of Annual Information** (See instructions.)

Provide the following information with respect to all shares of the PFIC held by the shareholder:

1   Description of each class of shares held by the shareholder: **common**
     ☐ Check if shares jointly owned with spouse.

2   Date shares acquired during the taxable year, if applicable: **0**

3   Number of shares held at the end of the taxable year: **1**

4   Value of shares held at the end of the taxable year (check the appropriate box, if applicable):
     (a) ☑ $0-50,000   **(b)** ☐ $50,001-100,000   **(c)** ☐ $100,001-150,000   **(d)** ☐ $150,001-200,000
     (e) If more than $200,000, list value: _____

5   Type of PFIC and amount of any excess distribution or gain treated as an excess distribution
     under section 1291, inclusion under section 1293, or inclusion or deduction under section 1296:

     (a) ☑ Section 1291 $ _____ **2,000**
     (b) ☐ Section 1293 (Qualified Electing Fund) $ _____
     (c) ☐ Section 1296 (Mark to Market) $ _____

Part II   **Elections** (See instructions.)

A ☐ **Election To Treat the PFIC as a QEF.** I, a shareholder of a PFIC, elect to treat the PFIC as a QEF. *Complete lines 6a through 7c of Part III.*

B ☐ **Election To Extend Time For Payment of Tax.** I, a shareholder of a QEF, elect to extend the time for payment of tax on the undistributed earnings and profits of the QEF until this election is terminated. *Complete lines 8a through 9c of Part III to calculate the tax that may be deferred.*

     Note: *If any portion of line 6a or line 7a of Part III is includible under section 951, you may **not** make this election. Also, see sections 1294(c) and 1294(f) and the related regulations for events that terminate this election.*

C ☐ **Election To Mark-to-Market PFIC Stock.** I, a shareholder of a PFIC, elect to mark-to-market the PFIC stock that is marketable within the meaning of section 1296(e). *Complete Part IV.*

D ☐ **Deemed Sale Election.** I, a shareholder on the first day of a PFIC's first tax year as a QEF, elect to recognize gain on the deemed sale of my interest in the PFIC. *Enter gain or loss on line 15f of Part V.*

E ☐ **Deemed Dividend Election.** I, a shareholder on the first day of a PFIC's first tax year as a QEF that is a controlled foreign corporation (CFC), elect to treat an amount equal to my share of the post-1986 earnings and profits of the CFC as an excess distribution. *Enter this amount on line 15e of Part V. If the excess distribution is greater than zero, also complete line 16 of Part V.*

F ☐ **Election To Recognize Gain on Deemed Sale of PFIC.** I, a shareholder of a former PFIC or a PFIC to which section 1297(d) applies, elect to treat as an excess distribution the gain recognized on the deemed sale of my interest in the PFIC on the last day of its last tax year as a PFIC under section 1297(a). *Enter gain on line 15f of Part V.*

G ☐ **Deemed Dividend Election With Respect to a Section 1297(e) PFIC.** I, a shareholder of a section 1297(e) PFIC, within the meaning of Regulations section 1.1297-3(a), elect to make a deemed dividend election with respect to the Section 1297(e) PFIC. My holding period in the stock of the Section 1297(e) PFIC includes the CFC qualification date, as defined in Regulations section 1.1297-3(d). *Enter the excess distribution on line 15e, Part V. If the excess distribution is greater than zero, also complete line 16, Part V.*

H ☐ **Deemed Dividend Election With Respect to a Former PFIC.** I, a shareholder of a former PFIC, within the meaning of Regulations section 1.1298-3(a), elect to make a deemed dividend election with respect to the former PFIC. My holding period in the stock of the former PFIC includes the termination date, as defined in Regulations section 1.1298-3(d). *Enter the excess distribution on line 15e, Part V. If the excess distribution is greater than zero, also complete line 16, Part V.*

For Disclosure, Privacy Act, and Paperwork Reduction Act Notice, see separate instructions.   Cat. No. 64174H   Form **8621** (Rev. 12-2014)

¶504

Form 8621 (Rev. 12-2014)   Page **2**

Part III   **Income From a Qualified Electing Fund (QEF).** All QEF shareholders complete lines 6a through 7c. If you are making Election B, also complete lines 8a through 9c. (See instructions.)

6a	Enter your pro rata share of the ordinary earnings of the QEF	**6a**	
b	Enter the portion of line 6a that is included in income under section 951 or that may be excluded under section 1293(g)	**6b**	
c	Subtract line 6b from line 6a. Enter this amount on your tax return as ordinary income		**6c**
7a	Enter your pro rata share of the total net capital gain of the QEF	**7a**	
b	Enter the portion of line 7a that is included in income under section 951 or that may be excluded under section 1293(g)	**7b**	
c	Subtract line 7b from line 7a. This amount is a net long-term capital gain. Enter this amount in Part II of the Schedule D used for your income tax return. (See instructions.)		**7c**
8a	Add lines 6c and 7c		**8a**
b	Enter the total amount of cash and the fair market value of other property distributed or deemed distributed to you during the tax year of the QEF. (See instructions.)	**8b**	
c	Enter the portion of line 8a not already included in line 8b that is attributable to shares in the QEF that you disposed of, pledged, or otherwise transferred during the tax year	**8c**	
d	Add lines 8b and 8c		**8d**
e	Subtract line 8d from line 8a, and enter the difference (if zero or less, enter amount in brackets)		**8e**

Important: *If line 8e is greater than zero, and no portion of line 6a or 7a is includible in income under section 951, you may make Election B with respect to the amount on line 8e.*

9a	Enter the total tax for the tax year (See instructions.)	**9a**	
b	Enter the total tax for the tax year determined without regard to the amount entered on line 8e	**9b**	
c	Subtract line 9b from line 9a. **This is the deferred tax, the time for payment of which is extended by making Election B. See instructions**		**9c**

Part IV   **Gain or (Loss) From Mark-to-Market Election** (See instructions.)

10a	Enter the fair market value of your PFIC stock at the end of the tax year		**10a**
b	Enter your adjusted basis in the stock at the end of the tax year		**10b**
c	Subtract line 10b from line 10a. If a gain, do not complete lines 11 and 12. Include this amount as ordinary income on your tax return. If a loss, go to line 11		**10c**
11	Enter any unreversed inclusions (as defined in section 1296(d))		**11**
12	Enter the loss from line 10c, but only to the extent of unreversed inclusions on line 11. Include this amount as an ordinary loss on your tax return		**12**
13	**If you sold or otherwise disposed of any section 1296 stock (see instructions) during the tax year:**		
a	Enter the fair market value of the stock on the date of sale or disposition		**13a**
b	Enter the adjusted basis of the stock on the date of sale or disposition		**13b**
c	Subtract line 13b from line 13a. If a gain, do not complete line 14. Include this amount as ordinary income on your tax return. If a loss, go to line 14		**13c**
14a	Enter any unreversed inclusions (as defined in section 1296(d))		**14a**
b	Enter the loss from line 13c, but only to the extent of unreversed inclusions on line 14a. Include this amount as an ordinary loss on your tax return. If the loss on line 13c exceeds unreversed inclusions on line 14a, complete line 14c		**14b**
c	Enter the amount by which the loss on line 13c exceeds unreversed inclusions on line 14a. Include this amount on your tax return according to the rules generally applicable for losses provided elsewhere in the Code and regulations		**14c**

Note. See instructions in case of multiple sales or dispositions.

Form **8621** (Rev. 12-2014)

Part V	**Distributions From and Dispositions of Stock of a Section 1291 Fund** (See instructions.) *Complete a **separate** Part V for each excess distribution and disposition (see instructions).*		
15a	Enter your total distributions from the section 1291 fund during the current tax year with respect to the applicable stock. If the holding period of the stock began in the current tax year, see instructions	15a	3,000
b	Enter the total distributions (reduced by the portions of such distributions that were excess distributions but not included in income under section 1291(a)(1)(B)) made by the fund with respect to the applicable stock for each of the 3 years preceding the current tax year (or if shorter, the portion of the shareholder's holding period before the current tax year)	15b	0
c	Divide line 15b by 3. (See instructions if the number of preceding tax years is less than 3.)	15c	0
d	Multiply line 15c by 125% (1.25)	15d	0
e	Subtract line 15d from line 15a. This amount, if more than zero, is the excess distribution with respect to the applicable stock. If there is an excess distribution, complete line 16. If zero or less and you did not dispose of stock during the tax year, **do not** complete the rest of Part V. See instructions if you received more than one distribution during the current tax year. Also, see instructions for rules for reporting a nonexcess distribution on your income tax return	15e	3,000
f	Enter gain or loss from the disposition of stock of a section 1291 fund or former section 1291 fund. If a gain, complete line 16. If a loss, show it in brackets and **do not** complete line 16	15f	0
16a	If there is a positive amount on line 15e or 15f (or both), attach a statement for each excess distribution and disposition. Show your holding period for each share of stock or block of shares held. Allocate the excess distribution or gain to each day in your holding period. Add all amounts that are allocated to days in each tax year.		
b	Enter the total of the amounts determined in line 16a that are allocable to the current tax year and tax years before the foreign corporation became a PFIC (pre-PFIC years). Enter these amounts on your income tax return as other income	16b	1,000
c	Enter the aggregate increases in tax (before credits) for each tax year in your holding period (other than the current tax year and pre-PFIC years). (See instructions.)	16c	800
d	Foreign tax credit. (See instructions.)	16d	0
e	Subtract line 16d from line 16c. Enter this amount on your income tax return as "additional tax." (See instructions.) .	16e	800
f	Determine interest on each net increase in tax determined on line 16e using the rates and methods of section 6621. Enter the aggregate amount of interest here. (See instructions.)	16f	49.44

Part VI	**Status of Prior Year Section 1294 Elections and Termination of Section 1294 Elections** *Complete a separate column for each outstanding election. Complete lines 25 and 26 only if there is a partial termination of the section 1294 election.*						
		(i)	**(ii)**	**(iii)**	**(iv)**	**(v)**	**(vi)**
17	Tax year of outstanding election						
18	Undistributed earnings to which the election relates .						
19	Deferred tax						
20	Interest accrued on deferred tax (line 19) as of the filing date						
21	Event terminating election .						
22	Earnings distributed or deemed distributed during the tax year						
23	Deferred tax due with this return						
24	Accrued interest due with this return						
25	Deferred tax outstanding after partial termination of election .						
26	Interest accrued after partial termination of election . .						

Statement for Part IV, Line 11a

	Dates of Holding	Allocation of Distribution
20X1	January 1 to December 31	$1,000
20X2	January 1 to December 31	$1,000

Chapter 6

Foreign Currency Translation and Transactions

¶ 601   Introduction
¶ 602   Foreign Currency Translation
¶ 603   Foreign Currency Transactions

¶ 601   INTRODUCTION

The foreign branches and subsidiaries of U.S. companies generally conduct business and maintain their books and records in the currency of the host country. This creates a currency translation issue for the domestic parent corporation, which must compute its taxable income and foreign tax credit in U.S. dollars. Tax attributes that require translation include the taxable income or loss of a foreign branch, foreign income taxes paid on branch income, remittances from a foreign branch, dividends and Subpart F inclusions from a foreign corporation, and the foreign income taxes deemed paid by a domestic shareholder of a foreign corporation. In addition to translation issues, transactional issues arise when a domestic corporation engages in transactions with customers, suppliers, lenders and borrowers that are denominated in a foreign currency, and the exchange rate fluctuates between the time the transaction is entered into and the time the transaction closes. Translation issues are discussed in the section entitled "Foreign Currency Translation," and transactional issues are discussed in the section entitled "Foreign Currency Transactions."

¶ 602   FOREIGN CURRENCY TRANSLATION

The currency translation rules are based on the concepts of a *qualified business unit* and *functional currency*.

.01   *Qualified Business Unit*

A taxpayer and each qualified business unit (QBU) generally must make all of its tax determinations in its functional currency.[1] A QBU is any separate and clearly identified unit of a trade or business of a taxpayer that maintains separate books and records.[2] A corporation is automatically a QBU.[3] In addition, a branch of a corporation qualifies as a QBU if the branch is a separate and clearly identified unit

---

[1] Code Sec. 985(a) and Reg. § 1.985-1.

[2] Code Sec. 989(a).

[3] Reg. § 1.989(a)-1(b)(2)(i).

of a trade or business of the corporation for which separate books and records are maintained.[4]

Whether a branch operation constitutes a separate trade or business of the corporation is a question of fact. For this purpose, a trade or business is a specific unified group of activities that constitutes an independent economic activity carried on for profit. This group of activities ordinarily includes every operation which is part of the process by which an enterprise earns a profit, including the collection of income and the payment of expenses. It is not necessary that the trade or business carried out by the branch be of a different type than that carried out by other QBUs of the taxpayer. For example, a sales branch that is located in a different geographic market than the home office sales operation can constitute a separate trade or business. However, activities that are merely ancillary to a trade or business of the corporation do not constitute a separate trade or business.[5]

Example 6.1: [6] USAco, a domestic corporation, manufactures goods for sale both in the United States and abroad. USAco sells goods in the United Kingdom through a branch office located in London. The London office has its own employees who solicit and process orders. USAco maintains separate books and records for all of the transactions entered into by the London office. USAco qualifies as a QBU because of its corporate status. The branch sales office in London also qualifies as a separate QBU because its sales operation constitutes a separate trade or business for which USAco maintains separate books and records.

---

[4] Code Sec. 989(a) and Reg. §1.989(a)-1(b)(2)(ii). A separate set of books and records generally includes books of original entry and ledger accounts, both general and subsidiary. Reg. §1.989(a)-1(d).

[5] Reg. §1.989(a)-1(c). An activity of a foreign person which produces income effectively connected with the conduct of a U.S. trade or business is always treated as a separate QBU. Reg. §1.989(a)-1(b)(3).

[6] Compare Reg. §1.989(a)-1(e), Example 1.

***Example* 6.2:** [7] USAco, a domestic corporation, incorporates a wholly-owned subsidiary in Switzerland to market its products in Europe. In addition to its sales operation located in Switzerland, the Swiss subsidiary has branch sales offices in France and Germany that are responsible for all marketing operations in those countries. Each branch has its own employees, solicits and processes orders, and maintains a separate set of books and records. USAco and the Swiss subsidiary are both QBUs because of their corporate status. The French and German branches also are QBUs of the Swiss subsidiary because each sales operation constitutes a separate trade or business for which separate books and records are maintained.

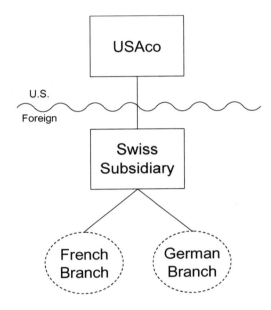

Unlike a corporation, an individual is not a QBU.[8] Moreover, activities of an individual conducted as an employee do not constitute a QBU.[9] However, activities of an individual conducted as a sole proprietor do constitute a QBU if they satisfy the separate trade or business and separate books and records requirements discussed above.[10] As with a corporation, a partnership, trust, or estate is automatically considered to be a QBU of the partner or beneficiary, regardless of the scope of the entity's activities or whether the entity keeps separate books and records.[11] In addition, each different activity of a partnership, trust, or estate also can qualify as a separate QBU if it satisfies the separate trade or business and separate books and records requirements.[12]

---

[7] Compare Reg. § 1.989(a)-1(e), Example 2.

[8] Reg. § 1.989(a)-1(b)(2)(i).

[9] Reg. § 1.989(a)-1(c).

[10] Reg. § 1.989(a)-1(b)(2)(ii).

[11] Reg. § 1.989(a)-1(b)(2)(i).

[12] Reg. § 1.989(a)-1(b)(2)(ii).

.02 Functional Currency

Each QBU makes all of its determinations, such as computing its taxable income or its earnings and profits, in its functional currency.[13] A QBU's functional currency is the U.S. dollar, unless the QBU conducts a significant part of its activities in an economic environment in which a foreign currency is used and the QBU maintains its books and records in that foreign currency.[14] For this purpose, a QBU is presumed to keep its books and records in the currency of the economic environment in which a significant part of its activities are conducted.[15] The taxpayer must consider all of the facts and circumstances in identifying the relevant economic environment, including the currency of the country in which the QBU is a resident, as well as the currencies in which the QBU realizes its cash flows, generates its revenues, incurs its expenses, borrows and lends, sells its products, and makes its pricing and other financial decisions.[16] If a QBU has more than one currency that satisfies these requirements, then the QBU may choose any of those currencies as its functional currency.[17]

The adoption of a functional currency is treated as a method of accounting. As a consequence, the functional currency used in the year of adoption must be used for all subsequent tax years unless permission to change is granted by the IRS.[18] Permission to change functional currencies generally is not granted unless significant changes in the facts and circumstances of the QBU's economic environment occur. The QBU's functional currency for U.S. financial reporting purposes is a relevant factor in this regard.[19]

.03 Foreign Branches

Code Sec. 987 governs translation issues related to foreign branches. In 2006, the Treasury Department issued proposed regulations which provide some guidance as to the IRS's position.

If a foreign branch is a QBU that has a functional currency other than the U.S. dollar, the taxable income or loss of the branch is computed in its functional currency, and is then translated into U.S. dollars using the average exchange rate for the year, unless the spot rate is required (e.g., the basis in an asset is based on the spot rate).[20] The average exchange rate for the year means the simple average of the daily exchange rates, excluding weekends, holidays, and any other nonbusiness days for the tax year.[21]

---

[13] Code Sec. 985(a).

[14] Code Sec. 985(b)(1) and Reg. § 1.985-1(c)(1). Activities of a foreign person which produce income effectively connected with the conduct of a U.S. trade or business are always treated as a separate QBU, with the U.S. dollar as its functional currency. Reg. § 1.985-1(b)(1)(v). Special rules also apply to a foreign corporation with two or more QBUs that do not have the same functional currency. Reg. § 1.985-1(d).

[15] Reg. § 1.985-1(c)(3).

[16] Reg. § 1.985-1(c)(2)(i). Other relevant factors include the duration of the QBU's business operations and the significance or volume of the QBU's independent activities.

[17] Reg. § 1.985-1(c)(4).

[18] Reg. § 1.985-4(a).

[19] Reg. § 1.985-4(b). If a QBU is granted permission to change its functional currency, adjustments may be required. Reg. § 1.985-5.

[20] Code Sec. 987 and Prop. Reg. §§ 1.987-3(b) and 1.987-1(c).

[21] Reg. § 1.989(b)-1.

¶602.02

Example 6.3: [22] USAco is a domestic corporation with the U.S. dollar ($) as its functional currency. On November 1, 20Y1, USAco establishes a sales branch in France, which qualifies as a QBU with the euro (€) as its functional currency. The spot rate is used to determine the cost basis in the branch's inventory, and the average exchange rate is used to translate the gross receipts from the branch's inventory sales.[23]

Assume that the branch purchased 300 units of inventory on November 1 for € 1.50 per unit, when the spot rate is € 1 = $1.08. Thus, the branch's basis in these units is $486 [(300 units × € 1.50) × $1.08]. Assume the branch sold all 300 units by the end of the year at a price of € 3 per unit, and the average exchange rate for 20Y1 is € 1 = $1.05. USAco's gross receipts from the inventory sales are $945 [(300 units× € 3) × $1.05], its costs of goods sold is $486 [basis], and its gross income is $459 [$945 – $486].

The U.S. parent recognizes a foreign currency gain or loss ("section 987 gain or loss") if the branch remits foreign currency or other property to the U.S. parent, and the U.S. dollar value of the distribution differs from the U.S. parent's basis in the branch's accumulated earnings, as determined by prior year income inclusions.[24] The rationale behind these rules is that foreign currency is property, and that the taxpayer should recognize gain or loss on its repatriation when the value of the remittance differs from its basis. The section 987 gain or loss equals the branch's "net unrecognized section 987 gain or loss"[25] multiplied by the ratio of the remittance to the adjusted basis of branch's total assets, including the remittance.[26]

Example 6.4: [27] USAco is a domestic corporation with the U.S. dollar as its functional currency. USAco has a sales branch in the United Kingdom, which is a QBU with the British pound as its functional currency. In prior years, USAco recognized $420,000 of branch income, none of which has been

---

[22] Compare Prop. Reg. § 1.987-3(f), Example 1.

[23] Prop. Reg. § 1.987-3(b)(2)(ii)(B). The proposed regulations refer to the spot rate as the "historic exchange rate."

[24] Code Sec. 987(3) and Prop. Reg. § 1.987-5. The incorporation or other termination of a branch also triggers

recognition of a foreign currency gain or loss. Prop. Reg. § 1.987-8(d).

[25] Prop. Reg. § 1.987-4.

[26] Prop. Reg. § 1.987-5.

[27] Compare Prop. Reg. § 1.987-5(g), Example 1.

repatriated. Based on the current exchange rate, the branch's accumulated earnings now have a value of $500,000, resulting in a net unrecognized section 987 gain of $80,000.[28] During the current year, the branch remits $500,000 worth of British pounds to USAco. At the time of the remittance, USAco's basis in the assets of the branch, including the remittance, was $5 million.

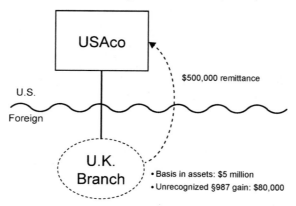

As a result of the remittance, USAco must recognize a section 987 gain of $8,000 [$80,000 net unrecognized section 987 gain × ($500,000 remittance ÷ $5 million total assets, including remittance)].

A section 987 gain or loss is treated as ordinary income that is sourced by reference to the source of income giving rise to the branch's accumulated earnings.[29]

.04 Foreign Corporations

Dividend distributions. The translation rules for computing the U.S. tax consequences of receiving a dividend distribution from a foreign corporation are as follows:

(i) *Dividend*—If a foreign corporation pays a dividend in a foreign currency, the U.S. shareholder translates the dividend income into U.S. dollars using the spot rate for the date on which the dividend was included in the taxpayer's income.[30]

(ii) *Foreign withholding taxes*—Accrual-basis taxpayers generally translate foreign withholding taxes imposed on a dividend into U.S. dollars using the average exchange rate for the tax year to which the taxes relate (the translation rules for foreign income taxes are discussed in detail below).[31]

(iii) *Deemed paid foreign tax credit*—For purposes of computing the deemed paid foreign tax credit, accrual-basis taxpayers generally translate a foreign corporation's post-1986 foreign income taxes into U.S. dollars using the average exchange rate for the tax year to which the taxes

---

[28] Prop. Reg. § 1.987-4(d)(2)(ii)(A).

[29] Code Sec. 987(3)(A) and (B); *see also* Prop. Reg. § 1.987-6.

[30] Code Secs. 986(b)(2) and 989(b)(1).

[31] Code Sec. 986(a).

relate (see Foreign Income Taxes, below).[32] On the other hand, the foreign corporation's dividend distribution and post-1986 undistributed earnings are not translated into U.S. dollars, but are instead maintained in the foreign corporation's functional currency.[33]

Example 6.5: USAco, a domestic corporation, owns 100% of the stock of EURco. EURco is a calendar year, Dutch corporation with the euro (€) as its functional currency. During its first year of operations, EURco derives € 10 million of taxable income, pays € 2 million in foreign income taxes, and distributes a € 4 million dividend to USAco on December 31. The spot rate on December 31 was € 1 = $1.15, and the average exchange rate was € 1 = $1.14. Therefore, the € 4 million dividend translates into $4,600,000 [€ 4 million × $1.15], and EURco's foreign income taxes are $2,280,000 [€ 2 million × $1.14]. EURco's earnings and profits are € 8 million [€ 10 million of taxable income − € 2 million of foreign income taxes]. As a result, EURco's dividend pulls out deemed paid taxes of $1,140,000 [$2,280,000 of foreign income taxes × (€ 4 million dividend ÷ € 8 million of earnings and profits)], and USAco must recognize dividend income of $5,740,000 [$4,600,000 dividend + $1,140,000 gross-up].

Subpart F inclusions. The translation rules for computing the U.S. tax consequences of a U.S. shareholder's Subpart F inclusion from a controlled foreign corporation (or CFC) are as follows:

(i) *Subpart F inclusion*—The appropriate exchange rate for computing an income inclusion under Subpart F varies with the type of inclusion. An inclusion of Subpart F income is translated into U.S. dollars using the average exchange rate for the CFC's tax year. Inclusions for investments in U.S. property are computed using the spot rate for the last day of the CFC's tax year.[34]

(ii) *Deemed paid foreign tax credit*—For purposes of computing the deemed paid credit, the CFC's Subpart F inclusion and post-1986 undistributed

---

[32] Code Sec. 986(a).

[33] Code Sec. 986(b)(1).

[34] Code Secs. 986(b)(2) and 989(b).

earnings and profits are not translated into U.S. dollars, but are instead maintained in the CFC's functional currency.[35] On other hand, accrual-basis taxpayers generally translate a CFC's post-1986 foreign income taxes into U.S. dollars using the average exchange rate for the tax year to which the taxes relate (see Foreign Income Taxes, below).[36]

(iii) *Distributions of previously taxed income*—For purposes of tracing actual dividend distributions to previously taxed income, the taxpayer measures the CFC's earnings in its functional currency.[37] Later, when receiving a distribution of previously taxed income, the U.S. shareholder must recognize a foreign currency gain or loss equal to the difference between:

(a) The U.S. dollar value of the distribution as determined using the spot rate for the date of the distribution and

(b) The U.S. shareholder's basis in the distribution as determined by the U.S. dollar amount at which the taxpayer previously included the earnings in U.S. taxable income.[38]

Foreign currency gains and losses are treated as ordinary income that has the same source as the associated income inclusion.[39]

Example 6.6: USAco, a domestic corporation, owns 100% of the stock of FORco, which was organized in year 1. FORco is a calendar year, foreign corporation with the euro (€) as its functional currency. FORco's tax attributes for its first two years of operations are as follows:

	Year 1	Year 2
Taxable income......................	€ 50 million	None
Foreign income taxes	€ 10 million	None
Current year E&P	€ 40 million	None
Subpart F income (net of foreign income taxes)	€ 20 million	None
Investments in U.S. property............	€ 5 million	None
Dividend distribution on December 31	None	€ 4 million

---

[35] Code Sec. 986(b)(1).
[36] Code Sec. 986(a).
[37] Code Sec. 986(b)(1).

[38] Code Sec. 986(c)(1) and Notice 1988-71.
[39] Code Sec. 986(c)(1).

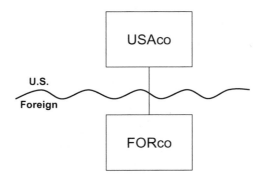

The average exchange rate for year 1 was € 1 = $1.10, and the spot rate was € 1 = $1.20 on December 31 of year 1 and € 1 = $1.40 on December 31 of year 2. USAco's Subpart F income inclusion for year 1 is $28 million [(€ 20 million of Subpart F income × $1.10) + (€ 5 million investment in U.S. property × $1.20)]. With respect to the deemed paid credit, FORco has foreign income taxes of $11 million [€ 10 million × $1.10] and undistributed earnings and profits of € 40 million [€ 50 million of taxable income – € 10 million of foreign income taxes]. Therefore, USAco's deemed paid taxes are $6,875,000 [$11 million of foreign income taxes × (€ 25 million total Subpart F inclusion ÷ € 40 million of undistributed earnings)].

USAco can exclude from income the € 4 million dividend received in year 2 because it is traced to FORco's previously taxed income from year 1. For this purpose, USAco measures FORco's earnings in euros and traces the distribution to FORco's € 5 million investment of earnings in U.S. property from year 1.[40] However, the dividend does trigger the recognition of a foreign currency gain produced as a result of the euro strengthening against the dollar. The gain equals $800,000, which represents the excess of the distribution's value of $5.6 million [€ 4 million dividend × $1.40] over USAco's basis in the previously taxed earnings of $4.8 million [€ 4 million × $1.20].

Passive foreign investment company inclusions. A U.S. person translates his or her pro rata share of the undistributed earnings and profits of a qualified electing fund (or QEF) into U.S. dollars using the average exchange rate for the QEF's tax year (the same average exchange rate as for Subpart F income).[41] For purposes of tracing subsequent actual dividend distributions to the QEF's previously taxed income, the taxpayer measures the QEF's earnings in its functional currency.[42] In addition, a U.S. person who receives a distribution of a QEF's previously taxed income must recognize a foreign currency gain or loss equal to the difference between:

---

[40] Code Sec. 959(c).
[41] Code Secs. 986(b)(2) and 989(b)(3).

[42] Code Sec. 986(b)(1).

    (i) The U.S. dollar value of the actual distribution as determined using the spot rate for the date of the distribution and

    (ii) The taxpayer's basis in the distribution as determined by the U.S. dollar amount at which the taxpayer previously included the earnings in U.S. taxable income.[43]

Foreign currency gains and losses are treated as ordinary income that has the same source as the associated income inclusion.[44]

.05 Foreign Income Taxes

Accrual-basis taxpayers generally translate foreign income taxes into U.S. dollars using the average exchange rate for the tax year to which the taxes relate. However, such taxpayers must use the spot rate (i.e., the exchange rate on the date of payment) to translate (i) foreign taxes actually paid more than two years from the close of such tax year, (ii) foreign taxes paid in a tax year prior to the year to which they relate, and (iii) foreign taxes paid in a hyperinflationary currency. In addition, any adjustment to the amount of the taxes is translated using the spot rate when the adjusted taxes are paid to the foreign country. In the case of any refund of foreign taxes, taxpayers must use the spot rate when the original payment of the foreign taxes was made.[45]

In lieu of using the average exchange rate for the year, an accrual-basis taxpayer may elect to translate foreign income taxes into U.S. dollars using the spot rate, but this election can be made only for foreign income taxes that are denominated in a currency other than the taxpayer's functional currency.[46] This election may ease the administrative burden for taxpayers that earn income subject to withholding taxes. Once made, the taxpayer may revoke the election only with the consent of the IRS.

Cash-basis taxpayers translate foreign income taxes into U.S. dollars using the spot rate.[47]

.06 Special Rules for Hyperinflationary Currencies

Special rules apply to any QBU that would otherwise be required to use a hyperinflationary currency as its functional currency. A hyperinflationary currency is the currency of a foreign country in which there is a cumulative compounded rate of inflation of at least 100% during the 36-month period immediately preceding the first day of the current calendar year.[48] The rates of inflation are generally determined by reference to the consumer price index of the country as listed in the monthly issues of "International Financial Statistics" or a successor publication of the International Monetary Fund.[49]

Hyperinflationary currency creates significant problems with the conventional methods for translating the results of a foreign operation into U.S. dollars. For

---

[43] Code Sec. 986(c)(1).

[44] Code Sec. 986(c)(1).

[45] Code Sec. 986(a). However, the IRS has the authority to issue regulations that would allow these foreign tax payments to be translated into U.S. dollar amounts using an average exchange rate for a specified period.

[46] Code Sec. 986(a)(1)(D). This election may apply to foreign income taxes attributable to a QBU in accordance with any regulations the IRS promulgates.

[47] Code Sec. 986(a)(2)(A).

[48] Reg. § 1.985-1(b)(2)(ii)(D).

[49] *Id.* If a country's currency is not listed in such publication, a QBU may use any other reasonable method consistently applied for determining the country's consumer price index.

example, in a hyperinflationary environment, the conventional methods result in a mismatch of costs and revenues, because the deflated costs of prior-year investments in inventory and equipment are offset against the inflated revenues from current year sales.

A QBU that would otherwise be required to use a hyperinflationary currency must use the U.S. dollar as its functional currency and must compute its taxable income (and earnings and profits) using the dollar approximate separate transactions method (or "DASTM").[50] The DASTM attempts to mitigate the distortions caused by a hyperinflationary currency by translating the QBU's taxable income (and earnings and profits) on at least a monthly basis,[51] and by annually recognizing certain unrealized foreign currency gains and losses.[52] The DASTM is generally applied by preparing an income statement for the QBU in its hyperinflationary currency with certain adjustments (e.g., conforming to U.S. generally accepted accounting principles and U.S. tax accounting principles), converting the adjusted amounts into U.S. dollars, and making an adjustment for the DASTM gain or loss.

A QBU that has been required to use the U.S. dollar as its functional currency and the DASTM because its otherwise functional currency was hyperinflationary must use that functional currency once it ceases to be hyperinflationary.[53]

> ***Example 6.7:*** [54] Forco is a corporation incorporated under the laws of Foronia, a country whose local currency, the Foro, has experienced annual inflation rates for the past three years of 29%, 25% and 30%. The cumulative inflation rate for this three-year period is 109.625% [$(1.29 \times 1.25 \times 1.30) - 1.0 = 109.625$]. As such, Forco must use the U.S. dollar as its functional currency (and not the Foro) and the DASTM until the Foro ceases to be a hyperinflationary currency.

¶ 603 FOREIGN CURRENCY TRANSACTIONS

.01 Applicable Transactions

Code Sec. 988 provides rules governing the determination of the amount, timing, character, and source of foreign currency gains and losses associated with Code Sec. 988 transactions. Code Sec. 988 transactions include the following:

(i) Dispositions of a nonfunctional currency, and

(ii) The following three categories of transactions where the amount the taxpayer is entitled to receive or required to pay is denominated in a nonfunctional currency:[55]

---

[50] Reg. §§ 1.985-1(b)(2)(ii)(A) and 1.985-3. There are exceptions for foreign corporations other than CFCs and certain QBU branches of foreign corporations. Reg. § 1.985-1(b)(2)(ii)(B).

[51] Reg. § 1.985-3(b)(3) and (c)(7). The conventional approach is to translate taxable income on an annual basis.

[52] Reg. § 1.985-3(b)(4) and (d)(1).

[53] Reg. § 1.985-1(b)(2)(ii)(E). Note that this change can result in the need for certain adjustments. *See* Reg. § 1.985-5.

[54] *Compare* Reg. § 1.985-1(b)(2)(ii)(D).

[55] In addition to being denominated in a nonfunctional currency, the amount may also be determined by reference to a nonfunctional currency.

    (a) *Debt instruments*—This includes transactions where the taxpayer lends or borrows funds through the use of a bond, debenture, note, certificate, or other evidence of indebtedness.

    (b) *Receivables and payables*—This includes transactions where the taxpayer accrues an item of income or expense that will be received or paid at a future date, including a payable or receivable relating to a capital expenditure.

    (c) *Forward, futures, and option contracts*—This includes transactions where the taxpayer enters into a forward contract, futures contract, currency option, or similar financial instrument.[56]

Code Sec. 988 transactions do not include any transaction entered into by an individual unless the transaction is related to a business or investment activity[57] and certain transactions between or among a taxpayer and/or QBUs of that taxpayer.[58]

The entire amount of gain or loss arising from a disposition of functional currency or from entering into a currency forward, futures, or option contract is treated as an foreign currency gain or loss.[59]

In contrast, a gain or loss arising from a foreign currency transaction involving a debt instrument, receivable, or payable is treated as a foreign currency gain or loss only to the extent it is attributable to a change in exchange rates that occurs between the transaction's booking date and the payment date.[60] In other words, foreign currency gains and losses arising from a foreign currency transaction involving debt instruments, receivables, or payables generally are accounted for separately from the gain or loss on the underlying transaction. For this purpose, the payment date is the date on which payment is made or received,[61] whereas the booking date is the date on which funds are borrowed or lent in the case of a debt instrument[62] or the date on which the item is accrued in the case of a receivable or payable.[63]

A special rule applies to simplify the accounting for trade receivables and trade payables. If an average exchange rate is consistent with the taxpayer's financial accounting, the taxpayer can elect to use that average exchange rate, based on intervals of one quarter year or less, to both accrue and record the receipt and payment of amounts in satisfaction of trade receivables and payables that are denominated in a nonfunctional currency. For example, a taxpayer may use the average exchange rate for the first quarter to accrue all payables and receivables incurred during the first quarter. The same average rate also would be used to

---

[56] Code Sec. 988(c)(1)(A), (B), and (C), and Reg. § 1.988-1(a)(1) and (a)(2). A forward contract is an agreement to buy or sell a given amount of foreign currency on a future date at a specified exchange rate. A futures contract is an agreement to buy or sell foreign currency that is traded on a futures exchange. A currency option gives the holder the right to buy or sell a given amount of currency at a specified exchange rate prior to the contract's expiration date.

[57] Code Sec. 988(e) and Reg. § 1.988-1(a)(9).

[58] Reg. § 1.988-1(a)(10). Code Sec. 988 transactions also do not include either regulated futures contracts or non-equity options, which would be marked to market under Code Sec. 1256 if held on the last day of the tax year.

[59] Code Secs. 988(b)(3) and (c)(1)(C)(i)(II).

[60] Code Sec. 988(b)(1) and (2).

[61] Code Sec. 988(c)(3).

[62] Code Sec. 988(c)(2)(A).

[63] Code Sec. 988(c)(2)(B).

record all payments made and amounts received in satisfaction of payables and receivables during the first quarter.[64]

.02 Tax Consequences

Amount and timing of foreign currency gains and losses. The taxation of foreign currency gains and losses is based on the premise that, for U.S. tax purposes, only U.S. dollars are money. As a consequence, currencies other than the U.S. dollar are treated as "property" that has a tax basis independent of its specific denomination. One implication of this approach is that foreign currency gains and losses arising from a Code Sec. 988 transaction involving debt instruments, receivables, or payables generally are accounted for separately from the gain or loss on the underlying transaction.[65] For example, if a domestic corporation with the U.S. dollar as its functional currency makes a sale on account that is denominated in a foreign currency, the gross profit from the sale is recognized separately from any foreign currency gain or loss arising from an account receivable that is denominated in the foreign currency.

> **Example 6.8:** USAco is an accrual-basis, domestic corporation with the U.S. dollar as its functional currency. On January 1, USAco makes an export sale denominated in Norwegian krone (kr). The sales price is kr2,000. The foreign customer remits the kr2,000 on April 1 and USAco converts the kr2,000 into U.S. dollars on April 10. The spot rates for converting kroner to U.S. dollars is $1.50 on January 1, $1.45 on April 1, and $1.43 on April 10. Therefore, on January 1, USAco recognizes sales revenues of $3,000 [kr2,000 × $1.50]. In addition, because the krone weakened against the dollar between the booking date of January 1 and the payment date of April 1, USAco recognizes a foreign currency loss on the collection of the receivable. The loss is $100, which represents the difference between the value of the kroner received in payment of $2,900 [kr2,000 × $1.45] and USAco's basis in the related account receivable of $3,000 [kr2,000 × $1.50].[66] USAco also must recognize a foreign currency loss upon converting the kroner into dollars. The loss is $40, which represents the difference between the amount realized from the sale of the kroner of $2,860 [kr2,000 × $1.43] and USAco's basis in the kroner of $2,900 [kr2,000 × $1.45].[67]

Character and source of foreign currency gains and losses. Foreign currency gains and losses attributable to a Code Sec. 988 transaction are treated as ordinary income or loss,[68] and are sourced by reference to the residence of the taxpayer or the QBU of the taxpayer on whose books the underlying asset, liability, or item of income or expense is properly reflected.[69] For purposes of this source

---

[64] Reg. § 1.988-1(d)(3). A taxpayer cannot change the use of a convention without the consent of the Commissioner once it has been adopted.

[65] Code Sec. 988(a)(1)(A) and Reg. § 1.988-1(e). However, the foreign currency gain or loss realized on transactions involving debt instruments is limited to the total gain or loss realized on the transaction. Reg. § 1.988-2(b)(8).

[66] Reg. § 1.988-2(c)(2).

[67] Reg. § 1.988-2(a)(2)(i).

[68] Code Sec. 988(a)(1)(A). However, a taxpayer can elect to characterize foreign currency gains or losses on certain identified currency forward, futures, or option contracts as capital gains or losses. Code Sec. 988(a)(1)(B) and Reg. § 1.988-3(b).

[69] Code Sec. 988(a)(3)(A). However, any foreign currency gain or loss realized by a foreign person from the conduct of a U.S. trade or business is treated as U.S. source income. Reg. § 1.988-4(c).

¶603.02

rule, a U.S. resident is any corporation, partnership, trust, or estate that is a U.S person, as well as any individual who has a tax home in the United States.[70] An individual's tax home is his or her regular or principal place of business, provided that he or she is not treated as having a tax home in a foreign country during any period in which his or her abode is in the United States.[71] A foreign resident is any corporation, partnership, trust, or estate that is a foreign person, as well as any individual who has a tax home in a foreign country.[72] The residence of any QBU of the taxpayer (e.g., a branch of a domestic corporation) is the country in which the QBU's principal place of business is located.[73]

For purposes of the foreign tax credit limitation, net gains from foreign currency transactions generally are passive category income. An exception applies to gains or losses arising from foreign currency transactions that are "directly related to the business needs" of the taxpayer.[74]

.03 Hedging Transactions

U.S. companies routinely employ a variety of financial instruments, such as currency forward, futures and options contracts, to reduce the currency exchange risk associated with a business transaction.

> ***Example 6.9:*** USAco is an accrual-basis, calendar year domestic corporation with the dollar as its functional currency. On February 1, USAco enters into a contract with a Mexican supplier to purchase raw materials for 600,000 pesos for delivery and payment on July 1. Also on February 1, USAco hedges against the currency exchange risk associated with this purchase agreement by entering into a currency forward agreement with a bank to buy 600,000 pesos for $100,000 on July 1. The forward contract effectively eliminates the currency exchange risk component of the purchase agreement by fixing the purchase price of the raw materials in U.S. dollars at $100,000.

---

[70] Code Sec. 988(a)(3)(B)(i)(I) and (II).

[71] Code Secs. 988(a)(3)(B)(i)(I) and Code Sec. 911(d)(3), and Reg. §1.911-2(b). An individual's abode is in the United States if that is where his or her economic, social, and personal ties are closest. For example, *see J.T. Lemay,* CA-5, 88-1 USTC ¶ 9182, 837 F2d 681 (5th Cir. 1988). Aff'g 53 TCM 862, Dec. 43,931(M), TC Memo. 1987-256; *and D.P. Lansdown,* 68 TCM 680, Dec. 50,114(M), TC Memo. 1994-452. Aff'd, 73 F3d 373 (10th

Cir. 1995)). An individual who does not have a tax home is treated as a U.S. resident if such individual is a U.S. citizen or resident alien and as a foreign resident if such individual is not a U.S. citizen or resident alien. Code Sec. 988(a)(3)(B)(i).

[72] Code Sec. 988(a)(3)(B)(i)(I) and (III).

[73] Code Sec. 988(a)(3)(B)(ii).

[74] Code Secs. 904(d)(2)(A) and (B) and 954(c)(1)(D); and Reg. § 1.954-2(g).

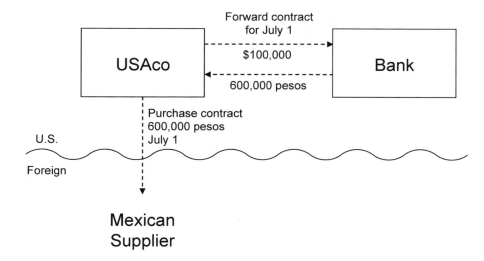

Because there is no currency exchange risk associated with a fully hedged transaction, in certain circumstances a taxpayer is allowed to integrate the accounting for the hedge with the accounting for the underlying hedged transaction. This approach reflects the reality that a fully hedged transaction is, in substance, a transaction denominated in the hedge security (in Example 6.9, the U.S. dollar).

A hedge and hedged transaction qualify for integration treatment only if they meet the definitional requirements of a Code Sec. 988 hedging transaction.[75] If these requirements are met, the taxpayer can ignore the nonfunctional currency aspect of the transaction and account for the transaction as if it were denominated in the hedge currency, in which case no foreign currency gain or loss is recognized. Code Sec. 988 includes the following three categories of hedging transactions:

    (i) *Hedged debt instruments*—These include hedges associated with transactions in which the taxpayer lends or borrows funds through the use of a bond, debenture, note, certificate, or other evidence of indebtedness (but not accounts payable, accounts receivable, or similar items of income and expense).[76]

    (ii) *Hedged executory contracts for goods and services*—These include hedges involving executory contracts to pay or receive nonfunctional currency in the future with respect to the sale or purchase of property or services in the ordinary course of the taxpayer's business.[77]

    (iii) *Hedge for the period between the trade and settlement dates on the purchase or sale of a publicly traded stock or security.*[78]

    Example 6.10: [79] USAco is an accrual-basis, calendar year domestic corporation with the dollar as its functional currency. On June 1, USAco enters

---

[75] Code Sec. 988(d).
[76] Reg. § 1.988-5(a). *See also* Temp. Reg. § 1.988-5T.
[77] Reg. § 1.988-5(b).

[78] Reg. § 1.988-5(c).
[79] Compare Reg. § 1.988-5(b)(4), Example 6(v).

into a contract with a German steel manufacturer to purchase steel for 200,000 euros (€) for delivery and payment on November 1. Also on June 1, USAco hedges against the currency exchange risk associated with this purchase agreement by purchasing € 195,000 at the spot rate of € 1 = $1.30 (total cost of $253,500). USAco deposits the € 195,000 in a separate bank account that will make a € 5,000 interest payment on the deposited funds on November 1. On November 1, USAco withdraws the principal and interest of € 200,000 from the bank account and makes payment in exchange for delivery of the steel. The spot rate on November 1 is € 1 = $1.35.

The contract to purchase the steel and the simultaneous purchase of euros are part of a single economic transaction. As such, USAco may treat them as an integrated transaction if USAco satisfies certain requirements (e.g., USAco identifies the transaction as a hedged executory contract and deposits the euros in a separate account).[80]

Under this approach, USAco treats the $253,500 paid under the hedge as an amount paid directly for the steel and recognizes *no* gain or loss for the exchange rate fluctuation between June 1 and November 1. USAco treats the € 5,000 of interest as part of the hedge[81] and, using the spot rate for the date of the interest payment,[82] USAco recognizes interest income of $6,750 [€ 5,000 × $1.35]. However, because the interest is part of the hedge, USAco recognizes *no* foreign currency gain or loss when the interest is used to purchase the steel. USAco's basis in the steel is $260,250 [$253,500 + $6,750].

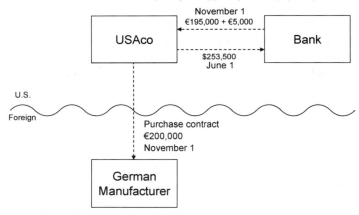

.04 De Minimis Rule for Personal Transactions Entered Into by Individuals

Foreign currency gains realized by an individual from the disposition of foreign currency in a personal transaction are not taxable, provided that the gain does not exceed $200. Note that the threshold is $200 per transaction, as opposed to cumulative gains of $200 per year. Transactions entered into in connection with business travel are treated as personal transactions under this provision. This rule eliminates the need to report gains arising from the exchanges of currency that are small in amount and that are associated with personal or business travel.[83]

---

[80] Reg. § 1.988-5(b).
[81] Reg. § 1.988-5(b)(2)(iii)(E).
[82] Reg. § 1.988-2(b)(1).
[83] Code Sec. 988(e).

Chapter 7

Export Benefits

¶ 701 THE EXPORT BENEFITS SAGA

Congress has always loved exporters because they create manufacturing jobs in the United States. However, the history of export benefits that Congress has created has continually changed the last forty-five years.

In 1971, Congress enacted the domestic international sales corporation (DISC) regime to attempt to stimulate U.S. exports. A DISC allowed a U.S. exporter to avoid U.S. tax on a portion of its export profits by allocating those profits to a special type of U.S. subsidiary known as a DISC. A DISC was a domestic corporation that was little more than a paper corporation. In the mid-1970s, major trading partners of the United States began complaining that the DISC provisions were an illegal export subsidy in violation of the General Agreement on Tariffs and Trade (GATT).

Congress tried to end the controversy in 1984 by enacting the foreign sales corporation (FSC) regime to replace the DISC regime, while also creating a vestige of the old DISC, the Interest Charge-DISC (IC-DISC) regime. The FSC regime responded to the GATT controversy by requiring U.S. exporters to establish a foreign corporation that performs certain activities abroad in order to obtain a U.S. tax benefit. However, these foreign activities were typically negligible. Therefore, similar to a DISC, a FSC was little more than a paper corporation. A domestic corporation that established a FSC allocated a portion of its qualified export profits to its FSC, which were exempt from U.S. tax. The net effect of this arrangement was a permanent exclusion from U.S. tax on a portion of a U.S. corporation's export profits at both the FSC and U.S. shareholder levels. Due to the lack of a permanent tax benefit, the IC-DISC regime saw little use when initially legislated.

In 1998, the European Union complained to the World Trade Organization (WTO) asserting that the FSC regime, as with its predecessor, the DISC regime, was an illegal export subsidy in violation of GATT. In 1999, the WTO released its report on the European Union's complaint, ruling that the FSC regime was indeed an illegal export subsidiary and ruled for its elimination by 2000.

In response to the WTO's ruling, the United States enacted into law the FSC Repeal and Extraterritorial Income Exclusion Act of 2000. The extraterritorial income (ETI) exclusion provided U.S. exporters (either U.S. or foreign corporations) with essentially the same tax benefit as the old FSC regime without even having to form a new corporation. As a consequence, the enactment of the ETI exclusion did not put an end to the trade controversy. The WTO ruled that the ETI exclusion was similarly an illegal export subsidiary and ruled for elimination of the ETI exclusion.

As a result, in the American Jobs Creation Act of 2004 (the "2004 Act"), Congress phased out a repeal of the ETI exclusion while phasing in a domestic production deduction. Although the domestic production activities deduction does not require an export sale, a later paragraph of this chapter will discuss the domestic production activities deduction because it replaces an export benefit, the ETI exclusion and, despite its name, may involve some foreign manufacturing. Nevertheless, as this chapter will show, the current export benefit is the longstanding IC-DISC, which has become favored as a result of the lower rate of tax on dividends received from domestic corporations at the 20 percent capital gains rate.[1] In the past several years, Congress has discussed eliminating the IC-DISC benefit, but has never passed such legislation.

If a rate differential between dividends and ordinary income ceases to exist, much of the current planning with IC-DISCs will end. This almost occurred at the end of 2012 before Congress made the rate differential permanent in the American Taxpayer Relief Act of 2012.

¶ 702 INTRODUCTION TO THE IC-DISC

.01 Taxation of an IC-DISC and Its Shareholders

Congress designed the IC-DISC as a means by which a U.S. exporter could borrow funds from the U.S. Treasury. An IC-DISC must be a U.S. corporation with a single class of stock that has a minimum par value of $2,500.[2] More importantly, an IC-DISC is not subject to the regular U.S. corporate income tax.[3] The lack of a corporate income tax on an IC-DISC combined with the 20% tax rate on qualified dividends, results in owners of U.S. pass-through entities saving 20% of tax on a portion of their export income.[4]

> **Example 7.1:** U.S. individual wholly owns USAco, an S corporation that manufactures and exports widgets. U.S. individual forms an IC-DISC. On its export of widgets, USAco pays IC-DISC a commission of $240,000. The $240,000 commission is a deduction against USAco's taxable income that flows through to U.S. individual, reducing income subject to tax at approximately a

---

[1] Code Sec. 1(h)(11).
[2] Code Sec. 992(a)(1)(C).
[3] Code Sec. 991.

[4] The IRS has not issued guidance as to whether an individual must pay the net investment income tax of 3.8% under Code Sec. 1411 on a dividend received from an IC-DISC.

40% rate. The IC-DISC does not pay tax on the commission, but distributes it as a qualified dividend to the U.S. individual, who pays tax at a 20% rate. The U.S. individual has an income tax savings of 20 percentage points.

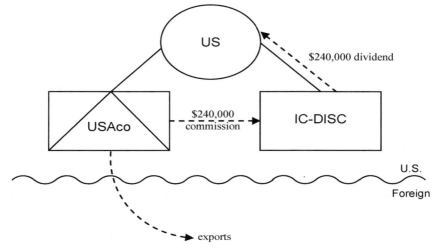

In addition to incurring tax on actual dividend distributions, U.S. shareholders are subject to tax on deemed dividend distributions from the IC-DISC.[5] The deemed distributions do not include income derived from the first $10 million of qualified export receipts each year.[6] Therefore, an IC-DISC allows a U.S. shareholder to defer paying U.S. tax on the income derived from up to $10 million of qualified export receipts each year. The IC-DISC may defer, accordingly, $10 million of its most profitable export sales.[7] Most U.S. shareholders of flow-through entities declare dividends to lock in tax savings due to the rate differential.

However, if a U.S. shareholder fails to take a dividend (actual or deemed), the U.S. shareholder must pay an interest charge on its IC-DISC-related deferred tax liability. That liability equals the difference between the shareholder's tax for the year computed with and without the accumulated IC-DISC income of the shareholder that has been deferred.[8] Therefore, a U.S. shareholder must continue to pay interest on deferred IC-DISC income until that income is either actually distributed or deemed distributed by the IC-DISC. The interest rate is the current market rate for 52-week Treasury bills.[9] That rate is adjusted annually and applies for the fiscal year ending September 30. The rates for the last several years are as follows:

---

[5] Code Sec. 995(a) and (b).

[6] Code Sec. 995(b)(1)(E). It is not possible to circumvent the $10 million limitation by creating multiple IC-DISCs. Code Sec. 995(b)(4)(B).

[7] Reg. § 1.995-8(b).

[8] Code Sec. 995(f)(2).

[9] Code Sec. 995(f)(4).

Year ending September 30	Interest Rate
2007	4.87%[10]
2008	2.48%[11]
2009	0.63%[12]
2010	0.34%[13]
2011	0.22%[14]
2012	0.16%[15]
2013	0.14%[16]
2014	0.11%[17]

IC-DISC shareholders compute the interest charge on Form 8404, Computation of Interest Charge on DISC-Related Deferred Tax Liability (a completed copy of which is in the Appendix) and the interest is due on the same date as the shareholder's regular tax return, without any extensions.[18] The IC-DISC regime does not require any estimated tax payments with respect to the interest charge.[19]

Example 7.2: Uncle Sam, a U.S. citizen, wholly owns USAco, a manufacturer of widgets. Due to burgeoning export sales, Uncle Sam forms an IC-DISC that receives a commission on $9 million of qualified export receipts. Should Uncle Sam decide not to receive a dividend of the cash representing the commission on $9 million of qualified export receipts (and pay tax at only the 20% capital gains rate on qualified dividends), the IC-DISC would pay an interest charge to the U.S. government based on the difference between the hypothetical amount of tax due if Uncle Sam had received a dividend of the commission and Uncle Sam's actual U.S. tax due.

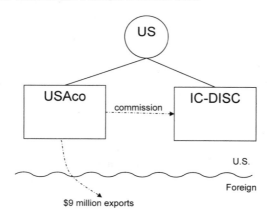

---

[10] Rev. Rul. 2007-64, 2007-2 CB 953.

[11] Rev. Rul. 2008-51, 2008-2 CB 1171.

[12] Rev. Rul. 2009-36, 2009-2 CB 650.

[13] Rev. Rul. 2010-28, 2010-2 CB 804.

[14] Rev. Rul. 2011-30, 2011-2 CB 826.

[15] Rev. Rul. 2012-22, 2012-48 IRB 565.

[16] Rev. Rul. 2013-24, 2013-49 IRB 594.

[17] Rev. Rul. 2014-33, 2014-52 IRB 957.

[18] Reg. § 1.995(f)-1(j)(3)(i).

[19] Reg. § 1.995(f)-1(a)(2)(iii).

If the IC-DISC distributes cash representing all its income as a dividend (as most do to ensure current taxation at the preferential 20% rate), the interest charge is inapplicable.

.02 Tests to Qualify as an IC-DISC

To qualify as an IC-DISC, the domestic corporation must pass both a gross receipts test and an export assets test.

The gross receipts test states that 95 percent of the gross receipts of the IC-DISC must constitute qualified gross receipts.[20] Qualified gross receipts include the following:

(i) Gross receipts from the sale, exchange, or other disposition of export property;

(ii) Gross receipts from the lease or rental of export property for use outside the United States;

(iii) Gross receipts for services that are related to or are subsidiary to any exchange of property;

(iv) Interest on any obligation that is a qualified export asset;

(v) Gross receipts for engineering or architectural services for construction projects located outside the United States;

(vi) Gross receipts for the managerial services for furtherance of production or other qualified export receipts; and

(vii) Commissions received for any of the transactions listed above in (i) through (vi).

Example 7.3: Uncle Sam, a U.S. citizen, wholly owns USAco, a manufacturer of widgets. Due to burgeoning export sales, Uncle Sam forms an IC-DISC whose only activity results in receiving a commission on $9 million of qualified export receipts. Because 100% of the IC-DISC's gross receipts constitute commissions, the IC-DISC satisfies the gross receipts test.

---

[20] Code Secs. 992(a)(1) and 993(d) and (f).

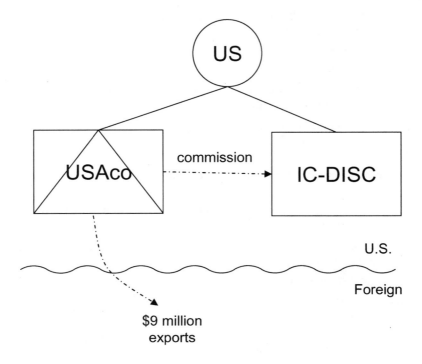

The qualified export assets test states that 95 percent of the assets of the corporation must be qualified export assets.[21] Qualified export assets include the following:

    (i) Accounts receivable,

    (ii) Temporary investments,

    (iii) Export property,

    (iv) Assets used primarily in connection with the production of qualified export receipts, and

    (v) Loans to producers.

    Example 7.4: Uncle Sam, a U.S. citizen, wholly owns USAco, a manufacturer of widgets. Uncle Sam forms an IC-DISC that receives a commission on $9 million of qualified export receipts. The IC-DISC, instead of distributing a dividend to Uncle Sam, loans the cash representing the commission back to USAco. Assuming the loan to USAco constitutes a qualified export asset as a producers loan, 100% of the IC-DISC's assets constitute qualified export assets. Consequently, the IC-DISC passes the qualified export assets test.

---

[21] Code Secs. 992(a)(1)(A) and 993(b).

¶702.02

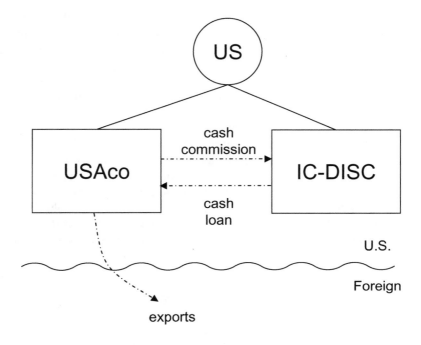

¶ 703 SALES OF EXPORT PROPERTY

Although exporters often think of newly manufactured property as export property, the property can be used equipment or even scrap. There are three requirements for an IC-DISC to receive income from a sale of export property:[22]

(i) The property must be manufactured, produced, grown or extracted in the United States by a person other than the IC-DISC;

(ii) The export property must be held primarily for sale, lease or rental for direct use, consumption or disposition outside the United States; and

(iii) The export property must have a minimum of 50 percent U.S. content.

.01 The Manufacturing Requirement

The IC-DISC may not manufacture the export property. The export property must be manufactured (minor assembly is insufficient)[23] in the United States by a U.S. person other than the IC-DISC.[24] Generally, the shareholders of a U.S. manufacturing entity will form an IC-DISC to benefit from export sales. The IC-DISC will typically receive a commission for the export sales (with a corresponding commission deduction by the U.S. manufacturing entity).[25] Property is manufactured within the United States if either (i) a safe-harbor of 20 percent of its conversion costs are incurred in the United States, (ii) there is a substantial transformation in the United

---

[22] Code Sec. 993(c).

[23] Reg. § 1.993-3(c)(2)(i).

[24] Code Sec. 993(c)(1)(A).

[25] Although not as common, an IC-DISC may be a "buy-sell" IC-DISC, whereby the IC-DISC will actually buy and take title to the export property from the U.S. manufacturing entity before the export sale occurs.

States, or (iii) the operations in the United States are generally considered to constitute manufacturing.[26] These three tests are identical to the first three tests to satisfy the manufacturing exception to foreign base company sales income under Subpart F. (See ¶ 501.06).

For the 20% safe-harbor, the conversion costs counts both direct labor and factory burden, which for this test only, includes packaging and assembly.[27]

> **Example 7.5:** USAco sells lime-green leisure suits with wide white belts. In order to make these hideous-looking suits attractive to consumers, USAco packages them in gold-plated cardboard and plastic boxes and exports them for $100 a suit. USAco pays contract manufacturers in China $30 for each suit, but the gold-plated packaging adds $10 to the cost of goods sold. Because the $10 cost in the United States constitutes at least 20% (25%) of the total cost of goods sold of $40 ($30 + $10), USAco has conducted manufacturing under the safe-harbor.

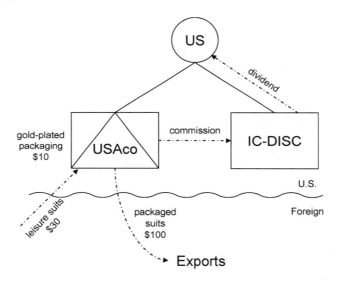

Manufacturing occurs under the substantial transformation test when the product looks substantially different before the process than after the process.[28]

> **Example 7.6:** USAco operates a metal processing shop. USAco purchases steel rods and converts them to screws and nails. The conversion is a substantial transformation and, therefore, USAco has manufactured the screws and nails.

---

[26] Reg. § 1.993-3(c). The IRS will not rule on whether a product is manufactured. Rev. Proc. 2008-7, 2008-1 IRB 229.

[27] Reg. § 1.993-3(c)(2)(iv).

[28] Reg. § 1.993-3(c)(2)(ii).

¶703.01

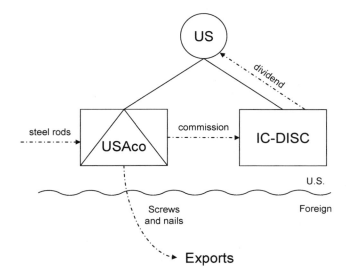

Taxpayers satisfy the generally considered manufacturing test when U.S. operations are substantial in nature.[29] This is somewhat of an ambiguous standard and can produce unexpected results.

Example 7.7: USAco separately purchases the frames, wings, tinted lenses, and little screws that can be put together to make sunglasses. USAco pays minimum wages to low-skilled employees who put together approximately 20 sunglasses each hour. Assuming that these conversion costs are less than 20% of the costs of goods sold and there is a not a substantial transformation of the sunglass components in the sunglasses, manufacturing is satisfied *only if* this process is generally considered to constitute manufacturing.[30]

---

[29] Reg. § 1.993-3(c)(2)(iii).

[30] This example is based on *Bausch & Lomb v. Commissioner,* T.C. Memo. 1996-57, which involved similar facts under the same test for manufacturing to avoid foreign base company sales income.

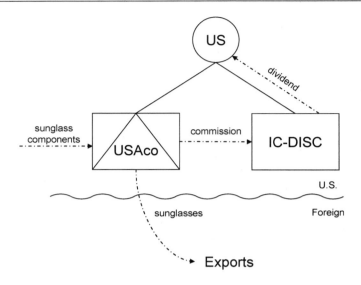

.02 The Destination Test

The export property must satisfy a destination test, which means it must be held for sale, lease or rental in the ordinary course of business for direct use, disposition or consumption outside the United States.[31]

Property satisfies the destination test if it is delivered to a freight forwarder for ultimate shipment abroad.[32] Property also satisfies the destination test if it is sold to a purchaser in the United States, provided the property does not undergo further manufacturing or use by the purchaser prior to export, and the property is shipped to a foreign destination within one year.[33] Under this destination test, what may seemingly be domestic sales could qualify as export sales. The domestic purchasers of an exporter's product will have to provide the exporter with information showing that the product was exported within one year of manufacturing by providing the IC-DISC with documentation of ultimate shipment outside the United States.

Example 7.8: USAco sells widgets to a widget distributor in Buffalo, New York. One of the Buffalo distributor's biggest customers is a Toronto-based company. If properly documented, the widgets re-sold by Buffalo distributor to a Toronto-based company satisfy the destination test.

---

[31] Code Sec. 993(c)(1)(B).
[32] Reg. § 1.993-3(d)(2)(i)(a).

[33] Reg. § 1.993-3(d)(2)(i)(b).

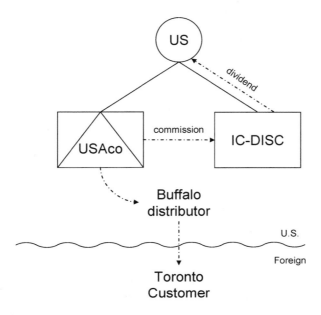

If the domestic purchaser conducts further manufacturing, the original seller has not satisfied the destination test because a different product is leaving the United States. The definition for manufacturing is identical to the alternative tests for manufacturing discussed in the previous section. In *General Electric Co.,*[34] the Tax Court denied an export benefit, finding that the jet engines General Electric manufactured were subject to further manufacturing (under the generally considered manufacturing test) when they were attached to Boeing's jet planes for delivery overseas. However, the Second Circuit Court of Appeals reversed, finding in favor of General Electric that: (i) the airplane industry recognizes aircraft and engines as legally distinct and separate and (ii) affixing a completed product to another does not constitute manufacturing or use.[35]

***Example* 7.9:** TireCo, a U.S. corporation, manufactures automobile tires in the United States with U.S. materials. TireCo, through its IC-DISC, sells its tires to Big3co, a Detroit auto manufacturer, which affixes the tires to its new automobiles that are exported to Canada. TireCo's IC-DISC can benefit from the sale of its tires to Big3co because the final destination of the automobiles is outside the United States. Furthermore, affixing tires to automobiles does not appear to be further manufacturing by Big3Co.

---

[34] 70 TCM 39, Dec. 50,743(M), TC Memo. 1995-306.

[35] *General Electric Co.,* CA-2, 2001-1 USTC ¶ 50,329, 245 F.3d 149.

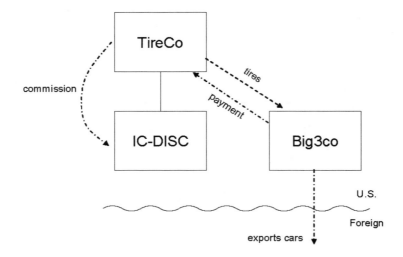

An exporter can receive an IC-DISC benefit on sales to a foreign subsidiary. However, only the amount earned by the IC-DISC (and not its foreign subsidiary) qualifies.

Five types of property are ineligible to be qualified export property.[36] Ineligible property consists of (i) property rented for use by a related party, (ii) intellectual property other than films, tapes, records, or computer software, (iii) unprocessed softwood timber, (iv) products, such as oil or coal, for which a depletion deduction is allowable, and (v) property the President designates as being in short supply.

.03 The Maximum of 50 Percent Foreign Content Requirement

No more than 50% of the fair market value of export property may be attributable to the fair market value of articles imported into the United States.[37] The fair market value of the foreign content is determined by the dutiable value of any foreign components.[38]

> *Example* **7.10:** Willie, a U.S. citizen, wholly owns PAPco, a manufacturer of paper products that is a C corporation. Due to burgeoning export sales, Willie forms an IC-DISC that receives commissions on PAPco's sales of $200 per paper product. The materials to manufacture the paper products are wood pulp, which is purchased from companies located in the United States, and kryptonite, which is purchased from a kryptonite mine in Mexico. The dutiable value of the kryptonite is $80 per paper product. Because less than half the content constitutes materials purchased outside the United States, the paper products satisfy the content requirement. However, should the cost of kryptonite ever rise to the extent that it exceeds 50% of the value of the paper products, the paper products would have too much foreign content and would not qualify as export property.

---

[36] Code Sec. 993(c)(2).
[37] Code Sec. 993(c)(1)(C).

[38] Reg. § 1.993-3(e)(4)(i).

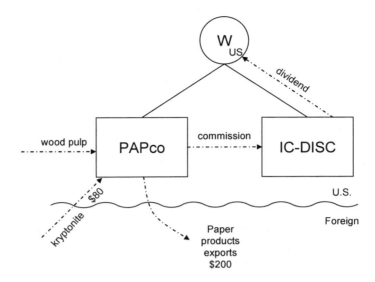

¶ 704 DETERMINING THE IC-DISC BENEFIT

The income of an IC-DISC from sales of export property is in an amount constituting:

- 4 percent of qualified export receipts,[39]

- 50 percent of the combined taxable income from qualified export receipts,[40] or

- The arm's-length amount determined under the transfer pricing principles of section 482.[41]

These methods to determine the IC-DISC's income apply regardless of whether the IC-DISC is a "commission" IC-DISC or a "buy-sell" IC-DISC. Any of these transfer pricing methods for the IC-DISC combined with the 20 percent rate of tax on qualified dividends by domestic corporations to U.S. individual shareholders, creates tax savings from this export benefit.[42] Taxpayers rarely use the section 482 transfer pricing method to determine the arm's-length amount of income for the IC-DISC because the IC-DISC's functions performed and risks assumed are minimal.

The qualified export receipts method allocates 4 percent of the qualified export receipts from the export sales to the IC-DISC.

Example 7.11: Uncle Sam, a U.S. citizen, owns USAco, a U.S. S corporation. USAco has qualifying export sales of $6 million of low-margin products

---

[39] Code Sec. 994(a)(1).

[40] Code Sec. 994(a)(2).

[41] Code Sec. 994(a)(3).

[42] Code Sec. 246(d). C corporations are not tax-advantaged owners of IC-DISCs because the dividends received deduction does not apply to dividends received from an IC-DISC. However, the shareholders of the C corporation can either directly own the IC-DISC's shares or be beneficiaries of a trust that owns the IC-DISC shares.

through its IC-DISC. Using 4% of the qualified export receipts method, USAco will exclude a commission of $240,000 of gross receipts, resulting in a tax reduction of $96,000 (40% of $240,000). If USAco's IC-DISC distributes the cash representing this income as a dividend to Uncle Sam, Uncle Sam would pay U.S. tax of $48,000 ($240,000 at the 20% capital gains rate for qualified dividends). As a result, the impact of the 4% of qualified gross receipts method combined with the 20% capital gains rate for qualified dividends is an income tax savings of $48,000 ($96,000 less $48,000).

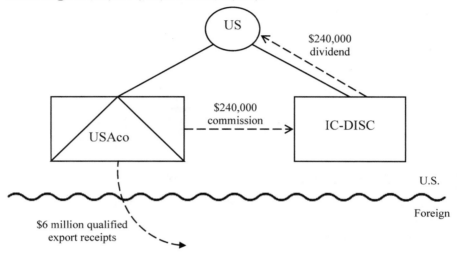

The combined taxable income method allocates 50 percent of the taxable income from the export sales to the IC-DISC.

Example 7.12: Uncle Sam, a U.S. citizen, owns USAco, a U.S. S corporation. USAco earns $1 million of taxable income from the export of high margin products through its IC-DISC. Using the 50% of combined taxable income method, USAco pays $500,000 as a commission to its IC-DISC, resulting in a tax reduction of $200,000 (40% of $500,000). If the IC-DISC distributes the $500,000 of cash representing the income as a dividend to Uncle Sam, that $500,000 would be subject to a capital gains rate on qualified dividends of $100,000 (20% of $500,000). As a result, the impact of the 50% of combined taxable income with the 20% capital gains rate for qualified dividends is an income tax savings of $100,000 ($200,000 less $100,000).

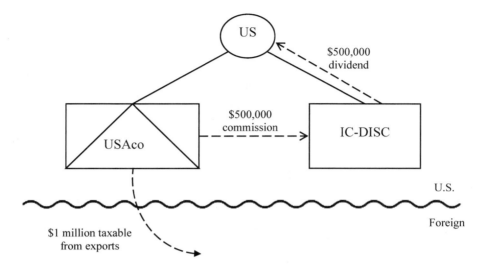

Very few taxpayers determine the IC-DISC's income using the transfer pricing principles of section 482 because IC-DISC's generally have little economic activity and, consequently, lower income under those principles than under the other two methods.

¶ 705 MAXIMIZING THE IC-DISC INCOME

An exporter can use any of the methods described in the previous section to achieve the greatest IC-DISC income possible. The IC-DISC rules permit the use of different methods to different sales based on product lines, recognized industry or trade usage, and even by transaction.[43] In practice, most of the decisions will be between the qualified export receipts and combined taxable income methods. The combined taxable income method results in the largest IC-DISC income when exports have a net pre-tax margin greater than 8 percent. On the other hand, the qualified export receipts method provides the largest IC-DISC income when the net pre-tax margin on exports is less than 8 percent. If the net pre-tax margin on exports is lower than worldwide net pre-tax margins, which often occurs due to the extra shipping and administrative expenses of foreign sales, the marginal costing of combined taxable income may result in the largest commission. Also, by apportioning expenses away from export sales towards domestic sales, an exporter may increase its combined taxable income. Finally, an exporter can maximize the IC-DISC's income by ignoring loss sales.[44]

.01 Grouping

Grouping refers to the exporter's maximizing the IC-DISC's commission by separating high-margin sales from low-margin sales.

Example 7.13: USAco, a domestic corporation, exports domestically produced red and white wines. The annual gross receipts and combined taxable income from these export sales are as follows:

---

[43] Reg. § 1.994-1(c)(7).   [44] Reg. § 1.994-1(e)(1).

	Qualified Export receipts	Combined taxable income	Net pre-tax margin
Red wine	$500,000	$100,000	20%
White wine	$500,000	$20,000	4%
Total export sales	$1,000,000	$120,000	12%

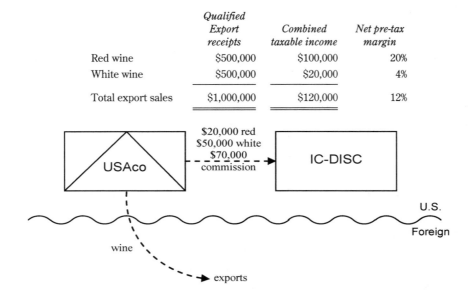

By using the 4% of qualified export receipts method, the commission would be $40,000 (4% of $1,000,000). By using the 50% of combined taxable income method, the commission would be $60,000 (50% of $120,000). However, through product grouping, USAco can use the 50% of combined taxable income method for sales of red wine for a $50,000 commission [50% of $100,000]. At the same time, USAco can use the 4% of qualified export receipts method for sales of white wine, for a $20,000 commission [4% of $500,000]. As a result, separate groupings for sales of red wine from sales of white wine increase the total amount of the IC-DISC's commission to $70,000.

Exporters have considerable flexibility in grouping. An exporter's product or product line grouping will be accepted if the groupings conform to recognized trade or industry usage or the two-digit major groups (or inferior classifications) of Standard Industrial Classification codes.[45] In addition, within the same taxable year, an exporter can use grouping for one product line and the transaction-by-transaction method for another product line.[46] The availability of specialized software designed to optimize the IC-DISC's income generated by transactional pricing (as well as marginal costing and expense allocations, as discussed below) has greatly enhanced the ability of exporters to take advantage of grouping techniques.

.02 Marginal Costing

Marginal costing can increase the IC-DISC's combined taxable income.[47] Under the general rule, combined taxable income equals the excess of the qualified export receipts over the total direct and indirect costs related to exports.[48] However, if the exporter elects marginal costing, the exporter only accounts for marginal

---

[45] Reg. § 1.994-1(c)(7)(ii).
[46] Reg. § 1.994-1(c)(7)(iii).

[47] Code Sec. 994(b)(2) and Reg. § 1.994-2(c).
[48] Reg. § 1.994-1(c)(3).

costs in computing combined taxable income. Therefore, marginal costing allows a taxpayer to increase combined taxable income by not deducting the amount of the fixed costs related to export sales. Marginal costs include only the direct material and direct labor costs, as other costs, such as selling, general, and administrative expenses and interest expense, are ignored for purposes of computing combined taxable income under marginal costing.[49]

However, an overall profit percentage limitation restricts the combined taxable income under marginal costing to an amount equal to export sales multiplied by the ratio of taxable income to total sales (domestic and foreign).[50]

Example **7.14:** USAco, a U.S. corporation, exports products through its IC-DISC that constitute export property. During the current year, USAco's results from operations are as follows:

	Export sales	*U.S. sales*	*Total sales*
Sales	$10 million	$15 million	$25 million
Direct material and labor	– 6 million	– 7 million	– 13 million
Marginal costing CTI	$ 4 million	$ 8 million	$12 million
Indirect expenses	– 3 million	– 3 million	– 6 million
Full costing CTI	$ 1 million	$ 5 million	$ 6 million

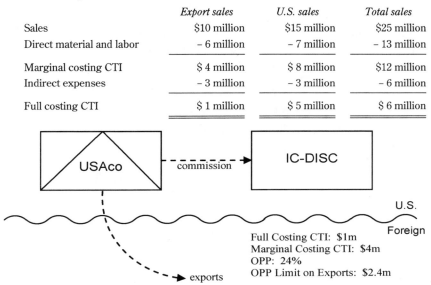

The marginal costing profit margin on export sales of 40% ($4 million ÷ $10 million) exceeds the overall profit percentage of 24% ($6 million ÷ $25 million). Therefore, the overall profit limitation restricts combined taxable income to $2.4 million (24% of $10 million of export sales). Marginal costing limited by the overall profit percentage to $2.4 million is still preferable to full costing, however, because full costing produces only $1 million of combined taxable income.

.03 Expense Allocations

Another technique to increase the combined taxable income is to increase the expenses allocated to domestic sales. As discussed above, combined taxable income equals the excess of qualified export receipts over the total costs of the

---

[49] Reg. § 1.994-2(b)(2).   [50] Reg. § 1.994-2(b)(3).

exporter, which includes deductions that are definitely related to export sales (e.g., cost of goods sold) and a ratable portion of any deductions that are not definitely related to any specific class of gross income (e.g., selling, general, and administrative expenses).[51] Therefore, a taxpayer can increase combined taxable income and, in turn, the amount of its IC-DISC's commission income, by developing defensible apportionment bases that allocate fewer deductions against qualified export receipts.[52]

Example 7.15: DomCo, a domestic corporation, sells $36 million of widgets in both the United States and foreign markets. For its exports, DomCo has $24 million of sales and a $12 million gross profit. For its domestic sales, DomCo has $12 million of sales and a $4 million gross profit. DomCo incurs $10 million of indirect expenses. If DomCo allocates the indirect expenses based on gross profit, $7.5 million ($10 million of indirect expenses times [$12 million of gross profit on exports divided by $16 million of total gross profit]) would be allocated to exports. However, if DomCo allocates the indirect expenses based on sales, only $6.7 million ($10 million of indirect expenses times [$24 million of exports divided by the $36 million of total sales]) would be allocated to exports. By allocating fewer indirect expenses to exports via an allocation based on sales ($6.7 million instead of $7.5 million), the combined taxable income and, presumably, the commission should be greater.

Allocation Based on Gross Profit

	Sales	Gross Profit	Expense Allocation	CTI
Foreign	$24 million	$12 million	$7.5 million	$4.5 million
Domestic	$12 million	$4 million	$2.5 million	$1.5 million

Allocation Based on Sales

	Sales	Gross Profit	Expense Allocation	CTI
Foreign	$24 million	$12 million	$6.7 million	$5.3 million
Domestic	$12 million	$4 million	$3.3 million	$0.7 million

.04 Loss Sales

Exporters should not include sales that result in losses when determining qualified export receipts. As a result of eliminating loss sales, commissions should be higher under the combined taxable income method than the qualified export receipts method.[53]

¶ 706 IC-DISC COMPREHENSIVE EXAMPLE

EXPORTco, a U.S. corporation, manufactures products for sale in the United States and abroad. During the current year, EXPORTco's qualified export receipts

---

[51] Reg. § 1.994-1(c)(6)(iii).

[52] For an example in the context of research and development expenditures, *see St. Jude Medical, Inc.*, CA-8, 94-2 USTC ¶ 50,459, 34 F.3d 1394.

[53] Reg. § 1.994-1(e)(1).

are $6 million and the related cost of goods sold is $5 million. With respect to domestic sales, EXPORTco's gross receipts are $19 million and its related cost of goods sold is $15 million for a $4 million gross profit. EXPORTco must allocate $2.5 million of administrative expenses and, because exports have a lower gross profit than domestic sales (which is typical), EXPORTco apportions the administrative expenses on the basis of gross profits instead of sales so that fewer administrative expenses are allocated to exports. Accordingly, EXPORTco apportions $500,000 of administrative expenses against its gross profit from exports ($2.5 million of administrative expenses × [$1 million export gross profit / $5 million total gross profit]). In sum, EXPORTco's results for the year are as follows (before the IC-DISC commission):

	Total receipts	Qualified export receipts	Domestic receipts
Gross receipts	$25 million	$6 million	$19 million
Cost of goods sold (direct material and labor)	(20 million)	(5 million)	(15 million)
Gross profit	5 million	1 million	4 million
Administrative expenses	(2.5 million)	(.5 million)	(2 million)
Net income	$2.5 million		

Therefore, USAco's combined taxable income equals $500,000, computed as follows:

	Combined taxable income
Qualified export receipts	$6 million
Cost of goods sold	(5 million)
Gross profit	1 million
Administrative expenses	(.5 million)
Combined taxable income	$0.5 million

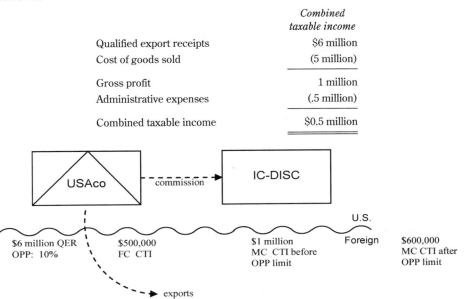

Now assume, for example, that EXPORTco has an IC-DISC. The two primary methods to calculate a commission, produce the following amounts:

¶706

    (i) $240,000 (4% × $6 million of qualified export receipts), or

    (ii) $250,000 (50% × $500,000 of combined taxable income).

If the exporter elects marginal costing, the combined taxable income would exclude the allocated $500,000 of administrative expenses and preliminarily be $1 million. However, the overall profit percentage of 10% ($2.5 million of net income divided by $25 million of total sales) on $6 million of qualified export receipts limits marginal costing combined taxable income to $600,000. Even with marginal costing combined taxable income limited by this overall profit percentage to $600,000, a 50% commission would be $300,000, which is greater than a commission of $250,000 based on full costing combined taxable income.

¶ 707 THE DOMESTIC PRODUCTION DEDUCTION

The domestic production deduction equals 9 percent of the lesser of taxable income or qualified production activities income of the taxpayer. Although the domestic production deduction applies to domestic as well as foreign sales, Congress enacted it to replace the extraterritorial income inclusion.

    Example 7.16: USman, a U.S. corporation, manufactures widgets. Because the widget manufacturing process comprises entirely U.S.-source components and activities, USman's taxable income of $1 million is the same as its qualified production activities income. Further assume that all other requirements for the domestic production deduction are satisfied. USman should receive a domestic production deduction of $90,000.

<table>
<tr><td>USman</td><td>$1 million taxable income

$1 million qualified production activities income</td></tr>
</table>

In determining the amount of the deduction, a manufacturer must analyze the following items:

- Domestic production gross receipts,

- Costs allocated to domestic production gross receipts, and

- Total wages on Forms W-2.

Domestic production gross receipts are receipts from any sale, exchange, or other disposition of qualifying production property that is manufactured, produced, grown, or extracted by the taxpayer in the United States. Once the domestic production gross receipts are determined, the taxpayer subtracts the allocable costs (the cost of goods sold deduction and other deductions allocable to the receipts) from them to determine qualified production activities income. Finally, the domestic production deduction is limited to 50 percent of the taxpayer's W-2 wages paid that are related to domestic production gross receipts.

.01 Determining Domestic Production Gross Receipts

Domestic production gross receipts are generally any sale, exchange, or other disposition of qualifying production property (including, *inter alia,* tangible personal property) that is manufactured, produced, grown, or extracted by the taxpayer "in whole or in significant part within the United States."[54]

> **Example 7.17:** USman, a U.S. corporation, manufactures widgets, which are tangible personal property. Because USman's manufactured products constitute qualifying production property, their sale constitutes domestic production gross receipts.

Definition of "qualifying production property." Because qualifying production property must be manufactured "in significant part within the United States," some manufacturing may occur outside the United States. Pursuant to regulations issued by the IRS, property is produced "in significant part within the United States" if the production activity in the United States is substantial in nature. A safe harbor states that property is substantial in nature if at least 20 percent of the cost of goods sold of the property is attributed to U.S. activity.[55]

> **Example 7.18:** USman, a U.S. C corporation, manufactures widgets for sale to customers in the ordinary course of business. USman engages contract manufacturers in Mexico and Canada to manufacture a portion of the widgets. Of the final cost of good sold of widgets, 30% is attributable to Canadian activities, 30% is attributable to Mexican activities, and 40% is attributable to U.S. activities. By incurring more than 20% of the cost of goods sold in the United States (even though U.S. costs are less than half of the cost of goods sold), the U.S. activities constitute a significant part of the manufacturing process, the sale of the widgets constitutes the sale of qualifying production property, and USman has domestic production gross receipts that would qualify for the domestic production deduction.

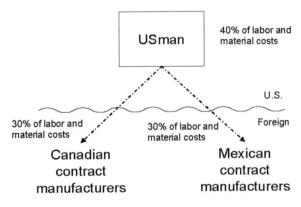

If the 20 percent safe harbor does not apply, there is a facts and circumstances test to determine if the U.S. activity is substantial in nature. However, the mere

---

[54] Code Sec. 199(c)(4)(A)(i)(I).

[55] Reg. § 1.199-3(g)(3).

development of intangibles in the United States for use by a foreign contract manufacturer does not constitute "substantial" activity in the United States.[56]

Example 7.19: ResearchCo, a U.S. C corporation, conducts research and development activities. ResearchCo develops designs for the super widget. Instead of licensing the super widget design, ResearchCo desires to sell the super widgets itself. Without any manufacturing facilities, ResearchCo engages a contract manufacturer, CANco, a Canadian corporation with manufacturing facilities in Toronto, to manufacture the super widgets as designed by ResearchCo. Although the key economic factor behind the value of the super widget is the design that ResearchCo previously developed in the United States, engaging a foreign contract manufacturer does not constitute manufacturing by ResearchCo.

Broad definition of production activity. Qualifying production property also includes the sale of electricity, natural gas, potable water, engineering or architectural services performed in the United States for construction projects located in the United States, musical CDs, software, and the sale or license of a qualified film the taxpayer produces (more than 50 percent of the compensation of which is paid for services that are performed in the United States).[57]

As a result, the domestic production deduction offers a planning opportunity for filmmakers to bring some of their production back to the United States.[58]

Example 7.20: FilmCo, a U.S. C corporation, is a major motion picture studio. A recent script requires that the track film "Crazylegs" be set in San Francisco. However, wanting to take advantage of decreased production costs, the head of FilmCo, Harold Hecuba, seeks to shoot the movie in Vancouver, Canada. His controller informs him that if his costs of services performed in the United States by actors, production personnel, directors, and producers are at least 50% of compensation costs, FilmCo's investors will be much happier because the film "Crazylegs" will produce domestic production gross receipts that are eligible for the domestic production deduction. As a result, Harold

---

[56] Reg. § 1.199-3(g)(5)(Ex. 9).
[57] Code Sec. 199(c)(4) and (5).

[58] Code Sec. 199(c)(6).

Hecuba decides to shoot only the exterior scenes in Vancouver, with the rest shot in San Francisco to satisfy this requirement.

.02 Allocable Costs and Qualified Production Gross Income

After determining domestic production gross receipts, the taxpayer arrives at qualified production activities income by subtracting allocable costs—the cost of goods sold deduction and other deductions allocable to these receipts.[59]

Example 7.21: USAco, a U.S. C corporation, manufactures widgets for sale to customers in the ordinary course of business. USAco earns domestic production gross receipts of $10 million and incurs $9 million in cost of goods sold and other deductions allocable to those domestic production gross receipts. As a result, USAco has $1 million of qualified production activities income.

$10 million of domestic production gross receipts

$9 million of cost of goods sold and other deductions

Special rules determine costs when the manufacturing of the qualifying production property includes some foreign activity. To maintain the integrity of any cost allocation, any item or service shall be treated as purchased for a cost equal to its dutiable value when it enters the United States.[60]

Example 7.22: USman, a U.S. C corporation, manufactures widgets for sale to customers in the ordinary course of business. A key component of each widget is a pound of the material kronos, which sells at the fair market value in the United States at $10 per pound. In a bankruptcy sale in Mexico, USman purchases a year's supply of kronos for $4 per pound. Because the fair market value of the kronos in the United States is $10 per pound, when determining

---

[59] Code Sec. 199(c)(1)(B) and (2); Reg. § 1.199-4(c).   [60] Code Sec. 199(c)(3)(A).

the U.S. allocable cost of goods sold (as well as whether a significant part of manufacturing occurs in the United States), USman allocates a $10 cost per widget to nondomestic expenses (instead of a $4 cost) to determine qualified production activities income.

Furthermore, if property is exported for further manufacturing abroad, when the property re-enters the United States, the costs of the further manufacturing abroad cannot exceed the difference between the value of the property when exported and the value of the property when re-entering the United States.[61] This rule effectively limits expenses allocable to foreign production activities, which prevents taxpayers from artificially increasing their qualified production activities income.

> **Example 7.23:** USman, a U.S. C corporation, manufactures widgets for sale to customers in the ordinary course of business. USman conducts a significant part of the manufacturing process within the United States. However, USman exports semifinished widgets with a value of $16 to Mexico for finishing before re-entering the United States with a value of $25. As a result, the cost allocable to Mexico, regardless of the costs incurred in Mexico, cannot exceed $9 per widget.

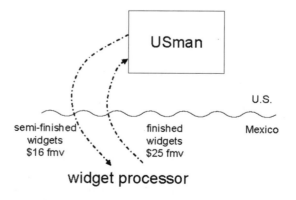

---

[61] Code Sec. 199(c)(3)(B).

.03 Deduction Limited to 50 Percent of W-2 Wages

The deduction is limited to 50 percent of the W-2 wages related to the taxpayer's domestic production gross receipts.[62] The policy behind tying the maximum deduction to an amount based on W-2 wages is to increase W-2 wages, which the taxpayer presumably pays to employees in manufacturing jobs.[63]

> ***Example 7.24:*** USman, a U.S. C corporation, manufactures widgets for sale to customers in the ordinary course of business. USman's taxable income is the same as its qualified production activities income of $1 million. Although USman is interested in taking a domestic production deduction of $90,000, constituting 9% of $1 million, USman only pays W-2 wages of $120,000 related to domestic production gross receipts. As a result, USman's domestic production deduction is limited to one half of its W-2 wages paid totaling $120,000, which is $60,000. To obtain the full domestic production deduction of $90,000, USman would have to increase its total W-2 wages paid to $180,000.

$1 million taxable income

$1 million qualified production activities income

$120,000 of W-2 wages related to domestic production gross receipts

The domestic production deduction is also available to S corporations, partnerships, and other pass-through entities, such as single-member limited liability companies, by determining the individual owner's proportionate share of the qualified production activities income of the pass-through entity. Although the deduction is taken by the individual owner, the Code applies that wage limitation at the entity level and the IRS has written regulations relating to the determination of compensation deductions at the individual owner level.[64] Furthermore, when determining the lesser of taxable income or qualified production activities income for individual owners, taxpayers use adjusted gross income instead of taxable income.[65]

---

[62] Code Sec. 199(b).
[63] Conf. Rep. No. 755, 108th Cong., 2d Sess. 11 (2004).

[64] Reg. § 1.199-9(c).
[65] Code Sec. 199(d).

¶ 708 APPENDIX

Betsy Ross, a U.S. citizen, wholly owns the shares of FLAGco, a U.S. S corporation that manufactures and exports flags. Due to growing exports, Betsy incorporates an IC-DISC effective January 1, 2014, with a capital contribution of $3,000. During the taxable year 2014, FLAGco exports $6 million of flags (the cost of good sold is $5 million and the other expenses allocable to exports are $520,000) and pays a commission to the IC-DISC of $240,000 that the IC-DISC distributes as a dividend through FLAGco to Betsy Ross on December 31, 2014. Betsy filed a Form 4876-A by March 30, 2014 (90 days after the start of the taxable year) electing IC-DISC status for FLAGco IC-DISC. FLAGco IC-DISC must file a Form 1120-IC-DISC. Betsy does not have to file a Form 8404 because the IC-DISC has distributed all of its income as a dividend as there is not any deferral.

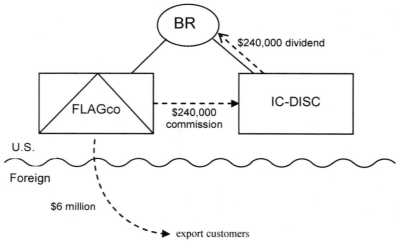

Form **4876-A** (Rev. December 2009) Department of the Treasury Internal Revenue Service	**Election To Be Treated as an Interest Charge DISC**	OMB No. 1545-0190

Part I The corporation named below elects to be treated as an interest charge domestic international sales corporation (IC-DISC) for income tax purposes. All of the corporation's shareholders must consent to this election.

Name of corporation **FLAGco IC-DISC**	**A** Employer identification number 89 : 6423781

Number, street, and room or suite no. (or P.O. box if mail is not delivered to street address) **239 Arch Street**	**B** Principal business classification (see instructions) 423990

City or town, state, and ZIP code **Philadelphia, PA 19106**	**D** Name of person who may be called for information: (optional)

C Tax year of IC-DISC: Must use tax year of shareholder (or shareholder group) with the highest percentage of voting power (see instructions). Enter ending month and day ▶ 12/31

E Election is to take effect for the tax year beginning (month, day, year) **January 1, 2014**	**F** Date corporation began doing business **January 1, 2014**	Telephone number: ( )

G Name and address (including ZIP code) of each shareholder (or expected shareholder) at the beginning of the tax year the election takes effect and when the election is filed.

	H Number of shares of stock held on— (Complete both columns for each shareholder.)		**I** Identifying number (see instructions)
	First day of year of election	Date consent is made	
1 Betsy Ross 239 Arch Street, Philadelphia, PA 19106	100	100	123-45-6789
2			
3			
4			
5			
6			
7			
8			
9			
10			
Total. Enter total shares for all shareholders (include shares of shareholders listed on any attachments)	100	100	

Under penalties of perjury, I declare that the corporation named above has authorized me to make this election for the corporation to be treated as an IC-DISC and that the statements made are to the best of my knowledge and belief true, correct, and complete.

Signature and Title of Officer ▶   Date

Part II Shareholders' Consent Statement. Part II may be used instead of attachments. For this election to be valid, each shareholder must sign and date below or attach a separate consent to this form (see instructions).

We, the undersigned shareholders, consent to the election of the corporation named above to be treated as an IC-DISC. Our consent is irrevocable and is binding upon all transferees of our shares in this corporation.

Signature of shareholder and date. (If consent involves transferred shares, attach a schedule showing the name and address of the holder of the shares at the beginning of the tax year and the number of shares for which the consent is made.)

1 Betsy Ross	**6**
2	**7**
3	**8**
4	**9**
5	**10**

For Paperwork Reduction Act Notice, see page 2.   Cat. No. 62075X   Form **4876-A** (Rev. 12-2009)

¶708

Form **1120-IC-DISC**

(Rev. December 2012)

Department of the Treasury
Internal Revenue Service

Interest Charge Domestic International Sales Corporation Return

(Please type or print.)

▶ Information about Form 1120-IC-DISC and its separate instructions is at *www.irs.gov/f1120icdisc.*

OMB No. 1545-0938

For calendar year 20 **14** , or tax year beginning   , 20   , and ending   , 20   .

A Date of IC-DISC election	Name

FLAGco IC-DISC

C Employer identification number

89-6423781

January 1, 2014   Number, street, and room or suite no. (or P.O. box if mail is not delivered to street address)

239 Arch Street

D Date incorporated

January 1, 2014

B Business activity code no. (See instructions.)

4 2 3 9 9 0   City or town, state, and ZIP code

Philadelphia, PA 19106

E Total assets (see instructions)

$ 3,000,000

F   Check applicable box(es): (1) ☑ Initial return   (2) ☐ Final return   (3) ☐ Name change   (4) ☐ Address change   (5) ☐ Amended return

G(1)   Did any corporation, individual, partnership, trust, or estate own, directly or indirectly, 50% or more of the IC-DISC's voting stock at the end of the IC-DISC's tax year? (See section 267(c) for rules of attribution.) . . . . .

      If "Yes," complete the following schedule. (If a foreign owner, see instructions.)

	Yes	**No**
	✓	

Name	Identifying number	Address	Voting stock owned	Total assets (corporations only)	Foreign owner	
					Yes	**No**
Betsy Ross	123-45-6789	239 Arch Street, Philadelphia, PA 19106	100 %			✓
			%			

(2)   Enter the following for any corporation listed in G(1) that will report the IC-DISC's income:

Tax year of first corporation	IRS Service Center where return will be filed
Tax year of second corporation	IRS Service Center where return will be filed

H(1)   Check the appropriate box(es) to indicate any intercompany pricing rules that were applied to 25% or more of gross income (line 1 below):

     ☐ 50-50 combined taxable income method   ☑ 4% gross receipts method   ☐ Section 482 method ("arm's length pricing")

(2)   Check here ☐ if the marginal costing rules under section 994(b)(2) were applied in figuring the combined taxable income for any transactions.

All Computations Must Reflect Intercompany Pricing Rules If Used (Section 994)
See separate Schedule P (Form 1120-IC-DISC).

Taxable Income

1	Gross income. Enter amount from Schedule B, line 4, column (e)	1	240,000
2	Cost of goods sold from Schedule A, line 8	2	
3	Total income. Subtract line 2 from line 1	3	240,000
4	Deductions. Enter amount from Schedule E, line 3	4	
5	Taxable income before net operating loss deduction and dividends-received deduction. Subtract line 4 from line 3	5	240,000
6a	Net operating loss deduction (attach statement)	6a	
b	Dividends-received deduction from Schedule C, line 9	6b	
c	Add lines 6a and 6b	6c	
7	**Taxable income.** Subtract line 6c from line 5	7	240,000
8	Refundable credit for federal tax paid on fuels (attach Form 4136)	8	

Sign Here

Under penalties of perjury, I declare that I have examined this return, including accompanying schedules and statements, and to the best of my knowledge and belief, it is true, correct, and complete. Declaration of preparer (other than taxpayer) is based on all information of which preparer has any knowledge.

▶ _____   _____ ▶ _____
    Signature of officer   Date   Title

Paid Preparer Use Only	Print/Type preparer's name	Preparer's signature	Date	Check ☐ if self-employed	PTIN
	Firm's name ▶			Firm's EIN ▶	
	Firm's address ▶			Phone no.	

For Paperwork Reduction Act Notice, see instructions.   Cat. No. 11473P   Form **1120-IC-DISC** (Rev. 12-2012)

¶708

Form 1120-IC-DISC (Rev. 12-2012) Page **2**

| Schedule A | **Cost of Goods Sold** (see instructions) |

If the intercompany pricing rules of section 994 are used, reflect **actual** purchases from a related supplier at the transfer price determined under such rules. See separate Schedule P (Form 1120-IC-DISC).

1	Inventory at beginning of the year	1	
2	Purchases	2	
3	Cost of labor	3	
4	Additional section 263A costs (attach statement)	4	
5	Other costs (attach statement)	5	
6	**Total.** Add lines 1 through 5	6	
7	Inventory at end of the year	7	
8	**Cost of goods sold.** Subtract line 7 from line 6. Enter here and on line 2, page 1	8	

9a Check all methods used for valuing closing inventory:

(i) ☐ Cost

(ii) ☐ Lower of cost or market

(iii) ☐ Other (Specify method used and attach statement.) ▶ _____

b Check if there was a writedown of subnormal goods . . . . ▶ ☐

c Check if the LIFO inventory method was adopted this tax year for any goods. (If checked, attach Form 970.) . . . . . ▶ ☐

d If the LIFO inventory method was used for this tax year, enter amount of closing inventory computed under LIFO . . . . | 9d | |

e If property is produced or acquired for resale, do the rules of section 263A apply to the corporation? . . . . ☐ Yes ☐ No

f Was there any change in determining quantities, cost, or valuations between the opening and closing inventory? (If "Yes," attach statement.) ☐ Yes ☐ No

| Schedule B | **Gross Income** (see instructions) |

(a) Type of receipts	Commission sales		(d) Other receipts	(e) Total (add columns (c) and (d))
	(b) Gross receipts	(c) Commission		
1 Qualified export receipts from sale of export property—				
a To unrelated purchasers:				
(i) Direct foreign sales	6,000,000	240,000		240,000
(ii) Foreign sales through a related foreign entity				
(iii) Persons in the United States (other than an unrelated IC-DISC)				
(iv) An unrelated IC-DISC				
b To related purchasers:				
(i) Direct foreign sales				
(ii) Persons in the United States				
c Total				240,000
2 Other qualified export receipts:				
a Leasing or renting of export property				
b Services related and subsidiary to a qualified export sale or lease				
c Engineering and architectural services				
d Export management services				
e Qualified dividends (Schedule C, line 15)				
f Interest on producer's loans				
g Other interest (attach statement)				
h Capital gain net income (attach Schedule D (Form 1120))				
i Net gain or (loss) from Part II, Form 4797 (attach Form 4797)				
j Other (attach statement)				
k Total				
3 Nonqualified gross receipts:				
a Ultimate use in United States				
b Exports subsidized by the U.S. Government				
c Certain direct or indirect sales or leases for use by the U.S. Government				
d Sales to other IC-DISCs in the same controlled group				
e Nonqualified dividends (Schedule C, line 16)				
f Other (attach statement)				
g Total				
4 **Total.** Add lines 1c, 2k, 3g, column (e). Enter here and on line 1, page 1				240,000

Form **1120-IC-DISC** (Rev. 12-2012)

Form 1120-IC-DISC (Rev. 12-2012)   Page **3**

Schedule C   **Dividends and Dividends-Received Deduction** (see instructions)

		(a) Dividends received	(b) %	(c) Dividends–received deduction: ((a) × (b))
1	Dividends from less-than-20%-owned domestic corporations (other than debt-financed stock)		70	
2	Dividends from 20%-or-more-owned domestic corporations (other than debt-financed stock)		80	
3	Dividends on debt-financed stock of domestic and foreign corporations . . .		see instructions	
4	Dividends on certain preferred stock of less-than-20%-owned public utilities . .		42	
5	Dividends on certain preferred stock of 20%-or-more-owned public utilities . .		48	
6	Dividends from less-than-20%-owned foreign corporations		70	
7	Dividends from 20%-or-more-owned foreign corporations		80	
8	Dividends from wholly owned foreign subsidiaries		100	
9	**Total.** Add lines 1 through 8. See instructions for limitation			
10	Dividends from foreign corporations not included on lines 3, 6, 7, or 8			
11	Income from controlled foreign corporations under subpart F (attach Form(s) 5471)			
12	IC-DISC and former DISC dividends not included on lines 1, 2, or 3			
13	Other dividends			
14	**Total dividends.** Add lines 1 through 13, column (a)			
15	Qualified dividends. Enter here and on Schedule B, line 2e, column (d)			
16	Nonqualified dividends. Subtract line 15 from line 14. Enter here and on Schedule B, line 3e, column (d)			

Schedule E   **Deductions** (Before completing, see **Limitations on Deductions** in the instructions.)

1	Export promotion expenses:		
a	Market studies	1a	
b	Advertising	1b	
c	Depreciation (attach Form 4562)	1c	
d	Salaries and wages	1d	
e	Rents	1e	
f	Sales commissions	1f	
g	Warehousing	1g	
h	Freight (excluding insurance)	1h	
i	Compensation of officers	1i	
j	Repairs and maintenance	1j	
k	Pension, profit-sharing, etc., plans	1k	
l	Employee benefit programs	1l	
m	Other (list): _____		
	_____	1m	
n	**Total.** Add lines 1a through 1m	1n	
2	Other expenses not deducted on line 1:		
a	Bad debts	2a	
b	Taxes and licenses	2b	
c	Interest	2c	
d	Contributions	2d	
e	Freight	2e	
f	Freight insurance	2f	
g	Other (list): _____		
	_____	2g	
h	**Total.** Add lines 2a through 2g	2h	
3	**Total deductions.** Add lines 1n and 2h. Enter here and on line 4, page 1	3	

Form **1120-IC-DISC** (Rev. 12-2012)

Form 1120-IC-DISC (Rev. 12-2012) Page **4**

Schedule J	**Deemed and Actual Distributions and Deferred DISC Income for the Tax Year**		
	Part I—Deemed Distributions Under Section 995(b)(1) (see instructions)		
1	Gross interest derived during the tax year from producer's loans (section 995(b)(1)(A))	1	
2	Gain recognized on the sale or exchange of section 995(b)(1)(B) property (attach statement)	2	
3	Gain recognized on the sale or exchange of section 995(b)(1)(C) property (attach statement)	3	
4	50% of taxable income attributable to military property (section 995(b)(1)(D)) (attach statement)	4	
5	Taxable income from line 7, Part II, below	5	
6	Taxable income of the IC-DISC (from line 7, page 1)	6	
7	Add lines 1 through 5	7	
8	Subtract line 7 from line 6	8	
9	If you have shareholders that are C corporations, enter one-seventeenth of line 8 (.0588235 times line 8)	9	
10	International boycott income (see instructions)	10	
11	Illegal bribes and other payments	11	
	Note: *Separate computations for lines 12–23 are required for shareholders that are C corporations and shareholders that are **not** C corporations. Complete lines 12, 14, 15, 17a, 18, 20, and 22 for shareholders that are **not** C corporations. Complete lines 13, 14, 16, 17b, 19, 21, and 23 for shareholders that **are** C corporations.*		
12	Add lines 7, 10, and 11	12	
13	Add lines 7, 9, 10, and 11	13	
14	Earnings and profits for the tax year (attach statement)	14	
15	Enter the smaller of line 12 or 14	15	
16	Enter the smaller of line 13 or 14	16	
17	Foreign investment attributable to producer's loans (attach statement):		
a	For shareholders other than C corporations	17a	
b	For shareholders that are C corporations	17b	
18	Add lines 15 and 17a	18	
19	Add lines 16 and 17b	19	
20	Enter percentage of stock owned by shareholders other than C corporations	20	%
21	Enter percentage of stock owned by shareholders that are C corporations	21	%
22	Multiply line 18 by line 20 (Allocate to shareholders other than C corporations)	22	
23	Multiply line 19 by line 21 (Allocate to C corporation shareholders)	23	
24	**Total deemed distributions under section 995(b)(1) for all shareholders.** Add lines 22 and 23	24	
	Part II—Section 995(b)(1)(E) Taxable Income (see instructions)		
1	Total qualified export receipts (see instructions)	1	
2	Statutory maximum	2	$10,000,000
3	Controlled group member's portion of the statutory maximum	3	
4	Enter smaller of **(a)** 1 or **(b)** number of days in tax year divided by 365 (or 366) (see instructions)	4	
5	Proration. Multiply line 2 or 3, whichever is applicable, by line 4	5	
6	Excess qualified export receipts. Subtract line 5 from line 1. (If line 5 exceeds line 1, enter -0- here and on line 7 below.)	6	
7	Taxable income attributable to line 6 receipts. Enter here and on line 5 of Part I above	7	
	Part III—Deemed Distributions Under Section 995(b)(2) (see instructions)		
1	Annual installment of distribution attributable to revocation of election in an earlier year	1	
2	Annual installment of distribution attributable to not qualifying as a DISC or IC-DISC in an earlier year	2	
3	**Total deemed distributions under section 995(b)(2).** Add lines 1 and 2	3	
	Part IV—Actual Distributions (see instructions)		
1	Distributions to meet qualification requirements under section 992(c) (attach computation statement)	1	
2	Other actual distributions	2	240,000
3	**Total.** Add lines 1 and 2	3	240,000
4	Amount on line 3 treated as distributed from:		
a	Previously taxed income	4a	
b	Accumulated IC-DISC income (including IC-DISC income of the current year)	4b	
c	Other earnings and profits	4c	
d	Other	4d	
	Part V—Deferred DISC Income Under Section 995(f)(3) (see instructions)		
1	Accumulated IC-DISC income (for periods after 1984) at end of computation year	1	
2	Distributions-in-excess-of-income for the tax year following the computation year to which line 1 applies	2	
3	Deferred DISC income under section 995(f)(3). Subtract line 2 from line 1	3	

Form **1120-IC-DISC** (Rev. 12-2012)

Form 1120-IC-DISC (Rev. 12-2012)   Page **5**

Schedule L		Balance Sheets per Books	(a) Beginning of tax year	(b) End of tax year
Assets	1	Qualified export assets:		
	a	Working capital (cash and necessary temporary investments)	3,000	3,000
	b	Funds awaiting investment (cash in U.S. banks in excess of working capital needs) in other qualified export assets		
	c	Export-Import Bank obligations		
	d	Trade receivables (accounts and notes receivable)		
		Less allowance for bad debts	( )	( )
	e	Export property (net) (including inventory and qualified property held for lease)		
	f	Producer's loans		
	g	Investment in related foreign export corporations		
	h	Depreciable assets		
		Less accumulated depreciation	( )	( )
	i	Other (attach statement)		
	2	Nonqualified assets (net) (list):		
	3	**Total assets.** Combine lines 1a through 2	3,000	3,000
Liabilities and Shareholders' Equity	4	Accounts payable		
	5	Other current liabilities (attach statement)		
	6	Mortgages, notes, bonds payable in 1 year or more		
	7	Other liabilities (attach statement)		
	8	Capital stock	3,000	3,000
	9	Additional paid-in capital		
	10	Other earnings and profits		
	11	Previously taxed income (section 996(f)(2))		
	12	Accumulated pre-1985 DISC income (see instructions)		
	13	Accumulated IC-DISC income (see instructions)		
	14	Less cost of treasury stock	( )	( )
	15	Total liabilities and shareholders' equity	3,000	3,000

Schedule M-1	Reconciliation of Income per Books With Income per Return			
1	Net income (loss) per books	240,000	6 Income recorded on books this year not included on this return (itemize):	
2	Excess of capital losses over capital gains			
3	Taxable income not recorded on books this year (itemize):		7 Deductions on this return not charged against book income this year (itemize):	
4	Expenses recorded on books this year and not deducted on this return (itemize):			
			8 Add lines 6 and 7	0
5	Add lines 1 through 4	240,000	9 Income (line 5, page 1)—line 5 less line 8	240,000

Schedule M-2	Analysis of Other Earnings and Profits (Line 10, Schedule L)			
1	Balance at beginning of year . . .		5 Distributions to qualify under section 992(c)	
2	Increases (itemize):		6 Other decreases (itemize):	
		240,000		(240,000)
3	Add lines 1 and 2	240,000	7 Add lines 4 through 6	(240,000)
4	Deficit in earnings and profits . .		8 Balance at end of year (line 3 less line 7)	0

Schedule M-3	Analysis of Previously Taxed Income (Line 11, Schedule L)			
1	Balance at beginning of year . . .	0	5 Deficit in earnings and profits	
2	Deemed distributions under section 995(b)		6 Distributions to qualify under section 992(c)	
3	Other increases (itemize):		7 Other decreases (itemize):	
			8 Add lines 5 through 7	0
4	Add lines 1 through 3	0	9 Balance at end of year (line 4 less line 8)	0

Schedule M-4	Analysis of Accumulated IC-DISC Income (Line 13, Schedule L)			
1	Balance at beginning of year . . .	0	6 Distributions to qualify under section 992(c)	
2	Increases (itemize):		7 Distributions upon disqualification (sec. 995(b)(2))	
		240,000	8 Other decreases (itemize):	
3	Add lines 1 and 2	240,000		240,000
4	Deficit in earnings and profits . . .	0	9 Add lines 4 through 8	240,000
5	Redemptions under section 996(d) . .		10 Balance at end of year (line 3 less line 9)	0

Form **1120-IC-DISC** (Rev. 12-2012)

Form 1120-IC-DISC (Rev. 12-2012)   Page **6**

Schedule N   **Export Gross Receipts of the IC-DISC and Related U.S. Persons** (see instructions)

1   See the instructions and enter the product code and percentage of total export gross receipts for **(a)** the largest and **(b)** 2nd largest product or service sold or provided by the IC-DISC:

(a) Code   229   Percentage of total   100 %   **(b)** Code _____   Percentage of total _____ %

2   **Export gross receipts for the current tax year**

(a) Export gross receipts of the IC-DISC	**Export gross receipts of related U.S. persons**	
	(b) Related IC-DISCs	**(c)** All other related U.S. persons
		6,000,000

3   If item 2(b) or 2(c) is completed, complete the following (if more space is needed, attach a statement following the format below):

(a) IC-DISCs in Your Controlled Group

Name	Address	Identifying number

(b) All Other Related U.S. Persons in Your Controlled Group

Name	Address	Identifying number
FlagCo	Boston, MA	89-1234567

Schedule O   **Other Information** (see instructions)

		Yes	No
1	See the instructions and enter the main:		
a	Business activity ▶ 423990 **b** Product or service ▶ flags		
2a	Did 95% or more of the IC-DISC's gross receipts for the tax year consist of qualified export receipts (defined in section 993(a))?	✓	
b	Did the adjusted basis of the IC-DISC's qualified export assets (as defined in section 993(b)) at the end of the tax year equal or exceed 95% of the sum of the adjusted basis of all the IC-DISC's assets at the end of the tax year?	✓	
c	If **a** or **b** is "No," did the IC-DISC make a pro rata distribution of property as defined in section 992(c)?		✓
3	Was the IC-DISC have more than one class of stock at any time during the tax year?		✓
4	Was the par or stated value of the IC-DISC's stock at least $2,500 on each day of the tax year (for a new corporation, this means on the last day for making an election to be an IC-DISC and for each later day)?	✓	
5	Did the IC-DISC keep separate books and records?	✓	
6a	Does the IC-DISC or any member of the IC-DISC's controlled group (as defined in section 993(a)(3)) have operations in or related to any country (or with the government, a company, or a national of that country) associated with carrying out the boycott of Israel that is on the list kept by the Secretary of the Treasury under section 999(a)(3)?		✓
b	Did the IC-DISC or any member of the controlled group of which the IC-DISC is a member have operations in any unlisted country that the IC-DISC knows or has reason to know requires participation in or cooperation with an international boycott against Israel?		✓
c	Did the IC-DISC or any member of the controlled group of which the IC-DISC is a member have operations in any country that the IC-DISC knows or has reason to know requires participation in or cooperation with an international boycott other than the boycott of Israel?		✓

If the answer to any of the questions in 6 is "Yes," see instructions and **Form 5713**, International Boycott Report.

7   Enter the amount of tax-exempt interest income received or accrued during the tax year ▶ $ _____

8   At any time during the tax year, did one foreign person own, directly or indirectly, at least 25% of
(a) the total voting power of all classes of stock of the corporation entitled to vote or
(b) the total value of all classes of stock of the corporation?
If "Yes," enter: a   Percentage owned ▶ _____ and
                    b   Owner's country ▶ _____
                    c   The corporation may have to file Form 5472, Information Return of a 25% Foreign-Owned U.S. Corporation or a Foreign Corporation Engaged in a U.S. Trade or Business. Enter number of Forms 5472 attached ▶ _____

Note: If the IC-DISC, at any time during the tax year, had assets or operated a business in a foreign country or U.S. possession, it may be required to attach **Schedule N (Form 1120)**, Foreign Operations of U.S. Corporations, to this return. See Schedule N for details.

Form **1120-IC-DISC** (Rev. 12-2012)

¶708

¶708

SCHEDULE K
(Form 1120-IC-DISC)

Department of the Treasury
Internal Revenue Service

Shareholder's Statement of IC-DISC Distributions—2014

For calendar year 2014 or tax year

beginning ___ January 1 ___, 2014, ending ___ January 1 ___, 20 __ 14

(Complete for each shareholder. See instructions on back of Copy C.)

OMB No. 1545-0123

COPY A – Attach to
Form 1120-IC-DISC

Part I   Taxable Distributions

1 Deemed distributions: **a** Under section 995(b)(1)	1a	
b Annual installment under section 995(b)(2)	1b	
c Total. Add lines 1a and 1b	1c	
2 Actual taxable distributions	2	240,000
3 **Total taxable distributions.** Add line 1c and line 2. Enter here and in Section A or B below	3	240,000

Section A—C Corporations

4a Part of line 3 above entitled to section 243 dividends-received deduction	4a	
b Part of line 3 above **not** entitled to section 243 dividends-received deduction	4b	

Section B—Shareholders Other Than C Corporations

5 Amount of taxable dividends included on line 3	5	240,000

Part II   Nontaxable Distributions

6 Actual distributions from previously taxed income and accumulated pre-1985 DISC income	6	
7 Other actual nontaxable distributions	7	
8 **Total nontaxable distributions.** Add lines 6 and 7	8	

Part III   Other Information

9 Accumulated IC-DISC income attributable to stock sold during the year	9	
10 Deferred DISC income. See instructions	10	

Name, employer identification number, and address (including ZIP code)
of IC-DISC, former DISC, or former IC-DISC

FLAGco IC-DISC
239 Arch Street
Philadelphia, PA 19106

Shareholder's name, identifying number, and address (including ZIP code)

Betsy Ross
123-45-6789
239 Arch Street
Philadelphia, PA 19106

For Paperwork Reduction Act Notice, see the Instructions for Form 1120-IC-DISC.   www.irs.gov/form1120icdisc   Cat. No. 11474A   **Schedule K (Form 1120-IC-DISC) 2014**

SCHEDULE P
(Form 1120-IC-DISC)
(Rev. December 2008)
Department of the Treasury
Internal Revenue Service

Intercompany Transfer Price or Commission

Attach a separate schedule for each transaction or group of transactions to which the intercompany pricing rules under section 994(a)(1) and (2) are applied.

For the calendar year 20 **14**, or fiscal year beginning_____, 20___, and ending _____, 20___

For amount reported on line _____, Schedule _____, Form 1120-IC-DISC

OMB No. 1545-0938

Name as shown on Form 1120-IC-DISC	Employer identification number	
FLAGco IC-DISC	89	6423781

Identify product or product line reported on this schedule. (Also, enter the Principal Business Activity code number, if used.) (See instructions.)

423990 Flags

This schedule is for a (check one):
Single transaction . . . . . . ☐
Group of transactions . . . . . ☐

Part I   IC-DISC Taxable Income

SECTION A—Combined Taxable Income

<table>
<tr><td colspan="3" align="center">Section A-1—If marginal costing is not used</td><td></td><td></td></tr>
<tr><td>1</td><td colspan="2">Gross receipts from transaction between IC-DISC (or related supplier) and third party . . . . .</td><td>1</td><td>6,000,000</td></tr>
<tr><td>2</td><td colspan="2">Less costs and expenses allocable to gross receipts from transaction:</td><td></td><td></td></tr>
<tr><td>a</td><td>Cost of goods sold from property if sold, or depreciation from property if leased</td><td>2a 5,000,000</td><td></td><td></td></tr>
<tr><td>b</td><td>Related supplier's expenses allocable to gross receipts from transaction . .</td><td>2b 520,000</td><td></td><td></td></tr>
<tr><td>c</td><td>IC-DISC export promotion expenses allocable to gross receipts from transaction</td><td>2c</td><td></td><td></td></tr>
<tr><td>d</td><td>Other IC-DISC expenses allocable to gross receipts from transaction . . .</td><td>2d</td><td></td><td></td></tr>
<tr><td>e</td><td>Add lines 2a through 2d</td><td></td><td>2e</td><td>5,520,000</td></tr>
<tr><td>3</td><td colspan="2">Combined taxable income. Subtract line 2e from line 1. If a loss, enter -0- . . . .</td><td>3</td><td>480,000</td></tr>
<tr><td colspan="3" align="center">Section A-2—If marginal costing is used</td><td></td><td></td></tr>
<tr><td>4</td><td colspan="2">Gross receipts from resale by IC-DISC (or sale by related supplier) to third party . . . .</td><td>4</td><td></td></tr>
<tr><td>5</td><td colspan="2">Costs and expenses allocable to gross receipts from sale:</td><td></td><td></td></tr>
<tr><td>a</td><td>Cost of direct material from property sold . . . .</td><td>5a</td><td></td><td></td></tr>
<tr><td>b</td><td>Cost of direct labor from property sold . . . .</td><td>5b</td><td></td><td></td></tr>
<tr><td>c</td><td>IC-DISC export promotion expenses allocable to gross receipts from sales that are claimed as promotional . . . .</td><td>5c</td><td></td><td></td></tr>
<tr><td>d</td><td>Add lines 5a through 5c . . . .</td><td></td><td>5d</td><td></td></tr>
<tr><td>6</td><td colspan="2">Combined taxable income or (loss) before application of overall profit percentage limitation. Subtract line 5d from line 4. If a loss, skip lines 7 through 11 and enter -0- on line 12 . . . . . .</td><td>6</td><td></td></tr>
<tr><td>7</td><td colspan="2">Gross receipts of related supplier and IC-DISC (or controlled group) from all foreign and domestic sales of the product or product line . . . .</td><td>7</td><td></td></tr>
<tr><td>8</td><td colspan="2">Costs and expenses of related supplier and IC-DISC (or controlled group) allocable to gross income from such sales:</td><td></td><td></td></tr>
<tr><td>a</td><td>Cost of goods sold from property sold . . . .</td><td>8a</td><td></td><td></td></tr>
<tr><td>b</td><td>Expenses allocable to gross receipts from such sales . . . .</td><td>8b</td><td></td><td></td></tr>
<tr><td>c</td><td>Add lines 8a and 8b . . . .</td><td></td><td>8c</td><td></td></tr>
<tr><td>9</td><td colspan="2">Subtract line 8c from line 7. If a loss, skip lines 10 and 11 and enter -0- on line 12. . . . .</td><td>9</td><td></td></tr>
<tr><td>10</td><td colspan="2">Overall profit percentage. Divide line 9 by line 7. Check if controlled group optional method is used . . . . ▶ ☐</td><td>10</td><td>%</td></tr>
<tr><td>11</td><td colspan="2">Overall profit percentage limitation. Multiply line 4 by line 10 . . . .</td><td>11</td><td></td></tr>
<tr><td>12</td><td colspan="2">Combined taxable income. Enter the smaller of line 6 or line 11. . . . .</td><td>12</td><td></td></tr>
</table>

SECTION B—50-50 Combined Taxable Income Method (Must be used if marginal costing is used. See instructions.)

13	Combined taxable income. Enter amount from line 3 or line 12	13	
14	Multiply line 13 by 50% (.50)	14	
15	Enter 10% (.10) of IC-DISC export promotion expenses allocable to gross income from transactions that are claimed as export promotion	15	
16	Add lines 14 and 15	16	
17	**IC-DISC taxable income.** Enter the smaller of line 13 or line 16	17	

SECTION C—4% Gross Receipts Method (Cannot be used if marginal costing is used.)

18	Gross receipts from transaction. Enter amount from line 1	18	6,000,000
19	Multiply line 18 by 4% (.04)	19	240,000
20	Multiply line 2c by 10% (.10)	20	
21	Add lines 19 and 20	21	240,000
22	Combined taxable income. Enter amount from line 3 or amount computed under special rule. If special rule is applied, check here ☐. See instructions.	22	480,000
23	**IC-DISC taxable income.** Enter the smaller of line 21 or line 22	23	240,000

For Paperwork Reduction Act Notice, see the Instructions for Form 1120-IC-DISC.   Cat. No. 11478S   Schedule P (Form 1120-IC-DISC) (Rev. 12-2008)

Schedule P (Form 1120-IC-DISC) (Rev. 12-2008)   Page **2**

Part II	**Transfer Price From Related Supplier to IC-DISC** (See instructions.)		
24	Gross receipts from transaction. Enter amount from line 1 or line 4, Part I	24	
25	Less reductions:		
a	IC-DISC taxable income (but not to exceed amount determined in Part I)	25a	
b	IC-DISC export promotion expenses allocable to gross income from transaction	25b	
c	Other IC-DISC expenses allocable to gross income from transaction	25c	
d	Add lines 25a through 25c	25d	
26	**Transfer price from related supplier to IC-DISC.** Subtract line 25d from line 24	26	
Part III	**IC-DISC Commission From Related Supplier** (See instructions.)		
27	IC-DISC taxable income (but not to exceed amount determined in Part I)	27	240,000
28	IC-DISC export promotion expenses allocable to gross receipts from transaction	28	
29	Other IC-DISC expenses allocable to gross receipts from transaction	29	
30	**IC-DISC commission from related supplier.** Add lines 27 through 29	30	240,000

Instructions

Section references are to the Internal Revenue Code unless otherwise noted.

Purpose of schedule. Use Schedule P to show the computation of taxable income used in computing (1) the transfer price from a related supplier to an IC-DISC (Part II) or (2) the IC-DISC commission from a related supplier (Part III).

Complete and attach a separate Schedule P to Form 1120-IC-DISC for each transaction or group of transactions to which the intercompany pricing rules of sections 994(a)(1) and (2) are applied.

IC-DISC taxable income. Generally, the intercompany pricing determinations are to be made on a transaction-by-transaction basis. However, the IC-DISC may make an annual election to determine intercompany pricing on the basis of groups consisting of products or product lines. If the group basis is elected, then all transactions for that product or product line must be grouped. Each group is limited to one type of transaction (i.e., sales, leases, or commissions).

A product or product line determination will be accepted if it conforms to either of the following standards: (1) a recognized industry or trade usage or (2) major product groups (or any subclassifications within a major product group) (see *Schedule P (Form 1120-IC-DISC) Codes for Principal Business Activity* on page 13 of the Instructions for Form 1120-IC-DISC). The corporation may choose a product grouping for one product and use the transaction-by-transaction method for another product within the same tax year.

Generally, the computation of taxable income under the intercompany pricing rules will not be permitted to the extent that their application would result in a loss to the related supplier.

Each of the following methods may be applied for sales, leases, and services. See the regulations under section 994.

50-50 combined taxable income method. The transfer price the related supplier charges the IC-DISC, or the related supplier's IC-DISC commission, is the amount that lowers the taxable income the IC-DISC derives from the

transaction to an amount that is no more than the sum of (1) 50% of the IC-DISC's and related supplier's combined taxable income attributable to the qualified export receipts from the transaction and (2) 10% of the IC-DISC's export promotion expenses (as defined in Regulations section 1.994-1(f)) attributable to the qualified export receipts. Do not include in combined taxable income (line 13) the discount amount reflected in receivables (on the sale of export property) that a related supplier transferred to the IC-DISC. See Regulations sections 1.994-1(c)(3) and (6)(v).

See Part I, Section A instructions below if marginal costing rules apply.

4% gross receipts method. The transfer price charged by the related supplier to the IC-DISC or IC-DISC commission from the related supplier is the amount that ensures that the taxable income derived by the IC-DISC from the transaction does not exceed the sum of (1) 4% of the qualified export receipts of the IC-DISC derived from the transaction and (2) 10% of the export promotion expenses (as defined in Regulations section 1.994-1(f)) of the IC-DISC attributable to the qualified export receipts.

Section 482 method. The transfer price the related supplier charged the IC-DISC, or IC-DISC commission from the related supplier, is the amount actually charged, but is subject to the arm's length standard of section 482. Do not complete Schedule P if the section 482 method is used.

Incomplete transactions. For the 50-50 and 4% methods, if the related supplier sells property to the IC-DISC during the year but the IC-DISC does not resell it during the year, the related supplier's transfer price to the IC-DISC must equal the related supplier's cost of goods sold. Do not complete Schedule P for incomplete transactions. The related supplier's transfer price to the IC-DISC must be recomputed for the year in which the IC-DISC resells the property and the transaction must then be reported on Schedule P for that year.

Part I, Section A—Combined Taxable Income. Complete Section A-1 only if marginal costing is not used.

For purposes of line 2d, be sure to include the appropriate apportionment of deductions that are not directly allocable such as interest expenses and stewardship expenses. See Temporary Regulations sections 1.861-11T(f) and 1.861-14T(f) for an explanation of appropriate apportionment.

Complete Section A-2 if marginal costing is used. The marginal costing rules may be used only for sales, or commissions on sales, of property if the 50-50 method is used.

Marginal costing cannot be used for (1) leasing of property, (2) performance of services, or (3) sales of export property that (in the hands of a purchaser related under section 954(d)(3) as foreign base company sales income as described in section 954(d) unless, for the purchaser's year in which it resells the property, section 954(b)(3)(A) applies or the income is under the exceptions in section 954(b)(4).

Line 22. The overall profit percentage may be computed under an optional method. See Regulations section 1.994-2(c)(2) for details.

Part I, Section B and Section C. Complete Section B or Section C. You must complete Section B if marginal costing is used.

Line 22. If IC-DISC taxable income on a sale is computed under the 4% method and the IC-DISC chooses to apply the special rule for transfer prices or commissions, check the box in line 22 and attach a separate computation of the limitation on IC-DISC taxable income determined under the special rule and enter the amount on line 22. Under the special rule, a transfer price or commission will not be considered to cause a loss for a related supplier if the IC-DISC's net profit on the sale does not exceed the IC-DISC's and related supplier's net profit percentage on all their sales of the product or product line. See Regulations section 1.994-1(e)(1)(ii) for details.

Reporting Part II and Part III amounts on Form 1120-IC-DISC. If the computed transfer price for sales, leases, or services (Part II) or IC-DISC commission (Part III) is entered on more than one line of Form 1120-IC-DISC, attach an explanation indicating the portion of the total that is applied to each line.

Schedule P (Form 1120-IC-DISC) (Rev. 12-2008)

Chapter 8
Planning for Foreign Operations

¶ 801 INTRODUCTION

This chapter discusses general planning issues with respect to a U.S. company's foreign operations. More specific planning issues are discussed throughout the book. For example, Chapter 4 (¶ 401) discusses strategies for eliminating excess foreign tax credits and planning for dividend repatriations from foreign subsidiaries, Chapter 12 (¶ 1201) discusses developing a transfer pricing strategy, and Chapter 7 (¶ 701) discusses techniques for maximizing certain export tax benefits.

¶ 802 EVOLUTION OF A U.S. EXPORTER

.01 Entering a Foreign Market

There are several options available to a U.S. company that wishes to sell its products abroad. For example, a U.S. company may initially export its products through independent brokers or distributors. Smaller U.S. exporters, in particular, may find it advantageous to use independent intermediaries to market their goods abroad as the exporters may lack expertise regarding foreign markets and international trade. There are costs to such an arrangement, however, including the need to share profits with the intermediary (either through commission costs or reduced sales revenues) and the loss of control over the sales and distribution functions.

As the exporter's sales volume grows and the exporter becomes more familiar with international trade, the exporter may wish to bring the foreign marketing function in-house by having U.S. employees travel abroad in order to identify customers, display inventory, negotiate sales agreements, and provide technical support. Alternatively, the exporter could employ residents of the foreign market to perform these functions.

The next logical step in the progression of a U.S. company's foreign marketing activities is to establish a liaison or branch sales office within the importing country. The activities of a liaison office usually are limited to advertising and promotion, storing or displaying merchandise, market research, and liaising with agents, distributors, and customers. As foreign sales volume increases, however, the U.S. company may wish to have its foreign office also negotiate and close sales agreements and distribute its products. These activities would elevate the status of the foreign operation to that a branch sales office. A foreign presence often is required in the case of export sales of services. For example, an export sale of construction services usually requires that U.S. engineers and technicians travel abroad in order to provide on-site management of the project.

Licensing and franchising are more indirect methods of entering a foreign market. A U.S. company that owns a patent, trademark, or other intangible property can license that intangible to a company located in a foreign country. In return, the licensor receives a percentage of the local sales of the licensed or franchised product in the form of a royalty. In essence, licensing and franchising are types of joint venture arrangements that permit a U.S. company to enter a foreign market quickly, but may not produce the same profit margins that are potentially available from more direct forms of exporting. Moreover, the U.S. company may lose some control over the quality and image of its product.

.02 Basic Tax Issues

Export sales. U.S. exporters that sell their products through independent distributors will not have a taxable presence within the importing country and, therefore, foreign tax reduction planning is a moot issue. Nevertheless, foreign tax credit planning may still be worthwhile since the U.S. exporter may be subject to foreign taxation in the future and excess foreign tax credits can be carried back one year. One potential strategy is to pass title abroad on export sales, in which case export sales will generate foreign-source income.

A U.S. exporter that sells its products using its own sales force faces the same tax issues (e.g., title passage) as those faced by companies that export through independent distributors. In addition, the presence of employees in the importing country may expose the U.S. exporter to foreign taxation. As discussed in the next section, whether the U.S. exporter will be subject to host country taxation depends on the internal tax laws of the host country and the provisions of any applicable tax treaties. Typically, the U.S. exporter will be subject to host country taxation only if it has a permanent establishment within the host country.

A U.S. exporter that establishes a foreign sales office must decide whether to structure the foreign sales operation as a branch or a subsidiary. In addition, assuming the sales office constitutes a taxable presence within the host country, the U.S. exporter must determine its taxable income for foreign tax purposes. The profit of a foreign sales office usually is computed based on the fiction that the office is an independent enterprise dealing at arm's length with the U.S. home office. Therefore, the more functions performed and the greater the risks assumed by the foreign sales office, the more profit it should earn (whether this profit is all foreign-source income for purposes of the foreign tax credit limitation is another matter). For example, if the office operates as a buy-sell distributor that assumes inventory risk, credit risk, and warranty risk, then its profit should be greater than a sales office that functions as a mere commission agent that never takes title to the goods.

Table 8.1 summarizes the primary tax issues associated with the different stages of foreign marketing activities.

TABLE 8.1. EXPORT SALES—BASIC TAX ISSUES

Export sales activities	*Basic tax issues*
Export through independent distributors	• Title passage
	• Export benefits
Export using employee salespersons	• Title passage and export benefits
	• Permanent establishment (PE)
Establish foreign sales office	• Title passage, export benefits, and PE
	• Branch versus subsidiary
	• Profit allocable to sales office

Licensing and franchising. A principal tax issue associated with entering into licensing and franchising arrangements with foreign persons is the appropriate foreign withholding tax rate on the U.S. company's royalty income. Most income tax treaties provide for reduced withholding tax rates on royalties derived by a foreign licensor. Typically, the rate is 10% or less and, in some treaties, varies with whether the payment is an industrial royalty (e.g., a payment for the use of a patent, trade secret, or formula), a motion picture or television royalty, or some other type of royalty, such as a payment for the use of a copyright on a book. Table 8.2 presents the royalty withholding tax rates for some of our major trading partners.

TABLE 8.2. TREATY WITHHOLDING TAX RATES ON ROYALTIES DERIVED BY U.S. RESIDENTS[1]

	Treaty withholding rate			
Foreign payer's country of residence	*Industrial*	*Patents*	*Film and TV*	*Copyrights*
Canada.	0%	0%	10%	0%
China.	10%	10%	10%	10%
France	0%	0%	0%	0%
Germany	0%	0%	0%	0%
Italy.	8%	8%	8%	0%
Japan	0%	0%	0%	0%
Mexico.	10%	10%	10%	10%
United Kingdom	0%	0%	0%	0%

[1] Taken from Table 1 of IRS Publication 515 (December 2014), which is reproduced in its entirety in the appendix to Chapter 13 (¶ 1305).

¶802.02

¶ 803 DETERMINANTS OF HOST COUNTRY TAXATION

A central tax issue for a U.S. exporter is whether its export profits will be subject to foreign taxation. Foreign taxation is an important issue for two reasons. First, complying with foreign tax laws entails administrative costs. Second, if the foreign income taxes paid or accrued exceed the taxpayer's foreign tax credit limitation, the resulting excess foreign tax credits represent an out-of-pocket tax cost. Whether a U.S. exporter's activities are subject to foreign taxation depends on several factors, including the nature of the taxpayer's activities within the foreign country, the internal tax laws of the foreign country, and the provisions of any income tax treaty between the foreign country and the United States.

As a general rule, most countries assert tax jurisdiction over all of the income derived from sources within their borders, regardless of the citizenship or residence of the person receiving that income. However, most tax treaties contain a permanent establishment provision under which a U.S. exporter's business profits are exempt from foreign taxation unless those profits are attributable to a permanent establishment located within the foreign country.[2] A permanent establishment includes a fixed place of business (e.g., a sales office), unless the fixed place of business is used solely for auxiliary functions (e.g., purchasing, storing, displaying, or delivering inventory), or activities of a preparatory nature (e.g., collecting information about potential customers).[3] A permanent establishment also exists if employees or other dependent agents habitually exercise in the foreign country an authority to conclude sales contracts in the taxpayer's name.[4] As a consequence, a U.S. exporter that sends executives or salespeople abroad to enter into contracts may create a permanent establishment even if those employees operate out of hotels and thus have no fixed place of business. Employees who limit their activities to auxiliary or preparatory activities, such as collecting information about potential customers, with sales concluded outside the foreign country (i.e., in the United States), will not create a permanent establishment. Marketing products abroad solely through independent foreign brokers or distributors also does not create a permanent establishment.[5]

¶ 804 STRUCTURING THE FOREIGN OPERATION

A U.S. company that engages in sales, service, or manufacturing activities abroad can structure that foreign operation as either a branch or a subsidiary. Therefore, a central tax issue in planning for foreign operations is determining the best legal structure.

.01 Branches

An unincorporated foreign branch is simply an extension of the domestic corporation, as opposed to a separate legal entity. Assuming the branch constitutes a permanent establishment, the branch will be subject to foreign country taxation. Branch taxable income usually is determined on the basis of a separate accounting,

---

[2] For example, *see* Article 7(1) of the U.S. Model Income Tax Treaty (¶ 1304.07).

[3] For example, *see* Article 5(1), (2), and (4) of the U.S. Model Income Tax Treaty (¶ 1304.05).

[4] For example, *see* Article 5(5) of the U.S. Model Income Tax Treaty (¶ 1304.05).

[5] For example, *see* Article 5(6) of the U.S. Model Income Tax Treaty (¶ 1304.05).

whereby the branch reports a profit equal to the amount it would have earned if it were an independent enterprise. Foreign countries usually allow a domestic corporation to allocate all direct costs, such as the cost of goods sold, against branch income. The host country also may allow charges against branch income for reasonable allocations of indirect expenses, such as interest expense and home office overhead.

From a U.S. tax perspective, the income derived by a foreign branch may represent foreign-source income earned directly by the domestic corporation. The branch's income is therefore subject to U.S. tax at the regular corporate rates, with a credit allowed for the lesser of the related foreign income taxes or the applicable foreign tax credit limitation. The taxpayer may owe a residual U.S. tax on the income of a branch operating in a low-tax foreign jurisdiction, whereas a branch operating in a high-tax foreign jurisdiction may create excess foreign tax credits.

The remittance of branch profits back to the U.S. home office is not a taxable event for U.S. tax purposes, except to the extent it triggers the recognition of a currency exchange gain or loss (see Chapter 6 (¶ 602)). Whether the remittance impacts the domestic corporation's foreign taxes depends on whether the host country has some type of branch profits tax. Most foreign countries impose withholding taxes on dividends paid by a local subsidiary to its U.S. parent. Some countries also have a branch profits tax, which is a withholding-type tax that is imposed on branch remittances.[6]

.02 Subsidiaries

A foreign subsidiary is a corporation organized under the laws of the foreign country and, therefore, is a separate legal entity from its U.S. parent. The subsidiary's earnings are usually subject to foreign country taxation by virtue of its foreign nationality or the source of its income. As with a branch, the subsidiary's taxable income should reflect the amount of income that the subsidiary would earn if it were an independent enterprise. To achieve this result, the U.S. parent corporation must use arm's length transfer prices for intercompany transactions. For example, if a foreign sales subsidiary purchases inventory from its U.S. parent for resale abroad, the transfer price should equal the sales price on comparable sales involving two unrelated entities.

The United States generally does not tax a U.S. parent corporation on the active foreign business profits earned through a foreign subsidiary until the subsidiary distributes those earnings to the U.S. parent as a dividend. This makes it possible for a domestic corporation to defer payment of the residual U.S. tax on the earnings of foreign subsidiaries operating in low-tax foreign jurisdictions.

Example **8.1**: USAco, a domestic corporation, earns $10 million of foreign-source income through a foreign sales office. Assume the U.S. tax rate is 35% and the foreign tax rate is 20%. If USAco structures the foreign sales office as a branch, the total tax burden on the $10 million of foreign-source income is

---

[6] For example, the United States imposes a branch profits tax on the dividend equivalent amounts of U.S. branches of foreign corporations. Code Sec. 884.

$3.5 million, consisting of foreign taxes of $2 million [20% × $10 million] and a residual U.S. tax of $1.5 million [$3.5 million pre-credit U.S. tax – $2 million foreign tax credit]. On the other hand, if USAco structures the foreign sales office as a subsidiary, the only current year tax due on the $10 million of foreign-source income is the foreign tax of $2 million [20% × $10 million]. Payment of the $1.5 million residual U.S. tax is deferred until the subsidiary distributes its earnings to USAco in the form of a dividend.

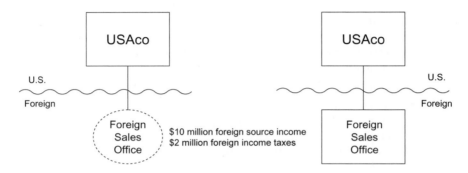

As discussed in Chapter 5 (¶ 501), certain types of unrepatriated income earned through a foreign subsidiary, such as passive investment income, are subject to immediate U.S. taxation.

One disadvantage of deferral is that net operating losses of foreign subsidiaries do not flow-through and offset the U.S. parent corporation's domestic profits. In contrast, a domestic corporation can deduct the losses of a foreign branch. A branch loss recapture rule prevents taxpayers from exploiting this advantage of the branch form by initially operating abroad as a branch and then converting to the subsidiary form when the foreign operation becomes profitable. Under the branch loss recapture rule, a domestic corporation must recognize a gain on the incorporation of a foreign branch to the extent it has previously deducted branch losses against its other taxable income.[7]

.03 Branch versus Subsidiary

The choice between the branch and subsidiary forms must take into account not only U.S. and foreign tax laws, but also general business considerations. There is no simple rule that dictates the best structure in all cases. Tax advantages of the subsidiary form include the following:

(i) A subsidiary generally allows a U.S. parent to defer the residual U.S. tax on low-tax foreign-source income.

(ii) The subsidiary form provides more control over the timing of income recognition for U.S. tax purposes, which may be useful in foreign tax credit planning. For example, a U.S. parent in an excess credit position may wish to avoid repatriating the earnings of a high-tax foreign subsidi-

---

[7] Code Sec. 367(a)(3)(C). The branch loss recapture rule is discussed in detail in Chapter 14 (¶ 1401).

ary and, thereby, store excess credits in that subsidiary until they can be used. This option is not available with a branch, because a branch's earnings are subject to immediate U.S. taxation.

(iii) Local tax incentives, such as a tax holiday, may be available only to a locally incorporated entity.

(iv) The sale of stock in a subsidiary results in a capital gain, which may be exempt from foreign taxation.

(v) The separate legal status of a subsidiary may make it easier to justify management fees and other intercompany charges (such as an allocation of indirect expenses) to foreign tax authorities.

Tax advantages of the branch form include the following:

(i) A domestic corporation can deduct the foreign losses of a branch against its U.S. profits. These losses are recaptured, however, if the branch later incorporates.[8]

(ii) The transfer of assets to a branch is a nontaxable event. In contrast, transfers of appreciated property to a foreign subsidiary can trigger gain recognition.[9]

(iii) S corporation shareholders, who are generally individuals, cannot claim a deemed paid credit for foreign taxes incurred by a foreign corporation.[10] However, these individuals can claim a direct credit for the foreign taxes paid directly on the income of a branch. This aspect of a branch form is also advantageous for individuals who are either partners in a U.S. partnership or members of a U.S. limited liability company that is classified as a partnership for U.S. tax purposes.

(iv) There may be no foreign taxes when a branch repatriates its profits, whereas dividends paid by a subsidiary generally attract foreign withholding taxes.

General business factors which should be considered when choosing between the branch and subsidiary form include:

(i) A subsidiary insulates the U.S. parent from legal liability issues in the foreign country.

(ii) A subsidiary may present a better local image to potential customers and employees.

(iii) A branch may be simpler to operate. For example, foreign business registration and financial reporting requirements of a branch may be less onerous than those for an incorporated subsidiary.

(iv) Foreign laws may require a subsidiary to have outside foreign shareholders or directors.

---

[8] Code Sec. 367(a)(3)(C).
[9] Code Sec. 367.

[10] Code Sec. 902(a) and 1373(a).

(v) A subsidiary may make it easier to involve foreign investors in the venture, because a subsidiary can issue additional shares to those foreign investors.

(vi) The use of a branch avoids the minimum capitalization requirements imposed by some countries.

.04 Hybrid Entities

A hybrid entity is a foreign business entity that is treated as a corporation for foreign tax purposes, but as a disregarded entity or partnership for U.S. tax purposes. Unless it is a "per se" corporation (see discussion below), a foreign business entity with two or more owners can elect to be treated as a corporation or a partnership, while an entity with only a single owner can elect to be treated as a corporation or a disregarded entity (in effect, an unincorporated branch). This regime is known as "check-the-box" because the entity's owner merely checks the box on a Form 8832 to classify the entity (Form 8832 is reproduced in the Appendix to this chapter).

A separate entity must actually exist before making a check-the-box election. U.S. federal tax law controls for purposes of determining what constitutes an entity.[11] Although federal law is determinative, the regulatory rules reflect the common law partnership definition of an entity as a group of participants carrying on a trade, business, financial operation, or venture and dividing the profits therefrom.[12] A cost sharing arrangement does not constitute an entity.[13]

About 80 types of foreign business entities are excluded from the elective system because the IRS has determined that they should be treated as "per se" corporations (see listing in Table 8.3).[14] However, the regulations grandfathered pre-existing classifications of foreign business entities that would otherwise be treated as per se corporations if certain conditions are met. For example, a per se entity that qualified as a partnership under the old regulations (pre-1997) may retain its status as a partnership under certain circumstances.[15] Furthermore, any foreign entity existing before the 1997 effective date of the regulations may retain its prior status if that prior status was relevant on a previously filed return.[16]

---

[11] Reg. §§ 301.7701-1(a)(1) and (a)(3).

[12] Reg. § 301.7701-1(a)(2). These factors are based on the case of *H.M. Luna*, 42 TC 1067, Dec. 26,967.

[13] Reg. §§ 301.7701-1(a)(2) and (c).

[14] Reg. § 301.7701-2(b)(8).

[15] Reg. § 301.7701-2(d).

[16] Reg. §§ 301.7701-3(b)(3)(ii) and -3(d).

TABLE 8.3. LIST OF PER SE CORPORATE ENTITIES

American Samoa, Corporation
Argentina, Sociedad Anonima
Australia, Public Limited Company
Austria, Aktiengesellschaft
Barbados, Limited Company
Belgium, Societe Anonyme
Belize, Public Limited Company
Bolivia, Sociedad Anonima
Brazil, Sociedade Anonima
Bulgaria, Aktsionerno Druzhestro
Canada, Corporation and Company
Chile, Sociedad Anonima
People's Republic of China, Gufen Youxian Gongsi
Republic of China (Taiwan), Ku-fen Yu-hsien Kung-szu
Colombia, Sociedad Anonima
Costa Rica, Sociedad Anonima
Cyprus, Public Limited Company
Czech Republic, Akciova Spolecnost
Denmark, Aktieselskab
Ecuador, Sociedad Anonima or Compania Anonima
Egypt, Sharikat Al-Mossahamah
El Salvador, Sociedad Anonima
Estonia, Aktsiaselts
European Union, Societas Europaea
Finland, Julkinen Osakeyhtio/Publikt Aktiebolag
France, Societe Anonyme
Germany, Aktiengesellschaft
Greece, Anonymos Etairia
Guam, Corporation
Guatemala, Sociedad Anonima
Guyana, Public Limited Company
Honduras, Sociedad Anonima
Hong Kong, Public Limited Company
Hungary, Reszvenytarsasag
Iceland, Hlutafelag

India, Public Limited Company
Indonesia, Perseroan Terbuka
Ireland, Public Limited Company
Israel, Public Limited Company
Italy, Societa per Azioni
Jamaica, Public Limited Company
Japan, Kabushiki Kaisha
Kazakstan, Ashyk Aktsionerlik Kogham
Republic of Korea, Chusik Hoesa
Latvia, Akciju Sabiedriba
Liberia, Corporation
Liechtenstein, Aktiengesellschaft
Lithuania, Akeine Bendroves
Luxembourg, Societe Anonyme
Malaysia, Berhad
Malta, Public Limited Company
Mexico, Sociedad Anonima
Morocco, Societe Anonyme
The Netherlands, Naamloze Vennootschap
New Zealand, Limited Company
Nicaragua, Compania Anonima
Nigeria, Public Limited Company
Northern Mariana Islands, Corporation
Norway, Allment Aksjeselskap
Pakistan, Public Limited Company
Panama, Sociedad Anonima
Paraguay, Sociedad Anonima
Peru, Sociedad Anonima
Philippines, Stock Corporation
Poland, Spolka Akcyjna
Portugal, Sociedade Anonima
Puerto Rico, Corporation
Romania, Societe pe Actiuni
Russia, Otkrytoye Aktsionernoy Obshchestvo
Saudi Arabia, Sharikat Al-Mossahamah
Singapore, Public Limited Company
Slovak Republic, Akciova Spolocnost

¶804.04

Slovenia, Delniska Druzba

South Africa, Public Limited Company

Spain, Sociedad Anonima

Surinam, Naamloze Vennootschap

Sweden, Publika Aktiebolag

Switzerland, Aktiengesellschaft

Thailand, Borisat Chamkad (Machachon)

Trinidad and Tobago, Limited Company

Tunisia, Societe Anonyme

Turkey, Anonim Sirket

Ukraine, Aktsionerne Tovaristvo Vidkritogo Tipu

United Kingdom, Public Limited Company

United States Virgin Islands, Corporation

Uruguay, Sociedad Anonima

Venezuela, Sociedad Anonima or Compania Anonima

Default classification rules apply if a foreign eligible entity does not make an election.[17] First, if the foreign entity has two or more owners and at least one owner does not have limited liability, the foreign entity is a partnership. Second, if all the owners have limited liability, the foreign entity is a corporation. Third, if the foreign entity has only one owner that does not have limited liability, the foreign entity is disregarded as an entity separate from its owner (i.e., a branch). An owner of a foreign entity has limited liability if ownership does not result in personal liability. This is purely a matter of the foreign country's local law, and requires a review of the foreign entity's organizational documents.[18]

A check-the-box election can have an effective date of up to 75 days prior to the election date and up to one year after the election date. Once elected, an owner cannot re-elect for five years.[19] Problems can arise when a U.S. taxpayer checks-the-box by filing a Form 8832 more than 75 days after the desired effective date, typically the date of organization of the foreign entity, which may result in a taxable liquidation.[20] Taxpayers may be able to obtain relief for a late entity classification election that is both (i) due to reasonable cause and (ii) either the entity has not filed a return for the year with the desired effective date or the return was filed consistent with the desired classification.[21]

Hybrid entities provide the tax advantages of the flow-through entity form (i.e., a branch or partnership), while still providing the U.S. parent corporation with limited liability and a "corporate" presence in the foreign country. For example, an entity that is considered a branch or a partnership for U.S. tax purposes allows foreign losses to flow-through and be deducted by the U.S. parent corporation. In contrast, losses of a foreign subsidiary are not deductible by the U.S. parent corporation. In addition, whereas noncorporate shareholders cannot claim a deemed paid foreign tax credit for the foreign income taxes incurred by a foreign

---

[17] Reg. § 301.7701-3(b). A different default rule applies for domestic business entities, treating the entity as a partnership if it has two or more owners and a disregarded entity if it has only a single owner.

[18] Reg. § 301.7701-3(b)(2)(ii).

[19] Reg. § § 301.7701-3(c)(1)(iii) and (iv).

[20] A liquidation pursuant to Code Sec. 331 results in capital gain and a liquidation by a domestic parent corporation of a foreign subsidiary pursuant to Code Sec. 332 results in a deemed dividend (*see* ¶ 1402).

[21] Rev. Proc. 2009-41, 2009-39 IRB 439.

¶804.04

corporation,[22] they can claim a direct credit for the foreign taxes incurred by a foreign branch or partnership.[23]

Example **8.2:** Uncle Sam, a U.S. citizen, is the sole member of a U.S. limited liability company, USAllc, which operates in Country H, a high-tax country, through a private limited company. If USAllc makes a check-the-box election to treat the private limited company as a disregarded entity (or branch), Uncle Sam can claim a direct foreign tax credit for foreign income taxes paid by the private limited company.

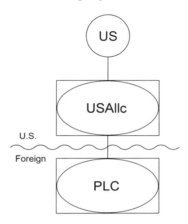

Although hybrid entities have a number of benefits, there are significant tax costs associated with converting an existing foreign subsidiary into a foreign branch or partnership. In particular, "hybridizing" an existing foreign subsidiary is a two-step transaction, involving the inbound liquidation of the foreign corporation, followed by a contribution of those assets to a foreign branch or partnership. Taxpayers must carefully analyze such transactions since inbound repatriating liquidations are taxable events,[24] and an outbound expatriating transfer to a foreign partnership may be subject to a special allocation of income.[25]

.05 Reverse Hybrid Entities

Reverse hybrid entities are foreign business entities that are treated as corporations for U.S. tax purposes, but as partnerships for foreign tax purposes. From a U.S. perspective, operating as a reverse hybrid offers several tax planning opportunities. A foreign subsidiary generally will allow a U.S. company to defer the residual U.S. tax on foreign profits. Furthermore, a foreign subsidiary offers more control over the timing of income recognition, which is useful in foreign tax credit planning. To take advantage of these opportunities, while avoiding local foreign tax, a U.S. company can create a reverse hybrid.

---

[22] Code Sec. 902(a) and 1373(a).
[23] Code Sec. 901(b)(5).

[24] Code Sec. 367(b). *See* discussion in Chapter 14 (¶ 1402).
[25] Code Sec. 721(c). *See* discussion in Chapter 14 (¶ 1401).

Example 8.3: In year 1, USAco organizes a foreign limited partnership, Limitada, in country L. USAco makes a check-the-box election to treat Limitada as a corporation for U.S. tax purposes. Limitada's earnings are not subject to country L corporate income tax because of its partnership status. In addition, because Limitada is treated as a corporation for U.S. tax purposes, its earnings are also not subject to U.S. tax until it distributes a dividend. If Limitada distributes all of its earnings to USAco in, say, year 5, USAco must pay U.S. tax on the dividend. Nevertheless, the use of a reverse hybrid entity would effectively defer the taxation of Limitada's earnings for 5 years.

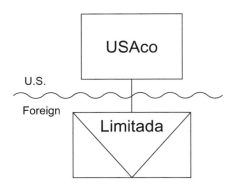

.06 Dual Consolidated Loss Rules

The United States determines the residency of a corporation based on where it is organized, whereas some foreign countries determine corporate residency based on where the corporation is managed. Consequently, a domestic corporation may be treated as a resident of both the U.S. and a foreign country. For example, if a corporation is organized in Delaware but has its seat of management in London, the corporation is treated as a domestic corporation for U.S. tax purposes, and may also be treated as a resident of the United Kingdom for U.K. tax purposes. As a result, such a corporation may have the opportunity to deduct losses incurred against income earned in both the United Kingdom and the United States.

To prevent a double tax benefit, the dual consolidated loss rules prohibit a dual-resident corporation ("DRC") from using a loss to reduce U.S. taxable income if the loss is also used to offset the income of a foreign affiliate.[26] DRCs include U.S. corporations subject to a foreign country's tax on either a worldwide income or residence basis, as well as foreign branches, partnerships and hybrid entities.[27] Specifically, a DRC may not deduct a "dual consolidated loss" in the United States,[28] unless the DRC elects and annually certifies for 15 years that the loss will not be used abroad.[29]

Example 8.4: U.S. Parent owns DRC (a corporation incorporated in the United States with its seat of management located in the United Kingdom),

---

[26] Code Sec. 1503(d).
[27] Reg. § 1.1503-2(c).

[28] Reg. § 1.1503-2(d).
[29] Reg. § 1.1503(d)-2(g).

which owns UKCo, a U.K. corporation. DRC files a U.S. consolidated tax return with U.S. Parent, and also files a U.K. consolidated tax return with UKCo. DRC borrows money from a bank and annually pays interest to the bank. Absent the dual consolidated loss rules, the interest may be deductible against the income of both U.S. Parent and UKCo. However, pursuant to the dual consolidated loss rules, the interest expense is not deductible in the U.S. unless DRC elects to not deduct the interest expense in the U.K. and annually certifies that the interest expense was not so deducted.

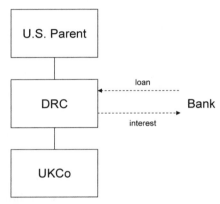

.07 Information Reporting for Foreign Partnerships

Foreign partnerships controlled by U.S. persons have information reporting requirements that are similar to the information reporting rules that apply to controlled foreign corporations. Under these provisions, a U.S. partner that controls a foreign partnership must file an annual information return.[30] A U.S. partner is considered to be in control of a foreign partnership if the U.S. partner holds, directly or indirectly, a greater than 50% interest in the capital, profits, or, to the extent provided in the regulations, deductions or losses of the partnership.[31] Where there is no single controlling partner, but the partnership is controlled by a number of U.S. persons each holding at least a 10% interest in the partnership, similar reporting is required of one or more of the 10% U.S. partners.[32] The penalty for failure to comply with these reporting obligations is $10,000, and may also include a reduction in the taxpayer's foreign tax credit.[33] In addition to the requirements for U.S. persons that "hold" interests in a controlled foreign partnership, U.S. persons that "acquire" or "dispose" of such interests are also subject to reporting requirements.[34] Moreover, there are reporting requirements for U.S. persons who transfer property to a foreign partnership.[35] This reporting requirement applies only if the U.S. person owns, directly or indirectly, at least a 10% interest in the partnership, or if the fair market value of the property transferred to the foreign partnership during a 12-month period exceeds $100,000.[36] As with the reporting requirements for

---

[30] Code Sec. 6038(a).
[31] Code Sec. 6038(e)(3).
[32] Code Sec. 6038(a)(5).
[33] Code Sec. 6038(b) and (c).

[34] Code Sec. 6046A.
[35] Code Sec. 6038B(a)(1)(B).
[36] Code Sec. 6038B(b)(1).

controlled foreign partnerships, the reporting of contributions to foreign partnerships parallels the reporting of similar transfers to foreign corporations. The penalty for a failure to report a contribution to a foreign partnership equals 10% of the fair market value of the property transferred, as well as gain recognition as if the property had been sold.[37]

The IRS has promulgated regulations implementing the reporting requirements on a Form 8865 for U.S. persons that hold interests in controlled foreign partnerships,[38] U.S. persons that acquire or dispose of an interest in a controlled foreign partnership,[39] and U.S. persons that transfer property to a foreign partnership.[40] A completed Form 8865 is reproduced in its entirety in the Appendix to this chapter.

¶ 805 BASICS OF OUTBOUND TAX PLANNING

Outbound tax planning involves the interplay of the tax laws of two or more countries. From a domestic corporation's perspective, the objective of outbound tax planning is to reduce the U.S. and foreign taxes on foreign-source income. Foreign income taxes increase a domestic corporation's total tax costs only to the extent they are not creditable for U.S. tax purposes. Taxpayers can reduce these excess credits either through foreign tax reduction planning or planning that increases the allowable credit for U.S. tax purposes. With respect to U.S. taxes, the United States generally collects any residual U.S. taxes on low-tax foreign-source income. Nevertheless, foreign-source income can give rise to opportunities to defer or even permanently reduce U.S. taxes. These issues are discussed in more detail below.

.01 Export Tax Benefits

Export tax benefits, such as the IC-DISC, are discussed in Chapter 7 (¶ 701).

.02 Operating in Low-Tax Foreign Jurisdictions

The United States generally does not tax foreign business profits earned through a foreign subsidiary until the subsidiary repatriates those earnings through a dividend. Therefore, a U.S. multinational corporation may be able to reduce its total tax costs by shifting income producing assets and activities to a foreign subsidiary located in a low-tax jurisdiction. There are limitations on the tax benefits of this strategy, however. First, shifting income to a low-tax foreign subsidiary does not permanently avoid the residual U.S. tax on low-tax foreign earnings, but instead merely defers those taxes until the subsidiary repatriates its earnings through a dividend distribution. In addition, the eventual repatriation of those earnings may be subject to foreign withholding taxes, which increases the total foreign tax rate on those earnings.

There also are significant constraints on the ability of U.S. multinationals to shift income to low-tax foreign subsidiaries. For example, a domestic parent corpo-

---

[37] Code Sec. 6038B(c). However, the penalty does not apply if the U.S. person can show that the failure to comply was due to reasonable cause and not to willful neglect. Moreover, the total penalty cannot exceed $100,000 unless the failure is due to intentional disregard of the reporting requirements.

[38] Reg. § 1.6038-3.

[39] Reg. § 1.6046A-1.

[40] Reg. § 1.6038B-2.

ration must use arm's length transfer prices to compute its share of income arising from related party transactions[41] and special penalties may apply if the IRS makes a significant transfer pricing adjustment.[42] Moreover, Congress has enacted a variety of anti-deferral provisions, including the Subpart F and passive foreign investment company provisions (see Chapter 5 (¶ 501)). Under these provisions, certain types of unrepatriated earnings of a foreign corporation, such as passive investment income, are subject to immediate U.S. taxation.

.03 Operating in High-Tax Foreign Jurisdictions

When a U.S. company conducts business in a high-tax foreign jurisdiction, the resulting excess foreign tax credits increase the total tax burden beyond what it would have been if only the United States had taxed the foreign-source income. One strategy for eliminating the excess credits is to increase the proportion of the taxpayer's worldwide income that is classified as foreign-source for U.S. tax purposes. For example, by arranging for the passage of title abroad, export sales will generate foreign-source income. Recharacterizing deductions also is an effective strategy for eliminating excess credits. Specifically, by using alternative apportionment bases for sourcing selling, general, and administrative expenses, a taxpayer may be able to reduce the amount of these deductions allocated and apportioned to foreign-source gross income.

Another strategy for reducing excess credits is to blend low-tax and high-tax foreign-source income within a single limitation. This allows the excess limitation on the low-tax foreign-source income to offset the excess credits on the high-tax foreign-source income. Separate limitations apply to passive limitation income and general limitation income,[43] which prevents cross-crediting. However, cross-crediting is still allowed with respect to the same type of income (passive category or general category) derived from different foreign countries. Look-through rules make cross-crediting possible with respect to dividends derived from foreign corporations located in low and high-tax foreign jurisdictions, as long as the underlying earnings are assigned to the same category of income.[44]

A final strategy for eliminating the excess credits on high-tax foreign-source income is foreign tax reduction planning.

.04 Foreign Tax Reduction Planning

Many of the techniques that a U.S. company can use to reduce foreign income taxes are similar to those used to reduce income taxes in a purely domestic context. Examples include realizing income in a form that is taxed at a lower rate (such as a preferential rate for capital gains), deferring the recognition of gross income, and accelerating the recognition of deductions. Other foreign tax reduction techniques are unique to the international context and include taking advantage of local tax incentives, debt financing, transfer pricing, and the use of tax treaties.

---

[41] Code Sec. 482.

[42] Code Sec. 6662. *See* discussion of transactional and net adjustment penalties in Chapter 12 (¶ 1204).

[43] Code Sec. 904(d)(1).

[44] Code Sec. 904(d)(3) and (d)(4).

Local tax incentives. One way to reduce foreign taxes is to take advantage of the special tax exemptions and holidays that various countries offer as an incentive to locate particular types of operations within their borders. For example, Singapore offers tax breaks for certain advanced technology companies, Puerto Rico grants tax breaks to companies that establish manufacturing operations in Puerto Rico, and Switzerland offers low-tax rates for holding companies and principal companies.

Debt financing. It may be advantageous to finance high-tax foreign subsidiaries in a way that maximizes interest deductions and minimizes dividend payments. The potential advantages of debt financing provided by a U.S. parent include a deduction in the high-tax foreign jurisdiction for interest paid to the U.S. parent, as well as the possibility of lower foreign withholding taxes on interest payments, as opposed to dividend distributions.

Assuming the foreign subsidiary is a controlled foreign corporation (or "CFC"), intercompany debt also increases the U.S. parent's foreign tax credit limitation by creating a stream of low-tax foreign-source income. Two special netting rules limit these benefits. First, interest paid by a CFC to a U.S. shareholder of that CFC is treated as passive income to the extent of the CFC's foreign personal holding company income.[45] This netting rule is designed to maintain the integrity of the separate category of income limitations by preventing a U.S. parent from artificially increasing its general limitation income by making a loan to a CFC, rather than purchasing foreign securities, merely as a device to recharacterize interest income as general limitation income. Second, the U.S. parent may be required to specifically allocate a portion of its third-party interest expense against the interest income received from a CFC.[46] This netting rule prevents a U.S. parent from borrowing money from third-party lenders and re-loaning the funds to its foreign subsidiaries (i.e., back-to-back loans) merely as a device to artificially increase the portion of worldwide income classified as foreign-source income. Absent this rule, back-to-back lending would create net foreign-source income for the U.S. parent because the entire amount of interest income would be foreign-source, whereas only of a portion of the interest expense would be apportioned against foreign-source income under the asset-based apportionment rules.[47]

To secure the benefits of debt financing, the U.S. parent corporation must ensure that any intercompany payments meant to be interest qualify as such under both U.S. tax law and foreign tax law.[48] The rules for determining whether an investment in a local subsidiary is treated as debt and not equity vary from country to country. Some countries employ relatively objective standards (for example, a maximum debt to equity ratio of 3 to 1),[49] while other countries employ more subjective facts and circumstances standards. To the extent that interest payments are limited by these standards, the taxpayer may wish to consider other methods of

---

[45] Code Sec. 954(b)(5).

[46] Reg. § 1.861-10(e).

[47] Code Sec. 864(e)(2).

[48] *See,* for example, *Hewlett-Packard Company,* TC Memo. 2012-135, CCH Dec. 59,055(M); and *Pepsico Puerto Rico, Inc.,* TC Memo. 2012-269, CCH Dec. 59,199(M).

[49] For example, pursuant to the anti-earnings provision of Code Sec. 163(j), a U.S. subsidiary may not deduct interest paid to a foreign parent if the U.S. subsidiary's debt to equity ratio exceeds 1.5 to 1 and certain other requirements are met (*see* ¶ 1003).

repatriating earnings that give rise to a deduction at the foreign subsidiary level, such as royalty payments.

Transfer pricing. By altering its transfer pricing policy, a U.S. multinational corporation may be able to allocate a higher portion of its worldwide profits to subsidiaries located in low-tax foreign jurisdictions. Examples include charging lower prices on inventory sales to foreign marketing subsidiaries, or charging higher prices on inventory sales to foreign manufacturing subsidiaries.

On the other hand, if the goal is to allocate less income to foreign subsidiaries located in high-tax foreign jurisdictions, one option is to charge the subsidiaries for the use of U.S.-owned manufacturing and marketing intangibles. If the subsidiary is a CFC, the resulting royalties also provide the U.S. parent with a stream of low-tax foreign-source income that has the same character for foreign tax credit limitation purposes as the underlying earnings of the CFC to which the royalty expense is properly allocable.[50] If a foreign jurisdiction does not allow a deduction for technology charges paid to a parent corporation, the taxpayer should consider using a cost-sharing arrangement (see discussion in Chapter 12 (¶ 1202)). Charging a foreign subsidiary for management services provided by the U.S. home office also reduces the foreign income taxes of the subsidiary.

As discussed in detail in Chapter 12 (¶ 1204), special penalties may apply if the IRS makes a significant transfer pricing adjustment.[51] Therefore, U.S. taxpayers must establish defensible positions for the transfer prices they use through contemporaneous documentation of their transfer pricing methodology or through an advance pricing agreement.

Tax treaties. Taxpayers also can reduce foreign taxes by making use of permanent establishment provisions and the reduced withholding tax rates provided by tax treaties. Under most tax treaties, a U.S. company's business profits are not subject to foreign taxation unless it conducts business through a permanent establishment located within the foreign country. A permanent establishment is a branch office, or the presence of dependent agents who habitually conclude sales contracts in the taxpayer's name. Marketing products abroad solely through independent brokers or distributors does not create a permanent establishment. Tax treaties also provide lower withholding tax rates on dividends, interest, and royalties derived from sources within the treaty country. As a consequence, a U.S. parent corporation may be able to reduce foreign withholding taxes by owning its foreign subsidiaries through strategically located holding companies (so-called "treaty shopping"). Chapter 13 (¶ 1302) discusses the restrictions on a taxpayer's ability to engage in treaty shopping.

.05 Tax-Efficient Supply Chain Management [52]

A U.S. company's supply chain is the system that moves goods and services from suppliers to customers. From a tax perspective, the key aspects of the supply

---

[50] Code Sec. 904(d)(3)(C) and Reg. § 1.904-5(c)(3).
[51] Code Sec. 6662.

[52] This discussion draws heavily on *Present Law and Background Related to Possible Income Shifting and Transfer Pricing*, Joint Committee on Taxation, JCX-37-10, July 22, 2010.

chain include (1) the types and location of the entities involved and (2) the contractual arrangements among those entities that govern the movement of goods and services from suppliers to customers. Arm's length transfer prices plays a critical role in ensuring that each entity in the supply chain reports the proper amount of taxable income for the contribution it makes (in terms of assets, functions and risks) to the production of the goods and services.

Many U.S. companies have reorganized their legal structures and contractual arrangements to provide more centralized management of the manufacturing, distribution, support services, and research functions. These restructurings often involve (1) creating regional principal companies, (2) centralizing ownership of intangible property, (3) converting manufacturing and distribution subsidiaries into limited-risk distributors and contract manufacturers, and (4) centralizing support services and R&D activities by creating shared services centers and research companies.

A principal company is the economic owner of the taxpayer's high-value intangible assets, is in-charge of business planning and strategy, and oversees the development, production, and sale of goods and services. By centralizing its key intangibles, functions, and risks in the principal company, a U.S. company can streamline its operations and create economies of scale.

A limited-risk distributor performs limited functions (hiring and training a local sales force and executing the local sales strategy) and bears limited risks (flash inventory ownership and local market risk). In contrast, a traditional distribution subsidiary contracts in its own name, holds title to its inventory, performs significant functions (advertising, logistics, pricing, technical services, etc.) and bears significant risks (credit, inventory, etc.). In a similar fashion, under a contract manufacturing arrangement, a principal company hires the manufacturer to produce its products according the specifications and production schedule the principal company provides. In contrast, a traditional manufacturing subsidiary holds title to inventory, performs significant functions (acquire and maintain facilities, hire and train workers, product design, procurement, quality control, etc.) and bears significant risks (capital investment, inventory, warranty, etc.).

The principal company reports high profits because it is the economic owner of the intangible assets and is responsible for the key functions and risks. On the other hand, the specialized operating entities, such as the limited-risk distributors, contract manufacturers, and shared service centers, do not own high-value intangibles, perform routine functions, and bear limited risks. Consequently, these operating entities report relatively low profits. The shifting of income to a principal company can create significant tax savings if the principal company is located in a low-tax jurisdiction.

.06 Foreign Holding Companies

A foreign holding company functions as the legal owner of a U.S. company's foreign subsidiaries, provides offshore cash management and financing, and facilitates the acquisition and disposition of foreign operating companies. Examples of popular locations for holding companies include Bermuda, Ireland, Luxembourg,

¶805.06

The Netherlands and Switzerland. To varying degrees, these countries offer low corporate tax rates, reduced withholding taxes on dividends, interest and royalties received from foreign subsidiaries or paid to the U.S. parent corporation, participation exemptions for dividends received from foreign subsidiaries, lenient CFC-type rules for taxing the income of foreign subsidiaries, and lenient thin capitalization rules that allow interest expense deductions.

.07 Check-the-Box Elections and Qualified Dividend Income Derived by U.S. Citizens and Resident Aliens

The check-the-box rules and the preferential tax rate for qualified dividend income have impacted outbound tax planning for closely-held businesses. Under the check-the-box rules, a U.S. citizen or resident alien can organize a foreign business entity that is treated as a corporation for foreign tax purposes, but as a disregarded entity for U.S. tax purposes (hybrid entity).[53] In addition, although U.S. citizens and resident aliens cannot claim a Code Sec. 902 deemed paid credit with respect to a dividend from a foreign corporation, they can take advantage of the 20% maximum U.S. income tax on qualified dividend income, which includes dividends received from foreign corporations that reside in countries who have entered into an income tax treaty with the United States.[54] Such dividends are also potentially subject to the 3.8% Medicare contribution tax on net investment income.[55]

The use of hybrid entities allows a U.S. citizen or resident alien to avoid U.S. taxation of dividends, as well as the flow-through of foreign losses.

> ***Example 8.5:*** Betsy Ross, a U.S. citizen, owns 100% of FLAGco, a business entity that is organized in country H and is treated as a corporation for both U.S. and country H tax purposes. In year 1, FLAGco has $1 million of taxable income, pays $400,000 of foreign income taxes, and distributes its entire $600,000 of earnings and profits to Betsy as a dividend. The dividend is exempt from withholding tax under the U.S.-country H tax treaty. The U.S. income tax on Betsy's dividend is $120,000 (20% × $600,000), resulting in a total effective income tax rate of 52% on FLAGco's $1 million of income [($400,000 + $120,000) ÷ $1,000,000].

---

[53] Reg. § 301.7701-3.
[54] Code Sec. 1(h)(11).

[55] Code Sec. 1411. A taxpayer may not claim a foreign tax credit against the net investment income tax. Reg. § 1.1411-1(e).

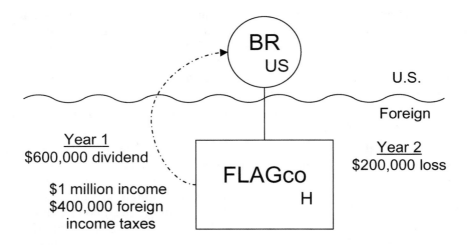

In year 2, FLAGco incurs a net operating loss of $200,000. The loss does not flow-through to Betsy and offset the other income on her U.S. tax return because FLAGco is treated as a corporation for U.S. tax purposes.

Example 8.6: Now assume that Betsy makes a check-the-box election to treat FLAGco as a disregarded entity. In year 1, FLAGco's taxable income and foreign income taxes would flow-through to Betsy, but the distribution would not be treated as a dividend. Assuming a 39.6% tax rate, no U.S. tax would be due on the $1 million of foreign-source taxable income because the $400,000 of foreign tax credits would fully offset the $396,000 pre-credit U.S. tax.

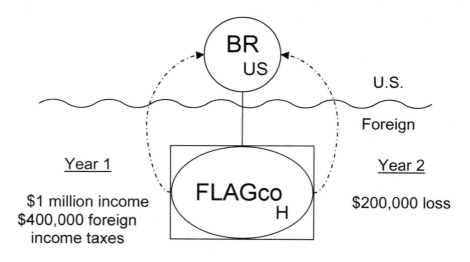

In year 2, the $200,000 foreign loss would flow-through to Betsy and potentially provide her with a U.S. tax benefit.

The use of a hybrid entity may not be the optimal strategy in a low-tax country that has entered into an income tax treaty with the United States. Instead, repatriating the foreign earnings through a dividend distribution may result in a lower overall effective tax rate.

Example 8.7: Betsy Ross, a U.S. citizen, owns 100% of BRITco, a corporation organized in the United Kingdom, which has a treaty with the United States. BRITco earns $400,000 on which it pays $80,000 of foreign income taxes. BRITco distributes a $320,000 cash dividend to Betsy, who pays U.S. tax of $64,000 (20% of $320,000).

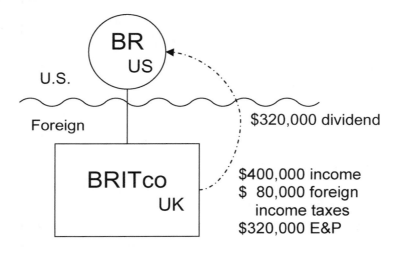

The total effective income tax rate on BRITco's $400,000 of earnings is 36% ([($80,000 + $64,000) ÷ $400,000], which is less than the top U.S. income tax rate of 39.6%.

.08 Operating in Tax Havens

U.S. taxpayers can achieve significant tax and nontax benefits from the use of tax havens. Although the meaning of the term "tax haven" varies from country-to-country, a common theme is that the tax haven offers a lower corporate tax rate. For example, in France, a tax haven is described as a country having a "privileged tax system," which is any country which levies a tax, equal to or less than two-thirds the tax France imposes.[56] The term tax haven, if applied literally, could include countries such as the United States, which does not tax interest earned by nonresident aliens on deposits in U.S. banks. It therefore constitutes a tax haven for those foreign investors who derive interest income from deposits in U.S. banks.

Although the U.S. Congress has passed laws to limit the use of tax havens and other offshore sites for tax-savings purposes (e.g., Subpart F, Code Sec. 367 and the PFIC provisions), there is no official U.S. definition of the term "tax haven."

---

[56] Code General des Impots Art. 238 A, paragraph 2.

In general, there are six principal characteristics of tax havens:

(i) A tax haven either imposes no income tax or imposes a tax on income that is low in comparison to the tax imposed by the taxpayer's home country.

(ii) A tax haven often protects the confidentiality of financial and commercial information. In so doing, the tax haven may adopt bank secrecy or similar internal laws that make it a crime to disclose this information to any person.

(iii) Financial institutions, such as banks, frequently assume a dominant role in the tax haven's trade or commerce, and its residents include those skilled in financial transactions, such as bankers, lawyers, and accountants.

(iv) A tax haven normally possesses modern communications facilities necessary to the conduct of financial and commercial affairs.

(v) A tax haven often does not impose currency controls or similar restrictions on foreign nationals.

(vi) If the tax haven has a treaty network, the haven may offer benefits such as reduced tax rates on income tax by its treaty partners.

Tax haven incentives. A tax haven jurisdiction typically imposes a low or zero rate of tax on all or some class of income. The following list describes the special incentives that selected tax havens generally offer:

(i) *Countries that impose zero tax*—These are jurisdictions that impose no tax on income, capital gains, gifts, inheritances, estates and trusts. Since these countries do not have treaty networks, they have no obligation to furnish tax information to other jurisdictions. Such countries generally charge an annual formation fee to registered companies. An example of this type of tax haven would be Bermuda.

(ii) *Countries that impose a low tax rate*—In order to compete with havens that impose a zero rate of tax, these jurisdictions offer a low rate of tax combined with a treaty network. The treaty networks are useful in adding some degree of flexibility to tax planning. An example of this type of tax haven would be Ireland.

(iii) *Countries that impose no tax on foreign source income*—These tax havens do not impose any tax on income earned from sources outside of the particular jurisdiction. These havens are especially attractive to the transportation industry when, for example, the jurisdiction allows the registration of foreign flagships. An example of this type of tax haven would be Hong Kong.

(iv) *Countries that impose a reduced rate of tax on offshore finance and trade-oriented businesses*—These countries usually impose a minimal or token tax to resident companies that do not conduct business or trade within the haven. An example of this type of tax haven would be the British Virgin Islands.

¶805.08

(v) *Countries that offer special inducements*—In order to attract certain companies, such as holding companies, some jurisdictions offer significant inducements that may include privileged treatment with respect to income taxes, import taxes, customs, duties, etc. In order to attract manufacturing facilities to their countries, some jurisdictions, such as Singapore, provide for various tax holidays on profits earned on products manufactured for export.

Non-tax factors. The laws of most countries provide for some degree of confidentiality with respect to banking and other commercial activities. However, most nations will not protect information from a legitimate inquiry initiated by a foreign government, especially if the request is made pursuant to a treaty provision. On the other hand, tax havens with stringent secrecy laws typically refuse to breach their secrecy rules even when serious violations of another nation's law may have occurred. To do otherwise may seriously impair the jurisdiction's tax haven status with those persons who wish to keep their finances confidential.

Many jurisdictions, in order to maintain or improve their competitive position as a tax haven, have enacted legislation providing for criminal sanctions for breach of the secrecy laws. An example is the Cayman Islands. The Cayman Islands, which have had stringent bank secrecy laws since the 1960s when it tightened its common law through statute, passed additional legislation providing for substantial sanctions against persons who either divulged or received confidential banking and commercial information.

Many tax havens have a dual currency control system that distinguishes between residents and nonresidents, and between local currency and foreign currency. Generally, residents are subject to currency controls while nonresidents are only subject to controls placed on the local currency. For currency control purposes, a company which is formed in the tax haven and which is beneficially owned by a resident and which conducts its business outside the haven is generally treated as a nonresident. Therefore, a tax haven company doing business solely in other jurisdictions cannot be subject to the tax haven's currency exchange controls provided it deals in the currency of other countries. These rules facilitate the use of a tax haven by a person wishing to establish a tax haven entity for purposes of doing business in other jurisdictions. The rules also offer the free movement of foreign currency abroad.

A tax haven enjoying a treaty network can provide a most attractive combination in the formation of a multi-national tax strategy. This combination offers increased flexibility in devising plans to reduce tax rates through treaty shopping. Many U.S. treaty partners have treaties with tax haven type countries.

Finally, in addition to selecting a particular tax haven for purposes such as low tax, secrecy, banking, currency control, communications, and treaty networks, taxpayers should also consider nontax factors. These factors include economic and political stability, geographic accessibility to markets, the availability of labor, the risk of nationalization of assets, and government cooperation.

¶805.08

¶ 806 FINANCIAL REPORTING IMPLICATIONS OF INTERNATIONAL TAX PLANNING

The globalization of U.S. business has increased the importance of understanding how a U.S. multinational corporation's foreign operations impact the effective tax rate it reports in its financial statements. Virtually all countries tax the income of corporations and, therefore, the profits of a U.S. multinational corporation are typically subject to income taxation in a number of countries. A firm's book effective tax rate provides a convenient metric for capturing the cumulative effect of these various income taxes on the corporation's profitability. For financial reporting purposes, a company's effective tax rate equals its GAAP provision for income taxes (which includes federal, state and foreign income taxes) divided by its GAAP income before income taxes. For example, if the income tax provision is $100 million, and pre-tax book income is $300 million, the company's book effective tax rate is 33 percent.

When evaluating a U.S. corporation's effective tax rate, the de facto benchmark is the U.S. statutory rate. For large U.S. corporations, the statutory tax rate has been 35% since 1993.[57] However, a U.S. company's foreign operations can cause its effective tax rate to diverge from 35 percent. For example, operations in high-tax foreign jurisdictions can give rise to excess foreign tax credits that increase a firm's effective tax rate. Likewise, operations in low-tax foreign jurisdictions can reduce a firm's reported effective tax rate if management intends to permanently reinvest those earnings abroad.

.01 Operations in High-Tax Foreign Jurisdictions

The foreign tax credit limitation prevents U.S. companies operating in high-tax jurisdictions from claiming a credit for foreign taxes in excess of the U.S. statutory tax rate. These excess credits can increase the total tax burden on a U.S. company's foreign earnings beyond what it would have been if only the United States had taxed the income. Excess credits can be carried back one year and carried forward ten years and taken as a credit in a year that the limitation exceeds the amount of creditable foreign taxes.[58] Therefore, excess credits increase the reported effective tax rate only to the extent they cannot be utilized in one of the carryback or carryforward years.[59] The financial statements of U.S. oil and gas companies illustrate the impact of excess credits on the effective tax rate of a U.S. multinational corporation. For example, in its annual report for calendar year 2014, Exxon Mobil Corporation reported an effective tax rate of 41% on its worldwide earnings. Oil-producing countries often impose special taxes the profits of oil companies. For example, in addition to its general corporate income tax of 27%, Norway imposes a special petroleum tax of 50% on income from oil and gas production.

---

[57] Code Sec. 11.

[58] Code Sec. 905.

[59] If a company carries back its excess credits, it obtains an immediate tax benefit that is reflected in a lower current year income tax expense. The tax provision for the current year is also reduced if the firm expects to use its excess credits in a carryforward year, in which case the firm establishes a deferred tax asset for the expected future tax benefit of the carryforward. FASB ASC 740, *Income Taxes*.

.02 Operations in Low-Tax Foreign Jurisdictions

The U.S. corporate income tax rate of 35%, plus any state tax add-ons, is higher than the tax rate in most other countries. For example, in 2014, the average corporate income tax rate in the 33 OECD countries other than the United States was only 24.8%.[60] Furthermore, a number of countries, such as Hong Kong, Ireland and Switzerland, offer corporate tax rates that are substantially below the U.S. rate of 35%. Because the United States generally does not tax the foreign profits of a foreign subsidiary until those earnings are remitted to the U.S. parent as a dividend, it is possible to defer payment of the "residual" U.S. tax on low-tax foreign earnings.

For financial reporting purposes, it is presumed that the U.S. parent will eventually repatriate all of a foreign subsidiary's undistributed foreign earnings, in which case the U.S. tax savings associated with deferral are accounted for as a temporary difference that has no effect on the firm's reported effective tax rate. In other words, the U.S. parent records a deferred tax liability for the future payment of the residual U.S. tax on the foreign earnings. For this purpose, the time value of money is ignored.

However, if sufficient evidence shows that the firm has or will reinvest a foreign subsidiary's undistributed foreign earnings "indefinitely," it is not necessary to include the residual U.S tax on undistributed low-tax foreign earnings in the income tax provision for the current year. This exception provides U.S. corporations with the ability to treat the benefit of operating in a low-tax foreign jurisdiction as a permanent difference that reduces both the income tax provision and the reported effective tax rate. In effect, the U.S. parent may assume that it will never pay any residual U.S. tax on its unrepatriated foreign earnings.

The financial statements of U.S. technology companies illustrate the impact of operations in low-tax jurisdiction on the effective tax rate of a U.S. multinational corporation. Unlike oil and gas companies, technology companies can manufacture their products and locate their high-value intellectual property in low-tax foreign jurisdictions. For example, in its annual report for the fiscal year ending December 31, 2014, Google Inc. reported an effective tax rate of 19.3% on its worldwide earnings. In its income tax footnote, Google indicated that the "foreign rate differential" reduced the company's book effective tax rate by 13.9 percentage points.

¶ 807 COMPREHENSIVE EXAMPLE

USAco, a domestic corporation, plans to locate a new factory in either country L or country H. USAco will structure the new facility as a wholly-owned foreign subsidiary, FORco, and finance FORco solely with an equity investment. USAco projects that in FORco's first year of operations, it will generate $10 million of taxable income, all from active foreign manufacturing activities. Assume that the U.S. corporate tax rate is 35%. To simplify the analysis, further assume that USAco's only item of income during the year is that derived from FORco.

---

[60] http://www.oecd.org/tax/tax-policy/tax-database.htm#C_CorporateCaptial.

The total tax rate on FORco earnings will vary significantly, depending on a number of factors, including:

(i) Whether FORco is located in a low-tax or high-tax foreign country,

(ii) The extent to which USAco repatriates FORco's earnings,

(iii) Whether USAco repatriates FORco's earnings through dividend distributions, as opposed to interest or royalty payments, and

(iv) The availability of favorable tax treaty withholding rates on dividends, interest, and royalty payments made by FORco to USAco.

The effect of these factors is illustrated below by computing the worldwide tax rate on FORco's earnings under a variety of assumptions.

Case 1: Low-tax country/No dividends. Country L has a corporate income tax rate of 25%, which is ten percentage points lower than the U.S. rate. If USAco locates FORco in country L and FORco pays no dividends, the total tax rate on its earnings is 25%, computed as follows:

Foreign income tax

FORco's taxable income	$10,000,000
Country L income tax rate	×25%
Country L income tax	$2,500,000
Foreign withholding taxes on repatriated earnings	$0
U.S. tax on repatriated earnings	$0
Total taxes [$2,500,000 + $0 + $0]	$2,500,000
Worldwide effective tax rate [$2,500,000 ÷ $10,000,000]	25%

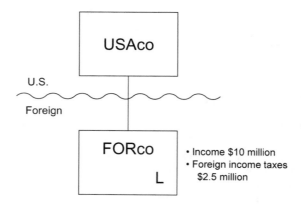

This example illustrates that USAco can reduce the current year worldwide tax rate on the new manufacturing facility below the U.S. tax rate of 35% by locating the factory in L, a low-tax foreign country, and not repatriating the foreign earnings.

¶807

Case 2: Low-tax country/Pays dividend/Tax treaty. Assume that country L has a tax treaty with the United States that provides a 10% withholding tax rate on dividends. If USAco locates FORco in country L and repatriates half of FORco's after-tax earnings through a dividend distribution, the total tax rate on its repatriated and unrepatriated earnings is 30%, computed as follows:

Foreign income tax

FORco's taxable income	$10,000,000
Country L income tax rate	×25%
Country L income tax	$2,500,000

Foreign withholding taxes on repatriated earnings

FORco's after-tax earnings [$10,000,000 – $2,500,000] . .	$7,500,000
Percentage repatriated through dividend	×50%
Dividend distribution	$3,750,000
Withholding tax rate (per treaty)	×10%
Country L withholding tax	$375,000

U.S. tax on repatriated earnings

Dividend from FORco	$3,750,000
Code Sec. 78 gross-up	+1,250,000
USAco's taxable income	$5,000,000
U.S. tax rate	×35%
Pre-credit U.S. tax	$1,750,000
Foreign tax credit	–1,625,000

> Foreign withholding taxes: $375,000
>
> Deemed paid taxes: $2,500,000 × [$3,750,000 ÷ $7,500,000] = $1,250,000
>
> Creditable foreign taxes: [$375,000 + $1,250,000] = $1,625,000
>
> General limitation: $1,750,000 × [$5,000,000 ÷ $5,000,000] = $1,750,000

U.S. income tax	$125,000
Total taxes [$2,500,000 + $375,000 + $125,000]	$3,000,000
Worldwide effective tax rate [$3,000,000 ÷ $10,000,000]	30%

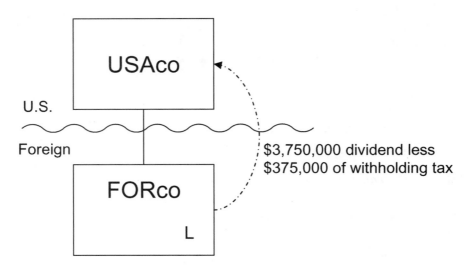

By repatriating half of FORco's earnings through a dividend distribution, USAco increases the worldwide tax rate on FORco's earnings from 25% in Case 1 to 30% in Case 2. The 30% rate is a blended rate, whereby the $5 million of income that USAco recognizes by virtue of the dividend is, in effect, taxed one time at the U.S. rate of 35% and FORco's remaining $5 million of earnings is taxed one time at the country L rate of 25%.

Case 3: Low-tax country/Pays dividend/No tax treaty. An important assumption in Case 2 is that country L had a tax treaty with the United States that provided for a 10% withholding tax rate on dividends. Now assume that there is no tax treaty between the United States and country L and that country L's statutory withholding rate on dividends is 30%. The lack of a favorable treaty withholding rate increases the total tax rate on FORco's repatriated and unrepatriated earnings from 30% in Case 2 to 36.25% in Case 3, computed as follows:

Foreign income tax

FORco's taxable income	$10,000,000
Country L income tax rate	× 25%
Country L income tax	$2,500,000

Foreign withholding taxes on repatriated earnings

FORco's after-tax earnings [$10,000,000 − $2,500,000] . .	$7,500,000
Percentage repatriated through dividend	× 50%
Dividend distribution	$3,750,000
Withholding tax rate (per statute)	× 30%
Country L withholding tax	$1,125,000

U.S. tax on repatriated earnings

Dividend from FORco	$3,750,000
Code Sec. 78 gross-up	+ 1,250,000
USAco's taxable income	$5,000,000
U.S. tax rate	×35%
Pre-credit U.S. tax	$1,750,000
Foreign tax credit	– 1,750,000

Foreign withholding taxes: $1,125,000

Deemed paid taxes: $2,500,000 × [$3,750,000 ÷ $7,500,000] = $1,250,000

Creditable foreign taxes: [$1,125,000 + $1,250,000] = $2,375,000

General limitation: $1,750,000 × [$5,000,000 ÷ $5,000,000] = $1,750,000

U.S. income tax	$0
Total taxes [$2,500,000 + $1,125,000 + $0]	$3,625,000
Worldwide effective tax rate [$3,625,000 ÷ $10,000,000]	36.25%

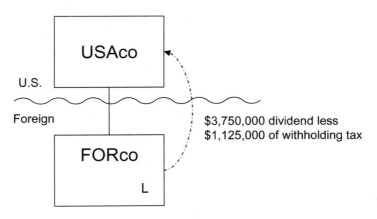

Case 3 shows that if USAco repatriates some of FORco's earnings through a dividend distribution, the availability of a favorable treaty withholding rate on dividends is critical to the ability of USAco to obtain the benefits of lower tax rates abroad.

Case 4: High-tax country/No dividends. Country H has a corporate income tax rate of 45%, which is ten percentage points higher than the U.S. rate. If USAco locates FORco in country H and FORco pays no dividends, the total tax rate on its earnings is 45%, computed as follows:

Foreign income tax

FORco's taxable income	$10,000,000
Country H income tax rate	× 45%
Country H income tax	$4,500,000

Foreign withholding taxes on repatriated earnings $0

U.S. tax on repatriated earnings $0

Total taxes [$4,500,000 + $0 + $0] $4,500,000

Worldwide effective tax rate [$4,500,000 ÷ $10,000,000] 45%

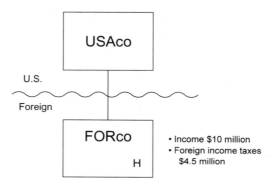

The 45% worldwide tax rate indicates that the total tax rate on USAco new manufacturing facility will exceed the U.S. tax rate of 35% if USAco locates the factory in H, a high-tax foreign country, and does not repatriate the foreign earnings.

Case 5: High-tax country/Pays dividend/Tax treaty. Assume that country H has a tax treaty with the United States that provides a 10% withholding tax rate on dividends. If USAco locates FORco in country H and repatriates half of FORco's after-tax earnings through a dividend distribution, the total tax rate on its repatriated and unrepatriated earnings is 47.75%, computed as follows:

Foreign income tax

FORco's taxable income	$10,000,000
Country H income tax rate.......................	× 45%
Country H income tax	$4,500,000

Foreign withholding taxes on repatriated earnings

FORco's after-tax earnings [$10,000,000 – $4,500,000] ..	$5,500,000
Percentage repatriated through dividend	× 50%
Dividend distribution	$2,750,000
Withholding tax rate (per treaty)	× 10%
Country H withholding tax	$275,000

¶807

U.S. tax on repatriated earnings

Dividend from FORco	$2,750,000
Code Sec. 78 gross-up	+ 2,250,000
USAco's taxable income	$5,000,000
U.S. tax rate	× 35%
Pre-credit U.S. tax	$1,750,000
Foreign tax credit	− 1,750,000

> Foreign withholding taxes: $275,000
>
> Deemed paid taxes: $4,500,000 × [$2,750,000 ÷ $5,500,000] = $2,250,000
>
> Creditable foreign taxes: [$275,000 + $2,250,000] = $2,525,000
>
> General limitation: $1,750,000 × [$5,000,000 ÷ $5,000,000] = $1,750,000

U.S. income tax	$0
Total taxes [$4,500,000 + $275,000 + $0]	$4,775,000
Worldwide effective tax rate [$4,775,000 ÷ $10,000,000]	47.75%

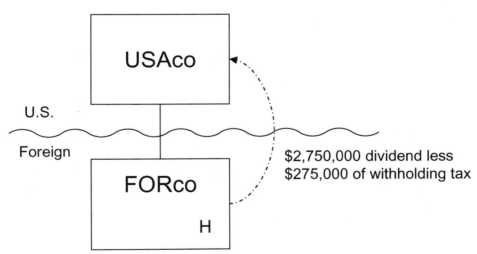

By repatriating half of FORco's earnings through a dividend distribution, USAco increases the worldwide tax rate on FORco's earnings from 45% in Case 4 to

47.75% in Case 5. The foreign withholding tax on the dividend distribution is responsible for the increase in the total tax rate.

Case 6: High-tax country/Pays dividend/No tax treaty. A comparison of Cases 4 and 5 indicates that repatriating half of FORco's earnings through a dividend distribution increases the worldwide tax rate on FORco's earnings from 45% to 47.75%. Now assume that there is no tax treaty between the United States and country H and that country H's statutory withholding rate on dividends is 30%. The lack of a favorable treaty withholding rate further increases the total tax rate on FORco's repatriated and unrepatriated earnings from 47.75% in Case 5 to 53.25% in Case 6, computed as follows:

Foreign income tax

FORco's taxable income	$10,000,000
Country H income tax rate	× 45%
Country H income tax	$4,500,000

Foreign withholding taxes on repatriated earnings

FORco's after-tax earnings [$10,000,000 – $4,500,000] . .	$5,500,000
Percentage repatriated through dividend	× 50%
Dividend distribution	$2,750,000
Withholding tax rate (per statute)	× 30%
Country H withholding tax	$825,000

U.S. tax on repatriated earnings

Dividend from FORco	$2,750,000
Code Sec. 78 gross-up	+ 2,250,000
USAco's taxable income	$5,000,000
U.S. tax rate	× 35%
Pre-credit U.S. tax	$1,750,000
Foreign tax credit	– 1,750,000

Foreign withholding taxes: $825,000

Deemed paid taxes: $4,500,000 × [$2,750,000 ÷ $5,500,000] = $2,250,000

Creditable foreign taxes: [$825,000 + $2,250,000] = $3,075,000

General limitation: $1,750,000 × [$5,000,000 ÷ $5,000,000] = $1,750,000

U.S. income tax	$0
Total taxes [$4,500,000 + $825,000 + $0]	$5,325,000
Worldwide effective tax rate [$5,325,000 ÷ $10,000,000]	53.25%

¶807

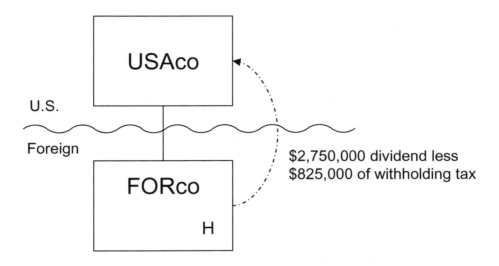

Case 7: High-tax country/Earnings stripping/Tax treaty. If USAco locates FORco in country H, one strategy for reducing the excess credits on FORco's earnings is to engage in earnings stripping, that is, to repatriate FORco's profits through deductible interest and royalty payments, rather than nondeductible dividend distributions. For example, assume that USAco modifies its plans for FORco, as follows:

    (i) Finance FORco with both debt and equity, such that FORco will pay USAco $3 million of interest each year,

   (ii) Charge FORco an annual royalty of $2 million for the use of USAco's patents and trade secrets, and

  (iii) Eliminate FORco's dividend distribution.

Assume that the applicable tax treaty withholding rate is 0% for both interest and royalties.

As the following computations indicate, debt financing and charges for technology transfers reduces the total tax rate on country H earnings from 47.75% in Case 5 to 40%, computed as follows:

Foreign income tax

FORco's income before interest and royalties	$10,000,000
Interest paid to USAco	– 3,000,000
Royalties paid to USAco	– 2,000,000
FORco's taxable income	$5,000,000
Country H income tax rate	× 45%
Country H income tax	$2,250,000

Foreign withholding taxes on repatriated earnings

Withholding tax on interest (per treaty)	$0
Withholding tax on royalties (per treaty)	0
Country H withholding taxes	$0

U.S. tax on repatriated earnings

Interest from FORco	$3,000,000
Royalties from FORco	+ 2,000,000
USAco's taxable income	$5,000,000
U.S. tax rate	× 35%
Pre-credit U.S. tax	$1,750,000
Foreign tax credit	– 0

> Foreign withholding taxes: $0
> Deemed paid taxes: $0 (no dividends)

U.S. income tax	$1,750,000
Total taxes [$2,250,000 + $0 + $1,750,000]	$4,000,000
Worldwide effective tax rate [$4,000,000 ÷ $10,000,000]	40%

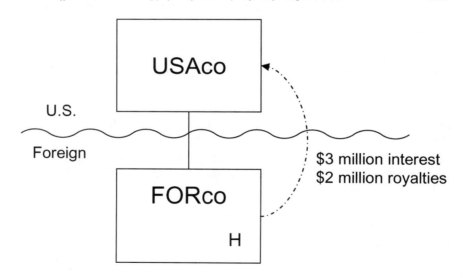

The 40% worldwide tax rate on the country H earnings is a blended rate, whereby the $5 million of interest and royalties paid to USAco are, in effect, taxed one time at the U.S. rate of 35% and the $5 million of unrepatriated earnings is taxed one time at the country H rate of 45%. Therefore, earnings stripping can be an effective method for reducing the worldwide tax rate on the earnings of a high-tax foreign subsidiary.

Case 8: Low-tax country/Earnings stripping/Tax treaty. In contrast to the benefits illustrated in Case 7, repatriating FORco's profits through deductible interest and royalty payments rather than a dividend distribution will have no effect on FORco's total tax rate if FORco is located in country L (the low-tax country). As in Case 2, where FORco repatriated its earnings through dividend distributions, the worldwide tax rate on FORco's repatriated and unrepatriated earnings is still 30%, computed as follows:

Foreign income tax

FORco's income before interest and royalties	$10,000,000
Interest paid to USAco	– 3,000,000
Royalties paid to USAco	– 2,000,000
FORco's taxable income	$5,000,000
Country L income tax rate	× 25%
Country L income tax	$1,250,000

Foreign withholding taxes on repatriated earnings

Withholding tax on interest (per treaty)	$0
Withholding tax on royalties (per treaty)	0
Country L withholding taxes	$0

U.S. tax on repatriated earnings

Interest from FORco	$3,000,000
Royalties from FORco	+ 2,000,000
USAco's taxable income	$5,000,000
U.S. tax rate	× 35%
Pre-credit U.S. tax	$1,750,000
Foreign tax credit	– 0
Foreign withholding taxes: $0	
Deemed paid taxes: $0 (no dividends)	
U.S. income tax	$1,750,000

Total taxes [$1,250,000 + $0 + $1,750,000]	$3,000,000
Worldwide effective tax rate [$3,000,000 ÷ $10,000,000]	30%

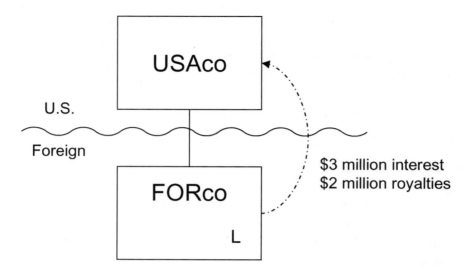

Case 9: Low-tax country/No dividends/Hybrid entity. Country L has a corporate income tax rate of 25%, which is ten percentage points lower than the U.S. rate. If USAco locates FORco in country L and elects to treat FORco as a disregarded entity for U.S. tax purposes, USAco is taxed on all of FORco's earnings even though FORco does not pay a dividend. Consequently, USAco cannot defer the residual U.S. tax on FORco's low-tax foreign earnings and the total tax rate on those earnings is 35%, computed as follows:

Foreign income tax

FORco's taxable income	$10,000,000
Country L income tax rate	× 25%
Country L income tax	$2,500,000

Foreign withholding taxes on repatriated earnings $0

U.S. tax on repatriated earnings

Earnings from FORco	$10,000,000
U.S. tax rate	× 35%
Pre-credit U.S. tax	$3,500,000
Foreign tax credit	− 2,500,000
U.S. income tax	$1,000,000

Total taxes [$2,500,000 + $0 + $1,000,000] $3,500,000

Worldwide effective tax rate [$3,500,000 ÷ $10,000,000] 35%

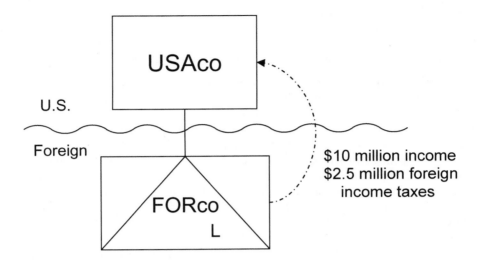

Summary. Table 8.4 summarizes the results of the nine case scenarios described above.

TABLE 8.4. COMPREHENSIVE EXAMPLE—SUMMARY

Case	U.S. tax rate	Foreign tax rate	Earnings repatriated	Repatriation method	Withholding tax rate	Effective tax rate
1	35%	25%	None	n.a	n.a	25.00%
2	35%	25%	50%	Dividend	10%	30.00%
3	35%	25%	50%	Dividend	30%	36.25%
4	35%	45%	None	n.a	n.a	45.00%
5	35%	45%	50%	Dividend	10%	47.75%
6	35%	45%	50%	Dividend	30%	53.25%
7	35%	45%	50%	Interest and royalties	0%	40.00%
8	35%	25%	50%	Interest and royalties	0%	30.00%
9 (HE)	35%	25%	100%	n.a	n.a	35.00%

¶ 808 FUTURE OF U.S. SYSTEM FOR TAXING U.S. MULTINATIONAL CORPORATIONS

In recent decades, most industrialized countries have significantly reduced their corporate income tax rates. For example, in 2014, the corporate tax rate was 21% in the United Kingdom, 25% in China, 26.5% in Canada, and the average was roughly 21% in the 34 countries that comprise the European Union. In contrast, the last time the U.S. reduced its corporate tax rate was in the late 1980s, when it lowered its 46%tax rate to 34%. In 1993, the U.S. increased the tax rate to 35%, and it has remained unchanged for over 20 years. In addition to the federal tax rate of 35%, most U.S.states also impose a corporate income tax, with rates generally ranging from 5% to 10%. Consequently, U.S. corporate income tax rates are currently much higher than nearly all of its major trading partners.

Another distinctive feature of the U.S. system for taxing multinational corporations is that U.S. corporations are eventually required to pay U.S. taxes on business profits earned abroad. Under this worldwide tax system, U.S. companies are able to defer U.S. taxation of foreign business profits earned through foreign subsidiaries, but only if the earnings are reinvested abroad. A U.S. tax is imposed, however, when the earnings are repatriated through dividend distributions. This system allows U.S. companies to compete abroad on a tax parity with foreign companies, but can impose a significant tax burden on U.S. companies that reinvest their foreign earnings back into the U.S. economy. In contrast, nearly all other industrialized countries use a territorial system for taxing the business profits of a domestic multinational corporation. Under a territorial tax system, a country taxes only those business profits that a domestic multinational corporation earns within the country's borders, and exempts a domestic multinational corporation's foreign earnings from domestic taxation.

The combination of a high corporate tax rate and a worldwide tax system has raised concerns about whether the U.S. corporate tax system is competitive with those of its major trading partners. In fact, the U.S. corporate tax climate has become so unattractive that some U.S.-based multinationals have moved their headquarters elsewhere through so-called "corporate inversion" transactions.

A corporate inversion is a transaction in which an established U.S. multinational corporation reorganizes its structure so that the parent company is a foreign corporation rather than a U.S. corporation. In effect, a foreign corporation acquires the established U.S. company, and the U.S. company becomes a subsidiary of a foreign parent corporation. A corporate inversion typically has little or no effect on the actual business operations of the company, but it can provide significant U.S. tax benefits. Because the parent corporation of the multinational company is no longer a U.S. corporation, the U.S. no longer taxes the foreign profits earned by the foreign subsidiaries and the new foreign parent can access those foreign earnings without triggering U.S. consequences.

U.S. lawmakers have made numerous proposals for improving the competitiveness of the U.S. corporate tax system, such as reducing the corporate tax rate to 25% and replacing the worldwide tax system with a territorial tax system. As of May 2015, however, none of these proposals have been enacted into law.

¶ 809 SURVEY OF FOREIGN ENTITY CLASSIFICATION

This survey (Tables 8.5, 8.6 and 8.7) lists entities in selected foreign countries, discusses whether the foreign country imposes an entity level tax, describes the treatment for U.S. tax purposes if an election is not made (whether the entity is a per se corporation or has default status as a corporation or pass-through entity), and considers the possibility for treatment as a hybrid or reverse hybrid entity. In each listed country, U.S. owners may operate as a sole proprietorship or a branch, which is not treated as a separate entity under the check-the-box rules.

For example, in Hong Kong, the principal business forms are limited liability companies, whether referred to as public or private, partnerships and limited partnerships, branches of foreign companies, and sole proprietors. A public limited liability company is easy to classify because it is the only Hong Kong entity on the per se list.[61] Therefore, the shareholders of a public limited liability company must treat it as a corporation for U.S. tax purposes. As a public limited liability company, it must pay a corporate tax in Hong Kong[62] and does not offer any hybrid planning opportunities.

A private limited liability company is an entity whose creditors are limited to pursuit of the company's assets.[63] As a result, the default rules treat the private limited liability company as a corporation. However, because the private limited liability company pays a Hong Kong corporate income tax,[64] it presents hybrid tax planning opportunities if its shareholders elect partnership or branch classification for U.S. tax purposes. The failure to elect will result in the default rules limiting planning opportunities.

Hong Kong law provides for both partnerships and limited partnerships. Under common law, a partnership constitutes a separate entity.[65] Since each partner is liable for all the debts and obligations of the partnership, the default rules treat the entity as a partnership for U.S. tax purposes. Similarly, the default rules also treat a Hong Kong limited partnership as a partnership because one or more partners have unlimited liability. Since Hong Kong taxes a partner's share of partnership income only once,[66] a reverse hybrid entity planning opportunity exists if the partnership's partners elect corporate classification for U.S. purposes. Failure to elect corporate status will result in a loss of this opportunity through partnership classification in both countries.

---

[61] Reg. § 301.7701-2(b)(8); Table 9.3.
[62] Chapter 112, Laws of Hong Kong, Section 41.
[63] Chapter 32, Laws of Hong Kong, Section 4(2)(a).

[64] Chapter 112, Laws of Hong Kong, Section 45.
[65] Chapter 112, Laws of Hong Kong, Section 22(1).
[66] Chapter 112, Laws of Hong Kong, Section 22(1).

TABLE 8.5. CLASSIFICATION OF ENTITIES IN ASIAN COUNTRIES

	Foreign country tax[67]	*Status without a check-the-box election*	*Hybrid or reverse hybrid opportunity*
Australia			
Public limited liability company	Yes	Per Se Corp	——
Private limited liability company	Yes	Corporation	Hybrid
Partnership	No	Pass-through	Reverse
Hong Kong			
Public limited liability company	Yes	Per Se Corp	——
Private limited liability company	Yes	Corporation	Hybrid
Partnerships	No	Pass-through	Reverse
Limited partnerships	No	Pass-through	Reverse
Japan			
Joint stock companies (kabushiki kaisha)	Yes	Per Se Corp	——
Limited liability company (yugen kaisha)	Yes	Corporation	Hybrid
Unlimited liability partnership company (gomei kaisha)	Yes	Pass-through	Hybrid
Limited liability partnership company (goshi kaisha)	Yes	Pass-through	Hybrid
General partnership (nin-i kumiai)	No	Pass-through	Hybrid
Silent partnership (tokumei kumiai)	No	Pass-through	Hybrid
Korea			
Stock corporation (chusik hoesa)	Yes	Per Se Corp	——
Limited liability company (yuhan hoesa)	Yes	Corporation	Hybrid
Unlimited membership enterprise (hapmyong hoesa)	No	Pass-through	Reverse
Limited partnership (hapja hoesa)	No	Pass-through	Reverse
Singapore			
Private limited company	Yes	Corporation	Hybrid
Public limited company	Yes	Per Se Corp	——
General partnership	No	Pass-through	Hybrid
Limited partnership	No	Pass-through	Hybrid
Limited liability partnership	No	Pass-through	Hybrid

---

[67] Many of the entities listed as not subject to foreign country tax do contain some type of mechanism, such as withholding to ensure collection of tax on a non-resident's share of income.

TABLE 8.6. CLASSIFICATION OF ENTITIES IN EUROPE

	Foreign country tax	Status without a check-the-box election	Hybrid or reverse hybrid opportunity
European Union			
Societas Europaea	No	Per Se Corp	——
European Economic Interest Grouping (EEIG)	No	Pass-through	Reverse
France			
Joint stock company "SA" (societe anonyme)	Yes	Per Se Corp	——
Limited liability company "SARL" (societe a responsabilite limitee)	Yes	Corporation	Hybrid
Simplified limited liability company "SAS" (societe par actions simplifiee)	Yes	Corporation	Hybrid
General partnership "SNC" (societe en nom collectif)	No	Pass-through	Reverse
Limited partnership "SCS" (societe en commandite simple)	No	Pass-through	Reverse
Partnership limited by shares "SCPA" (societe en commandite par actions)	No	Pass-through	Reverse
Germany			
Limited liability company "GmbH" (Gesellschaft mit beschrankter Haftung)	Yes	Corporation	Hybrid
Stock corporation "AG" (Aktiengesellschaft)	Yes	Per Se Corp	——
General commercial partnership "OHG" (Handelsgesellschaft)	No	Pass-through	Reverse
Limited partnership "KG" (Kommanditgesellschaft)	No	Pass-through	Reverse
Limited partnership with Transferable shares "KgaA" (Kommanditgesellschaft auf Aktien)	No	Pass-through	Reverse
Civil law partnership "GbR" (Gesellschaft burgerlichen Rechts)	No	Pass-through	Reverse
Silent partnership (Stile Gesellschaft)	No	Pass-through	Reverse
Ireland			
Private limited company	Yes	Corporation	Hybrid
Public limited company	Yes	Per Se Corp	——
General partnership	No	Pass-through	Reverse
Limited partnership	No	Pass-through	Reverse
Italy			
Corporation "SpA" (Societa per Azioni)	Yes	Per Se Corp	——
Limited liability company "SRL" (Societa a Responsabilita Limitata)	Yes	Corporation	Hybrid

¶809

	Foreign country tax	Status without a check-the-box election	Hybrid or reverse hybrid opportunity
General partnership "SNC" (Societa in Nome Collettivo)	No	Pass-through	Reverse
Limited partnership "Sas" (Societa in Accomandita Semplice)	No	Pass-through	Reverse
Limited share partnership "SapA" (Societa in Accomandita per Azioni)	No	Pass-through	Reverse
The Netherlands			
Private limited liability company "BV" (Besloten Vennootschap Mat Beperkte Aansprakelijkheid)	Yes	Corporation	Hybrid
Public limited liability company "NV" (Naamlooze Vennootschap)	Yes	Per Se Corp	——
General partnership "VOF" (Vennootschap Onder Firma)	No	Pass-through	Reverse
Limited partnership "CV" (Commanditaire Vennootschap)	No	Pass-through	Reverse
Switzerland			
Corporation "SA" (Societe Annonyme)	Yes	Per Se Corp	——
Limited liability company "Sarl" (Societe a Responsabilite Limitee)	Yes	Corporation	Hybrid
General partnership (Societe en nom Collectif)	No	Pass-through	Reverse
Limited partnership (Societe en Commandite)	No	Pass-through	Reverse
The United Kingdom			
Private limited company	Yes	Corporation	Hybrid
Public limited company	Yes	Per Se Corp	——
Partnership	No	Flow Through	Reverse
Limited partnership	No	Flow Through	Reverse

¶809

TABLE 8.7. CLASSIFICATION OF ENTITIES IN THE AMERICAS

	Foreign country tax	Status without a check-the-box election	Hybrid or reverse hybrid opportunity
Argentina			
Stock corporation (sociedad anonima)	Yes	Per Se Corp	——
Limited liability company (sociedad de responsabilidad limitada)	Yes	Corporation	Hybrid
General partnership (sociedad colectiva)	No	Pass-through	Reverse
Limited partnership (sociedad en comandita)	No	Pass-through	Reverse
Brazil			
Corporation (sociedade anonima)	Yes	Per Se Corp	——
Limited liability company (sociedade limitada)	Yes	Corporation	Hybrid
Partnership (sociedade simples)	No	Pass-through	Reverse
Limited partnership (sociedade em comandita poracoes)	No	Pass-through	Reverse
Silent partnership (sociedade em conta de participacao)	No	Pass-through	Reverse
Canada			
Corporation (federal and provincial)	Yes	Per Se Corp	——
Unlimited Liability Company (ULC)	Yes	Corporation	Hybrid
General partnership	No	Pass-through	Reverse
Limited partnership	No	Pass-through	Reverse
Mexico			
Corporation with fixed capital (sociedad anomima)	Yes	Per Se Corp	——
Corporation with variable capital (sociedad anomima de capital variable)	Yes	Per Se Corp	——
Limited liability company (sociedad responsabilidad limitada)	Yes	Corporation	Hybrid
Limited liability company with variable capital (sociedad responsabilidad limitada de capital variable)	Yes	Corporation	Hybrid
General partnerships (sociedad en nombre colectivo)	No	Pass-through	Reverse
Limited partnership with shares (sociedad en comandita simple)	No	Pass-through	Reverse
Limited partnership without shares (sociedad en comandita por acciones)	No	Pass-through	Reverse
Joint ventures (asociacion en participacion)	No	Pass-through	Reverse

¶809

¶ 810 APPENDIX

On January 1, 2014, Mark Twain, a U.S. citizen, forms the Twain Hong Kong Private Limited Company in Hong Kong. Mark Twain decides to "check-the-box" by filing a Form 8832 and does so on March 15, 2014. Because the election may be retroactive for up to 75 days, Mark Twain chooses to have the election effective January 1, 2014. Pursuant to the IRS's instructions with respect to Form 8832, Twain Hong Kong Private Limited Company had to have an Employer Identification number before its entity classification could be elected. It is insufficient to put "applied for" on the form for the Employer Identification number.

Form **8832**

(Rev. December 2013)

Department of the Treasury
Internal Revenue Service

Entity Classification Election

▶ Information about Form 8832 and its instructions is at *www.irs.gov/form8832.*

OMB No. 1545-1516

	Name of eligible entity making election	Employer identification number
Type or Print	Twain Hong Kong Private Limited Company	88-8888888
	Number, street, and room or suite no. If a P.O. box, see instructions.	
	City or town, state, and ZIP code. If a foreign address, enter city, province or state, postal code and country. Follow the country's practice for entering the postal code.	

▶ Check if: ☐ Address change ☐ Late classification relief sought under Revenue Procedure 2009-41
☐ Relief for a late change of entity classification election sought under Revenue Procedure 2010-32

Part I **Election Information**

1 **Type of election** (see instructions):

a ☑ Initial classification by a newly-formed entity. Skip lines 2a and 2b and go to line 3.

b ☐ Change in current classification. Go to line 2a.

2a Has the eligible entity previously filed an entity election that had an effective date within the last 60 months?

☐ **Yes.** Go to line 2b.
☑ **No.** Skip line 2b and go to line 3.

2b Was the eligible entity's prior election an initial classification election by a newly formed entity that was effective on the date of formation?

☐ **Yes.** Go to line 3.
☐ **No.** Stop here. You generally are not currently eligible to make the election (see instructions).

3 Does the eligible entity have more than one owner?

☐ **Yes.** You can elect to be classified as a partnership or an association taxable as a corporation. Skip line 4 and go to line 5.
☑ **No.** You can elect to be classified as an association taxable as a corporation or to be disregarded as a separate entity. Go to line 4.

4 If the eligible entity has only one owner, provide the following information:

a Name of owner ▶ Mark Twain

b Identifying number of owner ▶ 123-45-6789

5 If the eligible entity is owned by one or more affiliated corporations that file a consolidated return, provide the name and employer identification number of the parent corporation:

a Name of parent corporation ▶

b Employer identification number ▶

For Paperwork Reduction Act Notice, see instructions. Cat. No. 22598R Form **8832** (Rev. 12-2013)

10559492

Part I	**Election Information** (Continued)

6   **Type of entity** (see instructions):

a   ☐ A domestic eligible entity electing to be classified as an association taxable as a corporation.
b   ☐ A domestic eligible entity electing to be classified as a partnership.
c   ☐ A domestic eligible entity with a single owner electing to be disregarded as a separate entity.
d   ☐ A foreign eligible entity electing to be classified as an association taxable as a corporation.
e   ☐ A foreign eligible entity electing to be classified as a partnership.
f   ☑ A foreign eligible entity with a single owner electing to be disregarded as a separate entity.

7   If the eligible entity is created or organized in a foreign jurisdiction, provide the foreign country of
organization ▶ Hong Kong

8   Election is to be effective beginning (month, day, year) (see instructions) . . . . ▶   11/1/14

9 Name and title of contact person whom the IRS may call for more information	**10** Contact person's telephone number
Mark Twain	573-555-8765

Consent Statement and Signature(s) (see instructions)

Under penalties of perjury, I (we) declare that I (we) consent to the election of the above-named entity to be classified as indicated above, and that I (we) have examined this election and consent statement, and to the best of my (our) knowledge and belief, this election and consent statement are true, correct, and complete. If I am an officer, manager, or member signing for the entity, I further declare under penalties of perjury that I am authorized to make the election on its behalf.

Signature(s)	Date	Title

Form **8832** (Rev. 12-2013)

| **Part II** | **Late Election Relief** |

11 Provide the explanation as to why the entity classification election was not filed on time (see instructions).

_____

_____

_____

_____

_____

_____

_____

_____

_____

Under penalties of perjury, I (we) declare that I (we) have examined this election, including accompanying documents, and, to the best of my (our) knowledge and belief, the election contains all the relevant facts relating to the election, and such facts are true, correct, and complete. I (we) further declare that I (we) have personal knowledge of the facts and circumstances related to the election. I (we) further declare that the elements required for relief in Section 4.01 of Revenue Procedure 2009-41 have been satisfied.

Signature(s)	Date	Title

On January 1, 2014, Mark Twain, a U.S. citizen, contributes $15,000,000 U.S. to a Hong Kong private limited company called Twain Hong Kong Private Limited Company. Mark Twain timely files a Form 8832 to check-the-box for the Hong Kong entity.

The chartered accountant in Hong Kong provides you with the following account information in Hong Kong dollars for the year ended December 31, 2014.

Sales:	$25,000,000
Cost of Goods Sold:	$15,000,000
Compensation:	$ 2,000,000
Cash:	$31,400,000
Accounts Payable:	$15,000,000

The average exchange rate is $1.5 U.S. to $1 HK. Twain must prepare a Form 8858 for this foreign disregarded entity.

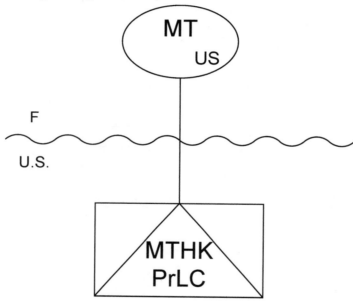

Form **8858**	**Information Return of U.S. Persons With Respect To Foreign Disregarded Entities**	OMB No. 1545-1910
(Rev. December 2013)	▶ Information about Form 8858 and its separate instructions is at *www.irs.gov/form8858.*	
Department of the Treasury Internal Revenue Service	Information furnished for the foreign disregarded entity's annual accounting period (see instructions) beginning _____ , 20 **14** , and ending _____ , 20 **14**	Attachment Sequence No. **140**

Name of person filing this return	Filer's identifying number
Mark Twain	123-45-6789

Number, street, and room or suite no. (or P.O. box number if mail is not delivered to street address)

City or town, state, and ZIP code

Hannibal, MO

Filer's tax year beginning	**January 1** , 20 **14** , and ending	**December 31** , 20 **14**

Important: *Fill in all applicable lines and schedules. All information **must** be in English. All amounts **must** be stated in U.S. dollars unless otherwise indicated.*

1a Name and address of foreign disregarded entity	**b(1)** U.S. identifying number, if any
	88-8888888
	b(2) Reference ID number (see instructions)

Twain Hong Kong Private Limited Company

c Country(ies) under whose laws organized and entity type under local tax law		**d** Date(s) of organization	**e** Effective date as foreign disregarded entity

Hong Kong

f If benefits under a U.S. tax treaty were claimed with respect to income of the foreign disregarded entity, enter the treaty and article number	**g** Country in which principal business activity is conducted	**h** Principal business activity	**i** Functional currency
	Hong Kong		**Hong Kong Dollars**

2 Provide the following information for the foreign disregarded entity's accounting period stated above.

a Name, address, and identifying number of branch office or agent (if any) in the United States	**b** Name and address (including corporate department, if applicable) of person(s) with custody of the books and records of the foreign disregarded entity, and the location of such books and records, if different

3 For the **tax owner** of the foreign disregarded entity (if different from the filer) provide the following (see instructions):

a Name and address	**b** Annual accounting period covered by the return (see instructions)
	c(1) U.S. identifying number, if any
	c(2) Reference ID number (see instructions)
	d Country under whose laws organized / **e** Functional currency

4 For the **direct owner** of the foreign disregarded entity (if different from the tax owner) provide the following (see instructions):

a Name and address	**b** Country under whose laws organized
	c U.S. identifying number, if any / **d** Functional currency

5 Attach an organizational chart that identifies the name, placement, percentage of ownership, tax classification, and country of organization of all entities in the chain of ownership between the tax owner and the foreign disregarded entity, and the chain of ownership between the foreign disregarded entity and each entity in which the foreign disregarded entity has a 10% or more direct or indirect interest. See instructions.

For Paperwork Reduction Act Notice, see the separate instructions.   Cat. No. 21457L   Form **8858** (Rev. 12-2013)

Form 8858 (Rev. 12-2013)   Page **2**

Schedule C   **Income Statement** (see instructions)

Important: *Report all information in functional currency in accordance with U.S. GAAP. Also, report each amount in U.S. dollars translated from functional currency (using GAAP translation rules or the average exchange rate determined under section 989(b)). If the functional currency is the U.S. dollar, complete only the U.S. Dollars column. See instructions for special rules for foreign disregarded entities that use DASTM.*
If you are using the average exchange rate (determined under section 989(b)), check the following box . . . . . . ☑

			Functional Currency	U.S. Dollars
1	Gross receipts or sales (net of returns and allowances)	1	25,000,000	12,500,000
2	Cost of goods sold	2	15,000,000	7,500,000
3	Gross profit (subtract line 2 from line 1)	3	10,000,000	5,000,000
4	Other income.	4		
5	Total income (add lines 3 and 4)	5	10,000,000	5,000,000
6	Total deductions	6	2,000,000	1,000,000
7	Other adjustments	7		
8	Net income (loss) per books	8	8,000,000	4,000,000

Schedule C-1   Section 987 Gain or Loss Information

			(a) Amount stated in functional currency of foreign disregarded entity	(b) Amount stated in functional currency of recipient
	Note. See the instructions if there are multiple recipients of remittances from the foreign disregarded entity.			
1	Remittances from the foreign disregarded entity	1		
2	Section 987 gain (loss) of recipient	2		

		Yes	No
3	Were all remittances from the foreign disregarded entity treated as made to the direct owner?		
4	Did the tax owner change its method of accounting for section 987 gain or loss with respect to remittances from the foreign disregarded entity during the tax year?.		

Schedule F   Balance Sheet

Important: *Report all amounts in U.S. dollars computed in functional currency and translated into U.S. dollars in accordance with U.S. GAAP. See instructions for an exception for foreign disregarded entities that use DASTM.*

	Assets		(a) Beginning of annual accounting period	(b) End of annual accounting period
1	Cash and other current assets	1		15,700,000
2	Other assets	2		
3	Total assets	3		15,700,000
	Liabilities and Owner's Equity			
4	Liabilities	4		7,500,000
5	Owner's equity	5		8,200,000
6	Total liabilities and owner's equity	6		15,700,000

Schedule G   Other Information

		Yes	No
1	During the tax year, did the foreign disregarded entity own an interest in any trust?.		✓
2	During the tax year, did the foreign disregarded entity own at least a 10% interest, directly or indirectly, in any foreign partnership?		✓
3	*Answer the following question only if the foreign disregarded entity made its election to be treated as disregarded from its owner during the tax year:* Did the tax owner claim a loss with respect to stock or debt of the foreign disregarded entity as a result of the election?		✓
4	If the interest in the foreign disregarded entity is a separate unit under Reg. 1.1503(d)-1(b)(4) or part of a combined separate unit under Reg. 1.1503(d)-1(b)(4)(ii) does the separate unit or combined separate unit have a dual consolidated loss as defined in Reg. 1.1503(d)-1(b)(5)(ii)?		

If "Yes," enter the amount of the dual consolidated loss ▶ $ Answer question 5a.

Form **8858** (Rev. 12-2013)

¶810

Form 8858 (Rev. 12-2013)   Page **3**

Schedule G	Other Information *(continued)*		
		Yes	**No**
5a	Was any portion of the dual consolidated loss in question 4 taken into account in computing consolidated taxable income for the year? If "Yes," go to 5b. If "No," skip 5b and 5c		✓
b	Was this a permitted domestic use of the dual consolidated loss under Reg. 1.1503(d)-6? If "Yes," see instructions and skip 5c. If "No," go to 5c		
c	If this was not a permitted domestic use, was the dual consolidated loss used to compute consolidated taxable income as provided under Reg. 1.1503(d)-4?		
	If "Yes," enter the separate unit's contribution to the cumulative consolidated taxable income ("cumulative register") as of the beginning of the tax year ▶ $_____ See instructions.		
6	During the tax year, did the foreign disregarded entity pay or accrue any foreign tax that was disqualified for credit under section 901(m)?		✓
7	During the tax year, did the foreign disregarded entity pay or accrue foreign taxes to which section 909 applies, or treat foreign taxes that were previously suspended under section 909 as no longer suspended?		✓
8	*Answer the following question only if the tax owner of the foreign disregarded entity is a controlled foreign corporation (CFC):* Were there any intracompany transactions between the foreign disregarded entity and the CFC or any other branch of the CFC during the tax year, in which the foreign disregarded entity acted as a manufacturing, selling, or purchasing branch?		

Schedule H	Current Earnings and Profits or Taxable Income (see instructions)		
Important: *Enter the amounts on lines 1 through 6 in functional currency.*			
1	Current year net income or (loss) per foreign books of account	**1**	8,000,000
2	Total net additions	**2**	
3	Total net subtractions	**3**	
4	Current earnings and profits (or taxable income—see instructions) (line 1 plus line 2 minus line 3) . .	**4**	8,000,000
5	DASTM gain or loss (if applicable)	**5**	
6	Combine lines 4 and 5.	**6**	
7	Current earnings and profits (or taxable income) in U.S. dollars (line 6 translated at the average exchange rate determined under section 989(b) and the related regulations (see instructions)) . . .	**7**	8,000,000
	Enter exchange rate used for line 7 ▶		

Form **8858** (Rev. 12-2013)

On January 1, 2014, Mark Twain, a U.S. citizen, contributes $14,850,000 to a United Kingdom partnership called Brit Partnership. The other 1% partner is Charles Phillip Arthur George, a subject of the United Kingdom, who contributes $150,000 for the remaining 1% interest.

The chartered accountant in Cambridge provides you with the following account information for the year ended December 31, 2014:

Sales:	£25,000,000
Cost of Goods Sold:	£15,000,000
Compensation:	£ 2,000,000
Taxes:	£ 2,000,000
Cash:	£16,000,000
Inventory:	£15,000,000
Accounts Payable:	£15,000,000

The British pound was worth $1.50 during each day of 2014.

When filing Form 8865, Mark Twain is a Category 1 filer because he controls a foreign partnership during the year. Twain is not a Category 2 filer because Category 1 filers are excluded from being Category 2 Filers. Twain is a Category 3 filer because he contributed property to the foreign partnership in excess of $100,000 and, in addition, his interest in the foreign partnership is greater than 10% (99%). Twain is a Category 4 filer because he acquired more than 10% of Brit Partnership during the year, but the additional filing requirements of Category 4 (Schedule P) are rendered unnecessary by the Category 3 filings.

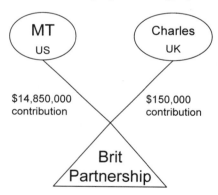

Form **8865**

Department of the Treasury
Internal Revenue Service

Return of U.S. Persons With Respect to Certain Foreign Partnerships

▶ Attach to your tax return.
▶ Information about Form 8865 and its separate instructions is at *www.irs.gov/form8865.*
Information furnished for the foreign partnership's tax year
beginning _____ , 2014, and ending _____ , 20 **14**

OMB No. 1545-1668

20**14**

Attachment
Sequence No. **118**

Name of person filing this return	Filer's identifying number
Mark Twain	123-45-6789

Filer's address (if you are not filing this form with your tax return)

1234 Main Street
Hannibal, MO 63401

A Category of filer (see **Categories of Filers** in the instructions and check applicable box(es)):
1 ☑   2 ☐   3 ☑   4 ☐

B Filer's tax year beginning _____ , 20 _____ , and ending _____ , 20 _____

C Filer's share of liabilities: Nonrecourse $ _____ 22,275,000 _____ Qualified nonrecourse financing $ _____ Other $ _____

D If filer is a member of a consolidated group but not the parent, enter the following information about the parent:

Name _____ EIN _____

Address _____

E Information about certain other partners (see instructions)

(1) Name	(2) Address	(3) Identifying number	(4) Check applicable box(es)		
			Category 1	Category 2	Constructive owner

F1 Name and address of foreign partnership	**2(a)** EIN (if any)
Brit Partnership Cambridge, England CB2 3AP	**2(b)** Reference ID number (see instr.) BRITP2014 **3** Country under whose laws organized United Kingdom

4 Date of organization	**5** Principal place of business	**6** Principal business activity code number	**7** Principal business activity	**8a** Functional currency	**8b** Exchange rate (see instr.)
1/1/14	United Kingdom	423910	sporting goods	Pound Sterling	$1 - €0.6667

G Provide the following information for the foreign partnership's tax year:

1 Name, address, and identifying number of agent (if any) in the United States

N/A

2 Check if the foreign partnership must file:
☐ Form 1042   ☐ Form 8804   ☐ Form 1065 or 1065-B
Service Center where Form 1065 or 1065-B is filed: _____

3 Name and address of foreign partnership's agent in country of organization, if any

Charles Philip Arthur George
Windsor, England

4 Name and address of person(s) with custody of the books and records of the foreign partnership, and the location of such books and records, if different

Charles Philip Arthur George, Windsor, England

5 Were any special allocations made by the foreign partnership? . . . . ▶ ☐ Yes ☑ No

6 Enter the number of Forms 8858, Information Return of U.S. Persons With Respect To Foreign Disregarded Entities, attached to this return (see instructions) . . . . ▶ _____ 0 _____

7 How is this partnership classified under the law of the country in which it is organized? ▶ Partnership

8a Does the filer have an interest in the foreign partnership, or an interest indirectly through the foreign partnership, that is a separate unit under Reg. 1.1503(d)-1(b)(4) or part of a combined separate unit under Reg. 1.1503(d)-1(b)(4)(ii)? If "No," skip question 8b. ▶ ☐ Yes ☑ No

b If "Yes," does the separate unit or combined separate unit have a dual consolidated loss as defined in Reg. 1.1503(d)-1(b)(5)(ii)? ▶ ☐ Yes ☐ No

9 Does this partnership meet **both** of the following requirements?
• The partnership's total receipts for the tax year were less than $250,000 and
• The value of the partnership's total assets at the end of the tax year was less than $1 million.
If "Yes," **do not** complete Schedules L, M-1, and M-2.
. . . . . ▶ ☐ Yes ☑ No

Sign Here Only If You Are Filing This Form Separately and Not With Your Tax Return.

Under penalties of perjury, I declare that I have examined this return, including accompanying schedules and statements, and to the best of my knowledge and belief, it is true, correct, and complete. Declaration of preparer (other than general partner or limited liability company member) is based on all information of which preparer has any knowledge.

▶ _____ ▶ _____
Signature of general partner or limited liability company member   Date

Paid Preparer Use Only

Print/Type preparer's name	Preparer's signature	Date	Check ☐ if self-employed	PTIN
Firm's name ▶			Firm's EIN ▶	
Firm's address ▶			Phone no.	

For Privacy Act and Paperwork Reduction Act Notice, see the separate instructions.   Cat. No. 25852A   Form **8865** (2014)

Form 8865 (2014)   Page **2**

Schedule A — Constructive Ownership of Partnership Interest.

Check the boxes that apply to the filer. If you check box **b**, enter the name, address, and U.S. taxpayer identifying number (if any) of the person(s) whose interest you constructively own. See instructions.

a ☑ Owns a direct interest   **b** ☐ Owns a constructive interest

Name	Address	Identifying number (if any)	Check if foreign person	Check if direct partner
Mark Twain	1234 Main Street, Hannibal, MO	123-45-6789		✓

Schedule A-1 — Certain Partners of Foreign Partnership (see instructions)

Name	Address	Identifying number (if any)	Check if foreign person

Does the partnership have any other foreign person as a direct partner? . . . . ☑ Yes   ☐ No

Schedule A-2 — Affiliation Schedule.

List all partnerships (foreign or domestic) in which the foreign partnership owns a direct interest or indirectly owns a 10% interest.

Name	Address	EIN (if any)	Total ordinary income or loss	Check if foreign partnership

Schedule B — Income Statement—Trade or Business Income

Caution. Include **only** trade or business income and expenses on lines 1a through 22 below. See the instructions for more information.

1a	Gross receipts or sales	**1a** 37,500,000	00	
b	Less returns and allowances	**1b**		**1c** 37,500,000 00
2	Cost of goods sold			**2** 22,500,000 00
3	Gross profit. Subtract line 2 from line 1c			**3** 15,000,000 00
4	Ordinary income (loss) from other partnerships, estates, and trusts (attach statement)			**4**
5	Net farm profit (loss) (attach Schedule F (Form 1040))			**5**
6	Net gain (loss) from Form 4797, Part II, line 17 (attach Form 4797)			**6**
7	Other income (loss) (attach statement)			**7**
8	**Total income (loss).** Combine lines 3 through 7			**8** 15,000,000 00
9	Salaries and wages (other than to partners) (less employment credits)			**9** 3,000,000 00
10	Guaranteed payments to partners			**10**
11	Repairs and maintenance			**11**
12	Bad debts			**12**
13	Rent			**13**
14	Taxes and licenses			**14**
15	Interest			**15**
16a	Depreciation (if required, attach Form 4562)	**16a**		
b	Less depreciation reported elsewhere on return	**16b**		**16c**
17	Depletion (**Do not** deduct oil and gas depletion.)			**17**
18	Retirement plans, etc.			**18**
19	Employee benefit programs			**19**
20	Other deductions (attach statement)			**20**
21	**Total deductions.** Add the amounts shown in the far right column for lines 9 through 20			**21** 3,000,000 00
22	**Ordinary business income (loss)** from trade or business activities. Subtract line 21 from line 8			**22** 12,000,000 00

Income (lines 1a–8)   *Deductions (see instructions for limitations)* (lines 9–22)

Form **8865** (2014)

¶810

Form 8865 (2014)   Page **3**

Schedule K		Partners' Distributive Share Items		Total amount	
Income (Loss)	1	Ordinary business income (loss) (page 2, line 22)	1	12,000,000	00
	2	Net rental real estate income (loss) (attach Form 8825)	2		
	3a	Other gross rental income (loss)	3a		
	b	Expenses from other rental activities (attach statement) . . .	3b		
	c	Other net rental income (loss). Subtract line 3b from line 3a	3c		
	4	Guaranteed payments	4		
	5	Interest income	5		
	6	Dividends: **a** Ordinary dividends	6a		
		b Qualified dividends	6b		
	7	Royalties	7		
	8	Net short-term capital gain (loss) (attach Schedule D (Form 1065)) . . .	8		
	9a	Net long-term capital gain (loss) (attach Schedule D (Form 1065))	9a		
	b	Collectibles (28%) gain (loss)	9b		
	c	Unrecaptured section 1250 gain (attach statement)	9c		
	10	Net section 1231 gain (loss) (attach Form 4797)	10		
	11	Other income (loss) (see instructions) Type ▶	11		
Deductions	12	Section 179 deduction (attach Form 4562)	12		
	13a	Contributions	13a		
	b	Investment interest expense	13b		
	c	Section 59(e)(2) expenditures: **(1)** Type ▶ _____ **(2)** Amount ▶	13c(2)		
	d	Other deductions (see instructions) Type ▶	13d		
Self-Employ-ment	14a	Net earnings (loss) from self-employment	14a		
	b	Gross farming or fishing income	14b		
	c	Gross nonfarm income	14c		
Credits	15a	Low-income housing credit (section 42(j)(5))	15a		
	b	Low-income housing credit (other)	15b		
	c	Qualified rehabilitation expenditures (rental real estate) (attach Form 3468)	15c		
	d	Other rental real estate credits (see instructions) Type ▶	15d		
	e	Other rental credits (see instructions) Type ▶	15e		
	f	Other credits (see instructions) Type ▶	15f		
Foreign Transactions	16a	Name of country or U.S. possession ▶			
	b	Gross income from all sources	16b	15,000,000	00
	c	Gross income sourced at partner level	16c		
		Foreign gross income sourced at partnership level			
	d	Passive category ▶ _____ **e** General category ▶ 15,000,000 **f** Other (attach statement) ▶	16f		
		Deductions allocated and apportioned at partner level			
	g	Interest expense ▶ _____ **h** Other . . . . ▶	16h		
		Deductions allocated and apportioned at partnership level to foreign source income			
	i	Passive category ▶ _____ **j** General category ▶ 3,000,000 **k** Other (attach statement) ▶	16k		
	l	Total foreign taxes (check one): ▶ ☐ Paid ☑ Accrued	16l	3,000,000	00
	m	Reduction in taxes available for credit (attach statement)	16m		
	n	Other foreign tax information (attach statement)			
Alternative Minimum Tax (AMT) Items	17a	Post-1986 depreciation adjustment	17a		
	b	Adjusted gain or loss	17b		
	c	Depletion (other than oil and gas)	17c		
	d	Oil, gas, and geothermal properties—gross income	17d		
	e	Oil, gas, and geothermal properties—deductions	17e		
	f	Other AMT items (attach statement)	17f		
Other Information	18a	Tax-exempt interest income	18a		
	b	Other tax-exempt income	18b		
	c	Nondeductible expenses	18c		
	19a	Distributions of cash and marketable securities	19a		
	b	Distributions of other property	19b		
	20a	Investment income	20a		
	b	Investment expenses	20b		
	c	Other items and amounts (attach statement)			

Form **8865** (2014)

¶810

Form 8865 (2014)   Page **4**

Schedule L	Balance Sheets per Books. (Not required if Item G9, page 1, is answered "Yes.")			
		Beginning of tax year		End of tax year	

	Assets	(a)	(b)	(c)	(d)
1	Cash		15,000,000		46,500,000
2a	Trade notes and accounts receivable				
b	Less allowance for bad debts				
3	Inventories				
4	U.S. government obligations				
5	Tax-exempt securities				
6	Other current assets (attach statement) . .				
7a	Loans to partners (or persons related to partners)				
b	Mortgage and real estate loans				
8	Other investments (attach statement) . . .				
9a	Buildings and other depreciable assets . .				
b	Less accumulated depreciation				
10a	Depletable assets				
b	Less accumulated depletion				
11	Land (net of any amortization)				
12a	Intangible assets (amortizable only) . . .				
b	Less accumulated amortization				
13	Other assets (attach statement)				
14	**Total** assets		15,000,000		46,500,000
	Liabilities and Capital				
15	Accounts payable				22,500,000
16	Mortgages, notes, bonds payable in less than 1 year				
17	Other current liabilities (attach statement) .				
18	All nonrecourse loans				
19a	Loans from partners (or persons related to partners)				
b	Mortgages, notes, bonds payable in 1 year or more				
20	Other liabilities (attach statement)				
21	Partners' capital accounts		15,000,000		24,000,000
22	**Total** liabilities and capital		15,000,000		46,500,000

Form **8865** (2014)

¶810

Form 8865 (2014)   Page **5**

Schedule M	**Balance Sheets for Interest Allocation**	**(a)** Beginning of tax year	**(b)** End of tax year
1	Total U.S. assets	0	0
2	Total foreign assets:		
a	Passive category		
b	General category	15,000,000	46,500,000
c	Other (attach statement)		

Schedule M-1	**Reconciliation of Income (Loss) per Books With Income (Loss) per Return.** (Not required if Item G9, page 1, is answered "Yes.")

1	Net income (loss) per books .	12,000,000		**6**	Income recorded on books this year not included on Schedule K, lines 1 through 11 (itemize):		
2	Income included on Schedule K, lines 1, 2, 3c, 5, 6a, 7, 8, 9a, 10, and 11 not recorded on books this year (itemize):			**a**	Tax-exempt interest $ _____		
3	Guaranteed payments (other than health insurance) . . .			**7**	Deductions included on Schedule K, lines 1 through 13d, and 16l not charged against book income this year (itemize):		
4	Expenses recorded on books this year not included on Schedule K, lines 1 through 13d, and 16l (itemize):			**a**	Depreciation $ _____		
a	Depreciation $ _____						
b	Travel and entertainment $_____			**8**	Add lines 6 and 7	0	00
				9	Income (loss). Subtract line 8 from line 5	12,000,000	00
5	Add lines 1 through 4 . . .	12,000,000	00				

Schedule M-2	**Analysis of Partners' Capital Accounts.** (Not required if Item G9, page 1, is answered "Yes.")

1	Balance at beginning of year	15,000,000	00	**6**	Distributions: **a** Cash . . .		
2	Capital contributed:				**b** Property . .		
	a Cash . . .			**7**	Other decreases (itemize): _____		
	b Property . .						
3	Net income (loss) per books .	12,000,000	00			3,000,000	00
4	Other increases (itemize): _____			**8**	Add lines 6 and 7	3,000,000	00
				9	Balance at end of year. Subtract line 8 from line 5	24,000,000	00
5	Add lines 1 through 4 . . .	27,000,000	00				

Form **8865** (2014)

¶810

Schedule N   **Transactions Between Controlled Foreign Partnership and Partners or Other Related Entities**

Important: Complete a separate Form 8865 and Schedule N for each controlled foreign partnership. Enter the totals for each type of transaction that occurred between the foreign partnership and the persons listed in columns (a) through (d).

	Transactions of foreign partnership	(a) U.S. person filing this return	(b) Any domestic corporation or partnership controlling or controlled by the U.S. person filing this return	(c) Any other foreign corporation or partnership controlling or controlled by the U.S. person filing this return	(d) Any U.S. person with a 10% or more direct interest in the controlled foreign partnership (other than the U.S. person filing this return)
1	Sales of inventory . . .				
2	Sales of property rights (patents, trademarks, etc.)				
3	Compensation received for technical, managerial, engineering, construction, or like services				
4	Commissions received .				
5	Rents, royalties, and license fees received				
6	Distributions received . .				
7	Interest received . . .				
8	Other				
9	Add lines 1 through 8 . .				
10	Purchases of inventory .	22,500,000			
11	Purchases of tangible property other than inventory				
12	Purchases of property rights (patents, trademarks, etc.)				
13	Compensation paid for technical, managerial, engineering, construction, or like services				
14	Commissions paid . . .				
15	Rents, royalties, and license fees paid				
16	Distributions paid . . .				
17	Interest paid				
18	Other				
19	Add lines 10 through 18 .	22,500,000			
20	Amounts borrowed (enter the maximum loan balance during the year). See instructions				
21	Amounts loaned (enter the maximum loan balance during the year). See instructions				

Form **8865** (2014)

¶810

| SCHEDULE O
(Form 8865)

Department of the Treasury
Internal Revenue Service | **Transfer of Property to a Foreign Partnership**
(under section 6038B)
▶ Attach to Form 8865. See Instructions for Form 8865.
▶ Information about Schedule O (Form 8865) and its separate instructions is at *www.irs.gov/form8865*. | OMB No. 1545-1668

20**14** |

Name of transferor		Filer's identifying number
Mark Twain		123-45-678

Name of foreign partnership	EIN (if any)	Reference ID number (see instructions)
Brit Partnership		BRITP2014

Part I Transfers Reportable Under Section 6038B

Type of property	(a) Date of transfer	(b) Number of items transferred	(c) Fair market value on date of transfer	(d) Cost or other basis	(e) Section 704(c) allocation method	(f) Gain recognized on transfer	(g) Percentage interest in partnership after transfer
Cash	1/1/14		$14,850,000				99%
Stock, notes receivable and payable, and other securities							
Inventory							
Tangible property used in trade or business							
Intangible property							
Other property							

Supplemental Information Required To Be Reported (see instructions):

Part II Dispositions Reportable Under Section 6038B

(a) Type of property	(b) Date of original transfer	(c) Date of disposition	(d) Manner of disposition	(e) Gain recognized by partnership	(f) Depreciation recapture recognized by partnership	(g) Gain allocated to partner	(h) Depreciation recapture allocated to partner

Part III Is any transfer reported on this schedule subject to gain recognition under section 904(f)(3) or section 904(f)(5)(F)? . . . . ▶ ☐ Yes ☑ No

For Paperwork Reduction Act Notice, see the Instructions for Form 8865.　　　Cat. No. 25909U　　　Schedule O (Form 8865) 2014

¶810

☐ Final K-1	☐ Amended K-1	OMB No. 1545-1668

Schedule K-1
(Form 8865)

Department of the Treasury
Internal Revenue Service

20 14

For calendar year 2014, or tax
year beginning _____, 2014
ending _____, 20 ___

Partner's Share of Income, Deductions,
Credits, etc. ► See back of form and separate instructions.

Part I	Information About the Partnership

A1 Partnership's employer identification number
N/A

A2 Reference ID number (see instr.)
BRITP2014

B Partnership's name, address, city, state, and ZIP code

Brit Partnership
Cambridge, England
CB2 3AP

Part II	Information About the Partner

C Partner's identifying number
123-45-678

D Partner's name, address, city, state, and ZIP code

Mark Twain
1234 Main Street
Hannibal, MO 53401

E Partner's share of profit, loss, capital, and deductions:
(see Partner's Instr. (Form 1065))

	Beginning	Ending
Profit	99 %	99 %
Loss	99 %	99 %
Capital	99 %	99 %
Deductions	99 %	99 %

F Partner's capital account analysis:

Beginning capital account	. . . . . $	14,850,000
Capital contributed during the year	. . . $	0
Current year increase (decrease)	. . . $	8,910,000
Withdrawals & distributions	. . . . $	(0)
Ending capital account	. . . . . $	23,760,000

☐ Tax basis   ☐ GAAP   ☐ Section 704(b) book
☐ Other (explain)

For IRS Use Only

Part III	Partner's Share of Current Year Income, Deductions, Credits, and Other Items

1	Ordinary business income (loss) 11,880,000	15	Credits 2,970,000
2	Net rental real estate income (loss)		
3	Other net rental income (loss)		
4	Guaranteed payments		
5	Interest income	16	Foreign transactions
6a	Ordinary dividends		
6b	Qualified dividends		
7	Royalties		
8	Net short-term capital gain (loss)		
9a	Net long-term capital gain (loss)		
9b	Collectibles (28%) gain (loss)		
9c	Unrecaptured section 1250 gain	17	Alternative minimum tax (AMT) items
10	Net section 1231 gain (loss)		
11	Other income (loss)		
		18	Tax-exempt income and nondeductible expenses
12	Section 179 deduction	19	Distributions
13	Other deductions		
		20	Other information
14	Self-employment earnings (loss)		

* See attached statement for additional information.

For Paperwork Reduction Act Notice, see Instructions for Form 8865.   IRS.gov/form8865   Cat. No. 28396B   **Schedule K-1 (Form 8865) 2014**

26784330

¶810

Chapter 9

Withholding on the Income of Foreign Persons in the United States

¶ 901 THE U.S. SYSTEM FOR TAXING FOREIGN PERSONS

.01 Overview

U.S. tax law contains the following two-pronged territorial system for taxing the U.S.-source income of nonresident alien individuals, foreign corporations, and other foreign persons:

   (i) *U.S.-source investment-type income*—If a nonresident alien individual or foreign corporation derives fixed, determinable, annual, or periodic income (primarily investment-type income) from sources within the United States, the U.S. taxes the gross amount of that income at a flat rate of 30%.[1] The person controlling the payment of the income must deduct and withhold the U.S. tax at a 30% rate.[2]

   (ii) *U.S. trade or business profits*—If a nonresident alien individual or foreign corporation is engaged in a trade or business within the United States, the net amount of effectively connected income with the conduct of that U.S. trade or business is taxed at the regular marginal rates.[3]

There are several major exceptions to the general rules for taxing foreign persons. For example, income tax treaties usually reduce the withholding tax rate on U.S.-source dividend, interest, and royalty income from the statutory rate of 30% to 15% or less. Capital gains also are generally exempt from U.S. taxation,[4] except for gains

---

[1] Code Secs. 871(a) and 881(a).
[2] Code Secs. 1441(a) and 1442(a).

[3] Code Secs. 871(b) and 882(a). The U.S. branch operations of a foreign corporation are also subject to the branch profits tax. Code Sec. 884.
[4] Reg. § 1.1441-2(b)(2).

¶901.01

on the sale of U.S. real property interests, which are taxed in the same manner as effectively connected income with the conduct of a U.S. trade or business.[5]

Example 9.1: NRA is a nonresident alien whose only connection with the United States is the ownership of the shares of a U.S. corporation, USSub. USSub has cash of $4 million and machinery with a fair market value of $6 million. If NRA sells the shares of USSub, NRA will not pay tax because a capital gain is neither FDAP nor ECI. Moreover, the source of income on the sale of shares of a U.S. corporation is foreign-source income. Foreign-source income of a foreign person is not within the U.S. taxing jurisdiction.

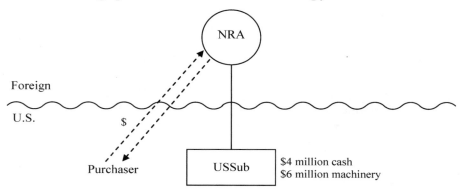

Chapter 9 discusses the U.S. system for taxing the U.S.-source fixed, determinable, annual, or period income of foreign persons (and other withholding aspects) and Chapter 10 (¶ 1001) discusses the U.S. system for taxing a foreign person's effectively connected income with the conduct of a U.S. trade or business.

.02 The Impact of U.S. Taxes on Total Tax Costs

The effect of U.S. taxation on a foreign person's total tax costs depends on the type of system that the foreign person's home country employs to mitigate international double taxation. For example, if a foreign person is a resident of a country that employs a territorial system, then the full amount of any U.S. taxes imposed on the taxpayer's U.S.-source income represents an out-of-pocket cost. In these situations, the foreign person's objective will be to minimize U.S. taxes, since every dollar of U.S. taxes saved reduces the foreign person's total tax costs by a dollar. On the other hand, if a foreign person is a resident of a home country that employs a credit system, then the foreign person's U.S. tax costs may be either partially or fully offset by the tax savings associated with the home country's foreign tax credit for U.S. taxes.

Example 9.2: FORco, a foreign corporation, has a branch sales office in the United States. FORco's effectively connected income to its U.S. trade or business is $100. FORco's home country allows FORco to claim a credit for the U.S. taxes paid on its U.S.-source income. Assuming the U.S. corporate tax rate

---

[5] Code Sec. 897(a)(1).

is 35% and FORco's home country rate is 40%, FORco can claim a credit for all of its U.S. income taxes, as follows.

Home country tax return		U.S. tax return	
Taxable income	$1 million	Taxable income	$1 million
Tax rate	× .40	U.S. tax rate	× .35
Pre-credit tax	400,000	U.S. tax	$ 350,000
Credit	– 350,000		
Home Tax	$ 50,000		

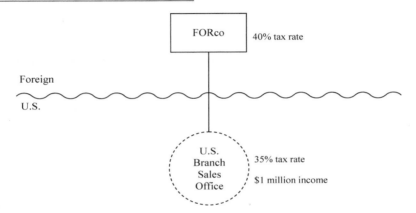

U.S. taxes do not represent an out-of-pocket tax cost in this case. For example, if FORco were able to reduce its U.S. tax from $350,000 to $340,000, the U.S. tax savings would be completely offset by an increase in home country taxes from $50,000 to $60,000.

Now, assume that FORco's home country only taxes income earned within its country. FORco does not pay any home country tax on the $1 million of U.S.-source income under the territorial system and pays only U.S. tax of $350,000 on the U.S.-source income, as follows.

Home country tax return		U.S. tax return	
Taxable income	$0	Taxable income	$1 million
Tax rate	× .40	U.S. tax rate	× .35
Home Tax	$0	U.S. Tax	$350,000

There are actually two U.S. withholding regimes with respect to investment-type income. First, the Foreign Account Tax Compliance Act of 2010 (FATCA)[6] imposes withholding for failure of foreign payees to provide information about

---

[6] Code Secs. 1471-1474.

beneficial U.S. recipients and is sometimes referred to Chapter 4 withholding. Second, the withholding regime for investment-type income imposes withholding on payments of fixed, determinable, annual or periodic income (FDAP) and is sometimes referred to as Chapter 3 withholding.

If the FATCA regime requires withholding on a particular payment, the FDAP regime does not apply. As a result, there will not be withholding under both the FATCA regime and the FDAP regime. However, because many of the FATCA withholding rules are the result of exceptions to the FDAP withholding rules, we will initially discuss the FDAP withholding rules.

¶ 902 WITHHOLDING ON U.S.-SOURCE FIXED, DETERMINABLE, ANNUAL, OR PERIODIC INCOME UNDER THE FDAP REGIME

.01 Introduction

As aforementioned, the FATCA regime under Chapter 4 threatens the withholding on U.S. source investment-type income and is more fully described in paragraph ¶ 903. This paragraph describes the more traditional withholding on U.S. source investment and compensation income under the regime for fixed, determinable, annual, or periodic income (FDAP) under Chapter 3, which applies only if the FATCA regime does not require withholding.

The United States taxes the gross amount of a foreign person's U.S.-source FDAP income, which is typically investment or compensation income, at a flat rate of 30%.[7] FDAP includes dividends, interest, royalties and, in contrast to the withholdable payment definition under the FATCA regime, includes compensation for personal services and excludes gains from the sales of income-producing assets.[8] Under the FDAP regime, the person controlling the payment of the income must deduct and withhold U.S. tax at the 30% rate.[9] Therefore, once the person controlling the payment withholds the appropriate amount of U.S. tax, a foreign recipient generally has no further U.S. tax obligations.[10] Withholding ensures the collection of taxes from foreign recipients, over whom the IRS would typically not have any collection jurisdiction. In order to withhold, the withholding agent must be able to readily ascertain both the tax base and the applicable tax rate. This explains both the gross basis taxation and the use of a flat tax rate because the withholding agent may not have any way of determining a foreign person's allocable expenses and appropriate tax bracket based on worldwide income.

.02 Income and Persons Subject to Withholding

Persons subject to withholding. The following lists the foreign persons[11] who are subject to U.S. withholding taxes:

   (i) Nonresident alien individuals,

   (ii) Foreign corporations,

---

[7] Code Secs. 871(a), 881(a), and 1441(a).
[8] Code Secs. 871(a) and 881(a).
[9] Code Secs. 1441(a) and 1442(a).

[10] An exception is services income, which is both FDAP and effectively connected income.
[11] *See also* ¶ 202.02.

(iii) Foreign partnerships,

(iv) Foreign estates, and

(v) Foreign trusts.[12]

A nonresident alien is an individual who is neither a citizen nor a resident of the United States.[13] An alien is a U.S. resident in any calendar year that he meets either the green card test or the substantial presence test.[14] A foreign corporation is a corporation organized or created under the laws of a foreign country or U.S. possession.[15] Likewise, a foreign partnership is a partnership organized or created under the laws of either a foreign country or a U.S. possession.[16] An estate is foreign if its foreign-source income, other than any effectively connected income with a U.S. trade or business, is not subject to U.S. taxation.[17] A trust is foreign if either no U.S. court is able to exercise primary supervision over the administration of the trust or no U.S. person has the authority to control all substantial decisions of the trust.[18]

Income subject to withholding. FDAP withholding under Chapter 3 is required with respect to any income that meets the following two tests:

(i) The income is fixed, determinable, annual, or periodic, and

(ii) The income is derived from sources within the United States.[19]

Fixed, determinable, annual, or periodic (FDAP) income includes dividends, interest (other than original issue discount), rents, royalties, salaries, wages, premiums, annuities, and other forms of compensation.[20] It is immaterial whether the income is received through a series of payments or in a single lump sum. For example, $60,000 in rental income is FDAP and subject to withholding whether it is paid in twelve payments of $5,000 each or in one payment of $60,000.[21] In addition, although the rules specifically exempt original issue discount from withholding, payors must withhold on certain accrued amounts on the sale or exchange of an original issue discount obligation[22] and on the imputed interest portion of an installment payment.[23]

Allowable deductions. No deductions are allowed for purposes of computing the amount of a foreign person's U.S.-source FDAP income subject to U.S. withholding taxes.[24] Otherwise, a potential abuse would result from the foreign recipients inflating the amount of their deductions. Moreover, allowing deductions would put the payor of the FDAP income in the awkward position of determining the veracity of the claimed deductions.

---

[12] Reg. §§ 1.1441-1(a) and 1.1441-3(f) and (g).

[13] Code Sec. 7701(b)(1)(B).

[14] Code Sec. 7701(b)(1)(A). The green card and substantial presence tests are discussed in Chapter 2 (¶ 202).

[15] Code Sec. 7701(a)(5).

[16] Code Sec. 7701(a)(5).

[17] Code Sec. 7701(a)(31)(A).

[18] Code Sec. 7701(a)(30)(E) and (a)(31)(B).

[19] Code. Sec. 1441(a) and (b). For this purpose, the United States includes the 50 states and the District of Columbia, but not U.S. possessions. Code Sec. 7701(a)(9).

[20] Code. Sec. 1441(b).

[21] Reg. § 1.1441-2(b)(1)(i).

[22] Code Secs. 871(a)(1)(C) and 881(a)(3).

[23] Reg. § 1.1441-2(a)(1) and Code Sec. 483(a).

[24] Reg. §§ 1.871-7(a)(3) and 1.881-2(a)(3).

Applicable tax rate. The statutory withholding rate on a foreign person's U.S.-source FDAP income is generally 30%.[25] However, as more fully described below, special statutory rates apply to certain types of income.

Withholding agent responsibilities. Any person having control, receipt, custody, disposal, or payment of an item of U.S.-source FDAP income to a foreign person is obligated to withhold U.S. tax.[26] Examples of withholding agents include corporations distributing dividends, debtors paying interest, tenants paying rents, and licensees paying royalties. A withholding agent who fails to withhold is liable for the uncollected tax.[27] Therefore, potential withholding agents must carefully monitor any payments made to foreign persons to ensure withholding of the appropriate amount of tax.

A withholding agent must deposit any taxes withheld with a Federal Reserve bank or an authorized financial institution through either using a federal tax deposit coupon or transferring funds electronically.[28] The withholding agent also must file an annual informational return, Form 1042, Annual Withholding Tax Return for U.S. Source Income of Foreign Persons. When filing Form 1042, the withholding agent must attach a separate Form 1042-S, Foreign Person's U.S. Source Income Subject to Withholding, for and to each foreign payee.[29] (Completed samples of Forms 1042 and 1042-S are included in the Appendix to this chapter.)

.03 Exemptions to Withholding and Special Rules

At first glance, it may appear that the United States imposes a significant tax burden on the U.S.-source FDAP income of foreign persons given the 30% tax rate and the stringent withholding requirements under Chapter 3. According to IRS statistics, however, the effective withholding tax rate on the U.S.-source investment income reported to the IRS in 2011 was less than 2% (see Table 9.1). This low effective tax rate is due to various exemptions, in particular, the portfolio interest exemption, and reduced treaty withholding rates for interest, dividends, and royalties.

TABLE 9.1. U.S.-SOURCE FDAP INCOME PAID TO FOREIGN PERSONS

Type of U.S.-source income	Amount (in billions)
Interest	$279.4
Dividends	109.6
Notional principal contract income	76.9
Other	102.6
Total U.S.-source taxable income	$568.5

---

[25] Code Secs. 1441(a) and 1442(a).
[26] Code Secs. 1441(a) and 1442(a).
[27] Code Sec. 1461.

[28] Reg. § 1.6302-2.
[29] Reg. § 1.1461-2(b) and (c). Form 1042 is due by March 15 of the year following the end of the calendar year in which the tax was required to be withheld.

U.S. withholding taxes	Amount (in billions)
Total income paid to foreign persons (A)	$568.5
Total U.S. tax withholding (B)	$8.9
Effective withholding tax rate (B ÷ A)	1.56%

Source: "Foreign Recipients of U.S. Income, 2011," *IRS Statistics on Income Division,* Winter 2015.

Effectively connected income is exempt from withholding. An exemption from withholding applies to any U.S.-source income that is effectively connected income (ECI) with the conduct of a U.S. trade or business.[30] Instead of withholding at a 30% rate for FDAP, ECI is subject to U.S. taxes at the regular marginal rates imposed on U.S. persons.[31] Even though the top marginal rates may be higher than the 30% gross withholding rate, foreign persons may prefer taxation at the higher marginal rates on ECI due to the availability of deductions that may result in lower tax. Interest, dividends, rents and royalties are treated as effectively connected income if the income is derived from assets used in or held for use in the conduct of a U.S. trade or business or if the activities of the U.S. trade or business are a material factor in the realization of the income (also known as the business activities test).[32]

Example 9.3: FORco, a foreign corporation, maintains a text-book distribution branch in the United States. Due to the nature of the business, the U.S. branch must typically hold large balances of cash from September 15 through December 15. Temporarily, the large cash balances are not necessary and FORco's U.S. branch invests the cash in 90-day notes. Because the notes have a direct relationship to the trade or business of FORco's U.S. branch, the interest on the 90-day notes is derived from an asset used in the trade or business. As a result, this interest is ECI and the borrowers do not have to withhold.[33]

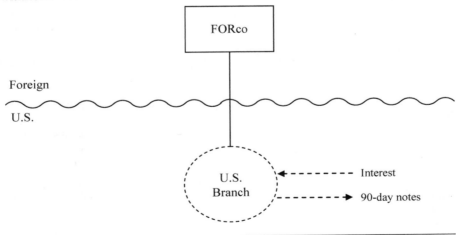

---

[30] Code Sec. 1441(c)(1), Reg. § 1.1441-4(a)(1).
[31] Code Secs. 871(b) and 882(a).

[32] Code Sec. 864(c)(2). *See* discussion in Chapter 10 (¶ 1001).
[33] Reg. § 1.864-4(c)(2)(iv)(Ex.4).

¶902.03

Example **9.4:** FORfund is a foreign corporation that manages portfolios for investing or trading in stocks and bonds worldwide. FORfund has a U.S. office that is engaged in the business of trading stocks and bonds in the United States. On occasion, U.S. companies, whose shares FORfund owns, will pay a dividend. Similarly, bonds may pay interest. Because the dividends and interest directly relate to the business activities of FORfund's U.S. branch, the dividends and interest are ECI to FORfund and are exempt from withholding.[34]

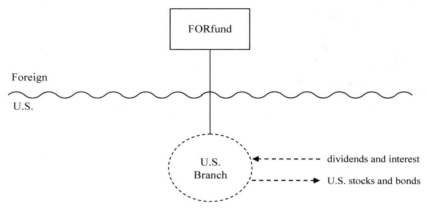

To obtain a withholding exemption for effectively connected income, the foreign person engaged in the U.S. trade or business must submit a Form W-8ECI, Certificate of Foreign Person's Claim for Exemption From Withholding on Income Effectively Connected With the Conduct of a Trade or Business in the United States, to each withholding agent from whom the foreign person expects to receive payment.[35] A sample of a completed Form W-8ECI is included in the Appendix of this chapter.

The exemption for ECI also applies to any income received by a foreign corporation or a foreign partnership for the performance of services. However, as discussed below, special rules apply to the effectively connected personal services income of a nonresident alien and the effectively connected income of a partnership (U.S. or foreign) that is allocable to a foreign partner.

Exception to the exemption for effectively connected personal services income. The withholding exemption for FDAP that is effectively connected income does not apply to the personal services income of a nonresident alien. The policy behind the exception is that the mobility of nonresident aliens offers them the opportunity to leave the United States and avoid the U.S. taxing jurisdiction by not filing a return and paying tax. Instead, the nonresident alien would incur either 30% withholding if the personal services are performed as an independent contractor[36] or wage withholding under Sections 3401 and 3402 if the personal services are performed as an employee.[37]

---

[34] Reg. § 1.864-4(c)(3)(ii)(Ex.1).
[35] Reg. § 1.1441-4(a)(2).

[36] Rev. Rul. 73-107, 1973-1 C.B. 376.
[37] Reg. § 31.3401(a)-1(a)(1).

¶902.03

Example 9.5: Norman Ray Allen (NRA), a nonresident alien, is engaged by USCo, a U.S. company, to perform personal services in the United States. Although NRA is engaged in the trade or business of performing services in the United States, withholding still applies. If NRA is not considered an employee of USCo (and, therefore, an independent contractor), USCo must withhold tax from NRA's wages at a 30% rate. However, if NRA is an employee of USCo, USCo must withhold pursuant to Code Sections 3401 and 3402 as it would withhold for employees who are U.S. citizens or residents.

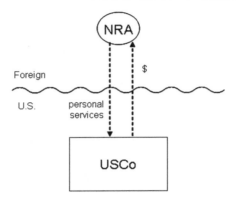

Withholding on income allocable to a foreign partner. Unlike any other type of withholding, partnerships with foreign partners must withhold on income received even if there is never a cash distribution. First, a partnership must withhold tax on a foreign partner's allocable share of the partnership's U.S.-source FDAP income, such as passive dividend and interest income.[38] Second, a partnership, regardless of residency, must withhold income tax on the portion of its effectively connected taxable income that is allocable to a foreign partner.[39] The amount of this special withholding tax equals the foreign partner's allocable share of ECI multiplied by the maximum U.S. tax rate applicable to the partner,[40] which is currently 35% for foreign corporations and approximately 40% for nonresident aliens.[41] The partnership must remit this withholding tax through quarterly installment tax payments.[42]

Example 9.6: T, a U.S. citizen would like to engage in a 50-50 joint venture in the United States with NRA, a nonresident alien. Because a nonresident alien may not be a member of an S corporation, T and NRA form a limited liability company (LLC) that is treated as a partnership for U.S. tax purposes. In year one, the LLC earns $200,000 of taxable income, for which both T and NRA have an allocable share of $100,000 of taxable income. Even if the LLC

---

[38] Reg. § 1.1441-3(f).

[39] Code Sec. 1446(a). This withholding requirement applies regardless of whether any distributions are actually made to such partners. The partnership must file a Form 8804 (Annual Return For Partnership Withholding Tax), Form 8805 (Foreign Partner's Information State-

ment), and a Form 8813 (Partnership Withholding Tax Payment), complete samples of which are included in the Appendix of this chapter.

[40] Code Sec. 1446(b).

[41] Code Secs. 1 and 11.

[42] Reg. § 1.1446-3(d)(1)(ii).

never distributes any cash to NRA, the LLC must withhold $40,000 of tax on NRA's allocable share [40% × $100,000].

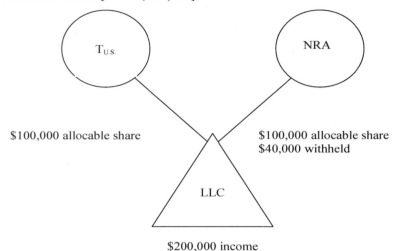

$200,000 income

The foreign partner will later file a U.S. income tax return and treat the withholding on ECI as a pre-payment of tax. Depending on the withholding amounts and the foreign partner's ultimate tax bracket, the foreign partner may receive a refund or owe additional tax.

Gains from the sale or exchange of property. Income derived from the sale in the United States of personal property is not subject to withholding under the FDAP regime because it is not FDAP income (in contrast, the proceeds could be withholdable payments subject to FATCA withholding). This provision applies to all types of gains, both capital and ordinary, but is intended to exempt from withholding on gains realized by foreign persons from the sale of U.S. stocks and securities (see Example 9.1). A policy for this exemption is the belief that the only way to enforce the taxation of passive foreign investors is through withholding and that withholding on capital gains is not feasible. Taxing the gross amount realized on a sale is unfair if the net gain is small and taxing the net gain may be impractical since the withholding agent may not have any way to determine the foreign person's basis in the property.[43]

Despite these administrative problems, withholding is required on the following types of gains:[44]

(i) Gains from the disposition of timber, coal, or domestic iron ore with a retained economic interest;[45]

(ii) Gains from the sale or exchange of original issue discount obligations attributable to certain accrued amounts;[46]

---

[43] *See* Example 9.1.
[44] Code Secs. 1441(b) and 1442(a). Reg. §1.1441-3(d) discusses the procedures for withholding on gains.

[45] Code Secs. 871(a)(1)(B), 881(a)(2), and 631(b) and (c).
[46] Code Secs. 871(a)(1)(C) and 881(a)(3).

(iii) Gains from dispositions of <u>U.S. real property interests</u>; and[47]

(iv) Gains from the sale or exchange of <u>intangibles</u> to the extent such gains are derived from <u>payments which are contingent on the productivity</u>, use, or disposition of the property (under the rationale that these are economically similar to royalties).[48]

Portfolio interest exemption. <u>Portfolio interest</u> received by foreign persons <u>is exempt</u> from U.S. withholding tax on FDAP.[49] Congress enacted the portfolio interest exemption, partly in resignation to the widespread avoidance of U.S. taxes on portfolio interest. Previously, passive foreign investors were able to avoid U.S. taxation of portfolio interest through treaty exemptions or, in the case of foreign investors from non-treaty countries, treaty shopping.

<u>Portfolio interest is any U.S.-source interest paid or accrued on debt obligations,</u> other than interest effectively connected with the conduct of a U.S. trade or business. However, Congress has enacted various restrictions in order to protect against the unauthorized use of the portfolio interest exemption by U.S. persons. These restrictions apply to holders of both registered and unregistered (or bearer) debt.

In the case of registered debt obligations, the exemption applies only if the U.S. withholding agent has received a statement that the beneficial owner of the obligation is a foreign person.[50] Because the owners of unregistered (or bearer) debt obligations are harder to track, the exemption applies only if the obligations satisfy the following requirements:

(i) There are arrangements reasonably designed to ensure that the obligation will be sold (or resold in connection with the original issue) only to foreign persons,

(ii) The obligor pays interest only to foreign persons resident outside the United States, and

(iii) There is a statement on the face of the obligation providing that any U.S. person who holds the obligation will be subject to the U.S. income tax laws.[51]

Consistent with the principle that the portfolio interest exemption is aimed at passive foreign investors, <u>interest received by the following types of foreign lenders does not qualify for the exemption:</u>

(i) *10% shareholders*—Interest received by a 10% owner does not qualify for the portfolio interest exemption.[52] In the case of an obligation issued by a corporation, a 10% shareholder is any person who owns, directly or constructively, 10% of more of the combined voting power of such a corporation.[53] Furthermore, in the case of an obligation issued by a

---

[47] Code Sec. 1445(a). *See* ¶ 905.

[48] Code Secs. 871(a)(1)(D), 881(a)(4) and 936(h)(3)(B).

[49] Code Secs. 1441(c)(9) and 1442(a).

[50] Code Secs. 871(h)(2)(B) and 881(c)(2)(B). *See* Code Sec. 871(h)(5) regarding the requirements for this state-

ment; Reg. §§ 1.871-14(c)(2)(i) and 1.1441-1(e)(1)(ii). *See* ¶ 1103.

[51] Code Secs. 871(h)(2)(A), 881(c)(2)(A), and 163(f)(2)(B).

[52] Code Secs. 871(h)(3)(A) and 881(c)(3)(B).

[53] Code Secs. 871(h)(3)(B)(i) and (h)(3)(C).

partnership, a 10% shareholder is any person who owns 10% of more of the capital or profits interest of such a partnership.[54]

(ii) *Foreign banks*—Any interest received by a foreign bank on a loan entered into in the ordinary course of its banking business (other than interest paid on an obligation of the U.S. government) does not qualify for the portfolio interest exemption.[55]

(iii) *Controlled foreign corporations*—Any interest received by a controlled foreign corporation (see ¶ 501.03) from a related person does not qualify for the portfolio interest exemption.[56]

Example 9.7: USCo is a U.S. corporation in which Norman Ray Allen, a nonresident alien, owns 8% of the shares. USCo issues bearer bonds only to foreign persons for $1,000 each that annually pay $70 of interest. Norman Ray Allen buys one of the bonds. As long as U.S. persons cannot own the bonds, the $70 of interest paid to foreign persons, such as Norman Ray Allen, is exempt from withholding under the portfolio interest exception.

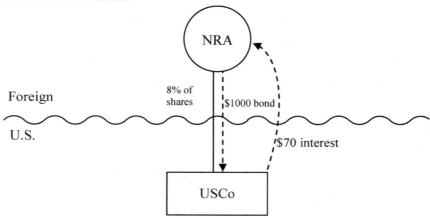

However, if Norman Ray Allen increases his ownership of USCo's shares to 10%, the portfolio interest exception will not apply and USCo will have to withhold $21 ($70 at 30%) of each interest payment.

 The portfolio interest exemption does not apply to payments of so-called "contingent interest," which are essentially dividend payments disguised as interest to obtain a deduction.[57] The United States taxes gains realized by foreign investors on the disposition of equity interests in U.S. real property.[58] Therefore, prior to the enactment of this special rule for contingent interest, shared appreciation mortgages and other hybrid debt instruments were used to obtain debt characterization for what were, in substance, equity interests in U.S. real estate. The contingent

---

[54] Code Sec. 871(h)(3)(B)(ii).

[55] Code Sec. 881(c)(3)(A).

[56] Code Sec. 881(c)(3)(C). Other special rules apply to portfolio interest received by a controlled foreign corporation (*see* Code Sec. 881(c)(5)).

[57] Code Secs. 871(h)(4) and 881(c)(4).

[58] Code Sec. 897(a)(1).

¶902.03

interest rules close this loophole by taxing the interest income associated with such an investment hybrid debt instrument. Contingent interest is defined as any interest whose amount is determined by reference to one of the following items:

(i) The receipts, sales, or other cash flows of the debtor;

(ii) Any income or profits of the debtor;

(iii) Any change in the value of any property of the debtor; or

(iv) Any dividend, partnership distribution, or similar payment made by the debtor.[59]

However, any contingent interest that is exempt under an existing U.S. tax treaty is not subject to the tax on contingent interest.[60]

Other exemptions for interest and dividends. In addition to the portfolio interest exemption, the following types of interest and dividend income also are exempt from the 30% withholding tax on FDAP income under Chapter 3:

(i) the active foreign business percentage of any dividend or interest paid by an 80/20 company that existed prior to 2011,[61]

(ii) the income derived by a foreign central bank of issue from banker's acceptances,[62] and

(iii) the U.S.-source interest either on bank deposits or on amounts held by an insurance company under an agreement to pay interest thereon (the policy is to support U.S. financial industry interests).[63]

Example 9.8: FORco is a corporation organized in a South American country with an unstable banking system and currency. As a result, FORco deposits all its cash reserves in the First National Bank of Florida, a U.S. bank. Although the U.S. bank pays FORco a significant amount of U.S. source interest, no U.S. withholding tax is due under the bank deposit interest exception.

Treaty reductions for dividends, interest, and royalties. Tax treaties usually reduce the 30% FDAP withholding tax rate under Chapter 3 on dividend, interest, and royalty income to 15% or less.

---

[59] Code Sec. 871(h)(4)(A). Various exceptions are provided in Code Sec. 871(h)(4)(C).

[60] Notice 94-39, 1994-1 CB 350.

[61] Code Secs. 871(i)(2)(B) and 871(l).

[62] Code Sec. 871(i)(2)(C).

[63] Code Secs. 871(i) and 881(d).

In the case of dividends, the rate often is lower for controlling shareholders (e.g., a shareholder owning 10% or more of the payor's stock) than for noncontrolling shareholders. For example, under Article 10(2) of the United States Model Income Tax Convention of November 15, 2006 (the "U.S. Model Treaty"), the withholding rate on dividends is 5% for a company that directly owns 10% or more of the voting stock of the payor and 15% for all other shareholders.

Interest and royalties often are exempt from withholding tax.[64] In some treaties, the withholding rate on royalties varies with whether the payment is an industrial royalty (such as a payment for the use of a patent, trade secret, or formula) or an entertainment-oriented royalty (such as a payment for the rights to a motion picture, television show, or book). The appendix in Chapter 13 (¶ 1305) lists treaty withholding rates for dividends, interest, and royalties, by country. Treaties generally do not reduce the withholding rate for rents.

Treaty exemptions for personal services income. Tax treaties usually provide a variety of tax exemptions from Chapter 3 withholding for personal services income. The Code eliminates tax by re-sourcing the compensation of nonresident aliens for *de minimis* U.S. services as foreign-source income (See ¶ 302.04). In contrast, under the U.S. Model Treaty, income derived by a nonresident alien individual from employment in the United States is exempt from U.S. taxation if the following requirements are satisfied:

(i) The employee is present in the United States for 183 days or less,

(ii) The employee's compensation is paid by, or on behalf of, an employer that is not a U.S. resident, and

(iii) The compensation is not borne by a permanent establishment or a fixed base that the employer maintains in the United States.[65]

Example 9.9: FORco is a company incorporated in country F, which has a treaty with the United States identical to the U.S. Model Treaty. FORco has a sales employee, who does not have final contracting authority, that spends 10 days each year traveling throughout the United States. The sales employee spends no more than a day in any locale and receives payment from FORco. The salary of the sales employee is not subject to tax because the sales employee is present in the United States for 183 days or less, the sales employee is paid by FORco (a foreign resident), and the compensation is not borne by a permanent establishment or fixed base that FORco maintains in the United States.

---

[64] For example, *see* Articles 11(1) and 12(1) (¶ 1304.11 and ¶ 1304.12) of the U.S. Model Treaty.

[65] Article 14(2) (¶ 1304.14) of the U.S. Model Treaty.

¶902.03

Traveling Sales Employee

Many older treaties contain a separate independent services provision to govern the taxation of personal services income earned by self-employed professionals. However, the current U.S. Model Treaty takes the position that the U.S. taxation of these professionals should occur only if they have a permanent establishment in the United States.[66]

Tax treaties usually contain special rules for specific types of personal services income. For example, under the U.S. Model Treaty, there are special rules governing income derived by crew members of ships and aircraft operated in international traffic,[67] directors' fees,[68] entertainers and athletes,[69] pensions, social security, annuities, alimony and child support,[70] pension funds,[71] government workers,[72] and students and trainees.[73] The Appendix to Chapter 13 (¶ 1305) provides a listing of the treaty provisions governing personal services income, by country.

To obtain a treaty exemption for independent or dependent services, a nonresident alien must submit a Form 8233, Exemption from Withholding on Compensation for Independent Personal Services of a Nonresident Alien Individual, to each withholding agent from whom amounts are to be received.[74] (A completed sample of Form 8233 is included in the Appendix to this chapter.)

Election to treat real property income as effectively connected income. A foreign corporation or nonresident alien individual who is a passive investor in a U.S. real property interest may elect to have the U.S.-source income derived from the investment taxed as if it were effectively connected income.[75] This election allows foreign persons to offset the gross income from investments in U.S. real property (e.g., gross rental income) with related deductions (e.g., depreciation, depletion, and interest expense) to compute their effectively connected income.[76] The election results in taxation of net income at marginal rates, which may be lower than the FDAP withholding tax on gross rents at 30%.

Example **9.10:** Landlord is a nonresident alien. Landlord purchases an office building located in the United States. Landlord does not manage the

---

[66] Article 5 of the U.S. Model Treaty of 2006. *See* ¶ 1304.5.

[67] For example, *see* Article 14(3) (¶ 1304.14) of the U.S. Model Treaty.

[68] Article 15 (¶ 1304.15) of the U.S. Model Treaty.

[69] For example, *see* Article 16 (¶ 1304.16) of the U.S. Model Treaty.

[70] Article 17 (¶ 1304.17) of the U.S. Model Treaty.

[71] Article 18 (¶ 1304.18) of the U.S. Model Treaty.

[72] For example, *see* Article 19 (¶ 1304.19) of the U.S. Model Treaty.

[73] For example, *see* Article 20 (¶ 1304.20) of the U.S. Model Treaty.

[74] Reg. § 1.1441-4(b)(2).

[75] Code Secs. 871(d)(1) and 882(d)(1).

[76] Reg. §§ 1.873-1(a)(1) and 1.882-4(b)(1).

property, but instead leases the building to an unrelated U.S. business on a net-lease basis. During the first year of operations, Landlord has rental income of $400,000 and operating expenses (including depreciation and interest expense) of $340,000. Because Landlord's U.S. activities are *de minimis*, Landlord probably is not engaged in a U.S. trade or business. Therefore, under the general rules, Landlord's U.S.-source rental income of $400,000 is subject to withholding tax at a 30% rate. As a consequence, Landlord's U.S. tax would be $120,000 [30% × $400,000] even though Landlord realizes only $60,000 of net income from the U.S. building. However, if Landlord elects to have its rental income taxed as if it were effectively connected income with a U.S. trade or business, then Landlord's net profit of $60,000 [$400,000 – $340,000] would incur U.S. tax of only $24,000 [40% × $60,000].

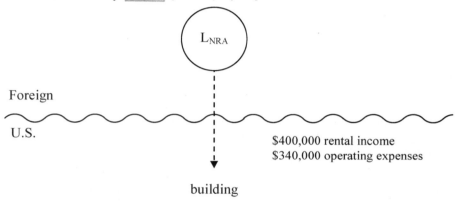

building

To qualify for the election, the foreign person must derive income from real property located within the United States and held for the production of income.[77] The foreign person elects trade or business status when filing its return and the election applies to all of the taxpayer's income from U.S. real property that would not otherwise be effectively connected income.[78] The election applies for all subsequent taxable years and may be revoked only with the consent of the IRS.[79] If the foreign person revokes the election, the foreign person may not re-elect for five years, unless the IRS consents to an early re-election.[80]

Foreign governments and international organizations. Income derived by a foreign government from investments in the United States in stocks, bonds, or other U.S. securities, financial instruments held in the execution of governmental financial or monetary policy, or interest on deposits in U.S. banks is exempt from U.S. tax.[81] In the case of an international organization, income from investments in

---

[77] This includes gains from the sale or exchange of real property, rents or royalties from mines, wells, or other natural deposits, and gains from the disposition of timber, coal, or domestic iron ore with a retained economic interest. Code Secs. 871(d)(1) and 882(d)(1).

[78] Reg. § 1.871-10(b)(1).

[79] Code Secs. 871(d)(1) and 882(d)(1). *See* Reg. § 1.871-10(d) regarding the procedures for making and revoking the election.

[80] Code Secs. 871(d)(2) and 882(d)(2).

[81] Code Sec. 892(a)(1). This exception does not apply to income derived by a foreign government from the conduct of a commercial activity, either directly or through a controlled commercial entity. Code Sec. 892(a)(2).

¶902.03

the United States in stocks, bonds, or other U.S. securities, or from interest on deposits in U.S. banks, is exempt from U.S. tax.[82] The compensation of nonresident aliens, who are employees of foreign governments or international organizations, is also exempt from U.S. tax under certain conditions.[83]

   ***Example* 9.11:** Country F sends one of its nationals, Rose, as its Ambassador to the United States in Washington. Rose's income is U.S.-source income because she is performing services in the United States and she is a nonresident alien because the days in the United States do not count for the substantial presence test.[84] However, Rose is exempt from U.S. tax because she works for a foriegn government in its diplomatic mission.

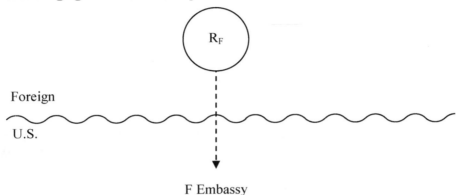

F Embassy

   Finally, any income earned by a foreign central bank from obligations of the United States or of any agency or instrumentality thereof, or from interest on bank deposits, is exempt from U.S. tax.[85]

   Foreign tax-exempt organizations. A foreign tax-exempt organization is subject to withholding on any receipts of unrelated business taxable income, unless such income is effectively connected with the conduct of a U.S. trade or business.[86] The gross U.S.-source investment income of a foreign private foundation also is subject to withholding taxes, but at a reduced rate of 4%.[87] However, if a tax treaty provides an exemption for the specific type of income (e.g., interest income), then the foreign private foundation's income will be exempt.[88]

   Social security benefits. Eighty-five percent of the social security benefits received by a nonresident alien individual are subject to the 30% withholding tax.[89] Moreover, the United States has entered Totalization Agreements with 26 foreign countries that detail the country to whom an individual would make social security contributions.

---

[82] Code Sec. 892(b).

[83] Code Sec. 893; *Abrahamsen v. Commissioner,* 142 T.C. No. 22 (2014).

[84] Code Sec. 7701(b)(5)(B).

[85] Code Sec. 895. This exception does not apply to an obligation or deposit held for, or used in connection with, the conduct of a commercial activity.

[86] Reg. § 1.1443-1(a).

[87] Reg. § 1.1443-1(b)(1)(i) and Code Sec. 4948(a).

[88] Reg. § 1.1443-1(b)(1)(ii).

[89] Code Sec. 871(a)(3).

Gambling winnings. Withholding is not required on proceeds from a wager placed by a nonresident alien individual in gambling on blackjack, baccarat, craps, roulette, or big-6 wheel.[90] Withholding is required on proceeds from horse or dog races occurring in the United States, unless the wager is placed outside the United States.[91] Other gambling winnings are subject to withholding tax if the amount of the winnings exceeds certain dollar thresholds.[92]

Scholarships and Fellowships. A 14% withholding rate applies to scholarships and fellowships received by a nonresident alien.[93]

Tax on gross transportation income. The U.S.-source gross transportation income of a foreign person is subject to a special 4% tax.[94] Transportation income is income derived from the use or lease of a vessel or aircraft (including any container used in connection with a vessel or aircraft) or from the performance of services directly related to the use of a vessel of aircraft.[95] A foreign person's U.S.-source gross transportation income equals 50% of the income from any transportation that begins in the United States and ends abroad or that begins abroad and ends in the United States.[96] The 4% tax does not apply to any effectively connected income with the conduct of a U.S. trade or business.[97]

¶ 903 THE THREAT OF WITHHOLDING ON U.S.-SOURCE WITHHOLDABLE PAYMENTS UNDER THE FATCA REGIME

.01 Introduction to the FATCA Regime Under Chapter 4

Some U.S. persons have invested in foreign entities (deposits in foreign banks, shares of foreign companies, etc.) without reporting or paying tax on their income earned from these foreign entities. At the same time, these foreign entities often earned FDAP income in the United States that was exempt from Chapter 3 withholding via either the Code or a tax treaty. The IRS was, in essence, whipsawed by U.S. taxpayers who did not report income earned by their foreign entities whose U.S.-source income did not incur U.S. tax. Despite the attempts of the IRS to use the exchange of information articles in tax treaties to try to obtain information about these foreign entities and U.S. persons,[98] these requests were often unfruitful. FATCA combats this problem via threatening the foreign entities (i.e., the foreign bank or the foreign company) with a 30% withholding tax on its U.S.-source withholding payments when the foreign entities do not provide information about U.S. persons on Form 8966, FATCA Report. A copy of a completed FATCA report is in the Appendix to this Chapter.

Example 9.12: U.S. individual deposits cash in an interest-bearing account with Swiss Bank. Swiss Bank owns 20% of USCo, a U.S. company, which

---

[90] Code Secs. 1441(c)(11) and 871(j).
[91] Code Sec. 872(b)(5).
[92] Code Sec. 3402(q).
[93] Code Sec. 1441(b).
[94] Code Sec. 887(a).
[95] Code Sec. 863(c)(3).

[96] Code Sec. 863(c)(2)(A). This rule generally does not apply to transportation income derived from personal services performed by the taxpayer. Code Sec. 863(c)(2)(B).
[97] Code Sec. 887(b)(2). Certain possessions income also is exempt. Code Sec. 887(b)(3).
[98] Article 26(1) of the U.S. Model Treaty of 2006. See ¶ 1302.11.

pays dividends. Under the Switzerland-U.S. Tax Treaty,[99] USCo would normally withhold tax of only 5% on dividends to Swiss Bank. However, if Swiss Bank does not provide Form 8936 to the IRS that contains information about its U.S. depositors, FATCA requires USCo to withhold 30% under Chapter 4 instead of 5% FDAP withholding under Chapter 3.

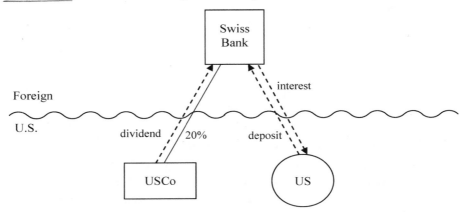

FATCA applies to foreign financial institutions[100] and non-financial foreign entities.[101] Foreign governments, international organizations, central banks, and certain retirement funds are exempt from the FATCA withholding requirements of Chapter 4.[102] FATCA does not apply to payments to nonresident aliens.

.02 Coordination of Withholding Between the FATCA and FDAP Regimes

As aforementioned, the FATCA regime of Chapter 4 imposes withholding before any analysis of the FDAP regime of Chapter 3. If there is withholding under the FATCA regime, the analysis ends and there is not any withholding under the FDAP regime. If withholding does not apply under the FATCA regime, the taxpayer must analyze the potential implications of withholding under the FDAP regime.[103]

> *Example 9.13:* Swiss Bank, a foreign financial institution, owns 20% of BigBlueCo, a U.S. company. Under the FATCA regime, if Swiss Bank does not provide information about its U.S. depositors to the IRS, BigBlueCo must withhold 30% on the payment of each dividend and any analysis of the FDAP regime is unnecessary. If Swiss Bank provides the information about its U.S. depositors to the IRS, withholding under the FATCA regime does not apply and withholding under the FDAP regime applies. Under the FDAP regime, assuming that Swiss Bank provides BigBlueCo a valid W-8BEN-E indicating Swiss residency, the dividend is subject to withholding tax of only 5% under the Swiss-U.S. Tax Treaty.

---

[99] Article 10 of the Switzerland-U.S. Tax Treaty.
[100] Code Sec. 1471.
[101] Code Sec. 1472.

[102] Code Secs. 1471(f) and 1472(c).
[103] Reg. § 1.1474-6(a) and (b).

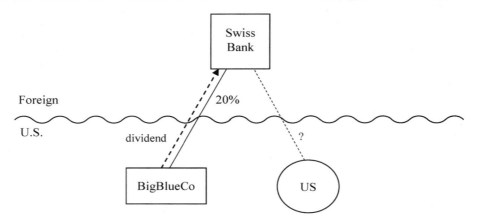

.03 FATCA Applies to Withholdable Payments

The threat of FATCA withholding under Chapter 4 induces the foreign entity to provide information to the IRS. Withholdable payments include interest, dividends, rents, royalties and, in contrast to the FDAP regime, any gross proceeds from the sale of property that can produce these types of income.[104]

Example 9.14: Swiss Bank, in an attempt to diversify its asset base, deposits $10 million in an interest-bearing account with U.S. Bank. Under the Chapter 3 withholding rules for FDAP, U.S. bank deposit interest is exempt from withholding. However, the interest is a withholdable payment and, unless Swiss Bank provides information about its U.S. depositers, FATCA applies to impose a 30% withholding tax.

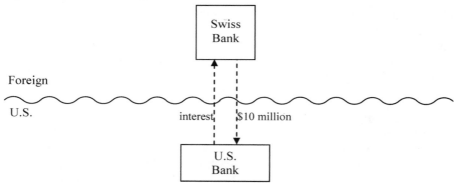

Example 9.15: Swiss Bank, in an attempt to diversify its asset base, purchases 20% of USCo's shares. Several years later, Swiss Bank sells the shares of USCo to a U.S. purchaser for $20 million. This transaction does not incur U.S. income tax as it does not produce either U.S.-source FDAP or effectively connected income.[105] However, the payment of the purchase price

---

[104] Reg. § 1.1471-1(a). FATCA only applies to gross proceeds from the sale of property that can produce withholdable payments beginning January 1, 2017.

[105] *See* Example 9.1.

¶903.03

for the shares (property that produces dividends) is a withholdable payment for FATCA. Accordingly, unless Swiss Bank provides information about its U.S. depositers, FATCA applies to impose a 30% withholding tax.

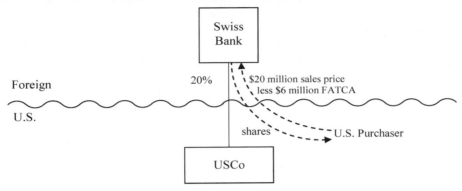

Payments for personal services,[106] unlike the FDAP rules, and all other forms of ECI to recipients, are not withholdable payments.[107]

Example 9.16: FORco, a foreign corporation, provides IT consulting services to USCo, a U.S. company in the United States. Because FORco is engaged in the trade or business of performing IT consulting services, its effectively connected income from USCo is not subject to FATCA.

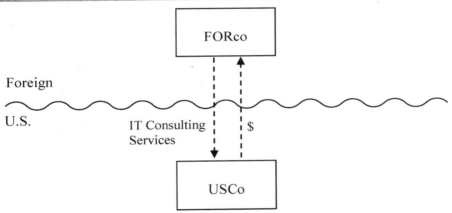

.04 FATCA Applies to Foreign Financial Institutions

The U.S. payor must withhold unless the foreign financial institution certifies that it does not have any accounts of $50,000 or more[108] held by U.S. persons.[109] The information required on the Form 8966 that the foreign financial institution must

---

[106] Reg. § 1.1473-1(a)(4)(ii).

[107] Code Sec. 1473(1)(B).

[108] Code Sec. 1471(a)(1)(B)(ii).

[109] A financial account is any depository account maintained at a foreign financial institution, any custodial account maintained at a foreign financial institution, and any equity on debt or debt interest in such foreign financial institution. Code Sec. 1471(d)(2).

provide the IRS includes the name, the address, the taxpayer identification number, and the account balance or value.[110]

Example 9.17: Carl, a U.S. citizen, has deposited $45,000 in an account with Swiss Bank. Because the account is less than $50,000, Carl is not a U.S. account holder. After winning $10,000 at Monte Carlo in roulette, Carl deposits the $10,000 in his account with Swiss Bank. As a result, Carl is now a U.S. account holder on whom Swiss Bank must report to the IRS.

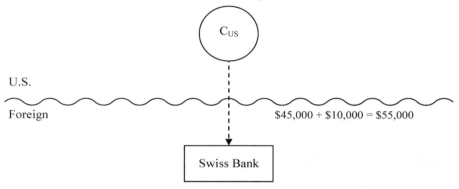

FATCA defines a foreign financial institution as a foreign entity that accepts deposits in the ordinary course of a banking business, holds financial assets for the accounts of others as a substantial portion of its business, or engages primarily in the business of investing, reinvesting, or trading in certain securities, partnership interests, or commodities.[111]

Example 9.18: Swiss Bank is organized in Switzerland and accepts deposits from customers worldwide in the ordinary course of a banking business. Swiss bank is a foreign financial institution.

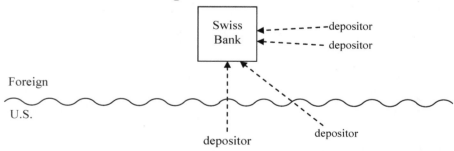

However, the definition of a foreign financial institution does not include foreign companies in non-financial groups that conduct holding company, treasury center, or captive financing functions.[112]

Example 9.19: FORco, a Country F multi-national company engaged in the widget business, has 50 subsidiaries world-wide. Foreign subsidiary 50 acts

---

[110] Code Sec. 1471(c).
[111] Code Sec. 1471(d)(5).

[112] Reg. § 1.1471-5(e)(5).

as a treasury center that is responsible for managing the risk of interest rate and currency exchange rate fluctuations. Because foreign subsidiary 50 engages in treasury center functions, foreign subsidiary 50 is excepted from FATCA compliance as a non-financial group entity.

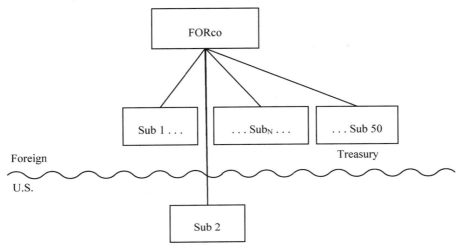

Foreign financial institutions are either participating, deemed-compliant, or non-compliant. Payors of witholdable payments to participating or deemed-compliant foreign finanical institutions do not have to withhold under FATCA. Payors of withholdable payments to non-compliant foreign financial institutions have to withhold under FATCA. A non-compliant foreign financial institution is one that fails to annually provide information about U.S. account holders to the IRS. More specifically, the foreign financial institution must satisfy due diligence procedures to identify U.S. account holders.[113]

> ***Example* 9.20:** Rural, Inc., a U.S. corporation, has bonds outstanding, some of which are owned by ForBank. If ForBank does not properly conduct due diligence to identify its U.S. account holders, ForBank is non-compliant. Under FATCA, Rural, Inc. must withhold 30% of the interest payments to ForBank.

---

[113] Code Sec. 1471(b)(1)(B).

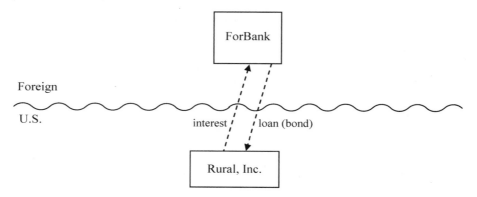

A participating[114] foreign financial institution may comply with FATCA by providing information pursuant to an InterGovernmental Agreement (IGA) between the foreign financial institiution's country and the United States. The United States has entered approximately 34 IGAs, primarily with our major trading partners and with Western and Central European countries, under one of two models. Under Model 1,[115] which is the most popular model (signatory countries include Canada, the United Kingdom, and Germany), the foreign financial institution reports to its foreign country, which collects the information for provision to the IRS. Under Model 2,[116] which is the less popular model (signatory countries include Switzerland), the foreign financial institution reports directly to the IRS.

> ***Example* 9.21:** Rural, Inc., a U.S. corporation, has bonds outstanding, some of which are owned by ForBank. If ForBank does not properly conduct due diligence to identify its U.S. account holders, Rural, Inc. must withhold 30% of the interest payments under FATCA. However, if ForBank's country has entered an IGA with the United States, ForBank can satisfy the IGA's information requirements to avoid incurring FATCA withholding on the interest.

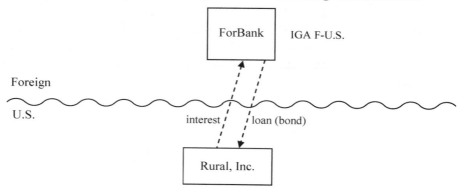

Some foreign financial institutions are deemed-compliant. The extensive list of those that are deemed-compliant includes local foreign financial institutions. Local

---

[114] Reg. § 1.1474-1T(b)(9).
[115] Reg. § 1.1471-1(b)(78).

[116] Reg. § 1.1471-1(b)(79).

foreign financial institutions have neither a fixed place of business outside its home country nor solicit customers outside its home country and have 98% of its account values from depositors in its home country.[117]

In addition, foreign financial institutions must perform 30% "passthru" withholding on U.S.-source withholdable payments to recalcitrant account holders and non-participating foreign financial institutions.[118]

> **Example 9.22:** Foreign Bank is organized in country F, which has entered an IGA with the United States. A U.S. depositor refuses to provide the necessary information for Foreign Bank to comply with the IGA. As a result, the Foreign Bank must withhold 30% of withholdable payments (presumably interest) to the U.S. depositor.

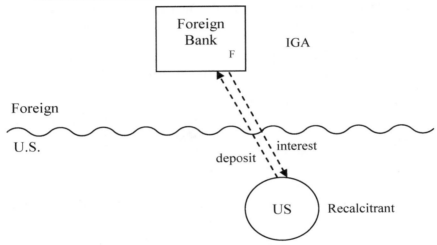

.05 FATCA Applies to Non-Financial Foreign Entities

FATCA similarly threatens imposing a 30% withholding tax under Chapter 4 on withholdable payments to non-financial foreign entities.[119] Withholding under the FATCA regime does not apply if the non-financial foreign entity provides the IRS information about its substantial U.S. owners (greater than 10% U.S. shareholders), such as their names, taxpayer identification numbers, and ownership percentages.[120]

> **Example 9.23:** SwissCo, a watch manufacturer, owns 20% of USCo. SwissCo sells the USCo shares to a U.S. Purchaser for $20 million. Unless SwissCo provides information about its 10% U.S. shareholders to the IRS, the U.S. Purchaser must withhold 30% of the sales proceeds. However, if U.S. Purchaser buys a watch from SwissCo, no withholding occurs because, as previously discussed, as a payment of ECI is not a withholdable payment.

---

[117] Reg. § 1.1471-5(f)(i)(A).
[118] Code Sec. 1471(b)(1)(D)(i).

[119] Any foreign entity other than a foreign financial institution. Code Sec. 1472(d).
[120] Code Sec. 1472(a) and (b).

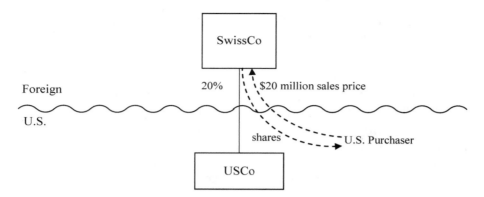

Alternatively, a non-financial foreign entity may elect to directly report information about its U.S. owners to the IRS instead of providing the information to the payor of the withholdable payment.[121]

Non-Financial Foreign Entities are either excepted or passive. Payors of witholdable payments to excepted non-finanical foreign entities do not have to withhold under FATCA. Payors of withholdable payments to passive non-financial foreign entities have to withhold under FATCA. To be excepted, a non-financial foreign entity must be either publicly-traded, an affiliate of a publicly-traded entity, or an active entity.[122] A non-financial foreign entity is active if less than 50% of both its gross income and assets are passive. All other non-financial foreign entities are passive and must provide information about their 10% U.S. owners to the IRS or incur FATCA withholding.

Example 9.24: FORco, a country F corporation, owned $100 million of operating assets in its manufacturing business. More specifically, FORco owned $40 million of assets that manufactured widgets and $60 million of assets that manufactured gadgets. Consequently, FORco was an active non-financial foreign entity that was excepted from FATCA. However, suppose FORco sells the gadget business for $60 million of proceeds that FORco reinvests in portfolio stocks. As a result, over half of FORco's assets are passive ($60 million divided by $100 million is 60%). Consequently, FORco is no longer an excepted entity because it is no longer an active entity, and is a passive entity that results in FATCA applying to any withholdable payments to FORco.

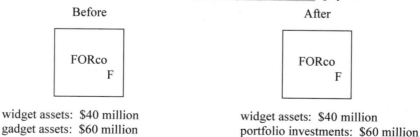

Before

After

widget assets: $40 million
gadget assets: $60 million

widget assets: $40 million
portfolio investments: $60 million

---

[121] Reg. § 1.1471-1T(c)(1)(vi).   [122] Reg. § 1.1472-1(c).

¶ 904 WITHHOLDING PROCEDURES UNDER THE FDAP AND FATCA REGIMES

.01 Introduction

Placing the burden on the U.S. payor to collect the proper withholding tax requires the payor to determine the country of residence and sometimes even the entity status of the payee. Pursuant to the former FDAP regulations, a U.S. corporation that paid a dividend could rely on the address of the payee to determine the country of residence, absent other actual knowledge of residence. Relying on the foreign address created opportunities for abuse by both U.S. and foreign persons.

> **Example 9.25:** USAco is a publicly held U.S. corporation with shareholders located worldwide. Uncle Sam, a U.S. citizen, would prefer not to provide USAco with his social security number because he does not want to pay U.S. tax and, accordingly, wants to avoid USAco reporting the payment to the IRS. He hopes that the IRS could not match the payment with his return. Uncle Sam obtains a mailing address in country F, whose treaty with the United States reduces the withholding tax on dividends to 10%. USAco pays a dividend to Uncle Sam. Not having any knowledge of Uncle Sam's residence, other than his mailing address, USAco withholds tax at a 10% rate. Uncle Sam does not report any of the dividend on his U.S. return and incurs a tax of only 10%.

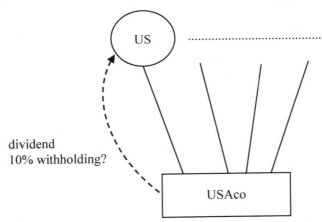

Similarly, residents of foreign countries that did not have a treaty with the United States often tried to obtain a mailing address in a treaty country.

> **Example 9.26:** USAco is a publicly held U.S. corporation that pays dividends to its shareholders worldwide. Norman Ray Allen (NRA) owns shares of USAco and is a resident of Argentina (which does not have an income tax treaty with the United States). NRA obtains a mailing address in Germany to try to take advantage of the lower 15% withholding rates of the Tax Treaty between the United States and Germany.

¶904.01

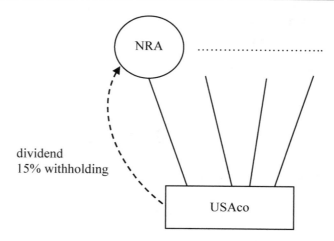

dividend
15% withholding

Examples such as these prompted the IRS to revise its withholding regulations.

The policy behind these withholding regulations is that reduced withholding tax rates under U.S. income tax treaties are available only to foreign beneficial owners that reside in a treaty country. A U.S. beneficial owner may be subject to back-up withholding at a rate of 28%.[123] A foreign beneficial owner that does not reside in a treaty country should incur FDAP withholding at a rate of 30%.[124]

.02 Determining the Beneficial Ownership

The withholding regulations focus on the documentation that the payee must provide to the payor. U.S. persons must provide Form W-9, which contains the U.S. person's taxpayer identification number. A U.S. person's taxpayer identification number is typically the social security number for individuals and the employer identification number for entities.

Foreign persons must file a type of Form W-8. There are four different types of Forms W-8,[125] including the Form W-8BEN, Certificate of Foreign Status of Beneficial Owner for United States Tax Withholding and Reporting (Individuals), a completed sample of which is included in the Appendix. A nonresident alien uses a Form W-8BEN to:

   (i) Establish foreign status,

   (ii) Claim beneficial ownership of the income for which the form is furnished,

   (iii) Claim a reduced rate of withholding under an income tax treaty, and

   (iv) Claim exemption from back-up withholding for income that is not subject to withholding under section 1441.

---

[123] Code Secs. 1(c) and 3406(a)(2).

[124] Code Secs. 1441 and 1442.

[125] In addition to the Forms W-8BEN and W-8BEN-E, other Forms W-8 include Form W-8ECI, Certificate of

Foreign Person's Claim for Exemption From Withholding on Income Effectively Connected With the Conduct of a Trade or Business in the United States and Form W-8EXP, Certificate of Foreign Government or Other Foreign Organization for United States Tax Withholding.

The payor can rely on receipt of valid documentation, such as a Form W-9 or Form W-8BEN (in the absence of actual knowledge that any statements in the form are inaccurate), when determining the appropriate withholding.[126]

Example 9.27: Norma Ray Allen (NRA) is a citizen and resident of a European country that has a treaty with the United States identical to the U.S. Model Treaty. NRA is a shareholder of USAco, a U.S. corporation that pays dividends and NRA provides USAco a Form W-8BEN indicating that she is an individual and resident of a European country. Unless USAco has actual knowledge that NRA is not a resident of that European country, USAco can rely on the Form W-8BEN and withhold at the treaty rate.

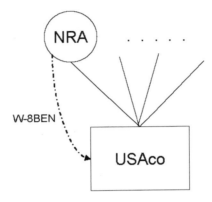

Similar to the Form W-8BEN for nonresident aliens, a foreign corporation uses the Form W-8BEN-E, Certificate of Foreign Status of Beneficial Owner for United States Tax Withholding and Reporting (Entities), to:

  (i) Establish foreign status,

  (ii) Claim beneficial ownership of the income for which the form is furnished,

  (iii) Claim a reduced rate of withholding under an income tax treaty,

  (iv) Claim exemption from back-up withholding for income that is not subject to withholding under section 1442, and

  (v) Establish status for FATCA withholding under Chapter 4.

Providing a Form W-8BEN-E is important to a foreign corporation that owns stock of a U.S. corporation. With respect to FDAP withholding under Chapter 3, most of the tax treaties that the United States has entered provide for reduced withholding on dividends paid by a U.S. corporation to a foreign company that has a substantial ownership interest in the U.S. corporation. For example, the U.S. Model Treaty reduces the withholding tax rate on dividends to only 5% if the foreign owner is a corporation that directly owns at least 10% of the voting stock of the U.S.

---

[126] Reg. § 1.1441-1 (b) (2) (vii) (A).

¶904.02

corporation.[127] With respect to FATCA withholding under Chapter 4, the Form W-8BEN-E has approximately thirty different categories based on FATCA withholding (a completed sample Form W-8BEN-E is attached to the Appendix to this Chapter). The withholding agent can rely on the category indicated on the Form W-8BEN-E unless the withholding agent knows that the Form W-8BEN-E is inaccurate.

> ***Example 9.28:*** FORco, a manufacturing corporation organized in country F, owns 10% of USAco. Country F has a treaty with the United States that is identical to the U.S. Model Treaty. Under the FDAP withholding principles of Chapter 3, if FORco provides a Form W-8BEN-E indicating that FORco is both a resident of country F and a corporation, USAco should withhold tax on any dividends paid at the special treaty rate of 5% instead of the general treaty rate of 15%.

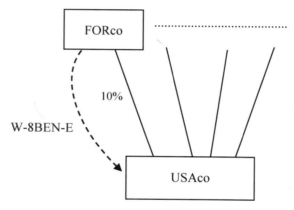

Moreover, FORco must designate its Chapter 4 status to avoid FATCA withholding. As a result, FORco must also designate on Form W-8BEN-E that is is an active non-financial foreign entity.

.03 Presumptions in the Absence of Documentation

If a payee fails to provide adequate documentation, such as a Form W-9 or a type of Form W-8, the payor of income must follow certain presumptions to determine the status of the payee.

The FDAP and FATCA withholding regulations generally presume that a payee is a U.S. person if the withholding agent cannot reliably associate a payment with documentation.[128]

> ***Example 9.29:*** USAco is a publicly-held U.S. corporation with shareholders located worldwide. Uncle Sam, a U.S. citizen, would prefer not to provide USAco with his social security number because he wants to avoid USAco reporting the dividend payment to the IRS, who could match the payment with the income he reports on his Form 1040. Because Uncle Sam has not provided

---

[127] Article 10(2)(a) (¶ 1304.10) of the U.S. Model Treaty.

[128] Reg. §§ 1.1441-1(b)(3)(iii) and 1.1471-3T(f)(3).

either a Form W-9 or W-8BEN, USAco presumes that Uncle Sam is a U.S. person and back-up withholds tax at a rate of 28%.

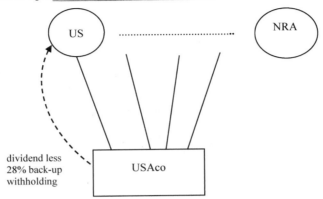

The FDAP and FATCA withholding regulations also provide a presumption to determine the classification of a recipient as an individual or an entity. If the payor cannot reliably associate a payment with valid documentation, the payor must presume that the payee is an individual, a trust, or an estate based on the payee's name. Otherwise, the payor may treat the payee as a corporation or a partnership.[129]

If the payor of the item of income cannot determine the appropriate FATCA category for a foreign entity, the regulations presume that the foreign entity is a non-compliant foreign financial institution.[130]

.04 Foreign Intermediaries

U.S. persons often pay items of U.S.-source income to foreign recipients through foreign intermediaries. Previously, U.S. persons were often uncertain as to the appropriate withholding rate. To resolve this issue, the withholding regulations provide specific rules for payments to foreign intermediaries.

The withholding regulations differentiate between a qualified intermediary (QI) and a nonqualified intermediary (NQI). A QI has qualified and registered with the Internal Revenue Service to be responsible for withholding on payments to the ultimate beneficiaries at the appropriate withholding rate under either the FDAP[131] or FATCA withholding regimes.[132] NQIs must provide the appropriate Forms W-9 and W-8s to the payor, who retains responsibility for withholding at the appropriate rate.[133]

> **Example 9.30:** FORbrok is a foreign brokerage that invests on behalf of its clients located in a variety of countries (including the United States) in U.S. stocks and bonds, many of which pay dividends and interest. If FORbrok has entered an agreement with the IRS to be a QI, FORbrok must obtain all the Forms W-8 and W-9 from its customers and withhold at the appropriate FDAP

---

[129] Reg. §§ 1.1441-1(b)(3)(ii)(B) and 1.1471-3T(f)(2).
[130] Reg. § 1.1471-3T(f)(4).
[131] Reg. § 1.1441-1(b)(2)(v).
[132] Code Sec. 1471(c)(3) and Reg. § 1.1471-3(b)(3).
[133] Reg. § 1.1441-1(b)(2)(vii)(B).

rates, considering any tax treaties between the United States and its customers, or the 30% FATCA rate.

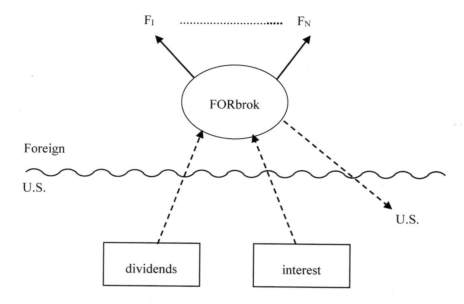

If FORbrok has not entered an agreement with the IRS, FORbrok is a NQI. Accordingly, FORbrok must provide the Forms W-8 and W-9 from its customers to the U.S. payors of dividends and interest, who will have to withhold on payments to FORbrok at the appropriate rates.

¶ 905 TAXATION AND WITHHOLDING ON SALES OF U.S. REAL PROPERTY INTERESTS

.01 Introduction

U.S. real estate has always been a popular investment for foreigner investors, in part because the United States previously did not tax foreign investors on any capital gains realized on the sale of U.S. real property interests. This became a U.S. political issue, and Congress responded by enacting the Foreign Investment in Real Property Tax Act (FIRPTA), which attempts to equate the tax treatment of real property gains realized by U.S. and foreign investors. Under FIRPTA, gains or losses realized by foreign corporations or nonresident alien individuals from any sale, exchange, or other disposition of a U.S. real property interest are taxed in the same manner as effectively connected income with the conduct of a U.S. trade or business.[134] This means that gains from dispositions of U.S. real property interests are taxed at the regular marginal rates with losses deductible against any other

---

[134] Code Sec. 897(a)(1). In addition, for purposes of computing a nonresident alien individual's alternative minimum tax, the taxable excess amount cannot be less than the individual's net U.S. real property gain for the taxable year. Code Sec. 897(a)(2).

effectively connected income.[135] Furthermore, FIRPTA ensures collection of some tax by requiring the purchaser to withhold 10% of the purchase price.[136]

Example 9.31: Norman Ray Allen (NRA) is a nonresident alien individual whose only connection with the United States is the ownership of some undeveloped land located in the United States. NRA holds the land as a passive investment. NRA eventually sells the land for a gain to a U.S. Purchaser. Prior to the enactment of FIRPTA, any gain realized by NRA on the sale of the land would be exempt from U.S. taxation. Under FIRPTA, the United States taxes NRA's gain on the sale of the land in the same manner as effectively connected income with the conduct of a U.S. trade or business, that is, on a net basis and at the regular marginal rates.

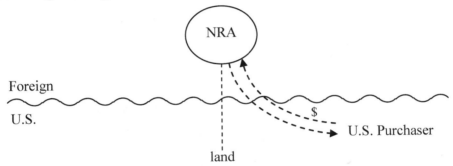

.02 U.S. Real Property Interests

A U.S. real property interest includes interests in any of the following types of property located within the United States:

(i) Land,

(ii) Buildings, including a personal residence,

(iii) Inherently permanent structures other than buildings (e.g., grain bins or broadcasting towers),

(iv) Mines, wells, and other natural deposits,

(v) Growing crops and timber, and

(vi) Personal property associated with the use of real property, such as mining equipment, farming equipment, or a hotel's furniture and fixtures.[137]

For this purpose, an "interest" in real property means any interest, other than an interest solely as a creditor. This includes fee ownership, co-ownership, a leasehold, an option to purchase or lease property, a time-sharing interest, a life estate,

---

[135] Code Secs. 871(b) and 882(a). However, a loss realized by a nonresident alien individual from the disposition of a U.S. real property interest held for personal use is deductible only if it arises from a fire, storm, or other casualty event. Code Secs. 897(b) and 165(c).

[136] Code Sec. 1445(a). As effectively connected income, gain from the sale of U.S. real estate is not subject to FATCA withholding. Code Sec. 1473(1)(b).

[137] Code Sec. 897(c)(1)(A)(i) and Reg. § 1.897-1(b).

remainder, or reversionary interest, and <u>any other direct or indirect right to share in the appreciation in value or proceeds from the sale of real property</u>.[138]

> **Example 9.32:** Lisa, a Hungarian, owns farmland on which there is a growing corn crop. The corn crop has an estimated value of $100,000 and the land has an estimated value of $1 million. Lisa sells the land with the growing crop to Mr. Haney for $1.1 million. If the corn is harvested before the sale, the U.S. real property interest is only the land with a fair market value of $1 million and results in withholding tax at a 10% rate for $100,000. If Mr. Haney purchases the land with the growing crop before harvest, Mr. Haney is purchasing a U.S. real property interest with a value of $1.1 million and must, therefore, withhold 10% for $110,000.

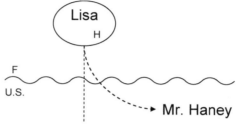

Farmland $1M

Corn Crop $100g

A U.S. real property interest also includes any interest (other than an interest solely as a creditor) in a U.S. corporation that was a U.S. real property holding corporation at any time during the five-year period ending on the date of sale or, if shorter, the period the foreign person held the interest.[139] This provision prevents foreign persons from avoiding the FIRPTA tax by incorporating their U.S. real estate investments and then realizing the resulting gains through stock sales, which ordinarily are exempt from U.S. taxation.[140] <u>A U.S. corporation is a U.S. real property holding corporation if the fair market value of its U.S. real property interests equals 50% or more of the fair market value of the sum of the corporation's following interests:</u>

(i) <u>U.S. real property interests</u> (including any interest in another U.S. real property holding corporation),

(ii) <u>Interests in foreign real property</u>, and

(iii) <u>Any other property of the corporation which is used or held for use in a trade or business</u>.[141]

> **Example 9.33:** NRA is a nonresident alien individual whose only connection with the United States is the ownership of the shares of a U.S. corporation,

---

[138] Code Sec. 897(c)(6)(A) and Reg. § 1.897-1(d)(2).
[139] Code Sec. 897(c)(1)(A)(ii).
[140] Reg. § 1.1441-2(a)(3).

[141] Code Sec. 897(c)(2). For this purpose, a U.S. real property holding corporation includes any interests in a foreign corporation that would qualify as a U.S. real property holding corporation if that foreign corporation were a domestic corporation. Code Sec. 897(c)(4)(A).

¶905.02

USSub. USSub has cash of $4 million and a parcel of undeveloped land located in the United States with a fair market value of $6 million. Under FIRPTA, USSub is a U.S. real property holding corporation because over 50% of the fair market value of its assets constitute a U.S. real property interest ($6 million divided by $10 million equals 60%). As a result, the United States imposes the FIRPTA tax on NRA's gain on the sale of shares of USSub in the same manner as if NRA had directly owned and sold the parcel of land. This is in contrast to Example 9.1, where the sale of shares of USSub, which was not a U.S. real property holding corporation, did not incur U.S. tax.

Now, suppose that USSub has a $3.5 million mortgage securing the land in the United States, decreasing the land's net fair market value to $2.5 million. USSub's only other asset is still the cash of $4 million such that USSub's fair market value is $6.5 million. USSub is no longer a U.S. real property holding corporation because less than 50% of the fair market value of its assets constitute a U.S. real property interest ($2.5 million divided by $6.5 million equals 38%). As a result, FIRPTA would not apply to USSub's sale.

The rule looking at whether a U.S. corporation was a U.S. real property holding corporation at any time during the previous five-year period prevents stuffing non-real property assets into a U.S. corporation.

Example **9.34**: ForCo, a foreign corporation, owns USSub, whose only asset for the last five years has been U.S. real estate with a basis of $1 million and a fair market value of $10 million. ForCo has a Buyer for USSub and, wanting to avoid any FIRPTA implications, ForCo contributes $10.1 million to USSub moments before selling the USSub shares to Buyer for $20.1 million. However, due to the 5-year look back, USSub is still a U.S. real property holding corporation, ForCo must report gain, and Buyer must withhold 10% of the sales proceeds of $20.1 million for $2.01 million.

¶905.02

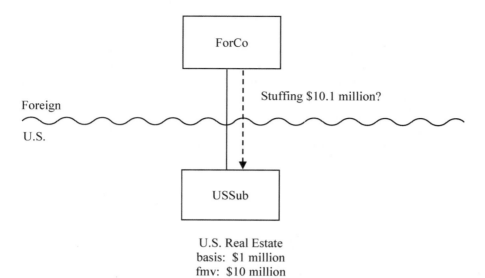

U.S. Real Estate
basis: $1 million
fmv: $10 million

For purposes of determining whether a U.S. corporation qualifies as a U.S. real property holding corporation, the U.S. corporation is treated as owning a proportionate share of the assets of any other corporation it controls and a proportionate share of the assets of any partnership, trust, or estate, in which it is a partner or beneficiary.[142]

Example 9.35: ForCo, a foreign corporation, owns 100% of US$_1$, a U.S. C corporation with net assets comprised of cash of $600,000 and U.S. real estate of $500,000. US$_1$ owns 50% of US$_2$, another U.S. C corporation, which has cash of $300,000 and U.S. real estate of $800,000. By merely looking at US$_1$'s tangible assets, US$_1$ is not a U.S. real property holding corporation. However, when adding 50% of US$_2$'s net assets—cash of $150,000 and U.S. real estate of $400,000—US$_1$ is now treated as having cash of $750,000 and U.S. real estate of $900,000. Because the $900,000 of U.S. real estate is greater than 50% of the combined net assets of $1,650,000, US$_1$ is a U.S. real property holding corporation.

---

[142] Code Sec. 897(c)(4)(B) and (c)(5).

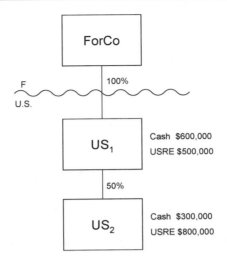

The following types of interests are exempted from the U.S. real property holding corporation taint:

(i) *Publicly traded corporations*—Stock that is regularly traded on an established securities market generally is not treated as a U.S. real property interest.[143] Without this exception, many major U.S. industrial companies would be treated as U.S. real property holding corporations, which would hinder trading.

(ii) *Domestically controlled real estate investment trusts*—An interest in a real estate investment trust is not a U.S. real property interest if foreign persons directly or indirectly own less than 50% of the value of the shares of the real estate investment trust.[144]

(iii) *Corporations that have disposed of all U.S. real property interests*—U.S. real property interests do not include an interest in a corporation that has previously disposed of all of its U.S. real property interests in transactions that recognized the full amount of gain, if any.[145]

Example **9.36:** ForCo, a foreign corporation, owns all the shares of USSub, which, because its only asset is a parcel of U.S. real estate, is a U.S. real property holding corporation. USSub sells its U.S. real estate to a third party at a gain on which USCo pays tax at marginal U.S. rates. If ForCo sells the shares of USSub, USSub is no longer a U.S. real property holding corporation.

---

[143] Code Sec. 897(c)(3). An exception applies to a person who owns, directly or constructively, more than 5% of the shares in question. Code Sec. 897(c)(3) and (c)(6)(C).

[144] Code Sec. 897(h)(2) and (h)(4)(B).
[145] Code Sec. 897(c)(1)(B).

¶**905.02**

.03 Special Rules for Certain Dispositions to Prevent Tax Avoidance

The Internal Revenue Code contains a variety of special rules in order to apply the FIRPTA tax to the following types of dispositions that would otherwise be tax-free:

  (i) A distribution by a foreign corporation of a U.S. real property interest to its shareholders as either a dividend, a redemption of stock, or a liquidation,[146]

  (ii) A disposition of a U.S. real property interest that would otherwise qualify as a nontaxable transaction (e.g., a like-kind exchange),[147]

  (iii) A sale or other disposition of an interest in a partnership, trust, or estate that holds a U.S. real property interest,[148]

  (iv) A distribution by a real estate investment trust that holds a U.S. real property interest,[149] and

  (v) A contribution of a U.S. real property interest to the capital of a foreign corporation.[150]

.04 Withholding Requirement of 10% of Proceeds

To ensure collection of the FIRPTA tax, any purchaser of a U.S. real property interest must deduct and withhold a tax equal to 10% of the amount realized.[151] The term purchaser includes any person, foreign or domestic, that acquires a U.S. real property interest by purchase, exchange, gift, or any other type of transfer.[152] The amount realized is the sum of the cash paid or to be paid (excluding interest), the market value of other property transferred, the amount of liabilities assumed by the purchaser, and the liabilities attached to the transferred property.[153] Withholding requirements also apply to both distributions made by a U.S. or foreign corporation,

---

[146] Code Sec. 897(d) and Temp. Reg. § 1.897-5T(c).

[147] Code Sec. 897(e) and Temp. Reg. § 1.897-6T.

[148] Code Sec. 897(g).

[149] Code Sec. 897(h)(1) and (h)(3).

[150] Code Sec. 897(j).

[151] Code Sec. 1445(a). A transferee must file Forms 8288 and 8288-A to report and deposit any tax withheld within 20 days of withholding. Reg. § 1.1445-1(c)(1).

[152] Reg. § 1.1445-1(g)(4). Withholding by a seller who is a foreign person poses a compliance problem.

[153] Reg. § 1.1445-1(g)(5).

partnership, estate, or trust, to the extent the distribution involves a U.S. real property interest and dispositions of interests in a partnership, trust, or estate that has a U.S. real property interest.[154]

    Example 9.37: Normal Ray Allen (NRA), a citizen of a foreign country, comes to the United States to begin a new job on September 1. NRA immediately purchases a house. However, on October 1, before NRA has become a resident under either the substantial presence test or the green card test, NRA is fired and leaves the United States. NRA sells the house for $500,000. The purchaser must withhold $50,000 of the sales price as 10% of the gross sales proceeds. If $50,000 exceeds the NRA's ultimate tax due, NRA can file a Form 1040NR seeking a refund. If NRA's ultimate tax due is greater than $50,000, NRA will owe additional tax.

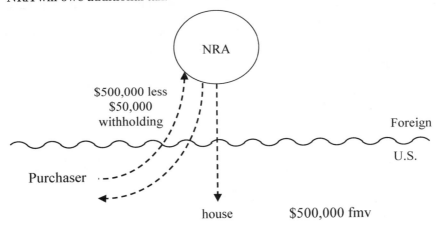

    As with withholding taxes in general, a purchaser that fails to withhold is liable for any uncollected taxes.[155] Therefore, any purchaser of U.S. real property must be careful to determine whether withholding is required. To ease the administrative burden, the following situations do not require withholding:

(i) The purchaser receives an affidavit from the transferor which states, under penalty of perjury, that the seller is not a foreign person or, in the case of the disposition of an interest in a U.S. corporation, that the U.S. corporation is not and has not been a U.S. real property holding company,

(ii) The seller obtains a withholding certificate issued by the IRS, which states that no (or reduced) withholding is required,

(iii) The purchaser receives a notice from the seller that no recognition of gain or loss on the transaction is required because a nonrecognition provision applies,

---

[154] Code Sec. 1445(e) and Reg. § 1.1445-5.

[155] Code Sec. 1461. However, the seller's liability for a failure to withhold the FIRPTA tax is limited to the seller's maximum tax liability. Code Sec. 1445(c)(1)(A).

(iv) The purchaser acquires the property for use as a personal residence and the purchase price does not exceed $300,000 (compare with the $500,000 price in the previous Example), or

(v) The purchaser acquires stock that is regularly traded on an established securities market.[156]

The administrative burden is also eased by a procedure whereby a foreign seller may obtain an early refund of any excess withholding taxes.[157]

Example 9.38: Norman Ray Allen (NRA), a citizen of a foreign country, comes to the United States to begin a new job on September 1. NRA immediately purchases a house. However, on October 1, before NRA has become a resident under either the substantial presence test or the green card test, NRA is fired and leaves the United States. NRA sells the house for $250,000. Because NRA sold the house for less than $300,000, this purchaser need not withhold any of the gross sales proceeds as tax. However, NRA should file a Form 1040NR to report any gain recognized and pay any tax due. Compare this to the previous Example, which required withholding because the purchase price was $500,000.

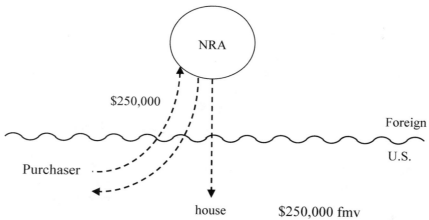

---

[156] Code Sec. 1445(b) and Reg. § 1.1445-2. An agent of either party, such as a real estate broker or attorney, who has actual knowledge that an affidavit regarding the status of the seller is false, but fails to notify the seller that it is false, may be liable for the withholding tax to the extent of the agent's compensation from the transaction. Code Sec. 1445(d) and Reg. § 1.1445-4.

[157] Reg. § 1.1445-3.

¶905.04

¶ 906 APPENDIX

USCo, a closely-held C corporation, has Norman Ray Allen (NRA) as one of its owners. NRA is a citizen and resident of the Cayman Islands, which does not have a tax treaty with the United States. USCo declares and pays dividends and withholds the following amounts of tax on the following three dates in 2014:

Date	Dividend	Withholding
March 31, 2014	$10,000	$3,000
June 30, 2014	$ 2,000	$ 600
September 30, 2014	$ 500	$ 150

USAco will complete a Form 1042-S for NRA and transmits to the IRS with a Form 1042-T (along with other Forms 1042-S, if there were any). USAco will file a Form 1042 that compiles all the annual withholding tax information for the IRS. Because the only withholdings were on the payments to NRA, the Form 1042 only lists withholding on his dividends.

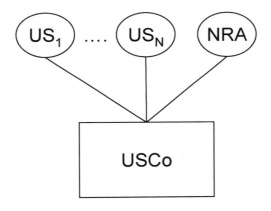

Form **1042-S**	Foreign Person's U.S. Source Income Subject to Withholding				OMB No. 1545-0096	
Department of the Treasury Internal Revenue Service	▶ Information about Form 1042-S and its separate instructions is at *www.irs.gov/form1042.*			2014	**Copy A** for Internal Revenue Service	
	AMENDED ☐	**PRO-RATA BASIS REPORTING** ☐				

1 Income code	2 Gross income	3 Chap. 3: ☐	4 Chap. 4: ☐	5 Withholding allowance		0
6	12,500	3a Exemption code	4a Exemption code	6 Net income		12,500
		3b Tax rate 30	4b Tax rate	7 Federal tax withheld		3,750
				Check if tax not deposited under escrow procedure ☐		

8 Tax withheld by other agents

9 Tax assumed by withholding agent   3,750

10 Total withholding credit

11 Amount repaid to recipient

12a Withholding agent's EIN 34-5678912	12b Ch. 3 status code 02	12c Ch. 4 status code	14e Primary Withholding Agent's Name (if applicable)

14f Primary Withholding Agent's EIN

13a Withholding agent's name   USCo

15a Intermediary or flow-through entity's EIN, if any	15b Ch. 3 status code	15c Ch. 4 status code

13b Withholding agent's Global Intermediary Identification Number (GIIN)

16a Intermediary or flow-through entity's name

13c Country code	13d Foreign taxpayer identification number, if any	16b Intermediary or flow-through entity's GIIN	
		16c Country code	16d Foreign tax identification number, if any

13e Address (number and street)

16e Address (number and street)

1234 Main Street

13f City or town, state or province, country, ZIP or foreign postal code

16f City or town, state or province, country, ZIP or foreign postal code

Las Vegas, NV

13g Recipient's U.S. TIN, if any

17 Recipient's GIIN

18 Recipient's foreign tax identification number, if any

13h Ch. 3 status code 19	13i Ch. 4 status code	19 Recipient's account number	20 Recipient's date of birth

14a Recipient's name

14b Recipient's country code   CJ

Norman Ray Allen

14c Address (number and street)	21 Payer's name	22 Payer's TIN	23 Payer's GIIN

14d City or town, state or province, country, ZIP or foreign postal code	24 State income tax withheld	25 Payer's state tax no.	26 Name of state

Georgetown, Grand Cayman

For Privacy Act and Paperwork Reduction Act Notice, see instructions.   Cat. No. 11386R   Form **1042-S** (2014)

273727323

¶906

DO NOT STAPLE

Form **1042-T**			
Department of the Treasury Internal Revenue Service	**Annual Summary and Transmittal of Forms 1042-S**		OMB No. 1545-0096
			20**14**

Name of withholding agent		02	1) Ch. 4 Status Code	Employer identification number
USCo		02	2) Ch. 3 Status Code	34-5678912

Number, street, and room or suite no.

City or town, state or province, country, and ZIP or foreign postal code

Las Vegas, NV

1a Type of paper Forms 1042-S attached (check only **one** box): ☑ Original   ☐ Amended

Also check here if pro-rata (see instructions) ▶ ☐

b Number of paper Forms 1042-S attached ▶ _____1_____

2 Total gross income reported on all paper Forms 1042-S (box 2) attached . . . . $ _____12,500

3 Total federal tax withheld on all paper Forms 1042-S attached:

a Total federal tax withheld under chapter 4 . . . . $ _____

b Total federal tax withheld under chapter 3 . . . . $ _____3,750

Caution: *If you have already filed a Form 1042 and an attached Form 1042-S causes the gross income or tax withheld information shown on your previously filed Form 1042 to change, you must file an amended Form 1042. See the instructions below.*

If this is your FINAL return, enter an "X" here (see instructions) ▶ ☒

Please return this entire page to the Internal Revenue Service.

Sign Here Under penalties of perjury, I declare that I have examined this return and accompanying documents and, to the best of my knowledge and belief, they are true, correct, and complete.

Your signature ▶ _____ | Title _____ | Date _____ | Daytime phone number _____

Instructions

Purpose of form. Use this form to transmit paper Forms 1042-S, Foreign Person's U.S. Source Income Subject to Withholding, to the Internal Revenue Service. Use a separate Form 1042-T to transmit each type of Form 1042-S (see the instructions for line 1a).

Electronic filing requirement. If you file 250 or more Forms 1042-S, you are required to submit them electronically. If you submit less than 250 Forms 1042-S, you are encouraged to file them electronically. If you are a financial institution you are required to submit Form 1042-S electronically irrespective of the number of Forms 1042-S you submit. If you submit Forms 1042-S electronically, do not use Form 1042-T. See the instructions for Form 1042 for the definition of financial institution.

Filing Forms 1042 and 1042-S. Use of this form to transmit paper Forms 1042-S does not affect your obligation to file Form 1042, Annual Withholding Tax Return for U.S. Source Income of Foreign Persons.

If you have not yet filed a Form 1042 for 2014, you may send in more than one Form 1042-T to submit paper Forms 1042-S prior to filing your Form 1042. You may submit amended Forms 1042-S even though changes reflect differences in gross income and tax withheld information of Forms 1042-S previously submitted with a Form 1042-T.

If you have already filed a Form 1042 for 2014 and an attached Form 1042-S caused the gross income or tax withheld information previously reported on line 62c or 63e of your Form 1042 to change, you must file an amended Form 1042.

Where and when to file. File Form 1042-T (and Copy A of the paper Forms 1042-S being transmitted) with the Ogden Service Center; P.O. Box 409101; Ogden, UT 84409; by March 16, 2015. Send the forms in a flat mailing (not folded).

Identifying information at top of form. The name, address, EIN, and chapter 4 and 3 status codes of the withholding agent named on this form must be the same as those you enter on Forms 1042 and 1042-S. See the instructions for Form 1042 for definitions of withholding agent. See the instructions for Form 1042 for the withholding agent codes for the chapter 3 and 4 status codes. See instructions for Forms 1042-S for the definition of withholdable payment to determine when a chapter 4 status code is required.

Line 1a. You must file a separate Form 1042-T for each type of paper Form 1042-S you are transmitting. Check only the Original or Amended box. If you are filing pro-rata Forms 1042-S (see Form 1042-S instructions), also check the pro-rata box. As a result, there are four possible types of Form 1042-S that may be transmitted:

- Original non pro-rata
- Original pro-rata
- Amended non pro-rata
- Amended pro-rata

Each type must be transmitted with a separate Form 1042-T. For example, you must transmit only original non pro-rata Forms 1042-S with one Form 1042-T.

Line 2. Enter the total of the gross income amounts shown on the Forms 1042-S (box 2) being transmitted with this Form 1042-T.

Line 3. Enter the total of the federal tax withheld amounts shown on all Forms 1042-S (total of boxes 7, 8, and 9) being transmitted with this Form 1042-T. Allocate withheld amounts between chapter 4 and chapter 3 on lines 3a and 3b.

Final return. If you will not be required to file additional Forms 1042-S, including amended Forms 1042-S for the 2014 year (on paper or electronically), enter an "X" in the "FINAL return" box.

Paperwork Reduction Act Notice. The time needed to complete and file this form will vary depending on individual circumstances. The estimated average time is 12 minutes.

For more information and the Privacy Act and Paperwork Reduction Act Notice, see Form 1042-S.   Cat. No. 28848W   Form **1042-T** (2014)

Form **1042**	Annual Withholding Tax Return for U.S. Source Income of Foreign Persons	OMB No. 1545-0096
Department of the Treasury Internal Revenue Service	▶ Information about Form 1042 and its separate instructions is at *www.irs.gov/form1042*.	20**14**

If this is an amended return, check here . . . . ▶ ☐

Name of withholding agent	Employer identification number	For IRS Use Only	
USCo	34-5678912	CC	FD
Ch. 3 Status Code 02 Ch. 4 Status Code 02		RD	FF
Number, street, and room or suite no. (if a P.O. box, see instructions)		CAF	FP
		CR	I
City or town, state or province, country, and ZIP or foreign postal code		EDC	SIC

Las Vegas, NV

If you do not expect to file this return in the future, check here ▶ ☐   Enter date final income paid ▶

Section 1   Record of Federal Tax Liability (Do not show federal tax deposits here)

Line No.	Period ending	Tax liability for period (including any taxes assumed on Form(s) 1000)	Line No.	Period ending	Tax liability for period (including any taxes assumed on Form(s) 1000)	Line No.	Period ending	Tax liability for period (including any taxes assumed on Form(s) 1000)
1	7		21	7		41	7	
2	Jan. 15		22	May 15		42	Sept. 15	
3	22		23	22		43	22	
4	31		24	31		44	30	150
5	Jan. total		25	May total		45	Sept. total	150
6	7		26	7		46	7	
7	Feb. 15		27	June 15		47	Oct. 15	
8	22		28	22		48	22	
9	28		29	30	600	49	31	
10	Feb. total		30	June total	600	50	Oct. total	
11	7		31	7		51	7	
12	Mar. 15		32	July 15		52	Nov. 15	
13	22		33	22		53	22	
14	31	3,000	34	31		54	30	
15	Mar. total	3,000	35	July total		55	Nov. total	
16	7		36	7		56	7	
17	Apr. 15		37	Aug. 15		57	Dec. 15	
18	22		38	22		58	22	
19	30		39	31		59	31	
20	Apr. total		40	Aug. total		60	Dec. total	

61   No. of Forms 1042-S filed: a On paper _____ 1 _____   **b** Electronically _____

62   Total gross amounts reported on all Forms 1042-S and 1000:

a	Total U.S. source FDAP income (other than U.S. source substitute payments) reported	62a	12,500
b	Total U.S. source substitute payments reported:		
	(1) Total U.S. source substitute dividend payments reported	62b(1)	
	(2) Total U.S. source substitute payments reported other than substitute dividend payments . . .	62b(2)	
c	**Total gross amounts reported** (Add lines 62a-b)	62c	12,500
d	Enter gross amounts actually paid if different from gross amounts reported	62d	

Third Party Designee   Do you want to allow another person to discuss this return with the IRS (see instructions)? ☐ Yes. Complete the following. ☐ No

Designee's name ▶ _____   Phone no. ▶ _____   Personal identification number (PIN) ▶ _____

Sign Here   Under penalties of perjury, I declare that I have examined this return, including accompanying schedules and statements, and to the best of my knowledge and belief, it is true, correct, and complete. Declaration of preparer (other than withholding agent) is based on all information of which preparer has any knowledge.

Your signature ▶ _____   Date _____   Capacity in which acting ▶ _____   Daytime phone number ▶ _____

Paid Preparer Use Only	Print/Type preparer's name	Preparer's signature	Date	Check ☐ if self-employed	PTIN
	Firm's name ▶			Firm's EIN ▶	
	Firm's address ▶			Phone no.	

For Privacy Act and Paperwork Reduction Act Notice, see instructions.   Cat. No. 11384V   Form **1042** (2014)

Form 1042 (2014)   Page **2**

63	Total tax reported as withheld or assumed on all Forms 1042-S and 1000:		
a	Taxes withheld by withholding agent	63a	3,750
b	Taxes withheld by other withholding agents:		
	(1) For payments other than substitute dividends	63b(1)	
	(2) For substitute dividends	63b(2)	
c	Reimbursements	63c	( )
d	Tax assumed by withholding agent	63d	
e	**Total tax reported as withheld or assumed** (Add lines 63a-d)	63e	3,750
64	Total net tax liability		
a	Adjustments of underwithheld tax on corporate distributions made during the calendar year . . .	64a	3,750
b	Total net tax liability under chapter 3	64b	3,750
c	Total net tax liability under chapter 4	64c	
d	Excise tax on specified federal procurement payments (Total payments made x 2%)	64d	
e	**Total net tax liability** (Add lines 64 a-d)	64e	3,750
65	Total paid by electronic funds transfer (or with a request for extension of time to file)	65	3,750
66	Enter overpayment applied as credit from 2013 Form 1042	66	
67	Credit for amounts withheld by other withholding agents:		
a	For payments other than substitute dividend payments	67a	
b	For substitute dividend payments	67b	
68	**Total payments.** Add lines 65 through 67	68	3,750
69	If line 64e is larger than line 68, enter balance due here	69	
70a	Enter overpayment attributable to overwithholding on U.S. source income of foreign persons . . .	70a	
b	Enter overpayment attributable to excise tax on specified federal procurement payments	70b	
71	Apply overpayment (sum of lines 70a and 70b) to **(check one)**:		
	☐ Credit on 2015 Form 1042 or ☐ Refund		

Section 2   **Reconciliation of Payments of U.S. Source FDAP Income-Optional**

1	Total U.S. source FDAP income required to be withheld upon under chapter 4	1	
2	Total U.S. source FDAP income required to be reported under chapter 4 but not required to be withheld upon under chapter 4 because:		
a	Amount of income paid to recipients whose chapter 4 status established no withholding is required .	2a	
b	Amount of excluded nonfinancial payments (see instructions)	2b	
c	Amount of income paid with respect to grandfathered obligations	2c	
d	Amount of income effectively connected with the conduct of a trade or business in the U.S.	2d	
e	Amount of excluded offshore payment	2e	
f	Total U.S. source FDAP income required to be reported under chapter 4 but not required to be withheld upon under chapter 4 (Add lines 2a-e)	2f	
3	Total U.S. source FDAP income reportable under chapter 4 (Add lines 1 and 2f)	3	
4	Total U.S. source FDAP income reported on all Forms 1042-S (from line 62a, (b)(1), and (b)(2)) . . .	4	
5	Total variance, subtract line 3 from line 4, if amount other than 0 provide explanation on line 6 . . .	5	
6	_____		
	_____		
	_____		
	_____		

Section 3   **Notional principal contract payments and other payments on derivative contracts that reference (in whole or in part) a U.S. security**

Check here if any payments (including gross proceeds) were made by the withholding agent under notional principal contracts or other derivatives contracts that reference (in whole or in part) a U.S. security (see instructions) . . . . ☐

Form **1042** (2014)

Uncle Sam, a U.S. citizen, and Norman Ray Allen (NRA), a resident of the Cayman Islands, each own 50% of U.S. Partnership. During 2014, U.S. Partnership earns $100,000 of ordinary income each quarter for annual ordinary income of $400,000. NRA's share of the ordinary income is $50,000 per quarter, which would result in quarterly withholding at a top 40% rate of $20,000. U.S. Partnership would tender a Form 8813 with the quarterly withholding, issue a Form 8805 to NRA (with a copy to the IRS) that details the annual withholding, and file an annual return with respect to the amount of annual withholdings to the IRS on a Form 8804. The attached Form 8813 is for the first quarter of 2014.

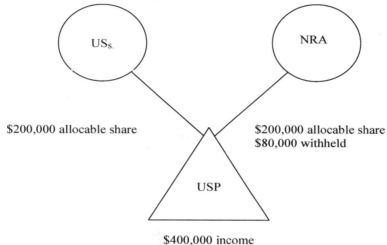

Form **8813**

(Rev. December 2008)

Department of the Treasury
Internal Revenue Service

Partnership Withholding Tax Payment Voucher (Section 1446)

▶ **See separate Instructions for Forms 8804, 8805, and 8813.**

OMB No. 1545-1119

For calendar year **2014** , or tax year beginning _____ , 20 ____ , and ending _____ , 20 ____

1 Partnership's U.S. employer identification number

98 ┊ 7654321

2 Amount of this payment

$ **20,000**

3 PARTNERSHIP'S name, address, (number, street, and room or suite no.), city, state, and ZIP code. If a P.O. box or foreign address, see instructions.

U.S. Partnership
Anytown, USA

Mail this voucher with a check or money order payable to the "United States Treasury." Write the partnership's employer identification number, tax year, and "Form 8813" on the check or money order.

▶ **Do not staple or attach this voucher to your payment.**

▶ **Do not send cash.**

▶ **If you have applied the provisions of Regulations section 1.1446-6, attach all required Forms 8804-C and computations (see instructions).**

For Paperwork Reduction Act Notice, see separate Instructions for Forms 8804, 8805, and 8813.   Cat. No. 10681H   Form **8813** (Rev. 12-2008)

31871918

Form **8805**

Department of the Treasury
Internal Revenue Service

**Foreign Partner's Information Statement
of Section 1446 Withholding Tax**

▶ Information about Form 8805 and its instructions is at *www.irs.gov/form8805*.

For partnership's calendar year 2014, or tax year beginning   , 2014, and ending   , 20

OMB No. 1545-0123

2014

Copy A for Internal Revenue Service
Attach to Form 8804.

1a Foreign partner's name

NRA

b U.S. identifying number

c Address (if a foreign address, see instructions)

Georgetown, Grand Cayman
Cayman Islands

5a Name of partnership

U.S. Partnership

b U.S. EIN

88-7654321

c Address (if a foreign address, see instructions)

2 Account number assigned by partnership (if any)

6 Withholding agent's name. If partnership is also the withholding agent, enter "SAME" and do not complete line 7.

3 Type of partner (specify—see instructions) ▶ Individual

4 Country code of partner (enter two-letter code; see instructions)

CJ

7 Withholding agent's U.S. employer identification number

8a Check if the partnership identified on line 5a owns an interest in one or more partnerships . . . . ▢
b Check if any of the partnership's effectively connected taxable income (ECTI) is exempt from U.S. tax for the partner identified on line 1a . ▢

9 Partnership's ECTI allocable to partner for the tax year (see instructions) . . . . . **Individual and corporate partners:** | **9** | 200,000 | 00

10 Total tax credit allowed to partner under section 1446 (see instructions). Claim this amount as a credit against your U.S. income tax on Form 1040NR, 1120-F, etc. . . . . . . | **10** | 80,000 | 00

Schedule T—Beneficiary Information (see instructions)

11a Name of beneficiary

b U.S. identifying number of beneficiary

c Address (if a foreign address, see instructions)

12 Amount of ECTI on line 9 to be included in the beneficiary's gross income (see instructions) . . . . | **12**

13 Amount of tax credit on line 10 that the beneficiary is entitled to claim on its return (see instructions) | **13**

For Paperwork Reduction Act Notice, see separate Instructions for Forms 8804, 8805, and 8813.   Cat. No. 10078E   Form **8805** (2014)

27114883

¶906

Form **8804**	**Annual Return for Partnership Withholding Tax (Section 1446)**	OMB No. 1545-0123
Department of the Treasury Internal Revenue Service	▶ Attach Form(s) 8804-C and 8805. ▶ Information about Form 8804 and its instructions is at *www.irs.gov/form8804*. For calendar year 2014 or tax year beginning , 2014, and ending , 20	20**14**

Check this box if the partnership keeps its records and books of account outside the United States and Puerto Rico . . . . ▶ ☐

Part I   **Partnership**

1a Name of partnership	**b U.S. employer identification number (EIN)**		
U.S. Partnership	98-7654321		
c Number, street, and room or suite no. If a P.O. box, see instructions.	**For IRS Use Only**		
	CC		FD
	RD		FF
d City or town, state or province, country, and ZIP or foreign postal code. If a foreign address, see instructions.	CAF		FP
	CR		I
Anytown, USA	EDC		

Part II   **Withholding Agent**

2a Name of withholding agent. If partnership is also the withholding agent, enter "SAME" and do not complete lines 2b, 2c, or 2d.	**b Withholding agent's U.S. EIN**
SAME	

c Number, street, and room or suite no. If a P.O. box, see instructions.

d City or town, state or province, country, and ZIP or foreign postal code.

Part III   **Section 1446 Tax Liability and Payments**

3a	Enter number of foreign partners . . . . ▶				
b	Enter number of Forms 8805 attached to this Form 8804 . . . . . ▶				
c	Enter number of Forms 8804-C attached to Forms 8805 . . . . . ▶				
4	Total effectively connected taxable income (ECTI) allocable to foreign partners (see instructions):				
a	Total ECTI allocable to corporate partners	**4a**	200,000	00	
b	Reduction to line 4a for state and local taxes under Regulations section 1.1446-6(c)(1)(iii)	**4b**	(	)	
c	Reduction to line 4a for certified foreign partner-level items submitted using Form 8804-C	**4c**	(	)	
d	Combine lines 4a, 4b, and 4c	**4d**	200,000	00
e	Total ECTI allocable to non-corporate partners other than on lines 4i, 4m, and 4q	**4e**			
f	Reduction to line 4e for state and local taxes under Regulations section 1.1446-6(c)(1)(iii)	**4f**	(	)	
g	Reduction to line 4e for certified foreign partner-level items submitted using Form 8804-C	**4g**	(	)	
h	Combine lines 4e, 4f, and 4g	**4h**	0	00
i	28% rate gain allocable to non-corporate partners	**4i**			
j	Reduction to line 4i for state and local taxes under Regulations section 1.1446-6(c)(1)(iii)	**4j**	(	)	
k	Reduction to line 4i for certified foreign partner-level items submitted using Form 8804-C	**4k**	(	)	
l	Combine lines 4i, 4j, and 4k	**4l**	0	00
m	Unrecaptured section 1250 gain allocable to non-corporate partners	**4m**			
n	Reduction to line 4m for state and local taxes under Regulations section 1.1446-6(c)(1)(iii)	**4n**	(	)	
o	Reduction to line 4m for certified foreign partner-level items submitted using Form 8804-C	**4o**	(	)	
p	Combine lines 4m, 4n, and 4o	**4p**	0	00

For Paperwork Reduction Act Notice, see separate **Instructions for Forms 8804, 8805, and 8813.**   Cat. No. 10077T   Form **8804** (2014)

Form 8804 (2014) | Page **2**

q	Adjusted net capital gain (including qualified dividend income and net section 1231 gain) allocable to non-corporate partners	**4q**				
r	Reduction to line 4q for state and local taxes under Regulations section 1.1446-6(c)(1)(iii)	**4r**	(	)		
s	Reduction to line 4q for certified foreign partner-level items submitted using Form 8804-C	**4s**	(	)		
t	Combine lines 4q, 4r, and 4s				**4t**	
5	Gross section 1446 tax liability:					
a	Multiply line 4d by 35% (.35)	**5a**	80,000	00		
b	Multiply line 4h by 39.6% (.396)	**5b**				
c	Multiply line 4l by 28% (.28)	**5c**				
d	Multiply line 4p by 25% (.25)	**5d**				
e	Multiply line 4t by 20% (.20)	**5e**				
f	Add lines 5a through 5e				**5f**	80,000	00
6a	Payments of section 1446 tax made by the partnership identified on line 1a during its tax year (or with a request for an extension of time to file) and amount credited from 2013 Form 8804	**6a**	800,000	00		
b	Section 1446 tax paid or withheld by another partnership in which the partnership identified on line 1a was a partner during the tax year (enter only amounts reported on Form(s) 8805 and attach the Form(s) 8805 to Form 8804)	**6b**				
c	Section 1446 tax paid or withheld by another partnership in which the partnership identified on line 1a was a partner during the tax year (enter only amounts reported on Form(s) 1042-S and attach the Form(s) 1042-S to Form 8804)	**6c**				
d	Section 1445(a) or 1445(e)(1) tax withheld from or paid by the partnership identified on line 1a during the tax year for a disposition of a U.S. real property interest (enter only amounts reported on Form(s) 8288-A and attach the Form(s) 8288-A to Form 8804)	**6d**				
e	Section 1445(e) tax withheld from the partnership identified on line 1a during the tax year for a disposition of a U.S. real property interest (enter only amounts reported on Form(s) 1042-S and attach the Form(s) 1042-S to Form 8804)	**6e**				
7	**Total payments.** Add lines 6a through 6e				**7**	80,000	00
8	Estimated tax penalty (see instructions). Check if Schedule A (Form 8804) is attached ☐				**8**	
9	Add lines 5f and 8				**9**	80,000	00
10	**Balance due.** If line 7 is smaller than line 9, enter balance due. Attach a check or money order for the full amount payable to "United States Treasury." Write the partnership's U.S. EIN, tax year, and "Form 8804" on it				**10**	
11	**Overpayment.** If line 7 is more than line 9, enter amount overpaid				**11**	
12	Amount of line 11 you want **refunded to you** ▶				**12**	
13	Amount of line 11 you want **credited to next year's Form 8804**	**13**				

Sign Here

Under penalties of perjury, I declare that I have examined this return, including accompanying schedules and statements, and to the best of my knowledge and belief, it is true, correct, and complete. Declaration of preparer (other than general partner, limited liability company member, or withholding agent) is based on all information of which preparer has any knowledge.

▶

Signature of general partner, limited liability company member, or withholding agent | Title | Date

Paid Preparer Use Only

Print/Type preparer's name	Preparer's signature	Date	Check ☐ if self-employed	PTIN
Firm's name ▶			Firm's EIN ▶	
Firm's address ▶			Phone no.	

Form **8804** (2014)

Kris Kringle, a merry old soul who is a resident of Finland, works in the United States as an independent contractor and makes personal appearances at various locations during the Christmas season. Although Kris has a U.S. trade or business in the United States, Kris is exempt from tax under the independent services article of the U.S.-Finland Tax Treaty. Kris must provide a Form 8233 with respect to his various engagements.

Form **8233** (Rev. March 2009) Department of the Treasury Internal Revenue Service	**Exemption From Withholding on Compensation for Independent (and Certain Dependent) Personal Services of a Nonresident Alien Individual** ▶ See separate instructions.	OMB No. 1545-0795

Who Should Use This Form?	**IF** you are a nonresident alien individual who is receiving . . .	**THEN,** if you are the beneficial owner of that income, use this form to claim . . .
Note: *For definitions of terms used in this section and detailed instructions on required withholding forms for each type of income, see* **Definitions** *on pages 1 and 2 of the instructions.*	Compensation for independent personal services performed in the United States	A tax treaty withholding exemption (Independent personal services, Business profits) for part or all of that compensation and/or to claim the daily personal exemption amount.
	Compensation for dependent personal services performed in the United States	A tax treaty withholding exemption for part or all of that compensation. **Note: Do not** use Form 8233 to claim the daily personal exemption amount.
	Noncompensatory scholarship or fellowship income **and** personal services income **from the same withholding agent**	A tax treaty withholding exemption for part or all of **both** types of income.
DO NOT Use This Form. . .	**IF** you are a beneficial owner who is . . .	**INSTEAD,** use . . .
	Receiving compensation for dependent personal services performed in the United States **and** you are **not** claiming a tax treaty withholding exemption for that compensation	Form W-4 (See page 2 of the Instructions for Form 8233 for how to complete Form W-4.)
	Receiving noncompensatory scholarship or fellowship income **and** you are **not** receiving any personal services income **from the same withholding agent**	Form W-8BEN or, if elected by the withholding agent, Form W-4 for the noncompensatory scholarship or fellowship income
	Claiming only foreign status or treaty benefits with respect to income that is **not** compensation for personal services	Form W-8BEN

This exemption is applicable for compensation for calendar year _____ , or other tax year beginning _____ and ending _____ .

Part I	**Identification of Beneficial Owner** (See instructions.)	
1 Name of individual who is the beneficial owner **Kris Kringle**	2 U.S. taxpayer identifying number **912-25-1225**	3 Foreign tax identifying number, if any (optional)

4 Permanent residence address (street, apt. or suite no., or rural route). **Do not use a P.O. box.**

1234 Christmas Lane

City or town, state or province. Include postal code where appropriate. **Rovaniemi**	Country (do not abbreviate) **Finland**

5 Address in the United States (street, apt. or suite no., or rural route). **Do not use a P.O. box.**

varies

City or town, state, and ZIP code

Note: *Citizens of Canada or Mexico are not required to complete lines 7a and 7b.*

6 U.S. visa type **H1B**	7a Country issuing passport **USA**	7b Passport number **1225**
8 Date of entry into the United States **November 16, 20X1**	9a Current nonimmigrant status	9b Date your current nonimmigrant status expires **November 1, 20X5**

10 If you are a foreign student, trainee, professor/teacher, or researcher, check this box . . . . ▶ ☐

Caution: *See the line 10 instructions for the required additional statement you must attach.*

For Privacy Act and Paperwork Reduction Act Notice, see separate instructions.   Cat. No. 62292K   Form **8233** (Rev. 3-2009)

¶906

Form 8233 (Rev. 3-2009)   Page **2**

Part II   **Claim for Tax Treaty Withholding Exemption and/or Personal Exemption Amount**

11   Compensation for independent (and certain dependent) personal services:

  a   Description of personal services you are providing Taxpayer participates in numerous Christmas activities playing the
role of a jolly elderly gentleman who spreads joy

  b   Total compensation you expect to be paid for these services in this calendar or tax year $ _____ 10,000

12   If compensation is exempt from withholding based on a tax treaty benefit, provide:

  a   Tax treaty **and treaty article** on which you are basing exemption from withholding U.S.-Finnish Tax Treaty, Article 14

  b   Total compensation listed on line 11b above that is exempt from tax under this treaty $ _____ 10,000

  c   Country of permanent residence Finland

> **Note:** *Do not complete lines 13a through 13c unless you also received compensation for personal services from the same withholding agent.*

13   Noncompensatory scholarship or fellowship income:

  a   Amount $ _____

  b   Tax treaty **and treaty article** on which you are basing exemption from withholding

  c   Total income listed on line 13a above that is exempt from tax under this treaty $

14   Sufficient facts to justify the exemption from withholding claimed on line 12 and/or line 13 (see instructions)
Kris travels from function to function as an independent contractor. His activities are not attributable to any
fixed base regularly available to him. His vagabond-like activities cumulate in visiting the homes of many good
girls and boys the night before Christmas.

> **Note:** *Lines 15 through 18 are to be completed only for certain independent personal services (see instructions).*

15 Number of personal exemptions claimed ▶	**16** How many days will you perform services in the United States during this tax year? ▶

17   Daily personal exemption amount claimed (see instructions) ▶

18   Total personal exemption amount claimed. Multiply line 16 by line 17 ▶

Part III   **Certification**

Under penalties of perjury, I declare that I have examined the information on this form and to the best of my knowledge and belief it is true, correct, and complete. I further certify under penalties of perjury that:

● I am the beneficial owner (or am authorized to sign for the beneficial owner) of all the income to which this form relates.

● The beneficial owner is not a U.S. person.

● The beneficial owner is a resident of the treaty country listed on line 12a and/or 13b above within the meaning of the income tax treaty between the United States and that country.

Furthermore, I authorize this form to be provided to any withholding agent that has control, receipt, or custody of the income of which I am the beneficial owner or any withholding agent that can disburse or make payments of the income of which I am the beneficial owner.

Sign Here ▶ _____   _____
          Signature of beneficial owner (or individual authorized to sign for beneficial owner)   Date

Part IV   **Withholding Agent Acceptance and Certification**

Name	**Employer identification number**

Address (number and street) (Include apt. or suite no. or P.O. box, if applicable.)

City, state, and ZIP code	Telephone number

Under penalties of perjury, I certify that I have examined this form and any accompanying statements, that I am satisfied that an exemption from withholding is warranted, and that I do not know or have reason to know that the nonresident alien individual is not entitled to the exemption or that the nonresident alien's eligibility for the exemption cannot be readily determined.

Signature of withholding agent ▶   Date ▶

Form **8233** (Rev. 3-2009)

Norman Ray Allen (NRA), a resident of the Cayman Islands, purchases an apartment building located in the United States. NRA comes to the United States to manage the apartment building where he is responsible for maintenance. On the first day of each month, NRA collects ten rent checks of $1,000 each for a total of $10,000. NRA provides a Form W-8ECI to each tenant to claim that the income is effectively connected with the conduct of a trade or business in the United States so that the tenants do not have to withhold 30%. After the end of his first taxable year, NRA will have to file a Form 1040NR and pay tax on his net rental income.

Form **W-8ECI**	**Certificate of Foreign Person's Claim That Income Is Effectively Connected With the Conduct of a Trade or Business in the United States**	
(Rev. February 2014)	▶ Section references are to the Internal Revenue Code.	OMB No. 1545-1621
Department of the Treasury Internal Revenue Service	▶ Information about Form W-8ECI and its separate instructions is at *www.irs.gov/formw8eci*. ▶ Give this form to the withholding agent or payer. Do not send to the IRS.	

Note. *Persons submitting this form must file an annual U.S. income tax return to report income claimed to be effectively connected with a U.S. trade or business (see instructions).*

Do not use this form for:	Instead, use Form:
• A beneficial owner solely claiming foreign status or treaty benefits	W-8BEN or W-8BEN-E
• A foreign government, international organization, foreign central bank of issue, foreign tax-exempt organization, foreign private foundation, or government of a U.S. possession claiming the applicability of section(s) 115(2), 501(c), 892, 895, or 1443(b)	W-8EXP

Note. *These entities should use Form W-8ECI if they received effectively connected income and are not eligible to claim an exemption for chapter 3 or 4 purposes on Form W-8EXP.*

• A foreign partnership or a foreign trust (unless claiming an exemption from U.S. withholding on income effectively connected with the conduct of a trade or business in the United States)	W-8BEN-E or W-8IMY
• A person acting as an intermediary	W-8IMY

Note. *See instructions for additional exceptions.*

Part I   **Identification of Beneficial Owner** (see instructions.)

1 Name of individual or organization that is the beneficial owner	2 Country of incorporation or organization
Norman Ray Allen	Cayman Islands

3   Name of disregarded entity receiving the payments (if applicable)

4   Type of entity (check the appropriate box):

☐ Partnership   ☐ Simple trust   ☑ Individual   ☐ Corporation
☐ Government   ☐ Grantor trust   ☐ Complex trust   ☐ Estate
☐ Private foundation   ☐ International organization   ☐ Central bank of issue   ☐ Tax-exempt organization

5   Permanent residence address (street, apt. or suite no., or rural route). **Do not use a P.O. box or in-care-of address.**
321 High Street

City or town, state or province. Include postal code where appropriate.	Country
Georgetown, Grand Cayman	Cayman Islands

6   Business address in the United States (street, apt. or suite no., or rural route). **Do not use a P.O. box or in-care-of address.**
1234 Main Street

City or town, state, and ZIP code
Springfield, USA

7 U.S. taxpayer identification number (required—see instructions).	8 Foreign tax identifying number
☑ SSN or ITIN ☐ EIN 999-99-9999	

9 Reference number(s) (see instructions)	10 Date of birth (MM-DD-YYYY)
	02-30-1910

11   Specify each item of income that is, or is expected to be, received from the payer that is effectively connected with the conduct of a trade or business in the United States. (attach statement if necessary)   Norman Ray Allen is in the first year of the trade or business of renting the residential real estate located at 1234 Main Street, Springfield, USA. Moreover, when he files his form 1040NR to pay tax at marginal rates on this rental income, he intends to make a protective election to be treated as a trade or business under Treas. Reg. Section 1.871-10. Therefore, withholding on rental payments is inappropriate.

Part II   **Certification**

Under penalties of perjury, I declare that I have examined the information on this form and to the best of my knowledge and belief it is true, correct, and complete. I further certify under penalties of perjury that:

• I am the beneficial owner (or I am authorized to sign for the beneficial owner) of all the payments to which this form relates,

• The amounts for which this certification is provided are effectively connected with the conduct of a trade or business in the United States,

• The income for which this form was provided is includible in my gross income (or the beneficial owner's gross income) for the taxable year, **and**

• The beneficial owner is not a U.S. person.

Sign Here

Furthermore, I authorize this form to be provided to any withholding agent that has control, receipt, or custody of the payments of which I am the beneficial owner or any withholding agent that can disburse or make payments of the amounts of which I am the beneficial owner.

I agree that I will submit a new form within 30 days if any certification made on this form becomes incorrect.

Signature of beneficial owner (or individual authorized to sign for the beneficial owner)	Print name	Date (MM-DD-YYYY)

☐ I certify that I have the capacity to sign for the person identified on line 1 of this form.

For Paperwork Reduction Act Notice, see separate instructions.   Cat. No. 25045D   Form **W-8ECI** (Rev. 2-2014)

¶906

Reijo Salo, a resident of Finland, owns 10,000 shares of MagnaSoft, a U.S. corporation. MagnaSoft declares a $100,000 dividend to Reijo Salo. By providing the Form W-8BEN to MagnaSoft, MagnaSoft will only withhold at a treaty rate on dividends to individuals under the U.S.-Finnish Tax Treaty of 15% (for $15,000 of withholding) instead of the non-treaty rate of 30%.

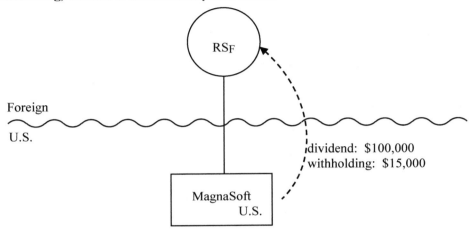

Form **W-8BEN**

(Rev. February 2014)

Department of the Treasury
Internal Revenue Service

Certificate of Foreign Status of Beneficial Owner for United States Tax Withholding and Reporting (Individuals)

▶ For use by individuals. Entities must use Form W-8BEN-E.
▶ Information about Form W-8BEN and its separate instructions is at *www.irs.gov/formw8ben.*
▶ Give this form to the withholding agent or payer. Do not send to the IRS.

OMB No. 1545-1621

Do NOT use this form if:	**Instead, use Form:**
• You are NOT an individual	W-8BEN-E
• You are a U.S. citizen or other U.S. person, including a resident alien individual	W-9
• You are a beneficial owner claiming that income is effectively connected with the conduct of trade or business within the U.S. (other than personal services)	W-8ECI
• You are a beneficial owner who is receiving compensation for personal services performed in the United States	8233 or W-4
• A person acting as an intermediary	W-8IMY

Part I   **Identification of Beneficial Owner** (see instructions)

1 Name of individual who is the beneficial owner	2 Country of citizenship
Reijo	Finland

3   Permanent residence address (street, apt. or suite no., or rural route). **Do not use a P.O. box or in-care-of address.**

4321 Finnish White Wine Way

City or town, state or province. Include postal code where appropriate.	Country
Espoo	Finland

4   Mailing address (if different from above)

City or town, state or province. Include postal code where appropriate.	Country

5 U.S. taxpayer identification number (SSN or ITIN), if required (see instructions)	6 Foreign tax identifying number (see instructions)
977-77-7777	

7 Reference number(s) (see instructions)	8 Date of birth (MM-DD-YYYY) (see instructions)
	03-03-1961

Part II   **Claim of Tax Treaty Benefits** (for chapter 3 purposes only) (see instructions)

9   I certify that the beneficial owner is a resident of Finland within the meaning of the income tax treaty between the United States and that country.

10   **Special rates and conditions** (if applicable—see instructions): The beneficial owner is claiming the provisions of Article 10 of the treaty identified on line 9 above to claim a 15 % rate of withholding on (specify type of income): dividends

Explain the reasons the beneficial owner meets the terms of the treaty article: The beneficial owner is an individual who is a resident of Finland and, therefore, entitled to the benefits of Article X of the U.S.-Finnish Tax Treaty.

Part III   **Certification**

Under penalties of perjury, I declare that I have examined the information on this form and to the best of my knowledge and belief it is true, correct, and complete. I further certify under penalties of perjury that:

- I am the individual that is the beneficial owner (or am authorized to sign for the individual that is the beneficial owner) of all the income to which this form relates or am using this form to document myself as an individual that is an owner or account holder of a foreign financial institution,

- The person named on line 1 of this form is not a U.S. person,

- The income to which this form relates is:

  (a) not effectively connected with the conduct of a trade or business in the United States,

  (b) effectively connected but is not subject to tax under an applicable income tax treaty, or

  (c) the partner's share of a partnership's effectively connected income,

- The person named on line 1 of this form is a resident of the treaty country listed on line 9 of the form (if any) within the meaning of the income tax treaty between the United States and that country, and

- For broker transactions or barter exchanges, the beneficial owner is an exempt foreign person as defined in the instructions.

Furthermore, I authorize this form to be provided to any withholding agent that has control, receipt, or custody of the income of which I am the beneficial owner or any withholding agent that can disburse or make payments of the income of which I am the beneficial owner. **I agree that I will submit a new form within 30 days if any certification made on this form becomes incorrect.**

Sign Here ▶

Signature of beneficial owner (or individual authorized to sign for beneficial owner)	Date (MM-DD-YYYY)

Print name of signer	Capacity in which acting (if form is not signed by beneficial owner)

For Paperwork Reduction Act Notice, see separate instructions.   Cat. No. 25047Z   Form **W-8BEN** (Rev. 2-2014)

¶906

Shorty, a resident of the Netherlands, owns real estate known as Blackacre, which is a parcel of land located in Nashville, Tennessee. On February 28, 20X1, Shorty sells Blackacre for a price of $1 million to Betsy Ross, a U.S. citizen. Betsy must withhold $100,000, which is 10% of the purchase price of Blackacre. By March 20, 20X1, 20 days after the purchase, Betsy must file a Form 8288 with the IRS along with a copy of Form 8288-A (which is also provided to Shorty) and tender the $100,000 of tax withheld.

Form **8288**	U.S. Withholding Tax Return for Dispositions by Foreign Persons of U.S. Real Property Interests	OMB No. 1545-0902

(Rev. August 2013)
Department of the Treasury
Internal Revenue Service

▶ Information about Form 8288 and its separate instructions is at *www.irs.gov/form8288.*

Complete Part I **or** Part II. Also complete and attach Copies A and B of Form(s) 8288-A.
(Attach additional sheets if you need more space.)

Part I   To Be Completed by the Buyer or Other Transferee Required To Withhold Under Section 1445(a)

1 Name of buyer or other transferee responsible for withholding (see instructions)

Betsy Ross

Identifying number

123-41-1234

Street address, apt. or suite no., or rural route. Do not use a P.O. box.

234 Arch Street

City or town, province or state, country, and ZIP or foreign postal code

Philadelphia, PA 19108

Phone number (optional)

2 Description and location of property acquired   Blackacre is located at 1313 21st Avenue South, Nashville, TN 37205

3 Date of transfer	**4** Number of Forms 8288-A attached	**5** Amount realized on the transfer
February 28, 20XI	1	$1,000,000

6 Check applicable box.

7 Amount withheld

a Withholding is at 10% ☑

b Withholding is of a reduced amount ☐ $100,000

Part II   To Be Completed by an Entity Subject to the Provisions of Section 1445(e)

1 Name of entity or fiduciary responsible for withholding (see instructions)

Identifying number

Street address, apt. or suite no., or rural route. Do not use a P.O. box.

City or town, province or state, country, and ZIP or foreign postal code

Phone number (optional)

2 Description of U.S. real property interest transferred or distributed

3 Date of transfer	**4** Number of Forms 8288-A attached

5 Complete all items that apply.

6 Total amount withheld

a Amount subject to withholding at 35%

b Amount subject to withholding at 10%

c Amount subject to withholding at reduced rate

d Large trust election to withhold at distribution ☐

Sign Here Under penalties of perjury, I declare that I have examined this return, including accompanying schedules and statements, and to the best of my knowledge and belief, it is true, correct, and complete. Declaration of preparer (other than taxpayer) is based on all information of which preparer has any knowledge.

▶ Signature of withholding agent, partner, fiduciary, or corporate officer   Title (if applicable)   Date

Paid Preparer Use Only	Print/Type preparer's name	Preparer's signature	Date	Check ☐ if self-employed	PTIN
	Firm's name ▶			Firm's EIN ▶	
	Firm's address ▶			Phone no.	

For Privacy Act and Paperwork Reduction Act Notice, see the instructions.   Cat. No. 62260A   Form **8288** (Rev. 8-2013)

Statement of Withholding on Dispositions by Foreign Persons of U.S. Real Property Interests

OMB No. 1545-0902

Copy A
For Internal Revenue Service Center

For Privacy Act and Paperwork Reduction Act Notice, see the Instructions for Form 8288.

Withholding agent's name, street address, city, state, and ZIP code

Betsy Ross
239 Arch Street
Philadelphia, PA 19108

1 Date of transfer	
February 28, 20X1	
2 Federal income tax withheld	
	$100,000

Withholding agent's Federal identification number	Identification number of foreign person subject to withholding (see instructions)	3 Amount realized	4 Gain recognized by foreign corporation
123-41-1234	966-66-6666	$1,000,000	

5 Description of property transferred

Blackacre

Name of person subject to withholding

Shorty

6 Person subject to withholding is: An individual ☑
A corporation ☐   Other (specify) ▶

Foreign address (number, street, and apt. or suite no.)	7 Country code
	NL

Mailing address of person subject to withholding (if different)

City, province or state, postal code, and country (not U.S.)

Amsterdam, The Netherlands

Attach Copies A and B to Form 8288

Form **8288-A** (Rev. 6-2011)   Cat. No. 62261L   Department of the Treasury - Internal Revenue Service

¶906

Judge Aloha, a resident of Ceylon, sells Green Acre, a parcel of land located in Sadstone, Michigan, to Oliver Douglas, a U.S. citizen. Judge Aloha's adjusted basis in Green Acre is $450,000 and the sales price is $500,000, resulting in gain to Judge Aloha of $50,000. Because the tax on the $50,000 gain will be less than the $50,000 withheld under FIRPTA (10% of the purchase price of $500,000), Judge Aloha files a Form 8288-B with the IRS to request a certificate for a reduced amount of withholding at the close.

Form **8288-B** (Rev. August 2013) Department of the Treasury Internal Revenue Service	**Application for Withholding Certificate for Dispositions by Foreign Persons of U.S. Real Property Interests** ▶ Please type or print.	OMB No. 1545-1060

1 Name of transferor (attach additional sheets if more than one transferor)	**Identification number**
Judge Aloha	955-55-5555

Street address, apt. or suite no., or rural route. Do not use a P.O. box.

City, state or province, and country (if not U.S.). Include ZIP code or postal code where appropriate.

Ceylon

2 Name of transferee (attach additional sheets if more than one transferee)	**Identification number**
Oliver Douglas	482-37-4743

Street address, apt. or suite no., or rural route. Do not use a P.O. box.

City, state or province, and country (if not U.S.). Include ZIP code or postal code where appropriate.

Hooterville, USA

3 Applicant is: Transferor ☑ Transferee ☐

4a Name of withholding agent (see instructions)	**b Identification number**
Oliver Douglas	555-55-5555
c Name of estate, trust, or entity (if applicable)	**d Identification number**

5 Address where you want withholding certificate sent (street address, apt. or suite no., P.O. box, or rural route number)	Phone number (optional)

City, state or province, and country (if not U.S.). Include ZIP code or postal code where appropriate.

Hooterville, USA

6 Description of U.S. real property transaction:

a Date of transfer (month, day, year) (see inst.) ___12/25/XI___ **b** Contract price $ ___500,000___

c Type of interest transferred: ☑ Real property ☐ Associated personal property
☐ Domestic U.S. real property holding corporation

d Use of property at time of sale: ☐ Rental or commercial ☑ Personal ☐ Other (attach explanation)

e Adjusted basis $ ___450,000___

f Location and general description of property (for a real property interest), description (for associated personal property), or the class or type and amount of the interest (for an interest in a U.S. real property holding corporation). See instructions.

Green Acres is a farmhouse and farm located at 4321 Main Street, Sadstone, MI

g For the 3 preceding tax years:

(1) Were U.S. income tax returns filed relating to the U.S. real property interest? . . . . ☐ Yes ☑ No
If "Yes," when and where were those returns filed? ▶

(2) Were U.S. income taxes paid relating to the U.S. real property interest? . . . . ☐ Yes ☑ No
If "Yes," enter the amount of tax paid for each year ▶

7 Check the box to indicate the reason a withholding certificate should be issued. See the instructions for information that must be attached to Form 8288-B.

a ☐ The transferor is exempt from U.S. tax or nonrecognition treatment applies.

b ☑ The transferor's maximum tax liability is less than the tax required to be withheld.

c ☐ The special installment sales rules described in section 7 of Rev. Proc. 2000-35 allow reduced withholding.

8 Does the transferor have any unsatisfied withholding liability under section 1445? . . . . ☐ Yes ☑ No
See the instructions for information required to be attached.

9 Is this application for a withholding certificate made under section 1445(e)? . . . . ☐ Yes ☑ No
If "Yes," check the applicable box in **a** and the applicable box in **b** below.

a Type of transaction: ☐ 1445(e)(1) ☐ 1445(e)(2) ☐ 1445(e)(3) ☐ 1445(e)(5) ☐ 1445(e)(6)

b Applicant is: ☑ Taxpayer ☐ Other person required to withhold. Specify your title (e.g., trustee) ▶ ___

Under penalties of perjury, I declare that I have examined this application and accompanying attachments, and, to the best of my knowledge and belief, they are true, correct, and complete.

Signature	Title (if applicable)	Date

For Privacy Act and Paperwork Reduction Act Notice, see the instructions.   Cat. No. 10128Z   Form **8288-B** (Rev. 8-2013)

GERco, a German company that manufactures widgets, wholly owns USCo, which sells GERco's widgets in the United States. USCo distributes a dividend to GERco, on which GERco is exempt from U.S. withholding tax under the German-U.S. Tax Treaty. GERco must provide a Form W-8BEN-E indicating that it is a corporation entitled to treaty benefits to avoid FDAP withholding under Chapter 3. GERco must also indicate on Form W-8BEN-E that it is an active non-financial foreign entity to avoid FATCA withholding under Chapter 4.

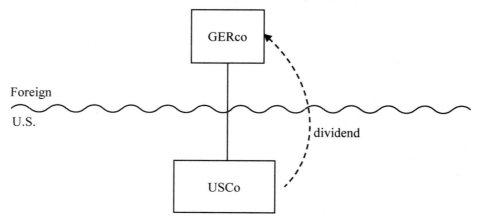

Form **W-8BEN-E**

(February 2014)
Department of the Treasury
Internal Revenue Service

Certificate of Status of Beneficial Owner for United States Tax Withholding and Reporting (Entities)

▶ For use by entities. Individuals must use Form W-8BEN. ▶ Section references are to the Internal Revenue Code.
▶ Information about Form W-8BEN-E and its separate instructions is at *www.irs.gov/formw8bene*.
▶ Give this form to the withholding agent or payer. Do not send to the IRS.

OMB No. 1545-1621

Do NOT use this form for:	**Instead use Form:**
• U.S. entity or U.S. citizen or resident	W-9
• A foreign individual	W-8BEN (Individual)
• A foreign individual or entity claiming that income is effectively connected with the conduct of trade or business within the U.S. (unless claiming treaty benefits).	W-8ECI
• A foreign partnership, a foreign simple trust, or a foreign grantor trust (unless claiming treaty benefits) (see instructions for exceptions) .	W-8IMY
• A foreign government, international organization, foreign central bank of issue, foreign tax-exempt organization, foreign private foundation, or government of a U.S. possession claiming that income is effectively connected U.S. income or that is claiming the applicability of section(s) 115(2), 501(c), 892, 895, or 1443(b) (unless claiming treaty benefits) (see instructions)	W-8ECI or W-8EXP
• Any person acting as an intermediary	W-8IMY

Part I	**Identification of Beneficial Owner**

1 Name of organization that is the beneficial owner

GERco

2 Country of incorporation or organization

Germany

3 Name of disregarded entity receiving the payment (if applicable)

4 Chapter 3 Status (entity type) (Must check one box only): ☑ Corporation　☐ Disregarded entity　☐ Partnership
☐ Simple trust　☐ Grantor trust　☐ Complex trust　☐ Estate　☐ Government
☐ Central Bank of Issue　☐ Tax-exempt organization　☐ Private foundation

If you entered disregarded entity, partnership, simple trust, or grantor trust above, is the entity a hybrid making a treaty claim? If "Yes" complete Part III.　☐ Yes　☐ No

5 Chapter 4 Status (FATCA status) (Must check one box only unless otherwise indicated). (See instructions for details and complete the certification below for the entity's applicable status).

☐ Nonparticipating FFI (including a limited FFI or an FFI related to a Reporting IGA FFI other than a registered deemed-compliant FFI or participating FFI).

☐ Participating FFI.

☐ Reporting Model 1 FFI.

☐ Reporting Model 2 FFI.

☐ Registered deemed-compliant FFI (other than a reporting Model 1 FFI or sponsored FFI that has not obtained a GIIN).

☐ Sponsored FFI that has not obtained a GIIN. Complete Part IV.

☐ Certified deemed-compliant nonregistering local bank. Complete Part V.

☐ Certified deemed-compliant FFI with only low-value accounts. Complete Part VI.

☐ Certified deemed-compliant sponsored, closely held investment vehicle. Complete Part VII.

☐ Certified deemed-compliant limited life debt investment entity. Complete Part VIII.

☐ Certified deemed-compliant investment advisors and investment managers. Complete Part IX.

☐ Owner-documented FFI. Complete Part X.

☐ Restricted distributor. Complete Part XI.

☐ Nonreporting IGA FFI (including an FFI treated as a registered deemed-compliant FFI under an applicable Model 2 IGA). Complete Part XII.

☐ Foreign government, government of a U.S. possession, or foreign central bank of issue. Complete Part XIII.

☐ International organization. Complete Part XIV.

☐ Exempt retirement plans. Complete Part XV.

☐ Entity wholly owned by exempt beneficial owners. Complete Part XVI.

☐ Territory financial institution. Complete Part XVII.

☐ Nonfinancial group entity. Complete Part XVIII.

☐ Excepted nonfinancial start-up company. Complete Part XIX.

☐ Excepted nonfinancial entity in liquidation or bankruptcy. Complete Part XX.

☐ 501(c) organization. Complete Part XXI.

☐ Nonprofit organization. Complete Part XXII.

☐ Publicly traded NFFE or NFFE affiliate of a publicly traded corporation. Complete Part XXIII.

☐ Excepted territory NFFE. Complete Part XXIV.

☑ Active NFFE. Complete Part XXV.

☐ Passive NFFE. Complete Part XXVI.

☐ Excepted inter-affiliate FFI. Complete Part XXVII.

☐ Direct reporting NFFE.

☐ Sponsored direct reporting NFFE. Complete Part XXVIII.

6 Permanent residence address (street, apt. or suite no., or rural route). **Do not use a P.O. box or in-care-of address** (other than a registered address).

Reinhold Schneider Str. 32/0003

City or town, state or province. Include postal code where appropriate.

79117 Freiburg

Country

Germany

7 Mailing address (if different from above)

City or town, state or province. Include postal code where appropriate.

Country

8 U.S. taxpayer identification number (TIN), if required | **9a** ☐ GIIN | **b** ☐ Foreign TIN | **10** Reference number(s) (see instructions)

Note. Please complete remainder of the form including signing the form in Part XXIX.

For Paperwork Reduction Act Notice, see separate instructions.　　Cat. No. 59689N　　Form **W-8BEN-E** (2-2014)

Form W-8BEN-E (2-2014)   Page **2**

Part II	**Disregarded Entity or Branch Receiving Payment.** (Complete only if disregarded entity or branch of an FFI in a country other than the FFI's country of residence.)

11   Chapter 4 Status (FATCA status) of disregarded entity or branch receiving payment

☐ Limited Branch.   ☐ Reporting Model 1 FFI.   ☐ U.S. Branch.

☐ Participating FFI.   ☐ Reporting Model 2 FFI.

12   Address of disregarded entity or branch (street, apt. or suite no., or rural route). **Do not use a P.O. box or in-care-of address** (other than a registered address).

City or town, state or province. Include postal code where appropriate.

Country

13   GIIN (if any)

Part III	**Claim of Tax Treaty Benefits** (if applicable). (For chapter 3 purposes only)

14   I certify that (check all that apply):

a   ☑ The beneficial owner is a resident of   Germany   within the meaning of the income tax treaty between the United States and that country.

b   ☐ The beneficial owner derives the item (or items) of income for which the treaty benefits are claimed, and, if applicable, meets the requirements of the treaty provision dealing with limitation on benefits (see instructions).

c   ☐ The beneficial owner is claiming treaty benefits for dividends received from a foreign corporation or interest from a U.S. trade or business of a foreign corporation and meets qualified resident status (see instructions).

15   Special rates and conditions (if applicable—see instructions): The beneficial owner is claiming the provisions of Article   10-3   of the treaty identified on line 14a above to claim a   0%   % rate of withholding on (specify type of income): **dividend**   .

Explain the reasons the beneficial owner meets the terms of the treaty article: GERco is a public company that wholly owns USCo

Part IV	**Sponsored FFI That Has Not Obtained a GIIN**

16   Name of sponsoring entity:

17   **Check whichever box applies.**

☐ I certify that the entity identified in Part I:

• Is an FFI solely because it is an investment entity;

• Is not a QI, WP, or WT; **and**

• Has agreed with the entity identified above (that is not a nonparticipating FFI) to act as the sponsoring entity for this entity.

☐ I certify that the entity identified in Part I:

• Is a controlled foreign corporation as defined in section 957(a);

• Is not a QI, WP, or WT;

• Is wholly owned, directly or indirectly, by the U.S. financial institution identified above that agrees to act as the sponsoring entity for this entity; **and**

• Shares a common electronic account system with the sponsoring entity (identified above) that enables the sponsoring entity to identify all account holders and payees of the entity and to access all account and customer information maintained by the entity including, but not limited to, customer identification information, customer documentation, account balance, and all payments made to account holders or payees.

Part V	**Certified Deemed-Compliant Nonregistering Local Bank**

18   ☐ I certify that the FFI identified in Part I:

• Operates and is licensed solely as a bank or credit union (or similar cooperative credit organization operated without profit) in its country of incorporation or organization;

• Engages primarily in the business of receiving deposits from and making loans to, with respect to a bank, retail customers unrelated to such bank and, with respect to a credit union or similar cooperative credit organization, members, provided that no member has a greater than five percent interest in such credit union or cooperative credit organization;

• Does not solicit account holders outside its country of organization;

• Has no fixed place of business outside such country (for this purpose, a fixed place of business does not include a location that is not advertised to the public and from which the FFI performs solely administrative support functions);

• Has no more than $175 million in assets on its balance sheet and, if it is a member of an expanded affiliated group, the group has no more than $500 million in total assets on its consolidated or combined balance sheets; **and**

• Does not have any member of its expanded affiliated group that is a foreign financial institution, other than a foreign financial institution that is incorporated or organized in the same country as the FFI identified in Part I and that meets the requirements set forth in this Part V.

Form **W-8BEN-E** (2-2014)

Part VI	**Certified Deemed-Compliant FFI with Only Low-Value Accounts**

19 ☐ I certify that the FFI identified in Part I:

- Is not engaged primarily in the business of investing, reinvesting, or trading in securities, partnership interests, commodities, notional principal contracts, insurance or annuity contracts, or any interest (including a futures or forward contract or option) in such security, partnership interest, commodity, notional principal contract, insurance contract or annuity contract;

- No financial account maintained by the FFI or any member of its expanded affiliated group, if any, has a balance or value in excess of $50,000 (as determined after applying applicable account aggregation rules); **and**

- Neither the FFI nor the entire expanded affiliated group, if any, of the FFI, have more than $50 million in assets on its consolidated or combined balance sheet as of the end of its most recent accounting year.

Part VII	**Certified Deemed-Compliant Sponsored, Closely Held Investment Vehicle**

20 Name of sponsoring entity: _____

21 ☐ I certify that the entity identified in Part I:

- Is an FFI solely because it is an investment entity described in §1.1471-5(e)(4);

- Is not a QI, WP, or WT;

- Has a contractual relationship with the above identified sponsoring entity that agrees to fulfill all due diligence, withholding, and reporting responsibilities of a participating FFI on behalf of this entity; **and**

- Twenty or fewer individuals own all of the debt and equity interests in the entity (disregarding debt interests owned by U.S. financial institutions, participating FFIs, registered deemed-compliant FFIs, and certified deemed-compliant FFIs and equity interests owned by an entity if that entity owns 100 percent of the equity interests in the FFI and is itself a sponsored FFI).

Part VIII	**Certified Deemed-Compliant Limited Life Debt Investment Entity**

22 ☐ I certify that the entity identified in Part I:

- Was in existence as of January 17, 2013;

- Issued all classes of its debt or equity interests to investors on or before January 17, 2013, pursuant to a trust indenture or similar agreement; **and**
- Is certified deemed-compliant because it satisfies the requirements to be treated as a limited life debt investment entity (such as the restrictions with respect to its assets and other requirements under § 1.1471-5(f)(2)(iv)).

Part IX	**Certified Deemed-Compliant Investment Advisors and Investment Managers**

23 ☐ I certify that the entity identified in Part I:

- Is a financial institution solely because it is an investment entity described in §1.1471-5(e)(4)(i)(A); **and**
- Does not maintain financial accounts.

Part X	**Owner-Documented FFI**

Note. This status only applies if the U.S. financial institution or participating FFI to which this form is given has agreed that it will treat the FFI as an owner-documented FFI (see instructions for eligibility requirements). In addition, the FFI must make the certifications below.

24a ☐ (All owner-documented FFIs check here) I certify that the FFI identified in Part I:

- Does not act as an intermediary;

- Does not accept deposits in the ordinary course of a banking or similar business;

- Does not hold, as a substantial portion of its business, financial assets for the account of others;

- Is not an insurance company (or the holding company of an insurance company) that issues or is obligated to make payments with respect to a financial account;

- Is not owned by or in an expanded affiliated group with an entity that accepts deposits in the ordinary course of a banking or similar business, holds, as a substantial portion of its business, financial assets for the account of others, or is an insurance company (or the holding company of an insurance company) that issues or is obligated to make payments with respect to a financial account; **and**
- Does not maintain a financial account for any nonparticipating FFI.

Form **W-8BEN-E** (2-2014)

Part X	Owner-Documented FFI *(continued)*

Check box 24b or 24c, whichever applies.

b ☐ I certify that the FFI identified in Part I:

    • Has provided, or will provide, an FFI owner reporting statement that contains:

        • The name, address, TIN (if any), chapter 4 status, and type of documentation provided (if required) of every individual and specified U.S. person that owns a direct or indirect equity interest in the owner-documented FFI (looking through all entities other than specified U.S. persons);

        • The name, address, TIN (if any), chapter 4 status, and type of documentation provided (if required) of every individual and specified U.S. person that owns a debt interest in the owner-documented FFI (including any indirect debt interest, which includes debt interests in any entity that directly or indirectly owns the payee or any direct or indirect equity interest in a debt holder of the payee) that constitutes a financial account in excess of $50,000 (disregarding all such debt interests owned by participating FFIs, registered deemed-compliant FFIs, certified deemed-compliant FFIs, excepted NFFEs, exempt beneficial owners, or U.S. persons other than specified U.S. persons); **and**

    • Any additional information the withholding agent requests in order to fulfill its obligations with respect to the entity.

c ☐ I certify that the FFI identified in Part I has provided, or will provide, an auditor's letter, signed within four years of the date of payment, from an independent accounting firm or legal representative with a location in the United States stating that the firm or representative has reviewed the FFI's documentation with respect to all of its owners and debt holders identified in §1.1471-3(d)(6)(iv)(A)(2), and that the FFI meets all the requirements to be an owner-documented FFI. The FFI identified in Part I has also provided, or will provide, an FFI owner reporting statement of its owners that are specified U.S. persons and Form(s) W-9, with applicable waivers.

Check box 24d if applicable.

d ☐ I certify that the entity identified in line 1 is a trust that does not have any contingent beneficiaries or designated classes with unidentified beneficiaries.

Part XI	Restricted Distributor

25a ☐ (All restricted distributors check here) I certify that the entity identified in Part I:

    • Operates as a distributor with respect to debt or equity interests of the restricted fund with respect to which this form is furnished;

    • Provides investment services to at least 30 customers unrelated to each other and less than half of its customers are related to each other;

    • Is required to perform AML due diligence procedures under the anti-money laundering laws of its country of organization (which is an FATF-compliant jurisdiction);

    • Operates solely in its country of incorporation or organization, has no fixed place of business outside of that country, and has the same country of incorporation or organization as all members of its affiliated group, if any;

    • Does not solicit customers outside its country of incorporation or organization;

    • Has no more than $175 million in total assets under management and no more than $7 million in gross revenue on its income statement for the most recent accounting year;

    • Is not a member of an expanded affiliated group that has more than $500 million in total assets under management or more than $20 million in gross revenue for its most recent accounting year on a combined or consolidated income statement; **and**

    • Does not distribute any debt or securities of the restricted fund to specified U.S. persons, passive NFFEs with one or more substantial U.S. owners, or nonparticipating FFIs.

Check box 25b or 25c, whichever applies.

I further certify that with respect to all sales of debt or equity interests in the restricted fund with respect to which this form is furnished that are made after December 31, 2011, the entity identified in Part I:

b ☐ Has been bound by a distribution agreement that contained a general prohibition on the sale of debt or securities to U.S. entities and U.S. resident individuals and is currently bound by a distribution agreement that contains a prohibition of the sale of debt or securities to any specified U.S. person, passive NFFE with one or more substantial U.S. owners, or nonparticipating FFI.

c ☐ Is currently bound by a distribution agreement that contains a prohibition on the sale of debt or securities to any specified U.S. person, passive NFFE with one or more substantial U.S. owners, or nonparticipating FFI and, for all sales made prior to the time that such a restriction was included in its distribution agreement, has reviewed all accounts related to such sales in accordance with the procedures identified in §1.1471-4(c) applicable to preexisting accounts and has redeemed or retired any, or caused the restricted fund to transfer the securities to a distributor that is a participating FFI or reporting Model 1 FFI securities which were sold to specified U.S. persons, passive NFFEs with one or more substantial U.S. owners, or nonparticipating FFIs.

Part XII	Nonreporting IGA FFI

26 ☐ I certify that the entity identified in Part I:

    • Meets the requirements to be considered a nonreporting financial institution pursuant to an applicable IGA between the United States and _____ .

    • Is treated as a _____ under the provisions of the applicable IGA (see instructions); **and**

    • If you are an FFI treated as a registered deemed-compliant FFI under an applicable Model 2 IGA, provide your GIIN: _____

Form **W-8BEN-E** (2-2014)

Part XIII	**Foreign Government, Government of a U.S. Possession, or Foreign Central Bank of Issue**

27 ☐ I certify that the entity identified in Part I is the beneficial owner of the payment and is not engaged in commercial financial activities of a type engaged in by an insurance company, custodial institution, or depository institution with respect to the payments, accounts, or obligations for which this form is submitted (except as permitted in §1.1471-6(h)(2)).

Part XIV	**International Organization**

Check box 28a or 28b, whichever applies.

28a ☐ I certify that the entity identified in Part I is an international organization described in section 7701(a)(18).

b ☐ I certify that the entity identified in Part I:

• Is comprised primarily of foreign governments;

• Is recognized as an intergovernmental or supranational organization under a foreign law similar to the International Organizations Immunities Act;

• The benefit of the entity's income does not inure to any private person;

• Is the beneficial owner of the payment and is not engaged in commercial financial activities of a type engaged in by an insurance company, custodial institution, or depository institution with respect to the payments, accounts, or obligations for which this form is submitted (except as permitted in §1.1471-6(h)(2)).

Part XV	**Exempt Retirement Plans**

Check box 29a, b, c, d, e, or f, whichever applies.

29a ☐ I certify that the entity identified in Part I:

• Is established in a country with which the United States has an income tax treaty in force (see Part III if claiming treaty benefits);

• Is operated principally to administer or provide pension or retirement benefits; **and**

• Is entitled to treaty benefits on income that the fund derives from U.S. sources (or would be entitled to benefits if it derived any such income) as a resident of the other country which satisfies any applicable limitation on benefits requirement.

b ☐ I certify that the entity identified in Part I:

• Is organized for the provision of retirement, disability, or death benefits (or any combination thereof) to beneficiaries that are former employees of one or more employers in consideration for services rendered;

• No single beneficiary has a right to more than 5% of the FFI's assets;

• Is subject to government regulation and provides annual information reporting about its beneficiaries to the relevant tax authorities in the country in which the fund is established or operated; **and**

• Is generally exempt from tax on investment income under the laws of the country in which it is established or operates due to its status as a retirement or pension plan;

• Receives at least 50% of its total contributions from sponsoring employers (disregarding transfers of assets from other plans described in this part, retirement and pension accounts described in an applicable Model 1 or Model 2 IGA, other retirement funds described in an applicable Model 1 or Model 2 IGA, or accounts described in §1.1471-5(b)(2)(i)(A));

• Either does not permit or penalizes distributions or withdrawals made before the occurrence of specified events related to retirement, disability, or death (except rollover distributions to accounts described in §1.1471-5(b)(2)(i)(A) (referring to retirement and pension accounts), to retirement and pension accounts described in an applicable Model 1 or Model 2 IGA, or to other retirement funds described in this part or in an applicable Model 1 or Model 2 IGA); **or**

• Limits contributions by employees to the fund by reference to earned income of the employee or may not exceed $50,000 annually.

c ☐ I certify that the entity identified in Part I:

• Is organized for the provision of retirement, disability, or death benefits (or any combination thereof) to beneficiaries that are former employees of one or more employers in consideration for services rendered;

• Has fewer than 50 participants;

• Is sponsored by one or more employers each of which is not an investment entity or passive NFFE;

• Employee and employer contributions to the fund (disregarding transfers of assets from other plans described in this part, retirement and pension accounts described in an applicable Model 1 or Model 2 IGA, or accounts described in §1.1471-5(b)(2)(i)(A)) are limited by reference to earned income and compensation of the employee, respectively;

• Participants that are not residents of the country in which the fund is established or operated are not entitled to more than 20 percent of the fund's assets; **and**

• Is subject to government regulation and provides annual information reporting about its beneficiaries to the relevant tax authorities in the country in which the fund is established or operates.

d ☐ I certify that the entity identified in Part I is formed pursuant to a pension plan that would meet the requirements of section 401(a), other than the requirement that the plan be funded by a trust created or organized in the United States.

e ☐ I certify that the entity identified in Part I is established exclusively to earn income for the benefit of one or more retirement funds described in this part or in an applicable Model 1 or Model 2 IGA, accounts described in §1.1471-5(b)(2)(i)(A) (referring to retirement and pension accounts), or retirement and pension accounts described in an applicable Model 1 or Model 2 IGA.

Form **W-8BEN-E** (2-2014)

¶906

Part XV	**Exempt Retirement Plans** (Continued)

f   ☐ I certify that the entity identified in Part I:

- Is established and sponsored by a foreign government, international organization, central bank of issue, or government of a U.S. possession (each as defined in §1.1471-6) or an exempt beneficial owner described in an applicable Model 1 or Model 2 IGA to provide retirement, disability, or death benefits to beneficiaries or participants that are current or former employees of the sponsor (or persons designated by such employees); **or**

- Is established and sponsored by a foreign government, international organization, central bank of issue, or government of a U.S. possession (each as defined in §1.1471-6) or an exempt beneficial owner described in an applicable Model 1 or Model 2 IGA to provide retirement, disability, or death benefits to beneficiaries or participants that are not current or former employees of such sponsor, but are in consideration of personal services performed for the sponsor.

Part XVI	**Entity Wholly Owned by Exempt Beneficial Owners**

30   ☐ I certify that the entity identified in Part I:

- Is an FFI solely because it is an investment entity;

- Each direct holder of an equity interest in the investment entity is an exempt beneficial owner described in §1.1471-6 or in an applicable Model 1 or Model 2 IGA;

- Each direct holder of a debt interest in the investment entity is either a depository institution (with respect to a loan made to such entity) or an exempt beneficial owner described in §1.1471-6 or an applicable Model 1 or Model 2 IGA.

- Has provided an owner reporting statement that contains the name, address, TIN (if any), chapter 4 status, and a description of the type of documentation provided to the withholding agent for every person that owns a debt interest constituting a financial account or direct equity interest in the entity; **and**

- Has provided documentation establishing that every owner of the entity is an entity described in §1.1471-6(b), (c), (d), (e), (f) and/or (g) without regard to whether such owners are beneficial owners.

Part XVII	**Territory Financial Institution**

31   ☐ I certify that the entity identified in Part I is a financial institution (other than an investment entity) that is incorporated or organized under the laws of a possession of the United States.

Part XVIII	**Excepted Nonfinancial Group Entity**

32   ☐ I certify that the entity identified in Part I:

- Is a holding company, treasury center, or captive finance company and substantially all of the entity's activities are functions described in §1.1471-5(e)(5)(i)(C) through (E);

- Is a member of a nonfinancial group described in §1.1471-5(e)(5)(i)(B);

- Is not a depository or custodial institution (other than for members of the entity's expanded affiliated group); **and**

- Does not function (or hold itself out) as an investment fund, such as a private equity fund, venture capital fund, leveraged buyout fund, or any investment vehicle with an investment strategy to acquire or fund companies and then hold interests in those companies as capital assets for investment purposes.

Part XIX	**Excepted Nonfinancial Start-Up Company**

33   ☐ I certify that the entity identified in Part I:

- Was formed on (or, in the case of a new line of business, the date of board resolution approving the new line of business) _____ (date must be less than 24 months prior to date of payment);

- Is not yet operating a business and has no prior operating history or is investing capital in assets with the intent to operate a new line of business other than that of a financial institution or passive NFFE;

- Is investing capital into assets with the intent to operate a business other than that of a financial institution; **and**

- Does not function (or hold itself out) as an investment fund, such as a private equity fund, venture capital fund, leveraged buyout fund, or any investment vehicle whose purpose is to acquire or fund companies and then hold interests in those companies as capital assets for investment purposes.

Part XX	**Excepted Nonfinancial Entity in Liquidation or Bankruptcy**

34   ☐ I certify that the entity identified in Part I:

- Filed a plan of liquidation, filed a plan of reorganization, or filed for bankruptcy on _____ ;

- During the past 5 years has not been engaged in business as a financial institution or acted as a passive NFFE;

- Is either liquidating or emerging from a reorganization or bankruptcy with the intent to continue or recommence operations as a nonfinancial entity; **and**

- Has, or will provide, documentary evidence such as a bankruptcy filing or other public documentation that supports its claim if it remains in bankruptcy or liquidation for more than three years.

Part XXI	**501(c) Organization**

35   ☐ I certify that the entity identified in Part I is a 501(c) organization that:

- Has been issued a determination letter from the IRS that is currently in effect concluding that the payee is a section 501(c) organization that is dated _____ ; **or**

- Has provided a copy of an opinion from U.S. counsel certifying that the payee is a section 501(c) organization (without regard to whether the payee is a foreign private foundation).

Part XXII Non-Profit Organization

36 ☐ I certify that the entity identified in Part I is a non-profit organization that meets the following requirements:

- The entity is established and maintained in its country of residence exclusively for religious, charitable, scientific, artistic, cultural or educational purposes;
- The entity is exempt from income tax in its country of residence;
- The entity has no shareholders or members who have a proprietary or beneficial interest in its income or assets;
- Neither the applicable laws of the entity's country of residence nor the entity's formation documents permit any income or assets of the entity to be distributed to, or applied for the benefit of, a private person or non-charitable entity other than pursuant to the conduct of the entity's charitable activities or as payment of reasonable compensation for services rendered or payment representing the fair market value of property which the entity has purchased; **and**
- The applicable laws of the entity's country of residence or the entity's formation documents require that, upon the entity's liquidation or dissolution, all of its assets be distributed to an entity that is a foreign government, an integral part of a foreign government, a controlled entity of a foreign government, or another organization that is described in this Part XXII or escheats to the government of the entity's country of residence or any political subdivision thereof.

Part XXIII Publicly Traded NFFE or NFFE Affiliate of a Publicly Traded Corporation

Check box 37a or 37b, whichever applies.

37a ☐ I certify that:

- The entity identified in Part I is a foreign corporation that is not a financial institution; **and**
- The stock of such corporation is regularly traded on one or more established securities markets, including _____ (name one securities exchange upon which the stock is regularly traded).

b ☐ I certify that:

- The entity identified in Part I is a foreign corporation that is not a financial institution;
- The entity identified in Part I is a member of the same expanded affiliated group as an entity the stock of which is regularly traded on an established securities market;
- The name of the entity, the stock of which is regularly traded on an established securities market, is _____ ; **and**
- The name of the securities market on which the stock is regularly traded is _____ .

Part XXIV Excepted Territory NFFE

38 ☐ I certify that:

- The entity identified in Part I is an entity that is organized in a possession of the United States;
- The entity identified in Part I:
  - Does not accept deposits in the ordinary course of a banking or similar business,
  - Does not hold, as a substantial portion of its business, financial assets for the account of others, or
  - Is not an insurance company (or the holding company of an insurance company) that issues or is obligated to make payments with respect to a financial account; **and**
- All of the owners of the entity identified in Part I are bona fide residents of the possession in which the NFFE is organized or incorporated.

Part XXV Active NFFE

39 ☑ I certify that:

- The entity identified in Part I is a foreign entity that is not a financial institution;
- Less than 50% of such entity's gross income for the preceding calendar year is passive income; **and**
- Less than 50% of the assets held by such entity are assets that produce or are held for the production of passive income (calculated as a weighted average of the percentage of passive assets measured quarterly) (see instructions for the definition of passive income).

Part XXVI Passive NFFE

40a ☐ I certify that the entity identified in Part I is a foreign entity that is not a financial institution (other than an investment entity organized in a possession of the United States) and is not certifying its status as a publicly traded NFFE (or affiliate), excepted territory NFFE, active NFFE, direct reporting NFFE, or sponsored direct reporting NFFE.

Check box 40b or 40c, whichever applies.

b ☐ I further certify that the entity identified in Part I has no substantial U.S. owners, or

c ☐ I further certify that the entity identified in Part I has provided the name, address, and TIN of each substantial U.S. owner of the NFFE in Part XXX.

Part XXVII Excepted Inter-Affiliate FFI

41 ☐ I certify that the entity identified in Part I:

- Is a member of an expanded affiliated group;
- Does not maintain financial accounts (other than accounts maintained for members of its expanded affiliated group);
- Does not make withholdable payments to any person other than to members of its expanded affiliated group that are not limited FFIs or limited branches;
- Does not hold an account (other than a depository account in the country in which the entity is operating to pay for expenses) with or receive payments from any withholding agent other than a member of its expanded affiliated group; **and**
- Has not agreed to report under §1.1471-4(d)(2)(ii)(C) or otherwise act as an agent for chapter 4 purposes on behalf of any financial institution, including a member of its expanded affiliated group.

| Part XXVIII | **Sponsored Direct Reporting NFFE** |

42   Name of sponsoring entity: _____

43   ☐ I certify that the entity identified in Part I is a direct reporting NFFE that is sponsored by the entity identified in line 42.

| Part XXIX | **Certification** |

Under penalties of perjury, I declare that I have examined the information on this form and to the best of my knowledge and belief it is true, correct, and complete. I further certify under penalties of perjury that:

- The entity identified on line 1 of this form is the beneficial owner of all the income to which this form relates, is using this form to certify its status for chapter 4 purposes, or is a merchant submitting this form for purposes of section 6050W,

- The entity identified on line 1 of this form is not a U.S. person,

- The income to which this form relates is: (a) not effectively connected with the conduct of a trade or business in the United States, (b) effectively connected but is not subject to tax under an income tax treaty, or (c) the partner's share of a partnership's effectively connected income, **and**

- For broker transactions or barter exchanges, the beneficial owner is an exempt foreign person as defined in the instructions.

Furthermore, I authorize this form to be provided to any withholding agent that has control, receipt, or custody of the income of which the entity on line 1 is the beneficial owner or any withholding agent that can disburse or make payments of the income of which the entity on line 1 is the beneficial owner.

I agree that I will submit a new form within 30 days if any certification on this form becomes incorrect.

Sign Here ▶

--   --------------------------------   ----------------------
Signature of individual authorized to sign for beneficial owner   Print Name   Date (MM-DD-YYYY)

☐ **I certify that I have the capacity to sign for the entity identified on line 1 of this form.**

| Part XXX | **Substantial U.S. Owners of Passive NFFE** |

As required by Part XXVI, provide the name, address, and TIN of each substantial U.S. owner of the NFFE. Please see instructions for definition of substantial U.S. owner.

Name	Address	TIN

Form **W-8BEN-E** (2-2014)

HAVENbank is a bank organized in a country that does not have an InterGovernmental Agreement with the United States. HAVENbank has a deposit with a U.S. Bank. To avoid FATCA withholding on any interest earned at U.S. Bank, HAVENbank must provide a Form 8966 that contains information about its sole U.S. depositor, Mr. Haney, who has a deposit in excess of $50,000.

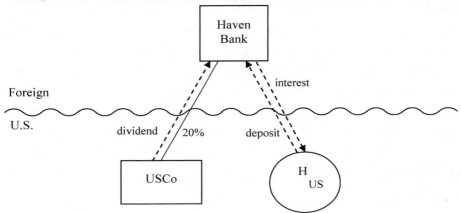

Form **8966**	**FATCA Report**	OMB No. 1545-2246
Department of the Treasury Internal Revenue Service	▶ Information about Form 8966 and its separate instructions is at *www.irs.gov/form8966.*	20**14**

Check if report is being corrected, amended, or voided

Corrected report ☐   Amended report ☐   Voided report ☐

Part I   Identification of Filer

1   Name of Filer

Swiss Bank

2   Number, street, and room or suite no. (if P.O. box, see instructions)

3a City or town	**3b** State/Province/Region	**3c** Country (including postal code)
Zurich	Zurich	Switzerland

4   Global Intermediary Identification Number (GIIN)

5   TIN

6   Name of Sponsored Entity or Intermediary, if applicable

7   Number, street, and room or suite no. (if P.O. box, see instructions)

8a City or town	**8b** State/Province/Region	**8c** Country (including postal code)

9   GIIN

10   TIN

Part II   Account Holder or Payee Information

1   Name of Account Holder or Payee

Eustace Charleston Haney

2   Number, street, and room or suite no. (if P.O. box, see instructions)

1234 Pixley Highway

3a City or town	**3b** State/Province/Region	**3c** Country (including postal code)
Hooterville		USA

4   TIN

273454747

5   If account holder or payee is an entity, check applicable box to specify the entity's type:

☐ Owner-Documented FFI with specified U.S. owner(s)   ☐ Passive NFFE with substantial U.S. owner(s)

☐ Non-Participating FFI   ☐ Specified U.S. Person

☐ Direct Reporting NFFE

Part III   Identifying Information of U.S. Owners that are specified U.S. Persons

1   Name of Owner

2   Number, street, and room or suite no. (if P.O. box, see instructions)

3a City or town	**3b** State/Province/Region	**3c** Country (including postal code)

4   TIN of Owner

Part IV   Financial Information

1 Account Number	**2** Currency Code
XYZ1234	USD

3   Account Balance

$1 million

4a Interest	**4c** Gross proceeds/Redemptions
$50,000	
4b Dividends	**4d** Other

For Paperwork Reduction Act Notice, see separate instructions.   Cat. No. 55748F   Form **8966** (2014)

Part V	**Pooled Reporting Type**

1 Check applicable Pooled Reporting Type (check only one):

☐ Recalcitrant account holders with U.S. Indicia   ☐ Recalcitrant account holders without U.S. Indicia

☐ Dormant Accounts   ☐ Non-participating FFI

☐ Recalcitrant account holders that are U.S. persons   ☐ Recalcitrant account holders that are passive NFFEs

2 Number of Accounts	**3** Aggregate payment amount
4 Aggregate account balance	**5** Currency Code

Form **8966** (2014)

Chapter 10
Foreign Persons Doing Business in the United States

¶ 1001 TAXATION OF EFFECTIVELY CONNECTED INCOME TO A U.S. TRADE OR BUSINESS

The previous Chapter described the first prong of the two-prong U.S. system for taxing foreign persons—taxation of fixed, determinable, annual, or periodic income (primarily investment and service income) via 30% withholding by the payor of the item of income. This Chapter describes the second prong for taxing foreign persons—taxation of effectively connected income to their U.S. trade or business.

A threshold issue for a foreign business entering the U.S. market is whether the foreign business' U.S. activities are subject to U.S. taxation. As discussed below, the answer to this question depends on both U.S. tax law and the provisions of any income tax treaty between the United States and the foreign business' home country.

.01 Determinants of U.S. Taxation

U.S. trade or business. The United States taxes foreign persons on the net amount of their income effectively connected with the conduct of a trade or business within the United States.[1] Therefore, under the Internal Revenue Code, the existence of a U.S. trade or business is the touchstone of U.S. taxation of a foreign person's U.S. business profits. Despite its importance, there is not any comprehensive definition of the term "trade or business" in the Code or the Regulations. The relevant case law suggests that a U.S. trade or business exists only if the activities of either the taxpayer or the taxpayer's dependent agents (e.g., an employee) within the United States are considerable, continuous, and regular,[2]

---

[1] Code Secs. 871(b) and 882(a). For this purpose, the United States includes the 50 states and the District of Columbia, but not U.S. possessions. Code Sec. 7701(a)(9).

[2] For example, *see I. Balanovski,* CA-2, 56-2 USTC ¶ 9832, 236 F2d 298 (2nd Cir., 1956); *De Amediov,* 34 TC 894, Dec. 24,315. Aff'd, CA-3, 62-1 USTC ¶ 9283, 299 F2d 623 (3rd Cir.1962). It is the author's analysis that U.S.

which is a low level of economic penetration. This determination is made based on the facts and circumstances of each case.

> *Example* **10.1** *:* FORco, a foreign corporation operates a branch office in the United States that sells its widgets to U.S. customers. Operating a branch sales office is a considerable, continuous, and regular activity in the United States. Therefore, FORco has a U.S. trade or business on which FORco will have to report and pay U.S. tax on a Form 1120-F.

[handwritten margin note: Form 1120-F]

[handwritten margin note: INDEPENDENT AGENT]

The conduct of a U.S. trade or business by an independent agent is generally not imputed to the principal.[3] An independent agent is one who is both legally and economically independent of the principal—able and willing to act on behalf of more than one principal. Likewise, the conduct of a U.S. trade or business by a U.S. corporation is not imputed to a foreign shareholder, even if the shareholder owns 100% of the stock of the U.S. corporation.

[handwritten margin note: CORPORATION IN US ↓ TAX ONLY WHEN REPATRIATE (DIVIDENDS)]

> *Example* **10.2** *:* FORco, a foreign corporation, owns all the shares of USCo, a U.S. corporation that operates a sales office. FORco sells widgets to USCo for resale to U.S. customers. The mere activity of FORco owning the shares of USCo does not create a U.S. trade or business. USCo will file its own Form 1120 that reports any income USCO earns. FORco will incur U.S. tax at a 30% rate on any amounts repatriated, typically in the form of a dividend.

(Footnote Continued)

courts often interpret the considerable, continuous, and regular standard in favor of the IRS.

[3] For example, *see British Timken, Ltd.*, 12 TC 880, Dec. 16,992, A. 1949-2 CB 1, and *E. Higgins*, 312 US 212, 1941.

¶1001.01

However, if a partnership, estate, or trust is engaged in a U.S. trade or business, then each partner or beneficiary is considered to be engaged in a U.S. trade or business.[4]

   ***Example* 10.3:** FORco, a foreign corporation, owns 99.9% of the interests of USP, a U.S. partnership. FORco sells widgets to USP for resale to U.S. customers. USP's operation of a sales office is a considerable, continuous, and regular activity in the United States that is attributed to FORco, to whom 99% of the effectively connected income will be allocated. Therefore, FORco has a U.S. trade or business on which FORco will have to report and pay U.S. tax on a Form 1120-F.

   A U.S. trade or business ordinarily includes the performance of personal services in the United States.[5] As discussed in ¶ 902.02 (Example 9.5), personal services income is also fixed, determinable, annual, or periodic income. As a result,

---

[4] Code Sec. 875. *See* ¶ 902.02 (Example 9.7) for taxation of a foreign partner's allocable share of effectively connected income.

[5] Code Sec. 864(b).

"DE MINIMIS"

30% withholding occurs before the foreign person files a return and pays tax on effectively connected income with the withholding tax treated as a pre-payment credit.[6] However, under a *de minimis* rule, the performance of dependent personal services (i.e., employment) by a nonresident alien individual does not constitute a U.S. trade or business if the following requirements are met:

CUMULATIVE REQUIREMENTS

(i) the nonresident alien is present in the United States for 90 days or less during the taxable year;

(ii) the nonresident alien receives no more than $3,000 for his or her U.S. services; and

(iii) the nonresident alien works as an employee or under contract for either a foreign person who is not engaged in a U.S. trade or business or the foreign office of a U.S. person.[7]

Example 10.4: FORacc is an accounting firm located in country F. FORacc sends a manager to the United States for a brief meeting with management of one of its client's U.S. subsidiaries. Immediately following the half-day meeting, the manager returns to the foreign country. FORacc receives $2,500 from the U.S. subsidiary for attending the meeting. Because the foreign manager was in the United States for 90 days or less, she received less than $3,000 for her U.S. services, and FORacc was not otherwise engaged in a U.S. trade or business, the manager does not have a U.S. trade or business.

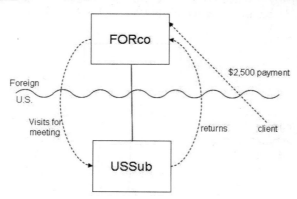

This exception allows nonresident aliens to make short business trips to the United States free of U.S. taxes. As discussed later in this chapter, income tax treaties often contain more generous exemptions that allow for longer stays and increase or eliminate the limitation on earnings for business travelers from treaty countries.

SAFE HARBOR

In addition to the *de minimis* rule for dependent personal services, the following safe harbor exceptions are provided for foreign persons engaged in the trading of stocks, securities, and certain commodities:[8]

---

[6] *See also*, Example 10.13.

[7] Code Sec. 864(b)(1) and Reg. § 1.864-2(b). The compensation of a nonresident alien who meets these requirements has foreign-source income. Code Sec. 861(a)(3).

[8] Code Sec. 864(b)(2). These exceptions apply only to commodities of the kind customarily dealt in on an organized commodity exchange (e.g., grain), and then only to transactions of the kind customarily consummated at

(i) *Broker-dealers*—Trading for the account of another through an independent agent located in the United States does not constitute a U.S. trade or business.[9] This exception does not apply, however, if, at any time during the taxable year, the taxpayer has an office or other fixed place of business in the United States through which, or by the direction of which, the trades are made.[10]

    Example **10.5:** Norman Ray Allen (NRA), a nonresident alien, trades lamb chop futures on the Chicago Mercantile Exchange through E.F. Mutton, a brokerage in the United States. Because E.F. Mutton is an independent agent, NRA does not have a U.S. trade or business. However, if NRA's trading volume becomes so large that E.F. Mutton specially designates and reserves an office for NRA, NRA would have a U.S. trade or business.

futures trading

(ii) *Trading for own account*—Trading by taxpayers for their own account does not constitute a U.S. trade or business, regardless of whether the trades are made by the taxpayer, the taxpayer's employee, or an independent agent. This exception does not apply to dealers,[11] who are defined as foreign persons that regularly buy and sell to customers for a profit.[12]

Foreign persons whose trading activities do not qualify for one of these safe harbor provisions are not automatically treated as engaged in a U.S. trade or business. Instead, that determination is made based on the facts and circumstances of each case and focuses on whether that activity is considerable, continuous, and regular.[13]

    Permanent establishments. Income tax treaties to which the United States is a party ordinarily contain a provision that exempts a foreign person's business profits from U.S. income tax, unless those profits are attributable to a permanent

---

(Footnote Continued)

such an exchange (e.g., futures). Code Sec. 864(b)(2)(B)(iii).

[9] Code Sec. 864(b)(2)(A)(i) and (b)(2)(B)(i). For purposes of this exception, the volume of stock, security, or commodity transactions effected during the taxable year is irrelevant. Reg. § 1.864-2(c)(1).

[10] Code Sec. 864(b)(2)(C).

[11] Code Sec. 864(b)(2)(A)(ii) and (b)(2)(B)(ii).

[12] Reg. § 1.864-2(c)(2)(iv).

[13] Reg. § 1.864-2(e). *See also*, footnote 2.

establishment that the foreign person maintains within the United States.[14] In contrast to the low level of economic activity for a U.S. trade or business, the permanent establishment standard requires a high level of economic activity before the foreign business is subject to U.S. tax. A permanent establishment includes a fixed place of business (e.g., a sales office), unless the fixed place of business is used solely for auxiliary functions (e.g., purchasing, storing, displaying, or delivering inventory) or activities of a preparatory nature (e.g., collecting information about potential customers).[15] A permanent establishment also exists if employees or other dependent agents (but not independent agents) habitually exercise in the United States an authority to conclude sales contracts in the foreign business' name.[16] As a consequence, a foreign business that sends executives or salespeople to the United States to enter into contracts may create a permanent establishment even if those employees do not operate out of a formal sales office.

> **Example 10.6:** FORco is a country F corporation that manufactures widgets. FORco employs a country F citizen and resident that spends three months a year traveling throughout the United States and soliciting widget purchase orders from U.S. customers. The sales employee has the customers sign purchase orders, which she forwards to FORco's home office in country F for final approval. Under the non-treaty U.S. trade or business standard, the activities of the sales employee would constitute a trade or business of FORco in the United States. However, if foreign country F had a treaty with the United States similar to the U.S. Model Treaty, FORco would not be subject to U.S. taxes as FORco would not have a permanent establishment in the United States due to the sales employee's lack of final contracting authority.

Employees who limit their U.S. activities to auxiliary or preparatory functions, with sales concluded from a foreign country, will not create a permanent establishment. Marketing products in the United States solely through independent U.S. brokers or distributors also does not create a permanent establishment.[17] The

---

[14] For example, Article 7(1) (¶ 1304.07) of the United States Model Income Tax Convention of November 15, 2006 (or U.S. Model Treaty).

[15] For example, *see* Article 5(1) and (4) (¶ 1304.05) of the U.S. Model Treaty.

[16] For example, *see* Article 5(5) (¶ 1304.05) of the U.S. Model Treaty.

[17] For example, *see* Article 5(6) (¶ 1304.05) of the U.S. Model Treaty.

standards for the existence of a permanent establishment are more thoroughly discussed in ¶ 13.02.

Comparable to the aforementioned exemption in the Code from taxation for the performance of personal services that are *de minimis*, tax treaties usually provide greater exemptions from the taxation of personal services income. These provisions allow nonresident alien individuals to perform personal services within the United States and avoid U.S. taxation as long as their U.S. activities do not exceed a specified level of intensity. A common approach is to exempt income derived by nonresident alien individuals from dependent services performed in the United States that satisfy the following requirements:

(i) the employee is present in the United States for 183 days or less,

(ii) the employee's compensation is paid by an employer that is not a U.S. resident, and

CUMULATIVE REQUIREMENTS

(iii) the compensation is not borne by a permanent establishment that the employer maintains in the United States.[18]

Example **10.7:** FORco is a company incorporated in foreign country F, which has a treaty with the United States similar to the U.S. Model Treaty. FORco is in the refrigeration business. Due to the high demand for air conditioning repair services in the United States during June, July, and August, FORco sends Norman Ray Allen (NRA), a citizen and resident of country F, to serve customers. During that week, NRA helps repair air conditioning for 15 different customers of FORco. The compensation that FORco pays NRA is $20,000.

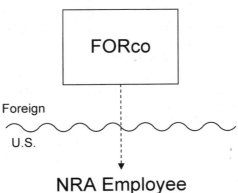

NRA is not taxed on his $20,000 of compensation for services he performs in the United States pursuant to the Treaty because (i) NRA is in the United States for only 92 days (less than 183 days), (ii) NRA's compensation is paid by FORco, which is not a resident of the United States, and (iii) NRA's compensation is not borne by a permanent establishment or a fixed base that FORco has in the United States.

---

[18] For example, *see* Article 14(2) (¶ 1304.14) of the U.S. Model Treaty.

Some older tax treaties also contain a separate independent personal services article that governs personal services income earned by self-employed professionals, such as accountants, doctors, engineers, and lawyers. Such income ordinarily is exempt from U.S. taxation unless the services are performed in the United States and the income is attributable to an office or other fixed place of business that is both located in the United States and regularly available to the taxpayer to perform the services. The current U.S. Model Treaty does not contain a separate independent personal services article. Instead, such activities are governed by the permanent establishment article.

Finally, tax treaties often contain special rules governing personal services income derived by crew members of ships and aircraft operated in international traffic,[19] entertainers and athletes,[20] government workers,[21] and students and trainees.[22] The appendix to Chapter 13 (¶ 1305) provides a listing of the treaty provisions by country that govern personal services income.

Differentiating between the U.S. trade or business and permanent establishment standards. Distinguishing between the Internal Revenue Code standard of a U.S. trade or business and the treaty standard of a permanent establishment is often a matter of degree.

> *Example* **10.8**: FORecq is a foreign corporation that breeds and races thoroughbred horses. FORecq ships a horse, K-Lair, to race in the Kentucky Derby. Immediately after winning the Kentucky Derby, FORecq ships K-Lair back to the foreign country. FORecq's entering a horse in a single race constitutes a U.S. trade or business under the non-treaty standard and FORecq's winnings would be taxable as effectively connected income.[23]. However, if FORecq is a resident in a foreign country that has a tax treaty with the United States (similar to the U.S. Model Treaty), the winnings would not incur U.S. tax because FORecq would not have a U.S. permanent establishment. Further assuming that FORecq, operating under the treaty standard, kept K-Lair in the United States to race in the Preakness Stakes and the Belmont Stakes, FORecq may then have a permanent establishment and its winnings would be subject to U.S. tax.[24]

---

[19] For example, *see* Article 15(3) (¶ 1304.15) of the U.S. Model Treaty.

[20] For example, *see* Article 16 (¶ 1304.16) of the U.S. Model Treaty.

[21] For example, *see* Article 19 (¶ 1304.19) of the U.S. Model Treaty.

[22] For example, *see* Article 20 (¶ 1304.20) of the U.S. Model Treaty.

[23] Code Sec. 882.

[24] Rev. Rul. 58-63, 1958-1 CB 624; Rev. Rul. 60-249, 1960-2 CB 264.

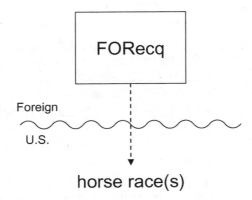

The activities of an independent salesperson typically do not result in either a U.S. trade or business or a permanent establishment for the foreign company.[25] However, the activities of dependent salespersons are treated differently, depending on the applicable standard.

> *Example* **10.9**: FORco sends its sales employee to meet with a U.S. customer at the food court at Chicago's O'Hare Airport. Between their first and second Chicago-style hot dogs, the U.S. customer signs a purchase order that will bind FORco only if approved by FORco management back in country F. If FORco is located in a treaty country, FORco does not have a permanent establishment in the United States and does not have a U.S. tax liability. However, if FORco is located in a non-treaty country, FORco has a U.S. trade or business and will have to pay U.S. tax on its effectively connected income.

.02 Effectively Connected Income

Overview. A foreign person engaged in a U.S. trade or business is subject to U.S. taxation on the income effectively connected with the conduct of its U.S. trade or business.[26] Effectively connected income (ECI) includes the following four categories of income:

---

[25] *Taisei Fire & Marine Ins. Co.*, 104 TC 535, Dec. 50,620. Acq. 1995-20 CB 1.

[26] Code Secs. 871(b) and 882(a).

    (i) most U.S.-source income,[27]

    (ii) certain types of foreign-source income attributable to a U.S. office,[28]

    (iii) certain types of deferred income that is recognized in a year that the foreign person is not engaged in a U.S. trade or business, but which would have been effectively connected income if the recognition of the income had not been postponed,[29] and

    (iv) income from an interest in U.S. real property that a passive foreign investor has elected to treat as effectively connected income.[30]

Categories (i), (ii), and (iii) are discussed in detail below and category (iv) is discussed in Chapter 9 (¶ 905).

    U.S.-source income. Effectively connected income includes all of the U.S.-source income of a foreign person engaged in a U.S. trade or business under a force of attraction principle, other than most U.S.-source fixed, determinable, annual, or periodic income, which ordinarily incurs tax at a 30% withholding tax.[31] Common examples of ECI include income derived by a U.S. branch from the sale of inventory or from providing services. Whether the U.S.-source income is actually derived from the taxpayer's U.S. trade or business is irrelevant for this purpose.[32]

    ***Example* 10.10:** FORco, a foreign corporation operates a branch office in the United States that sells its widgets to U.S. customers and, therefore, has a U.S. trade or business. Several times a year, U.S. customers will purchase gadgets directly from FORco's home office with title passing at the U.S. customer's loading lock. FORco's ECI includes both the profits from the sale of widgets and, under the force of attraction principle, the profits from the sale of gadgets.

---

[27] Code Sec. 864(c)(2) and (3).

[28] Code Sec. 864(c)(4).

[29] Code Sec. 864(c)(6) and (7).

[30] Code Secs. 871(d) and 882(d).

[31] Code Sec. 864(c)(3). Chapter 9 (¶ 902) discusses the types of U.S.-source income ordinarily subject to the 30% withholding tax on fixed, determinable, annual, or periodic income.

[32] Reg. §1.864-4(b). This is known as the force of attraction rule. However, tax treaty provisions regarding permanent establishments usually prohibit the United States from taxing all of a foreign person's U.S. business profits unless those profits are attributable to a permanent establishment. For example, *see* Article 7(1) (¶ 1304.07) of the U.S. Model Treaty.

U.S.-source dividends, interest, rents, and royalties are also included in effectively connected income if the item of income meets one of the following tests:

(i) *Assets-use test*—The income is derived from assets used in or held for use in the conduct of the U.S. trade or business.

(ii) *Business-activities test*—The activities of the U.S. trade or business were a material factor in the realization of the income.[33]

Both tests are designed to include in ECI any interest, dividends, rents, and royalties that are in substance business income. Examples include interest income derived from an account or note receivable arising from the trade or business, dividends and interest derived by a dealer in securities, and rents or royalties derived from an active leasing or licensing business.[34]

Example **10.11**: FORco is a foreign corporation that has a U.S. office for purposes of investing in U.S. stocks and bonds. On occasion, the U.S. stocks may pay dividends and the U.S. bonds may pay interest. Because the activities of the U.S. office were a material factor in the realization of the income, that income would be considered effectively connected income to a U.S. trade or business and not fixed, determinable, annual or periodic income.[35]

---

[33] Code Sec. 864(c)(2). In determining whether an item of income satisfies either the asset-use and business-activities tests, due regard is given to how the asset or income is reflected in the foreign corporation's books and records. Code Sec. 864(c)(2) and Reg. § 1.864-4(c)(4).

[34] Reg. § 1.864-4(c)(2) and (c)(3). Special rules apply to foreign persons engaged in a banking, financing, or similar business within the United States. Reg. § 1.864-4(c)(5).

[35] *See also* Example 9.3.

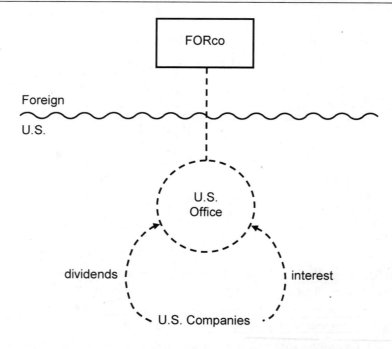

Compensation for <u>personal service performed in the United States</u> is U.S.-source income, as described more fully in ¶ 902.03. <u>This income includes fixed, determinable, annual, or periodic income withholding</u> (but not FATCA withholding) and is ECI. <u>The foreign service provider will have to file a return and pay tax on the ECI and treat the withholding as a pre-payment of tax.</u>

Example 10.12: Norman Ray Allen (NRA), a nonresident alien, is engaged by USCo, a U.S. company, to perform personal services in the United States. Because NRA is an independent contractor), USCo must withhold tax from NRA's wages at a 30% rate. NRA is in the U.S. trade or busines of providing services. Accordingly, NRA must file a <u>Form 1040-NR</u> that reports his wages as ECI and pay tax at marginal rates, for which the withholding is a pre-payment of tax.

[handwritten: FORM 1040-NR]

[handwritten: PERSONAL SERVICES IN US → FDAP + ECI → WHT (PRE PAYMENT) + TAX !]

¶1001.02

Foreign-source income attributable to a U.S. office. In addition to U.S.-source income,[36] ECI includes foreign-source income if the foreign person maintains an office or other fixed base in the United States and the U.S. office is both a material factor in producing the income and regularly carries on activities of the type that produce such income.[37] This inclusion applies to the following types of foreign-source income and their economic equivalents:

(i) rents or royalties for the use of any intangibles[38] derived from the active conduct of a U.S. trade or business and

(ii) dividend and interest income derived from the active conduct of a banking, financing, or similar business within the United States or received by a corporation whose principal business is trading in stocks and securities for its own account.[39]

Example **10.13:** EURco is a financial services company incorporated in a European country. EURco has a branch office in Chicago staffed with 10 employees. As the base for EURco's North American operations, EURco's Chicago branch accepts and confirms various letters of credit from businesses located in Canada, earning income. This income is equivalent to foreign-source interest. Consequently, the foreign-source interest income earned from accepting or confirming letters of credit is ECI to EURco's U.S. trade or business.

---

[36] Code Sec. 864(c)(4)(A).

[37] Code Sec. 864(c)(4)(B).

[38] Code Sec. 936(h)(3)(B).

[39] Code Sec. 864(c)(4)(B). However, effectively connected income does not include any Subpart F income, or any dividend, interest, or royalty income derived from a foreign corporation in which the taxpayer owns directly, indirectly, or constructively more than 50% of the combined voting power of all voting stock. Code Sec. 864(c)(4)(D).

Look-back rules for deferred income. Generally, only income recognized in the year that the foreign person is engaged in a U.S. trade or business is treated as ECI.[40] However, there are two exceptions to prevent foreign persons from avoiding the ECI taint by deferring income. Under the first exception, income that is recognized in one taxable year, but is attributable to a disposition of property or the performance of services in a prior taxable year (e.g., deferred compensation), is treated as ECI if the income would have been ECI in the prior taxable year.[41] An example of such income is a deferred gain from an installment sale of business equipment in the last taxable year in which the foreign person was engaged in a U.S. trade or business.

Example 10.14: EURco is a European media conglomerate that publishes a U.S. newspaper for European nationals living and working in the United States. To print the paper, EURco operates a printing press in the United States at its U.S. offices. EURco decides to terminate the U.S. newspaper and sells the printing press on an installment basis. In future years, even though EURco does not have a U.S. trade or business, EURco must pay U.S. tax on the portion of the installment sale proceeds representing gain as ECI because the printing press was sold while EURco had a U.S. trade or business.

---

[40] Code Sec. 864(c)(1)(B).   [41] Code Sec. 864(c)(6).

¶1001.02

Under the second exception, a gain from the sale of property that was withdrawn from a U.S. trade or business and is disposed of within 10 years after its withdrawal is treated as ECI if it would have been ECI had the sale occurred in the year of withdrawal.[42]

> **Example 10.15:** The facts are the same as in the previous Example, except that instead of terminating the U.S. newspaper, EURco decides to engage a contract printer to publish the paper and retires the printing press. Five years later, EURco sells the printing press. Even though the printing press is no longer an asset used in a U.S. trade or business, EURco must report effectively connected income from the gain on the sale of the printing press.

Gains on sale of a U.S. business. A foreign corporation does not have a U.S. trade or business due to its ownership of shares of a U.S. subsidiary. Just as the sale of shares is not FDAP income (see Example 9.1), the sale of shares is not ECI.[43] This applies to all types of gains, both capital and ordinary, but is intended to exempt from withholding any capital gains realized by foreign persons from their sale of U.S. stocks and securities. A policy for this exemption is the belief that the only way to enforce the taxation of passive foreign investors is through withholding and that withholding on capital gains is not feasible. Taxing the gross amount realized on a sale is unfair if the net gain is small and taxing the net gain may be impractical since the withholding agent may not have any way to determine the foreign person's basis in the property.

> **Example 10.16:** FORco, a foreign corporation, owns all the shares of USCo, a U.S. corporation that operates a sales office. FORco wants to exit the U.S. market and sells the shares of USCo for a gain. The gain on the sale of USCo's shares is not ECI.

---

[42] Code Sec. 864(c)(7).

[43] However, the sale of shares of a U.S. subsidiary is ECI if the U.S. subsidiary is a U.S. Real Property Holding Corporation. Code Sec. 897(c)(1)(A)(ii). *See* ¶ 905.

However, the income a foreign person earns from a U.S. parternship is ECI. Moreover, the foreign person's sale of an interest in a U.S. partnership is ECI under the rationale that the foreign person is selling its interest in the U.S. partnership's assets used in the U.S. trade or business.[44]

> **Example 10.17:** FORco, a foreign corporation, owns 99.9% of the interests of USP, a U.S. partnership. FORco wants to exit the U.S. market and sells its interest in USP for a gain. In contrast to the sale of shares in the previous Example, the gain on the sale of USP's interests is ECI.

Allowable deductions. A foreign corporation or nonresident alien individual engaged in the conduct of a U.S. trade or business can claim the following deductions against its effectively connected gross income:

> (i) expenses, losses, and other deductions that are directly related to effectively connected gross income (e.g., cost of goods sold), as well as a ratable portion of any deductions that are not definitely related to any specific item of gross income (e.g., interest expense);[45]

---

[44] Rev. Rul. 91-32, 199-1 CB 107; Code Sec. 875.

[45] Reg. §§ 1.873-1(a)(1), 1.882-4(b)(1), and 1.861-8.

¶1001.02

(ii) foreign income taxes imposed on either foreign-source ECI or U.S.-source ECI that incurs foreign taxation by reason of the income's source rather than the taxpayer's citizenship, residence, or domicile;[46]

(iii) charitable contributions made to U.S. charitable organizations;[47] and

(iv) in the case of a nonresident alien individual, casualty and theft losses with respect to personal property located within the United States, and a personal exemption deduction.[48]

Example 10.18: FORco, a foreign corporation, operates a branch sales office that constitutes a U.S. trade or business. FORco has $20 million of gross profit worldwide, $5 million of which is effectively connected to the U.S. trade or business. If FORco has $2 million of general and administrative expenses, FORco can aportion those expenses based on gross profit or another reasonable method. An allocation of 25% would result in a $500,000 deduction against the gross profit effectively connected to a U.S. trade or business. As a result, FORco's effectively connected income to a U.S. trade or business would be $4.5 million.

Foreign corporations have an incentive to apportion interest expense deductions, as with other expense deductions, to their U.S. trade or business to reduce ECI. However, special rules under Reg. § 1.882-5 govern the allocation of a foreign corporation's interest expense to determine ECI. Under these rules, the interest expense deduction is generally computed using a three-step process based on the value of the corporation's U.S. assets, its worldwide debt-to-assets ratio, and the liabilities recorded on the books of the U.S. business. These regulations are based on the principle that money is fungible and, as a result, a corporation that operates in two or more countries can artificially book debt and the related interest expense in the country with the higher tax rate. Consequently, Reg. § 1.882-5 adopts an

---

[46] Code Secs. 873(a) and 882(c)(1)(A), as modified by Code Sec. 906(b)(1).

[47] Code Secs. 873(b)(2) and 882(c)(1)(B).

[48] Reg. § 1.873-1(b)(2)(ii) and (b)(3). Residents of Mexico or Canada may qualify for an additional exemption deduction.

objective, formulary approach for computing interest expense deductions, as follows:

   (i) Step one: compute the value of the foreign corporation's U.S. assets.

   (ii) Step two: compute the total amount of the foreign corporation's U.S. connected liabilities. This is accomplished by multiplying the value of the foreign corporation's U.S. assets (determined in step one) by its world-wide debt-to-asset ratio for the year. The corporation's debt-to-asset ratio equals the total amount of the foreign corporation's worldwide liabilities divided by the total value of its worldwide assets. In lieu of determining its actual ratio, a foreign corporation may elect to use a fixed ratio of 50%, which is increased to 95% in the case of a foreign corporation that is a bank.

   (iii) Step three: compare the amount of the foreign corporation's U.S. connected liabilities (determined in step two) to its U.S. booked liabilities (those liabilities that are booked on the records of the foreign corporation's U.S. trade or business). If the foreign corporation's U.S. booked liabilities exceed its U.S. connected liabilities, the foreign corporation's U.S. interest expense equals the interest on its U.S. books reduced by the ratio of U.S. connected liabilities to U.S. booked liabilities. However, if the foreign corporation's U.S. booked liabilities are less than its U.S. connected liabilities, then the foreign corporation can increase its interest expense deduction for interest on the excess amount of connected liabilities.[49]

Example 10.19: FORco is a foreign corporation that actively conducts a real estate business in the United States through a U.S. branch. FORco's books indicate the following:

	Asset Value	
Foreign parcel	$100,000	
U.S. parcel	$100,000	
	Booked Liabilities	Booked Interest
Liability 1 (Foreign)	$20,000	$1,000
Liability 2 (U.S.)	$40,000	$4,000

Liability 1 is a booked liability in FORco's home country F and Liability 2 is a booked liability of the U.S. branch.

---

[49] Reg. § 1.882-5. In *National Westminster Bank, PLC v. U.S.*, CA-FC, 2008-1 USTC ¶ 50,140 512 F3d 1347, the court ruled that Article 7 of the U.S.-U.K. treaty overrides the formulary approach of Reg. § 1.882-5 insofar as the U.S. branch of a banking corporation is concerned.

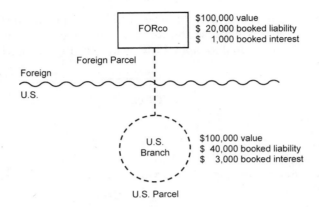

(i) Step One. The total value of U.S. assets is $100,000, the value of the U.S. parcel.

(ii) Step Two. The amount of FORco's U.S. connected liabilities is determined by multiplying $100,000 (the value of U.S. assets determined under Step One) by its worldwide debt-to-asset ratio. The worldwide debt-to-asset ratio is the amount of FORco's worldwide liabilities divided by the value of FORco's worldwide assets. Adding the two liabilities, the numerator is $60,000 (U.S. liability of $40,000 plus foreign liability of $20,000). The denominator comprises worldwide assets of $200,000 (U.S. parcel of $100,000 plus Foreign parcel of $100,000). Therefore, the worldwide debt-to-asset ratio is 30% ($60,000 over $200,000) and the amount of U.S. connected liabilities is $30,000 ($100,000 of U.S. assets times 30%).

(iii) Step Three. Because FORco's U.S. booked liabilities ($40,000) exceed the U.S. connected liabilities ($30,000) determined in Step Two, FORco determines its branch's interest deduction by multiplying the interest expense on U.S. booked liabilities ($3,000) times the ratio of U.S. connected liabilities ($30,000) to U.S. booked liabilities ($40,000). As a result, FORco reduces the U.S. branch's interest deduction to $2,250 [$3,000 × ($30,000 ÷ $40,000)].

Profits attributable to a permanent establishment. In lieu of paying U.S. tax on effectively connected income, a foreign corporation in a treaty country pays U.S. tax only on profits attributable to a permanent establishment. The profits attributable standard is vague and little guidance exists. Some foreign corporations will follow the effectively connected income rules (less the income not directly related to the activity causing the permanent establishment because the force of attraction principle does not apply).

Example 10.20: FORco, a foreign corporation operates a branch office in the United States that sells widgets to U.S. customers and, therefore, has a U.S. trade or business. Several times a year, U.S. customers will purchase gadgets directly from FORco's home office with title passing at the U.S. customer's loading lock. FORco's profits attributable to a permanent establish-

¶1001.02

ment include the profits from the sale of widgets, but excludes the profits from the sale of gadgets because the force of attraction principle does not apply. This is in contrast to Example 10.10, whereby the profits from the sale of gadgets would constitute ECI.

Other foreign corporations will apply transfer pricing rules (see Chapter 12) with the U.S. permanent establishment treated as an independent entity that earns income pursuant to its functions performed, risks assumed, and resources employed (e.g., assets used).[50]

.03 Applicable Tax Rates

The progressive rate schedules applicable to U.S. persons also apply to the ECI of foreign persons.[51] Therefore, the applicable rates range from 15% to 35% for foreign corporations[52] and 10% to 39.6% for nonresident aliens.[53] For nonresident aliens, the applicable schedules include those for single taxpayers, married individuals filing separately, and surviving spouses.[54] Nonresident aliens generally cannot use the head of household or married filing jointly rate schedules.[55]

.04 Foreign Tax Credit

A foreign corporation or nonresident alien individual engaged in a U.S. trade or business can, in lieu of a deduction, claim a credit for any foreign income taxes imposed on the following two types of income:

(i) foreign-source ECI and

(ii) U.S.-source ECI that is subject to foreign taxation by reason of the income's source rather than the taxpayer's citizenship, residence, or place of incorporation.[56]

---

[50] Footnote to Article 7, paragraph 3 (¶ 1304.07) of the U.S. Model Treaty.

[51] Code Secs. 871(b)(1) and 882(a)(1).

[52] Code Sec. 11.

[53] 39.6%. Code Sec. 1.

[54] Reg. § 1.1-1(a)(1).

[55] Code Secs. 2(b)(3)(A) and 6013(a)(1).

[56] Code Sec. 906(a) and (b)(1). A foreign corporation which receives a dividend from a 10%-or-more-owned foreign corporation also may qualify for a deemed paid

Foreign persons can take the foreign tax credit only against U.S. taxes on ECI and cannot offset U.S. withholding taxes or the branch profits tax.[57] In addition, a foreign person should only consider its ECI when computing the foreign tax credit limitation.[58]

.05 Alternative Minimum Tax

The ECI of a foreign person is subject to the alternative minimum tax if the foreign person's tentative minimum tax exceeds the regular tax for the year.[59] A corporate taxpayer's tentative minimum tax equals 20% (for individual taxpayers, a two-tiered rate schedule of 26% and 28% applies) of the taxpayer's alternative minimum taxable income less an exemption amount and is reduced by the alternative minimum foreign tax credit, if applicable.[60] Alternative minimum taxable income equals a taxpayer's regular taxable income, determined with certain adjustments, and increased by the amount of the taxpayer's tax preferences.[61]

¶ 1002 THE BRANCH TAXES

There are three branch taxes - the branch profits tax and two potentially applicable branch taxes on interest.

.01 The Branch Profits Tax

Overview. Prior to the enactment of the branch profits tax, there was a substantial disparity between the tax treatment of earnings repatriations from U.S. branches and U.S. subsidiaries. Foreign corporations incurred U.S. withholding taxes on dividend distributions from a U.S. subsidiary, but did not incur a secondary-level U.S. tax on earnings repatriated from a U.S. branch to the home office of the foreign corporation. Therefore, foreign corporations often avoided the secondary-level U.S. tax on their U.S.-source business profits merely by operating in the United States through a branch rather than a subsidiary.

> **Example 10.21:** FORco, a foreign corporation, owns 100% of the shares of USAco, a U.S. corporation that derives all of its income from U.S. business operations. During its first year of operations, USAco has taxable income of $10 million and distributes all of its after-tax earnings to FORco as a dividend. Assume the U.S. corporate tax rate is 35% and that the applicable treaty withholding rate for U.S.-source dividends is 5%.

USAco pays $3.5 million of U.S. income tax on its $10 million of taxable income and then distributes a dividend to FORco of $6.5 million [$10 million of taxable income – $3.5 million of U.S. income tax]. The dividend incurs $325,000 of U.S. withholding tax [$6.5 million dividend × 5% withholding tax rate], which makes the total U.S. tax burden on USAco's repatriated earnings equal to $3,825,000 [$3.5 million of U.S. income tax + $325,000 of U.S. withholding tax].

(Footnote Continued)

foreign tax credit if the dividend is ECI with the recipient's U.S. trade or business.

[57] Code Sec. 906(b)(3) and (7).

[58] Code Sec. 906(b)(2).

[59] Code Secs. 871(b)(1), 882(a)(1), and 55.

[60] Code Sec. 55(b)(1).

[61] Code Sec. 55(b)(2).

If FORco had structured its U.S. operation as a branch rather than as a subsidiary, FORco would still pay $3.5 million of U.S. income tax on its $10 million of income effectively connected with the U.S. branch operation. However, ignoring the branch profits tax, the repatriation of branch profits would be an internal fund transfer not subject to U.S. withholding tax. Therefore, without a branch profits tax, FORco would avoid $325,000 of U.S. withholding taxes merely by operating in the United States through a branch rather than through a subsidiary.

The branch profits tax better equates the tax treatment of the U.S. branch and U.S. subsidiary operations by imposing a tax equal to 30% of a foreign corporation's dividend equivalent amount for the taxable year, subject to treaty reductions.[62] The dividend equivalent amount approximates the amount of U.S. earnings and profits that a U.S. branch remits to its foreign home office during the year. Therefore, similar to the withholding tax imposed on a U.S. subsidiary's dividend distributions, the branch profits tax represents a second layer of U.S. taxes imposed on a foreign corporation's U.S.-source business profits (see Figure 10.1).

---

[62] Code Sec. 884(a).

Figure 10.1 Policy of the branch profits tax

U.S. subsidiary operations

U.S. branch operations

***Example* 10.22:** The facts are the same as in the previous Example, except now FORco must account for the effects of the branch profits tax. If FORco had structured its U.S. operation as a branch rather than as a subsidiary, it would pay $3.5 million of U.S. income tax on its $10 million of ECI [$10 million × 35% U.S. tax rate]. In addition, assuming the U.S. branch's dividend equivalent amount equals the branch's after-tax earnings of $6.5 million [$10 million of taxable income – $3.5 million of U.S. income taxes], FORco also would be subject to a branch profits tax of $325,000 [$6.5 million dividend equivalent amount × 5% tax rate]. Therefore, the branch profits tax creates a shareholder-level U.S. tax that is equivalent to the U.S. withholding tax imposed on dividends.

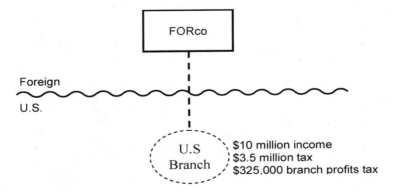

The foreign corporation pays the branch profits tax in the same manner as its corporate income tax (see ¶ 1004), except that the branch profits tax does not require estimated tax payments.[63]

Dividend equivalent amount. The tax base for the branch profits tax is the dividend equivalent amount, which estimates the amount of U.S. earnings and profits that a branch remits to its foreign home office during the year. Such an estimate accounts for the earnings and profits generated by the U.S. branch during the year. Consistent with this reasoning, a foreign corporation's dividend equivalent amount for a taxable year is computed using the following two-step procedure:[64]

Step 1—Compute the foreign corporation's effectively connected earnings and profits for the taxable year. Effectively connected earnings and profits equals the earnings and profits attributable to ECI with the foreign corporation's U.S. trade or business, before any reductions for dividend distributions, the branch profits tax, or the tax on excess interest.[65]

Step 2—Adjust the effectively connected earnings and profits amount for any changes in the foreign corporation's U.S. net equity during the year. Reduce the effectively connected earnings and profits amount from Step 1 by the amount of any increase in U.S. net equity for the year (but not below zero) under the theory that an increase in U.S. net equity is a reinvestment of earnings and profits in the U.S. branch operation. On the other hand, increase the effectively connected earnings and profits by the amount of any reduction in U.S. net equity for the year under the theory that a reduction is US. net equity is a repatriation of earnings and profits, which is similar to a dividend.[66]

Example **10.23:** FORco, a foreign corporation, operates a branch sales office in the United States. During its first year of operations, FORco earns effectively connected earnings and profits of $250,000 and its U.S. net equity is $500,000 at the beginning of the year and $750,000 at the end of the year. Therefore, FORco's dividend equivalent amount for year 1 is $0 and the branch profits tax is $0. In theory, the U.S. branch has reinvested its profits in the United States instead of repatriating the profits to FORco's home office:

(A) *Effectively connected earnings and profits* $250,000

(B) *Increase in U.S. net equity:*

End of the year U.S. net equity	$750,000	
Beginning of the year U.S. net equity	$500,000	
Increase in U.S. net equity		$250,000

Dividend equivalent amount [A – B] . . . .   None

---

[63] Reg. § 1.884-1(a).

[64] Code Sec. 884(b).

[65] Code Sec. 884(d)(1) and Reg. § 1.884-1(f)(1). A corporation's earnings and profits equal its taxable income, plus or minus various adjustments designed to make earnings and profits a better measure of the corporation's economic income. Examples of common adjustments include federal income taxes, ADS depreciation (Code Sec. 312(k)), and the LIFO recapture amount (Code Sec. 312(n)(4)). Certain types of earnings and profits are excluded from effectively connected earnings and profits (*see* Code Sec. 884(d)(2)).

[66] Code Sec. 884(b). An adjustment for a reduction in U.S. net equity for the year cannot exceed an amount equal to the excess of the aggregate amount of effectively connected earnings and profits accumulated over the aggregate amount of dividend equivalent amounts from prior taxable years. Code Sec. 884(b)(2)(B). This limitation prevents the taxation of returns of capital.

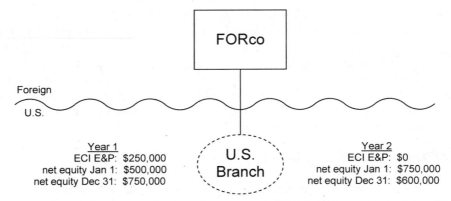

During year 2, FORco has no effectively connected earnings and profits and its U.S. net equity is $750,000 at the beginning of the year and $600,000 at the end of the year. Therefore, FORco's dividend equivalent amount for year 2 is $150,000, which results in a branch profits tax of $45,000 (30% of $150,000). Theoretically, the U.S. branch has repatriated the profits to FORco's home office.

(A) *Effectively connected earnings and profits* . . . . $ 0

(B) *Decrease in U.S. net equity:*

Beginning of the year U.S. net equity	$750,000	
End of the year U.S. net equity	$600,000	
Decrease in U.S. net equity		$150,000
Dividend equivalent amount [A + B]		$150,000

A foreign corporation determines its U.S. net equity as of the last day of the taxable year.[67] U.S. net equity equals the aggregate amount of money and the adjusted basis of the property of the foreign corporation connected with the U.S. trade or business reduced (including below zero) by the amount of U.S. connected liabilities.[68] The amount of U.S.-connected liabilities is determined the same way the foreign corporation determines its interest expense deduction discussed earlier in this chapter, except that the asset value and liability amounts are based on year end totals rather than annual averages.[69] In general, an asset is considered "connected" with a U.S. trade or business to the extent the income produced by the asset or a gain from the disposition of the asset is ECI. Regulations provide for applying this principle to specific types of assets, such as depreciable property, inventory, installment obligations, accounts receivable, bank deposits, and debt instruments.[70]

---

[67] Reg. § 1.884-1(c)(3).

[68] Code Sec. 884(c).

[69] Reg. §§ 1.884-1(e)(1) and 1.882-5. An election is available whereby the foreign corporation can reduce its

U.S.-connected liabilities by the excess of the formulary amount over a books and records amount. Reg. § 1.884-1(e)(3).

[70] Reg. § 1.884-1(c)(2) and (d).

Special rules apply to computing the branch profits tax for a taxable year in which a termination occurs. A termination includes the incorporation of a branch, the repatriation of all branch assets, a sale of all branch assets, or the liquidation or reorganization of the foreign corporation. The policy behind these provisions is to mimic the tax consequences that the foreign corporation would experience if it had structured its U.S. operations as a subsidiary rather than as a branch.[71] For example, a foreign corporation does not incur the branch profits tax in the year that the foreign corporation terminates its U.S. branch.[72]

.02 Treaty Reductions and Exemptions

Some tax treaties provide a specific exemption or rate reduction for the branch profits tax.[73] If the applicable treaty does not provide a specific exemption or rate reduction, the treaty rate for the branch profits tax is the rate that applies to dividends paid to the foreign corporation by a wholly-owned U.S. subsidiary.[74]

.03 Taxes on Branch Interest

Branch interest withholding tax. As with the branch profits tax, the policy supporting the branch interest withholding tax is to place U.S. branch and subsidiary operations on a tax parity. Under the branch interest withholding tax, any interest paid by a foreign corporation's U.S. branch is treated as if it were paid by a U.S. corporation.[75] The effect of this rule is to recharacterize the foreign-source interest paid as U.S.-source income and, thereby, subject the interest received by a foreign person to the 30% withholding tax that ordinarily applies to U.S.-source interest income.[76] Generally speaking, interest is considered to be "paid by" a U.S. branch if the foreign corporation books the underlying liability as a branch liability. Examples include a liability that is reflected in the books and records of the U.S. trade or business, a liability secured predominantly by a U.S. asset, or a liability specifically identified by the taxpayer as a liability of the U.S. trade or business.[77]

> **Example 10.24:** FORco is a foreign corporation that actively conducts a real estate business through a U.S. branch, as in Example 10.19. The amount of interest expense booked by the U.S. branch and paid to a foreign person is $3,000. Even though the U.S. branch determines that it must reduce the amount of the interest deduction, pursuant to Reg. § 1.882-5, to $2,250, the entire amount of interest paid of $3,000 is subject to the branch interest withholding tax.

---

[71] Reg. § 1.884-2 and Temp Reg. § 1.884-2T.

[72] Reg. § 1.884-2T(a)(1).

[73] Code Sec. 884(e)(2) and Reg. § 1.884-1(g)(1) and (g)(2). Typically, the reduction is found in the dividend article of a treaty. *See,* for example, Article 10(8) (¶ 1304.10) of the U.S. Model Treaty.

[74] Code Sec. 884(e)(2)(A)(ii) and Reg. § 1.884-1(g)(4)(i)(A).

[75] Code Sec. 884(f)(1)(A).

[76] Reg. § 1.884-4(a)(1). Unlike the branch profits tax, the branch interest withholding tax is borne by the foreign person receiving the interest income, not the foreign corporation making the interest payment.

[77] Reg. § 1.884-4(b). Interest is also considered to be "paid by" a U.S. branch if the liability has a particular connection with the branch operation.

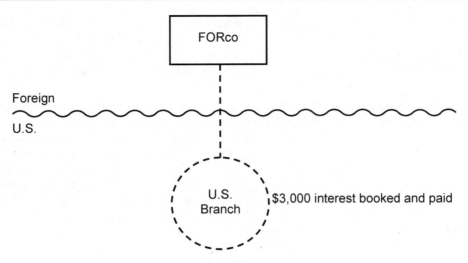

The branch interest withholding tax <u>is not imposed</u> on interest that qualifies for one of the following withholding tax exemptions from <u>investment-type income</u> (each of which is discussed in Chapter 9 (¶ 902)):[78]

(i) the <u>portfolio interest exemption</u>,[79]

(ii) the <u>exemption for interest paid on a U.S. bank deposit</u>,[80]

(iii) the <u>exemption for interest income that is ECI with the conduct of a U.S. trade or business</u>, or[81]

(iv) the <u>reduced withholding (or exemption) offered by an applicable treaty</u>.[82]

Tax on excess interest. In addition to the branch interest withholding tax, the branch tax regime also imposes a <u>tax on excess interest</u>. The rationale behind the excess interest tax is that <u>any interest expense that is deductible against the branch's U.S. taxable income also should give rise to an income inclusion, which is analogous to what happens when a U.S. subsidiary corporation makes an interest payment that incurs withholding tax</u>. A foreign corporation's excess interest equals the excess of:

(i) <u>the amount of the interest expense that is deducted against the U.S. branch's ECI</u> (e.g., interest expense on U.S.-connected liabilities) over

(ii) <u>the amount of the interest expense booked on the U.S. books and records for the branch interest withholding tax</u> (e.g., interest expense on U.S.-booked liabilities).

Under this provision, on the last day of its taxable year, the foreign corporation is deemed to have received a payment of interest from a wholly-owned U.S. corporation equal to the foreign corporation's excess interest.[83] The effect of this provision is to subject the foreign corporation's excess interest to the 30% withholding tax

---

[78] Reg. § 1.884-4(a)(1).

[79] Code Secs. 871(h) and 881(c).

[80] Code Secs. 871(i)(2)(A) and 881(d).

[81] Code Sec. 1441(c)(1).

[82] Code Sec. 884(f)(3) and Reg. § 1.884-4(b)(8).

[83] Code Sec. 884(f)(1)(B) and Reg. § 1.884-4(a)(2). A special exemption applies to interest on deposits with U.S. branches of foreign banks.

¶1002.03

that ordinarily applies to U.S.-source interest income.[84] However, if a U.S. tax treaty with the foreign corporation's country exempts or reduces the withholding rate for interest income, that treaty applies.[85] In all cases, the foreign corporation must report the tax due on excess interest on its income tax return and estimated tax payments are required.[86]

> **Example 10.25:** [87] FORco, a foreign manufacturer of industrial equipment, has a branch sales office in the United States. During the current year, FORco apportions $120,000 of interest expense under Reg. § 1.882-5 against its U.S. branch's ECI. However, only $100,000 of this amount is booked as paid by FORco's U.S. branch as a U.S. debt on its books and records for purposes of the branch interest withholding tax. Therefore, FORco has excess interest of $20,000 [$120,000 – $100,000]. FORco's tax on this excess interest is $6,000 [$20,000 of excess interest × 30% statutory withholding rate], assuming a tax treaty does not reduce the withholding rate for interest.

¶ 1003 ANTI-EARNINGS STRIPPING PROVISIONS

.01 What Is Earnings Stripping?

Determining the most tax-efficient way for a foreign parent corporation to repatriate profits from its U.S. subsidiary requires an analysis of U.S. taxes at both the subsidiary-level and the parent-level. At the subsidiary level, the U.S. subsidiary's total taxable income incurs U.S. taxation at the regular marginal rates. At the foreign parent level, any earnings that are repatriated through a dividend incur U.S. withholding taxes at either the 30% statutory rate or a reduced treaty rate. Therefore, the total U.S. tax burden on the earnings of a U.S. subsidiary that are repatriated through a dividend distribution equals the sum of the subsidiary-level corporate income tax and the parent-level withholding tax. In contrast to a dividend distribution, repatriating a U.S. subsidiary's earnings through interest payments raises the possibility of both a deduction at the subsidiary level and a lower treaty

---

[84] Unlike the branch interest withholding tax, the tax on excess interest is borne by the foreign corporation operating the U.S. branch.

[85] Reg. § 1.884-4(c)(3)(i).

[86] Reg. § 1.884-4(a)(2)(iv).

[87] Compare Reg. § 1.884-4(a)(4), Example 1.

withholding tax rate at the shareholder level. Therefore, by "stripping" the earnings of a U.S. subsidiary through intercompany interest payments, a foreign parent may be able to reduce or eliminate both levels of U.S. taxation.

Example **10.26:** FORco, a foreign corporation, owns 100% of USAco, a U.S. corporation that derives all of its income from U.S. business operations. During its first year of operations, USAco has taxable income of $10 million. Assume the U.S. corporate tax rate is 35% and that the applicable treaty withholding rate is 5% for dividends and 0% for interest.

Case 1—Repatriate earnings through dividend distribution: Given the 35% U.S. tax rate, USAco pays $3.5 million of U.S. tax on its $10 million of taxable income, leaving $6.5 million of earnings and profits ($10 million of pre-tax earnings - $3.5 million of corporate income tax). As a consequence, if FORco repatriates all of USAco's after-tax earnings through a dividend, FORco would receive a $6.5 million dividend and would incur $325,000 of U.S. withholding tax ($6.5 million dividend × 5% treaty withholding rate). Therefore, the total effective U.S. tax on USAco's repatriated profits is 38.25% [($3.5 million of corporate income tax + $325,000 of withholding tax) ÷ $10 million of taxable income].

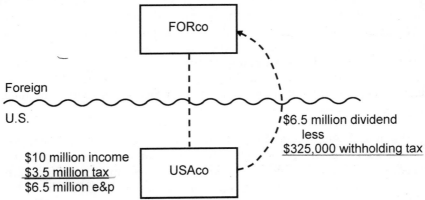

Case 2—Repatriate earnings through interest payments: Now assume that FORco has a bona-fide creditor interest in USAco such that USAco makes annual interest payments of $10 million to FORco. Ignoring the anti-earnings stripping provisions, the $10 million of interest expense would reduce USAco's net taxable income and U.S. tax liability to $0. In addition, FORco does not incur U.S. withholding taxes on the interest payments because of the treaty exemption. As a result, by repatriating USAco's earnings through interest payments rather than a dividend distribution, FORco is able to reduce the total effective U.S. tax rate on USAco's repatriated earning from 38.25% to 0%.

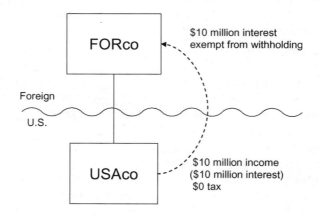

Foreign parent corporations engaging in earnings stripping must ensure that any intercompany payments meant to be interest qualify as such under U.S. tax laws. Historically, the IRS's only alternatives for attacking earnings stripping schemes were to attempt to recharacterize a portion of the U.S. subsidiary's intercompany debt as disguised equity[88] or to argue that the rate of interest paid on the intercompany debt did not represent an arm's-length rate.[89] Congress became concerned that foreign corporations financed their U.S. subsidiaries with excessive debt so that interest would erode income taxable in the United States. As a result, Congress enacted the anti-earnings stripping provision to reduce the deductibility of interest.

When analyzing the tax implications of planning for foreign businesses in the United States, the foreign business must consider both the U.S. and foreign tax consequences. More specifically, the foreign business must consider the efficiency of methods for a foreign parent to repatriate profits from a U.S. subsidiary. Interest payments received by a foreign parent from a U.S. subsidiary generally incur tax in a foreign parent's home country, while dividends are often exempt from tax in the foreign parent's country. Therefore, although interest payments may be the optimal approach to minimize U.S. taxes, a foreign parent must determine whether higher foreign taxes offset these U.S. tax savings. The prudent U.S. tax planner must consult with the foreign parent's tax advisor.

.02 Calculating the Non-Deductible Interest

The purpose of the Section 163(j) anti-earnings stripping provision is to limit a U.S. corporation's deductions for interest payments to related foreign lenders whose interest income is exempt from U.S. withholding tax. The calculation of the non-deductible interest requires the following multi-step analysis:

---

[88] Code Sec. 385.   [89] Code Sec. 482; Reg. § 1.482-2(a).

¶1003.02

(i) The debt-to-equity ratio of the U.S. corporation must exceed 1.5 to 1.[90] The U.S. corporation computes this ratio by comparing the cost basis of the total liabilities to the total assets, less the total liabilities.[91]

(ii) The U.S. corporation must have a net interest expense, which is the amount by which its interest expense exceeds its interest income.[92]

(iii) The U.S. corporation must have an excess interest expense, which equals the excess of the U.S. corporation's net interest expense (step (ii)) over 50% of the U.S. corporation's adjusted taxable income.[93] Adjusted taxable income is the U.S. corporation's taxable income with numerous adjustments designed to produce a better measure of the U.S. corporation's net cash flow from operations before interest income or interest expense. Examples of the required adjustments to taxable income include adding back any net interest expense, net operating losses, depreciation, amortization, and depletion.[94]

(iv) The U.S. corporation must pay or accrue interest to a related person who does not incur U.S. withholding tax on the interest income.[95] More specifically, these payments include the following two types of interest:

- *Related-person debt*—Interest paid or accrued by a U.S. corporation (directly or indirectly) to a related person (usually foreign) that does not incur U.S. withholding tax.

- *Guaranteed debt*—Interest paid or accrued by the U.S. corporation to an unrelated person that does not incur U.S. withholding tax if a related foreign person guarantees the debt.[96]

For purposes of both related person debt and guaranteed debt, interest whose withholding rate is reduced by a treaty is not subject to U.S. tax in proportion to the treaty's reduction. For example, if the statutory withholding rate is 30% and the treaty withholding rate is 10%, then two-thirds of the interest is interest not subject to U.S. tax.[97]

(v) The provision disallows interest expense to the extent of the lower of either excess interest expense (iii) or payments of interest to related parties that do not incur U.S. withholding tax on the interest (iv).

The U.S. corporation may indefinitely carry forward any disallowed interest deduction and deduct it in a year that the U.S. subsidiary has an excess limitation.[98]

---

[90] Code Sec. 163(j)(2)(A)(ii). Members of an affiliated group are generally treated as a single corporation. Prop. Reg. §1.163(j)-5.

[91] Code Sec. 163(j)(2)(C).

[92] Code Sec. 163(j)(6)(B).

[93] Code Sec. 163(j)(2)(B)(i) and (j)(6)(B).

[94] Code Sec. 163(j)(6)(A). Prop. Reg. §1.163(j)-2(f) lists 21 adjustments.

[95] Code Sec. 163(j)(3)(A). A related person includes any lender that owns more than 50% of the corporate debtor. Code Secs. 163(j)(4) and 267(b). The term of art for the amount in this step is "disqualified interest." However, the authors have chosen not to use this term of art as the term suggests that the step (iv) amount is not deductible when the non-deductible amount is determined in step (v).

[96] Guaranteed debt also arises from a guarantee by a related tax-exempt entity. Code Secs. 163(j)(3)(B) and (j)(6)(D)(i). Exceptions apply (i) if the corporation paying the interest owns a controlling interest in the guarantor or (ii) in any circumstances identified by regulations, where the interest would incur net-basis U.S. taxation if the interest had been paid to the guarantor. Code Sec. 163(j)(6)(D)(ii).

[97] Code Sec. 163(j)(5)(B) and Prop. Reg. §1.163(j)-4(b).

[98] Code Sec. 163(j)(1)(B).

¶1003.02

A U.S. corporation has an excess limitation in any year that its net interest expense is less than 50% of its adjusted taxable income.[99] In addition, a U.S. corporation can carry forward an excess limitation for three years to reduce excess interest expense in a carryforward year.[100]

Example **10.27:** FORco, a foreign corporation, owns 100% of USAco, a domestic corporation that derives all of its income from U.S. business operations. FORco also has a creditor interest in USAco, such that USAco's debt-to-equity ratio is 2 to 1 and USAco makes annual interest payments of $20 million to FORco. The results from USAco's operations are as follows:

Gross profit	$60 million
Interest income	$ 2 million
Interest expense (all paid to FORco)	($20 million)
Depreciation expense	($10 million)
Other operating expenses	($27 million)
Pre-tax income	$ 5 million

Assume the U.S. corporate tax rate is 35% and that the applicable treaty exempts interest income from withholding tax.

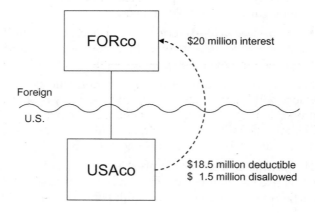

An analysis of the deductibility of interest is as follows:

   (i) USAco's debt to equity ratio is 2 to 1, which exceeds 1.5 to 1.

  (ii) USAco has a net interest expense of $18 million ($2 million of interest income less $20 million of interest expense).

 (iii) USAco's excess interest expense equals its net interest expense of $18 million less 50% of its adjusted taxable income of $33 million ($5 million of pre-tax income + $18 million of net interest expense + $10 million of depreciation). Therefore, the excess interest expense is $1.5 million [$18 million – (50% × $33 million)].

---

[99] Code Sec. 163 (j) (2) (B) (iii).   [100] Code Sec. 163 (j) (2) (B) (i) and (ii).

¶1003.02

    (iv) USAco pays the entire amount of interest expense of $20 million to a related party (FORco) that does not incur U.S. withholding tax on the interest income due to the treaty exemption.

    (v) The disallowed interest deduction is $1.5 million, which is the lesser of excess interest expense of $1.5 million (from iii) or the $20 million of interest paid to parties that do not incur U.S. withholding on the interest (from iv). Therefore, USAco can deduct only $18.5 million of the interest. USAco can carry forward the $1.5 million of disallowed interest and deduct it in a year that an excess limitation exists.

.03 Timing Restriction on Deductions of U.S. Subsidiaries

    Previously, an accrual-basis U.S. subsidiary could deduct an accrued expense for an amount owed to its cash-basis foreign parent, but the foreign parent did not include the amount in income until the U.S. subsidiary actually made the payment. As a result, the group received a timing benefit. However, section 267(a)(3) and its regulations postpone the deduction until the U.S. subsidiary actually pays the amount due to a related foreign person.[101]

    Example **10.28:** USAco is a U.S. subsidiary of FORco, a country F corporation. USAco is an accrual-basis taxpayer while FORco is a cash-basis taxpayer. In 20Y1, FORco makes a loan to USAco. On December 31, 20Y1, USAco accrues $1 million of interest expense, but USAco does not make the $1 million payment to FORco until 20Y2. Despite being an accrual-basis taxpayer, USAco may not deduct the $1 million of interest expense until January 1, 20Y2, which is the year in which FORco recognizes the $1 million of interest income for country F purposes.[102]

---

[101] Reg. § 1.267(a)-3.

[102] Reg. § 1.267(a)-3; *Tate & Lyle, Inc.,* 96-2 USTC ¶ 50,340, 87 F3d 99 (3rd Cir. 1996); *Square D,* 2006-1 USTC ¶ 50,162, 438 F.3d 739 (7th Cir. 2006).

¶ 1004 RETURNS AND PAYMENT OF TAX

A foreign corporation that is engaged in a U.S. trade or business at any time during a taxable year must file Form 1120-F, U.S. Income Tax Return of a Foreign Corporation. This requirement applies even if the foreign corporation does not have any ECI or U.S.-source income or is exempt from U.S. tax by reason of a treaty provision.[103] A foreign corporation that is not engaged in a U.S. trade or business, but that has income subject to U.S. withholding taxes, must also file Form 1120-F, unless its liability for the year is fully satisfied by the withholding tax.[104] (A sample of a completed Form 1120-F is included in the Appendix to this chapter.[105]) A foreign corporation engaged in a U.S. trade or business must make quarterly estimated tax payments of its income tax liability,[106] but not for a branch profits tax liability.[107]

A nonresident alien individual who is engaged in a U.S. trade or business must file Form 1040NR, U.S. Nonresident Alien Income Tax Return. This requirement applies even if the nonresident alien does not have any ECI or U.S.-source income or is exempt from U.S. tax by reason of a treaty provision.[108] A nonresident alien who is not engaged in a U.S. trade or business, but who has income that is subject to U.S. withholding taxes, must also file Form 1040NR, unless the withholding tax fully satisfied his or her liability for the year.[109] (A sample of a completed Form 1040NR is included in the Appendix to this chapter.[110]) A nonresident alien whose tax exceeds the amount of any withholding must make estimated tax payments.[111]

Any partnership engaged in a U.S. trade or business, or that has income from U.S. sources, is required to file Form 1065, U.S. Partnership Return of Income, which is an informational return.[112] As discussed in Chapter 9 (¶ 902.03), the partnership must also withhold on a foreign partner's allocable share of effectively connected income and fixed, determinable, annual, or periodic income. The partnership must file a Form 8804 (Annual Return For Partnership Withholding Tax), Form 8805 (Foreign Partner's Information Statement), and a Form 8813 (Partnership Withholding Tax Payment). A foreign partnership that is not engaged in a U.S. trade or business and does not have any U.S.-source income need not file either a Form 1065 or any other type of partnership return.[113]

---

[103] Reg. § 1.6012-2(g)(1)(i). A foreign corporation must timely file a true and accurate Form 1120-F in order to claim a deduction or credit. Reg. § 1.882-4(a)(2). For an example, *see InverWorld Inc.,* 71 TCM 3231, Dec. 51,428(M), TC Memo. 1996-301; *Swallows Holding, Ltd. v. United States,* 515 F.3d 162 (3d Cir. 2008), rev'g 126 TC 96, Dec. 56,417 (2006).

[104] Reg. § 1.6012-2(g)(2).

[105] Form 1120-F is due by the 15th day of the third month following the close of the taxable year if the foreign corporation has a U.S. office and, by the 15th day of the sixth month following the close of the taxable year, if the foreign corporation does not have a U.S. office. Reg. § 1.6072-2(a) and (b). However, a foreign corporation can obtain a six-month extension of time for filing Form 1120-F. Reg. § 1.6081-3(a).

[106] Code Sec. 6655.

[107] Reg. § 1.884-1(a).

[108] Reg. § 1.6012-1(b)(1)(i). A nonresident alien individual must timely file a true and accurate Form 1040NR in order to claim a deduction or credit. Reg. § 1.874-1(a).

[109] Reg. § 1.6012-1(b)(2).

[110] Form 1040NR is due by the 15th day of the sixth month following the close of the taxable year, unless the income includes wages subject to withholding, in which case the return is due by the 15th day of the fourth month following the close of the taxable year. Reg. § 1.6072-1(c). A nonresident alien can obtain a six-month extension of time for filing Form 1040NR. Reg. § 1.6081-4(a).

[111] Code Sec. 6654.

[112] Reg. § 1.6031(a)-1(c). Form 1065 generally is due by the 15th day of the fourth month after the close of the partnership's taxable year. Reg. § 1.6031(a)-1(e)(2).

[113] Reg. § 1.6031(a)-1(d)(1).

¶ 1005 APPENDIX

Louis LeBeau is a <u>French national</u> who is a technical consultant on movies produced at Hollywood Studio Company, where LeBeau <u>has an office.</u> For his consulting services performed in the United States during the taxable year, Lebeau earns $100,000 on which the Studio withholds $30,000. Lebeau is single and is entitled to one exemption. He must file a <u>Form 1040NR</u> as attached and pay tax at marginal rates on his ECI of $100,000.

Form **1040NR**	**U.S. Nonrecident Alien Income Tax Return**	OMB No. 1545-0074
Department of the Treasury Internal Revenue Service	▶ Information about Form 1040NR and its separate instructions is at *www.irs.gov/form1040nr.* For the year January 1–December 31, 2014, or other tax year beginning , 2014, and ending , 20	**20 14**

Please print or type	Your first name and initial Louis	Last name Labeau		Identifying number (see instructions)
	Present home address (number, street, and apt. no., or rural route). If you have a P.O. box, see instructions.		Check if:	☑ Individual ☐ Estate or Trust
	City, town or post office, state, and ZIP code. If you have a foreign address, also complete spaces below (see instructions). Paris			
	Foreign country name France	Foreign province/state/county		Foreign postal code

Filing Status

Check only one box.

1 ☐ Single resident of Canada or Mexico or single U.S. national			4 ☐ Married resident of South Korea
2 ☑ Other single nonresident alien			5 ☐ Other married nonresident alien
3 ☐ Married resident of Canada or Mexico or married U.S. national			6 ☐ Qualifying widow(er) with dependent child (see instructions)

If you checked box 3 or 4 above, enter the information below.

(i) Spouse's first name and initial	(ii) Spouse's last name	(iii) Spouse's identifying number

Exemptions

If more than four dependents, see instructions.

7a ☑	**Yourself.** If someone can claim you as a dependent, **do not** check box 7a					Boxes checked on 7a and 7b	1
b ☐	**Spouse.** Check box 7b only if you checked box 3 or 4 above **and** your spouse **did not** have any U.S. gross income					No. of children on 7c who:	

c Dependents: (see instructions)		(2) Dependent's identifying number	(3) Dependent's relationship to you	(4) ✔ if qualifying child for child tax credit (see instr.)	
(1) First name	Last name			☐	• lived with you
				☐	• did not live with you due to divorce or separation (see instructions)
				☐	
				☐	Dependents on 7c not entered above

d Total number of exemptions claimed	Add numbers on lines above ▶	1

Income Effectively Connected With U.S. Trade/ Business

Attach Form(s) W-2, 1042-S, SSA-1042S, RRB-1042S, and 8288-A here. Also attach Form(s) 1099-R if tax was withheld.

8 Wages, salaries, tips, etc. Attach Form(s) W-2	8	100,000
9a Taxable interest	9a	
b Tax-exempt interest. **Do not** include on line 9a	9b	
10a Ordinary dividends	10a	
b Qualified dividends (see instructions)	10b	
11 Taxable refunds, credits, or offsets of state and local income taxes (see instructions) . .	11	
12 Scholarship and fellowship grants. Attach Form(s) 1042-S or required statement (see instructions)	12	
13 Business income or (loss). Attach Schedule C or C-EZ (Form 1040)	13	
14 Capital gain or (loss). Attach Schedule D (Form 1040) if required. If not required, check here ☐	14	
15 Other gains or (losses). Attach Form 4797	15	
16a IRA distributions 16a	16b Taxable amount (see instructions)	16b	
17a Pensions and annuities 17a	17b Taxable amount (see instructions)	17b	
18 Rental real estate, royalties, partnerships, trusts, etc. Attach Schedule E (Form 1040) . .	18	
19 Farm income or (loss). Attach Schedule F (Form 1040)	19	
20 Unemployment compensation	20	
21 Other income. List type and amount (see instructions) _____	21	
22 Total income exempt by a treaty from page 5, Schedule OI, Item L (1)(e) 22		
23 Combine the amounts in the far right column for lines 8 through 21. This is your **total effectively connected income** . . . . ▶	23	100,000

Adjusted Gross Income

24 Educator expenses (see instructions)	24	
25 Health savings account deduction. Attach Form 8889 . . .	25	
26 Moving expenses. Attach Form 3903	26	
27 Deductible part of self-employment tax. Attach Schedule SE (Form 1040)	27	
28 Self-employed SEP, SIMPLE, and qualified plans	28	
29 Self-employed health insurance deduction (see instructions)	29	
30 Penalty on early withdrawal of savings	30	
31 Scholarship and fellowship grants excluded	31	
32 IRA deduction (see instructions)	32	
33 Student loan interest deduction (see instructions) . . .	33	
34 Domestic production activities deduction. Attach Form 8903 .	34	
35 Add lines 24 through 34 . . . . ▶	35	
36 Subtract line 35 from line 23. This is your **adjusted gross income** . . . . . . ▶	36	100,000

For Disclosure, Privacy Act, and Paperwork Reduction Act Notice, see instructions. Cat. No. 11364D Form **1040NR** (2014)

¶1005

Form 1040NR (2014)   Page **2**

Tax and Credits

37	Amount from line 36 (adjusted gross income)	37	100,000
38	**Itemized deductions** from page 3, Schedule A, line 15	38	
39	Subtract line 38 from line 37	39	100,000
40	Exemptions (see instructions)	40	3,950
41	**Taxable income.** Subtract line 40 from line 39. If line 40 is more than line 39, enter -0-	41	96,050
42	**Tax** (see instructions). Check if any tax is from: **a**☐ Form(s) 8814 **b**☐ Form 4972	42	20,063
43	**Alternative minimum tax** (see instructions). Attach Form 6251	43	
44	Excess advance premium tax credit repayment. Attach Form 8962	44	
45	Add lines 42, 43 and 44 ▶	45	20,063
46	Foreign tax credit. Attach Form 1116 if required	46	
47	Credit for child and dependent care expenses. Attach Form 2441	47	
48	Retirement savings contributions credit. Attach Form 8880	48	
49	Child tax credit. Attach Schedule 8812, if required	49	
50	Residential energy credits. Attach Form 5695	50	
51	Other credits from Form: **a**☐ 3800 **b**☐ 8801 **c**☐	51	
52	Add lines 46 through 51. These are your **total credits**	52	
53	Subtract line 52 from line 45. If line 52 is more than line 45, enter -0- ▶	53	20,063

Other Taxes

54	Tax on income not effectively connected with a U.S. trade or business from page 4, Schedule NEC, line 15	54	
55	Self-employment tax. Attach Schedule SE (Form 1040)	55	
56	Unreported social security and Medicare tax from Form: **a**☐ 4137 **b**☐ 8919	56	
57	Additional tax on IRAs, other qualified retirement plans, etc. Attach Form 5329 if required	57	
58	Transportation tax (see instructions)	58	
59a	Household employment taxes from Schedule H (Form 1040)	59a	
b	First-time homebuyer credit repayment. Attach Form 5405 if required	59b	
60	Taxes from: **a** ☐ Form 8959 **b** ☐ Instructions; enter code(s) _____	60	
61	Add lines 53 through 60. This is your **total tax** ▶	61	20,063

Payments

62	Federal income tax withheld from:		
	a Form(s) W-2 and 1099	62a	
	b Form(s) 8805	62b	
	c Form(s) 8288-A	62c	
	d Form(s) 1042-S	62d	30,000
63	2014 estimated tax payments and amount applied from 2013 return	63	
64	Additional child tax credit. Attach Schedule 8812	64	
65	Net premium tax credit. Attach Form 8962	65	
66	Amount paid with request for extension to file (see instructions)	66	
67	Excess social security and tier 1 RRTA tax withheld (see instructions)	67	
68	Credit for federal tax paid on fuels. Attach Form 4136	68	
69	Credits from Form: **a**☐ 2439 **b**■ Reserved **c**■ Reserved **d**☐ ___	69	
70	Credit for amount paid with Form 1040-C	70	
71	Add lines 62a through 70. These are your **total payments** ▶	71	30,000

Refund
Direct deposit?
See instructions.

72	If line 71 is more than line 61, subtract line 61 from line 71. This is the amount you **overpaid**	72	9,937
73a	Amount of line 72 you want **refunded to you.** If Form 8888 is attached, check here . ▶☐	73a	9,937
b	Routing number _____ ▶ **c** Type: ☐ Checking ☐ Savings		
d	Account number _____		
e	If you want your refund check mailed to an address outside the United States not shown on page 1, enter it here		
74	Amount of line 72 you want **applied to your 2015 estimated tax** ▶	74	

Amount You Owe

75	**Amount you owe.** Subtract line 71 from line 61. For details on how to pay, see instructions ▶	75	
76	Estimated tax penalty (see instructions)	76	

Third Party Designee

Do you want to allow another person to discuss this return with the IRS (see instructions)? ☐ **Yes.** Complete below. ☐ No

Designee's name ▶   Phone no. ▶   Personal identification number (PIN) ▶ ☐☐☐☐☐

Sign Here
Keep a copy of this return for your records.

Under penalties of perjury, I declare that I have examined this return and accompanying schedules and statements, and to the best of my knowledge and belief, they are true, correct, and complete. Declaration of preparer (other than taxpayer) is based on all information of which preparer has any knowledge.

Your signature ▶   Date   Your occupation in the United States   If the IRS sent you an Identity Protection PIN, enter it here (see inst.)

Paid Preparer Use Only

Print/Type preparer's name   Preparer's signature   Date   Check ☐ if self-employed   PTIN

Firm's name ▶   Firm's EIN ▶

Firm's address ▶   Phone no.

Form **1040NR** (2014)

¶1005

Form 1040NR (2014)   Page **3**

Schedule A—Itemized Deductions (see instructions)   07

Taxes You Paid	**1**	State and local income taxes	**1**	
Gifts to U.S. Charities		**Caution:** *If you made a gift and received a benefit in return, see instructions.*		
	2	Gifts by cash or check. If you made any gift of $250 or more, see instructions	**2**	
	3	Other than by cash or check. If you made any gift of $250 or more, see instructions. You **must** attach Form 8283 if the amount of your deduction is over $500	**3**	
	4	Carryover from prior year	**4**	
	5	Add lines 2 through 4	**5**	
Casualty and Theft Losses	**6**	Casualty or theft loss(es). Attach Form 4684. See instructions	**6**	
Job Expenses and Certain Miscellaneous Deductions	**7**	Unreimbursed employee expenses—job travel, union dues, job education, etc. You **must** attach Form 2106 or Form 2106-EZ if required. See instructions ▶ _____	**7**	
	8	Tax preparation fees	**8**	
	9	Other expenses. See instructions for expenses to deduct here. List type and amount ▶ _____	**9**	
	10	Add lines 7 through 9	**10**	
	11	Enter the amount from Form 1040NR, line 37 . . . . . | **11** |		
	12	Multiply line 11 by 2% (.02)	**12**	
	13	Subtract line 12 from line 10. If line 12 is more than line 10, enter -0-	**13**	
Other Miscellaneous Deductions	**14**	Other—see instructions for expenses to deduct here. List type and amount ▶ _____	**14**	
Total Itemized Deductions	**15**	Is Form 1040NR, line 37, over the amount shown below for the filing status box you checked on page 1 of Form 1040NR:		
		• $305,050 if you checked box 6,		
		• $254,200 if you checked box 1 or 2, or		
		• $152,525 if you checked box 3, 4, or 5?		
		☐ **No.** Your deduction is not limited. Add the amounts in the far right column for lines 1 through 14. Also enter this amount on Form 1040NR, line 38.		
		☐ **Yes.** Your deduction may be limited. See the Itemized Deductions Worksheet in the instructions to figure the amount to enter here and on Form 1040NR, line 38.	**15**	

Form **1040NR** (2014)

¶1005

Form 1040NR (2014)   Page **4**

Schedule NEC—Tax on Income Not Effectively Connected With a U.S. Trade or Business (see instructions)

Enter amount of income under the appropriate rate of tax (see instructions)

Nature of income		(a) 10%	(b) 15%	(c) 30%	(d) Other (specify)	
					%	%
1 Dividends paid by:						
a U.S. corporations	1a					
b Foreign corporations	1b					
2 Interest:						
a Mortgage	2a					
b Paid by foreign corporations	2b					
c Other	2c					
3 Industrial royalties (patents, trademarks, etc.)	3					
4 Motion picture or T.V. copyright royalties	4					
5 Other royalties (copyrights, recording, publishing, etc.)	5					
6 Real property income and natural resources royalties	6					
7 Pensions and annuities	7					
8 Social security benefits	8					
9 Capital gain from line 18 below	9					
10 Gambling—Residents of Canada only. Enter net income in column (c).						
If zero or less, enter -0-.						
a Winnings						
b Losses	10c					
11 Gambling winnings—Residents of countries other than Canada. **Note.** Losses not allowed	11					
12 Other (specify) ▶	12					
13 Add lines 1a through 12 in columns (a) through (d)	13					
14 **Multiply line 13 by rate of tax at top of each column**	14					
15 **Tax on income not effectively connected with a U.S. trade or business.** Add columns (a) through (d) of line 14. Enter the total here and on Form 1040NR, line 54					▶ **15**	

Capital Gains and Losses From Sales or Exchanges of Property

16	(a) Kind of property and description (if necessary, attach statement of descriptive details not shown below)	(b) Date acquired (mo., day, yr.)	(c) Date sold (mo., day, yr.)	(d) Sales price	(e) Cost or other basis	(f) LOSS If (e) is more than (d), subtract (d) from (e)	(g) GAIN If (d) is more than (e), subtract (e) from (d)

17 Add columns (f) and (g) of line 16   17 ( )   18

18 **Capital gain.** Combine columns (f) and (g) of line 17. Enter the net gain here and on line 9 above (if a loss, enter -0-) ▶ **18**

Enter only the capital gains and losses from property sales or exchanges that are from sources within the United States and not effectively connected with a U.S. business. Do not include a gain or loss on disposing of a U.S. real property interest; report these gains and losses on Schedule D (Form 1040).

Report property sales or exchanges that are effectively connected with a U.S. business on Schedule D (Form 1040), Form 4797, or both.

Form **1040NR** (2014)

Form 1040NR (2014)   Page **5**

Schedule OI—Other Information (see instructions)
Answer all questions

A Of what country or countries were you a citizen or national during the tax year? France

B In what country did you claim residence for tax purposes during the tax year? France

C Have you ever applied to be a green card holder (lawful permanent resident) of the United States? . . . . . . ☐ Yes ☑ No

D Were you ever:
    1. A U.S. citizen? . . . . ☐ Yes ☑ No
    2. A green card holder (lawful permanent resident) of the United States? . . . . ☐ Yes ☑ No
    If you answer "Yes" to (1) or (2), see Pub. 519, chapter 4, for expatriation rules that apply to you.

E If you had a visa on the last day of the tax year, enter your visa type. If you did not have a visa, enter your U.S. immigration status on the last day of the tax year. B-1

F Have you ever changed your visa type (nonimmigrant status) or U.S. immigration status? . . . . ☐ Yes ☑ No
    If you answered "Yes," indicate the date and nature of the change. ▶

G List all dates you entered and left the United States during 2014 (see instructions).
    Note. If you are a resident of Canada or Mexico AND commute to work in the United States at frequent intervals,
    check the box for Canada or Mexico and skip to item H . . . . ☐ Canada ☐ Mexico

Date entered United States mm/dd/yy	Date departed United States mm/dd/yy		Date entered United States mm/dd/yy	Date departed United States mm/dd/yy
09/01/14	11/30/14			

H Give number of days (including vacation, nonworkdays, and partial days) you were present in the United States during:
    2012   0   , 2013   0   , and 2014   91   .

I Did you file a U.S. income tax return for any prior year? . . . . ☐ Yes ☑ No
    If "Yes," give the latest year and form number you filed . . ▶

J Are you filing a return for a trust? . . . . ☐ Yes ☑ No
    If "Yes," did the trust have a U.S. or foreign owner under the grantor trust rules, make a distribution or loan to a
    U.S. person, or receive a contribution from a U.S. person? . . . . ☐ Yes ☐ No

K Did you receive total compensation of $250,000 or more during the tax year? . . . . ☐ Yes ☑ No
    If "Yes," did you use an alternative method to determine the source of this compensation? . . . . ☐ Yes ☑ No

L Income Exempt from Tax—If you are claiming exemption from income tax under a U.S. income tax treaty with a foreign country, complete (1) and (2) below. See Pub. 901 for more information on tax treaties.
    1. Enter the name of the country, the applicable tax treaty article, the number of months in prior years you claimed the treaty benefit, and the amount of exempt income in the columns below. Attach Form 8833 if required (see instructions).

(a) Country	**(b)** Tax treaty article	**(c)** Number of months claimed in prior tax years	**(d)** Amount of exempt income in current tax year

(e) **Total.** Enter this amount on Form 1040NR, line 22. Do not enter it on line 8 or line 12 . . . . . .
    2. Were you subject to tax in a foreign country on any of the income shown in 1(d) above? . . . . ☐ Yes ☐ No

Form **1040NR** (2014)

¶1005

Kingman Private Limited <u>Company is</u> a distributor of foundry manufacturing equipment worldwide and is <u>based in Hong Kong</u>, which is <u>not entitled to the treaty</u> benefits afforded by the U.S.-China Income Tax Treaty. The Company <u>operates in the United States</u> through a <u>sales office</u> headed primarily by Dave Kong. With respect to its U.S. operations, the Company <u>sells $20 million</u> of products and <u>purchases $16 million</u> of products. Kong, who earns an annual <u>salary of $1 million</u>, spends approximately <u>half his time in the United States</u>, where he supervises a staff whose combined <u>wages total $500,000</u> and incurs <u>advertising expenses of $1 million</u>. For the year, the accounts with respect to the U.S. branch include the following amounts:

Cash (at start of year)	$1 million
Cash (at end of year)	$1 million
Inventory (at start of year)	$2 million (at cost)
Inventory (at end of year)	$2 million (at cost)
Land	$2 million
Booked Liability	$1 million ~bank loan~
Retained Earnings (at start of year)	$4 million
Retained Earnings (at end of year)	$4 million
Tax Payments (during the year)	$1 million ~Estimated tax payments (pre-pay)~

The booked liability of $1 million is a <u>bank loan</u> on which the U.S. operations incur simple interest at an <u>annual rate of 5% for $50,000</u>. The Company also incurs simple interest at an <u>annual rate of 5% on its $4 million of non-U.S. booked liabilities.</u>

Kingman Private Limited Company will file a <u>Form 1120-F showing income tax, branch profits tax, and the tax on excess interest</u>. The Company has made <u>estimated tax payments of $1 million.</u>

¶1005

Form **1120-F**	**U.S. Income Tax Return of a Foreign Corporation**	OMB No. 1545-0123

Department of the Treasury
Internal Revenue Service

For calendar year 2014, or tax year beginning _____ , 2014, and ending _____ , 20 _____

▶ Information about Form 1120-F and its separate instructions is at *www.irs.gov/form1120f.*

2014

			Employer identification number
Type or Print	Name **Kingman Private Limited Cmpany**		
	Number, street, and room or suite no. (see instructions)		Check box(es) if: ☑ Initial return
			☐ Name or address change ☐ Final return
	City or town, state or province, country, and ZIP or foreign postal code		☐ First post-merger return ☐ Amended return
	Hong Kong		☐ Schedule M-3 attached ☐ Protective return

				Yes	No
A	Country of incorporation **Hong Kong**	**H**	Did the corporation's method of accounting change from the preceding tax year?		✓
B	Foreign country under whose laws the income reported on this return is also subject to tax **N/A**		If "Yes," attach a statement with an explanation.		
C	Date incorporated **01/01/14**	**I**	Did the corporation's method of determining income change from the preceding tax year?		✓
D	(1) Location of corporation's primary books and records (city, province or state, and country) **Hong Kong**		If "Yes," attach a statement with an explanation.		
	(2) Principal location of worldwide business **Hong Kong**	**J**	Did the corporation file a U.S. income tax return for the preceding tax year?		✓
	(3) If the corporation maintains an office or place of business in the United States, check here . . . . ▶ ☐	**K**	(1) At any time during the tax year, was the corporation engaged in a trade or business in the United States?	✓	
E	If the corporation had an agent in the United States at any time during the tax year, enter:		(2) If "Yes," is taxpayer's trade or business within the United States solely the result of a section 897 (FIRPTA) sale or disposition?		✓
	(1) Type of agent **Sales Employee**				
	(2) Name **Dave Kong**	**L**	Did the corporation have a permanent establishment in the United States for purposes of any applicable tax treaty between the United States and a foreign country?		✓
	(3) Address **1234 Main Street**				
	Los Angeles, CA		If "Yes," enter the name of the foreign country:		
F	See the instructions and enter the corporation's principal:				
	(1) Business activity code number ▶ **311500**	**M**	Did the corporation have any transactions with related parties?		✓
	(2) Business activity ▶ **Dairy Product Manufacturing**		If "Yes," Form 5472 may have to be filed (see instructions).		
	(3) Product or service ▶ **Frozen Custard**		Enter number of Forms 5472 attached ▶		
G	Check method of accounting: (1) ☑ Cash (2) ☐ Accrual		*Note: Additional information is required on page 2.*		
	(3) ☐ Other (specify) ▶				

Computation of Tax Due or Overpayment

1	Tax from Section I, line 11, page 2	**1**		
2	Tax from Section II, Schedule J, line 9, page 4	**2**	637,330	
3	Tax from Section III (add lines 6 and 10 on page 5)	**3**	393,801	
4	**Total tax.** Add lines 1 through 3	**4**		1,031,131
5a	2013 overpayment credited to 2014 . . .	**5a**		
b	2014 estimated tax payments	**5b**	1,000,000	
c	Less 2014 refund applied for on Form 4466 .	**5c** (	)	
d	Combine lines 5a through 5c	**5d**		
e	Tax deposited with Form 7004	**5e**		
f	Credit for tax paid on undistributed capital gains (attach Form 2439). . . .	**5f**		
g	Credit for federal tax paid on fuels (attach Form 4136). See instructions	**5g**		
h	Refundable credit from Form 8827, line 8c	**5h**		
i	U.S. income tax paid or withheld at source (add line 12, page 2, and amounts from Forms 8288-A and 8805 (attach Forms 8288-A and 8805))	**5i**		
j	Total payments. Add lines 5d through 5i	**5j**		1,000,000
6	Estimated tax penalty (see instructions). Check if Form 2220 is attached . . . . ▶ ☐	**6**		31,131
7	**Amount owed.** If line 5j is smaller than the total of lines 4 and 6, enter amount owed	**7**		
8a	**Overpayment.** If line 5j is larger than the total of lines 4 and 6, enter amount overpaid	**8a**		
b	Amount of overpayment on line 8a resulting from tax deducted and withheld under Chapters 3 and 4 (from Schedule W, line 7, page 7)	**8b**		
9	Enter portion of line 8a you want **Credited to 2015 estimated tax** ▶	Refunded ▶ **9**		

Sign Here

Under penalties of perjury, I declare that I have examined this return, including accompanying schedules and statements, and to the best of my knowledge and belief, it is true, correct, and complete. Declaration of preparer (other than taxpayer) is based on all information of which preparer has any knowledge.

▶ Signature of officer	Date	▶ Title	May the IRS discuss this return with the preparer shown below (see instructions)? ☐ Yes ☐ No

Paid Preparer Use Only

Print/Type preparer's name	Preparer's signature	Date	Check ☐ if self-employed	PTIN
Firm's name ▶			Firm's EIN ▶	
Firm's address ▶			Phone no.	

For Paperwork Reduction Act Notice, see separate instructions.

Cat. No. 11470I

Form **1120-F** (2014)

¶1005

Form 1120-F (2014)   Page **2**

Additional Information *(continued from page 1)*

		Yes	No
N	Is the corporation a controlled foreign corporation? (See section 957(a) for definition.)		✓
O	Is the corporation a personal service corporation? (See instructions for definition.)		✓
P	Enter tax-exempt interest received or accrued during the tax year (see instructions) ▶ $ _____		
Q	At the end of the tax year, did the corporation own, directly or indirectly, 50% or more of the voting stock of a U.S. corporation? (See section 267(c) for rules of attribution.) . . . . If "Yes," attach a statement showing **(1)** name and EIN of such U.S. corporation; **(2)** percentage owned; and **(3)** taxable income or (loss) before NOL and special deductions of such U.S. corporation for the tax year ending with or within your tax year.		✓
R	If the corporation has an NOL for the tax year and is electing to forego the carryback period, check here . . . . ▶ ☐		
S	Enter the available NOL carryover from prior tax years. (Do not reduce it by any deduction on line 30a, page 3.) ▶ $ _____		
T	Is the corporation a subsidiary in a parent-subsidiary controlled group? . . . . 'If "Yes," enter the parent corporation's:	✓	
	(1) EIN ▶ _____		
	(2) Name ▶ _____		
U	**(1)** Is the corporation a dealer under section 475? . .		✓
	(2) Did the corporation mark to market any securities or commodities other than in a dealer capacity?		✓

		Yes	No
V	At the end of the tax year, did any individual, partnership, corporation, estate, or trust own, directly or indirectly, 50% or more of the corporation's voting stock? (See section 267(c) for rules of attribution.) If "Yes," attach a statement showing the name and identifying number. (Do not include any information already entered in item **T**.) Enter percentage owned ▶ _____		✓
W	Is the corporation taking a position on this return that a U.S. tax treaty overrules or modifies an Internal Revenue law of the United States, thereby causing a reduction of tax? . If "Yes," the corporation is generally required to complete and attach Form 8833. See Form 8833 for exceptions. **Note:** *Failure to disclose a treaty-based return position may result in a $10,000 penalty (see section 6712).*		✓
X	During the tax year, did the corporation own any entity that was disregarded as an entity separate from its owner under Regulations sections 301.7701-2 and 301.7701-3? . . If "Yes," attach a statement listing the name, country under whose laws the entity was organized, and EIN (if any) of each such entity.		✓
Y	**(1)** Did a partnership allocate to the corporation a distributive share of income from a directly owned partnership interest, any of which is ECI or treated as ECI by the partnership or the partner? . . . . If "Yes," attach Schedule P. See instructions.		✓
	(2) During the tax year, did the corporation own directly or indirectly, at least a 10% interest, in any foreign partnership? If "Yes," see instructions for required attachment.		✓
Z	**(1)** Has the corporation engaged in any transactions the results of which are subject to the arm's length standard under section 482 and its regulations?		✓
	(2) Has the corporation recognized any interbranch amounts? If "Yes," attach statement (see instructions).		✓
AA	Is the corporation required to file Schedule UTP (Form 1120), Uncertain Tax Position Statement (see instructions)? If "Yes," complete and attach Schedule UTP.		✓

SECTION I— Income From U.S. Sources Not Effectively Connected With the Conduct of a Trade or Business in the United States—Do not report items properly withheld and reported on Form 1042-S. See instructions.

Report all gross transportation income subject to 4% tax on line 9. Report other column (a) income items only if not properly withheld and reported on Form 1042-S. The rate of tax on these **gross** income items is 30% or such lower rate specified by tax treaty. No deductions are allowed against these types of income. Enter treaty rates where applicable. **If the corporation is claiming a lower treaty rate, also complete item W above.** If multiple treaty rates apply to a type of income (e.g., subsidiary and portfolio dividends or dividends received by disregarded entities), attach a statement showing the amounts, tax rates, and withholding for each.

Name of treaty country, if any ▶

(a) Class of income (see instructions)	(b) Gross amount	(c) Rate of tax (%)	(d) Amount of tax liability	(e) Amount of U.S. income tax paid or withheld at the source
1 Interest				
2 Dividends				
3 Rents				
4 Royalties				
5 Annuities				
6 Gains from disposal of timber, coal, or domestic iron ore with a retained economic interest (attach supporting statement) . .				
7 Gains from sale or exchange of patents, copyrights, etc.				
8 Fiduciary distributions (attach supporting statement)				
9 Gross transportation income (see instructions)		4		
10 Other items of income				
_____				
_____				
11 Total. Enter here and on line 1, page 1 . . . . ▶				
12 Total. Enter here and include on line 5i, page 1 . . . . ▶				

13 Is the corporation fiscally transparent under the laws of the foreign jurisdiction with respect to any item of income listed above? ☐ Yes ☑ No

If "Yes," attach a statement that provides the information requested above with respect to each such item of income.

Form **1120-F** (2014)

SECTION II—Income Effectively Connected With the Conduct of a Trade or Business in the United States (see instructions)

Important: *Fill in all applicable lines and schedules. If you need more space, see **Assembling the Return** in the instructions.*

Income	1a	Gross receipts or sales [　] **b** Less returns and allowances [　] **c** Bal ▶	1c	20,000,000
	2	Cost of goods sold (attach Form 1125-A)	2	16,000,000
	3	Gross profit (subtract line 2 from line 1c)	3	
	4	Dividends (Schedule C, line 14)	4	
	5	Interest	5	
	6	Gross rents	6	
	7	Gross royalties	7	
	8	Capital gain net income (attach Schedule D (Form 1120))	8	
	9	Net gain or (loss) from Form 4797, Part II, line 17 (attach Form 4797)	9	
	10	Other income (see instructions—attach statement)	10	
	11	**Total income.** Add lines 3 through 10 . . . . ▶	11	4,000,000
Deductions (See instructions for limitations on deductions.)	12	Compensation of officers (see instructions—attach Form 1125-E)	12	500,000
	13	Salaries and wages (less employment credits)	13	500,000
	14	Repairs and maintenance	14	
	15	Bad debts (for bad debts over $500,000, attach a list of debtors and amounts) . . .	15	
	16	Rents	16	
	17	Taxes and licenses	17	
	18	Interest expense from Schedule I, line 25 (see instructions)	18	125,000
	19	Charitable contributions	19	
	20	Depreciation from Form 4562 not claimed on Form 1125-A or elsewhere on return (attach Form 4562) .	20	
	21	Depletion	21	
	22	Advertising	22	1,000,000
	23	Pension, profit-sharing, etc., plans	23	
	24	Employee benefit programs	24	
	25	Domestic production activities deduction (attach Form 8903)	25	
	26	Deductions allocated and apportioned to ECI from Schedule H, line 20 (see instructions)	26	
	27	Other deductions (attach statement)	27	
	28	**Total deductions.** Add lines 12 through 27 . . . . ▶	28	2,125,000
	29	Taxable income before NOL deduction and special deductions (subtract line 28 from line 11) . . ▶	29	1,875,000
	30	**Less:** **a** Net operating loss deduction (see instructions) . . . . ⎹ 30a ⎹		
		b Special deductions (Schedule C, line 15) . . . . . . ⎹ 30b ⎹		
		c Add lines 30a and 30b	30c	
	31	Taxable income or (loss). Subtract line 30c from line 29	31	1,875,000

Form **1120-F** (2014)

Form 1120-F (2014)   Page **4**

SECTION II—Income Effectively Connected With the Conduct of a Trade or Business in the United States *(Continued)*

Schedule C	Dividends and Special Deductions (see instructions)	(a) Dividends received	(b) %	(c) Special deductions: (a) × (b)
1	Dividends from less-than-20%-owned domestic corporations (other than debt-financed stock)		70	
2	Dividends from 20%-or-more-owned domestic corporations (other than debt-financed stock)		80	
3	Dividends on debt-financed stock of domestic and foreign corporations (section 246A)		see instructions	
4	Dividends on certain preferred stock of less-than-20%-owned public utilities		42	
5	Dividends on certain preferred stock of 20%-or-more-owned public utilities .		48	
6	Dividends from less-than-20%-owned foreign corporations		70	
7	Dividends from 20%-or-more-owned foreign corporations		80	
8	**Total.** Add lines 1 through 7. See instructions for limitation			
9	Dividends from foreign corporations not included on lines 3, 6, or 7 . . .			
10	Foreign dividend gross-up (section 78)			
11	IC-DISC and former DISC dividends not included on lines 1, 2, or 3 (section 246(d))			
12	Other dividends			
13	Deduction for dividends paid on certain preferred stock of public utilities .			
14	**Total dividends.** Add lines 1 through 12. Enter here and on line 4, page 3 .			
15	**Total special deductions.** Add lines 8 and 13. Enter here and on line 30b, page 3 . . . . ▶			

Schedule J	Tax Computation (see instructions)				
1	Check if the corporation is a member of a controlled group (attach Schedule O (Form 1120)) . . . ▶ ☐				
2	Income tax. Check if a qualified personal service corporation (see instructions) . . . . . . ▶ ☐		**2**	637,330	
3	Alternative minimum tax (attach Form 4626)		**3**		
4	Add lines 2 and 3		**4**		
5a	Foreign tax credit (attach Form 1118)	5a			
b	General business credit (attach Form 3800)	5b			
c	Credit for prior year minimum tax (attach Form 8827)	5c			
d	Bond credits from Form 8912	5d			
6	**Total credits.** Add lines 5a through 5d		**6**		
7	Subtract line 6 from line 4		**7**		
8	Other taxes. Check if from: ☐ Form 4255 ☐ Form 8611 ☐ Form 8697 ☐ Form 8866 ☐ Form 8902 ☐ Other (attach statement) .		**8**		
9	**Total tax.** Add lines 7 and 8. Enter here and on line 2, page 1		**9**	637,330	

Form **1120-F** (2014)

¶**1005**

Form 1120-F (2014)   Page **5**

SECTION III—Branch Profits Tax and Tax on Excess Interest

Part I—Branch Profits Tax (see instructions)

1	Enter the amount from Section II, line 29	1	1,875,000
2	Enter total adjustments to line 1 to get effectively connected earnings and profits. (Attach required statement showing the nature and amount of adjustments.) (See instructions.)	2	(637,330)
3	Effectively connected earnings and profits. Combine line 1 and line 2	3	1,237,670
4a	Enter U.S. net equity at the end of the current tax year. (Attach required statement.)	4a	4,000,000
b	Enter U.S. net equity at the end of the prior tax year. (Attach required statement.)	4b	4,000,000
c	Increase in U.S. net equity. If line 4a is greater than or equal to line 4b, subtract line 4b from line 4a. Enter the result here and skip to line 4e	4c	
d	Decrease in U.S. net equity. If line 4b is greater than line 4a, subtract line 4a from line 4b	4d	
e	Non-previously taxed accumulated effectively connected earnings and profits. Enter excess, if any, of effectively connected earnings and profits for preceding tax years beginning after 1986 over any dividend equivalent amounts for those tax years	4e	
5	Dividend equivalent amount. Subtract line 4c from line 3. If zero or less, enter -0-. If no amount is entered on line 4c, add the lesser of line 4d or line 4e to line 3 and enter the total here	5	1,237,670
6	**Branch profits tax.** Multiply line 5 by 30% (or lower treaty rate if the corporation is a qualified resident or otherwise qualifies for treaty benefits). (See instructions.) Enter here and include on line 3, page 1. **Also complete item W on page 2**	6	371,301

Part II—Tax on Excess Interest (see instructions for this Part and for Schedule I (Form 1120-F))

7 a	Enter the interest from Section II, line 18	7a	125,000
b	Enter the inverse of the total amount deferred, capitalized, and disallowed from Schedule I, line 24d (i.e., if line 24d is negative, enter as a positive number; if line 24d is positive, enter as a negative number)	7b	
c	Combine lines 7a and 7b (amount must equal Schedule I, line 23)	7c	125,000
8	**Branch Interest** (see instructions for definition): Enter the sum of Schedule I, line 9, column (c), and Schedule I, line 22. If the interest paid by the foreign corporation's U.S. trade or business was increased because 80% or more of the foreign corporation's assets are U.S. assets, check this box . . . . ▶ ☐	8	50,000
9 a	Excess interest. Subtract line 8 from line 7c. If zero or less, enter -0-	9a	75,000
b	If the foreign corporation is a bank, enter the excess interest treated as interest on deposits (see instructions for rules for computing this amount). Otherwise, enter -0-.	9b	
c	Subtract line 9b from line 9a	9c	75,000
10	**Tax on excess interest.** Multiply line 9c by 30% or lower treaty rate (if the corporation is a qualified resident or otherwise qualifies for treaty benefits). (See instructions.) Enter here and include on line 3, page 1. **Also complete item W on page 2**	10	22,500

Part III—Additional Information

		Yes	No
11	Is the corporation claiming a reduction in, or exemption from, the branch profits tax due to:		
a	A complete termination of all U.S. trades or businesses?		✓
b	The tax-free liquidation or reorganization of a foreign corporation?		✓
c	The tax-free incorporation of a U.S. trade or business?		✓

If **11a** or **11b** applies and the transferee is a domestic corporation, attach Form 8848. If **11c** applies, attach the statement required by Temporary Regulations section 1.884-2T(d)(5).

Form **1120-F** (2014)

Form 1120-F (2014)   Page **6**

Note. *Check if completing on* ▶   ☐ U.S. basis or   ☐ Worldwide basis.

Schedule L   **Balance Sheets per Books**

	Assets	Beginning of tax year (a)	Beginning of tax year (b)	End of tax year (c)	End of tax year (d)
1	Cash		1,000,000		1,000,000
2a	Trade notes and accounts receivable				
b	Less allowance for bad debts	( )		( )	
3	Inventories		2,000,000		2,000,000
4	U.S. government obligations				
5	Tax-exempt securities (see instructions)				
6a	Interbranch current assets*				
b	Other current non-U.S. assets*				
c	Other current U.S. assets*				
7	Loans to shareholders				
8	Mortgage and real estate loans				
9a	Other loans and investments—non-U.S. assets*				
b	Other loans and investments—U.S. assets*				
10a	Buildings and other depreciable assets				
b	Less accumulated depreciation	( )		( )	
11a	Depletable assets				
b	Less accumulated depletion	( )		( )	
12	Land (net of any amortization)		2,000,000		2,000,000
13a	Intangible assets (amortizable only)				
b	Less accumulated amortization	( )		( )	
14	Assets held in trust				
15	Other non-current interbranch assets*				
16a	Other non-current non-U.S. assets*				
b	Other non-current U.S. assets*				
17	Total assets		5,000,000		5,000,000
	Liabilities				
18	Accounts payable				
19	Mortgages, notes, bonds payable in less than 1 year:				
a	Interbranch liabilities*				
b	Third-party liabilities*				
20	Other current liabilities*				
21	Loans from shareholders				
22	Mortgages, notes, bonds payable in 1 year or more:				
a	Interbranch liabilities*				
b	Third-party liabilities*		1,000,000		1,000,000
23	Liabilities held in trust				
24a	Other interbranch liabilities*				
b	Other third-party liabilities*				
	Equity				
25	Capital stock: a Preferred stock				
	b Common stock				
26	Additional paid-in capital				
27	Retained earnings—Appropriated*				
28	Retained earnings—Unappropriated		4,000,000		4,000,000
29	Adjustments to shareholders' equity*				
30	Less cost of treasury stock		( )		( )
31	Total liabilities and shareholders' equity		5,000,000		5,000,000

Form **1120-F** (2014)

*Attach statement—see instructions.

Form 1120-F (2014)   Page **7**

Schedule W	Overpayment Resulting From Tax Deducted and Withheld Under Chapters 3 and 4		

1 Total Chapter 3 and 4 payments. Enter the amount from page 1, line 5i **1**

2 Enter the tax amount from page 1, line 1 . . . . **2**

3 Enter the portion of the tax amount shown on page 1, line 2 pertaining to
income associated with amounts deducted and withheld under sections 1445
and 1446 (see instructions for general guidelines) **3**

4 Total Chapter 3 and 4 tax. Combine lines 2 and 3 . . . . **4**

5 Tentative overpayment resulting from tax deducted and withheld under Chapters 3 and 4.
Subtract line 4 from line 1 . . . . **5**

6 Enter the amount from page 1, line 8a **6**

7 Overpayment resulting from tax deducted and withheld under Chapters 3 and 4.
Enter the smaller of line 5 or line 6. Enter the result here and on page 1, line 8b **7**

Form **1120-F** (2014)

¶**1005**

SCHEDULE H (Form 1120-F)	Deductions Allocated To Effectively Connected Income Under Regulations Section 1.861-8	OMB No. 1545-0123
Department of the Treasury Internal Revenue Service	▶ Attach to Form 1120-F. ▶ Information about Schedule H (Form 1120-F) and its separate instructions is at *www.irs.gov/form1120f.*	2014
Name of corporation		Employer identification number

Part I — Home Office Deductible Expenses Definitely Related Solely to ECI or Non-ECI

Note. Enter all amounts on lines 1a through 13 in only U.S. dollars or in only functional currency. If U.S. dollars, check box ☐. Otherwise, specify currency ▶

1a	Total expenses on the books of the home office	**1a**	
b	Check the applicable box below to indicate the accounting convention used to compute the amount on line 1a:		
	☐ U.S. GAAP ☐ Home Country GAAP		
	☐ IFRS ☐ Other (specify) ▶ _____		
2	Adjustments for U.S. tax principles (attach statement - see instructions) . .	**2**	
3	Total deductible expenses on the books of the home office. Combine lines 1a and 2	**3**	
4	Interest expense included on line 3	**4**	
5	Bad debt expense included on line 3	**5**	
6	Total of interest expense and bad debt expense. Add lines 4 and 5	**6**	
7	Remaining deductible expenses to be allocated and apportioned between ECI and non-ECI. Subtract line 6 from line 3	**7**	
8	Deductible expenses definitely related solely to non-ECI from subsidiaries .	**8**	
9	Deductible expenses definitely related solely to other non-ECI booked in the home country	**9**	
10	Deductible expenses definitely related solely to other non-ECI booked in other countries (including the United States)	**10**	
11	Deductible expenses definitely related solely to ECI	**11**	
12	Total deductible expenses definitely related solely to ECI or non-ECI. Add lines 8 through 11 . . .	**12**	

Part II — Home Office Deductible Expenses Allocated and Apportioned to ECI

Note. Enter the amounts on lines 15 through 20 in U.S. dollars.

13	Remaining deductible expenses on the books of the home office not definitely related solely to ECI or non-ECI. Subtract line 12 from line 7	**13**	
14	Average exchange rate used to convert amounts to U.S. dollars (see instructions)	**14**	
15	Enter the amount from line 13. If line 13 is stated in functional currency, divide line 13 by line 14 . .	**15**	
16	Remaining home office deductible expenses on line 15 allocated and apportioned under Regulations section 1.861-8 to ECI (attach computation)	**16**	
17	Enter the amount from line 11. If line 11 is stated in functional currency, divide line 11 by line 14 . .	**17**	
18	Total home office deductible expenses allocated and apportioned to ECI. Add lines 16 and 17 . . .	**18**	
19	Total deductible expenses from other non-U.S. locations allocated and apportioned to ECI	**19**	
20	**Total deductible expenses allocated and apportioned to ECI.** Add lines 18 and 19 and enter the amount here and on Form 1120-F, Section II, line 26	**20**	

Part III — Allocation and Apportionment Methods and Financial Records Used to Complete Parts I and II

Note. Enter the amounts in Part III, lines 21a, 21b, 22a, and 22b in U.S. dollars.

- If one or more methods used are different than in prior year, check box . . . . ☐
- If any amount on line 20 is recorded as an interbranch amount on books and records used to prepare Form 1120-F, Schedule L, include the amount on Part IV, line 35 and check this box . . . . ☐

21	Gross income ratio:				
a	Gross ECI	**21a**			
b	Worldwide gross income	**21b**			
c	Divide line 21a by line 21b		**21c**		%
22	Asset ratio:				
a	Average U.S. assets from Schedule I, line 5, column (d)	**22a**			
b	Worldwide assets (if applicable, from Schedule I, line 6b)	**22b**			
c	Divide line 22a by line 22b		**22c**		%
23	Number of personnel ratio:				
a	Personnel of U.S. trade or business	**23a**			
b	Worldwide personnel	**23b**			
c	Divide line 23a by line 23b		**23c**		%

		Yes	No
24	Did the corporation use any ratio-based methods (other than those indicated on lines 21 through 23 above) in Parts I and II? If "Yes," attach statement (see instructions)		✓
25	Did the corporation use any other methods (e.g., time-spent analysis or estimates) in Parts I and II? If "Yes," attach statement (see instructions).	✓	

For Paperwork Reduction Act Notice, see the Instructions for Form 1120-F.   Cat. No. 49679V   Schedule H (Form 1120-F) 2014

Part III	**Allocation and Apportionment Methods and Financial Records Used to Complete Parts I and II** *(continued)*

Note. Indicate whether the corporation used any of the following financial and other records in Parts I and II to identify deductible expenses allocated and apportioned to ECI.

		Yes	No
26a	Published or other non-public audited financial statements		✓
b	Non-audited financial statements		✓
27	Home office management or other departmental cost accounting reports		✓
28	Other (e.g., home country regulatory reports or written, contemporaneous functional analyses) (attach statement)		✓

Part IV	**Allocation and Apportionment of Expenses on Books and Records Used to Prepare Form 1120-F, Schedule L**

Note. Enter all amounts in Part IV in U.S. dollars.

29	Total expenses per books and records used to prepare Form 1120-F, Schedule L	**29**	1,000,000
30	Adjustments for U.S. tax principles (attach statement – see instructions) . .	**30**	
31	Total deductible expenses. Combine lines 29 and 30	**31**	1,000,000
32a	Third-party interest expense included on line 31	**32a**	
b	Interbranch interest expense included on line 31	**32b**	
33	Bad debt expense included on line 31	**33**	
34	Other third-party deductible expenses not allocated or apportioned to ECI and non-ECI under Regulations section 1.861-8 included on line 31 (attach statement).	**34**	
35	Interbranch expenses per books and records included on line 31 and not included on line 32b (attach statement)	**35**	
36	Add lines 32a through 35	**36**	
37	Deductible expenses on books and records allocated and apportioned to ECI or non-ECI under Regulations section 1.861-8. Subtract line 36 from line 31	**37**	500,000

Reconciliation of allocation and apportionment of deductible expenses to ECI and non-ECI on books and records under Regulations section 1.861-8 (from line 37)		**(a)** ECI Amounts	**(b)** Non-ECI Amounts	**(c)** Total: Add columns (a) and (b)
38a	Derivative transaction deductible expenses definitely related to ECI or non-ECI under Regulations section 1.861-8 (from line 37)			
b	Other deductible expenses definitely related to ECI or non-ECI (from line 37)			
39	Total deductible expenses definitely related to ECI or non-ECI. Add lines 38a and 38b			
40	Other deductible expenses on books and records not definitely related to ECI or non-ECI that are allocated and apportioned to ECI and non-ECI (from line 37)	500,000		500,000
41	Total deductible expenses on books and records allocated and apportioned to ECI and non-ECI. Add lines 39 and 40. Column (c) must equal line 37	500,000		500,000

Note. Line 41, column (a) is the total of the deductions reported on Form 1120-F, Section II, lines 12, 13, 14, 16, 17, 19 through 25, and 27.

Statement—Expenses were apportioned based on a time-spent analysis.

SCHEDULE I (Form 1120-F) Department of the Treasury Internal Revenue Service	**Interest Expense Allocation Under Regulations** **Section 1.882-5** ▶ **Attach to Form 1120-F.** ▶ Information about Schedule I (Form 1120-F) and its separate instructions is available at *www.irs.gov/form1120f.*	OMB No. 1545-0123 2014

Name of corporation	Employer identification number
Kingman private Limited Company	98-7654321

A Check here if the corporation is a foreign bank as defined in Regulations section 1.882-5(c)(4) . . . . ▶ ☐

B This Schedule I is being completed with respect to *(check one):*
- ☑ Adjusted U.S. booked liabilities method under Regs. sec. 1.882-5(d). **Complete lines 1 through 15 and 21 through 25.**
- ☐ Separate currency pools method under Regs. sec. 1.882-5(e). **Complete lines 1 through 9 and 16a through 25.**

Step 1 **Average U.S. Assets for the Tax Year: Regulations Section 1.882-5(b)**

		(a) Set(s) of Books that Give Rise to U.S. Booked Liabilities (see inst.)	(b) Partnership Interests	(c) Set(s) of Books Other than those Described in Columns (a) and (b)	(d) **Totals.** Add columns (a) through (c)
1	Specify the method used to determine the value of the corporation's U.S. assets on lines 2 through 5 below *(check one):*				
	☐ Adjusted basis method: Regs. sec. 1.882-5(b)(2)(i)				
	☐ Fair market value method: Regs. sec. 1.882-5(b)(2)(ii)				
2	Total assets per books	5,000,000			
3a	Total interbranch assets				
b	Total non-ECI assets under section 864(c)(4)(D)				
c	Total other non-ECI assets (attach statement-see instructions)				
d	Adjustments for amounts from partnerships and certain disregarded entities included on line 2, column (a) . .				
e	Adjustments for assets that give rise to direct interest expense allocations under Regs. sec. 1.882-5(a)(1)(ii) . .				
f	Other adjustments to average assets included in line 2 (e.g., mark-to-market differences)				
4	Combine lines 3a through 3f				
5	Total value of U.S. assets for the tax year	5,000,000			5,000,000

Column (a): Subtract line 4 from line 2.
Column (b): See instructions for amount to enter.
Column (c): See instructions for amount to enter.

Step 2 **U.S.-Connected Liabilities for the Tax Year: Regulations Section 1.882-5(c)**

6	Specify the method used to determine the amounts in Step 2 *(check one):*		
	☐ Actual ratio under Regs. sec. 1.882-5(c)(2). **Complete lines 6a through 6c below.**		
	☐ Fixed ratio under Regs. sec. 1.882-5(c)(4). **Complete line 6d below.**		
a	Average worldwide liabilities		
b	Average worldwide assets		
c	Divide line 6a by line 6b		%
d	Fixed ratio under Regs. sec. 1.882-5(c)(4). If the corporation is a foreign bank as defined in Regs. sec. 1.882-5(c)(4), enter 95% on line 6d. If the corporation is not a foreign bank or an insurance company, enter 50% on line 6d		50%
e	Enter the ratio from line 6c or 6d, as applicable		50 %
7a	U.S.-connected liabilities before Regs. sec. 1.884-1(e)(3) election(s). Multiply line 5, column (d) by line 6e		2,500,000
b	U.S. liability reduction under Regs. sec. 1.884-1(e)(3) election		
c	**U.S.-Connected Liabilities.** Subtract line 7b from line 7a . . . . ▶		2,500,000

Step 3 **Interest Expense Paid or Accrued on Average U.S. Booked Liabilities: Regulations Section 1.882-5(d)**

		(a) Set(s) of Books that Give Rise to U.S. Booked Liabilities (see inst.)	(b) Partnership Interests	(c) **Totals.** Add columns (a) and (b)
8	Total average amount of U.S. booked liabilities as defined in Regs. sec. 1.882-5(d)(2) (see instructions)	1,000,000		1,000,000

Column (a): Do not include amounts that give rise to directly allocable interest under Regs. sec. 1.882-5(a)(1)(ii) or from partnerships includible in column (b).
Column (b): Enter the portion of the total from Schedule P, line 18 that constitutes U.S. booked liabilities.

For Paperwork Reduction Act Notice, see the Instructions for Form 1120-F.   Cat. No. 49680W   Schedule I (Form 1120-F) 2014

Schedule I (Form 1120-F) 2014   Page **2**

Step 3 (cont.)	Interest Expense Paid or Accrued on Average U.S. Booked Liabilities: Regulations Section 1.882-5(d)		
	(a) Set(s) of Books that Give Rise to U.S. Booked Liabilities (see inst.)	**(b)** Partnership Interests	**(c)** Totals. Add columns (a) and (b)
9 Total interest paid or accrued during the tax year on line 8 amount	50,000		50,000

Column (a): Do not include amounts that give rise to directly allocable interest under Regs. sec. 1.882-5(a)(1)(ii) or from partnerships includible in column (b).
Column (b): Enter the portion of the total from Schedule P, line 15c that is interest on U.S. booked liabilities.

Step 3 (cont.)	Adjusted U.S. Booked Liabilities Method: Regulations Section 1.882-5(d)

If line 7c is greater than line 8, column (c), complete lines 10 through 13 below and skip lines 14a and 14b.
If line 7c is less than or equal to line 8, column (c), skip lines 10 through 13 and complete lines 14a and 14b.

10	If the corporation is a foreign bank which is making a current-year election to use the published average 30-day LIBOR (see instructions), check the box on this line, skip lines 10a through 10c, and enter the rate on line 10d ▶ ☐			
a	Total interest paid or accrued during the tax year on U.S. dollar liabilities that are **not** U.S. booked liabilities included on line 8	**10a**	200,000	
b	Average U.S. dollar denominated liabilities that are **not** U.S. booked liabilities included on line 8	**10b**	4,000,000	
c	Divide line 10a by line 10b	**10c**	5%	
d	Enter the 30-day LIBOR, if elected under Regs. sec. 1.882-5(d)(5)(ii)(B)	**10d**	%	
e	Enter the rate from line 10c or, if elected, the 30-day LIBOR on line 10d			**10e** 5 %
11	**Excess U.S.-connected liabilities.** Subtract line 8, column (c), from line 7c ▶			**11** 1,500,000
12	**Excess interest.** Multiply line 10e by line 11 ▶			**12** 75,000
13	Add lines 9, column (c) and 12			**13** 125,000
14a	**Scaling ratio.** Divide line 7c by line 8, column (c)			**14a** %
b	Multiply line 9, column (c) by line 14a. See instructions for hedging amounts			**14b**
15	**Interest expense allocable to ECI under the adjusted U.S. booked liabilities method.** Enter the result from line 13 or line 14b here and on line 21 ▶			**15** 125,000

Step 3 (cont.)	Separate Currency Pools Method: Regulations Section 1.882-5(e)			
	(a) U.S. Dollar Denominated	**(b)** Home Country Currency. Specify: ▶	**(c)** Other Currency. Specify: ▶	**(d)** Other Currency. Specify: ▶
16a **U.S. assets.** Enter the corporation's U.S. assets, using the methodology in Regs. sec. 1.882-5(e)(1)(i). If more columns are needed, attach statement (see instructions)				
b Check here if a less than 3% currency election was made ▶ ☐				
17a Enter the percentage from line 6e	%	%	%	%
b **U.S.-connected liabilities.** Multiply line 16a by line 17a, or, if a liability reduction election is made, see instructions				
18a Enter the total interest expense paid or accrued for the tax year with respect to the foreign corporation's worldwide liabilities denominated in that foreign currency (enter in functional currency)				
b Enter the corporation's average worldwide liabilities (whether interest bearing or not) denominated in that foreign currency (enter in functional currency)				
c **Borrowing rate:** Divide line 18a by line 18b	%	%	%	%
19 **Interest expense allocation by separate currency pool.** Multiply line 17b by line 18c				
20 **Interest expense allocable to ECI under the separate currency pools method.** Total the amounts on line 19, columns (a) through (d), and amounts from attached statement, if any, and enter the result here and on line 21				

Schedule I (Form 1120-F) 2014

SUMMARY—Interest Expense Allocation and Deduction under Regulations Section 1.882-5

21	Amount from line 15 or line 20, as applicable	**21**	125,000			
22	Enter the corporation's interest expense directly allocable under Regs. sec. 1.882-5(a)(1)(ii). (Include total from Schedule P, line 15b.)	**22**				
23	**Interest expense allocable to ECI under Regs. sec. 1.882-5.** Add lines 21 and 22 . . . . . . ▶			**23**	125,000	
24a	Amount of line 23 that is disallowed as a deduction under section 265, 163(f)(2), etc. or under an income tax treaty (attach statement—see instructions) . . .	**24a**	(	)		
b	Deferred interest expense under section 163(e)(3), 163(j), 267(a)(3), etc. (attach statement—see instructions)	**24b**				
c	Amount of line 23 that is capitalized under section 263A (attach statement—see instructions)	**24c**	(	)		
d	Combine lines 24a through 24c				**24d**		
25	**Total interest expense deduction under Regs. sec. 1.882-5.** Combine lines 23 and 24d and enter here and on Form 1120F, Section II, line 18. The amount entered on line 25 may not exceed the total interest expense paid or accrued by the foreign corporation . . . . ▶			**25**	125,000	

¶1005

SCHEDULES M-1 and M-2 (Form 1120-F) Department of the Treasury Internal Revenue Service	Reconciliation of Income (Loss) and Analysis of Unappropriated Retained Earnings per Books ▶ Information about Schedules M-1 and M-2 (Form 1120-F) and its instructions is at www.irs.gov/form1120f. ▶ Attach to Form 1120-F.	OMB No. 1545-0123 2014

Name of corporation	Employer identification number

Schedule M-1   Reconciliation of Income (Loss) per Books With Income per Return
Note. The corporation may be required to file Schedule M-3 (see instructions).

1	Net income (loss) per books	1,875,000	7	Income recorded on books this year not included on this return (itemize):	
2	Federal income tax per books		a	Tax-exempt interest $	
3	Excess of capital losses over capital gains		b	Other (itemize):	
4	Income subject to tax not recorded on books this year (itemize):				
			8	Deductions on this return not charged against book income this year (itemize):	
5	Expenses recorded on books this year not deducted on this return (itemize):		a	Depreciation . . $	
a	Depreciation . . . $		b	Charitable contributions $	
b	Charitable contributions $		c	Other (itemize):	
c	Travel and entertainment $				
d	Other (itemize):		9	Add lines 7 and 8	
6	Add lines 1 through 5	1,875,000	10	Income—line 6 less line 9	1,875,000

Schedule M-2   Analysis of Unappropriated Retained Earnings per Books

1	Balance at beginning of year	4,000,000	5	Distributions:	a	Cash	1,875,000
2	Net income (loss) per books	1,875,000			b	Stock	
3	Other increases (itemize):				c	Property . . .	
			6	Other decreases (itemize):			
			7	Add lines 5 and 6			
4	Add lines 1, 2, and 3	5,875,000	8	Balance at end of year (line 4 less line 7) .			4,000,000

What's New

Effective for tax years ending December 31, 2014 and later, foreign corporations that **(a)** are required to file a Schedule M-3 (Form 1120-F) and have less than $50 million in total assets at the end of the tax year or **(b)** are not required to file a Schedule M-3 (Form 1120-F) and voluntarily file a Schedule M-3 (Form 1120-F) must either **(1)** complete Schedule M-3 (Form 1120-F) entirely or **(2)** complete Schedule M-3 (Form 1120-F) through Part I and complete Schedule M-1 instead of completing Parts II and III of Schedule M-3 (Form 1120-F). If the foreign corporation chooses **(2)**, then Schedule M-1, line 1 must equal Schedule M-3 (Form 1120-F), Part I, line 11. See the Instructions for Schedule M-3 (Form 1120-F) for more information.

Who Must File

Generally, any foreign corporation that is required to complete Form 1120-F, Section II must complete Schedules M-1 and M-2 (Form 1120-F). However, under some circumstances, a foreign corporation is required to complete (or may voluntarily complete) Schedule M-3 (Form 1120-F) in lieu of Schedule M-1.

Complete Schedule M-3 in lieu of Schedule M-1 if total assets at the end of the tax year that are reportable on

Schedule L are $10 million or more. A corporation filing Form 1120-F that is not required to file Schedule M-3 may voluntarily file Schedule M-3 instead of Schedule M-1. See the Instructions for Schedule M-3 (Form 1120-F) for more information.

Note. If Schedule M-3 is completed in lieu of Schedule M-1, the corporation is still required to complete Schedule M-2.

Do not complete Schedules M-1, M-2, and M-3 if total assets at the end of the tax year (Schedule L, line 17, column (d)) are less than $25,000.

Specific Instructions

Schedule M-1

Line 1. Net income (loss) per books. The foreign corporation must report on line 1 of Schedule M-1 the net income (loss) per the set or sets of books taken into account on Schedule L.

Line 5c. Travel and entertainment expenses. Include any of the following:

• Meal and entertainment expenses not deductible under section 274(n).

• Expenses for the use of an entertainment facility.

• The part of business gifts over $25.

• Expenses of an individual over $2,000 that are allocable to conventions on cruise ships.

• Employee achievement awards over $400.

• The cost of entertainment tickets over face value (also subject to the 50% limit under section 274(n)).

• The cost of skyboxes over the face value of nonluxury box seat tickets.

• The part of luxury water travel expenses not deductible under section 274(m).

• Expenses for travel as a form of education.

• Other nondeductible travel and entertainment expenses.

Line 7a. Tax-exempt interest. Report any tax-exempt interest received or accrued, including any exempt-interest dividends received as a shareholder in a mutual fund or other regulated investment company. Also report this same amount in item P at the top of page 2 of Form 1120-F.

Schedule M-2

Line 1. Beginning balance of unappropriated retained earnings. Enter the beginning balance of unappropriated retained earnings per the set(s) of books taken into account on Schedule L.

Note. For additional information for Schedule M-2 reporting, see the Instructions for Schedule M-3 (Form 1120-F).

For Paperwork Reduction Act Notice, see the Instructions for Form 1120-F.   Cat. No. 49678K   Schedules M-1 and M-2 (Form 1120-F) 2014

Form **1125-A**		
(Rev. December 2012)	**Cost of Goods Sold**	OMB No. 1545-2225
Department of the Treasury Internal Revenue Service	▶ Attach to Form 1120, 1120-C, 1120-F, 1120S, 1065, or 1065-B. ▶ Information about Form 1125-A and its instructions is at *www.irs.gov/form1125a.*	

Name	Employer identification number
Kingman Private Limited Company	

1	Inventory at beginning of year	**1**	2,000,000	00
2	Purchases	**2**	16,000,000	00
3	Cost of labor	**3**		
4	Additional section 263A costs (attach schedule)	**4**		
5	Other costs (attach schedule)	**5**		
6	**Total.** Add lines 1 through 5	**6**	18,000,000	00
7	Inventory at end of year	**7**	2,000,000	00
8	**Cost of goods sold.** Subtract line 7 from line 6. Enter here and on Form 1120, page 1, line 2 or the appropriate line of your tax return (see instructions)	**8**	16,000,000	00

9a Check all methods used for valuing closing inventory:

    (i) ☑ Cost

    (ii) ☐ Lower of cost or market

    (iii) ☐ Other (Specify method used and attach explanation.) ▶ --

  b   Check if there was a writedown of subnormal goods . . . . ▶ ☐

  c   Check if the LIFO inventory method was adopted this tax year for any goods (if checked, attach Form 970) . . . . . . ▶ ☐

  d   If the LIFO inventory method was used for this tax year, enter amount of closing inventory computed under LIFO . . . . | **9d** |

  e   If property is produced or acquired for resale, do the rules of section 263A apply to the entity (see instructions)? . . ☐ Yes ☑ No

  f   Was there any change in determining quantities, cost, or valuations between opening and closing inventory? If "Yes," attach explanation . . . . ☐ Yes ☑ No

Section references are to the Internal Revenue Code unless otherwise noted.

General Instructions

Purpose of Form

Use Form 1125-A to calculate and deduct cost of goods sold for certain entities.

Who Must File

Filers of Form 1120, 1120-C, 1120-F, 1120S, 1065, or 1065-B, must complete and attach Form 1125-A if the applicable entity reports a deduction for cost of goods sold.

Inventories

Generally, inventories are required at the beginning and end of each tax year if the production, purchase, or sale of merchandise is an income-producing factor. See Regulations section 1.471-1. If inventories are required, you generally must use an accrual method of accounting for sales and purchases of inventory items.

Exception for certain taxpayers. If you are a qualifying taxpayer or a qualifying small business taxpayer (defined below), you can adopt or change your accounting method to account for inventoriable items in the same manner as materials and supplies that are not incidental.

Under this accounting method, inventory costs for raw materials purchased for use in producing finished goods and merchandise purchased for resale are deductible in the year the finished goods or merchandise are sold (but not before the year you paid for the raw materials or merchandise, if you are also using the cash method).

If you account for inventoriable items in the same manner as materials and supplies that are not incidental, you can currently deduct expenditures for direct labor and all indirect costs that would otherwise be included in inventory costs. See the instructions for lines 2 and 7.

For additional guidance on this method of accounting, see Pub. 538, Accounting Periods and Methods. For guidance on adopting or changing to this method of accounting, see Form 3115, Application for Change in Accounting Method, and its instructions.

Qualifying taxpayer. A qualifying taxpayer is a taxpayer that, (a) for each prior tax year ending after December 16, 1998, has average annual gross receipts of $1 million or less for the 3 prior tax years and (b) its business is not a tax shelter (as defined in section 448(d)(3)). See Rev. Proc. 2001-10, 2001-2 I.R.B. 272.

Qualifying small business taxpayer. A qualifying small business taxpayer is a taxpayer that, (a) for each prior tax year

ending on or after December 31, 2000, has average annual gross receipts of $10 million or less for the 3 prior tax years, (b) whose principal business activity is not an ineligible activity, and (c) whose business is not a tax shelter (as defined in section 448 (d)(3)). See Rev. Proc. 2002-28, 2002-18 I.R.B. 815.

Uniform capitalization rules. The uniform capitalization rules of section 263A generally require you to capitalize, or include in inventory, certain costs incurred in connection with the following.

• The production of real property and tangible personal property held in inventory or held for sale in the ordinary course of business.

• Real property or personal property (tangible and intangible) acquired for resale.

• The production of real property and tangible personal property by a corporation for use in its trade or business or in an activity engaged in for profit.

See the discussion on section 263A uniform capitalization rules in the instructions for your tax return before completing Form 1125-A. Also see Regulations sections 1.263A-1 through 1.263A-3. See Regulations section 1.263A-4 for rules for property produced in a farming business.

For Paperwork Reduction Act Notice, see instructions.   Cat. No. 55988R   Form **1125-A** (Rev. 12-2012)

11599767

Form **1125-E**	**Compensation of Officers**	OMB No. 1545-2225
(Rev. December 2013) Department of the Treasury Internal Revenue Service	▶ Attach to Form 1120, 1120-C, 1120-F, 1120-REIT, 1120-RIC, or 1120S. ▶ Information about Form 1125-E and its separate instructions is at *www.irs.gov/form1125e.*	

Name	Employer identification number
Kingman Private Limited Company	98-7654321

Note. Complete Form 1125-E only if total receipts are $500,000 or more. See instructions for definition of total receipts.

(a) Name of officer	(b) Social security number (see instructions)	(c) Percent of time devoted to business	Percent of stock owned		(f) Amount of compensation
			(d) Common	(e) Preferred	
1 Dave Kong	98-123-4567	50 %	0 %	0 %	500,000
		%	%	%	
		%	%	%	
		%	%	%	
		%	%	%	
		%	%	%	
		%	%	%	
		%	%	%	
		%	%	%	
		%	%	%	
		%	%	%	
		%	%	%	
		%	%	%	
		%	%	%	
		%	%	%	
		%	%	%	
		%	%	%	
		%	%	%	
		%	%	%	
		%	%	%	
		%	%	%	

2	Total compensation of officers	**2**	500,000
3	Compensation of officers claimed on Form 1125-A or elsewhere on return	**3**	0
4	Subtract line 3 from line 2. Enter the result here and on Form 1120, page 1, line 12 or the appropriate line of your tax return	**4**	500,000

For Paperwork Reduction Act Notice, see separate instructions.   Cat. No. 55989C   Form **1125-E** (Rev. 12-2013)

¶1005

Chapter 11
Planning for Foreign-Owned United States Operations

¶ 1101 INTRODUCTION

This chapter discusses general planning issues with respect to foreign-owned U.S. operations. More specific planning issues are discussed throughout this book. For example, Chapter 12 (¶ 1205) discusses transfer pricing strategies to reduce taxable income, Chapter 13 (¶ 1301) discusses the use of tax treaties to avoid double taxation, Chapter 9 (¶ 903) discusses exemptions from the U.S. withholding taxes on investment-type income, and Chapter 10 (¶ 1001) discusses the taxation of a U.S. trade or business.

¶ 1102 EVOLUTION OF A FOREIGN-OWNED U.S. BUSINESS

.01 Entering the United States

There is a natural progression of market penetration by a foreign company that wishes to sell its products in the United States. For example, a foreign company may initially import its products through independent brokers or distributors. Smaller foreign companies, in particular, may find it advantageous to use independent intermediaries to market their goods in the United States since they often lack expertise regarding local U.S. markets. There are costs to such an arrangement, however, including the need to share profits with the intermediary (either through commissions or reduced sales revenues), and the loss of control over the sales and distribution functions.

As the foreign company's sales volume grows and the foreign company becomes more familiar with marketing in the United States, the foreign company may wish to bring the U.S. marketing function in-house by having its foreign employees travel to the United States to identify customers, display inventory, negotiate sales agreements, and provide technical support. Alternatively, the foreign company could employ U.S. residents to perform those functions.

The next logical step in the progression of a foreign company's U.S. marketing activities is to establish a branch sales office in the United States. The activities of a branch sales office would include negotiating and closing sales agreements and distributing the foreign company's products. A United States presence often is required when importing services. For example, construction services usually require that foreign engineers and technicians travel to the United States in order to provide on-site management of the project.

Licensing and franchising are more indirect methods of entering the United States market. A foreign company that owns a patent, trademark, or other intangible property can license that intangible to a U.S. company. In return, the foreign company receives a percentage of the U.S. sales of the licensed or franchised product in the form of a royalty. In essence, licensing and franchising are types of joint venture arrangements that permit a foreign company to enter the United States quickly, but may not produce the same profit margins that are potentially available from more direct forms of importing. Moreover, the foreign company may lose some control over the quality and image of its product.

.02 Determinants of U.S. Taxation

A central tax issue for a foreign company is whether its activities in the United State are subject to U.S. taxation. Complying with the U.S. tax laws always involves administrative costs and, depending on how the foreign company's home country taxes its income, any U.S. taxes paid may represent an out-of-pocket tax cost. Whether a foreign company's activities are subject to U.S. taxation depends on several factors, including the precise nature of the foreign company's activities within the United States, the U.S. laws with respect to that trade or business, and the applicability of any income tax treaty between the foreign company's home country and the United States.

As a general rule, the United States asserts tax jurisdiction over all of the trade or business income derived from sources within its borders, regardless of the citizenship or residence of the person or entity receiving that income. However, most tax treaties contain a permanent establishment article, under which a foreign company's business profits are exempt from U.S. taxation unless those profits are attributable to a permanent establishment located within the United States.[1] A permanent establishment includes a fixed place of business (e.g. a sales office), unless the fixed place of business is used solely for auxiliary functions (e.g., purchasing, storing, displaying, or delivering inventory) or activities of a preparatory nature (e.g., collecting information about potential customers).[2] A permanent establishment also exists if employees or other dependent agents habitually exercise in the United States an authority to conclude sales contracts in the foreign company's name.[3] As a consequence, a foreign company that sends executives or salespeople to the United States to enter contracts may create a permanent establishment even if those employees operate out of hotels and do not have a fixed

---

[1] For example, *see* Article 7(1) (¶ 1304.07) of the U.S. Model Treaty.

[2] For example, *see* Article 5(1), (2), and (4) (¶ 1304.05) of the U.S. Model Treaty.

[3] For example, *see* Article 5(5) (¶ 1304.05) of the U.S. Model Treaty.

place of business. Employees who limit their activities to auxiliary or preparatory activities, such as collecting information about potential customers, with sales concluded in the foreign company's home country, will not create a permanent establishment. Marketing products in the United States solely through independent U.S. brokers or independent distributors also does not create a permanent establishment.[4]

¶ 1103 CHOICE OF ENTITY FOR U.S. OPERATIONS

A foreign company that engages in sales, service, or manufacturing activities in the United States can structure the U.S. operation as either a branch or a subsidiary. If a foreign company forms a limited liability company in the United States, under the U.S. entity classification regulations,[5] the foreign company will have to choose whether it will treat the limited liability company as a subsidiary or as a branch for U.S. tax purposes. The option of forming a domestic hybrid entity or a reverse domestic hybrid entity is also available.

.01 Branches

An unincorporated U.S. branch is simply an extension of the foreign corporation, as opposed to a separate legal entity. Assuming the branch constitutes a U.S. trade or business or a permanent establishment, the branch income will be subject to U.S. income taxation at graduated rates ranging from 15% to 35%.[6] The United States permits a foreign corporation to deduct against branch income all direct costs, such as the cost of goods sold by the branch, and indirect expenses, such as interest expense and home office overhead.[7] However, a U.S. branch cannot deduct payments made to its foreign parent corporation's headquarters office, such as management fees or royalties.

To better equate the tax treatment of U.S. branch and U.S. subsidiary operations, the United States imposes the following additional taxes on U.S. branches of foreign corporations:

(i) **Branch profits tax.** A U.S. branch's dividend equivalent amount is subject to tax at a 30% rate, subject to treaty reductions.[8]

(ii) **Branch interest withholding tax.** Interest paid by a U.S. branch is treated as if it were paid by a domestic corporation, which generally makes the interest U.S.-source income and potentially subject to U.S. withholding tax.[9]

(iii) **Tax on excess interest.** If the amount of interest expense deducted against effectively connected income exceeds the amount of interest paid by the branch for purposes of the branch interest withholding tax, the excess is subject to tax at a 30% rate, subject to treaty reductions.[10]

If the foreign corporation expects the U.S. branch to report losses in its first few years of operations, depending on the tax laws of the foreign corporation's

---

[4] For example, *see* Article 5(6) (¶ 1304.05) of the U.S. Model Treaty.

[5] Reg. § 301.7701-1 through -3.

[6] Code Sec. 11.

[7] Code Sec. 882(c).

[8] Code Sec. 884(a).

[9] Code Sec. 884(f)(1)(A).

[10] Code Sec. 884(f)(1)(B).

home country, the use of the branch form may permit the foreign corporation to deduct the U.S. losses against its other taxable income for purposes of computing the home country tax.

.02 Subsidiaries

A U.S. subsidiary is a corporation organized under the laws of one of the U.S. states or the District of Columbia. The United States taxes the worldwide income of domestic corporations at graduated rates ranging from 15% to 35%.[11] The U.S. subsidiary can deduct payments made to the foreign parent corporation for royalties and interest, which are generally subject to a U.S. withholding tax, and management fees, which do not incur a withholding tax as long as the management fees are for services performed outside the United States. The United States also generally imposes a withholding tax on dividends paid by a U.S. subsidiary to its foreign parent corporation.

The foreign parent corporation must avoid inadvertantly creating a permanent establishment of its own (or U.S. trade or business if there is not an applicable treaty), because that would result in the United States taxing any business profits of the foreign parent that are attributable to the inadvertant permanent establishment. For example, activities of the foreign parent's employees in the United States may inadvertently create a permanent establishment. This parent-level U.S. tax would be in addition to the U.S. taxes on the subsidiary. Consequently, it is important that all U.S. business activities be performed by the U.S. subsidiary, and that employees of the foreign parent not engage in selling or other activities at an office of the U.S. subsidiary.

An inadvertent permanent establishment may also result from the foreign parent corporation giving the contracting authority of an agent to its own employees operating in the United States.[12] Under the agency test, a dependent agent (e.g., an employee) of the foreign parent may constitute a permanent establishment if the dependent agent has the authority to contract on behalf of the foreign corporation in the United States and the agent habitually exercises that authority. Although the treaty does not define habitual exercise, the exercise of authority to negotiate and enter into contracts once or twice is probably habitual. The more the employee exercises this authority, the more likely the United States would deem it habitual.

In addition to avoiding an inadvertent permanent establishment, a foreign parent corporation should ensure that its U.S. subsidiary does not have any transfer pricing exposure.[13] Transfer pricing refers to the charges for controlled transactions, such as intercompany inventory sales, as well as intercompany licensing, services or financing arrangements (see Chapter 12). Transfer pricing receives substantial scrutiny from the IRS's International Examiners, who may impose additional tax and a 20% or 40% penalty if prices are not at arm's-length.[14] The best way to avoid transfer pricing adjustments by the IRS is to document the pricing practices as required by the regulations[15] or to enter into an advance pricing

---

[11] Code Sec. 11.

[12] For example, *see* Article 5(5) (¶ 1304.05) of the U.S. Model Treaty.

[13] Code Sec. 482; Reg. § 1.482-1 to -9.

[14] Code Sec. 6662.

[15] Reg. § 1.6662-6(d)(2)(iii).

¶1103.02

agreement.[16] In addition to protecting the U.S. subsidiary from a transfer pricing adjustment, foreign corporations should consider using transfer pricing as a tool for repatriating U.S. profits in a tax-efficient manner.

.03 Branch versus Subsidiary

The choice between the branch and subsidiary forms must take into account not only U.S. and foreign tax laws, but also general business considerations. There is no simple rule that dictates the best structure in all cases. Potential tax advantages of the subsidiary form include the following:

(i) The subsidiary form provides more control over the timing of income recognition of the secondary tax as withholding occurs when dividends are paid instead of the formulary approach of the Code Sec. 884 branch profits tax.

(ii) The sale of stock in a subsidiary is generally exempt from U.S. taxation.

(iii) The separate legal status of a subsidiary may make it easier to justify to the IRS the management fees and other intercompany charges paid to the foreign corporation.

Potential tax advantages of the branch form include the following:

(i) A foreign corporation may be able to deduct the losses of a U.S. branch against its other profits.

(ii) The transfer of assets to a branch is generally a nontaxable event.

Examples of general business factors that should be considered when choosing between the branch and the subsidiary form include:

(i) A subsidiary insulates the foreign corporation from legal liability issues in the United States. On the other hand, a foreign corporation may obtain limited liability with respect to its U.S. branch operation by structuring the branch as a limited liability company that is treated as a disregarded entity for U.S. tax purposes.

(ii) A subsidiary may present a better local image to potential U.S. customers and employees.

(iii) A subsidiary may make it easier to involve U.S. persons in the venture, since it can issue additional shares to those U.S. investors.

.04 Domestic Hybrid Entities

A domestic hybrid entity is a domestic legal entity (e.g., a limited liability company organized under U.S. law) that is treated as a disregarded entity or partnership for U.S. tax purposes, but a corporation for foreign tax purposes. With the exception of an entity that has per se corporate status (i.e., a business entity organized and referred to as a "corporation" under U.S. federal or state law), all U.S. business entities with at least two members can elect to be treated as a corporation or a partnership, and U.S. business entities with only a single member can elect to be treated as a corporation or a disregarded entity.[17] This regime is

---

[16] Rev. Proc. 2008-31, IRB 2008-23.

[17] Reg. § 301.7701-3(b)(1).

known as "check-the-box" because the entity's owner merely checks the box on a Form 8832 to classify the entity (a sample of a completed Form 8832 is attached to the Appendix to Chapter 8 (¶ 810). If an eligible entity fails to make an election, default rules treat the entity as a partnership if it has two or more owners and as a disregarded entity if it has only a single owner.[18]

Code Sec. 894(c) denies a foreign parent corporation the benefit of a reduced withholding tax rate under an income tax treaty with respect to certain U.S.-source investment-type income derived by the foreign corporation through a domestic hybrid entity.[19]

> **Example 11.1:** FORco is a country X corporation that owns 100% of USAco, a domestic corporation. FORco forms a U.S. limited liability company ("LLC") and contributes its USAco stock and cash to the LLC. The LLC is treated as a disregarded entity for U.S. tax purposes, but a corporation for country X tax purposes. The LLC lends the contributed cash to USAco. For U.S. tax purposes, the loan is treated as coming directly from FORco and USAco's interest payments to the LLC are treated as being made directly to FORco, which provides USAco with a U.S. tax deduction. For country X tax purposes, any payments that FORco receives from the LLC are treated as dividends which are exempt from tax. Absent Code Sec. 894, FORco's interest income would be eligible for a reduced U.S. withholding tax under the U.S.-country X tax treaty. Code Sec. 894 denies FORco the benefits of the treaty, however, in which case its interest income is subject to U.S. withholding tax at the statutory rate of 30%.

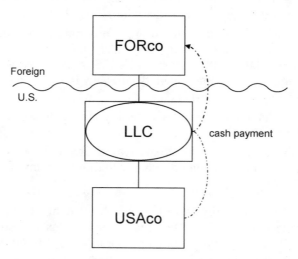

.05 Domestic Reverse Hybrid Entities

Domestic reverse hybrid entities are business entities that are treated as corporations for U.S. tax purposes, but as partnerships for foreign tax purposes. A

---

[18] Reg. § 301.7701-3(b).   [19] Reg. § 1.894-1.

domestic reverse hybrid entity is useful to a foreign corporation that wants pass-through treatment in its home country while avoiding any U.S. repatriation costs in the form of either a withholding tax or a branch tax. A popular form of domestic reverse hybrid entity is a U.S. limited partnership for which the foreign owner has filed a Form 8832 that checks-the-box for U.S. corporate tax status.

> **Example 11.2:** FORco operates in country F, where it currently incurs losses and anticipates continuing to incur losses in the near future. FORco considers the United States to be a potential market for its products, but wants to limit its liability in the United States. As a result, FORco forms a domestic reverse hybrid entity in the United States (USDRH), which is a corporation for U.S. tax purposes and a limited partnership for country F purposes. FORco can use the income that passes through its U.S. structure against its country F losses. As long as the domestic reverse hybrid entity does not distribute a dividend, neither a U.S. withholding tax nor a branch tax would apply.

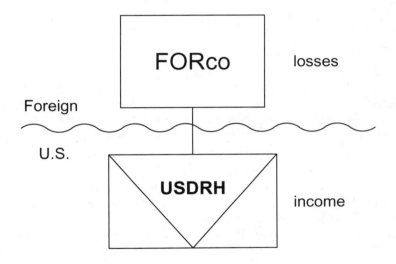

Domestic reverse hybrid entities have been a popular vehicle for "double dip" financing structures, whereby the interest is deductible against the income of both the U.S. subsidiary and the foreign parent.

> **Example 11.3:** FORco, a corporation incorporated in country F, operates in the United States through a U.S. subsidiary, USAco. FORco contributes its stock in USAco to a domestic reverse hybrid entity (USDRH), which is a partnership for country F tax purposes and a corporation for U.S. tax purposes. USDRH borrows money from a U.S. bank to which USDRH must pay interest. For U.S. tax purposes, USDRH and USAco file a consolidated return, which permits USDRH to deduct its interest expense against the operating income of USAco. A double dip occurs because the pass through nature of USDRH for country F tax purposes permits FORco to also deduct the interest expense on FORco's country F tax return.

¶1103.05

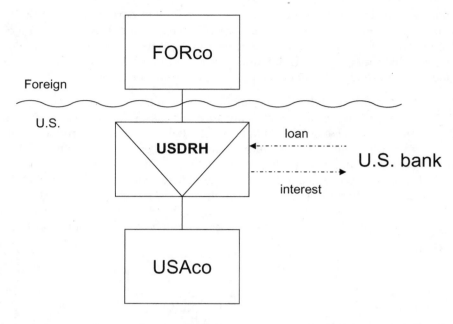

Due to the use of some abusive financing structures, the IRS has promulgated regulations under Code Sec. 894 that recharacterize an interest payment as a dividend when the domestic reverse hybrid makes a deductible payment to a related foreign owner for which a treaty reduces the withholding tax.[20]

Example 11.4: FORco, a corporation incorporated in country F, operates in the United States through a U.S. subsidiary, USAco. FORco contributes its stock in USAco to a domestic reverse hybrid entity (USDRH), which is a partnership for country F tax purposes, but a corporation for U.S. tax purposes. For U.S. tax purposes, FORco lends cash to the USDRH, which contributes the cash as equity to USAco. The treaty between the U.S. and country F exempts interest payments (but not dividends) from withholding tax. Because USDRH and USAco file a consolidated return in the United States, USDRH may deduct the interest expense against the operating income of USAco. Before the IRS issued the regulations, USDRH's interest payment to FORco was exempt from U.S. withholding tax under the treaty, while the interest income would not be reported in country F because it is an intracompany transaction. However, the IRS regulations recharacterize the interest payments in this example from interest to dividends, resulting in a withholding tax at the typically higher dividend rate.[21]

---

[20] Reg. § 1.894-1(d).   [21] Reg. § 1.894-1(d).

¶1103.05

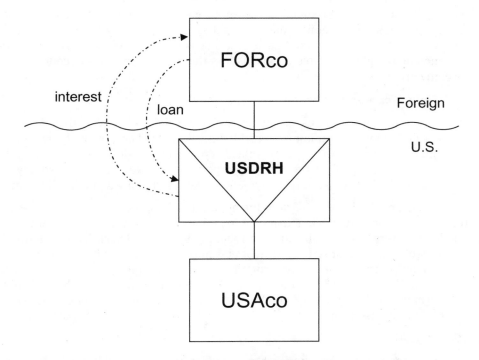

¶ 1104 BASICS OF INBOUND TAX PLANNING

Inbound tax planning involves the interplay of the tax laws of two or more countries. From a foreign corporation's perspective, the objective of inbound tax planning is to reduce the U.S. and foreign taxes on U.S.-source income. U.S. taxes increase a foreign corporation's total tax costs only to the extent they are not creditable for foreign tax purposes.

A major concern of foreign corporations operating in the United States is repatriation—sending money back to the foreign corporation at the lowest possible tax cost. The remainder of this section will focus on methods to repatriate funds.

.01 Dividends

Dividends are a common method of repatriating funds from a U.S. subsidiary to a foreign corporation. Unlike some other repatriation methods, dividends paid by the U.S. subsidiary are merely the distribution of its earnings and profits to the foreign corporation, and do not result in a deduction for the U.S. subsidiary. An advantage of a dividend is that many foreign countries use a territorial system that exempts from taxation the dividends received by a parent corporation from its subsidiaries in other countries, such as the United States.

The primary drawback of a dividend is the U.S. withholding tax. Although most tax treaties reduce the withholding rate on dividends to 15% or less, only a handful of treaties provide an exemption for dividends. If the foreign parent's home country uses a territorial system that exempts the dividend from taxation, the U.S.

withholding tax is non-creditable and represents an out-of-pocket cash cost. If the foreign parent's home country uses a credit system, generally the withholding tax still represents an out-of-pocket cash cost unless the effective U.S. tax rate (corporate income tax plus withholding tax) is less than the tax rate in the country of the foreign corporation.

.02 Debt Financing

It may be advantageous to finance a U.S. subsidiary in a way that maximizes interest deductions and minimizes dividend payments. The potential advantage of debt financing provided to a U.S. subsidiary includes a deduction in the United States for interest paid to the foreign corporation, as well as the possibility of a lower withholding tax on interest payments as opposed to dividend distributions.

To secure the benefits of debt financing, the foreign corporation must ensure that any intercompany payments meant to be interest qualify as such under the U.S. tax laws. There are no objective, bright-line tests for determining whether an investment in a U.S. subsidiary is debt and not equity.[22] In addition, Congress has enacted anti-earnings stripping provisions that may defer the interest expense deduction (see ¶ 1003).[23] To the extent that interest payments are limited by the anti-earnings stripping provisions, the taxpayer may wish to consider other methods of repatriating earnings that give rise to a deduction for the U.S. subsidiary.

.03 Royalties

A foreign corporation choosing to manufacture and/or sell in the United States often makes technology and other intangible assets available to its U.S. subsidiary. These intangibles include patents, copyrights, trademarks, trade names, unpatented know-how, etc. In return for benefiting from the use of the intangibles, the U.S. subsidiary agrees to pay royalties.

Royalties may be a tax efficient means of repatriating funds from a U.S. subsidiary for the use of intangibles. The deduction permitted to the paying U.S. subsidiary will help reduce the U.S. effective tax rate. Furthermore, royalty amounts can be substantial, particularly in light of the super-royalty provision in the last sentence of Section 482. Under this super-royalty provision, a payer of royalties must adjust the amount of royalties from time to time on the basis of the actual profit earned by the U.S. subsidiary and not just on the facts available at the time of the original transfer.

.04 Fees for Services

Foreign parent corporations often charge their U.S. subsidiaries fees for providing managerial, administrative or technical services. Service fees paid to a foreign corporation are typically not subject to U.S. withholding tax as long as the services are performed outside the United States. If the services are performed within the United States, the foreign corporation should be concerned that either (1) withholding should occur at a 30% rate[24] or (2) the foreign corporation will be

---

[22] *See,* for example, *NA General Partnership*, TC Memo. 2012-172, CCH Dec. 59,094(M).

[23] Code Sec. 163(j).

[24] Code Sec. 1442.

considered to be engaged in a U.S. trade or business or to have created a permanent establishment.[25]

The U.S. subsidiary's deduction for the service fees provides a U.S. tax benefit, and the payment of the fee may provide a convenient way for the foreign parent to repatriate its U.S. profits, possibly at a tax cost that is lower than the U.S. income tax savings. Service fees reduce the U.S. subsidiary's taxable income while increasing the foreign corporation's taxable income. Consequently, the service fees will reduce the group's worldwide effective tax rate if the foreign tax rate is lower than the U.S. tax rate.

To determine the amount of service fees the foreign corporation can charge its U.S. subsidiary, the foreign corporation should consider both the direct cost of providing the services and a reasonable allocation of the indirect costs (e.g., overhead). A central cost allocation agreement is a formal contract between the parties that establishes the fees for services to be performed. The challenge is to ensure that the charges for the services provided meet the arm's-length standard of transfer pricing.

.05 Transfer Pricing

With the exception of dividends, all of the above-mentioned repatriation techniques involve an element of transfer pricing. A foreign corporation may charge no more than an arm's length rate of interest on any loans to its U.S. subsidiary. The foreign corporation may shift income by charging its U.S. subsidiary a royalty for the use of foreign-owned manufacturing and marketing intangibles, but only if the royalty rate is an arm's length amount. In addition, any service fee must be at arm's length. Because transfer pricing is so ingrained in repatriation, transfer pricing is almost always raised by the IRS on audit. Therefore, it is imperative for taxpayers to establish defensible positions for the transfer prices charged through contemporaneous documentation of their transfer pricing methodology or through an advance pricing agreement.

By altering its transfer pricing policy, a foreign corporation may be able to allocate a smaller portion of its worldwide profits to its U.S. subsidiary. For example, a foreign corporation can allocate a smaller share of the gross profit from intercompany inventory sales by charging its U.S. subsidiary a higher price, as long as the higher price is within the arm's length range of acceptable transfer prices. The lower profit allocation provides a current U.S. tax benefit, and also limits future U.S. withholding taxes on dividend repatriations.

> ***Example 11.5:*** ASIAco is organized in a country that has a 16% corporate tax rate. ASIAco owns 100% of USAco, a domestic corporation that purchases gadgets from ASIAco for resale in the United States. The U.S. corporate tax rate is 35% and any dividends paid by USAco to ASIAco are subject to a 30% withholding tax, resulting in a total U.S. tax rate on repatriated profits of 54.5% [35% + (30% × {1 − 35%})]. Consequently, ASIAco and USAco can save 38.5 cents of tax on every dollar of income that can be shifted from USAco (54.5% tax rate) to ASIAco (16% tax rate) by increasing the transfer price for gadget sales.

---

[25] Code Sec. 882.

¶ 1105 COMPREHENSIVE EXAMPLE

FORco, a foreign corporation located in country F, plans to locate a new factory in the United States. FORco will structure the new facility as a wholly-owned U.S. subsidiary, USSub. FORco will finance USSub solely with an equity investment. FORco projects that in USSub's first year of operations, USSub will generate $10 million of taxable income, all from active U.S. manufacturing activities. In conducting this analysis, further assume the following:

(i) The U.S. corporate tax rate is 35%,

(ii) FORco's only item of income during the year is that derived from USSub, and

(iii) Country F generally taxes residents on their worldwide income, and allows residents to claim a credit for income taxes paid to other countries. However, country F provides an exemption for dividends received from subsidiaries that reside in other countries. Although country F offers a direct credit for income taxes paid in countries outside of foreign country F, a credit is not available for taxes paid to other countries related to dividends received from companies resident in other countries (either the underlying income taxes or any withholding taxes).

The total tax rate on USSub earnings will vary significantly, depending on a number of factors, including:

(i) Whether country F is a low-tax or high-tax foreign country,

(ii) Whether FORco repatriates USSub's earnings,

(iii) Whether FORco repatriates USSub's earnings through dividend distributions, as opposed to interest or royalty payments or higher transfer prices,

(iv) Whether a favorable tax treaty exists that reduces the withholding tax rates on dividends, interest, and royalties paid by USSub to FORco, and

(v) Whether FORco conducts its U.S. operations as a corporation, a domestic hybrid entity or a domestic reverse hybrid entity.

The effect of these factors is illustrated by computing the worldwide tax rate on USSub's earnings under a variety of assumptions.

Case 1: No dividends. If USSub does not pay any dividends, the total tax rate on its earnings is 35%, computed as follows:

U.S. income tax

USSub's taxable income	$10,000,000
U.S. income tax rate	× 35%
U.S. income tax	$3,500,000
U.S. withholding taxes on repatriated earnings	$0
F tax on repatriated earnings	$0
Total taxes [$3,500,000 + $0 + $0]	$3,500,000
Worldwide effective tax rate [$3,500,000 ÷ $10,000,000]	35%

This example illustrates that if USSub does not repatriate any of its earnings to FORco, the total tax rate on the U.S. operations will be the same as the U.S. corporate income tax rate. By not paying any dividends, the worldwide effective tax rate is 35% regardless of whether country F is a high-tax country (a corporate tax rate above the 35% U.S. corporate tax rate) or a low-tax country (a corporate tax rate below the 35% U.S. corporate tax rate).

Case 2: Pays dividend/Tax treaty. Assume that country F has a tax treaty with the United States that provides a 10% withholding tax rate on dividends. If FORco repatriates half of USSub's after-tax earnings through a dividend distribution, the total tax rate on USSub's repatriated and unrepatriated earnings is 38.25%, computed as follows:

U.S. income tax

USSub's taxable income	$10,000,000
U.S. income tax rate	× 35%
U.S. income tax	$3,500,000

U.S. withholding taxes on repatriated earnings

USSub's after-tax earnings [$10,000,000 – $3,500,000]	$6,500,000
Percentage repatriated through dividend	× 50%
Dividend distribution	$3,250,000
Withholding tax rate (per treaty)	× 10%
U.S. withholding tax	$325,000

F tax on repatriated earnings	$0
Total taxes [$3,500,000 + $325,000 + $0]	$3,825,000
Worldwide effective tax rate [$3,825,000 ÷ $10,000,000]	38.25%

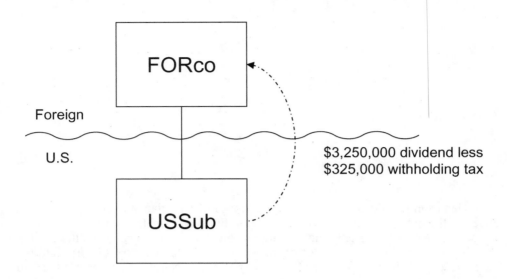

Therefore, by repatriating half of USSub's earnings through a dividend distribution, FORco increases the total tax rate on USSub's earnings from 35% in Case 1 to 38.25% in Case 2. The higher total tax rate is due to the 10% withholding tax. Country F does not tax the repatriated earnings due to its exemption for dividends.

Case 3: Pays dividend/No tax treaty. An important assumption in Case 2 is that country F had a tax treaty with the United States that provided for a 10% withholding tax rate on dividends. Now assume that there is no tax treaty between the United States and country F, in which case the U.S.'s statutory withholding rate on dividends of 30% applies. The lack of a favorable treaty withholding rate increases the total tax rate on USSub's repatriated and unrepatriated earnings from 38.25% in Case 2 to 44.75% in Case 3, computed as follows:

U.S. income tax

USSub's taxable income	$10,000,000
U.S. income tax rate	× 35%
U.S. income tax	$3,500,000

U.S. withholding taxes on repatriated earnings

USSub's after-tax earnings [$10,000,000 – $3,500,000]	$6,500,000
Percentage repatriated through dividend	× 50%
Dividend distribution	$3,250,000
Withholding tax rate (non-treaty)	× 30%
U.S. withholding tax	$975,000

F tax on repatriated earnings	$0
Total taxes [$3,500,000 + $975,000,000 + $0]	$4,475,000
Worldwide effective tax rate [$4,475,000 ÷ $10,000,000]	44.75%

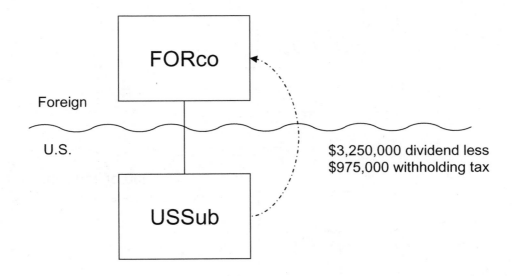

FORco

Foreign

U.S.

$3,250,000 dividend less
$975,000 withholding tax

USSub

Therefore, assuming FORco repatriates some of USSub's earnings through a dividend distribution, the availability of a favorable treaty withholding rate on dividends is critical to lowering the worldwide effective tax rate. As in Case 1 and Case 2, because country F does not tax dividends received from companies in other countries, the corporate tax rate in country F is irrelevant.

Case 4: Low-tax parent country/No dividends/Higher transfer price. Assume that USSub conducts a transfer pricing study and determines that it can increase its transfer price for goods and services paid to FORco by $3,250,000 (half of its previous after-tax income) and still remain within the arm's length range of acceptable transfer prices. Assume the country F corporate tax rate is 25%. The total tax rate on the U.S. earnings is 31.75%, computed as follows:

U.S. income tax

USSub's previous taxable income	$10,000,000
Additional cost of goods sold	– 3,250,000
USSub's taxable income	$6,750,000
U.S. income tax rate	× 35%
U.S. income tax	$2,362,500

U.S. withholding taxes on repatriated earnings $0

F tax on repatriated earnings

FORco's additional taxable income	$3,250,000
F tax rate	× 25%
F income tax	$812,500

Total taxes [$2,362,500 + $0 + $812,500] $3,175,000

Worldwide effective tax rate [$3,175,000 ÷ $10,000,000] 31.75%

¶1105

By repatriating $3,250,000 without a withholding tax, USSub has reduced the effective tax rate on the $3,250,000 of repatriated earnings from 35% (the U.S. rate) to 25% (the country F tax rate). When blended with the effective tax rate on the unrepatriated U.S. earnings taxed at the 35%, the worldwide effective tax rate decreases to 31.75%.

Case 5: High-tax parent country/No dividends/Higher transfer price. Again, assume that USSub conducts a transfer pricing study and determines that it can increase its transfer price for goods and services paid to FORco by $3,250,000 (half of its previous after-tax income) and still remain within the arm's length range of acceptable transfer prices. Assume the country F corporate tax rate is 45%. The total tax rate on the U.S. earnings is 38.25%, computed as follows:

U.S. income tax

USSub's previous taxable income	$10,000,000
Additional cost of goods sold	− 3,250,000
USSub's taxable income	$6,750,000
U.S. income tax rate	× 35%
	$2,362,500

U.S. withholding taxes on repatriated earnings $0

F tax on repatriated earnings

FORco's additional taxable income	$3,250,000
F tax rate	× 45%
F income tax	$1,462,500
Total taxes [$2,362,500 + $0 + $1,462,500]	$3,825,000
Worldwide effective tax rate [$3,825,000 ÷ $10,000,000]	38.25%

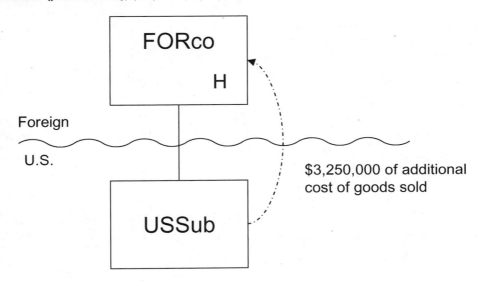

By using transfer pricing techniques to repatriate funds, USSub avoids U.S. withholding taxes on the repatriation of the $3,250,000. Although the change in transfer pricing policy will subject the $3,250,000 to the higher country F corporate tax rate, the lack of a withholding tax provides a worldwide effective tax rate of 38.25%, which is as low as paying dividends with a treaty (Case 2) and lower than paying dividends without a treaty (Case 3), but not as low as not repatriating (Case 1).

Case 6: Low-tax foreign parent/Earnings stripping/Tax treaty. A strategy for reducing the withholding taxes on USSub's earnings is to engage in earnings stripping, that is, to repatriate USSub's profits through deductible interest and royalty payments, rather than nondeductible dividend distributions. For example, assume that FORco, which pays tax at a 25% rate in country F, modifies its plans for USSub, as follows: (i) finance USSub with both debt and equity, such that USSub will pay FORco $2 million of interest each year, (ii) charge USSub an annual royalty of $1.25 million for the use of FORco's patents and trade secrets, and (iii) eliminate USSub's dividend distribution. Further assume that the applicable tax treaty withholding rate is zero percent for both interest and royalties.

As the following computations indicate, debt financing and charges for technology transfers totaling $3.25 million reduce the total effective tax rate on the earnings to 31.75%, computed as follows:

¶1105

U.S. income tax

USSub's income before interest and royalties	$10,000,000
Interest paid to FORco	– 2,000,000
Royalties paid to FORco	– 1,250,000
USSub's taxable income	$6,750,000
U.S. income tax rate	× 35%
U.S. income tax	$2,362,500

U.S. withholding taxes on repatriated earnings

Withholding tax on interest (per treaty)	$0
Withholding tax on royalties (per treaty)	0
U.S. Withholding taxes	$0

F tax on repatriated earnings

Interest from USSub	$2,000,000
Royalties from USSub	+ 1,250,000
FORco's taxable income	$3,250,000
F tax rate	× 25%
Pre-credit F tax	$812,500
F's credit	– 0
F's income tax	$812,500

Total taxes [$2,362,500 + $0 + $812,500] $3,175,000

Worldwide effective tax rate [$3,175,000 ÷ $10,000,000] 31.75%

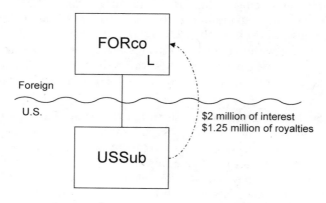

The 31.75% worldwide effective tax rate on the U.S. earnings is a blended rate, whereby the $3,250,000 of interest and royalties paid to FORco are, in effect, taxed at the country F rate of 25% and the unrepatriated U.S. earnings are taxed at the U.S. rate of 35%. This Case 6 has the same result as when FORco, a low-tax foreign parent, increases its transfer prices (Case 4), which are the two cases with the lowest worldwide effective tax rates of the cases in which FORco is in a low-tax country.

¶1105

Case 7: High-tax foreign parent/Earnings stripping/Tax treaty. Assume the same facts as in Case 6 (interest of $2 million and royalties of $1.25 million), except that country F is a high-tax country with a tax rate of 45%. As the following computations indicate, debt financing and charges for technology transfers result in a total tax rate on country F earnings to 38.25%, computed as follows:

U.S. income tax

USSub's income before interest and royalties	$10,000,000
Interest paid to FORco	– 2,000,000
Royalties paid to FORco	– 1,250,000
USSub's taxable income	$6,750,000
U.S. income tax rate	× 35%
U.S. income tax	$2,362,500

U.S. withholding taxes on repatriated earnings

Withholding tax on interest (per treaty)	$0
Withholding tax on royalties (per treaty)	0
U.S. Withholding taxes	$0

F tax on repatriated earnings

Interest from USSub	$2,000,000
Royalties from USSub	+ 1,250,000
FORco's taxable income	$3,250,000
F tax rate	× 45%
Pre-credit F tax	$1,462,500
F's credit	– 0
F's income tax	$1,462,500

Total taxes [$2,362,500 + $0 + $1,462,500]	$3,825,000
Worldwide effective tax rate [$3,825,000 ÷ $10,000,000]	38.25%

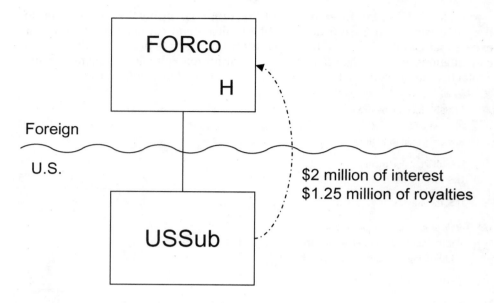

The 38.25% worldwide tax rate on USSub's earnings is a blended rate, whereby the $3,250,000 of interest and royalties paid to FORco are, in effect, taxed at the country F rate of 45% and the unrepatriated U.S. earnings are taxed at the U.S. rate of 35%. This is the same result as when FORco, a high-tax foreign parent, increases its transfer pricing (Case 5). These two cases result in the lowest worldwide effective tax rate (38.25%) of the cases in which FORco is in a high-tax country and repatriates from USSub.

Case 8: Low-tax foreign parent/No dividends/Domestic reverse hybrid. Assume country F has a 25% tax rate, and FORco operates in the United States through a limited partnership[26] that is treated as a corporation for U.S. tax purposes (i.e., a domestic reverse hybrid entity, or USDRH). USDRH does not pay any dividends. The total tax rate on USDRH's earnings is 35% computed as follows:

U.S. income tax

USDRH's taxable income	$10,000,000
U.S. income tax rate	× 35%
U.S. income tax	$3,500,000
U.S. withholding taxes on repatriated earnings	$0

---

[26] For this case and other cases involving partnerships, we will assume that FORco has formed a pass-through entity, such as an LLC, to be the other partner.

F tax on earnings

Earnings from USDRH	$10,000,000
F tax rate	× 25%
Pre-credit F tax	$2,500,000
F's credit (assume limited to country F tax on U.S.-source income)	− 2,500,000
F income tax	$0
Total taxes [$3,500,000 + $0 + $0]	$3,500,000
Worldwide effective tax rate [$3,500,000 ÷ $10,000,000]	35%

This example illustrates that regardless of whether the U.S. entity is a corporation under a state's corporate law or a domestic reverse hybrid entity, the worldwide effective tax rate remains 35% as long as (i) the U.S. entity does not distribute any dividends subject to withholding tax and (ii) the country F tax rate is less than the U.S. tax rate.

Case 9: Low-tax foreign parent/Pays dividend/Tax treaty/Domestic reverse hybrid. The facts are the same as in Case 8, except that USDRH distributes a $3,250,000 dividend that is subject to withholding tax at a 10% treaty rate. The dividend does not constitute income to FORco, but USDRH's $10 million of income is taxable to FORco. FORco may claim a credit for the U.S. income tax, but not the U.S. withholding tax. The total effective tax rate on the U.S. earnings is 38.25%, computed as follows:

U.S. income tax

USDRH's taxable income	$10,000,000
U.S. income tax rate	× 35%
U.S. income tax	$3,500,000

U.S. withholding taxes on repatriated earnings

USDRH's after-tax earnings [$10,000,000 − $3,500,000]	$6,500,000
Percentage repatriated through dividend	× 50%
Dividend distribution	$3,250,000
Withholding tax rate (per treaty)	× 10%
U.S. withholding tax	$325,000

¶1105

F tax on earnings

Earnings from USDRH	$10,000,000
F tax rate	× 25%
Pre-credit F tax	$2,500,000
F's credit	− 2,500,000
F income tax	$0

Total taxes [$3,500,000 + $325,000 + $0] $3,825,000

Worldwide effective tax rate [$3,825,000 ÷ $10,000,000] 38.25%

By creating a domestic reverse hybrid entity, FORco controls the timing of the U.S. withholding taxes on repatriated earnings at a treaty rate of 10%, but incurs a slight increase of the worldwide effective tax rate because the U.S. withholding taxes are not creditable.

Case 10: Domestic hybrid entity/Tax treaty. Assume FORco operates in the United States through a limited liability company, which is treated as a disregarded entity for U.S. tax purposes, but a corporation for country F tax purposes (i.e., a domestic hybrid entity, or USDH). USDH reinvests half of its earnings in the United States, and remits the other half to FORco. The remittance is subject to the U.S. branch profits tax, but is exempt from country F tax because country F does not tax dividends. The U.S. branch profits tax is not creditable for country F tax purposes. The total tax rate on the earnings is 38.25%, computed as follows:

U.S. income tax

USDH's taxable income	$10,000,000
U.S. income tax	× 35%
	$3,500,000

U.S. branch profits tax on dividend equivalent amount

USDH's after-tax earnings [$10,000,000 – $3,500,000]	$6,500,000
Percentage of earnings reinvested	× 50%
Increase in U.S. net equity	$3,250,000
Dividend equivalent amount [$6,500,000 - $3,250,000]	$3,250,000
Branch tax rate	× 10%
U.S. branch tax	$325,000

F tax on repatriated earnings	$0
Total taxes [$3,500,000 + $325,000 + $0]	$3,825,000
Worldwide effective tax rate [$3,825,000 ÷ $10,000,000]	38.25%

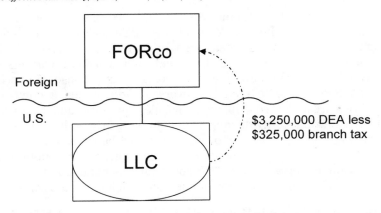

Because foreign country F does not tax the repatriated earnings of USDH, the total effective tax rate is not affected by whether country F is a low-tax or high-tax country.

TABLE 11.1. COMPREHENSIVE EXAMPLE—SUMMARY

Case	U.S.tax rate	Foreign tax rate	Amount repatriated	Repatriation method	Withholding tax rate	Effective tax rate
1	35%	n.a.	None	n.a.	n.a.	35.00%
2	35%	n.a.	$3,250,000	Dividend	10%	38.25%
3	35%	n.a.	$3,250,000	Dividend	30%	44.75%
4	35%	25%	$3,250,000	Transfer pricing	n.a.	31.75%
5	35%	45%	$3,250,000	Transfer pricing	n.a.	38.25%

Case	U.S. tax rate	Foreign tax rate	Amount repatriated	Repatriation method	Withholding tax rate	Effective tax rate
6	35%	25%	$3,250,000	Interest and royalties	0%	31.75%
7	35%	45%	$3,250,000	Interest and royalties	0%	38.25%
8 (DRH)	35%	25%	None	n.a.	n.a.	35.00%
9 (DRH)	35%	25%	$3,250,000	Dividend	10%	38.25%
10 (DH)	35%	n.a.	$3,250,000	Branch remittance	10%	38.25%

¶ 1106 SURVEY OF U.S. ENTITY CLASSIFICATION

This survey (Table 11.2) summarizes the U.S. tax classification of domestic business entities if a check-the-box election is not made, as well as which domestic business entities can elect to be treated as a hybrid entity or a reverse hybrid entity. General partnerships, limited partnerships, and limited liability partnerships are generally treated as pass-through entities for foreign tax purposes. Consequently, they offer the opportunity to be treated as reverse hybrid entities. In contrast, many foreign countries treat limited liability companies as corporations. As a result, limited liability companies offer the opportunity to be hybrid entities. An entity that is a "corporation" under U.S. federal or state law must be treated as a corporation for U.S. tax purposes. Therefore, they do not offer either hybrid entity or reverse hybrid entity planning opportunities. An S corporation is not option for inbound tax planning because a foreign person may not be a shareholder of an S corporation.[27]

TABLE 11.2. CLASSIFICATION OF U.S. BUSINESS ENTITIES

Entity	Status if no check-the-box election is made	Hybrid or reverse hybrid opportunity
Corporation	Corporation	n.a.
General partnership	Partnership	Reverse hybrid
Limited partnership	Partnership	Reverse hybrid
Limited liability partnership	Partnership	Reverse hybrid
Limited liability company	Disregarded entity or partnership	Hybrid or reverse hybrid

Note: A "hybrid entity" is a business entity that is treated as a disregarded entity or partnership for U.S. tax purposes, but a corporation for foreign tax purposes. A "reverse hybrid" is a business entity that is treated as corporation for U.S. tax purposes, but as a disregarded entity or a partnership for foreign tax purposes.

---

[27] Code Sec. 1361(b).

Chapter 12
Transfer Pricing

¶ 1201 WHAT IS TRANSFER PRICING?

The operating units of a multinational corporation usually engage in a variety of intercompany transactions. For example, a U.S. parent corporation may market its manufactured products abroad through foreign marketing subsidiaries. The same U.S. parent corporation also may provide managerial, technical, and administrative services for its subsidiaries. Another common arrangement is for a U.S. parent corporation to license its manufacturing and marketing intangibles to its foreign subsidiaries for commercial exploitation abroad. The U.S. parent corporation and its subsidiaries must determine a "transfer price" for these controlled transactions in order to satisfy various financial reporting, tax, and other regulatory requirements. Although transfer prices do not affect the combined income of a controlled group of corporations, they do affect how that income is allocated among the countries to which the group members belong.

> *Example* **12.1:** USAco, a U.S. corporation, manufactures engines for sale both in the United States and abroad. Foreign sales are made through FORco, a wholly-owned foreign corporation. On a per-unit basis, USAco's engines cost $600 to manufacture and sell abroad for $1,000. Regardless of the transfer price used for sales by USAco to FORco, the combined gross profit from a foreign sale is $400 per engine [$1,000 final sales price – $600 manufacturing cost]. However, transfer prices do affect the allocation of that combined profit between USAco and FORco.

At one extreme, a transfer price of $600 would allocate the combined gross profit of $400 entirely to FORco, as follows.

Transaction	Effect on USAco	Effect on FORco
Manufacture engine	Cost of goods sold = $600	
Controlled sale	Sales revenue = $600	Cost of goods sold = $600
Sale to foreign customer		Sales revenue = $1,000
	Gross profit = $0	Gross profit = $400

At the other extreme, a transfer price of $1,000 would allocate the combined gross profit of $400 entirely to USAco, as follows.

Transaction	Effect on USAco	Effect on FORco
Manufacture engine	Cost of goods sold = $600	
Controlled sale	Sales revenue = $1,000	Cost of sales = $1,000
Sale to foreign customer		Sales revenue = $1,000
	Gross profit = $400	Gross profit = $0

The arm's length price is somewhere between these two extremes. More specifically, multinational corporations must set a price to allocate their worldwide profits among the various countries in which they operate. The ideal allocation would permit each country to tax an appropriate portion of the taxpayer's total profit, while avoiding taxation of the same income by more than one country. The mechanism for allocating a multinational's worldwide profits between its U.S. and foreign affiliates is the transfer price used for intercompany transactions. When tax rates vary across countries, transfer pricing can significantly impact the taxpayer's total tax costs.

For example, a U.S. manufacturer may be able to reduce a foreign marketing subsidiary's share of worldwide profits by using higher prices for controlled inventory sales.

Example 12.2: The facts are the same as in the previous Example. Assume that the U.S. tax rate is 35%, the applicable foreign tax rate is 45%, and that operating expenses are negligable. Given the rate differential, the USAco group can reduce its worldwide taxes by using higher transfer prices for its outbound controlled sales. Assuming there are not any operating expenses, if a transfer price of $600 is used for a sale by USAco to FORco, the $400 gross profit is allocated entirely to FORco and the total tax equals the foreign tax of $180 [$400 of income × 45% foreign tax rate]. If, at the other extreme, a transfer price of $1,000 is used for the controlled sale, the $400 gross profit is allocated entirely to USAco and the total tax decreases to $140 [$400 of income × 35% U.S. tax rate].

Transfer pricing is also relevant for U.S. companies with operations in low-tax foreign jurisdictions. In these situations, a U.S. parent corporation has an incentive to shift income to its low-tax foreign subsidiary by, for example, using lower transfer prices for its outbound controlled sales. Although shifting income to a low-tax foreign subsidiary does not permanently avoid the residual U.S. tax on those low-taxed foreign earnings, shifting income does defer that tax until the foreign subsidiary repatriates those earnings through a dividend distribution.

Example **12.3:** The facts are the same as in the previous two Examples. Assume that the U.S. tax rate is 35%, the applicable foreign tax rate is 25%, and the operating expenses are negligible. Given this rate differential, the USAco group may reduce its worldwide taxes by using lower transfer prices for its controlled sale. Again assuming there are not any operating expenses, if a transfer price of $600 is used for a sale by USAco to FORco, the $400 gross profit is allocated entirely to FORco and the total tax equals $100 [$400 of income × 25% foreign tax rate]. If the related parties charge a transfer price of $1,000, the $400 gross profit is allocated entirely to USAco and the total tax increases to $140 [$400 of income × 35% U.S. tax rate].

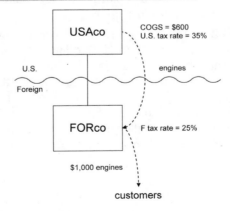

In the case of a foreign-owned U.S. corporation, transfer prices affect not only the amount of income reported by the U.S. subsidiary, but can also serve as a method by which the foreign parent company can repatriate cash without paying a dividend that would incur withholding taxes. This is particularly important for a foreign parent company that is a resident of a country that does not have an income tax treaty with the United States, in which case the dividend withholding tax rate is 30%.

Example 12.4: HKo is a trading company organized in Hong Kong, which has a corporate tax rate of only 16.5% and does not have a tax treaty with the United States. HKo's U.S. subsidiary, USDist, purchases widgets from HKo for resale in the United States. In addition to a 35% corporate-level U.S. tax, any dividends paid to HKo are also subject to a shareholder-level U.S. withholding tax of 30%. Therefore, the total effective U.S. tax rate on USDist's repatriated earnings to HKo is 54.5% [35% + 30% (1 – 35%)]. As a result, to the extent HKo can justify charging a higher transfer price on its widget sales to USDist, every dollar of income shifted from USDist (54.5% tax rate) to HKo (16.5% tax rate) results in a tax savings of 38¢.

Even if the U.S. corporate tax rate is lower than the foreign country's tax rate, the withholding tax on a dividend repatriation may make transfer pricing a cost-efficient method to repatriate to a foreign parent.

Example 12.5: ITALco is an Italian corporation wiht a U.S. subsidiary (USSub). ITALco sells gadgets to USSub for distribution to customers in the United States. The tax rate in Italy is 36%, the tax rate in the United States is 35%, and the withholding rate on the dividend under the Italian-U.S. tax Treaty is 5%. Therefore, the total effective U.S. tax rate on USSub's earnings repatriated as a dividend to ITALco is 38.25% [35% + 5%(1-35%)]. As a result, to the extent ITALco can justify a higher transfer price on its gadget sales to USSub, every dollar of income shifted from USSub (38.25%) to ITALco (36%) results in tax savings of 2.25%.

Multinational companies are often surprised by the large number of intercompany transactions that they must analyze. Even relatively simple scenarios for conducting cross-border business may result in numerous intercompany transactions.

***Example* 12.6:** CANco, a Canadian company, manufactures and sells widgets in the United States. Due to increased widget orders from U.S. customers, CANco decides to form a U.S. distribution subsidiary (USSub) to buy and resell widgets. Although USSub does not have any manufacturing functions, USSub employs its own administrative and sales staff while using CANco's proprietary distribution software. In an effort to ensure that USSub is financially solvent, USSub has payment terms on its trade receivables to CANco of six months (USSub's average collection period is one month). If USSub's customers do not pay, USSub enjoys the use of CANco's collection staff. Finally, USSub uses CANco's storage racks.

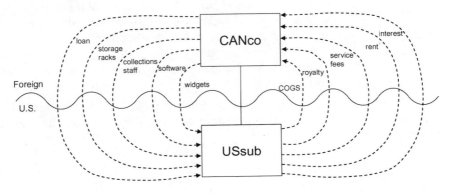

This inbound example illustrates <u>five intercompany transactions</u> for which USSub must pay CANco at arm's length. First, the purchase of widgets constitutes a <u>purchase of tangible property</u>. Second, the use of the proprietary distribution software constitutes a <u>transfer of intangible property</u> for which USSub must pay a royalty. Third, the generous payment terms constitute a <u>loan</u> on which USSub must pay an arm's length rate of interest. Fourth, the provision of the collection staff constitutes a <u>service</u> for which USSub must pay an arm's length amount. Fifth, for USSub's use of the storage racks, USAco must pay CANco an arm's length <u>rental</u> fee. An outbound example could pose five similar intercompany transactions.

¶ 1202 TRANSFER PRICING METHODS

.01 Basic Principles

The purpose of <u>Code Sec. 482</u> is to ensure that taxpayers report and pay tax on their <u>actual share of income arising from controlled transactions</u>.[1] To this end, the Regulations under Code Sec. 482 adopt an <u>arm's length standard</u> for evaluating the appropriateness of a transfer price. Under this standard, a taxpayer should realize a <u>similar amount of income from a controlled transaction as an uncontrolled party</u> would have realized from a similar transaction under similar circumstances.[2]

To arrive at an arm's length result, the taxpayer must select and apply the method that provides the <u>most reliable estimate of an arm's length price</u>.[3] Therefore, the primary focus in selecting a transfer pricing method is the <u>reliability of the result</u>, not its theoretical accuracy. The reliability of a pricing method is determined by the <u>degree of comparability between the controlled and uncontrolled transactions</u>, as well as the <u>quality of the data</u> and the <u>assumptions</u> used in the analysis.[4] The principal factors to consider in assessing the comparability of controlled and uncontrolled transactions include the following:[5]

- <u>Functions performed</u>—The functional analysis identifies and compares the <u>economically significant activities undertaken</u>. These activities would include, for example, <u>research and development, manufacturing or production, marketing and distribution, transportation and warehousing</u>, and administrative functions. From an economic perspective, the <u>related party performing more functions should receive more of the income</u>.[6]

- <u>Risks assumed</u>—This analysis requires a comparison of the <u>significant risks that could affect the prices to be charged</u>. For example, risk associated with the <u>success or failure of research and development, financial</u> (such as <u>fluctuations in foreign currency and interest rates</u>), <u>credit and collection, product liability, and market fluctuation</u>. From an economic perspective, the <u>related party assuming more risks should receive greater rewards</u>.[7]

- <u>Contractual terms</u>—Significant contractual terms could affect the economic analysis of two similarly-priced transactions. For example, the <u>quantity of</u>

---

[1] Reg. § 1.482-1(a)(1).
[2] Reg. § 1.482-1(b)(1).
[3] Reg. § 1.482-1(c)(1).
[4] Reg. § 1.482-1(c)(2).

[5] Reg. § 1.482-1(d)(1).
[6] Reg. § 1.482-1(d)(1)(i).
[7] Reg. § 1.482-1(d)(1)(iii).

the items purchased or sold, the form of the consideration (paid in U.S. dollars or foreign currency), the scope of any warranties, the rights to any updates or modifications, the duration of the contract, the extent of any collateral transactions between the parties, and the extension of any credit or payment terms may have an economic effect on the transaction. Ostensibly comparable transactions are often uncomparable after considering contractual terms.[8]

- Economic conditions and markets—This comparability factor focuses on the economic conditions that could affect the prices charged. This includes the similarity of geographic markets, the level of the market (e.g., wholesale or retail), the extent of competition in each market, the economic conditions of the particular industry, and the alternatives realistically available to either party (e.g., manufacture or purchase inventory). As with evaluating contract terms, seemingly comparable transactions are uncomparable after analyzing economic conditions and markets.[9]

- Nature of the property or services transferred in the transaction—As further discussed later in this chapter, the comparability of property sold or services provided is more relevant to the transaction-based methods than the profit-based methods.[10]

Example **12.7:** USAco, a U.S. subsidiary of ASIAco, a Japanese parent corporation, purchases televisions from ASIAco that USAco markets in the United States. If it were to use one of the transaction-based methods, USAco must compare prices charged for wholesale-level sales of televisions. However, if the taxpayer chooses a profit-based method, such as the comparable profits method, USAco must merely find companies comparable to itself with respect to the type of functions performed and risks assumed.

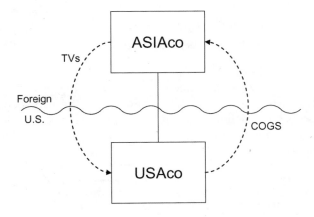

---

[8] Reg. § 1.482-1(d)(1)(ii).

[9] Reg. § 1.482-1(d)(1)(iv).

[10] Reg. § 1.482-1(d)(1)(v).

Related parties must adjust for any material differences between the controlled and uncontrolled transactions, assuming the effect of the differences can be ascertained with enough accuracy to improve the reliability of the results.[11]

As a practical matter, comparable transactions often are not readily available for the types of transactions entered into by affiliates of a vertically integrated multinational corporation. For example, inventory sales between affiliated companies often involve component parts and semifinished goods that are unique and are not sold in public markets. As a consequence, information about comparable transactions may not be available or appropriate.

The concept of an arm's length range permits a taxpayer to use two or more comparable uncontrolled transactions (of similar comparability and reliability) to establish an arm's length range of prices, which is the inter-quartile range of the companies. If the taxpayer's transfer prices lie within the arm's length range, the IRS will not make an adjustment.[12] If the taxpayer's transfer prices lie outside the arm's length range, then the IRS will make an adjustment, generally using the median of the range as the benchmark price.[13] Taxpayers also are allowed, under certain circumstances, to satisfy the arm's length requirement by showing that the average result for a multiple-year period is comparable to that of uncontrolled transactions for the same period (e.g., three years).[14] The use of multiple-year data helps reduce the effects of short-term variations in prices, such as the effects of an industry business cycle that are unrelated to transfer pricing.

.02 Transfers of Tangible Property

Introduction. A transfer of tangible property is the type of transaction traditionally considered when evaluating a company's transfer pricing practices. There are five specified methods for estimating an arm's length charge for transfers of tangible property:

    (i) the comparable uncontrolled price method,

    (ii) the resale price method,

    (iii) the cost plus method,

    (iv) the comparable profits method, and

    (v) the profit split method(s).[15]

The taxpayer must select and apply the method that provides the most reliable measure of an arm's length price.[16] In addition to the five specified methods, the taxpayer also has the option of using an unspecified method. However, a taxpayer can use an unspecified method only if it provides the most reliable estimate of an arm's length price.[17]

---

[11] Reg. § 1.482-1(d)(2).

[12] Reg. § 1.482-1(e)(1) and (e)(2)(i). All comparable uncontrolled transactions are included in the range if adjustments can be made for all of the material differences between the controlled and uncontrolled transactions. If adjustments cannot be made for all material differences, then the range is limited by statistical techniques, such as restricting the range to those comparable uncontrolled transactions which fall within the 25th and 75th percentiles of the range. Reg. § 1.482-1(e)(2)(iii).

[13] Reg. § 1.482-1(e)(3).

[14] Reg. § 1.482-1(f)(2)(iii).

[15] Reg. § 1.482-3(a).

[16] Reg. § 1.482-1(c)(1).

[17] Reg. § 1.482-3(e)(1).

When the transfer involves tangible property with embedded intangibles, such as a controlled sale of inventory where the related seller attaches its trademark to the goods, a separate arm's length charge for the intangible is unnecessary if the purchaser does not acquire the right to exploit the intangible other than in connection with the resale of the property. As with the use of a method for intangibles, the embedded intangible must be taken into account for purposes of determining the arm's length price for the sale of the related tangible property.[18]

> **Example 12.8:** CANco sells hockey pucks to USSub for distribution in the United States. Each puck contains the valuable "CANco" brand name. As long as USSub cannot exploit the "CANco" brand name (e.g., placing the brand name on other products), the "CANco" brand name is an embedded intangible. Therefore, the brand name may increase the price that USSub may pay CANco for the pucks, but USSub does not have to pay a royalty.

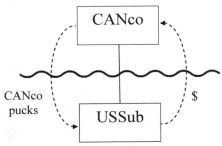

The first three methods are transaction-based methods, which focus on the comparability of products, contractual terms, and economic conditions.

Comparable uncontrolled price method. Under the comparable uncontrolled price (CUP) method, the arm's length price is the price charged for comparable goods in transactions between uncontrolled parties, adjusted for any material differences that exist between the controlled and uncontrolled transactions.[19] The CUP method ordinarily is the most reliable method for estimating an arm's length price if there are only minor differences (e.g., contractual terms) between the controlled and uncontrolled transactions for which appropriate adjustments can be made.[20]

> **Example 12.9:** USAco, a U.S. corporation, owns 100% of MEXSub, a Mexican corporation. USAco manufactures telecommunications equipment at a cost of $500 per unit and sells the equipment to an unrelated foreign distributor at a price of $750 per unit. USAco also sells the equipment to MEXSub, which then resells the goods to unrelated foreign customers for $850 each. The conditions of USAco's sales to MEXSub are substantially equivalent to those of the sales made to unrelated foreign distributors. Because information is available regarding comparable uncontrolled sales, USAco and MEXSub should use the CUP method. Under the CUP method, the arm's length price is $750.

---

[18] Reg. § 1.482-3(f).
[19] Reg. § 1.482-3(b)(1) and (b)(2)(ii)(B).
[20] Reg. § 1.482-3(b)(2)(ii)(A).

In assessing the comparability of controlled and uncontrolled sales for purposes of the CUP method, the most important factor is product similarity. Other significant factors include the similarity of contractual terms and economic conditions.[21] Because contractual terms and economic conditions often vary, the CUP method is usually difficult to apply in practice.

Example 12.10: USAco, a U.S. corporation, owns 100% of MEXSub, a Mexican corporation. USAco manufactures telecommunications equipment at a cost of $500 per unit and sells the equipment to an unrelated foreign distributor at a price of $750 per unit. USAco also sells the equipment to MEXSub, which then resells the goods to unrelated foreign customers for $850 each. However, MEXSub purchases only 20 units of equipment while the unrelated foreign distributor purchases 100 units. Moreover, the units MEXSub purchases have the valuable "USAco" brand name stamped on the equipment while the units the unrelated foreign distributor purchases are unbranded. Finally, USAco provides a three-year warranty on the equipment sold to MEXSub, but does not provide any warranty on the equipment sold to the unrelated foreign distributor. Any of the three differences - volume, branding, or warranties - could be a material difference that renders the CUP method inapplicable. As a result, MEXSub should pay more than $750 a unit.

---

[21] Reg. § 1.482-3 (b) (2) (ii) (A).

Resale price method. The type of transaction envisioned by the resale price method is a controlled sale of finished goods followed by the related distributor's resale of the goods to unrelated customers.[22] Under this method, the arm's length price is the resale price charged by the related distributor, reduced by the arm's length gross profit margin for such resales and adjusted for any material differences that exist between the controlled and uncontrolled transactions. The gross profit margin realized by either the independent distributors or the related distributor on similar uncontrolled sales provides an estimate of the arm's length gross profit, which is expressed as a percentage of the resale price.[23]

Example 12.11: USAco, a U.S. corporation, owns 100% of CANco, a Canadian corporation. USAco manufactures medical equipment at a cost of $1,000 per unit and sells the equipment to CANco, which resells the goods (without any further processing) to unrelated foreign customers for $1,500 each. Independent foreign distributors typically earn returns of 10% (expressed as a percentage of the resale price) on the purchase and resale of products comparable to those produced by USAco. Under the resale price method, the arm's length price is $1,350 [$1,500 – (10% × $1,500)].

---

[22] Reg. § 1.482-3(c)(1).   [23] Reg. § 1.482-3(c)(2) and (c)(3)(ii)(C).

Resale price = $1,500

CANco   Unrelated customers

Transfer price = ?

USAco

Cost = $1,000

As with the CUP method, when assessing the comparability of controlled and uncontrolled transactions for purposes of the resale price method, the parties should focus on contractual terms and economic conditions (see Example 12.10) as well as the ability to obtain reliable information.[24] Consistency between the accounting methods used to compute the gross profit for the controlled and uncontrolled transactions is also important.[25]

Cost plus method. The type of controlled transaction envisioned by the cost plus method is the manufacture, assembly, or other production of goods that are sold to related parties.[26] Under the cost plus method, the arm's length price is the manufacturing cost incurred by the related manufacturer, increased by the arm's length gross profit markup for such manufacturers and adjusted for any material differences that exist between the controlled and uncontrolled transactions. The gross profit realized by either independent manufacturers or the related manufacturer on similar uncontrolled sales provides an estimate of the arm's length gross profit markup, which is expressed as a percentage of the manufacturing costs.[27]

Example **12.12:** USAco, a domestic corporation, owns 100% of FORco, a foreign corporation. FORco manufactures power tools at a cost of $60 each and sells them to USAco. USAco attaches its trade name to the power tools (which has a significant effect on their resale price) and resells them to unrelated customers in the United States for $100 each. Independent foreign manufacturers producing similar power tools typically earn a gross profit markup of 20%. Under the cost plus method, the arm's length price is $72 [$60 + (20% × $60)].

---

[24] Reg. § 1.482-3(c)(3)(ii)(A) and (B).
[25] Reg. § 1.482-3(c)(3)(iii)(B).

[26] Reg. § 1.482-3(d)(1).
[27] Reg. § 1.482-3(d)(2) and (d)(3)(ii)(C).

As with the CUP and the resale price methods, when assessing the comparability of controlled and uncontrolled transactions for purposes of the cost plus method, the parties should focus on contractual terms and economic conditions (see Example 12.10) as well as the ability to obtain reliable information.[28] Consistency between the accounting methods used to compute the markup for the controlled and uncontrolled transactions is also important.[29]

The last two methods are profit based methods, which focus on the functions performed and the risks assumed.

Comparable profits method. The comparable profits method looks to the profits of uncontrolled entities, rather than the prices used in uncontrolled transactions, to determine an arm's length allocation of profit between two related corporations. Under this method, the profitability of comparable companies is used as a benchmark for determining an arm's length profit for one of the controlled parties (the "tested party") and then a transfer price is established that leaves the tested party with that amount of profit.[30]

The methodology for developing an arm's length profit involves the following seven steps:

(1) *Determine the tested party*—The tested party should be the participant in the controlled transaction for which the most reliable data regarding comparable companies can be located. This is likely to be the least complex of the controlled parties—the controlled party that does not own valuable intangible property or unique assets that distinguish it from potential uncontrolled comparable companies.[31]

---

[28] Reg. § 1.482-3(d)(3)(ii)(A) and (B).
[29] Reg. § 1.482-3(d)(3)(iii)(B).

[30] Reg. § 1.482-5(b)(1).
[31] Reg. § 1.482-5(b)(2)(i).

(2) *Search for comparable companies and obtain their financial data*—The key factors in assessing the comparability of the tested party to comparable companies are the functions performed, risks assumed, and resources employed (e.g., assets used).[32] Another important factor is the consistency between the accounting methods used by the tested and comparable companies to compute their operating profits.[33] Taxpayers must adjust for any differences between the tested party and the comparable companies that would materially affect the profitability measures used.[34]

(3) *Select a profit level indicator (PLI)*—Examples of PLIs that taxpayers can use include the ratio of operating profit to operating assets, the ratio of operating profit to sales, and the ratio of gross profit to operating expenses (also known as the "Berry Ratio"). To enhance the reliability of a PLI, the taxpayer should perform a multiple-year analysis which generally should encompass at least the taxable year under review and the two preceding years.[35]

(4) *Develop an arm's length range of PLIs*—The arm's length range of PLIs is the interquartile range (the middle 50%) of the PLIs of the comparable companies. The interquartile range is the range from the 25% to 75% percentile.[36]

(5) *Develop an arm's length range of comparable operating profits*—To construct an arm's length range of comparable operating profits, the selected PLI (e.g., the ratio of operating profits to operating assets) for the comparable companies in the arm's length range is applied to the tested party's most narrowly identifiable business activity for which data incorporating the controlled transaction is available (e.g., the operating income from the sale of inventory).[37]

(6) *Determine if an adjustment must be made*—An adjustment is required if the tested party's reported profit lies outside the arm's length range of comparable operating profits developed in step 5.[38]

(7) *Adjust the transfer price used for the controlled transaction*— If the tested party's reported profit lies outside the arm's length range, an adjustment is made equal to the difference between the tested party's reported profit and the benchmark arm's length profit.[39] All adjustment by the IRS would be to the mean or the median of the arm's length range of comparable operating profits.[40]

---

[32] Reg. § 1.482-5(c)(2)(ii).

[33] Reg. § 1.482-5(c)(3)(ii).

[34] Reg. § 1.482-5(c)(2)(iv).

[35] Reg. § 1.482-5(b)(4). However, any required adjustments are made on a year-by-year basis. Reg. § 1.482-5(e), Example 2.

[36] Reg. § 1.482-1(e)(2)(iii)(C). If, for example, there are eight comparable companies, the range is from an average between the second and third lowest to an average of the sixth and seventh lowest. If the number of compara-

ble companies is not divisible by four, the 25th percentile is the PLI for the lowest comparable company that at least 25% of the PLIs for the comparable companies are at or below. The 75th percentile is the PLI for the lowest comparable company that at least 75% of the PLIs for the comparable companies are at or below.

[37] Reg. § 1.482-5(b)(1).

[38] Reg. § 1.482-5(b)(1).

[39] Reg. § 1.482-5(b)(1).

[40] Reg. § 1.482-1(e)(3).

¶1202.02

***Example* 12.13:** [41] EURco, a foreign corporation, owns 100% of USAco, a U.S. corporation. EURco manufactures consumer products for worldwide distribution. USAco imports EURco's finished goods for resale in the United States.

USAco's average financial results for the last three years are as follows:

Sales	$50 million
Cost of goods sold	($40 million)
Operating expenses	($ 9 million)
Operating profit	$ 1 million

USAco is selected as the tested party because it engages in activities that are less complex than those of EURco. An analysis of seven comparable uncontrolled U.S. distributors indicates that the ratio of operating profits to sales is the most appropriate PLI. After adjustments have been made to account for material differences between USAco and the uncontrolled distributors, the average ratio of operating profit to sales for each uncontrolled distributor is as follows: 3%, 4%, 4.5%, 5%, 5%, 6%, and 7%.

The arm's length range of PLIs is from 4% to 6% (the interquartile range includes the PLI for the comparable companies at which 25% and 75% of the PLIs for the comparable companies are at or below) with the median PLI of 5%. The PLI of operating profits to sales for USAco is only 2% ($1 million of operating profits ÷ $50 million of sales), which is below the low part of the range. Applying these percentages to USAco's sales of $50 million yields an arm's length range of comparable operating profits of $2 million to $3 million with a median income of $2.5 million.

---

[41] This example is based on Reg. § 1.482-5(e), Example 2.

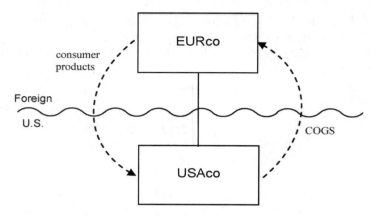

Because USAco's reported operating profit of $1 million lies below the arm's length range, an adjustment is required. The median of the interquartile range of comparable operating profits (i.e., $2.5 million) is determined to be the arm's length profit for USAco. Therefore, the IRS could reduce the transfer price that USAco pays EURco for its inventory by $1.5 million, which equals the difference between USAco's reported profit of $1 million and the arm's length profit of $2.5 million. This adjustment increases USAco's taxable income by $1.5 million per year.

Profit split method(s). The profit split method(s) evaluate whether the allocation of the combined operating profit attributable to a controlled transaction is arm's length by reference to the relative value of each controlled taxpayer's contribution to that combined profit.[42] The relative value of each controlled taxpayer's contribution is determined using either the comparable profit split method or the residual profit split method.

Under the comparable profit split method, the allocation of the combined operating profit between two controlled taxpayers is based on how uncontrolled taxpayers engaged in similar activities under similar circumstances allocate their joint profits.[43] However, the challenge of finding two companies that are functionally comparable to each of the two related parties and the challenge of obtaining from the two comparable companies the financial information regarding the transaction in issue render this method difficult to apply.

Under the residual profit split method, the related parties must determine a return for the routine activities each performs. Routine activities ordinarily include contributions of tangible property and services. After allocating profit based on the return for the routine activities each performs, the two parties split the residual profit on the basis of the relative value of the intangible property contributed by each party.[44]

> *Example* 12.14: FORco, a foreign corporation, manufactures liquid soap, using its proprietary manufacturing intangibles that have a fair market value of

---

[42] Reg. § 1.482-6(a).
[43] Reg. § 1.482-6(c)(2).

[44] Reg. § 1.482-6(c)(3).

$3 million. FORco sells the liquid soap to its USSub, which, due to an extensive advertising campaign, owns marketing intangibles with a fair market value of $1 million. Accordingly, FORco owns 75% of the group's intangibles and USSub owns 25% of the group's intangibles. Before paying FORco, USSub earns a return on sales of 20%.

An economist determines that a routine manufacturer (without any manufacturing intangibles) would earn a return on sales of 7% and that a routine distributor (without any marketing intangibles) would earn a return on sales of 5%. After allocating these routine returns totaling 12% to each party, the residual of 8% is split based on the relative value of the intangibles with 6% (75% of the 8%) going to FORco and 2% (25% of the 8%) going to USSub. Therefore, USSub must pay FORco an amount so that USSub earns only a return on sales of 7% (5% for routine distribution functions and 2% for its marketing intangibles).

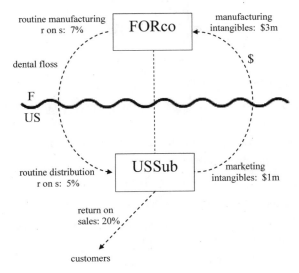

Ceiling on transfer price for imported goods. There is a statutory ceiling on the transfer prices used for property imported into the United States. Examples of such transactions include a U.S. parent corporation purchasing goods from a foreign manufacturing subsidiary or a U.S. marketing subsidiary purchasing goods from its foreign parent corporation. In these cases, the transfer price used by the controlled purchaser for income tax purposes (which becomes the controlled purchaser's cost basis for computing the gain on resale) cannot exceed the value amount taken into account for purposes of determining custom duties.[45] This ceiling is designed to prevent taxpayers from simultaneously avoiding U.S. custom duties by using a low transfer price for customs purposes and avoiding U.S. income taxes by using a high price for income tax purposes.

---

[45] Code Sec. 1059A.

Example 12.15: HKo, a Hong Kong corporation, owns 100% of USDist, a U.S. corporation. USDist imports widgets that HKo procures in Asia. For customs purposes, USDist declares a value per widget of $100. As a result, even if USDist determines that the arm's length price of a widget is $120, USDist cannot deduct a cost of goods sold for transfer pricing purposes of more than $100 per widget.

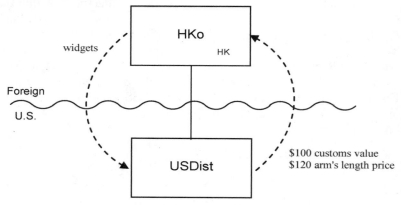

.03 Transfers of Intangible Property

Introduction. For transfer pricing purposes, an "intangible" includes any of the following items:

   (i) patents, inventions, formulae, processes, designs, patterns, or know-how,

  (ii) copyrights and literary, musical, or artistic compositions,

 (iii) trademarks, trade names, or brand names,

 (iv) franchises, licenses, or contracts,

  (v) methods, programs, systems, procedures, campaigns, surveys, studies, forecasts, estimates, customer lists, or technical data, and

 (vi) other similar items.[46]

However, as a practical matter, many economists classify intangibles by whether they are product intangibles, manufacturing intangibles, or marketing intangibles.

Determining the ownership of the intangible is critical to understanding whether there is a transfer of intangible property. The owner of an intangible for tax purposes ordinarily is the taxpayer who owns the legally protected rights (by registration or contract) to exploit that intangible in a jurisdiction as long as those rights are consistent with the economic substance of the transaction.[47] However, if the rights are either not legally protected or are inconsistent with the substance of the transaction, the sole consideration in determining ownership for tax purposes is the relative control over the intangible, which is a facts and circumstances test.[48]

---

[46] Reg. § 1.482-4(b).

[47] Reg. § 1.482-4(f)(3)(i).

[48] Reg. § 1.482-4(f)(3)(i)(A). If any other controlled party contributed to the development of the intangible,

There are three specified methods for estimating an arm's length charge for transfers of intangibles:

    (i) the comparable uncontrolled transaction method,

    (ii) the comparable profits method, and

    (iii) the profit split method(s).[49]

The taxpayer must select and apply the method which provides the most reliable estimate of an arm's length price.[50] In addition to using the three specified methods, the taxpayer can use an unspecified method only if it provides the most reliable measure of an arm's length price.[51]

Comparable uncontrolled transaction method. The comparable uncontrolled transaction (CUT) method is analogous to the comparable uncontrolled price method used for transfers of tangible property. Therefore, under the CUT method, the arm's length charge for the transfer of an intangible is the amount charged for the same or comparable intangibles in transactions between uncontrolled parties, adjusted for any material differences that exist between the controlled and uncontrolled transactions.[52] In order for the intangibles involved in the uncontrolled transaction to be considered comparable to the intangible involved in the controlled transaction, both intangibles must be used in connection with similar products or processes within the same general industry or market and must have similar profit potential.[53] The CUT method ordinarily is the most reliable method for estimating an arm's length price if there are only minor differences between the controlled and uncontrolled transactions for which reasonably ascertainable adjustments can be made.[54] Because information regarding comparable uncontrolled transactions is usually not available regarding intangible assets such as patents and trademarks, taxpayers often have difficulty applying the CUT method.[55]

    Example **12.16:** USAco, a domestic corporation, is a pharmaceutical company that develops a new drug. USAco licenses the formula to an unrelated pharmaceutical company in California for a royalty of 10% of sales. USAco also licenses the formula to its Canadian production and marketing subsidiary (CANco). If all the comparability factors between the two licenses are identical, CANco should pay USAco a royalty of 10% of sales under the CUT method. However, if the two licenses are not comparable in a manner for which the parties cannot make reasonably ascertainable adjustments, the 10% return on sales royalty is not a comparable uncontrolled transaction.

(Footnote Continued)

the owner must allocate an arm's length compensation to that party. Reg. § 1.482-4(f)(4)(i).

[49] Reg. § 1.482-4(a).

[50] Reg. § 1.482-1(c)(1).

[51] Reg. § 1.482-4(d)(1).

[52] Reg. § 1.482-4(c)(1).

[53] Reg. § 1.482-4(c)(2)(iii)(B)(1).

[54] Reg. § 1.482-4(c)(2)(ii).

[55] *See Veritas Software Corp.*, 133 TC 297 (2009), for an example of the use of the comparable uncontrolled transaction method.

Comparable profits method. The same comparable profits method used to determine arm's length prices for transfers of tangible property also can be used to determine arm's length royalty rates for transfers of intangible property.

> *Example* **12.17:** EURpharm, a European pharmaceutical company, owns 100% of USpharm, a domestic corporation. EURpharm develops a pharmaceutical "ColdAway," a cure for the common cold. EURpharm licenses the ColdAway formula with the rights to use the ColdAway trade name in the United States to USpharm.

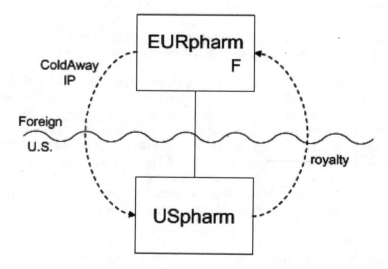

Without considering the appropriate arm's length royalty rate that USpharm must pay EURpharm, USpharm's average financial results for the last three years are as follows:

¶1202.03

Sales	$20 million
Cost of goods sold	($12 million)
Operating expenses	($ 4 million)
Operating profit	$ 4 million

USpharm is selected as the tested party as a result of engaging in relatively routine manufacturing and sales activities, whereas EURpharm engages in a variety of complex activities involving unique and valuable intangibles. Because USpharm's manufacturing activities are not complex, the ratio of operating profits to sales is the most appropriate PLI.

After adjustments have been made to account for material differences between USpharm and a sample of eight comparable companies for which data is available (routine manufacturers of generic drugs), the average ratio of operating profit to sales for the comparable companies is as follows: 5%, 6%, 8%, 9%, 10%, 15%, 15%, and 18%. Consequently, the arm's length range (the interquartile range) is 7% to 15% (the average of the second and third lowest PLIs and the average of the sixth and seventh lowest PLIs).

Before paying any royalty, USpharm's return on sales is 20% ($4 million of operating profit ÷ by $20 million of sales) and the high profitability is attributable to USpharm's use of EURpharm's intellectual property. Therefore, in order to report a return on sales that is within the arm's length range of 7% to 15%, USpharm should pay a royalty on sales of between 5% (20% – 5% = 15%) and 13% (20% – 13% = 7%).

As aforementioned, the comparable profits method can be used for tangible property as well as intangible property. The comparable profits method is particularly suitable for multiple transactions between two related parties as they need only conduct one analysis.[56]

    ***Example* 12.18:** USAco is a U.S. pharmaceutical company that develops a drug to soothe mosquito bites. USAco owns a subsidiary in the British Virgin Islands (BVI). USAco provides the formula to BVI and also sells the chemicals used in the formula to BVI. BVI produces the drug and sells the pills back to USAco. As opposed to testing each of the three intercompany transactions in this round-trip scenario (the provision of the formula, the sale of the chemicals, and the purchase of the pill), the parties merely have to conduct one comparable profits method analysis for BVI.

---

[56] Reg. § 1.482-1(f)(2)(i).

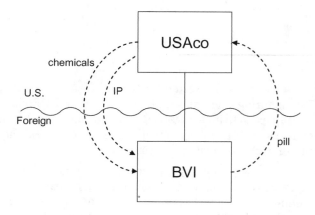

Profit split method(s). As with its use for transfers for tangible property, under the comparable profit split method(s), the allocation of the combined operating profit between two controlled taxpayers is based on how uncontrolled taxpayers engaged in similar activities under similar circumstances allocate their joint profits.[57] However, the challenge of finding two companies that are functionally comparable to each of the two related parties that license comparable intangibles and the challenge of obtaining the financial information regarding the two comparable companies render this method relatively inapplicable.

Under the residual profit split method, the related parties must determine a return for the routine activities each performs. Routine activities ordinarily include contributions of tangible property and services. After allocating profit based on the return for the routine activities each performs, the two parties split the residual profit on the basis of the relative value of the intangible property contributed by each party.[58] The price of the royalty would be the price that results in the parties earning their split amounts.

> **Example 12.19:** FORcola, a foreign corporation, has its research and development laboratory create its cola syrup (a product intangible). FORcola licenses the cola syrup formula to its USSub for bottling and sale in the United States. The cola syrup formula has a fair market value of $3 million. Due to an extensive advertising campaign, USSub owns marketing intangibles with a fair market value of $1 million. Accordingly, FORcola owns 75% of the group's intangibles and USSub owns 25% of the group's intangibles. Before paying FORcola, USSub earns a return on sales of 20%.
>
> An economist determines that a routine R&D lab (without any product intangibles) would earn a return on sales of 7% and that a routine bottler (without any marketing intangibles) would earn a return on sales of 5%. After allocating these routine returns totaling 12% to each party, the residual of 8% is

---

[57] Reg. § 1.482-6(c)(2).   [58] Reg. § 1.482-6(c)(3).

¶1202.03

split based on the relative value of the intangibles with 6% (75% of the 8%) going to FORcola and 2% (25% of the 8%) going to USSub. Therefore, USSub must pay FORcola an amount so that USSub earns only a return on sales of 7% (5% for routine bottling functions and 2% for its marketing intangibles).

Commensurate with income requirement. Many U.S. companies have moved operations to foreign countries offering low-cost labor, low tax rates, less government regulation, and new markets. These U.S. companies typically transfer manufacturing and marketing intangibles to their foreign subsidiaries. For example, a foreign manufacturing subsidiary might manufacture a good under a license from its domestic parent corporation and then sell its entire output to the parent at a markup. If the foreign subsidiary is located in a low-tax country, its U.S. parent will defer U.S. taxes to the extent the intercompany royalty rate understates the economic value of the intangible.

In response to this problem, Congress enacted a requirement that transfer prices for sales or licenses of intangibles must be "commensurate with the income attributable to the intangible."[59] In other words, transfer prices must reflect the actual profit experience realized subsequent to the transfer. To meet this requirement, the parties must annually adjust the original sales price or royalty rate to reflect any unanticipated changes in the income actually generated by the intangible.[60] For example, if a new patent leads to a product that turns out to be far more successful than was expected at the time the patent was licensed, the taxpayer must increase the intercompany royalty payments to reflect that unanticipated profitability. A determination in an earlier year that the royalty was arm's length does not preclude the IRS from making an adjustment in a subsequent year in which the unanticipated profitability occurs.[61]

---

[59] Code Sec. 482.
[60] Reg. § 1.482-4 (f) (2) (i).

[61] Reg. § 1.482-4 (f) (2) (i).

Example 12.20: USAco, a pharmaceutical company, licenses the rights to a balm that soothes burns to its British Virgin Islands company (BVI) for what is considered an arm's length royalty rate of 5% of sales. Four years later, an Indian scientist determines that the balm is the key ingredient in his cure for skin cancer. As a result, BVI earns a highly profitable return on sales of 60%. Even though BVI originally agreed to pay what was considered an arm's length royalty to USAco for the balm, the IRS can make an adjustment to reflect the unanticipated profitability.

The need to make periodic adjustments places a significant administrative burden on taxpayers. This burden is mitigated somewhat by the following exceptions:

    (i) *De minimis exception*—Periodic adjustments are not required if the total profits actually realized by the controlled licensee from the use of the intangible are between 80% and 120% of the profits that were foreseeable when the agreement was entered into and there have been no substantial changes in the functions performed by the licensee since the agreement was executed, except for changes required by unforeseeable events. The *de minimis* exception also requires a written royalty agreement and the preparation of contemporaneous supporting documentation. In addition, if the requirements of the *de minimis* exception are met for each of five consecutive taxable years, then no further periodic adjustments are required under any conditions.[62]

    (ii) *Extraordinary event exception*—Even if the total profits actually realized by the controlled licensee from the use of the intangible are less than 80% or more than 120% of the profits that were foreseeable when the parties entered the agreement, the parties need not make periodic adjustments if the unexpected variation in profits is due to extraordinary

---

[62] Reg. § 1.482-4(f)(2)(ii)(C). A slightly different set of requirements applies if the arm's length amount was determined under the comparable uncontrolled transaction method. Reg. § 1.482-4(f)(2)(ii)(B) and (E).

events that are beyond the parties' control and that they could not reasonably anticipate. In order to use this exception, the parties must satisfy all of the requirements of the *de minimis* exception, other than the 80% to 120% requirement.[63]

(iii) *Same intangible exception*—No periodic adjustments are required if the following requirements are met: (i) the same intangible was transferred to an uncontrolled taxpayer under circumstances similar to those of the controlled transaction, (ii) the uncontrolled transaction serves as the basis for the application of the comparable uncontrolled transaction method, and (iii) an arm's length charge is made in the first taxable year of the transfer.[64]

Cost sharing arrangements. One way for controlled parties to avoid the administrative burden and uncertainties associated with transfer pricing for intangibles is to enter into a cost sharing arrangement. For example, a U.S. parent corporation and a foreign subsidiary may agree to equally share the costs of developing a new product. Under such an agreement, the parent might own the rights to manufacture and market the new product in the United States, while the subsidiary might own the rights to manufacture and market the new product abroad. The advantage of a cost sharing arrangement is that the foreign subsidiary's ownership of the foreign rights to the intangible negates the need to have that foreign subsidiary pay a royalty to its U.S. parent. A bona fide cost sharing transaction must allocate intangible development costs in proportion to the reasonably anticipated benefits to each controlled party, which must bear a portion of the costs incurred at each stage of the development of both successful and unsuccessful intangibles.[65]

> **Example 12.21:** USAco, a maker of sailboat sails, believes that there is a market for a significantly more durable sail for use in both the Great Lakes and the Caribbean Sea and anticipates spending $1 million this year on research and development of such a durable sail. USAco believes that 60% of the market for a new durable sail would be in the Caribbean, which is served by its British Virgin Islands subsidiary (BVI). USAco has two alternatives for the taxation of this product intangible. First, USAco may deduct all the R&D expenses for the new product on its U.S. return and license the ultimate product intangible to BVI for a royalty. Second, USAco could enter a cost sharing arrangement with BVI and charge BVI $600,000 (the 60% anticipated share of the market × the $1 million of research and development expenses incurred). By entering into the cost sharing arrangement, BVI would own the Caribbean rights to the new product and not have to pay a royalty in the future for use of that product intangible.

---

[63] Reg. § 1.482-4(f)(2)(ii)(D).
[64] Reg. § 1.482-4(f)(2)(ii)(A).

[65] Reg. § 1.482-7(a)(2). *See also Veritas Software Corp.*, 133 TC 297, Dec. 58,016 (2009); and *Xilinx, Inc.*, CA-9, 2010-1 USTC ¶ 50,302.

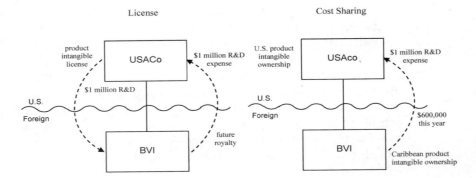

To the extent that a party brings existing intangibles to the arrangement, that party must be compensated an arm's length amount for what is defined as a platform contribution transaction.[66] A platform contribution transaction occurs when a party brings any resource, capability, or right to the development of cost shared intangibles.[67]

> *Example 12.22:* As in the previous Example, USAco, a maker of sailboat sails, believes that there is a market for a significantly more durable sail for use in both the Great Lakes and the Caribbean Sea and anticipates spending $1 million this year on research and development of such a durable sail. USAco believes that 60% of the market for a new durable sail would be in the Caribbean, which is served by its British Virgin Islands subsidiary (BVI). USAco enters a cost sharing arrangement with BVI and charge BVI $600,000 (the 60% anticipated share of the market × the $1 million of research and development expenses incurred). By entering into the cost sharing arrangement, BVI would own the Caribbean rights to the new product and not have to pay a royalty in the future for use of that product intangible.
>
> However, when conducting its research, USAco uses the design it developed for the sail USAco currently sells for use in the Great Lakes. The use of this pre-existing design is a resource to the development of the new design and is, therefore, a platform contribution. As a result, BVI must pay USAco for this platform contribution transaction in addition to paying its share of the development costs for the new sail design.

---

[66] Reg. § 1.482-7(a)(2).   [67] Reg. § 1.482-7(c)(1).

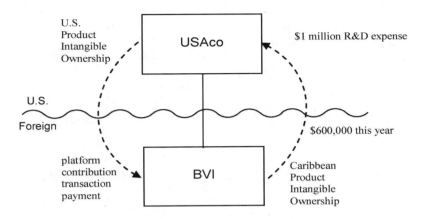

U.S.
Product
Intangible
Ownership

$1 million R&D expense

USAco

U.S.

Foreign

$600,000 this year

platform
contribution
transaction
payment

BVI

Caribbean
Product
Intangible
Ownership

.04 Loans and Advances

Controlled entities generally must charge each other an arm's length rate of interest on any intercompany loans or advances.[68] There is an exception, however, for intercompany trade receivables, which are debts that arise in the ordinary course of business and are not evidenced by a written agreement requiring the payment of interest.[69] If the controlled borrower is located outside the United States, the U.S. lender does not have to charge interest on an intercompany trade receivable until the first day of the fourth month following the month in which the receivable arises.[70] If the controlled borrower is located within the United States, the interest-free period only extends to the first day of the third month following the month in which the receivable arises.[71] This exception reflects the common business practice of not charging interest on trade receivables.

> **Example 12.23:** USAco, a domestic corporation, owns 100% of ASIAco, a foreign corporation. On November 1, ASIAco purchases $1 million of inventory on account from USAco. The $1 million debt, on which ASIAco pays no interest, is still outstanding on December 31, which is the end of USAco's taxable year. Since the $1 million intercompany trade receivable was outstanding for only two months, USAco does not have to recognize any interest income. However, if the $1 million debt were still outstanding on February 1 of the following year, ASIAco would begin owing USAco interest from that date forward because it will have been outstanding for 90 days.

---

[68] Reg. § 1.482-2(a)(1)(i).
[69] Reg. § 1.482-2(a)(1)(iii)(A).
[70] Reg. § 1.482-2(a)(1)(iii)(C).
[71] Reg. § 1.482-2(a)(1)(iii)(B).

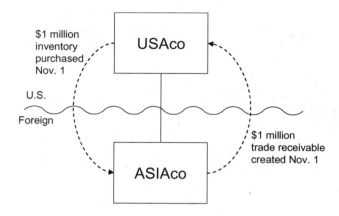

Longer interest-free periods are possible if the controlled lender ordinarily allows unrelated parties a longer interest-free period[72] or if a controlled borrower purchases the goods for resale in a foreign country and the average collection period for its sales is longer than the 90-day interest-free period.[73]

Intercompany debt other than a trade receivable generally must bear an arm's length interest rate.[74] To determine the arm's length rate, the taxpayer must consider all relevant factors, including the amount and duration of the loan, the security involved, the credit standing of the borrower, and the interest rate prevailing at the situs of the lender for comparable loans between uncontrolled parties.[75] If an arm's length rate is not readily determinable, the taxpayer can still protect itself against an IRS adjustment by satisfying the requirements of a safe-harbor provision. Under this safe harbor, an interest rate is deemed to be an arm's length rate if the rate is between 100% and 130% of the applicable federal rate.[76] The applicable federal rate is the average interest rate on obligations of the federal government with maturities similar to the term on the intercompany loan.[77]

> **Example 12.24:** EURco, a foreign corporation, owns 100% of USAco, a domestic corporation. During the current year, USAco borrows $1 million from EURco. The loan is denominated in U.S. dollars and has a four-year term. At the time of the loan, the applicable federal rate for a mid-term obligation is 8%. Under the safe-harbor provision, an interest rate of between 8% (100% of the applicable federal rate) and 10.4% (130% of the applicable federal rate) is automatically acceptable to the IRS. EURco and USAco can only use a rate lower than 8% or higher than 10.4% if they can establish that the rate is an arm's length rate, taking into account all of the relevant facts and circumstances.

---

[72] Reg. § 1.482-2(a)(1)(iii)(D).

[73] Reg. § 1.482-2(a)(1)(iii)(E).

[74] Reg. § 1.482-2(a)(1)(i).

[75] Reg. § 1.482-2(a)(2)(i).

[76] Reg. § 1.482-2(a)(2)(iii)(B). Controlled taxpayers use the short-term rate for demand loans and loans with

maturities of up to three years, the mid-term rate for loans with maturities of greater than three years to nine years, and the long-term rate for loans with maturities greater than nine years.

[77] Code Sec. 1274(d).

The safe harbor is not available if the intercompany debt is denominated in a foreign currency[78] or if the controlled lender is in the business of making loans to unrelated parties.[79]

A special rule applies if the controlled lender locally borrows the funds used to make the intercompany loan in the borrower's country. In these back-to-back loans, the controlled lender is treated as a mere conduit for the loan entered into with the unrelated lender. Therefore, the arm's length rate on such pass-through loans is assumed to be equal to the rate paid by the controlled lender on the original loan, increased by any associated borrowing costs, unless the taxpayer can establish that a different rate is more appropriate under the general rules.[80]

> *Example* 12.25: USAco, a domestic corporation, owns 100% of GERco, a German corporation. During the current year, USAco borrows $10 million from a German bank at a 10% rate and then relends the funds to GERco. The arm's length rate on the intercompany loan is deemed to be equal to 10% plus any borrowing costs incurred by USAco in securing the original loan. The parties can use a rate other than 10% if USAco can establish that such a rate is at arm's length, taking into account all of the relevant facts and circumstances.

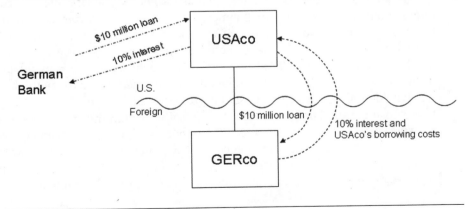

---

[78] Reg. § 1.482-2(a)(2)(iii)(E).
[79] Reg. § 1.482-2(a)(2)(iii)(D).
[80] Reg. § 1.482-2(a)(2)(ii).

.05 Performance of Services

A party must charge an arm's length fee when performing services for the benefit of, or on behalf of, another related party. This arm's length fee includes all costs—direct and indirect (i.e., an allocation of overhead) and must generally include a markup.[81]

However, under a safe-harbor provision known as the services cost method, an arm's length charge is equal to the total services costs incurred by the related party (direct and indirect costs) in providing the service without a markup.[82] This safe harbor reflects the reality that many intercompany services, such as payroll, human resources, and legal services, are provided for administrative convenience rather than profit.

The covered services that are eligible for the services cost method include both specified covered services (a listing of routine, back office, support-type services that the IRS identifies in a revenue procedure[83]) and low-margin covered services (defined as a markup of 7% or less). To further qualify for the services cost method, the covered service must meet several requirements. First, the covered service must not contribute significantly to key competitive advantages, core capabilities, or fundamental risks of success or failure in one or more trades or business of the controlled group. Second, the taxpayer must maintain adequate books and records. Third, the covered service must not be one of the following excluded activities: (1) manufacturing; (2) production; (3) extraction, exploration, or processing of natural resources; (4) construction; (5) reselling, distribution, acting as a sales or purchasing agent or acting under a commission or other similar arrangement; (6) research, development, or experimentation; (7) engineering or scientific; (8) financial transactions; and (9) insurance.[84]

> **Example 12.26:** USAco is a wholly-owned subsidiary of ASIAco, a multinational manufacturing conglomerate. USAco acts as a contract manufacturer for ASIAco, performs all of ASIAco's accounting services, and transports ASIAco's products sold in the United States. USAco must receive an arm's length markup on the costs of providing manufacturing services as manufacturing services are specifically excluded from the services cost method. The IRS has identified and listed accounting services as routine and, accordingly, USAco can merely charge ASIAco the cost of providing these services. If the transportation services, which the IRS has not listed, have a median comparable markup of 7% or less, USAco does not have to charge a markup. However, if the median comparable markup on the cost of providing these transportation services exceeds 7%, USAco must charge ASIAco an arm's length markup.

---

[81] Reg. § 1.482-9(j) and (k).
[82] Reg. § 1.482-9(b)(1).

[83] Rev. Proc. 2007-13, 2007-1 CB 295.
[84] Reg. § 1.482-9(b).

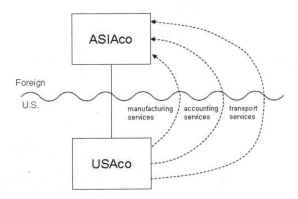

In situations in which the services cost method does not apply, the regulations provide other specific methods to determine the arm's length price. These methods, which are analogous to the methods for the transfers of tangible property, include the following:

(i)   the comparable uncontrolled services price method,[85] which is analogous to the CUP method;

(ii) the gross services margin method,[86] which is analogous to the resale price method;

(iii) the cost of services plus method,[87] which is analogous to the cost plus method;

(iv) the comparable profits method;[88] and

(v)   the profits split method(s).[89]

***Example* 12.27:** USAco is the wholly-owned U.S. subsidiary of ASIAco, a multinational conglomerate. USAco performs transportation services for ASIAco. USAco also performs transportation services in a functionally identical manner for unrelated companies by charging its costs (direct expenses and an allocation of indirect expenses) plus a 10% markup. Under the cost of services plus method, which is analogous to the cost plus method for tangible property, USAco must charge ASIAco its costs (direct and indirect) plus 10% of those costs for the transportation services.

---

[85] Reg. § 1.482-9(c).
[86] Reg. § 1.482-9(d).
[87] Reg. § 1.482-9(e).

[88] Reg. § 1.482-9(f).
[89] Reg. § 1.482-9(g).

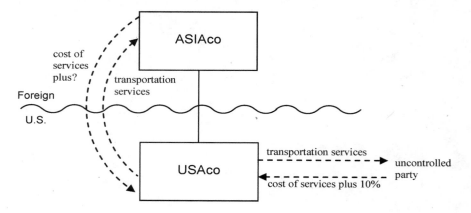

.06 Use of Tangible Property

Intercompany leases of tangible property generally must bear an arm's length rental charge.[90] The arm's length rental is the amount that unrelated parties under similar circumstances would have charged for the same or similar property. All relevant factors must be considered in determining the arm's length rental, including the period and location of the property's use, the owner's investment in the property, the owner's maintenance expenses, and the type and condition of the property.[91]

Example 12.28: MineCo is a U.S. corporation that buys, sells, and rents mining equipment. MineCo typically charges $5,000 a day for the use of its equipment. MineCo's Canadian subisidary, CanMine, rents a unit of mining equipment. As long as all the circumstances are similar between MineCo's leases to unrelated parties and MineCo's lease to CanMine, CanMine must pay MineCo $5,000 a day.

A special rule applies if the controlled lessor first leased the property from an unrelated person and then subleased it to the controlled lessee. In these sub-leases,

---

[90] Reg. § 1.482-2(c)(1).   [91] Reg. § 1.482-2(c)(2)(i).

the controlled lessor is treated as a mere conduit for the lease entered into with the unrelated lessor. Therefore, the arm's length rental for such pass-through leases is equal to the rental paid by the controlled lessor on the original lease, increased by any associated rental costs (e.g., maintenance, repairs, utilities, and managerial expenses).[92] This rule does not apply if either the controlled lessor or controlled lessee is regularly engaged in the business of leasing the type of property in question to unrelated persons or if the taxpayer establishes a more appropriate rental rate under the general rules, as a markup would be required.[93]

.07 Correlative Adjustments

When the IRS increases the taxable income of a related party through a transfer pricing adjustment, the IRS will also reduce the income of the other related party for U.S. purposes.

> **Example 12.29:** USAco sells machinery to FORco, its foreign subsidiary. The IRS makes a transfer pricing adjustment, increasing the income of USAco on the sale of machinery by $1 million. The IRS will correlatively decrease both the income and the earnings and profits of FORco by $1 million. The earnings and profits of FORco can affect numerous U.S. tax attributes of USAco, including its dividend income, deemed paid foreign tax credits, and Subpart F inclusions. The IRS may also permit USAco to establish an account receivable so that FORco's payment of cash in the amount of the adjustment will not result in additional income to USAco.

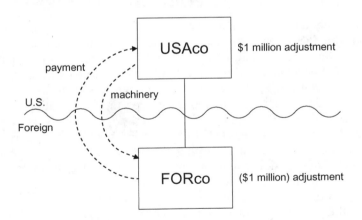

.08 Setoffs

The IRS will generally permit a taxpayer to offset a negative transfer pricing adjustment with a favorable transfer pricing adjustment provided that the adjustments are for the same two related parties.

> **Example 12.30:** USAco sells machinery to FORco, its foreign subsidiary. The IRS makes a transfer pricing adjustment, increasing the income of

---

[92] Reg. § 1.482-2(c)(2)(iii)(A).   [93] Reg. § 1.482-2(c)(2)(iii)(B).

¶1202.08

USAco on the sale of machinery by $1 million. If the IRS also determines that USAco should have paid FORco an additional $600,000 for services, the adjustments are offset for a net adjustment of $400,000.

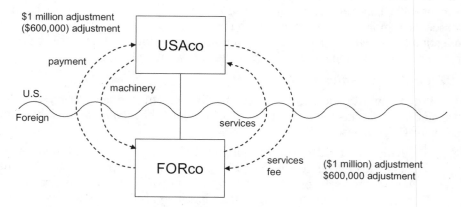

If, however, the IRS makes the adjustment for USAco's sales of machinery to FORco and a negative transfer pricing adjustment for the services received from ASIAco (another of USAco's foreign subsidiaries), USAco could not offset the adjustments.

¶ 1203 INFORMATION REPORTING REQUIREMENTS

To effectively audit the transfer prices used by a U.S. subsidiary of a foreign corporation, the IRS often must examine the books and records of the foreign parent corporation. As a result, each year certain reporting corporations must (i) file Form 5472, Information Return of a 25% Foreign-Owned U.S. Corporation or a Foreign Corporation Engaged in a U.S. Trade or Business and (ii) maintain certain books and records.[94] A U.S. corporation is a reporting corporation if, at any time during the taxable year, 25% or more of its stock, by vote or value, is owned directly or indirectly by one foreign person.[95] In filing a Form 5472, the reporting corporation must provide information regarding its foreign shareholders, certain other related parties, and the dollar amounts of intercompany transactions entered into during the year with foreign related parties.[96] A separate Form 5472 is filed for each related party with which the reporting corporation engaged in reportable transactions during the year.[97] The practical importance of Form 5472 is that the IRS often uses this form as a starting point for conducting a transfer pricing examination.[98] A completed Form 5472 is included in the Appendix to this chapter.

In addition to filing Form 5472, a reporting corporation also must maintain permanent books and records sufficient to establish the correctness of the report-

---

[94] *See generally,* Code Secs. 6038A and 6038C.

[95] Reg. § 1.6038A-1(c). A foreign corporation is a reporting corporation if, at any time during the taxable year, the foreign corporation is engaged in a U.S. trade or business and 25% or more of its stock, by vote or value, is owned directly or indirectly by one foreign person.

[96] Reg. § 1.6038A-2(b).

[97] Reg. § 1.6038A-2(a).

[98] *See* Internal Revenue Manual, International Audit Guidelines Handbook, April 1, 2002, 4.61.3.

ing corporation's U.S. tax liability, with an emphasis on transactions with related parties.[99] Certain reporting corporations are exempt from these special record maintenance requirements, but still must file Form 5472. These exemptions are for (i) reporting corporations whose U.S. gross receipts are less than $10 million[100] and (ii) reporting corporations whose annual payments to and from foreign related persons with respect to related party transactions are not more than $5 million and are less than 10% of the reporting corporation's U.S. gross income.[101] Any reporting corporation that fails to either file Form 5472 or maintain the requisite records may be subject to an annual penalty of $10,000.[102]

Information reporting also is required with respect to the foreign subsidiaries of domestic corporations.[103] Specifically, each year a U.S. person who owns more than 50% or more of the stock, by vote or value, of a foreign corporation must file a Form 5471, Information Return of U.S. Persons With Respect to Certain Foreign Corporations.[104] In the Form 5471, the U.S. shareholder must provide much of the information regarding the controlled foreign corporation that it would report on a Form 1120, plus the dollar amounts of intercompany transactions it entered into with related parties.[105] Any U.S. person who fails to furnish the required information may be subject to an annual penalty of $10,000, as well as a reduction in the taxpayer's foreign tax credit.[106] As with Form 5472, the practical importance of Form 5471 is that the IRS often uses this form as a starting point for conducting a transfer pricing examination.[107] A completed Form 5471 is included in the Appendix to Chapter 5 (¶ 504).

¶ 1204 TRANSFER PRICING PENALTIES AND DOCUMENTATION

Despite the information reqporting requirements described above, the IRS had trouble obtaining transfer pricing information from related parties abroad. To assist the IRS in obtaining this information, Congrtess instituted a special transfer pricing penalty with documentation requirements.[108]

More specifically, Congress strived to promote more voluntary compliance with the arm's length standard via either the transactional penalty and the net adjustment penalty. Either penalty equals 20% of the tax underpayment related to a transfer pricing adjustment made by the IRS.[109] The transactional penalty applies if the transfer price used by the taxpayer is 200% or more (or 50% or less) of the arm's length amount.[110] The net adjustment penalty applies if the net increase to taxable income exceeds the lesser of $5 million or 10% of the taxpayer's gross receipts.[111] Both penalties increase to 40% of the related tax underpayment if the transfer price used by the taxpayer is 400% or more (or 25% or less) of the arm's length amount or

---

[99] Reg. § 1.6038A-3(a)(1).

[100] Reg. § 1.6038A-1(h).

[101] Reg. § 1.6038A-1(i).

[102] Reg. § 1.6038A-4(a).

[103] *See generally,* Code Sec. 6038.

[104] Reg. § 1.6038-2(a) and (b).

[105] Reg. § 1.6038-2(f).

[106] Code Sec. 6038(b) and (c).

[107] *See* Internal Revenue Manual, International Audit Guidelines Handbook, May 1, 2006, 4.61.3.4.1.

[108] Code Sec. 6662(d); Reg. § 1.6662-6.

[109] Code Sec. 6662(a) and (b)(3).

[110] Code Sec. 6662(e)(1)(B)(i).

[111] Code Sec. 6662(e)(1)(B)(ii) and (e)(3)(A).

if the net increase to taxable income exceeds the lesser of $20 million or 20% of the taxpayer's gross receipts.[112]

    Example **12.31:** FORco is a foreign corporation that manufactures size AAA batteries. FORco sells the AAA batteries to its U.S. distribution subsidiary (USDist) for resale in the United States. During the taxable year, FORco sells 100 million AAA batteries at $1 per battery to USDist. If the IRS determines that the arm's length price is actually 90¢ per battery, the IRS will make a total adjustment of $10 million (10¢ per unit × 100 million batteries). Assuming a 35% tax rate, this results in $3.5 million of additional U.S. taxes. Because the net adjustment to taxable income of $10 million exceeds $5 million, USDist is subject to a Code Sec. 6662(e) penalty of $700,000 (20% of the $3.5 million of additional taxes).

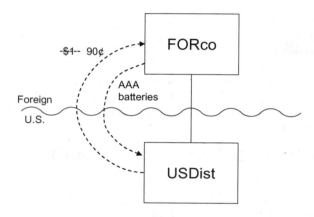

    The transactional and net adjustment penalties apply automatically whenever an IRS adjustment exceeds the numerical thresholds. The only way to avoid the penalty in such cases is to satisfy certain safe-harbor requirements. In the case of the transactional penalty, the penalty is waived only if the taxpayer can demonstrate that it had reasonable cause and acted in good faith.[113] In the case of the net adjustment penalty, the reasonable cause and good faith requirements can be met only if the taxpayer can demonstrate, through contemporaneous documentation provided to the IRS within 30 days of a request that the taxpayer acted reasonably in selecting and applying a transfer pricing method.[114] These added requirements for avoiding the net adjustment penalty force taxpayers to develop and have waiting for the IRS all of the documentation that the IRS ordinarily would need to review in a transfer pricing examination. In addition to providing protection against the transfer pricing penalty, the documentation may also persuade the IRS that a transfer pricing adjustment is not necessary. The IRS's Large Business and Interna-

---

[112] Code Sec. 6662(h).
[113] Reg. § 1.6662-6(b)(3) and Reg. § 1.6664-4(a).

[114] Code Sec. 6662(e)(3)(B)(i). Documentation is considered contemporaneous if it exists when the taxpayer timely files a tax return. Reg. § 1.6662-6(d)(2)(iii)(A).

tional Division (LB&I) has mandated that all LB&I agents should request documentation during audits.[115]

A taxpayer cannot reasonably conclude that the specified method selected provided the most reliable measure of an arm's length result unless the taxpayer has made a reasonable effort to evaluate the potential application of the other specified methods.[116] If the taxpayer used an unspecified method, the taxpayer must demonstrate that none of the specified methods would provide a result that clearly reflected income and that the unspecified method is likely to clearly reflect income.[117]

.01 Preparing Transfer Pricing Documentation

The principal supporting documents that a taxpayer normally must include in its contemporaneous documentation are as follows:

(i) an overview of the taxpayer's business, including an analysis of the economic and legal factors that affect the pricing of its property and services,

(ii) a description of the organizational structure (including an organization chart) covering all related parties engaged in potentially relevant transactions,

(iii) a description of the controlled transactions;

(iv) a functional analysis describing the functions performed, the risks assumed, and the intangible assets employed;

(v) a description of the pricing method selected and an explanation of why that method was selected as the best method,

(vi) a description of the alternative methods that were considered and an explanation of why they were not selected as the best method,

(vii) a description of the comparables used, how comparability was evaluated, and what adjustments were made, including any internal data used to analyze the controlled transactions,

(viii) an explanation of the economic analyses and projections relied on in developing the pricing method,

(ix) any documentation explicitly required by the Regulations under Code Sec. 482, and

(x) a general index of the principal and background documents along with a description of the recordkeeping system used for cataloging and accessing those documents.[118]

The process of preparing some of this documentation is described in more detail below.

---

[115] Memorandum for LMSB Executives, Managers, and Agents, January 22, 2003. LMSB was the predecessor to the current LB&I Division.

[116] Reg. § 1.6662-6(d)(2)(ii).
[117] Reg. § 1.6662-6(d)(3)(ii).
[118] Reg. § 1.6662-6(d)(2)(iii)(B).

.02 Information Gathering

The information gathering stage is usually the most time-consuming aspect of preparing transfer pricing documentation. The taxpayer will typically have to interview operational personnel on both sides of the intercompany transaction to obtain the factual information necessary to prepare a business description and a functional analysis. In addition, the taxpayer will also have to obtain relevant financial information, including internal cost accounting and profit margin analysis for the transactions at issue and the latest financial statements for recent years. Finally, the taxpayer will have to identify unrelated party transactions, which may be between either two unrelated parties or one of the related parties and an unrelated party.

> **Example 12.32:** USAco sells cheese to FORco, its foreign parent, and wants to apply the comparable uncontrolled price method to determine the appropriate transfer price. USAco has to interview the appropriate personnel to determine the price USAco charges unrelated parties in comparable cheese sales. In addition, USAco also needs to identify, to the extent available, the price charged on comparable sales of cheese by other cheese wholesalers.

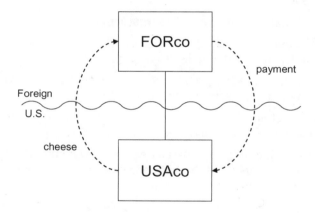

.03 Identification of the Best Method

The regulations require the taxpayer to apply the "best method" to its intercompany transactions. This requires choosing one of the methods prescribed in the regulations and developing the requisite support that the chosen method is the best method. At the same time, the taxpayer must explain why the other specified methods are not applicable. The taxpayer must review accurate and reliable data for application of the method; the degree of comparability between controlled and uncontrolled transactions or companies to which the methods are applied; and the number, magnitude, and accuracy of adjustments required to apply the method.[119]

---

[119] Reg. § 1.482-1(d)(2).

.04 Economic Analysis

The taxpayer should conduct economic analysis to evaluate the transactional data and obtain information concerning comparable companies from reliable databases.

> **Example 12.33:** USAco, a U.S. subsidiary, purchases software from ASIAco, a Singapore parent corporation, for resale in the United States. USAco wants to apply the comparable profits method to determine the appropriate transfer price. USAco must find companies comparable to itself with respect to the type of functions performed and the risks assumed. As a result, the economist will search for potentially comparable companies based, for example, on Form 10-K disclosures made to the Securities and Exchange Commission.

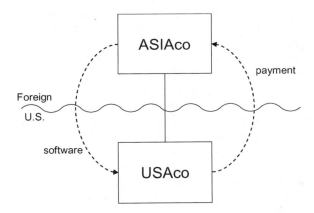

The economic analysis should further compare the financial results of the tested party to the financial results of the comparable transactions or companies. In addition to assuring functional comparability, an economist may also examine financial ratios such as return on costs, return on sales, and return on assets. Where appropriate, an economist may make adjustments for differences in relevant factors. The taxpayer's goal is to prepare an economic analysis that shows the related parties are at arm's length.

¶ 1205 DEVELOPING A TRANSFER PRICING STRATEGY

A corporation's transfer pricing strategy is driven, in part, by the need to develop an effective defense against the transactional and net adjustment penalties. The first step in developing a defense against these penalties is to assess the amount of risk associated with the taxpayer's current position. One major determinant of risk is the aggregate dollar value of controlled transactions between U.S. and foreign affiliates. Another major determinant of risk is the relative profitability of U.S. and foreign operations, in particular, the percentage of the taxpayer's worldwide profits that is allocated to low-tax foreign countries.

As a practical matter, the transactional penalty is likely to arise only in the unique circumstance where the taxpayer does not provide for a transfer price. For example, if a U.S. parent corporation transfers an intangible to a foreign subsidiary and does not provide for any royalty payments, then any price adjustment would exceed the 200% threshold. In contrast, any large corporation with a significant volume of cross-border transactions could conceivably exceed the $5 million net adjustment threshold. For example, a company with $100 million of cross-border controlled transactions is potentially subject to the 20% penalty if its transfer prices are off by just 5%.

One strategy to guard against the net adjustment penalty is to demonstrate, through contemporaneous documentation provided to the IRS within 30 days of a request, that the taxpayer acted reasonably in selecting and applying a transfer pricing method. As a consequence, a taxpayer can avoid the net adjustment penalty by using transfer prices that are supported by sufficient documentation and allocating to each affiliate a reasonable profit that reflects the economic realities of the parties' contractual relations. In this regard, reliance on a transfer pricing study done by a professional qualified to conduct such an analysis, such as an attorney, is a relevant factor in determining whether the taxpayer selected and applied a transfer pricing method in a reasonable manner.[120] Therefore, a formal transfer pricing study, whether prepared internally by the taxpayer's employees or externally by outside consultants, is an important factor in establishing defensible transfer pricing positions in terms of avoiding a penalty and persuading against an adjustment.

In addition to U.S. transfer pricing concerns, the same issue exists in the foreign country of the related party. Most of the trading partners of the United States have either specifically legislated transfer pricing rules or adopted the transfer pricing guidelines promulgated by the Organizatin for Economic Cooperation and Development (OECD).[121] A methodology and transfer price that the IRS may accept may not necessarily be acceptable to a foreign country's tax authority. Many foreign countries have a preference for the transaction-based methods (e.g., the CUP method) as opposed to the profit-based methods (e.g., the comparable profits method).

> ***Example* 12.34:** USSub, a U.S. subsidiary of CANco, a Canadian corporation, purchases oil from CANco for distribution in the United States. USSub properly applies the comparable profits method to justify to the IRS the transfer price of $100 a barrel. The Canada Revenue Agency audits CANco, disregards the comparable profits method analysis, and applies a CUP method to support an adjustment to CANco that increases the transfer price to $120 a barrel.

---

[120] Reg. § 1.6662-6 (d) (2) (iii) (D).

[121] Organization for Economic Cooperation and Development, *Transfer Pricing Guidelines for Multi-National Enterprises and Tax Administration,* 2010.

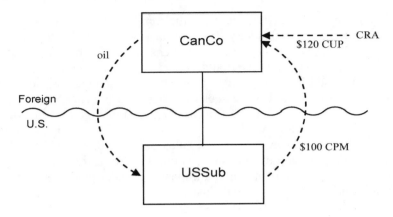

To try to coordinate between different countries, the OECD has promulgated a three-prong approach to transfer pricing documentation.[122] First, a multinational group must prepare a master file containing standardized information relevant for all the group's members. Second, a multinational group must prepare a local file referring specifically to material transactions of the local taxpayer. Third, a multinational group must prepare a Country-by-Country (CbC) report containing certain information relating to the global allocation of the group's income and taxes paid together with certain indicators of the location of economic activity within the group. The IRS has not currently issued any official guidance with respect to CbC.

An alternative strategy for avoiding both a transfer pricing penalty and an adjustment is to obtain an advance pricing agreement (APA). Under the APA procedure, the IRS reviews and agrees to the taxpayer's transfer pricing method for a prospective year.[123] An APA spells out the factual nature of the related party transactions, an appropriate pricing method, and the expected range of results by applying the agreed-on method to the transactions. If the taxpayer faithfully applies the agreed-on methodology, the IRS will not adjust the taxpayer's transfer prices in any future audits. A taxpayer seeking transfer pricing protection in both countries to a transaction may seek a bilateral APA.

Therefore, the advantages of an APA include the certainty of results for the taxpayer, as well as the possibility of reduced record keeping because the taxpayer knows in advance what information the IRS considers to be relevant. The disadvantages include the cost of developing the documentation needed to obtain an APA, as well as the up-front disclosure of information to the IRS. Disclosure may be only a timing issue, however, for large multinational corporations that the IRS routinely audits. Although taxpayers may have some concern that they are disclosing information about their company to potential competitors, the disclosure of the written APAs and any background documents is prohibited.[124]

---

[122] *Action 13: Guidance on the Implementation of Transfer Pricing Documentation and Country-by-Country Reporting,* Organization for Economic Cooperation and Development, 2015.

[123] Rev. Proc. 2006-9, 2006-2 IRB 292, and Announcement 2011-22, IRB 2011-16.

[124] Code Secs. 6103 and 6110.

***Example* 12.35:** NORDco, a Nordic company, manufactures widgets and sells them to its U.S. subsidiary (USDist) for resale in the United States. When evaluating USDist's transfer pricing practices, the economist determines in the documentation that USDist should report an arm's length return on sales between 3.1% and 5.3%. Desiring to avoid the expense of annual documentation for the next five years, USDist seeks an APA with the IRS. Subsequently, the IRS and USDist agree that, barring any material changes to the way USDist operates, USDist will annually report a cost of goods sold and, accordingly, a gross profit resulting in a return on sales between 3.1% and 5.3%. Assuming that USDist reports a return on sales within this range, the IRS will not make a transfer pricing adjustment, will not impose a transfer pricing penalty, and will not even audit the transfer pricing issue.

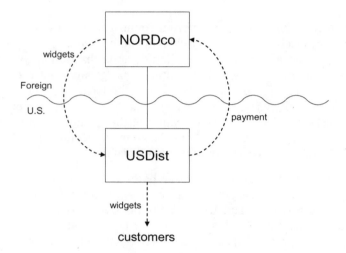

¶ 1206 APPENDIX

USACo, Inc. is 100% owned by ForCo Holdings AB, a holding company resident in Sweden, which is publicly held. ForCo Holdings AB wholly owns ForSub AB, an operating company that is resident in Sweden. USACo, Inc. purchases $20 million of forestry equipment from ForSub AB for distribution to its U.S. customers. In addition, USACo, Inc. pays $1 million to ForCo Holdings AB for management services performed in Sweden. When filing its U.S. Form 1120, USACo, Inc. must attach two Forms 5472 that detail its relationship with both ForCo Holdings AB and ForSub AB as well as identify the related party transactions.

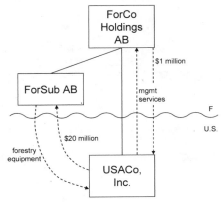

1. USACo, Inc. is a Reporting Corporation.

2. ForCo Holdings AB is a 25% Foreign Shareholder.

3. Both ForCo Holdings AB and ForSub AB are Related Parties to USACo, Inc.

4. Reportable Transactions of USACo, Inc. are its intercompany transactions: $1 million of consideration for management services from ForCo Holdings AB and purchases of $20 million of inventory from ForSub AB.

Form **5472** (Rev. December 2012) Department of the Treasury Internal Revenue Service	**Information Return of a 25% Foreign-Owned U.S. Corporation or a Foreign Corporation Engaged in a U.S. Trade or Business** **(Under Sections 6038A and 6038C of the Internal Revenue Code)** ▶ Information about Form 5472 and its separate instructions is at *www.irs.gov/form5472.* For tax year of the reporting corporation beginning January 1 , 2014 , and ending December 31 , 2014 **Note.** *Enter all information in English and money items in U.S. dollars.*	OMB No. 1545-0805

Part I   **Reporting Corporation** (see instructions). All reporting corporations must complete Part I.

1a Name of reporting corporation	**1b Employer identification number**
USCo, Inc.	34-5678901
Number, street, and room or suite no. (if a P.O. box, see instructions)	**1c** Total assets
City or town, state, and ZIP code (if a foreign address, see instructions) Chicago, IL 60609	$ 25,000,000

1d Principal business activity ▶ support activities for forestry	**1e** Principal business activity code ▶ 115310

1f Total value of gross payments made or received (see instructions) reported on **this** Form 5472	**1g** Total number of Forms 5472 filed for the tax year	**1h** Total value of gross payments made or received (see instructions) reported on **all** Forms 5472
$ 1,000,000	2	$ 21,000,000

1i Check here if this is a consolidated filing of Form 5472 ▶ ☐	**1j** Country of incorporation USA	**1k** Country(ies) under whose laws the reporting corporation files an income tax return as a resident USA	**1l** Principal country(ies) where business is conducted USA

2   Check here if, at any time during the tax year, any foreign person owned, directly or indirectly, at least 50% of **(a)** the total voting power of all classes of the stock of the reporting corporation entitled to vote, or **(b)** the total value of all classes of stock of the reporting corporation ▶ ☑

Part II   **25% Foreign Shareholder** (see instructions)

1a Name and address of direct 25% foreign shareholder ForCo Holdings AB Stockholm, Sweden	**1b(1)** U.S. identifying number, if any NA **1b(2)** Reference ID number (see instructions) S1

1c Principal country(ies) where business is conducted Sweden	**1d** Country of citizenship, organization, or incorporation Sweden	**1e** Country(ies) under whose laws the direct 25% foreign shareholder files an income tax return as a resident Sweden

2a Name and address of direct 25% foreign shareholder	**2b(1)** U.S. identifying number, if any **2b(2)** Reference ID number (see instructions)

2c Principal country(ies) where business is conducted	**2d** Country of citizenship, organization, or incorporation	**2e** Country(ies) under whose laws the direct 25% foreign shareholder files an income tax return as a resident

3a Name and address of ultimate indirect 25% foreign shareholder	**3b(1)** U.S. identifying number, if any **3b(2)** Reference ID number (see instructions)

3c Principal country(ies) where business is conducted	**3d** Country of citizenship, organization, or incorporation	**3e** Country(ies) under whose laws the ultimate indirect 25% foreign shareholder files an income tax return as a resident

4a Name and address of ultimate indirect 25% foreign shareholder	**4b(1)** U.S. identifying number, if any **4b(2)** Reference ID number (see instructions)

4c Principal country(ies) where business is conducted	**4d** Country of citizenship, organization, or incorporation	**4e** Country(ies) under whose laws the ultimate indirect 25% foreign shareholder files an income tax return as a resident

For Paperwork Reduction Act Notice, see instructions.   Cat. No. 49987Y   Form **5472** (Rev. 12-2012)

Form 5472 (Rev. 12-2012)   Page **2**

Part III Related Party (see instructions)

Check applicable box: Is the related party a ☑ foreign person or ☐ U.S. person?
All reporting corporations must complete this question and the rest of Part III.

1a Name and address of related party	1b(1) U.S. identifying number, if any
ForCo Holdings AB **Stockholm, Sweden**	**NA** 1b(2) Reference ID number (see instructions) **S1**

1c Principal business activity ▶ **offices of other holding companies**	1d Principal business activity code ▶ **55112**

1e Relationship—Check boxes that apply: ☑ Related to reporting corporation ☐ Related to 25% foreign shareholder ☑ 25% foreign shareholder

1f Principal country(ies) where business is conducted	1g Country(ies) under whose laws the related party files an income tax return as a resident
Sweden	Sweden

Part IV Monetary Transactions Between Reporting Corporations and Foreign Related Party (see instructions)

Caution: Part IV **must** be completed if the "foreign person" box is checked in the heading for Part III.

If estimates are used, check here ▶ ☐

1	Sales of stock in trade (inventory)	**1**	
2	Sales of tangible property other than stock in trade	**2**	
3	Platform contribution transaction payments received	**3**	
4	Cost sharing transaction payments received	**4**	
5a	Rents received (for other than intangible property rights)	**5a**	
b	Royalties received (for other than intangible property rights)	**5b**	
6	Sales, leases, licenses, etc., of intangible property rights (e.g., patents, trademarks, secret formulas)	**6**	
7	Consideration received for technical, managerial, engineering, construction, scientific, or like services	**7**	
8	Commissions received	**8**	
9	Amounts borrowed (see instructions) **a** Beginning balance _____ **b** Ending balance or monthly average ▶	**9b**	
10	Interest received	**10**	
11	Premiums received for insurance or reinsurance	**11**	
12	Other amounts received (see instructions)	**12**	
13	**Total.** Combine amounts on lines 1 through 12	**13**	
14	Purchases of stock in trade (inventory)	**14**	
15	Purchases of tangible property other than stock in trade	**15**	
16	Platform contribution transaction payments paid	**16**	
17	Cost sharing transaction payments paid	**17**	
18a	Rents paid (for other than intangible property rights)	**18a**	
b	Royalties paid (for other than intangible property rights)	**18b**	
19	Purchases, leases, licenses, etc., of intangible property rights (e.g., patents, trademarks, secret formulas)	**19**	
20	Consideration paid for technical, managerial, engineering, construction, scientific, or like services	**20**	1,000,000
21	Commissions paid	**21**	
22	Amounts loaned (see instructions) **a** Beginning balance _____ **b** Ending balance or monthly average ▶	**22b**	
23	Interest paid	**23**	
24	Premiums paid for insurance or reinsurance	**24**	
25	Other amounts paid (see instructions)	**25**	
26	**Total.** Combine amounts on lines 14 through 25	**26**	1,000,000

Part V Nonmonetary and Less-Than-Full Consideration Transactions Between the Reporting Corporation and the Foreign Related Party (see instructions)

Describe these transactions on an attached separate sheet and check here. ▶ ☐

Part VI Additional Information

All reporting corporations must complete Part VI.

1	Does the reporting corporation import goods from a foreign related party?	☑ Yes ☐ No
2a	If "Yes," is the basis or inventory cost of the goods valued at greater than the customs value of the imported goods?	☐ Yes ☑ No
	If "No," **do not** complete **b** and **c** below.	
b	If "Yes," attach a statement explaining the reason or reasons for such difference.	
c	If the answers to questions 1 and 2a are "Yes," were the documents used to support this treatment of the imported goods in existence and available in the United States at the time of filing Form 5472?	☐ Yes ☐ No
3	During the tax year, was the foreign parent corporation a participant in any cost sharing arrangement?	☐ Yes ☑ No
4	During the course of the tax year, did the foreign parent corporation become a participant in any cost sharing arrangement?	☐ Yes ☑ No

Form **5472** (Rev. 12-2012)

¶1206

Form **5472** (Rev. December 2012)	**Information Return of a 25% Foreign-Owned U.S. Corporation or a Foreign Corporation Engaged in a U.S. Trade or Business** (Under Sections 6038A and 6038C of the Internal Revenue Code) ▶ Information about Form 5472 and its separate instructions is at *www.irs.gov/form5472.*	OMB No. 1545-0805

Department of the Treasury
Internal Revenue Service   For tax year of the reporting corporation beginning __January 1__, __2014__ , and ending __December 31__ , __2014__
Note. *Enter all information in English and money items in U.S. dollars.*

Part I	**Reporting Corporation** (see instructions). All reporting corporations must complete Part I.		

1a Name of reporting corporation	**1b Employer identification number**
USCo, Inc.	34-5678901

Number, street, and room or suite no. (if a P.O. box, see instructions)	**1c** Total assets

City or town, state, and ZIP code (if a foreign address, see instructions)	$
Chicago, IL 60609	25,000,000

1d Principal business activity ▶ support activities for forestry	**1e** Principal business activity code ▶ 115310

1f Total value of gross payments made or received (see instructions) reported on **this** Form 5472	**1g** Total number of Forms 5472 filed for the tax year	**1h** Total value of gross payments made or received (see instructions) reported on **all** Forms 5472
$ 20,000,000	2	$ 21,000,000

1i Check here if this is a consolidated filing of Form 5472 ▶ ☐	**1j** Country of incorporation USA	**1k** Country(ies) under whose laws the reporting corporation files an income tax return as a resident USA	**1l** Principal country(ies) where business is conducted USA

2 Check here if, at any time during the tax year, any foreign person owned, directly or indirectly, at least 50% of **(a)** the total voting power of all classes of the stock of the reporting corporation entitled to vote, or **(b)** the total value of all classes of stock of the reporting corporation ▶ ☑

Part II	**25% Foreign Shareholder** (see instructions)	

1a Name and address of direct 25% foreign shareholder	**1b(1)** U.S. identifying number, if any
ForCo Holdings AB Stockholm, Sweden	NA
	1b(2) Reference ID number (see instructions) S1

1c Principal country(ies) where business is conducted Sweden	**1d** Country of citizenship, organization, or incorporation Sweden	**1e** Country(ies) under whose laws the direct 25% foreign shareholder files an income tax return as a resident Sweden

2a Name and address of direct 25% foreign shareholder	**2b(1)** U.S. identifying number, if any
	2b(2) Reference ID number (see instructions)

2c Principal country(ies) where business is conducted	**2d** Country of citizenship, organization, or incorporation	**2e** Country(ies) under whose laws the direct 25% foreign shareholder files an income tax return as a resident

3a Name and address of ultimate indirect 25% foreign shareholder	**3b(1)** U.S. identifying number, if any
	3b(2) Reference ID number (see instructions)

3c Principal country(ies) where business is conducted	**3d** Country of citizenship, organization, or incorporation	**3e** Country(ies) under whose laws the ultimate indirect 25% foreign shareholder files an income tax return as a resident

4a Name and address of ultimate indirect 25% foreign shareholder	**4b(1)** U.S. identifying number, if any
	4b(2) Reference ID number (see instructions)

4c Principal country(ies) where business is conducted	**4d** Country of citizenship, organization, or incorporation	**4e** Country(ies) under whose laws the ultimate indirect 25% foreign shareholder files an income tax return as a resident

For Paperwork Reduction Act Notice, see instructions.   Cat. No. 49987Y   Form **5472** (Rev. 12-2012)

¶1206

Form 5472 (Rev. 12-2012)   Page **2**

Part III Related Party (see instructions)

Check applicable box: Is the related party a ☑ foreign person or ☐ U.S. person?
All reporting corporations must complete this question and the rest of Part III.

1a Name and address of related party	**1b(1)** U.S. identifying number, if any
ForSub AB Stockholm, Sweden	NA
	1b(2) Reference ID number (see instructions) S2

1c Principal business activity ▶ gathering of forest products	**1d** Principal business activity code ▶ 1113210

1e Relationship—Check boxes that apply: ☑ Related to reporting corporation ☐ Related to 25% foreign shareholder ☑ 25% foreign shareholder

1f Principal country(ies) where business is conducted	**1g** Country(ies) under whose laws the related party files an income tax return as a resident
Sweden	Sweden

Part IV Monetary Transactions Between Reporting Corporations and Foreign Related Party (see instructions)

Caution: *Part IV* ***must*** *be completed if the "foreign person" box is checked in the heading for Part III.*
If estimates are used, check here ▶ ☐

1	Sales of stock in trade (inventory)	**1**	
2	Sales of tangible property other than stock in trade	**2**	
3	Platform contribution transaction payments received	**3**	
4	Cost sharing transaction payments received	**4**	
5a	Rents received (for other than intangible property rights)	**5a**	
b	Royalties received (for other than intangible property rights)	**5b**	
6	Sales, leases, licenses, etc., of intangible property rights (e.g., patents, trademarks, secret formulas)	**6**	
7	Consideration received for technical, managerial, engineering, construction, scientific, or like services	**7**	
8	Commissions received	**8**	
9	Amounts borrowed (see instructions) **a** Beginning balance _____ **b** Ending balance or monthly average ▶	**9b**	
10	Interest received	**10**	
11	Premiums received for insurance or reinsurance	**11**	
12	Other amounts received (see instructions)	**12**	
13	**Total.** Combine amounts on lines 1 through 12	**13**	
14	Purchases of stock in trade (inventory)	**14**	20,000,000
15	Purchases of tangible property other than stock in trade	**15**	
16	Platform contribution transaction payments paid	**16**	
17	Cost sharing transaction payments paid	**17**	
18a	Rents paid (for other than intangible property rights)	**18a**	
b	Royalties paid (for other than intangible property rights)	**18b**	
19	Purchases, leases, licenses, etc., of intangible property rights (e.g., patents, trademarks, secret formulas)	**19**	
20	Consideration paid for technical, managerial, engineering, construction, scientific, or like services	**20**	
21	Commissions paid	**21**	
22	Amounts loaned (see instructions) **a** Beginning balance _____ **b** Ending balance or monthly average ▶	**22b**	
23	Interest paid	**23**	
24	Premiums paid for insurance or reinsurance	**24**	
25	Other amounts paid (see instructions)	**25**	
26	**Total.** Combine amounts on lines 14 through 25	**26**	20,000,000

Part V Nonmonetary and Less-Than-Full Consideration Transactions Between the Reporting Corporation and the Foreign Related Party (see instructions)

Describe these transactions on an attached separate sheet and check here. ▶ ☐

Part VI Additional Information

All reporting corporations must complete Part VI.

1	Does the reporting corporation import goods from a foreign related party?	☑ Yes	☐ No
2a	If "Yes," is the basis or inventory cost of the goods valued at greater than the customs value of the imported goods?	☐ Yes	☑ No
	If "No," **do not** complete **b** and **c** below.		
b	If "Yes," attach a statement explaining the reason or reasons for such difference.		
c	If the answers to questions 1 and 2a are "Yes," were the documents used to support this treatment of the imported goods in existence and available in the United States at the time of filing Form 5472?	☐ Yes	☐ No
3	During the tax year, was the foreign parent corporation a participant in any cost sharing arrangement?	☐ Yes	☑ No
4	During the course of the tax year, did the foreign parent corporation become a participant in any cost sharing arrangement?	☐ Yes	☑ No

Form **5472** (Rev. 12-2012)

¶1206

Chapter 13
Tax Treaties

¶ 1301   INTRODUCTION

The major purpose of an income tax treaty is to <u>mitigate international double taxation</u> through tax reductions or exemptions on certain types of income derived by residents of one treaty country from sources within the other treaty country. Because tax treaties often substantially modify U.S. and foreign tax consequences, the relevant treaty must be considered in order to fully analyze the income tax consequences of any outbound or inbound transaction. In addition to treaties governing income taxes, the United States has also entered into bilateral tax treaties governing social security taxes, estate and gift taxes, and international shipping and aircraft.

The United States currently has income tax treaties with approximately <u>69</u> countries, including most of our major trading partners. Table 13.1 presents the list of foreign countries with which an income tax treaty is currently in force.

TABLE 13.1. COUNTRIES WITH WHICH THE UNITED STATES HAS INCOME TAX TREATIES IN FORCE[a]

Australia	Hungary	Pakistan
Austria	Iceland	Philippines
Bangladesh	India	Poland
Barbados	Indonesia	Portugal
Belgium	Ireland	Romania
Bulgaria	Israel	Russia
Canada	Italy	Slovak Republic
China, Peoples Republic of[b]	Jamaica	Slovenia
Commonwealth of Independent States[c]	Japan	South Africa
	Kazakstan	Spain
Cyprus	Korea	Sri Lanka
Czech Republic	Latvia	Sweden
Denmark	Lithuania	Switzerland
Egypt	Luxembourg	Thailand
Estonia	Malta	Trinidad and Tobago
Finland	Mexico	Tunisia
France	Morocco	Turkey
Germany	Netherlands	Ukraine
Greece	New Zealand	United Kingdom
	Norway	Venezuela

[a] Taken from Table 3 of IRS Pub. No. 515 (Dec. 9, 2014), which is reproduced in its entirety in the appendix to this chapter.

[b] Does not apply to Hong Kong. Notice 97-40, 1997-28 IRB 6.

[c] The members of the Commonwealth of Independent States include: Armenia, Azerbaijan, Belarus, Georgia, Kyrgyzstan, Moldova, Tajikistan, Turkmenistan, and Uzbekistan.

The United States has also agreed to exchange information about taxpayers with approximately twenty additional countries pursuant to Tax Information and Exchange Agreements.

There are several basic treaty provisions, such as permanent establishment provisions and reduced withholding tax rates, that are common to most income tax treaties. In many cases, these provisions are patterned after or similar to the United States Model Income Tax Convention of November 15, 2006 (U.S. Model Treaty), which reflects the traditional baseline negotiating position of the United States in establishing income tax treaties with other countries. Because the U.S. Model Treaty reflects the general pattern of most treaties and, therefore, is used as the reference point for the following discussion of typical treaty provisions. However, each tax treaty is separately negotiated and, accordingly, unique. Moreover, the U.S. Treasury Department will typically issue a Technical Explanation for each treaty. As a consequence, to determine the impact of treaty provisions in any specific situation, the planner must consult the applicable treaty.

¶1301

In most foreign countries, a treaty provision will supercede the foreign country's domestic law. The term "treaty override" describes legislation that conflicts with an earlier enacted treaty. However, the supremacy clause of the U.S. Constitution treats treaties and federal legislation equally. Consequently, if a treaty provision conflicts with legislation, whichever is later enacted will prevail.[1] The U.S. courts often try to read treaties and federal legislation as consistent so that there is not an override.[2]

¶ 1302 COMMON TREATY PROVISIONS

.01 Definition of Resident

The tax exemptions and reductions that treaties provide are available only to residents of either treaty country. Under the U.S. Model Treaty, a resident is any person who, under a country's internal laws, incurs tax by reason of domicile, residence, citizenship, place of management, place of incorporation, or other criteria of a similar nature.[3] A resident does not include a person who is subject to tax in the country only with respect to income derived from sources in that country.

A person may qualify as a resident in more than one country because each country has its own unique definition of residence. For example, a foreign national who is a U.S. resident under the substantial presence test pursuant to U.S. tax law may simultaneously qualify as a resident of a foreign country under the foreign country's definition of residency. To resolve this issue, the United States has included tie-breaker provisions in most of its income tax treaties. Tie-breaker rules are hierarchical in nature: only if the superordinate rule fails to resolve the issue does the analyst consider a subordinate rule. For example, Article 4(3) of the U.S. Model Treaty provides the following tie-breaker rules for individuals:

(i) The taxpayer is a resident of the country in which he or she has available a permanent home.

(ii) If the taxpayer has a permanent home available in both countries, the taxpayer is a resident of the country in which his or her personal and economic relations are closer (center of vital interests).

(iii) If the taxpayer does not have a center of vital interests in either country, he or she is a resident of the country in which he or she has a habitual abode.

(iv) If the taxpayer has a habitual abode in both countries or in neither country, the taxpayer is a resident of the country in which he or she is a citizen.

(v) If the taxpayer is a citizen of both countries or of neither country, the competent authorities of the two countries will settle the matter by mutual agreement.

---

[1] *Reid v. Covert*, SCt, 354 US 1, 77 SCt 1222, 18 (1956); *Breard v. Greene*, 523 U.S. 371 (1998); *Lindsey v. Comm'r.*, 98 T.C. 672 (1992), aff'd without opinion, 15 F.3d 1160 (D.C. Cir. 1994). *See also* Code Sec. 894(a) and 7852(d).

[2] *Cook v. United States*, 288 U.S. 102 120 (1933). *Price v. Commissioner*, 84 T.C.M. 250 (2002).

[3] Article 4(1) (¶ 1304.04) of the U.S. Model Treaty. Income derived by a partnership or other pass-through entity is treated as derived by a resident of a treaty country to the extent the income is treated, under the internal laws of that country, as taxable to a person that qualifies as a resident of that treaty country.

Example **13.1:** Ray Allen is a citizen and resident of country F, which has a tax treaty with the United States identical to the U.S. Model Treaty. Ray Allen owns FORco, a company incorporated in country F that is opening a branch office in the United States. Ray is divorced and maintains an apartment in country F, where he spends every other weekend visiting his children. Ray's first wife, who kept their house in their divorce, has never left country F. Ray becomes a U.S. resident alien under the substantial presence test as a result of managing FORco's U.S. branch. In the United States, Ray owns a condominium where he lives with his second wife.

Because Ray Allen is considered a resident of both the United States and country F, Ray Allen must consider the Treaty tie-breaker rules to determine which country has primary taxing jurisdiction. With an apartment in country F and a condominium in the United States, he has a permanent home available in both countries. With his children and the corporate headquarters in country F, as opposed to his place of business and his second wife in the United States, Ray Allen does not have a center of vital interests in either country. Furthermore, because he regularly spends time in both countries, he arguably has a habitual abode in both countries. As a result, under the Treaty tie-breakers, Ray Allen should be considered a resident of country F because he is a citizen of country F.

Tie-breaker rules are also provided for corporations and other types of entities. The Model Treaty specifies the country of incorporation as a tie-breaker for corporations resident under the internal law of two countries.[4]

Example **13.2:** Hans, a citizen and resident of country F, which has a treaty with the United States similar to the Model Treaty, owns all the shares of ZappCo, a corporation incorporated in one of the United States. Hans is the President and CFO of ZappCo, which he operates from a palatial office tower in country F. Under internal U.S. law, ZappCo is a resident of the United States. Under internal country F law, ZappCo is a resident of country F because ZappCo's mind and management is headquartered in country F. Under the

---

[4] Article 4(4) (¶ 1304.04) of the U.S. Model Treaty.

treaty tie-breaker, ZappCo is a U.S. resident because ZappCo is intercorporated in the United States.

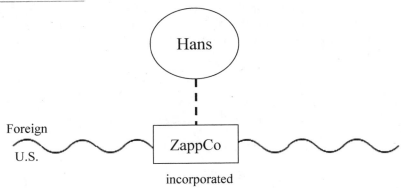

There is an exception to the principle that residence determines the availability of treaty benefits. Under so-called savings clause provisions, a treaty country saves the right to tax its own citizens and residents as though the treaty did not exist.[5] For example, under Article 11(1) of the income tax treaty between the United States and the United Kingdom, interest received by U.K. residents is exempt from U.S. taxation. However, under Article 1(4) of that treaty, the United States reserves the right to tax the payee if a U.K. resident also is a U.S. citizen or resident. As a consequence, the treaty does not impede the right of the United States to tax the worldwide income of U.S. persons.

.02 Business Profits and Permanent Establishments

A central tax issue for any company exporting its goods or services is whether it is subject to taxation in the importing country. Many countries assert jurisdiction over all of the income derived from sources within their borders, regardless of the citizenship or residence of the person receiving that income. This approach has its limits, however. For example, if the exporter's marketing activities within the importing country are *de minimis* (e.g., a company salesperson makes a few sales calls), the administrative costs of collecting the tax on those activities may exceed the related tax revenues. Moreover, a policy of imposing unreasonable compliance costs on foreign companies may inhibit a country's ability to benefit from international trade. These concerns have led countries to include permanent establishment provisions in their income tax treaties.

Under a permanent establishment provision, the business profits of a resident of one treaty country are exempt from taxation by the host treaty country unless those profits are attributable to a permanent establishment located within the host country.[6]

---

[5] Article 1(4) (¶ 1304.01) of the U.S. Model Treaty.

[6] Article 7(1) (¶ 1304.07) of the U.S. Model Treaty. A special exemption applies to the business profits of tax-payers that operate or rent ships, aircraft, or containers used in international traffic. Under Article 8 ¶ 1304.05 of the U.S. Model Treaty, such income generally is taxable only by the taxpayer's home country.

Example 13.3: USAco, a U.S. corporation, markets its products abroad by mailing catalogs to potential foreign customers, who then mail orders back to USAco's home office in the United States. Under the U.S. Model Treaty, the mere solicitation of orders through the mail does not constitute a permanent establishment. Therefore, USAco's export profits are not subject to foreign taxation.

Mail Order Sales

There are primarily two alternatives under which the IRS taxes a foreign person for having a permanent establishment: the fixed place of business test or the dependent sales agent test.

A permanent establishment includes a fixed place of business, such as a place of management, a branch, an office, a factory, a workshop, or a mine, well, quarry, or other place of natural resource extraction.[7]

Example 13.4: ForCo manufactures widgets at its plant in Chicago. The plant is a fixed place of business and, therefore, ForCo has a permanent establishment in the United States.

---

[7] Article 5(1) and (2) (¶ 1304.05) of the U.S. Model Treaty.

¶1302.02

A fixed base of business <u>does not</u> constitute a permanent establishment if it is used solely for <u>auxiliary functions</u> (e.g., <u>purchasing, storing, displaying, or delivering inventory</u>) or for <u>activities of a preparatory nature</u> (e.g., <u>collecting information about potential customers</u>). In particular, a permanent establishment <u>does not</u> include the following:

1. the use of facilities solely for the purpose of <u>storage, display, or delivery of goods, or merchandise</u> belonging to the foreign corporation;

2. the <u>maintenance</u> of a stock of goods or merchandise belonging to the foreign corporation solely for the purpose of <u>storage, display, or delivery</u>;

3. the <u>maintenance</u> of a stock of goods or merchandise belonging to the foreign corporation solely for the purpose of <u>processing by another enterprise</u>;

4. the <u>maintenance of a fixed place of business</u> solely for the purpose of <u>purchasing goods</u> or <u>merchandise</u> or of <u>collecting information</u> for the foreign corporation;

5. the <u>maintenance of a fixed place of business</u> solely for the purpose of carrying on, for the foreign corporation, any other activity of a <u>preparatory or auxiliary character</u> (e.g., collecting information about potential customers);

6. the <u>maintenance of a fixed place of business</u> solely for any combination of the activities mentioned above, provided that the overall activity of the fixed place of business resulting from this combination is of a <u>preparatory or auxiliary character</u>.[8]

Example **13.5:** USAco, a domestic corporation, decides to expand its foreign marketing activities by <u>leasing retail store space</u> in a major foreign city in order to <u>display its goods and keep an inventory from which to fill foreign orders</u>. Under the U.S. Model Treaty, USAco's business profits would still <u>not be subject to foreign taxation as long as USAco does not conclude any sales through its foreign office</u>. This may be possible in theory, but as a practical

---

[8] Article 5(4) (¶ 1304.05) of the U.S. Model Treaty.

matter, significant foreign sales may make it burdensome to conclude sales in this manner. If USAco's employees start concluding sales at the foreign office, USAco would have a permanent establishment in the foreign country.

In addition, a building or construction site is a permanent establishment only if it continues for more than a specified length of time.[9]

Example **13.6:** CanTract, a Canadian contractor, receives the contract to build Sav-On Arena. The project lasts eleven months, which is less than the twelve months permitted in Article V, paragraph 3 of the Canadian-U.S. tax Treaty. Therefore, Can Tract does not have a permanent establishment in the United States.

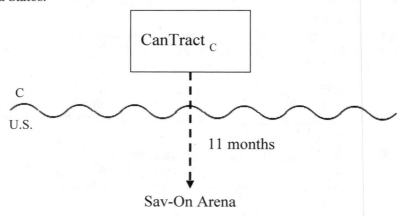

A permanent establishment also exists if employees or other dependent agents habitually exercise in the host country an authority to conclude sales contracts in the taxpayer's name.[10] As a consequence, an exporter that sends executives or salespeople abroad to enter into contracts may create a permanent establishment even if those employees do not operate out of a formal sales office.

---

[9] Article 5(3) (¶ 1304.05) of the U.S. Model Treaty.   [10] Article 5(5) (¶ 1304) of the U.S. Model Treaty.

¶ 1302.02

Example **13.7:** EurCo, a corporation incorporated in country F, employs a U.S. citizen and resident that spends three months a year traveling throughout the United States and soliciting purchase orders from U.S. customers. Although the sales employee solicits customers and has customers sign purchase orders, the sales employee does not sign purchase orders. Instead, the sales employee forwards the purchase orders to EurCo's home office in Europe for final approval. Under the appropriate tax treaty, EurCo would not be subject to U.S. taxes as EurCo would not have a permanent establishment in the United States due to the sales employee lacking final contracting authority.

Employees who limit their activities to auxiliary or preparatory functions, such as collecting information about potential customers, with sales concluded in the home country, will not create a permanent establishment. Marketing products abroad solely through independent brokers or distributors also does not create a permanent establishment, regardless of whether these independent agents conclude sales contracts in the exporter's name.[11] In addition, the mere presence within the importing country of a locally incorporated subsidiary does not create a permanent establishment for a parent company incorporated in another country, although the locally incorporated subsidiary will typically have to pay corporate income tax to the local country.[12]

If a resident of one treaty country has a permanent establishment in the other treaty country, the importing country may tax the taxpayer's business profits, but only to the extent those business profits are attributable to the permanent establishment.[13] The portion of an exporter's business profits that is attributable to a permanent establishment is computed based on the fiction that the permanent establishment is a distinct and independent enterprise dealing at arm's length with the home office.[14] Therefore, the more functions performed and the greater the risks assumed by the permanent establishment, the more income attributable to the permanent establishment. In making this determination, the taxpayer can allocate all direct costs, such as the cost of goods sold, against the permanent

---

[11] Article 5(6) (¶ 1304.05) of the U.S. Model Treaty.
[12] Article 5(7) (¶ 1304.05) of the U.S. Model Treaty.
[13] Article 7(1) (¶ 1304.07) of the U.S. Model Treaty.
[14] Article 7(2) (¶ 1304.07) of the U.S. Model Treaty.

establishment's income. The taxpayer also can make a reasonable allocation of indirect expenses, such as general and administrative expenses, research and development expenses, and interest expense, against the permanent establishment's income.[15]

In addition to the fixed place of business or the dependent agent with final contracting authority tests, a third test has emerged. More specifically, the Canadian-U.S. Tax Treaty deems a permanent establishment when, among other items, the foreign taxpayer operates in the host country for 183 days.[16]

.03 Personal Services Income

Treaty provisions covering personal services compensation are similar to the permanent establishment clauses covering business profits in that they create a higher threshold of activity for host country taxation. Generally, when an employee who is a resident of one treaty country derives income from services performed in the other treaty country, that income is usually taxable by the host country.[17] However, the employee's income is exempt from taxation by the host country if the employee's activities are less than the following standards:

(i) the employee is present in the host country for 183 days or less,

(ii) the employee's compensation is paid by, or on behalf of, an employer which is not a resident of the host country, and

(iii) the compensation is not borne by a permanent establishment that the employer has in the host country.[18]

Example **13.8:** FORco is a corporation organized in country F, which has a treaty with the United States identical to the U.S. Model Treaty. FORco is in the refrigeration business. Due to the high demand for air conditioning repair services in the United States in June, July and August, FORco sends Norman Ray Allen ("NRA"), a citizen and resident of country F, to serve customers. During that week, NRA helps repair air conditioning for many different customers of FORco. The compensation that FORco pays him is $20,000.

---

[15] Article 7(3) (¶ 1304.07) of the U.S. Model Treaty.
[16] Article V(9) of the Canadian-U.S. Tax Treaty.
[17] Article 14(1) (¶ 1304.14) of the U.S. Model Treaty.

[18] Article 14(2) (¶ 1304.14) of the U.S. Model Treaty. In contrast, the Internal Revenue Code has a *de minimis* standard that re-sources the income of a nonresident alien as foreign-source income. Code Sec. 861(a)(3).

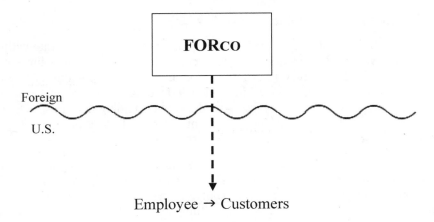

Employee → Customers

NRA is not taxed on his $20,000 of compensation for services he performs in the United States pursuant to the applicable treaty because (i) NRA is in the United States for only 7 days (less than 183 days), (ii) his compensation is paid by FORco, which is not a resident of the United States, and (iii) his compensation is not borne by a permanent establishment that FORco has in the United States.

Some older tax treaties contain a separate independent services provision that governs the taxation of personal services income derived by <u>self-employed professionals</u>, such as accountants, doctors, engineers, and lawyers. Such income is exempt from host country taxation unless the services are performed in the host country and the income is attributable to an office or other fixed base of business that is located in the host country and is regularly available to the taxpayer for purposes of performing the services. This provision allows self-employed professionals to provide services abroad without local taxation as long as they do not maintain an office or other fixed base of business within the host country. However, due to an emerging global consensus that little difference exists between a fixed base of business and a permanent establishment, the U.S. Model Treaty and more recent treaties do not contain a separate independent personal services article.

Tax treaties usually contain special rules for specific types of personal services income. For example, under the U.S. Model Treaty, there are special rules governing income derived by crew members of ships and aircraft operated in international traffic,[19] directors' fees,[20] entertainers and athletes,[21] pensions, social security, annuities, alimony and child support,[22] pension funds,[23] government workers,[24] and <u>students and trainees.</u>[25] A summary of the treaty provisions governing compensation for personal services can be found in the appendix to this chapter.

Although occasionally exempted from taxation as described above, <u>service income typically does not incur a reduced withholding rate under U.S. tax treaties.</u>

---

[19] Article 14(3) (¶ 1304.14) of the U.S. Model Treaty.
[20] Article 15 (¶ 1304.15) of the U.S. Model Treaty.
[21] Article 16 (¶ 1304.16) of the U.S. Model Treaty.
[22] Article 17 (¶ 1304.17) of the U.S. Model Treaty.
[23] Article 18 (¶ 1304.18) of the U.S. Model Treaty.
[24] Article 19 (¶ 1304.19) of the U.S. Model Treaty.
[25] Article 20 (¶ 1304.20) of the U.S. Model Treaty.

¶1302.03

.04 Dividends, Interest, and Royalties

As with the United States, most foreign countries impose flat rate withholding taxes on dividend, interest, and royalty income derived by offshore investors from sources within the country's borders. For example, the U.S. statutory withholding tax rate is 30% for both nonresident alien individuals and foreign corporations.[26] However, most tax treaties provide for reduced withholding tax rates, as long as the dividend, interest, or royalty income is not attributable to a permanent establishment of the taxpayer that is located within the host country.

In the case of dividends, the rate often is lower for controlling shareholders (e.g., a corporate shareholder owning 10% or more of the payor's stock) than for noncontrolling shareholders. For example, under the U.S. Model Treaty, the withholding rate on dividends is 5% for a company that directly owns 10% or more of the voting stock of the payer and 15% for all other shareholders. The U.S. treaties in a few countries provide for a 0% withholding tax rate for dividends paid by a subsidiary to its parent corporation. Table 13.2 presents the dividend withholding tax rates for selected countries.[27]

TABLE 13.2. TREATY WITHHOLDING TAX RATES ON DIVIDENDS PAID BY U.S. CORPORATIONS[a]

Payee's country of residence	Type of shareholder	
	Controlling	Noncontrolling
Canada	5%	15%
China	10%	10%
Finland	0%/5%	15%
France	0%/5%	15%
Germany	0%/5%	15%
Italy	5%	15%
Japan	0%/5%	10%
Mexico	0%/5%	10%
Netherlands	0%/5%	15%
United Kingdom	0%/5%	15%

[a] Taken from Table 1 of IRS Pub. No. 515 (Dec. 9, 2014), which is reproduced in its entirety in the appendix to this chapter.

Example 13.9: USAco is owned 40% by FORco (a corporation incorporated in country F), 40% by Norman Ray Allen (NRA, a citizen and resident of country F) and 20% by Kong (a citizen and resident of Hong Kong). Country F has a treaty with the United States identical to the U.S. Model Treaty. Hong Kong does not have a tax treaty with the United States. When USAco pays dividends to it shareholders, USAco will withhold 5% of the dividends paid to FORco because FORco is a controlling company pursuant to the Treaty, 15% to NRA because NRA is an individual resident of a treaty country, and the statutory rate of 30% to Kong because he is not a resident of a treaty country.

---

[26] Code Secs. 871(a) and 881(a).

[27] Article 10(2) (¶ 1304.10) of the U.S. Model Treaty.

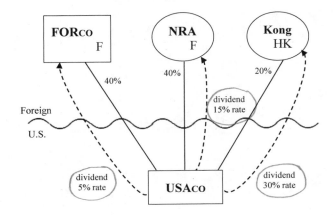

Tax treaties also usually reduce the withholding tax rate on interest to 15% or less. Under the U.S. Model Treaty, interest is exempt from withholding tax.[28] Table 13.3 presents the interest withholding tax rates for selected countries.

TABLE 13.3. TREATY WITHHOLDING TAX RATES ON INTEREST PAID BY U.S. PERSONS[a]

Payee's country of residence	Treaty withholding rate (general)
Canada	0%
China	10%
Finland	0%
France	0%
Germany	0%
Italy	10%
Japan	10%
Mexico	15%
Netherlands	0%
United Kingdom	0%

a Taken from Table 1 of IRS Pub. No. 515 (Dec. 9, 2014), which is reproduced in its entirety in the appendix to this chapter.

Example 13.10: USAco is owned 40% by FORco (a corporation organized in country F), 40% by Norman Ray Allen (NRA, a citizen and resident of country F) and 20% by Kong (a citizen and resident of Hong Kong). Country F has a treaty with the United States identical to the U.S. Model Treaty. FORco and Kong have also loaned money to USAco. Pursuant to the U.S. Model Treaty, the interest paid by USAco to FORco is exempt from tax. However, because Kong is a resident of Hong Kong, a non-treaty country, USAco must withhold the statutory rate of 30% from the interest income.

---

[28] Article 11(1) (¶ 1304.11) of the U.S. Model Treaty. When interest is paid by one related party to another, the treaty exemption applies only to an arm's-length amount of interest. Article 11(5) of the U.S. Model Treaty.

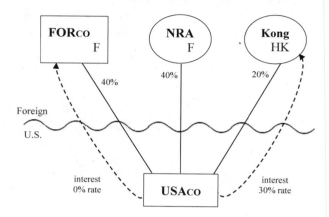

Most tax treaties also provide for lower withholding tax rates on royalties. Typically, the rate is 10% or less. Under the U.S. Model Treaty, all royalties are exempt from withholding.[29] The U.S. Model Treaty specifically defines a royalty as any payment for the use of, or the right to use, the following:

(i) any copyright of literary, artistic, or scientific work (including motion pictures or films or tapes used for television or radio broadcasting),

(ii) any patent, trademark, design, model, plan, secret formula or process, or other like right or property,

(iii) any information concerning industrial, commercial, or scientific experience, or

(iv) any gains derived from the disposition of any right or property described in (i) through (iii) where the proceeds are contingent on the future productivity, use, or disposition of that property.[30]

Example 13.11: FORco is a foreign corporation incorporated in country F, which has a tax treaty with the United States identical to the U.S. Model Treaty. FORco licenses the manufacturing process for the super-widget to unrelated licensees in the United States. Assuming that FORco is entitled to the benefits of the Treaty, the licensees do not have to withhold on the royalty payments to FORco.

---

[29] Article 12(1) (¶ 1304.12) of the U.S. Model Treaty. When a royalty is paid by one related party to another, the treaty exemption applies only to the arm's-length royalty amount. Article 12(4) of the U.S. Model Treaty.

[30] Article 12(2) (¶ 1304.12) of the U.S. Model Treaty.

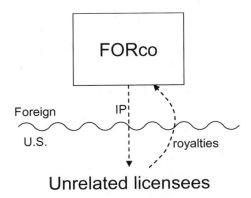

Table 13.4 presents the royalty withholding tax rates for selected countries.

TABLE 13.4. TREATY WITHHOLDING TAX RATES ON ROYALTIES PAID BY U.S. PERSONS[a]

Payee's country residence	Know-How/ Other	Patents	Film and TV	Copyrights
Canada	5%	0%	10%	0%
China	10%	10%	10%	10%
Finland	0%	0%	0%	0%
France	0%	0%	0%	0%
Germany	0%	0%	0%	0%
Italy	0%	8%	8%	0%
Japan	0%	0%	0%	0%
Mexico	10%	10%	10%	10%
Netherlands	0%	0%	0%	0%
United Kingdom	0%	0%	0%	0%

Type of royalty spans the four royalty-type columns.

[a]Taken from Table 1 of IRS Pub. No. 515 (Dec. 9, 2014), which is reproduced in its entirety in the appendix to this chapter.

A full listing of the treaty withholding rates for dividends, interest, and royalties can be found in the appendix to this chapter.

.05 Gains from the Disposition of Property

Under the U.S. Model Treaty, gains from the disposition of property, such as capital gains on the sale of stocks and securities, generally are taxable only by the country in which the seller resides.[31]

> **Example 13.12:** Bridgerock is a foreign corporation organized in country F, which has a tax treaty with the United States identical to the U.S. Model Treaty. Bridgerock owns all the shares of its U.S. subsidiary, Firerock. When

---

[31] Article 13(6) (¶ 1304.13) of the U.S. Model Treaty.

Bridgerock sells the Firerock shares to a purchaser, the Treaty does not permit the United States to tax the gain.

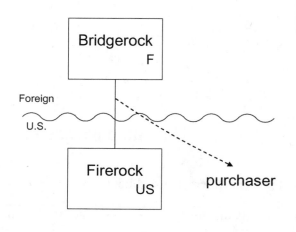

US MODEL TAXS GAIN ON REAL PROPERTY AND INVENTORY

However, the U.S. Model Treaty permits taxation of gains arising from the disposition of <u>real property, including gains from the disposition of shares of a corporation that has significant real property holdings and gains from the disposition of interests in a partnership, trust, or estate to the extent attributable to real property situated in a contracting state</u>.[32] The U.S. Model Treaty also permits the taxation of gains arising from the disposition of personal property, such as <u>inventory, that are attributable to a permanent establishment</u>.[33]

.06 Income from Real Property

Tax treaties typically do not provide tax exemptions or reductions for income from real property. Therefore, <u>both the home and the host country retain the right to tax real property income</u>, which includes income from agriculture and forestry.[34] <u>This rule applies to real property rental income</u>,[35] for which the Model Treaty does not reduce withholding rates, as well as gains from the sale of real property.[36]

Example **13.13:** Uncle Sam, a U.S. citizen and resident, owns appreciated real estate in country F, a country that has a tax treaty with the United States identical to the U.S. Model Treaty. Uncle Sam sells the appreciated real estate for substantial gain. <u>Country F can tax that gain</u> and, if it does, <u>Uncle Sam may claim a credit against his U.S. tax liability</u> for the country F income tax paid.

---

[32] Article 13(1) and (2) (¶ 1304.13) of the U.S. Model Treaty.

[33] Article 13(2)(c) (¶ 1304.13) of the U.S. Model Treaty.

[34] Article 6(1) (¶ 1304.06) of the U.S. Model Treaty. The home country may also retain the right to tax real property income.

[35] Article 6(3) (¶ 1304.06) of the U.S. Model Treaty.

[36] Article 13(1) and (2) (¶ 1304.13) of the U.S. Model Treaty.

If the real property income of a resident of one treaty country is taxed by the other treaty country, that taxpayer can elect to have its income taxed on a net basis at the normal marginal rates applicable to business profits, rather than having its income taxed on a gross basis through flat rate withholding taxes.[37] This election allows a taxpayer who owns rental property to offset the gross rental income with the related rental expenses, such as depreciation, interest, insurance, and maintenance expenses.

.07 Associated Enterprises Provisions

An associated enterprise treaty provision allows the United States and its treaty partners to allocate profits between two related business enterprises as if their financial relations were those of independent business enterprises. Treating related businesses as independent businesses resembles the arm's-length standard used to allocate income pursuant to Code Sec. 482.

    Example 13.14: USAco, a U.S. corporation, sells copper tubing to FORco, a wholly-owned country F subsidiary, at a price of $100 per tube. USAco sells the same tubing to independent distributors in country F at a price of $120 per tube. The U.S. and country F have entered a treaty with an associated enterprises provision identical to the U.S. Model Treaty.[38] As a result, the IRS can make a transfer pricing adjustment, increasing the price per tube sold from USAco to FORco to $120 per tube.

---

[37] Article 6(5) (¶ 1304.06) of the U.S. Model Treaty. Code Secs. 871(d) and 882(d) allow nonresident aliens and foreign corporations to make similar elections with respect to their U.S. real property interests.

[38] Article 9 (¶ 1304.09) of the U.S. Model Treaty.

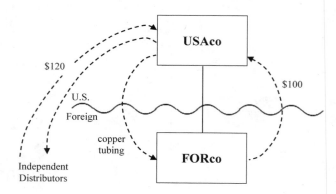

.08 Anti-treaty Shopping Provisions (Limitation on Benefits)

Because tax treaties provide lower withholding tax rates on dividend, interest, and royalty income, a multinational corporation may be able to reduce its foreign withholding taxes by owning its subsidiaries through strategically located holding companies. This practice is known as "treaty shopping."

> *Example* **13.15:** USAco is a U.S. corporation with a subsidiary in country X. The treaty between the United States and X provides a 15% withholding rate for dividends paid to a controlling shareholder. In contrast, the withholding rate on dividends paid to a controlling shareholder is 5% under the treaty between the United States and country Z and 0% under the treaty between countries Z and X. Country Z further exempts foreign dividends from Z's income tax. Therefore, USAco may be able to reduce the withholding tax rate on earnings repatriated from its country X subsidiary from 15% to 5% by interposing a Z holding company between itself and the X subsidiary.

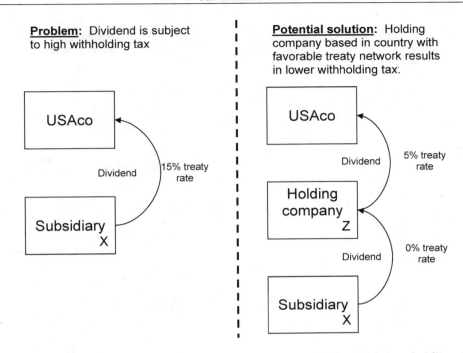

Problem: Dividend is subject to high withholding tax

USAco

Dividend   15% treaty rate

Subsidiary X

Potential solution: Holding company based in country with favorable treaty network results in lower withholding tax.

USAco

Dividend   5% treaty rate

Holding company Z

Dividend   0% treaty rate

Subsidiary X

Example 13.16: FORco is a country B corporation with a subsidiary in the United States. Country B does not have an income tax treaty with the United States. Accordingly, the U.S. withholding tax rate on any dividends received by FORco from its U.S. subsidiary is 30%. In contrast, the withholding tax rate on dividends is 0% under the treaty between the United States and country C and 10% under the treaty between countries C and B. Country C further exempts dividends from C's income tax. Therefore, FORco may be able to reduce the withholding tax rate on dividend distributions from its U.S. subsidiary from 30% to 10% by interposing a country C holding company between itself and the U.S. subsidiary.

¶1302.08

Problem: Dividend is subject to high statutory withholding tax rate.

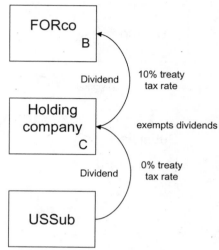

Potential solution: Holding company based in country with favorable treaty network.

Anti-treaty shopping provisions are formally known as limitation on benefits (or LOB) provisions. The principal target of a LOB provision is a corporation that is organized in a treaty country by a resident of a non-treaty country merely to obtain the benefits of that country's income tax treaty. A LOB provision denies such corporations the benefits of the treaty. Therefore, even if a corporation qualifies as a resident of the treaty country, that corporation is not entitled to treaty benefits unless it also satisfies the requirements of the treaty's LOB provision. For example, under the LOB provision found in Article 22 of the U.S. Model Treaty, a corporation that is a resident of a treaty country generally is entitled to treaty benefits only if the corporation meets one of the following additional requirements: (i) the corporation's shares are publicly traded,[39] (ii) the corporation is a subsidiary of a publicly traded corporation,[40] (iii) the corporation meets both a stock ownership test and a base erosion test,[41] or (iv) the corporation earns income that is related to an active trade or business.[42] Each of the four tests is discussed below in more detail. Resident individuals always satisfy the LOB provisions.

Shares publicly traded. A corporation is entitled to treaty benefits if both its principal class of shares is publicly traded on a recognized stock exchange and either (a) its principal class of shares is primarily traded on an exchange in its country of residence or (b) the company's primary place of management and

---

[39] Article 22(2)(c)(i) (¶1304.22) of the U.S. Model Treaty.

[40] Article 22(2)(c)(ii) (¶1304.22) of the U.S. Model Treaty.

[41] Article 22(2)(e) (¶1304.22) of the U.S. Model Treaty.

[42] Article 22(3) (¶1304.22) of the U.S. Model Treaty.

¶1302.08

control is in its country of residence.[43] The principal shares are the common shares of the company that constitute the majority of the voting power and value of the company. If no single class qualifies, then the principal class of shares means the class that in the aggregate represents the majority of the voting power and value. Although the recognized stock exchange for foreign country purposes will vary by treaty, the recognized stock exchanges in the United States are NASDAQ, any stock exchange registered with the U.S. Securities and Exchange Commission as a national securities exchange, and any other exchange agreed on by the United States and the foreign country.[44]

> ***Example* 13.17:** Foreign PubliCo is a foreign corporation whose principal class of shares regularly trade on a recognized stock exchange in country F, which has a tax treaty with the United States identical to the U.S. Model Treaty. Foreign PubliCo, a resident of country F, owns all the shares of USSub. USSub pays a dividend to Foreign PubliCo. Because Foreign PubliCo's shares are primarily and regularly traded on a recognized stock exchange in country F, the dividend Foreign PubliCo receives from USSub is subject to withholding at only the 5% treaty rate.

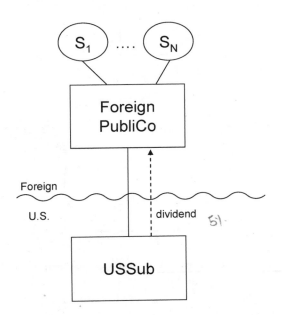

Subsidiary of publicly-traded corporation. A corporation is entitled to treaty benefits if over 50% of its shares are owned by five or fewer corporations entitled to treaty benefits. This test considers both direct and indirect owners, but is designed to provide benefits to an operating subsidiary incorporated in the country of a publicly-held holding company.

---

[43] Article 22(2)(c)(i) (¶ 1304.22) of the U.S. Model Treaty.

[44] Article 22(5)(a) (¶ 1304.22) of the U.S. Model Treaty.

Example **13.18:** Foreign PubliCo is a foreign corporation whose principal class of shares regularly trade on a recognized stock exchange in country F, which has a tax treaty with the United States identical to the U.S. Model Treaty. Foreign PubliCo, a resident of country F, owns all the shares of ForSub, a country F operating subsidiary that owns all the shares of USSub. USSub pays a dividend to ForSub. Although ForSub is not publicly traded, because Foreign PubliCo's shares are primarily and regularly traded on a recognized stock exchange in foreign country F and Foreign PubliCo owns all the shares of ForSub, the dividend ForSub receives is subject to withholding at only the 5% treaty rate.

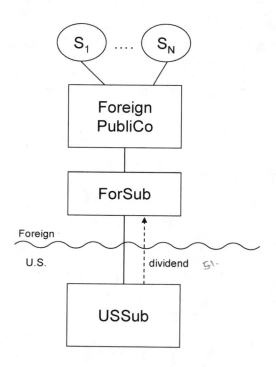

Stock ownership/base erosion test. A corporation qualifies for treaty benefits under this test if both at least 50% of the corporation's stock is owned by residents who are entitled to treaty benefits (the stock ownership test) and less than 50% of the corporation's gross income results in deductible payments to persons who are not residents of either treaty country (the base erosion test).[45]

Example **13.19:** Frank is a resident of country F, which has a tax treaty with the United States identical to the U.S. Model Treaty. Norman Ray Allen (NRA) is a resident of a country that does not have a treaty with the United States. Frank and NRA each own 50% of ForCo, a corporation organized in

---

[45] Article 22(2)(e) (¶ 1304.22) of the U.S. Model Treaty.

country F. ForCo owns all the shares of USCo, a domestic corporation. USCo pays a dividend to ForCo, which earns approximately $50,000 of gross income, before paying a salary to NRA of $20,000. Because at least 50% of the shares are owned by Frank and less than 50% of ForCo's gross income results in deductible payments to nonresidents of treaty countries, ForCo is entitled to treaty benefits. As a result, the dividend from USCo to ForCo is subject to withholding tax at the 5% treaty rate.

However, the dividend would not be entitled to treaty benefits and withholding would occur at the non-treaty rate of 30% if either: (i) NRA received a salary of $25,001 (over 50% of the $50,000 gross income of USCo), or (ii) Frank owned less than 50% of the shares of ForCo.

Active trade or business. Treaty benefits are extended to residents that do not otherwise qualify, but who are engaged in the active conduct of a trade or business in their country of residence. For this test, the benefits will extend only to income derived in connection with or incidental to that trade or business and only if that trade or business is substantial in relation to activities of that business in other countries. The substantiality test requires that the trade or business in the resident country is not merely a small portion of the income-generating activity in the source country.

Example **13.20:** Norman Ray Allen (NRA), a nonresident alien, wants to acquire USCo, a U.S. manufacturing company, that annually has $10 billion of active business income. Because the country in which NRA resides does not have a treaty with the United States, a 30% non-treaty withholding rate would apply to any dividends paid by USCo. Absent the substantiality requirement, NRA could take advantage of treaty benefits by acquiring USCo through ForCo (a corporation that is a resident of country F, which has a tax treaty with the

¶1302.08

United States identical to the U.S. Model Treaty) and then arranging for ForCo to have an outlet in country F that sells a relatively miniscule amount of manufactured products for $100,000 of active business income.

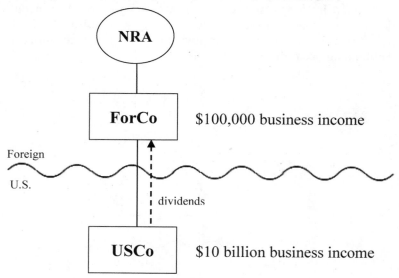

Derivative benefits. Although not currently in the U.S. Model Treaty, some of the recent treaties concluded with major U.S. trading partners reduce withholding tax rates on payments to corporations that satisfy the derivative benefits test. The policy behind the derivative benefits test is that treaty shopping does not occur when an intermediary receiving a payment is owned by a corporation in another country entitled to treaty benefits. For example, the U.S.-Canadian Treaty permits treaty rates on withholding when paid to a treaty resident corporation that has a 90% controlling ownership interest by persons who (i) are residents in a third country that has a comprehensive income tax treaty with the United States and are entitled to the same kind of benefits under that treaty, (ii) would be qualified persons eligible for treaty benefits if they were residents of the United States or Canada, (iii) would be entitled to a rate of tax in the United States under the third country treaty that is not lower than the tax rate in the U.S.-Canadian Treaty, and (iv) have less than 50% of the corporation's gross income paid directly or indirectly to persons who are not residents of either Canada or the United States.[46]

***Example* 13.21*:** UKCo is publicly traded on the London Stock Exchange and, if UKCo directly owned USCo, UKCo would be entitled to the benefit of a 5% withholding rate under the U.K.-U.S. Tax Treaty. However, UKCo prefers to operate in North America through a Canadian holding company ("CanCo"). CanCo does not make deductible payments to anyone outside of Canada. Even though CanCo does not satisfy any of the aforementioned limitation of benefits provisions, CanCo is entitled to derivative benefits under the U.S.-Canadian

---

[46] Article 29A(4) of the Tax Treaty between the United States and Canada.

¶1302.08

Tax Treaty. Therefore, a dividend from USCo to CanCo would be entitled to the preferential 5% U.S.-Canadian Tax Treaty withholding rate.

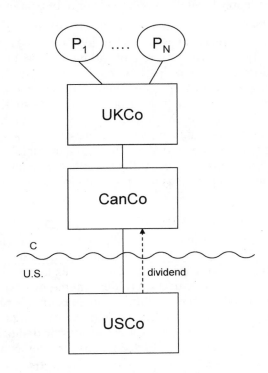

Many of the U.S. tax treaties with European countries require the ultimate owner to be an equivalent beneficiary, which usually requires residency in a European Union country.[47]

Case law and statutory provisions. In addition to the anti-treaty shopping provisions contained in treaties, the IRS has sought to disallow treaty benefits obtained through the use of intermediary entities by invoking the judicial doctrine of substance over form. The seminal case in this area is *Aiken Industries, Inc. v. Comm'r,*[48] in which the IRS successfully denied treaty benefits that the taxpayer attempted to obtain through the use of a back-to-back loan arrangement. The IRS has even collapsed back-to-back loans when there was a valid business purpose for the arrangement.[49]

In addition, Code Sec. 7701(l) gives the IRS the authority to disregard the existence of an intermediary or conduit entity with respect to treaty shopping that results in the avoidance of U.S. taxes. A multi-party financing arrangement is subject to recharacterization if a related intermediate entity participates in a back-to-

---

[47] *See,* for example, paragraphs 3-a and 7-d of Article 23 of the United Kingdom-U.S. Tax Treaty.

[48] 56 TC 925, Dec. 30,912, A. 1972-2 CB 1. *See also Northern Ind. Pub. Serv. Co.,* 105 TC 341, Dec. 50,979.

Aff'd, CA-7, 97-1 USTC ¶ 50,474, 115 F3d 506 (7th Cir., 1997).

[49] Rev. Rul. 84-152, 1984-2 CB 381; Rev. Rul. 84-153, 1984-2 CB 383.

back loan arrangement as part of a plan to avoid U.S. withholding taxes. These rules also apply to certain unrelated intermediaries, back-to-back leases, and licenses, but do not apply to equity investments or debt guarantees.[50]

Code Sec. 894(c) further limits the availability of reduced U.S. withholding tax under an income tax treaty for payments to hybrid entities. Specifically, a foreign person is not entitled to a reduced rate of withholding tax under a tax treaty on an item of income derived through a partnership (or other fiscally transparent entity) if all of the following apply: (i) the income item is not treated by the foreign country as an item of income to such foreign person, (ii) the foreign country does not impose tax on a distribution of the item by the U.S. entity to the foreign person, and (iii) the treaty does not contain a provision addressing the applicability of the treaty in the case of an item of income derived through a partnership.[51] Congress enacted Code Sec. 894(c) to primarily prevent the use of a tax planning strategy in which a U.S. limited liability company was interposed between a foreign parent corporation and its U.S. subsidiary.

.09 Non-Discrimination Provisions

Tax treaties generally include non-discrimination provisions, which are designed to prevent a treaty country from imposing a tax on residents of the other treaty country that is more burdensome than the tax imposed on its own residents. The U.S. Model Treaty specifically prohibits numerous types of discrimination. Examples include imposing a more burdensome tax on a permanent establishment of a foreign corporation than on a U.S. corporation carrying on the same activities, discriminating with respect to personal allowances or deductions based on family status, discriminating with respect to deductions for interest and royalty payments, and imposing a more burdensome tax on a U.S. corporation owned by foreign investors than on a similarly situated U.S. corporation owned by U.S. shareholders.[52]

> **Example 13.22:** FORco, a country Y parent corporation, owns all of the stock of USsub. USsub competes in the U.S. steel market with USAco, a domestic corporation wholly-owned by U.S. citizens. In order to protect the U.S. steel industry, Congress enacts legislation increasing the rate of income tax on all steel wholesalers that are foreign-owned from 35% to 45%. Subsequently, the U.S. and country Y enter into a treaty that contains an anti-discrimination provision identical to the U.S. Model Treaty, which includes a paragraph prohibiting tax discrimination based on capital ownership. As a result, USsub is exempt from the 45% rate, and will pay tax at the same 35% rate as USAco.

.10 Mutual Agreement Procedure

Tax treaties provide a mutual agreement procedure by which a resident of a treaty country can request assistance from the competent authority of that country in obtaining relief from actions of one or both treaty countries that the taxpayer

---

[50] Reg. § 1.881-3.

[51] Code Sec. 894(c) and Temp. Reg. § 1.894-1(a) and (b).

[52] Article 24 (¶ 1304.24) of the U.S. Model Treaty.

¶1302.09

believes are inconsistent with the treaty.[53] The competent authority is the governmental office that administers tax treaties. For example, if one or both treaty countries makes an adjustment to the intercompany transfer prices used by affiliated companies located within their respective countries, both countries might tax the same item of income. In such cases, the taxpayer may wish to seek relief from double taxation by petitioning the appropriate competent authority. Assuming the taxpayer's objections are justified, the competent authority of one treaty country is empowered to resolve the case by mutual agreement with the competent authority of the other treaty country. Other situations in which the taxpayer may wish to seek this mutual agreement procedure include conflicts regarding the proper characterization of an item of income, the application of a source-of-income rule, or the meaning of a term.[54] The various methods by which a U.S. taxpayer can request competent authority assistance are described in Chapter 16 (¶ 1606).

> **Example 13.23:** USAco is a subsidiary of EURco. USAco buys widgets from EURco for $200 and resells them in the United States for $210. The IRS argues that the arm's length price for the intercompany widget sales is $180 and assesses additional tax on USAco. As a consequence, despite EURco recognizing $200 on gross income with respect to each widget sale, USAco claims a cost of goods sold deduction of only $180. To obtain relief on this $20 of double taxation, either USAco or EURco can petition their respective competent authority.

.11 Exchanges of Information

In addition to the mutual agreement procedures outlined above, tax treaties also provide for exchanges of information regarding taxpayers as a mechanism for enhancing compliance with respect to international transactions. Under the U.S. Model Treaty, the competent authorities of the two treaty countries shall exchange such information as is necessary for enforcing provisions of the tax treaty, as well as the internal laws of the two countries concerning taxes covered by the treaty.[55]

---

[53] Article 25(1) and (2) (¶ 1304.25) of the U.S. Model Treaty.

[54] Article 25(3) (¶ 1304.25) of the U.S. Model Treaty. The procedures for requesting assistance from U.S. competent authorities are found in Rev. Proc. 2006-54, IRB 2006-38.

[55] Article 26(1) (¶ 1304.26) of the U.S. Model Treaty.

For example, the two treaty countries might share information regarding a taxpayer that both countries are auditing. Another example is an exchange of lists of residents of one treaty country deriving dividend, interest, or royalty income from sources within the other treaty country.

> ***Example* 13.24:** A distributor of candy, USAco is a subsidiary of ASIAco. USAco buys the candy from ASIAco for resale in the United States. The IRS's International Examiner conducts a transfer pricing audit of USAco. After USAco fails to respond to the International Examiner's IDR requesting all agreements between USAco and ASIAco, the International Examiner requests the information from ASIA country's tax authority pursuant to the exchange of information provision in the U.S.-ASIA country tax treaty.

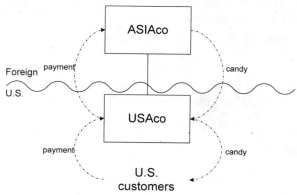

¶ 1303 DISCLOSURE OF TREATY-BASED RETURN POSITIONS

A taxpayer, U.S. or foreign, that claims the benefits of a treaty by taking a tax return position that is in conflict with the Internal Revenue Code must disclose the position.[56] A tax return position is considered to be in conflict with the Code and therefore treaty-based, if the U.S. tax liability under the treaty is different from the tax liability that would have to be reported in the absence of a treaty.[57] This reporting requirement is waived in various situations. A taxpayer reports treaty-based positions either by attaching a statement to its return or by using Form 8833 (a sample of a completed Form 8833 is reproduced in the Appendix to this chapter).[58] If a taxpayer fails to report a treaty-based return position, each such failure is subject to a penalty of $1,000 or a penalty of $10,000 in the case of a corporation.[59]

The regulations describe the items to be disclosed on a Form 8833. The disclosure statement typically requires six items:

---

[56] Code Sec. 6114.
[57] Reg. § 301.6114-1(a)(2)(i).

[58] Reg. § 301.6114-1(d) and Announcement 93-63, IRB 1993-16, 11.
[59] Code Sec. 6712.

¶1303

(i) the name and employer identification number of both the recipient and payor of the income at issue;

(ii) the type of treaty benefited item and its amount;

(iii) the facts and an explanation supporting the treaty position taken;

(iv) the specific treaty provisions on which the taxpayer bases its claims;

(v) the Internal Revenue Code provision exempted or reduced; and

(vi) an explanation of any applicable LOB provisions.

The disclosure regulations specify a non-exclusive list of treaty benefits that must always be disclosed.[60] The regulations also waive various treaty benefits from disclosure, but specify that if an issue is not on the wavier list, the issue must be disclosed.[61]

.01 Specific Disclosure Requirements

The regulations require disclosure of reduced withholding taxes on some payments to related persons. Examples include interest, dividend, rents, and royalties that a U.S. person pays to a related foreign person who is entitled to reduced rates of withholding tax under a treaty and the payment exceeds $500,000.[62]

Example 13.25: USSub, a U.S. corporation, is a subsidiary of FORco, a corporation organized in a country that has a tax treaty with the United States that is identical to the U.S. Model Treaty. USSub pays a $1 million dividend to FORco and withholds $50,000 pursuant to the treaty withholding rate on dividends of 5%. USSub must disclose the $1 million dividend to FORco and the reduced withholding on a Form 8833 and provide a Form 1042-S to both FORco and the IRS.

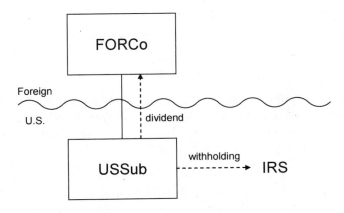

---

[60] Reg. § 301.6114-1(b).

[61] Reg. § 301.6114-1(c).

[62] Reg. § 301.6114-1(b)(4). For this purpose, a related foreign person includes a CFC in which the U.S. payer is a 10% or more U.S. shareholder, a foreign corporation controlled by the U.S. payer, a 25% or more foreign shareholder of the U.S. payer, or a foreign related party. This rule applies even though the foreign recipient may not otherwise have to file a U.S. income tax return.

Foreign persons claiming exemption from U.S. tax because their <u>trade or business does not constitute a permanent establishment</u> under a treaty <u>must disclose that position.</u>[63]

Example 13.26: FORco sells zinc to customers in the United States. FORco's only U.S. presence is a warehouse which FORco uses solely to store and deliver zinc. Without a tax treaty, FORco's sales in the United States combined with a U.S. warehouse would constitute carrying on a trade or business in the United States that would be subject to U.S. income tax. However, FORco is a resident of a country whose U.S. tax treaty excludes from the definition of a permanent establishment a warehouse used solely to store and deliver the taxpayer's own goods. Although FORco is not subject to tax in the United States under the treaty, <u>FORco must file a return disclosing the treaty position.</u>

How?
form 8033?

A foreign corporation operating in the United States through a branch may be subject to the branch profits tax. Some treaties provide exemptions or rate reductions to the <u>branch profits tax.</u>[64] <u>Any foreign corporation claiming such an exemption or reduction must disclose this position.</u>[65]

forms

Example 13.27: FORco, a country F corporation, sells paper to customers in the United States through its U.S. branch, which constitutes a permanent establishment under the tax treaty between the United States and country X. The treaty <u>reduces the branch profits tax from 30% to 5%.</u> FORco must disclose the reduced profits tax tax on its <u>Form 1120F with Form 8833.</u>

---

[63] Reg. § 301.6114-1(b)(5)(i).
[64] Code Sec. 884
[65] Reg. § 301.6114-1(b)(3).

¶**1303.01**

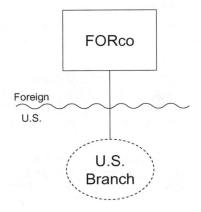

To the extent that a treaty may alter the sourcing of an item of income, a taxpayer must disclose this alteration.[66]

  ***Example* 13.28:** FORco is a corporation organized in country F, which has a treaty with the United States identical to the U.S. Model Treaty. FORco owns all the shares of USAco. Norman Ray Allen (NRA), a citizen and resident of country F, is the President of FORco. NRA is also on the Board of Directors of USAco, the U.S. subsidiary of FORco. Four times a year, NRA travels to the United States for the Board of Director meetings, for which he receives a total fee of $20,000. Although this personal services income is U.S.-source under Code Sec. 861(a)(3), Article 16 (¶ 1304.16) of the U.S. Model Treaty re-sources the income as foreign-source income. Due to the Treaty re-sourcing the item of income, NRA must disclose this alteration, although he will not have to pay any U.S. tax.

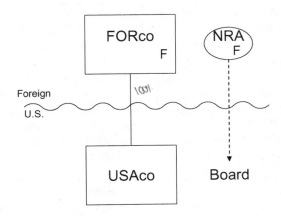

---

[66] Reg. § 301.6114-1(b)(6).

.02 Waiver of Disclosure Requirements

The disclosure regulations provide an exclusive list of issues that taxpayers do not have to disclose.

In contrast to payments in excess of $500,000 to related parties, <u>payments of interest, dividends, rents, or royalties by a U.S. person to an unrelated party are not subject to disclosure other than the withholding compliance procedures described in Chapter 9 (¶ 904).</u> As a result, an unrelated foreign recipient of U.S.-source fixed, determinable, annual, or periodic income <u>will not have a filing obligation, unless the taxpayer is engaged in a trade or business within the United States.</u>

> **Example 13.29:** FORco is a resident of a country that has a tax treaty with the United States that is identical to the U.S. Model Treaty. FORco owns only 1% of USCo, a U.S. corporation that pays FORco a $1 million dividend. The dividend is subject to withholding tax at the <u>15% treaty rate.</u> Because FORco's <u>percentage ownership of USCo is not high enough for FORco to be considered a related party,</u> disclosure to the IRS is specifically waived.

<u>The disclosure requirements also do not apply to a U.S. withholding agent.</u> These withholding agents already have reporting obligations in that they must file Forms 1042 and 1042S while retaining Form W-8BEN and do not have any further obligations with respect to reduced withholding pursuant to a treaty.[67]

No reporting is required when the treaty benefit is due to residency in a treaty partner country due to the tie-breaker rules when the individual receives, in the aggregate, amounts less than $100,000.[68] For example, suppose an individual is considered both a resident of the United States under the green card test and a resident of a treaty partner due to that treaty partner's internal laws. If, pursuant to the tie-breaker provisions in that treaty, the individual is classified a resident of the treaty partner, she does not have to file a U.S. return.

Nonresident aliens and foreign corporations may occasionally desire to make a protective tax return filing to avoid any penalties and to ensure that the statute of limitations begins to run. This would occur when it is uncertain whether the foreign corporation has a filing requirement.

---

[67] Reg. § 301.6114-1(c)(5). [68] Reg. § 301.6114-1(c)(2).

¶ 1304 UNITED STATES MODEL INCOME TAX CONVENTION OF NOVEMBER 15, 2006

UNITED STATES MODEL INCOME TAX CONVENTION OF NOVEMBER 15, 2006

**CONVENTION BETWEEN
THE GOVERNMENT OF THE UNITED STATES OF AMERICA
AND THE GOVERNMENT OF -------
FOR THE AVOIDANCE OF DOUBLE TAXATION
AND THE PREVENTION OF FISCAL EVASION
WITH RESPECT TO TAXES ON INCOME**

The Government of the United States of America and the Government of -----, desiring to conclude a Convention for the avoidance of double taxation and the prevention of fiscal evasion with respect to taxes on income, have agreed as follows:

2006 U.S. Model
Income Tax Convention

- 2 -

Article 1

GENERAL SCOPE

1.   This Convention shall apply only to persons who are residents of one or both of the Contracting States, except as otherwise provided in the Convention.

2.   This Convention shall not restrict in any manner any benefit now or hereafter accorded:

a)   by the laws of either Contracting State; or

b)   by any other agreement to which the Contracting States are parties.

3.   a)   Notwithstanding the provisions of subparagraph b) of paragraph 2 of this Article:

   i)   for purposes of paragraph 3 of Article XXII (Consultation) of the General Agreement on Trade in Services, the Contracting States agree that any question arising as to the interpretation or application of this Convention and, in particular, whether a taxation measure is within the scope of this Convention, shall be determined exclusively in accordance with the provisions of Article 25 (Mutual Agreement Procedure) of this Convention; and

   ii)   the provisions of Article XVII of the General Agreement on Trade in Services shall not apply to a taxation measure unless the competent authorities agree that the measure is not within the scope of Article 24 (Non-Discrimination) of this Convention.

b)   For the purposes of this paragraph, a "measure" is a law, regulation, rule, procedure, decision, administrative action, or any similar provision or action.

4.   Except to the extent provided in paragraph 5, this Convention shall not affect the taxation by a Contracting State of its residents (as determined under Article 4 (Resident)) and its citizens. Notwithstanding the other provisions of this Convention, a former citizen or former long-term resident of a Contracting State may, for the period of ten years following the loss of such status, be taxed in accordance with the laws of that Contracting State.

5.   The provisions of paragraph 4 shall not affect:

a)   the benefits conferred by a Contracting State under paragraph 2 of Article 9 (Associated Enterprises), paragraphs 1 b), 2, and 5 of Article 17 (Pensions, Social Security, Annuities, Alimony, and Child Support), paragraphs 1 and 4 of Article 18 (Pension Funds), and Articles 23 (Relief From Double Taxation), 24 (Non-Discrimination), and 25 (Mutual Agreement Procedure); and

- 3 -

b)   the benefits conferred by a Contracting State under paragraph 2 of Article 18 (Pension Funds), Articles 19 (Government Service), 20 (Students and Trainees), and 27 (Members of Diplomatic Missions and Consular Posts), upon individuals who are neither citizens of, nor have been admitted for permanent residence in, that State.

6.   An item of income, profit or gain derived through an entity that is fiscally transparent under the laws of either Contracting State shall be considered to be derived by a resident of a State to the extent that the item is treated for purposes of the taxation law of such Contracting State as the income, profit or gain of a resident.

- 4 -

Article 2

TAXES COVERED

1.   This Convention shall apply to taxes on income imposed on behalf of a Contracting State irrespective of the manner in which they are levied.

2.   There shall be regarded as taxes on income all taxes imposed on total income, or on elements of income, including taxes on gains from the alienation of property.

3.   The existing taxes to which this Convention shall apply are:

a)   in the case of ------:

b)   in the case of the United States: the Federal income taxes imposed by the Internal Revenue Code (but excluding social security and unemployment taxes), and the Federal excise taxes imposed with respect to private foundations.

4.   This Convention shall apply also to any identical or substantially similar taxes that are imposed after the date of signature of the Convention in addition to, or in place of, the existing taxes. The competent authorities of the Contracting States shall notify each other of any changes that have been made in their respective taxation or other laws that significantly affect their obligations under this Convention.

2006 U.S. Model
Income Tax Convention

- 5 -

Article 3

GENERAL DEFINITIONS

1. For the purposes of this Convention, unless the context otherwise requires:

a) the term "person" includes an individual, an estate, a trust, a partnership, a company, and any other body of persons;

b) the term "company" means any body corporate or any entity that is treated as a body corporate for tax purposes according to the laws of the state in which it is organized;

c) the terms "enterprise of a Contracting State" and "enterprise of the other Contracting State" mean respectively an enterprise carried on by a resident of a Contracting State, and an enterprise carried on by a resident of the other Contracting State; the terms also include an enterprise carried on by a resident of a Contracting State through an entity that is treated as fiscally transparent in that Contracting State;

d) the term "enterprise" applies to the carrying on of any business;

e) the term "business" includes the performance of professional services and of other activities of an independent character;

f) the term "international traffic" means any transport by a ship or aircraft, except when such transport is solely between places in a Contracting State;

g) the term "competent authority" means:

    i) in -----, --------------------------; and

    ii) in the United States: the Secretary of the Treasury or his delegate;

h) the term "--------" means ;

i) the term "United States" means the United States of America, and includes the states thereof and the District of Columbia; such term also includes the territorial sea thereof and the sea bed and subsoil of the submarine areas adjacent to that territorial sea, over which the United States exercises sovereign rights in accordance with international law; the term, however, does not include Puerto Rico, the Virgin Islands, Guam or any other United States possession or territory;

¶1304

2006 U.S. Model
Income Tax Convention
- 6 -

j)   the term "national" of a Contracting State means:

  i)   any individual possessing the nationality or citizenship of that State; and

  ii)   any legal person, partnership or association deriving its status as such from the laws in force in that State;

k)   the term "pension fund" means any person established in a Contracting State that is:

  i)   generally exempt from income taxation in that State; and

  ii)   operated principally either:

    A)   to administer or provide pension or retirement benefits; or

    B)   to earn income for the benefit of one or more persons described in clause A).

2.   As regards the application of the Convention at any time by a Contracting State any term not defined therein shall, unless the context otherwise requires, or the competent authorities agree to a common meaning pursuant to the provisions of Article 25 (Mutual Agreement Procedure), have the meaning which it has at that time under the law of that State for the purposes of the taxes to which the Convention applies, any meaning under the applicable tax laws of that State prevailing over a meaning given to the term under other laws of that State.

- 7 -

Article 4

RESIDENT

1.   For the purposes of this Convention, the term "resident of a Contracting State" means any person who, under the laws of that State, is liable to tax therein by reason of his domicile, residence, citizenship, place of management, place of incorporation, or any other criterion of a similar nature, and also includes that State and any political subdivision or local authority thereof. This term, however, does not include any person who is liable to tax in that State in respect only of income from sources in that State or of profits attributable to a permanent establishment in that State.

2.   The term "resident of a Contracting State" includes:

a)   a pension fund established in that State; and

b)   an organization that is established and maintained in that State exclusively for religious, charitable, scientific, artistic, cultural, or educational purposes,

notwithstanding that all or part of its income or gains may be exempt from tax under the domestic law of that State.

3.   Where, by reason of the provisions of paragraph 1, an individual is a resident of both Contracting States, then his status shall be determined as follows:

a)   he shall be deemed to be a resident only of the State in which he has a permanent home available to him; if he has a permanent home available to him in both States, he shall be deemed to be a resident only of the State with which his personal and economic relations are closer (center of vital interests);

b)   if the State in which he has his center of vital interests cannot be determined, or if he does not have a permanent home available to him in either State, he shall be deemed to be a resident only of the State in which he has an habitual abode;

c)   if he has an habitual abode in both States or in neither of them, he shall be deemed to be a resident only of the State of which he is a national;

d)   if he is a national of both States or of neither of them, the competent authorities of the Contracting States shall endeavor to settle the question by mutual agreement.

¶1304

2006 U.S. Model
Income Tax Convention

- 8 -

4.   Where by reason of the provisions of paragraph 1 a company is a resident of both Contracting States, then if it is created or organized under the laws of one of the Contracting States or a political subdivision thereof, but not under the laws of the other Contracting State or a political subdivision thereof, such company shall be deemed to be a resident of the first-mentioned Contracting State. In all other cases involving dual resident companies, the competent authorities of the Contracting States shall endeavor to determine the mode of application of the Convention to such company. If the competent authorities do not reach such an agreement, that company will not be treated as a resident of either Contracting State for purposes of its claiming any benefits provided by the Convention.

5.   Where by reason of the provisions of paragraphs 1 and 2 of this Article a person other than an individual or a company is a resident of both Contracting States, the competent authorities of the Contracting States shall by mutual agreement endeavor to determine the mode of application of this Convention to that person.

- 9 -

Article 5

PERMANENT ESTABLISHMENT

1.   For the purposes of this Convention, the term "permanent establishment" means a fixed place of business through which the business of an enterprise is wholly or partly carried on.

2.   The term "permanent establishment" includes especially:

    a)   a place of management;

    b)   a branch;

    c)   an office;

    d)   a factory;

    e)   a workshop; and

    f)   a mine, an oil or gas well, a quarry, or any other place of extraction of natural resources.

3.   A building site or construction or installation project, or an installation or drilling rig or ship used for the exploration of natural resources, constitutes a permanent establishment only if it lasts, or the exploration activity continues for more than twelve months.

4.   Notwithstanding the preceding provisions of this Article, the term "permanent establishment" shall be deemed not to include:

    a)   the use of facilities solely for the purpose of storage, display or delivery of goods or merchandise belonging to the enterprise;

    b)   the maintenance of a stock of goods or merchandise belonging to the enterprise solely for the purpose of storage, display or delivery;

    c)   the maintenance of a stock of goods or merchandise belonging to the enterprise solely for the purpose of processing by another enterprise;

    d)   the maintenance of a fixed place of business solely for the purpose of purchasing goods or merchandise, or of collecting information, for the enterprise;

    e)   the maintenance of a fixed place of business solely for the purpose of carrying on, for the enterprise, any other activity of a preparatory or auxiliary character;

- 10 -

f)   the maintenance of a fixed place of business solely for any combination of the activities mentioned in subparagraphs a) through e), provided that the overall activity of the fixed place of business resulting from this combination is of a preparatory or auxiliary character.

5.   Notwithstanding the provisions of paragraphs 1 and 2, where a person -- other than an agent of an independent status to whom paragraph 6 applies -- is acting on behalf of an enterprise and has and habitually exercises in a Contracting State an authority to conclude contracts that are binding on the enterprise, that enterprise shall be deemed to have a permanent establishment in that State in respect of any activities that the person undertakes for the enterprise, unless the activities of such person are limited to those mentioned in paragraph 4 that, if exercised through a fixed place of business, would not make this fixed place of business a permanent establishment under the provisions of that paragraph.

6.   An enterprise shall not be deemed to have a permanent establishment in a Contracting State merely because it carries on business in that State through a broker, general commission agent, or any other agent of an independent status, provided that such persons are acting in the ordinary course of their business as independent agents.

7.   The fact that a company that is a resident of a Contracting State controls or is controlled by a company that is a resident of the other Contracting State, or that carries on business in that other State (whether through a permanent establishment or otherwise), shall not be taken into account in determining whether either company has a permanent establishment in that other State.

- 11 -

Article 6

INCOME FROM REAL PROPERTY

1.   Income derived by a resident of a Contracting State from real property, including income from agriculture or forestry, situated in the other Contracting State may be taxed in that other State.

2.   The term "real property" shall have the meaning which it has under the law of the Contracting State in which the property in question is situated. The term shall in any case include property accessory to real property (including livestock and equipment used in agriculture and forestry), rights to which the provisions of general law respecting landed property apply, usufruct of real property and rights to variable or fixed payments as consideration for the working of, or the right to work, mineral deposits, sources and other natural resources. Ships and aircraft shall not be regarded as real property.

3.   The provisions of paragraph 1 shall apply to income derived from the direct use, letting, or use in any other form of real property.

4.   The provisions of paragraphs 1 and 3 shall also apply to the income from real property of an enterprise.

5.   A resident of a Contracting State who is liable to tax in the other Contracting State on income from real property situated in the other Contracting State may elect for any taxable year to compute the tax on such income on a net basis as if such income were business profits attributable to a permanent establishment in such other State. Any such election shall be binding for the taxable year of the election and all subsequent taxable years unless the competent authority of the Contracting State in which the property is situated agrees to terminate the election.

2006 U.S. Model
Income Tax Convention

- 12 -

Article 7

BUSINESS PROFITS

1.   The profits of an enterprise of a Contracting State shall be taxable only in that State unless the enterprise carries on business in the other Contracting State through a permanent establishment situated therein. If the enterprise carries on business as aforesaid, the profits of the enterprise may be taxed in the other State but only so much of them as are attributable to that permanent establishment.

2.   Subject to the provisions of paragraph 3, where an enterprise of a Contracting State carries on business in the other Contracting State through a permanent establishment situated therein, there shall in each Contracting State be attributed to that permanent establishment the profits that it might be expected to make if it were a distinct and independent enterprise engaged in the same or similar activities under the same or similar conditions. For this purpose, the profits to be attributed to the permanent establishment shall include only the profits derived from the assets used, risks assumed and activities performed by the permanent establishment.

3.   In determining the profits of a permanent establishment, there shall be allowed as deductions expenses that are incurred for the purposes of the permanent establishment, including executive and general administrative expenses so incurred, whether in the State in which the permanent establishment is situated or elsewhere.*

4.   No profits shall be attributed to a permanent establishment by reason of the mere purchase by that permanent establishment of goods or merchandise for the enterprise.

---

*   Protocol or Notes should include the following language:

It is understood that the business profits to be attributed to a permanent establishment shall include only the profits derived from the assets used, risks assumed and activities performed by the permanent establishment. The principles of the OECD Transfer Pricing Guidelines will apply for purposes of determining the profits attributable to a permanent establishment, taking into account the different economic and legal circumstances of a single entity. Accordingly, any of the methods described therein as acceptable methods for determining an arm's length result may be used to determine the income of a permanent establishment so long as those methods are applied in accordance with the Guidelines. In particular, in determining the amount of attributable profits, the permanent establishment shall be treated as having the same amount of capital that it would need to support its activities if it were a distinct and separate enterprise engaged in the same or similar activities. With respect to financial institutions other than insurance companies, a Contracting State may determine the amount of capital to be attributed to a permanent establishment by allocating the institution's total equity between its various offices on the basis of the proportion of the financial institution's risk-weighted assets attributable to each of them. In the case of an insurance company, there shall be attributed to a permanent establishment not only premiums earned through the permanent establishment, but that portion of the insurance company's overall investment income from reserves and surplus that supports the risks assumed by the permanent establishment.

¶1304

2006 U.S. Model
Income Tax Convention

- 13 -

5.   For the purposes of the preceding paragraphs, the profits to be attributed to the permanent establishment shall be determined by the same method year by year unless there is good and sufficient reason to the contrary.

6.   Where profits include items of income that are dealt with separately in other Articles of the Convention, then the provisions of those Articles shall not be affected by the provisions of this Article.

7.   In applying this Article, paragraph 6 of Article 10 (Dividends), paragraph 4 of Article 11 (Interest), paragraph 3 of Article 12 (Royalties), paragraph 3 of Article 13 (Gains) and paragraph 2 of Article 21 (Other Income), any income or gain attributable to a permanent establishment during its existence is taxable in the Contracting State where such permanent establishment is situated even if the payments are deferred until such permanent establishment has ceased to exist.

- 14 -

Article 8

SHIPPING AND AIR TRANSPORT

1.   Profits of an enterprise of a Contracting State from the operation of ships or aircraft in international traffic shall be taxable only in that State.

2.   For purposes of this Article, profits from the operation of ships or aircraft include, but are not limited to:

    a)   profits from the rental of ships or aircraft on a full (time or voyage) basis;

    b)   profits from the rental on a bareboat basis of ships or aircraft if the rental income is incidental to profits from the operation of ships or aircraft in international traffic; and

    c)   profits from the rental on a bareboat basis of ships or aircraft if such ships or aircraft are operated in international traffic by the lessee.

Profits derived by an enterprise from the inland transport of property or passengers within either Contracting State shall be treated as profits from the operation of ships or aircraft in international traffic if such transport is undertaken as part of international traffic.

3.   Profits of an enterprise of a Contracting State from the use, maintenance, or rental of containers (including trailers, barges, and related equipment for the transport of containers) shall be taxable only in that Contracting State, except to the extent that those containers are used for transport solely between places within the other Contracting State.

4.   The provisions of paragraphs 1 and 3 shall also apply to profits from participation in a pool, a joint business, or an international operating agency.

2006 U.S. Model
Income Tax Convention

- 15 -

Article 9

ASSOCIATED ENTERPRISES

1.   Where:

a)   an enterprise of a Contracting State participates directly or indirectly in the management, control or capital of an enterprise of the other Contracting State; or

b)   the same persons participate directly or indirectly in the management, control, or capital of an enterprise of a Contracting State and an enterprise of the other Contracting State,

and in either case conditions are made or imposed between the two enterprises in their commercial or financial relations that differ from those that would be made between independent enterprises, then any profits that, but for those conditions, would have accrued to one of the enterprises, but by reason of those conditions have not so accrued, may be included in the profits of that enterprise and taxed accordingly.

2.   Where a Contracting State includes in the profits of an enterprise of that State, and taxes accordingly, profits on which an enterprise of the other Contracting State has been charged to tax in that other State, and the other Contracting State agrees that the profits so included are profits that would have accrued to the enterprise of the first-mentioned State if the conditions made between the two enterprises had been those that would have been made between independent enterprises, then that other State shall make an appropriate adjustment to the amount of the tax charged therein on those profits. In determining such adjustment, due regard shall be had to the other provisions of this Convention and the competent authorities of the Contracting States shall if necessary consult each other.

- 16 -

Article 10

DIVIDENDS

1.   Dividends paid by a company that is a resident of a Contracting State to a resident of the other Contracting State may be taxed in that other State.

2.   However, such dividends may also be taxed in the Contracting State of which the company paying the dividends is a resident and according to the laws of that State, but if the dividends are beneficially owned by a resident of the other Contracting State, except as otherwise provided, the tax so charged shall not exceed:

    a)   5 percent of the gross amount of the dividends if the beneficial owner is a company that owns directly at least 10 percent of the voting stock of the company paying the dividends;

    b)   15 percent of the gross amount of the dividends in all other cases.

This paragraph shall not affect the taxation of the company in respect of the profits out of which the dividends are paid.

3.   Notwithstanding paragraph 2, dividends shall not be taxed in the Contracting State of which the company paying the dividends is a resident if:

    a)   the beneficial owner of the dividends is a pension fund that is a resident of the other Contracting State; and

    b)   such dividends are not derived from the carrying on of a trade or business by the pension fund or through an associated enterprise.

4.   a)   Subparagraph a) of paragraph 2 shall not apply in the case of dividends paid by a U.S. Regulated Investment Company (RIC) or a U.S. Real Estate Investment Trust (REIT). In the case of dividends paid by a RIC, subparagraph b) of paragraph 2 and paragraph 3 shall apply. In the case of dividends paid by a REIT, subparagraph b) of paragraph 2 and paragraph 3 shall apply only if:

        i)   the beneficial owner of the dividends is an individual or pension fund, in either case holding an interest of not more than 10 percent in the REIT;

        ii)   the dividends are paid with respect to a class of stock that is publicly traded and the beneficial owner of the dividends is a person holding an interest of not more than 5 percent of any class of the REIT's stock; or

¶1304

- 17 -

iii)   the beneficial owner of the dividends is a person holding an interest of not more than 10 percent in the REIT and the REIT is diversified.

b)   For purposes of this paragraph, a REIT shall be "diversified" if the value of no single interest in real property exceeds 10 percent of its total interests in real property. For the purposes of this rule, foreclosure property shall not be considered an interest in real property. Where a REIT holds an interest in a partnership, it shall be treated as owning directly a proportion of the partnership's interests in real property corresponding to its interest in the partnership.

5.   For purposes of this Article, the term "dividends" means income from shares or other rights, not being debt-claims, participating in profits, as well as income that is subjected to the same taxation treatment as income from shares under the laws of the State of which the payer is a resident.

6.   The provisions of paragraphs 2 through 4 shall not apply if the beneficial owner of the dividends, being a resident of a Contracting State, carries on business in the other Contracting State, of which the payer is a resident, through a permanent establishment situated therein, and the holding in respect of which the dividends are paid is effectively connected with such permanent establishment. In such case the provisions of Article 7 (Business Profits) shall apply.

7.   A Contracting State may not impose any tax on dividends paid by a resident of the other State, except insofar as the dividends are paid to a resident of the first-mentioned State or the dividends are attributable to a permanent establishment, nor may it impose tax on a corporation's undistributed profits, except as provided in paragraph 8, even if the dividends paid or the undistributed profits consist wholly or partly of profits or income arising in that State.

8.   a)   A company that is a resident of one of the States and that has a permanent establishment in the other State or that is subject to tax in the other State on a net basis on its income that may be taxed in the other State under Article 6 (Income from Real Property) or under paragraph 1 of Article 13 (Gains) may be subject in that other State to a tax in addition to the tax allowable under the other provisions of this Convention.

b)   Such tax, however, may be imposed:

i)   on only the portion of the business profits of the company attributable to the permanent establishment and the portion of the income referred to in subparagraph a) that is subject to tax under Article 6 or under paragraph 1 of Article 13 that, in the case of the United States, represents the dividend equivalent amount of such profits or income and, in the case of -------, is an amount that is analogous to the dividend equivalent amount; and

ii)   at a rate not in excess of the rate specified in paragraph 2 a).

- 18 -

Article 11

INTEREST

1.   Interest arising in a Contracting State and beneficially owned by a resident of the other Contracting State may be taxed only in that other State.

2.   Notwithstanding the provisions of paragraph 1:

a)   interest arising in ---------- that is determined with reference to receipts, sales, income, profits or other cash flow of the debtor or a related person, to any change in the value of any property of the debtor or a related person or to any dividend, partnership distribution or similar payment made by the debtor or a related person may be taxed in the Contracting State in which it arises, and according to the laws of that State, but if the beneficial owner is a resident of the other Contracting State, the interest may be taxed at a rate not exceeding 15 percent of the gross amount of the interest;

b)   interest arising in the United States that is contingent interest of a type that does not qualify as portfolio interest under United States law may be taxed by the United States but, if the beneficial owner of the interest is a resident of ----------, the interest may be taxed at a rate not exceeding 15 percent of the gross amount of the interest; and

c)   interest that is an excess inclusion with respect to a residual interest in a real estate mortgage investment conduit may be taxed by each State in accordance with its domestic law.

3.   The term "interest" as used in this Article means income from debt-claims of every kind, whether or not secured by mortgage, and whether or not carrying a right to participate in the debtor's profits, and in particular, income from government securities and income from bonds or debentures, including premiums or prizes attaching to such securities, bonds or debentures, and all other income that is subjected to the same taxation treatment as income from money lent by the taxation law of the Contracting State in which the income arises. Income dealt with in Article 10 (Dividends) and penalty charges for late payment shall not be regarded as interest for the purposes of this Convention.

4.   The provisions of paragraphs 1 and 2 shall not apply if the beneficial owner of the interest, being a resident of a Contracting State, carries on business in the other Contracting State, in which the interest arises, through a permanent establishment situated therein, and the debt-claim in respect of which the interest is paid is effectively connected with such permanent establishment. In such case the provisions of Article 7 (Business Profits) shall apply.

- 19 -

5.   Where, by reason of a special relationship between the payer and the beneficial owner or between both of them and some other person, the amount of the interest, having regard to the debt-claim for which it is paid, exceeds the amount which would have been agreed upon by the payer and the beneficial owner in the absence of such relationship, the provisions of this Article shall apply only to the last-mentioned amount. In such case the excess part of the payments shall remain taxable according to the laws of each State, due regard being had to the other provisions of this Convention.

- 20 -

Article 12

ROYALTIES

1.   Royalties arising in a Contracting State and beneficially owned by a resident of the other Contracting State may be taxed only in that other State.

2.   The term "royalties" as used in this Article means:

a)   payments of any kind received as a consideration for the use of, or the right to use, any copyright of literary, artistic, scientific or other work (including cinematographic films), any patent, trademark, design or model, plan, secret formula or process, or for information concerning industrial, commercial or scientific experience; and

b)   gain derived from the alienation of any property described in subparagraph a), to the extent that such gain is contingent on the productivity, use, or disposition of the property.

3.   The provisions of paragraph 1 shall not apply if the beneficial owner of the royalties, being a resident of a Contracting State, carries on business in the other Contracting State through a permanent establishment situated therein and the right or property in respect of which the royalties are paid is effectively connected with such permanent establishment. In such case the provisions of Article 7 (Business Profits) shall apply.

4.   Where, by reason of a special relationship between the payer and the beneficial owner or between both of them and some other person, the amount of the royalties, having regard to the use, right, or information for which they are paid, exceeds the amount which would have been agreed upon by the payer and the beneficial owner in the absence of such relationship, the provisions of this Article shall apply only to the last-mentioned amount. In such case the excess part of the payments shall remain taxable according to the laws of each Contracting State, due regard being had to the other provisions of the Convention.

- 21 -

Article 13

GAINS

1.   Gains derived by a resident of a Contracting State that are attributable to the alienation of real property situated in the other Contracting State may be taxed in that other State.

2.   For the purposes of this Article the term "real property situated in the other Contracting State" shall include:

   a)   real property referred to in Article 6 (Income from Real Property);

   b)   where that other State is the United States, a United States real property interest; and

   c)   where that other State is ------,

      i)   shares, including rights to acquire shares, other than shares in which there is regular trading on a stock exchange, deriving their value or the greater part of their value directly or indirectly from real property referred to in subparagraph a) of this paragraph situated in --------; and

      ii)   an interest in a partnership or trust to the extent that the assets of the partnership or trust consist of real property situated in --------, or of shares referred to in clause i) of this sub-paragraph.

3.   Gains from the alienation of movable property forming part of the business property of a permanent establishment that an enterprise of a Contracting State has in the other Contracting State, including such gains from the alienation of such a permanent establishment (alone or with the whole enterprise), may be taxed in that other State.

4.   Gains derived by an enterprise of a Contracting State from the alienation of ships or aircraft operated or used in international traffic or personal property pertaining to the operation or use of such ships or aircraft shall be taxable only in that State.

5.   Gains derived by an enterprise of a Contracting State from the alienation of containers (including trailers, barges and related equipment for the transport of containers) used for the transport of goods or merchandise shall be taxable only in that State, unless those containers are used for transport solely between places within the other Contracting State.

6.   Gains from the alienation of any property other than property referred to in paragraphs 1 through 5 shall be taxable only in the Contracting State of which the alienator is a resident.

- 22 -

Article 14

INCOME FROM EMPLOYMENT

1.   Subject to the provisions of Articles 15 (Directors' Fees), 17 (Pensions, Social Security, Annuities, Alimony, and Child Support) and 19 (Government Service), salaries, wages, and other similar remuneration derived by a resident of a Contracting State in respect of an employment shall be taxable only in that State unless the employment is exercised in the other Contracting State. If the employment is so exercised, such remuneration as is derived therefrom may be taxed in that other State.

2.   Notwithstanding the provisions of paragraph 1, remuneration derived by a resident of a Contracting State in respect of an employment exercised in the other Contracting State shall be taxable only in the first-mentioned State if:

    a)   the recipient is present in the other State for a period or periods not exceeding in the aggregate 183 days in any twelve month period commencing or ending in the taxable year concerned;

    b)   the remuneration is paid by, or on behalf of, an employer who is not a resident of the other State; and

    c)   the remuneration is not borne by a permanent establishment which the employer has in the other State.

3.   Notwithstanding the preceding provisions of this Article, remuneration described in paragraph 1 that is derived by a resident of a Contracting State in respect of an employment as a member of the regular complement of a ship or aircraft operated in international traffic shall be taxable only in that State.

- 23 -

Article 15

DIRECTORS' FEES

Directors' fees and other compensation derived by a resident of a Contracting State for services rendered in the other Contracting State in his capacity as a member of the board of directors of a company that is a resident of the other Contracting State may be taxed in that other Contracting State.

- 24 -

Article 16

ENTERTAINERS AND SPORTSMEN

1.   Income derived by a resident of a Contracting State as an entertainer, such as a theater, motion picture, radio, or television artiste, or a musician, or as a sportsman, from his personal activities as such exercised in the other Contracting State, which income would be exempt from tax in that other Contracting State under the provisions of Articles 7 (Business Profits) and 14 (Income from Employment) may be taxed in that other State, except where the amount of the gross receipts derived by such entertainer or sportsman, including expenses reimbursed to him or borne on his behalf, from such activities does not exceed twenty thousand United States dollars ($20,000) or its equivalent in ---------- for the taxable year of the payment.

2.   Where income in respect of activities exercised by an entertainer or a sportsman in his capacity as such accrues not to the entertainer or sportsman himself but to another person, that income, notwithstanding the provisions of Article 7 (Business Profits) or 14 (Income from Employment), may be taxed in the Contracting State in which the activities of the entertainer or sportsman are exercised unless the contract pursuant to which the personal activities are performed allows that other person to designate the individual who is to perform the personal activities.

¶1304

2006 U.S. Model
Income Tax Convention

- 25 -

Article 17

PENSIONS, SOCIAL SECURITY, ANNUITIES,
ALIMONY, AND CHILD SUPPORT

1.   a)   Pensions and other similar remuneration beneficially owned by a resident of a Contracting State shall be taxable only in that State.

b)   Notwithstanding subparagraph a), the amount of any such pension or remuneration arising in a Contracting State that, when received, would be exempt from taxation in that State if the beneficial owner were a resident thereof shall be exempt from taxation in the Contracting State of which the beneficial owner is a resident.

2.   Notwithstanding the provisions of paragraph 1, payments made by a Contracting State under provisions of the social security or similar legislation of that State to a resident of the other Contracting State or to a citizen of the United States shall be taxable only in the first-mentioned State.

3.   Annuities derived and beneficially owned by an individual resident of a Contracting State shall be taxable only in that State. The term "annuities" as used in this paragraph means a stated sum paid periodically at stated times during a specified number of years, or for life, under an obligation to make the payments in return for adequate and full consideration (other than services rendered).

4.   Alimony paid by a resident of a Contracting State to a resident of the other Contracting State shall be taxable only in that other State. The term "alimony" as used in this paragraph means periodic payments made pursuant to a written separation agreement or a decree of divorce, separate maintenance, or compulsory support, which payments are taxable to the recipient under the laws of the State of which he is a resident.

5.   Periodic payments, not dealt with in paragraph 4, for the support of a child made pursuant to a written separation agreement or a decree of divorce, separate maintenance, or compulsory support, paid by a resident of a Contracting State to a resident of the other Contracting State, shall be exempt from tax in both Contracting States.

2006 U.S. Model
Income Tax Convention

- 26 -

Article 18

PENSION FUNDS

1.   Where an individual who is a resident of one of the States is a member or beneficiary of, or participant in, a pension fund that is a resident of the other State, income earned by the pension fund may be taxed as income of that individual only when, and, subject to the provisions of paragraph 1 of Article 17 (Pensions, Social Security, Annuities, Alimony and Child Support), to the extent that, it is paid to, or for the benefit of, that individual from the pension fund (and not transferred to another pension fund in that other State).

2.   Where an individual who is a member or beneficiary of, or participant in, a pension fund that is a resident of one of the States exercises an employment or self-employment in the other State:

   a)   contributions paid by or on behalf of that individual to the pension fund during the period that he exercises an employment or self-employment in the other State shall be deductible (or excludible) in computing his taxable income in that other State; and

   b)   any benefits accrued under the pension fund, or contributions made to the pension fund by or on behalf of the individual's employer, during that period shall not be treated as part of the employee's taxable income and any such contributions shall be allowed as a deduction in computing the taxable income of his employer in that other State.

The relief available under this paragraph shall not exceed the relief that would be allowed by the other State to residents of that State for contributions to, or benefits accrued under, a pension plan established in that State.

3.   The provisions of paragraph 2 of this Article shall not apply unless:

   a)   contributions by or on behalf of the individual, or by or on behalf of the individual's employer, to the pension fund (or to another similar pension fund for which the first-mentioned pension fund was substituted) were made before the individual began to exercise an employment or self-employment in the other State; and

   b)   the competent authority of the other State has agreed that the pension fund generally corresponds to a pension fund established in that other State.

4.   a)   Where a citizen of the United States who is a resident of ------ exercises an employment in ------- the income from which is taxable in -------, the contribution is borne by an employer who is a resident of ------- or by a permanent establishment situated in -----, and the individual is a member or beneficiary of, or participant in, a pension plan established in ------,

- 27 -

i)   contributions paid by or on behalf of that individual to the pension fund during the period that he exercises the employment in --------, and that are attributable to the employment, shall be deductible (or excludible) in computing his taxable income in the United States; and

ii)   any benefits accrued under the pension fund, or contributions made to the pension fund by or on behalf of the individual's employer, during that period, and that are attributable to the employment, shall not be treated as part of the employee's taxable income in computing his taxable income in the United States.

b)   The relief available under this paragraph shall not exceed the lesser of:

i)   the relief that would be allowed by the United States to its residents for contributions to, or benefits accrued under, a generally corresponding pension plan established in the United States; and

ii)   the amount of contributions or benefits that qualify for tax relief in --------.

c)   For purposes of determining an individual's eligibility to participate in and receive tax benefits with respect to a pension plan established in the United States, contributions made to, or benefits accrued under, a pension plan established in ------ shall be treated as contributions or benefits under a generally corresponding pension plan established in the United States to the extent relief is available to the individual under this paragraph.

d)   This paragraph shall not apply unless the competent authority of the United States has agreed that the pension plan generally corresponds to a pension plan established in the United States.

- 28 -

Article 19

GOVERNMENT SERVICE

1.   Notwithstanding the provisions of Articles 14 (Income from Employment), 15 (Directors' Fees), 16 (Entertainers and Sportsmen) and 20 (Students and Trainees):

a)   Salaries, wages and other remuneration, other than a pension, paid to an individual in respect of services rendered to a Contracting State or a political subdivision or local authority thereof shall, subject to the provisions of subparagraph b), be taxable only in that State;

b)   such remuneration, however, shall be taxable only in the other Contracting State if the services are rendered in that State and the individual is a resident of that State who:

i)   is a national of that State; or

ii)   did not become a resident of that State solely for the purpose of rendering the services.

2.   Notwithstanding the provisions of paragraph 1 of Article 17 (Pensions, Social Security, Annuities, Alimony, and Child Support):

a)   any pension and other similar remuneration paid by, or out of funds created by, a Contracting State or a political subdivision or a local authority thereof to an individual in respect of services rendered to that State or subdivision or authority (other than a payment to which paragraph 2 of Article 17 applies) shall, subject to the provisions of subparagraph b), be taxable only in that State;

b)   such pension, however, shall be taxable only in the other Contracting State if the individual is a resident of, and a national of, that State.

3.   The provisions of Articles 14 (Income from Employment), 15 (Directors' Fees), 16 (Entertainers and Sportsmen) and 17 (Pensions, Social Security, Annuities, Alimony, and Child Support) shall apply to salaries, wages and other remuneration, and to pensions, in respect of services rendered in connection with a business carried on by a Contracting State or a political subdivision or a local authority thereof.

¶1304

2006 U.S. Model
Income Tax Convention

- 29 -

Article 20

STUDENTS AND TRAINEES

1.　　Payments, other than compensation for personal services, received by a student or business trainee who is, or was immediately before visiting a Contracting State, a resident of the other Contracting State, and who is present in the first-mentioned State for the purpose of his full-time education or for his full-time training, shall not be taxed in that State, provided that such payments arise outside that State, and are for the purpose of his maintenance, education or training. The exemption from tax provided by this paragraph shall apply to a business trainee only for a period of time not exceeding one year from the date the business trainee first arrives in the first-mentioned Contracting State for the purpose of training.

2.　　A student or business trainee within the meaning of paragraph 1 shall be exempt from tax by the Contracting State in which the individual is temporarily present with respect to income from personal services in an aggregate amount equal to $9,000 or its equivalent in [　　　　] annually. The competent authorities shall, every five years, adjust the amount provided in this subparagraph to the extent necessary to take into account changes in the U.S. personal exemption and the standard deduction.

3.　　For purposes of this Article, a business trainee is an individual:

a)　　who is temporarily in a Contracting State for the purpose of securing training required to qualify the individual to practice a profession or professional specialty; or

b)　　who is temporarily in a Contracting State as an employee of, or under contract with, a resident of the other Contracting State, for the primary purpose of acquiring technical, professional, or business experience from a person other than that resident of the other Contracting State (or a person related to such resident of the other Contracting State).

- 30 -

Article 21

OTHER INCOME

1.   Items of income beneficially owned by a resident of a Contracting State, wherever arising, not dealt with in the foregoing Articles of this Convention shall be taxable only in that State.

2.   The provisions of paragraph 1 shall not apply to income, other than income from real property as defined in paragraph 2 of Article 6 (Income from Real Property), if the beneficial owner of the income, being a resident of a Contracting State, carries on business in the other Contracting State through a permanent establishment situated therein and the income is attributable to such permanent establishment. In such case the provisions of Article 7 (Business Profits) shall apply.

2006 U.S. Model
Income Tax Convention

- 31 -

Article 22

LIMITATION ON BENEFITS

1.   Except as otherwise provided in this Article, a resident of a Contracting State shall not be entitled to the benefits of this Convention otherwise accorded to residents of a Contracting State unless such resident is a "qualified person" as defined in paragraph 2.

2.   A resident of a Contracting State shall be a qualified person for a taxable year if the resident is:

a)   an individual;

b)   a Contracting State, or a political subdivision or local authority thereof;

c)   a company, if:

    i)   the principal class of its shares (and any disproportionate class of shares) is regularly traded on one or more recognized stock exchanges, and either:

        A)   its principal class of shares is primarily traded on one or more recognized stock exchanges located in the Contracting State of which the company is a resident; or

        B)   the company's primary place of management and control is in the Contracting State of which it is a resident; or

    ii)   at least 50 percent of the aggregate vote and value of the shares (and at least 50 percent of any disproportionate class of shares) in the company is owned directly or indirectly by five or fewer companies entitled to benefits under clause i) of this subparagraph, provided that, in the case of indirect ownership, each intermediate owner is a resident of either Contracting State;

d)   a person described in paragraph 2 of Article 4 of this Convention, provided that, in the case of a person described in subparagraph a) of that paragraph, more than 50 percent of the person's beneficiaries, members or participants are individuals resident in either Contracting State; or

e)   a person other than an individual, if:

¶1304

2006 U.S. Model
Income Tax Convention

- 32 -

i)   on at least half the days of the taxable year, persons who are residents of that Contracting State and that are entitled to the benefits of this Convention under subparagraph a), subparagraph b), clause i) of subparagraph c), or subparagraph d) of this paragraph own, directly or indirectly, shares or other beneficial interests representing at least 50 percent of the aggregate voting power and value (and at least 50 percent of any disproportionate class of shares) of the person, provided that, in the case of indirect ownership, each intermediate owner is a resident of that Contracting State, and

ii)   less than 50 percent of the person's gross income for the taxable year, as determined in the person's State of residence, is paid or accrued, directly or indirectly, to persons who are not residents of either Contracting State entitled to the benefits of this Convention under subparagraph a), subparagraph b), clause i) of subparagraph c), or subparagraph d) of this paragraph in the form of payments that are deductible for purposes of the taxes covered by this Convention in the person's State of residence (but not including arm's length payments in the ordinary course of business for services or tangible property).

3.   a)   A resident of a Contracting State will be entitled to benefits of the Convention with respect to an item of income derived from the other State, regardless of whether the resident is a qualified person, if the resident is engaged in the active conduct of a trade or business in the first-mentioned State (other than the business of making or managing investments for the resident's own account, unless these activities are banking, insurance or securities activities carried on by a bank, insurance company or registered securities dealer), and the income derived from the other Contracting State is derived in connection with, or is incidental to, that trade or business.

b)   If a resident of a Contracting State derives an item of income from a trade or business activity conducted by that resident in the other Contracting State, or derives an item of income arising in the other Contracting State from a related person, the conditions described in subparagraph a) shall be considered to be satisfied with respect to such item only if the trade or business activity carried on by the resident in the first-mentioned Contracting State is substantial in relation to the trade or business activity carried on by the resident or such person in the other Contracting State. Whether a trade or business activity is substantial for the purposes of this paragraph will be determined based on all the facts and circumstances.

- 33 -

c)	For purposes of applying this paragraph, activities conducted by persons connected to a person shall be deemed to be conducted by such person. A person shall be connected to another if one possesses at least 50 percent of the beneficial interest in the other (or, in the case of a company, at least 50 percent of the aggregate vote and value of the company's shares or of the beneficial equity interest in the company) or another person possesses at least 50 percent of the beneficial interest (or, in the case of a company, at least 50 percent of the aggregate vote and value of the company's shares or of the beneficial equity interest in the company) in each person. In any case, a person shall be considered to be connected to another if, based on all the relevant facts and circumstances, one has control of the other or both are under the control of the same person or persons.

4.	If a resident of a Contracting State is neither a qualified person pursuant to the provisions of paragraph 2 nor entitled to benefits with respect to an item of income under paragraph 3 of this Article the competent authority of the other Contracting State may, nevertheless, grant the benefits of this Convention, or benefits with respect to a specific item of income, if it determines that the establishment, acquisition or maintenance of such person and the conduct of its operations did not have as one of its principal purposes the obtaining of benefits under this Convention.

5.	For purposes of this Article:

a)	the term "recognized stock exchange" means:

i)	the NASDAQ System owned by the National Association of Securities Dealers, Inc. and any stock exchange registered with the U.S. Securities and Exchange Commission as a national securities exchange under the U.S. Securities Exchange Act of 1934;

ii)	stock exchanges of -------; and

iii)	any other stock exchange agreed upon by the competent authorities;

b)	the term "principal class of shares" means the ordinary or common shares of the company, provided that such class of shares represents the majority of the voting power and value of the company. If no single class of ordinary or common shares represents the majority of the aggregate voting power and value of the company, the "principal class of shares" are those classes that in the aggregate represent a majority of the aggregate voting power and value of the company

c)	the term "disproportionate class of shares" means any class of shares of a company resident in one of the Contracting States that entitles the shareholder to disproportionately higher participation, through dividends, redemption payments or otherwise, in the earnings generated in the other State by particular assets or activities of the company; and

2006 U.S. Model
Income Tax Convention

- 34 -

d)   a company's "primary place of management and control" will be in the Contracting State of which it is a resident only if executive officers and senior management employees exercise day-to-day responsibility for more of the strategic, financial and operational policy decision making for the company (including its direct and indirect subsidiaries) in that State than in any other state and the staff of such persons conduct more of the day-to-day activities necessary for preparing and making those decisions in that State than in any other state.

- 35 -

Article 23

RELIEF FROM DOUBLE TAXATION

1.   In the case of -------, double taxation will be relieved as follows:

2.   In accordance with the provisions and subject to the limitations of the law of the United States (as it may be amended from time to time without changing the general principle hereof), the United States shall allow to a resident or citizen of the United States as a credit against the United States tax on income applicable to residents and citizens:

a)   the income tax paid or accrued to ------ by or on behalf of such resident or citizen; and

b)   in the case of a United States company owning at least 10 percent of the voting stock of a company that is a resident of -------- and from which the United States company receives dividends, the income tax paid or accrued to ------- by or on behalf of the payer with respect to the profits out of which the dividends are paid.

For the purposes of this paragraph, the taxes referred to in paragraphs 3 a) and 4 of Article 2 (Taxes Covered) shall be considered income taxes.

3.   For the purposes of applying paragraph 2 of this Article, an item of gross income, as determined under the laws of the United States, derived by a resident of the United States that, under this Convention, may be taxed in ----- shall be deemed to be income from sources in -----.

4.   Where a United States citizen is a resident of -------:

a)   with respect to items of income that under the provisions of this Convention are exempt from United States tax or that are subject to a reduced rate of United States tax when derived by a resident of ------ who is not a United States citizen, ------- shall allow as a credit against -------- tax, only the tax paid, if any, that the United States may impose under the provisions of this Convention, other than taxes that may be imposed solely by reason of citizenship under the saving clause of paragraph 4 of Article 1 (General Scope);

b)   for purposes of applying paragraph 2 to compute United States tax on those items of income referred to in subparagraph a), the United States shall allow as a credit against United States tax the income tax paid to -------- after the credit referred to in subparagraph a); the credit so allowed shall not reduce the portion of the United States tax that is creditable against the ----------- tax in accordance with subparagraph a); and

c)   for the exclusive purpose of relieving double taxation in the United States under subparagraph b), items of income referred to in subparagraph a) shall be deemed to arise in ------- to the extent necessary to avoid double taxation of such income under subparagraph b).

- 36 -

Article 24

NON-DISCRIMINATION

1.   Nationals of a Contracting State shall not be subjected in the other Contracting State to any taxation or any requirement connected therewith that is more burdensome than the taxation and connected requirements to which nationals of that other State in the same circumstances, in particular with respect to residence, are or may be subjected. This provision shall also apply to persons who are not residents of one or both of the Contracting States. However, for the purposes of United States taxation, United States nationals who are subject to tax on a worldwide basis are not in the same circumstances as nationals of --------- who are not residents of the United States.

2.   The taxation on a permanent establishment that an enterprise of a Contracting State has in the other Contracting State shall not be less favorably levied in that other State than the taxation levied on enterprises of that other State carrying on the same activities.

3.   The provisions of paragraphs 1 and 2 shall not be construed as obliging a Contracting State to grant to residents of the other Contracting State any personal allowances, reliefs, and reductions for taxation purposes on account of civil status or family responsibilities that it grants to its own residents.

4.   Except where the provisions of paragraph 1 of Article 9 (Associated Enterprises), paragraph 5 of Article 11 (Interest), or paragraph 4 of Article 12 (Royalties) apply, interest, royalties, and other disbursements paid by a resident of a Contracting State to a resident of the other Contracting State shall, for the purpose of determining the taxable profits of the first-mentioned resident, be deductible under the same conditions as if they had been paid to a resident of the first-mentioned State. Similarly, any debts of a resident of a Contracting State to a resident of the other Contracting State shall, for the purpose of determining the taxable capital of the first-mentioned resident, be deductible under the same conditions as if they had been contracted to a resident of the first-mentioned State.

5.   Enterprises of a Contracting State, the capital of which is wholly or partly owned or controlled, directly or indirectly, by one or more residents of the other Contracting State, shall not be subjected in the first-mentioned State to any taxation or any requirement connected therewith that is more burdensome than the taxation and connected requirements to which other similar enterprises of the first-mentioned State are or may be subjected.

6.   Nothing in this Article shall be construed as preventing either Contracting State from imposing a tax as described in paragraph 8 of Article 10 (Dividends).

7.   The provisions of this Article shall, notwithstanding the provisions of Article 2 (Taxes Covered), apply to taxes of every kind and description imposed by a Contracting State or a political subdivision or local authority thereof.

¶1304

- 37 -

Article 25

MUTUAL AGREEMENT PROCEDURE

1.   Where a person considers that the actions of one or both of the Contracting States result or will result for such person in taxation not in accordance with the provisions of this Convention, it may, irrespective of the remedies provided by the domestic law of those States, and the time limits prescribed in such laws for presenting claims for refund, present its case to the competent authority of either Contracting State.

2.   The competent authority shall endeavor, if the objection appears to it to be justified and if it is not itself able to arrive at a satisfactory solution, to resolve the case by mutual agreement with the competent authority of the other Contracting State, with a view to the avoidance of taxation which is not in accordance with the Convention. Any agreement reached shall be implemented notwithstanding any time limits or other procedural limitations in the domestic law of the Contracting States. Assessment and collection procedures shall be suspended during the period that any mutual agreement proceeding is pending.

3.   The competent authorities of the Contracting States shall endeavor to resolve by mutual agreement any difficulties or doubts arising as to the interpretation or application of the Convention. They also may consult together for the elimination of double taxation in cases not provided for in the Convention. In particular the competent authorities of the Contracting States may agree:

> a)   to the same attribution of income, deductions, credits, or allowances of an enterprise of a Contracting State to its permanent establishment situated in the other Contracting State;

> b)   to the same allocation of income, deductions, credits, or allowances between persons;

> c)   to the settlement of conflicting application of the Convention, including conflicts regarding:

>> i)   the characterization of particular items of income;

>> ii)   the characterization of persons;

>> iii)   the application of source rules with respect to particular items of income;

>> iv)   the meaning of any term used in the Convention;

>> v)   the timing of particular items of income;

2006 U.S. Model
Income Tax Convention

- 38 -

d)   to advance pricing arrangements; and

e)   to the application of the provisions of domestic law regarding penalties, fines, and interest in a manner consistent with the purposes of the Convention.

4.   The competent authorities also may agree to increases in any specific dollar amounts referred to in the Convention to reflect economic or monetary developments.

5.   The competent authorities of the Contracting States may communicate with each other directly, including through a joint commission, for the purpose of reaching an agreement in the sense of the preceding paragraphs.

2006 U.S. Model
Income Tax Convention

- 39 -

Article 26

EXCHANGE OF INFORMATION AND ADMINISTRATIVE ASSISTANCE

1.   The competent authorities of the Contracting States shall exchange such information as may be relevant for carrying out the provisions of this Convention or of the domestic laws of the Contracting States concerning taxes of every kind imposed by a Contracting State to the extent that the taxation thereunder is not contrary to the Convention, including information relating to the assessment or collection of, the enforcement or prosecution in respect of, or the determination of appeals in relation to, such taxes. The exchange of information is not restricted by paragraph 1 of Article 1 (General Scope) or Article 2 (Taxes Covered).

2.   Any information received under this Article by a Contracting State shall be treated as secret in the same manner as information obtained under the domestic laws of that State and shall be disclosed only to persons or authorities (including courts and administrative bodies) involved in the assessment, collection, or administration of, the enforcement or prosecution in respect of, or the determination of appeals in relation to, the taxes referred to above, or the oversight of such functions. Such persons or authorities shall use the information only for such purposes. They may disclose the information in public court proceedings or in judicial decisions.

3.   In no case shall the provisions of the preceding paragraphs be construed so as to impose on a Contracting State the obligation:

    a)   to carry out administrative measures at variance with the laws and administrative practice of that or of the other Contracting State;

    b)   to supply information that is not obtainable under the laws or in the normal course of the administration of that or of the other Contracting State;

    c)   to supply information that would disclose any trade, business, industrial, commercial, or professional secret or trade process, or information the disclosure of which would be contrary to public policy (ordre public).

4.   If information is requested by a Contracting State in accordance with this Article, the other Contracting State shall use its information gathering measures to obtain the requested information, even though that other State may not need such information for its own purposes. The obligation contained in the preceding sentence is subject to the limitations of paragraph 3 but in no case shall such limitation be construed to permit a Contracting State to decline to supply information because it has no domestic interest in such information.

2006 U.S. Model
Income Tax Convention

- 40 -

5.   In no case shall the provisions of paragraph 3 be construed to permit a Contracting State to decline to supply information requested by the other Contracting State because the information is held by a bank, other financial institution, nominee or person acting in an agency or a fiduciary capacity or because it relates to ownership interests in a person.

6.   If specifically requested by the competent authority of a Contracting State, the competent authority of the other Contracting State shall provide information under this Article in the form of depositions of witnesses and authenticated copies of unedited original documents (including books, papers, statements, records, accounts, and writings).

7.   Each of the Contracting States shall endeavor to collect on behalf of the other Contracting State such amounts as may be necessary to ensure that relief granted by the Convention from taxation imposed by that other State does not inure to the benefit of persons not entitled thereto. This paragraph shall not impose upon either of the Contracting States the obligation to carry out administrative measures that would be contrary to its sovereignty, security, or public policy.

8.   The requested State shall allow representatives of the requesting State to enter the requested State to interview individuals and examine books and records with the consent of the persons subject to examination.

8.   The competent authorities of the Contracting States may develop an agreement upon the mode of application of this Article, including agreement to ensure comparable levels of assistance to each of the Contracting States, but in no case will the lack of such agreement relieve a Contracting State of its obligations under this Article.

2006 U.S. Model
Income Tax Convention

- 41 -

Article 27

MEMBERS OF DIPLOMATIC MISSIONS AND CONSULAR POSTS

Nothing in this Convention shall affect the fiscal privileges of members of diplomatic missions or consular posts under the general rules of international law or under the provisions of special agreements.

2006 U.S. Model
Income Tax Convention

- 42 -

Article 28

ENTRY INTO FORCE

1.   This Convention shall be subject to ratification in accordance with the applicable procedures of each Contracting State, and instruments of ratification will be exchanged as soon thereafter as possible.

2.   This Convention shall enter into force on the date of the exchange of instruments of ratification, and its provisions shall have effect:

   a)   in respect of taxes withheld at source, for amounts paid or credited on or after the first day of the second month next following the date on which the Convention enters into force;

   b)   in respect of other taxes, for taxable periods beginning on or after the first day of January next following the date on which the Convention enters into force.

3.   Notwithstanding paragraph 2, the provisions of Article 26 (Exchange of Information and Administrative Assistance) shall have effect from the date of entry into force of this Convention, without regard to the taxable period to which the matter relates.

¶1304

- 43 -

Article 29

TERMINATION

This Convention shall remain in force until terminated by a Contracting State. Either Contracting State may terminate the Convention by giving notice of termination to the other Contracting State through diplomatic channels. In such event, the Convention shall cease to have effect:

> a) in respect of taxes withheld at source, for amounts paid or credited after the expiration of the 6 month period beginning on the date on which notice of termination was given; and

> b) in respect of other taxes, for taxable periods beginning on or after the expiration of the 6 month period beginning on the date on which notice of termination was given.

IN WITNESS WHEREOF, the undersigned, being duly authorized thereto by their respective Governments, have signed this Convention.

DONE at _____ in duplicate, in the English and ---------- languages, both texts being equally authentic, this __ day of _____, 20_.

FOR THE GOVERNMENT OF
THE UNITED STATES OF AMERICA:

FOR THE GOVERNMENT OF

¶1304

¶ 1305 APPENDIX

FORco is a foreign corporation that is incorporated in country F, a country with which the United States has a tax treaty similar to the U.S. Model Treaty. A publicly-held company on a recognized stock exchange in foreign country F, FORco occasionally sends sales employees to the United States to solicit customers, but the sales employees do not have final contracting authority. These sales employees are FORco's only contacts with the United States. FORco takes the position that it is not subject to U.S. tax because it does not have a permanent establishment in the United States due to the sales employees (dependent agents) not having final contracting authority. FORco files a Form 8833 with the IRS stating that FORco is not subject to U.S. tax even though it has a U.S. trade or business.

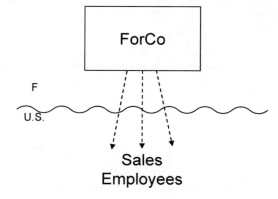

Form **8833**
(Rev. December 2013)
Department of the Treasury
Internal Revenue Service

Treaty-Based Return Position Disclosure
Under Section 6114 or 7701(b)
▶ Attach to your tax return.
▶ **Information about Form 8833 and its instructions is at** *www.irs.gov/form8833.*

OMB No. 1545-1354

Attach a separate Form 8833 for each treaty-based return position taken. Failure to disclose a treaty-based return position may result in a penalty of $1,000 ($10,000 in the case of a C corporation) (see section 6712).

Name	U.S. taxpayer identifying number	Reference ID number, if any (see instructions)
FORco	98-888888	
Address in country of residence	Address in the United States	
County F		

Check one or both of the following boxes as applicable:
- The taxpayer is disclosing a treaty-based return position as required by section 6114 . . . . ▶ ☑
- The taxpayer is a dual-resident taxpayer and is disclosing a treaty-based return position as required by
Regulations section 301.7701(b)-7 . . . . ▶ ☐

Note. If the taxpayer is a dual-resident taxpayer and a long-term resident, by electing to be treated as a resident of a foreign country for purposes of claiming benefits under an applicable income tax treaty, the taxpayer will be deemed to have expatriated pursuant to section 877A. For more information, see the instructions.

Check this box if the taxpayer is a U.S. citizen or resident or is incorporated in the United States . . . . ▶ ☐

1	Enter the specific treaty position relied on:	**3** Name, identifying number (if available to the taxpayer), and address in the United States of the payor of the income (if fixed or determinable annual or periodical). See instructions.
a	Treaty country Country F	
b	Article(s) 5(5)	
2	List the Internal Revenue Code provision(s) overruled or modified by the treaty-based return position	

I.R.C. section 882(a)

4 List the provision(s) of the limitation on benefits article (if any) in the treaty that the taxpayer relies on to prevent application
of that article ▶ Article 22(2)(c); publicly traded

5 Is the taxpayer disclosing a treaty-based return position for which reporting is specifically required pursuant
to Regulations section 301.6114-1(b)? . . . . ☑ Yes ☐ No

If "Yes," enter the specific subsection(s) of Regulations section 301.6114-1(b) requiring reporting . . . . ▶ (5)(i)
Also include the information requested in line 6.

6 Explain the treaty-based return position taken. Include a brief summary of the facts on which it is based. Also, list the nature and amount (or a reasonable estimate) of gross receipts, each separate gross payment, each separate gross income item, or other item (as applicable) for which the treaty benefit is claimed FORco periodically sends sales employees to the United States
to solicit a single customer that resulted in approximately $2 million of gross receipts during the taxable year. Although the sales
employees may constitute a trade or business in the United States, FORco is entitled to the benefits of the tax treaty between
Country F and the United States. More specifically, the treaty only permits the United States to tax a permanent establishment,
which FORco does not have, because its sales employees do not have final contracting authority.

For Paperwork Reduction Act Notice, see the instructions.   Cat. No. 14895L   Form **8833** (Rev. 12-2013)

16615271

¶1305

Evelyn Martin a U.S. citizen who annually files a timely Form 1040, wants to receive benefits of the U.S.-Spanish Income Tax Treaty in 20X3, which is the current year. More specifically, he wants reduced withholding on items of dividends, interest, and royalties he receives from a Spanish corporation. Martin should file a Form 8802, Application for United States Residency Certification to obtain a Form 6166 (Certificate of U.S. Tax Residency) that he can provide the Spanish corporation.

Form **8802** (Rev. April 2012) Department of the Treasury Internal Revenue Service	**Application for United States Residency Certification** ▶ **See separate instructions.**	OMB No. 1545-1817

Important. For applications filed after March 31, 2012, the user fee is $85 per application.

☐ **Additional request** (see instructions)   ☐ **Foreign claim form attached**

Electronic payment confirmation no. ▶

For IRS use only:
Pmt Amt $ _____
Deposit Date: ___ /___ /___
Date Pmt Vrfd: ___ /___ / ___

Applicant's name Evelyn Martin	Applicant's U.S. taxpayer identification number 283-59-7465
If a joint return was filed, spouse's name (see instructions)	If a joint return was filed, spouse's U.S. taxpayer identification number

If a separate certification is needed for spouse, check here ▶   ☐

1   Applicant's name and taxpayer identification number as it should appear on the certification if different from above

Evelyn Martin, 283-59-7465

2   Applicant's address during the calendar year for which certification is requested, including country and ZIP or postal code. If a P.O. box, see instructions.

1974 Rockfish Way
Malibu, CA

3a   Mail Form 6166 to the following address:

b   Appointee Information (see instructions):

Appointee Name ▶ _____   CAF No. ▶ _____

Phone No. ▶ (   ) _____   Fax No. ▶ (   ) _____

4   Applicant is (check appropriate box(es)):

a   ☑ Individual. Check all applicable boxes.
     ☑ U.S. citizen   ☐ U.S. lawful permanent resident (green card holder)   ☐ Sole proprietor
     ☐ Other U.S. resident alien. Type of entry visa ▶ _____
        Current nonimmigrant status ▶ _____ and date of change (see instructions) ▶ _____
     ☐ Dual-status U.S. resident (see instructions). From ▶ _____ to ▶ _____
     ☐ Partial-year Form 2555 filer (see instructions). U.S. resident from ▶ _____ to ▶ _____

b   ☐ Partnership. Check all applicable boxes.   ☐ U.S.   ☐ Foreign   ☐ LLC

c   ☐ Trust. Check if: ☐ Grantor (U.S.)   ☐ Simple   ☐ Rev. Rul. 81-100 Trust   ☐ IRA (for Individual)
                  ☐ Grantor (foreign)   ☐ Complex   ☐ Section 584   ☐ IRA (for Financial Institution)

d   ☐ Estate

e   ☐ Corporation. If incorporated in the United States only, go to line 5. Otherwise, continue.
     Check if: ☐ Section 269B   ☐ Section 943(e)(1)   ☐ Section 953(d)   ☐ Section 1504(d)
     Country or countries of incorporation ▶ _____
     If a dual-resident corporation, specify other country of residence ▶ _____
     If included on a consolidated return, attach page 1 of Form 1120 and Form 851.

f   ☐ S corporation

g   ☐ Employee benefit plan/trust. Plan number, if applicable ▶ _____
     Check if: ☐ Section 401(a)   ☐ Section 403(b)   ☐ Section 457(b)

h   ☐ Exempt organization. If organized in the United States, check all applicable boxes.
     ☐ Section 501(c)   ☐ Section 501(c)(3)   ☐ Governmental entity
     ☐ Indian tribe   ☐ Other (specify) ▶

i   ☐ Disregarded entity. Check if: ☐ LLC   ☐ LP   ☐ LLP   ☐ Other (specify) ▶ _____

j   ☐ Nominee applicant (must specify the type of entity/individual for whom the nominee is acting) ▶

For Privacy Act and Paperwork Reduction Act Notice, see separate instructions.   Cat. No. 10003D   Form **8802** (Rev. 4-2012)

¶1305

Form 8802 (Rev. 4-2012)   Page **2**

Applicant name:

5	Was the applicant required to file a U.S. tax form for the tax period(s) on which certification will be based?	
	Yes.	Check the appropriate box for the form filed and **go to line 7.**
		☐ 990 ☐ 990-T ☑ 1040 ☐ 1041 ☐ 1065 ☐ 1120 ☐ 1120S ☐ 3520-A ☐ 5227 ☐ 5500
		☐ Other (specify) ▶ _____
	No.	Attach explanation (see instructions). Check applicable box and go to line 6.
		☐ Minor child ☐ QSub ☐ U.S. DRE ☐ Foreign DRE ☐ Section 761(a) election
		☐ FASIT ☐ Foreign partnership ☐ Other ▶ _____

6 Was the applicant's parent, parent organization or owner required to file a U.S. tax form? **(Complete this line only if you checked "No" on line 5.)**

Yes. Check the appropriate box for the form filed by the parent.

☐ 990 ☐ 990-T ☐ 1040 ☐ 1041 ☐ 1065 ☐ 1120 ☐ 1120S ☐ 5500

☐ Other (specify) ▶ _____

Parent's/owner's name and address ▶ _____

and U.S. taxpayer identification number ▶ _____

No. Attach explanation (see instructions).

7 Calendar year(s) for which certification is requested.
Note. If certification is for the current calendar year or a year for which a tax return is not yet required to be filed, a penalties of perjury statement from Table 2 of the instructions must be entered on line 10 or attached to Form 8802 (see instructions).

20X3

8 Tax period(s) on which certification will be based (see instructions).

20X2

9 Purpose of certification. Must check applicable box (see instructions).
☑ Income tax   ☐ VAT (specify NAICS codes) ▶ _____
☐ Other (must specify) ▶ _____

10 Enter penalties of perjury statements and any additional required information here (see instructions).

Sign here

Evelyn Martin (283-59-7465) is a U.S. resident and will continue to be so throughout the current year.

Under penalties of perjury, I declare that I have examined this application and accompanying attachments, and to the best of my knowledge and belief, they are true, correct, and complete. If I have designated a third party to receive the residency certification(s), I declare that the certification(s) will be used only for obtaining information or assistance from that person relating to matters designated on line 9.

Keep a copy for your records. ▶

Applicant's signature (or individual authorized to sign for the applicant)   Applicant's daytime phone no.:

_____   _____   _____
Signature   Date

_____
Name and title (print or type)

_____
Spouse's signature. If a joint application, **both** must sign.

_____
Name (print or type)

Form **8802** (Rev. 4-2012)

¶1305

Form 8802 (Rev. 4-2012)   **Worksheet for U.S. Residency Certification Application**   Page **3**

Applicant Name	Applicant TIN
Evelyn Martin	283-59-7465

Appointee Name (If Applicable)

Calendar year(s) for which certification is requested (must be the same year(s) indicated on line 7)

20X3

11   Enter the number of certifications needed in the column to the right of each country for which certification is requested.

Note. If you are requesting certifications for more than one calendar year per country, enter the total number of certifications for all years for each country (see instructions).

Column A			Column B			Column C			Column D		
Country	**CC**	**#**	**Country**	**CC**	**#**	**Country**	**CC**	**#**	**Country**	**CC**	**#**
Armenia	AM		Finland	FI		Latvia	LG		South Africa	SF	
Australia	AS		France	FR		Lithuania	LH		Spain	SP	1
Austria	AU		Georgia	GG		Luxembourg	LU		Sri Lanka	CE	
Azerbaijan	AJ		Germany	GM		Mexico	MX		Sweden	SW	
Bangladesh	BG		Greece	GR		Moldova	MD		Switzerland	SZ	
Barbados	BB		Hungary	HU		Morocco	MO		Tajikistan	TI	
Belarus	BO		Iceland	IC		Netherlands	NL		Thailand	TH	
Belgium	BE		India	IN		New Zealand	NZ		Trinidad and Tobago	TD	
Bermuda	BD		Indonesia	ID		Norway	NO		Tunisia	TS	
Bulgaria	BU		Ireland	EI		Pakistan	PK		Turkey	TU	
Canada	CA		Israel	IS		Philippines	RP		Turkmenistan	TX	
China	CH		Italy	IT		Poland	PL		Ukraine	UP	
Cyprus	CY		Jamaica	JM		Portugal	PO		United Kingdom	UK	
Czech Republic	EZ		Japan	JA		Romania	RO		Uzbekistan	UZ	
Denmark	DA		Kazakhstan	KZ		Russia	RS		Venezuela	VE	
Egypt	EG		Korea, South	KS		Slovak Republic	LO				
Estonia	EN		Kyrgyzstan	KG		Slovenia	SI				
Column A - Total			**Column B - Total**			**Column C - Total**			**Column D - Total**		

12   Enter the total number of certifications requested (add columns A, B, C, and D of line 11) . . . . ▶ | **1**

Form **8802** (Rev. 4-2012)

¶**1305**

Table 1. **Withholding Tax Rates on Income Other Than Personal Service Income Under Chapter 3, Internal Revenue Code, and Income Tax Treaties**

► Taxpayers must meet the limitation on benefits provisions in the treaty, if any, to qualify for reduced withholding rates.

► In most cases, the Business Profits article, rather than a reduced withholding tax rate, applies if the income is attributable to a permanent establishment of the taxpayer in the United States.

Income Code Number		1	6	7	14
		Interest	Dividends		
Name	Code	Paid by U.S. Obligors— General	Paid by U.S. Corporations—Genera l[a]	Qualifying for Direct Dividend Rate[a, b]	Pensions and Annuities[d]
Australia	AS	10 g,k,nn	15 mm	5 mm,oo	0
Austria	AU	0 g,jj	15 w	5 w	0
Bangladesh	BG	10 g,bb,jj	15 mm	10 mm	0 f,q
Barbados	BB	5	15 w	5 w	0 f
Belgium	BE	0 g,jj	15 dd,mm	5 dd,mm,oo	0 f
Bulgaria	BU	5 g,dd,jj,nn	10 dd,mm	5 dd,mm	0 f
Canada	CA	0 g,jj	15 mm	5 mm	15
China, People's Rep. of	CH	10	10	10	0 t
Comm. of Independent States*		0 n	30	30	30
Cyprus	CY	10 nn	15	5	0 f
Czech Republic	EZ	0 g	15 w	5 w	0 f
Denmark	DA	0 g,kk	15 dd,mm	5 dd,mm,oo	30 c,t
Egypt	EG	15	15	5	0 f
Estonia	EN	10 g,kk	15 w	5 w	0 f
Finland	FI	0 g,kk	15 dd,mm	5 dd,mm,oo	0 f
France	FR	0 g,k	15 mm	5 mm,oo	30 t
Germany	GM	0 g,jj	15 dd,mm	5 dd,mm,oo	0 f
Greece	GR	0 r	30	30	0
Hungary	HU	0	15	5	0 t
Iceland	IC	0 g,kk	15 dd,mm	5 dd,mm	0
India	IN	15 z	25 w	15 w	0 f
Indonesia	ID	10	15	10	15 q
Ireland	EI	0 g,k	15 mm	5 mm	0 f
Israel	IS	17$\frac{1}{2}$ z	25 w	12$\frac{1}{2}$ w	0 f
Italy	IT	10 g,h	15 mm	5 mm	0 f
Jamaica	JM	12$\frac{1}{2}$	15	10	0 f,p
Japan	JA	10 e,g,dd,ee	10 dd,ee,mm	5 dd,ee,mm,oo	0
Kazakhstan	KZ	10 g	15 ff	5 ff	0 f
Korea, South	KS	12	15	10	0 f
Latvia	LG	10 g,kk	15 w	5 w	0 f

* Those countries to which the U.S.-U.S.S.R. income tax treaty still applies: Armenia, Azerbaijan, Belarus, Georgia, Kyrgyzstan, Moldova, Tajikistan, Turkmenistan, and Uzbekistan.

¶1305

Table 1.**Withholding Tax Rates on Income Other Than Personal Service Income Under Chapter 3, Internal Revenue Code, and Income Tax Treaties**

▶ Taxpayers must meet the limitation on benefits provisions in the treaty, if any, to qualify for reduced withholding rates.

▶ In most cases, the Business Profits article, rather than a reduced withholding tax rate, applies if the income is attributable to a permanent establishment of the taxpayer in the United States.

Income Code Number		10			11	12
		Royalties				
Name	Code	Industrial Equipment	Know-How/ Other Industrial Royalties	Patents	Film & TV	Copyrights
Australia	AS	30 u	5	5	5	5
Austria	AU	30 u	0	0	10	0
Bangladesh	BG	30 u	10	10	10	10
Barbados	BB	30 u	5	5	5	5
Belgium	BE	30 u	0	0	0	0
Bulgaria	BU	30 u	5	5	5	5
Canada	CA	30 u	0	0	10	0
China, People's Rep. of	CH	10 v	10	10	10	10
Comm. of Independent States		0	0	0	0	0
Cyprus	CY	30 u	0	0	0	0
Czech Republic	EZ	10	10	10	0	0
Denmark	DA	30 u	0	0	0	0
Egypt	EG	30 u	30 u	15	0	15
Estonia	EN	5	10	10	10	10
Finland	FI	30 u	0	0	0	0
France	FR	30 u	0	0	0	0
Germany	GM	30 u	0	0	0	0
Greece	GR	0	0	0	30 u	0
Hungary	HU	30 u	0	0	0	0
Iceland	IC	30 u	5	0	5	0
India	IN	10	15	15	15	15
Indonesia	ID	10	10	10	10	10
Ireland	EI	30 u	0	0	0	0
Israel	IS	30 u	15 u	15	10	10
Italy	IT	5	8	8	8	0
Jamaica	JM	30 u	10	10	10	10
Japan	JA	30 u	0 ee	0 ee	0 ee	0 ee
Kazakhstan	KZ	10	10	10	10	10
Korea, South	KS	30 u	15	15	10	10
Latvia	LG	5	10	10	10	10

¶1305

Table 1.**Withholding Tax Rates on Income Other Than Personal Service Income Under Chapter 3, Internal Revenue Code, and Income Tax Treaties**

► Taxpayers must meet the limitation on benefits provisions in the treaty, if any, to qualify for reduced withholding rates.

► In most cases, the Business Profits article, rather than a reduced withholding tax rate, applies if the income is attributable to a permanent establishment of the taxpayer in the United States.

Income Code Number		1	6	7	14
		Interest	Dividends		
Name	Code	Paid by U.S. Obligors—General	Paid by U.S. Corporations—General[a]	Qualifying for Direct Dividend Rate[a,b]	Pensions and Annuities
Lithuania	LH	10 g,kk	15 w	5 w	0 f
Luxembourg	LU	0 g,k	15 w	5 w	0
Malta	MT	10 g,jj	15 dd,mm	5 dd,mm	0 f
Mexico	MX	15 g,dd,ee,hh	10 dd,mm	5 dd,mm,oo	0
Morocco	MO	15	15	10	0 f
Netherlands	NL	0 g	15 pp	5 gg,oo,pp	0 f,pp
New Zealand	NZ	10 g,jj,nn	15 mm	5 mm,oo	0
Norway	NO	10 z	15	15	0 f
Pakistan	PK	30	30	15	0 j
Philippines	RP	15	25	20	30 q
Poland	PL	0	15	5	30
Portugal	PO	10 g,k	15 w	5 w	0 f
Romania	RO	10	10	10	0 f
Russia	RS	0 g	10 ff	5 ff	0 t
Slovak Republic	LO	0 g	15 w	5 w	0 f
Slovenia	SI	5 g	15 mm	5 mm	0 f
South Africa	SF	0 g,jj	15 w	5 w	15 l
Spain	SP	10	15 w	10 w	0 f
Sri Lanka	CE	10 g,jj	15 gg	15 gg	0 t
Sweden	SW	0 g	15 dd,mm	5 dd,mm,oo	0
Switzerland	SZ	0 g,jj	15 w	5 w	0
Thailand	TH	15 g,z	15 w	10 w	0 f
Trinidad & Tobago	TD	30	30	30	0 f
Tunisia	TS	15	20 w	14 w	0 f
Turkey	TU	15 g, m,z	20 w	15 w	0
Ukraine	UP	0 g	15 ff	5 ff	0
United Kingdom	UK	0 g,ee,kk	15 ee,mm	5 ee,mm,oo	0 f
Venezuela	VE	10 g,kk,ll	15 mm	5 mm	0 t
Other Countries		30	30	30	30

¶1305

Table 1. **Withholding Tax Rates on Income Other Than Personal Service Income Under Chapter 3, Internal Revenue Code, and Income Tax Treaties**

► Taxpayers must meet the limitation on benefits provisions in the treaty, if any, to qualify for reduced withholding rates.

► In most cases, the Business Profits article, rather than a reduced withholding tax rate, applies if the income is attributable to a permanent establishment of the taxpayer in the United States.

Income Code Number		10			11	12
		Royalties				
Name	Code	Industrial Equipment	Know-how/ Other Industrial Royalties	Patents	Film & TV	Copyrights
Lithuania	LH	5	10	10	10	10
Luxembourg	LU	30 u	0	0	0	0
Malta	MT	30 u	10	10	10	10
Mexico	MX	10	10	10	10	10
Morocco	MO	30 u	10	10	10	10
Netherlands	NL	30 u	0	0	0	0
New Zealand	NZ	30 u	5	5	5	5
Norway	NO	30 u	0	0	0	0
Pakistan	PK	30 u	0	0	30 u	0
Philippines	RP	30 u	15	15	15	15
Poland	PL	30 u	10	10	10	10
Portugal	PO	10	10	10	10	10
Romania	RO	30 u	15	15	10	10
Russia	RS	30 u	0	0	0	0
Slovak Republic	LO	10	10	10	0	0
Slovenia	SI	30 u	5	5	5	5
South Africa	SF	30 u	0	0	0	0
Spain	SP	8	10	10	8	5 aa
Sri Lanka	CE	30 u,y	10	10	10	10
Sweden	SW	30 u	0	0	0	0
Switzerland	SZ	30 u	0	0	30 u	0
Thailand	TH	8	15	15	5	5
Trinidad & Tobago	TD	30 u	15	15	30 u	0 cc
Tunisia	TS	10	15	15	15	15
Turkey	TU	5	10	10	10	10
Ukraine	UP	30 u	10	10	10	10
United Kingdom	UK	30 u	0 ee	0 ee	0 ee	0 ee
Venezuela	VE	5	10	10	10	10
Other Countries		30	30	30	30	30

¶1305

a   No U.S. tax is imposed on a percentage of any dividend paid by a U.S. corporation in existence on January 1, 2011, that received at least 80% of its gross income from an active foreign business for the 3-year period before the dividend is declared. (See sections 871(i)(2)(B) and 881(d) of the Internal Revenue Code.)

b   The reduced rate applies to dividends paid by a subsidiary to a foreign parent corporation that has the required percentage of stock ownership. In some cases, the income of the subsidiary must meet certain requirements (e.g., a certain percentage of its total income must consist of income other than dividends and interest).

c   In most cases, if the person was receiving pension distributions before March 31, 2000, the distributions continue to be exempt from U.S. tax.

d   In most cases, this rate applies only to pensions not paid by a government. See specific treaty rules for government pensions.

e   Interest is exempt if (a) paid to certain financial institutions or (b) paid on indebtedness from the sale on credit of equipment or merchandise.

f   Includes alimony.

g   Exemption or reduced rate does not apply to an excess inclusion for a residual interest in a real estate mortgage investment conduit (REMIC).

h   Interest paid or accrued on the sale of goods, merchandise, or services between enterprises is exempt. Interest paid or accrued on the sale on credit of industrial, commercial, or scientific property is exempt.

i   The rate is 5% for trademarks and any information for rentals of industrial, commercial, or scientific equipment.

j   Exemption is not available when paid from a fund under an employees' pension or annuity plan, if contributions to it are deductible under U.S. tax laws in determining taxable income of the employer.

k   The rate is 15% for interest determined with reference to the profits of the issuer or one of its associated enterprises.

l   Annuities purchased while the annuitant was not a resident of the United States are not taxable. The reduced rate applies if the distribution is not subject to a penalty for early withdrawal.

m   Contingent interest that does not qualify as portfolio interest is treated as a dividend and is subject to the rate under column 6 or 7.

n   The exemption applies only to interest on credits, loans, and other indebtedness connected with the financing of trade between the United States and the C.I.S. member. It does not include interest from the conduct of a general banking business.

o   The exemption applies only to gains from the sale or other disposition of property acquired by gift or inheritance.

p   The exemption does not apply if the applicable past employment was performed in the United states while such person was a resident of the United States, or if the annuity was purchased in the United States while such person was a resident of the United States.

q   Annuities paid in return for other than the recipient's services are exempt. For Bangladesh, exemption does not apply to annuity received for services rendered.

r   Exemption does not apply to such interest paid by a U.S. corporation to a Greek corporation controlling, directly or indirectly, more than 50 percent of the entire voting power in the paying corporation.

s   The rate for royalties with respect to tangible personal property is 7%.

t   Does not apply to annuities. For Denmark, annuities are exempt.

u   Depending on the facts, the rate may be determined by either the Business Profits article or the Other Income article.

v   Tax imposed on 70% of gross royalties for rentals of industrial, commercial, or scientific equipment.

w   The rate in column 6 applies to dividends paid by a regulated investment company (RIC) or a real estate investment trust (REIT). However, that rate applies to dividends paid by a REIT only if the beneficial owner of the dividends is an individual holding less than a 10% interest (25% in the case of Portugal, Spain, Thailand, and Tunisia) in the REIT.

x   Royalties not taxed at the 5% or 8% rate are taxed at a 10% rate, unless the royalty is attributable to a permanent establishment of the taxpayer in the United States.

y   The rate is 5% for the rental of tangible personal property.

z   The rate is 10% if the interest is paid on a loan granted by a bank or similar financial institution. For Norway, the interest described in the preceding sentences is exempt. For Thailand, the 10% rate also applies to interest from an arm's length sale on credit of equipment, merchandise, or services.

aa   The rate is 8% for copyrights of scientific work.

bb   The rate is 5% for interest (a) beneficially owned by a bank or similar financial institution (including an insurance company) or (b) paid due to a sale on credit of any industrial, commercial, or scientific equipment, or of any merchandise to an enterprise.

cc   The rate is 15% for copyrights of scientific work.

dd   Amounts paid to a pension fund that are not derived from the carrying on of a business, directly or indirectly, by the fund are exempt. This includes dividends paid by a REIT only if the conditions in footnote *mm* are met. For Sweden, to be entitled to the exemption, the pension fund must not sell or make a contract to sell the holding from which the dividend is derived within 2 months of the date the pension fund acquired the holding.

ee   Exemption or reduced rate does not apply to amount paid under, or as part of, a conduit arrangement.

ff   The rate in column 6 applies to dividends paid by a regulated investment company (RIC). Dividends paid by a real estate investment trust (REIT) are subject to a 30% rate.

gg   The rate applies to dividends paid by a real estate investment trust (REIT) only if the beneficial owner of the dividends is (a) an individual holding less than a 10% interest in the REIT, (b) a person holding not more than 5% of any class of the REIT's stock and the dividends are paid on stock that is publicly traded, or (c) a person holding not more than a 10% interest in the REIT and the REIT is diversified.

hh   The rate is 4.9% for interest derived from (1) loans granted by banks and insurance companies and (2) bonds or securities that are regularly and substantially traded on a recognized securities market. The rate is 10% for interest not described in the preceding sentence and paid (i) by banks or (ii) by the buyer of machinery and equipment to the seller due to a sale on credit.

ii   The exemption does not apply if (1) the recipient was a U.S. resident during the 5-year period before the date of payment, (2) the amount was paid for employment performed in the United States, and (3) the amount is not a periodic payment, or is a lump-sum payment in lieu of a right to receive an annuity.

jj   The rate is 15% (10% for Bulgaria; 30% for Austria, Germany and Switzerland) for contingent interest that does not qualify as portfolio interest. In most cases, this is interest based on receipts, sales, income, or changes in the value of property.

kk   The rate is 15% for interest determined with reference to (a) receipts, sales, income, profits or other cash flow of the debtor or a related person, (b) any change in the value of any property of the debtor or a related person, or (c) any dividend, partnership distribution, or similar payment made by the debtor or related person.

ll   The rate is 4.95% if the interest is beneficially owned by a financial institution (including an insurance company).

mm   The rate in column 6 applies to dividends paid by a regulated investment company (RIC) or real estate investment trust (REIT). However, that rate applies to dividends paid by a REIT only if the beneficial owner of the dividends is (a) an individual (or pension fund, in some cases) holding not more than a 10% interest in the REIT, (b) a person holding not more than 5% of any class of the REIT's stock and the dividends are paid on stock that is publicly traded, or (c) a person holding not more than a 10% interest in the REIT and the REIT is diversified.

nn   Interest received by a financial institution is exempt. In some cases, the exemption does not apply if the interest is paid as part of an arrangement involving back-to-back loans or other arrangement that is economically equivalent and intended to have a similar effect to back-to-back loans.

oo   Dividends received from an 80%-owned corporate subsidiary are exempt if certain conditions are met. For Japan, dividends received from a more than 50% owned corporate subsidiary are exempt if certain conditions are met.

pp   The rate in column 6 applies to dividends paid by a regulated investment company (RIC) or real estate investment trust (REIT). However, that rate applies to dividends paid by a REIT only if the beneficial owner of the dividends is (a) an individual holding not more than a 25% interest in the REIT, (b) a person holding not more than 5% of any class of the REIT's stock and the dividends are paid on stock that is publicly traded, or (c) a person holding not more than a 10% interest in the REIT and the REIT is diversified, or (d) a Dutch belegginginstelling.

Publication 515 (2015)

¶1305

Table 2. Compensation for Personal Services Performed in United States Exempt from U.S. Income Tax Under Income Tax Treaties

Country (1)	Code[1] (2)	Category of Personal Services — Purpose[22] (3)	Maximum Presence in U.S. (4)	Required Employer or Payer (5)	Maximum Amount of Compensation (6)	Treaty Article Citation (7)
Australia	16	Independent personal services[7]	183 days	Any contractor	No limit	14
	17	Dependent personal services[17]	183 days	Any foreign resident	No limit	15
	42	Public entertainment	No limit	Any U.S. or foreign resident	$10,000 p.a.[25]	17
	19	Studying and training: Remittances or allowances[11]	No limit	Any foreign resident	No limit	20
Austria	16	Independent personal services[7]	No limit	Any contractor	No limit	14
	17	Dependent personal services[17]	183 days	Any foreign resident	No limit	15
	42	Public entertainment	No limit	Any U.S. or foreign resident	$20,000 p.a.[25]	17
	19	Studying and training: Remittances or allowances[11]	3 years[45]	Any foreign resident	No limit	20
Bangladesh	15	Scholarship or fellowship grant[4]	2 years[45]	Any U.S. or foreign resident[6]	No limit	21(2)
	16	Independent personal services[7]	183 days	Any contractor	No limit	15
	17	Dependent personal services[17]	183 days	Any foreign resident	No limit	16
	42	Public entertainment	No limit	Any contractor	$10,000 p.a.[30]	18
	18	Teaching or research[4]	2 years	Any U.S. or foreign resident	No limit	21(1)
	19	Studying and training:[4] Remittances or allowances	2 years[45]	Any foreign resident	No limit	21(2)
		Compensation during study or training	2 years[45]	Any U.S. or foreign resident	$8,000 p.a.	21(2)
Barbados	16	Independent personal services[7, 8]	89 days	Any foreign contractor	No limit	14
	17	Dependent personal services[8, 17]	89 days	Any U.S. contractor	$5,000 p.a.	14
			183 days	Any foreign resident	$5,000 p.a.	15
	42	Public entertainment	183 days	Any U.S. or foreign resident	$250 per day or $4,000 p.a.[6, 50]	17
	19	Studying and training:[23] Remittances or allowances[11]	No limit	Any foreign resident	No limit	20
Belgium	16	Independent personal services[53]	183 days	Any foreign resident	No limit	7
	17	Dependent personal services[12, 17]	No limit	Any U.S. or foreign resident	$20,000 p.a.[25]	14
	42	Public entertainment	2 years	Any foreign resident	No limit	16
	18	Teaching[4]		Any U.S. educational or research institution		19(2)
	19	Studying and training:[11] Remittances or allowances	2 years[45]	Any foreign resident	No limit	19(1)(a)
		Compensation during study or training	2 years[45]	Any U.S. or foreign resident	$9,000 p.a.	19(1)(b)

¶1305

Country (1)	Code[1] (2)	Category of Personal Services — Purpose[22] (3)	Maximum Presence in U.S. (4)	Required Employer or Payer (5)	Maximum Amount of Compensation (6)	Treaty Article Citation (7)
Bulgaria	16	Independent personal services[53]	183 days	Any foreign resident	No limit	7
	17	Dependent personal services[8,17]	No limit	Any U.S. or foreign resident	$15,000 p.a.[25]	14
	42	Public entertainment	2 years	Any U.S. educational or research institution	No limit	16
	18	Teaching[4]			No limit	19(2)
	19	Studying and training: Remittances or allowances[11]	2 years[45]	Any foreign resident	No limit	19(1)(a)
		Compensation during study or training	2 years[45]	Any U.S. or foreign resident	$9,000 p.a.	19(1)(b)
Canada	16	Independent personal services[53]	No limit	Any U.S. or foreign resident	$10,000	VII
	17	Dependent personal services	183 days	Any foreign resident[17]	No limit[13]	XV
	42	Public entertainment[54]	No limit	Any U.S. or foreign resident	$15,000 p.a.[25]	XV
	19	Studying and training: Remittances or allowances[11]	No limit[52]	Any foreign resident	No limit	XVI
						XX
China, People's Rep. of	15	Scholarship or fellowship grant[15]	No specific limit	Any U.S. or foreign resident[6]	No limit	20(b)
	16	Independent personal services[7]	183 days	Any contractor	No limit	13
	17	Dependent personal services[8,17]	183 days	Any foreign resident	No limit	14
	42	Public entertainment[29]			No limit	16
	18	Teaching[4]	3 years	U.S. educational or research institute	No limit	19
	19	Studying and training: Remittances or allowances	No specific limit	Any foreign resident	No limit	20(a)
		Compensation during training or while gaining experience	No specific limit	Any U.S. or foreign resident	$5,000 p.a.	20(c)
Commonwealth of Independent States	15	Scholarship or fellowship grant	5 years	Any U.S. or foreign resident	Limited[19]	VI(1)
	16	Independent personal services	183 days	Any U.S. or foreign contractor	No limit	VI(2)
	17	Dependent personal services	183 days	Any U.S. or foreign resident	No limit	VI(2)
	18	Teaching[4,20]	2 years	Any U.S. educational or scientific institution	No limit	VI(1)
	19	Studying and training: Remittances or allowances	5 years	Any U.S. or foreign resident	Limited	VI(1)
		Compensation while gaining experience	1 year	C.I.S. resident	No limit[21]	VI(1)
		Compensation under U.S. Government program	1 year	Any U.S. or foreign resident	No limit	VI(1)

¶1305

Country (1)	Code[1] (2)	Category of Personal Services — Purpose[22] (3)	Maximum Presence in U.S. (4)	Required Employer or Payer (5)	Maximum Amount of Compensation (6)	Treaty Article Citation (7)
Cyprus	15	Scholarship or fellowship grant[15]	Generally, 5 years	Any U.S. or foreign resident[5]	No limit	21(1)
	16	Independent personal services[7]	182 days	Any contractor	No limit	17
	17	Dependent personal services[17]	182 days	Any foreign resident	No limit	18
	42	Public entertainment	No limit	Any U.S. or foreign resident	$500 per day or $5,000 p.a.[6]	19(1)
	19	Studying and training:				
		Remittances or allowances	Generally, 5 years	Any foreign resident	No limit	21(1)
		Compensation during training	Generally, 5 years	Any U.S. or foreign resident	$2,000 p.a.	21(1)
		Compensation while gaining experience[2]	1 year	Cyprus resident	$7,500	21(2)
		Compensation under U.S. Government program	1 year	U.S. Government or its contractor	$10,000	21(3)
Czech Republic	15	Scholarship or fellowship grant[4, 15]	5 years	Any U.S. or foreign resident[5]	No limit	21(1)
	16	Independent personal services[7]	183 days	Any contractor	No limit	14
	17	Dependent personal services[8, 17]	183 days	Any foreign resident	No limit	15
	42	Public entertainment	No limit	Any U.S. or foreign resident	$20,000 p.a.[30]	18
	18	Teaching[35]	2 years	Any U.S. educational or research institution	No limit	21(5)
	19	Studying and training:[4]				
		Remittances and allowances	5 years	Any foreign resident	No limit	21(1)
		Compensation during training	5 years	Any U.S. or foreign resident	$5,000 p.a.	21(1)
		Compensation while gaining experience[2]	12 consec. mos.	Czech resident	$8,000	21(2)
		Compensation under U.S. Government program	1 year	U.S. Government	$10,000	21(3)
Denmark	16	Independent personal services[7]	No limit	Any contractor	No limit	14
	17	Dependent personal services[8, 17]	183 days	Any foreign resident	No limit	15
	42	Public entertainment	No limit	Any U.S. or foreign resident	$20,000 p.a.[25]	17
	19	Studying and training:[4]				
		Remittances or allowances[11]	3 years[46]	Any foreign resident	No limit	20

Country (1)	Code[1] (2)	Category of Personal Services — Purpose[22] (3)	Maximum Presence in U.S. (4)	Required Employer or Payer (5)	Maximum Amount of Compensation (6)	Treaty Article Citation (7)
Egypt	15	Scholarship or fellowship grant[15]	Generally, 5 years	Any U.S. or foreign resident[6]	No limit	23(1)
	16	Independent personal services	89 days	Any contractor	No limit	15
	17	Dependent personal services[16,17]	89 days	Egyptian resident	No limit	16
	42	Public entertainment	No limit	Any U.S. or foreign resident	$400 per day[46]	17
	18	Teaching[4,13]	2 years	U.S. educational institution	No limit	22
	19	Studying and training:				
		Remittances or allowances	Generally, 5 years	Any foreign resident	No limit	23(1)
		Compensation during training	Generally, 5 years	U.S. or any foreign resident	$3,000 p.a.	23(1)
		Compensation while gaining experience[2]		Egyptian resident	$7,500	23(2)
		Compensation under U.S. Government program	12 consec. mos.	U.S. Government or its contractor	$10,000	23(3)
Estonia	15	Scholarship or fellowship grants[4]	5 years	Any U.S. or foreign resident[6]	No limit	20(1)
	16	Independent personal services[7]	183 days	Any contractor	No limit	14
	17	Dependent personal services[8,17]	183 days	Any foreign resident	No limit	15
	42	Public entertainment	No limit	Any U.S. or foreign resident	$20,000 p.a.[30]	17
	19	Studying and training:[4]				
		Remittances or allowances	5 years	Any foreign resident	No limit	20(1)
		Compensation during training	12 consec. mos.	Estonian resident	$8,000	20(2)
		Compensation while gaining experience[2]	5 years	Other foreign or U.S. resident	$5,000 p.a.	20(1)
		Compensation under U.S. Government program	12 consec. mos.	Estonian resident	$8,000	20(2)
			1 year	U.S. Government or its contractor	$10,000	20(3)
Finland	16	Independent personal services[7]	No limit	Any contractor	No limit	14
	17	Dependent personal services[17]	183 days	Any foreign resident	No limit	15
	42	Public entertainment	No limit	Any U.S. or foreign resident	$20,000 p.a.[25]	17
	19	Studying and training: Remittances or allowances[11]	No limit	Any U.S. or foreign resident	No limit	20
France	15	Scholarship or fellowship grant[15]	5 years[43]	Any U.S. or foreign resident[6]	No limit	21(1)
	16	Independent personal services[7]	No limit	Any contractor	No limit	14
	17	Dependent personal services[8,17]	183 days	Any foreign resident	No limit	15
	42	Public entertainment	No limit	Any U.S. or foreign resident	$10,000 p.a.[30]	17
	18	Teaching[4,44]	2 years[43]	U.S. educational or research institution	No limit	20
	19	Studying and training:[4]				
		Remittances or allowances	5 years[43]	Any foreign resident	No limit	21(1)
		Compensation during study or training	12 consec. mos.	French resident	$8,000	21(2)
		Compensation while gaining experience[2]	5 years[43]	Other foreign or U.S. resident	$5,000 p.a.	21(1)
			12 consec. mos.	French resident	$8,000	21(2)

¶1305

Country (1)	Category of Personal Services		Maximum Presence in U.S. (4)	Required Employer or Payer (5)	Maximum Amount of Compensation (6)	Treaty Article Citation (7)
	Code¹ (2)	Purpose²² (3)				
Germany	15	Scholarship or fellowship grant	No limit	Any U.S. or foreign resident⁶	No limit	20(3)
	16	Independent personal services⁵³				7
	17	Dependent personal services¹²,¹⁷	183 days	Any foreign resident	No limit	15
	42	Public entertainment	No limit	Any U.S. or foreign resident	$20,000 p.a.³⁰	17
	18	Teaching⁴,⁵⁵	2 years	U.S. educational or research institution	No limit	20(1)
	19	Studying and training:¹¹				
		Remittances or allowances	No limit	Any foreign resident	No limit	20(2)
		Compensation during study or training	4 years	Any U.S. or foreign resident	$9,000 p.a.	20(4)
		Compensation while gaining experience²	1 year	Any foreign resident	$10,000²⁸	20(5)
Greece	16	Independent personal services	183 days	Greek resident contractor	No limit	X
				Other foreign or U.S. resident contractor	$10,000 p.a.	X
	17	Dependent personal services	183 days	Greek resident	No limit	X
			183 days	Other foreign or U.S resident	$10,000 p.a.	X
	18	Teaching	3 years	U.S. educational institution	No limit	XII
	19	Studying and training: Remittances or allowances	No limit	Any foreign resident	No limit	XIII
Hungary	16	Independent personal services⁷	183 days	Any contractor	No limit	13
	17	Dependent personal services¹⁷	183 days	Any foreign resident	No limit	14
	18	Teaching⁴	2 years	U.S. educational institution	No limit	17
	19	Studying and training:²³ Remittances or allowances¹¹	No limit	Any foreign resident	No limit	18(1)
Iceland	15	Scholarship or fellowship grant	5 years	Any U.S. or foreign resident⁶	No limit	19(1)
	16	Independent personal services⁵³				7
	17	Dependent personal services⁶,¹⁷	183 days	Any foreign resident	No limit	14
	42	Public entertainment	No limit	Any U.S. or foreign resident	$20,000 p.a.²⁵	16
	19	Studying and training:				
		Remittances or allowances	5 years	Any foreign resident	No limit	19(1)
		Compensation during study or training	5 years	Any U.S. or foreign resident	$9,000 p.a.	19(1)
		Compensation while gaining experience	12 consec. mo.	Any U.S. or foreign resident²	$9,000	19(2)
		Compensation under U.S. Government program	1 year	U.S. Government or its contractor	$9,000	19(3)

¶1305

Country (1)	Code[22] (2)	Category of Personal Services — Purpose[22] (3)	Maximum Presence In U.S. (4)	Required Employer or Payer (5)	Maximum Amount of Compensation (6)	Treaty Article Citation (7)
India	16	Independent personal services[7,6]	89 days	Any contractor	No limit	15
	17	Dependent personal services[6,17]	183 days	Any foreign resident	No limit	16
	42	Public entertainment	No limit	Any U.S. or foreign resident	$1,500 p.a.[26,50]	18
	18	Teaching[4]	2 years	U.S. educational institution	No limit	22
	19	Studying and training: Remittances or allowances	Reasonable period	Any foreign resident[27]	No limit	21(1)
Indonesia	15	Scholarship and fellowship grant[15]	5 years	Any U.S. or foreign resident[6]	No limit	19(1)
	16	Independent personal services[7]	119 days	Any contractor	No limit	15
	17	Dependent personal services[17]	119 days	Any foreign resident	No limit	16
	42	Public entertainment	No limit	Any U.S. or foreign resident	$2,000 p.a.[26,50]	17
	18	Teaching[4,44]	2 years	U.S. educational institution	No limit	20
	19	Studying and training:				
		Remittances or allowances	5 years	Any foreign resident	No limit	19(1)
		Compensation during training	5 years	Any U.S. or foreign resident	$2,000 p.a.	19(1)
		Compensation while gaining experience	12 consec. mo.	Any U.S. or foreign resident	$7,500	19(2)
Ireland	16	Independent personal services[7]	No limit	Any contractor	No limit	14
	17	Dependent personal services[17,47]	183 days	Any foreign resident	No limit	15
	42	Public entertainment	No limit	Any U.S. or foreign resident	$20,000 p.a.[25]	17
	19	Studying and training: Remittances or allowances[11]	1 year[45]	Any foreign resident	No limit	20
Israel	15	Scholarship and fellowship grant	5 years	Any U.S. or foreign resident[6]	No limit	24(1)
	16	Independent personal services	182 days	Any contractor	No limit	16
	17	Dependent personal services[16,17]	182 days	Israeli resident	No limit	17
	42	Public entertainment	No limit	Any U.S. or foreign resident	$400 per day[37]	18
	18	Teaching[39]	2 years	U.S. educational institution	No limit	23
	19	Studying and training:				
		Remittances or allowances	5 years	Any foreign resident	No limit	24(1)
		Compensation during study or training	5 years	Any U.S. or foreign resident	$3,000 p.a.	24(1)
		Compensation while gaining experience[2]	12 consec. mo.	Israeli resident	$7,500	24(2)
		Compensation under U.S. Government program	1 year	U.S. Government or its contractor	$10,000	24(3)
Italy	16	Independent personal services[7]	No limit	Any foreign resident	No limit	14(1)
	17	Dependent personal services[6,17]	183 days	Any foreign resident	No limit	15(2)
	42	Public entertainment	90 days	Any U.S. or foreign resident	$20,000 p.a.[25]	17
	18	Teaching or research[4]	2 years	Any U.S. or foreign resident	No limit	20
	19	Studying and training: Remittances or allowances	No limit	Any foreign resident	No limit	21

¶1305

Country (1)	Code[1] (2)	Category of Personal Services — Purpose[22] (3)	Maximum Presence in U.S. (4)	Required Employer or Payer (5)	Maximum Amount of Compensation (6)	Treaty Article Citation (7)
Jamaica	16	Independent personal services[7]	89 days	Any foreign contractor	No limit	14
	17	Dependent personal services[17]	89 days	Any U.S. contractor	$5,000 p.a.	14
	42	Public entertainment	183 days	Any foreign resident	$5,000 p.a.	15
			No limit	Any U.S. or foreign resident	$400 per day or $5,000 p.a.[6]	18
	18	Teaching[4,44]	2 years	U.S. educational institution	No limit	22
	19	Studying and training:[23]				
		Remittances or allowances[11]	No limit	Any foreign resident	No limit	21(1)
		Compensation during study	12 consec. mo.	Jamaican resident	$7,500 p.a.	21(2)
		Compensation while gaining experience[2]	12 consec. mo.	Jamaican resident	$7,500 p.a.	21(2)
Japan	16	Independent personal services[8,53]	183 days	Any foreign resident	No limit	7
	17	Dependent personal services[8,17]	No limit	Any U.S. or foreign resident	No limit	14
	42	Public entertainment			$10,000 p.a.[25]	16
	18	Teaching or research[4]	2 years	Any U.S. educational institution	No limit	20
	19	Studying and training: Remittances or allowances[45]	1 year	Any foreign resident	No limit	19
Kazakhstan	15	Scholarship or fellowship grant[4,15,41]	5 years[31]	Any U.S. or foreign resident[5]	No limit	19
	16	Independent personal services[7]	183 days	Any contractor	No limit	14
	17	Dependent personal services[17,47]	183 days	Any foreign resident	No limit	15
	19	Studying and training: Remittances or allowances	5 years[31]	Any foreign resident	No limit	19
Korea, South	15	Scholarship or fellowship grant[15]	5 years	Any U.S. or foreign resident[5]	No limit	21(1)
	16	Independent personal services[7]	182 days	Any contractor	$3,000 p.a.	18
	17	Dependent personal services[17]	182 days	Korean resident[18]	$3,000 p.a.	19
	18	Teaching[4]	2 years	U.S. educational institution	No limit	20
	19	Studying and training:				
		Remittances or allowances	5 years	Any foreign resident	No limit	21(1)
		Compensation during training	5 years	Any foreign or U.S. resident	$2,000 p.a.	21(1)
		Compensation while gaining experience[2]	1 year	Korean resident	$5,000	21(2)
		Compensation under U.S. Government program	1 year	U.S. Government or its contractor	$10,000	21(3)

Country (1)	Category of Personal Services		Maximum Presence in U.S. (4)	Required Employer or Payer (5)	Maximum Amount of Compensation (6)	Treaty Article Citation (7)
	Code[1] (2)	Purpose[22] (3)				
Latvia	15	Scholarship or fellowship grants[4]	5 years	Any U.S. or foreign resident[6]	No limit	20(1)
	16	Independent personal services[7]	183 days	Any contractor	No limit	14
	17	Dependent personal services[8,17]	183 days	Any foreign resident	No limit	15
	42	Public entertainment	No limit	Any U.S. or foreign resident	$20,000 p.a.[30]	17
	19	Studying and training:[4]				
		Remittances or allowances	5 years	Any foreign resident	No limit	20(1)
		Compensation during training	12 consec. mos.	Latvian resident	$8,000	20(2)
		Compensation while gaining experience[2]	5 years	Other foreign or U.S. resident	$5,000 p.a.	20(1)
			12 consec. mos.	Latvian resident	$8,000	20(2)
		Compensation under U.S. Government program	1 year	U.S. Government or its contractor	$10,000	20(3)
Lithuania	15	Scholarship or fellowship grants[4]	5 years	Any U.S. or foreign resident[6]	No limit	20(1)
	16	Independent personal services[7]	183 days	Any contractor	No limit	14
	17	Dependent personal services[8,17]	183 days	Any foreign resident	No limit	15
	42	Public entertainment	No limit	Any U.S. or foreign resident	$20,000 p.a.[30]	17
	19	Studying and training:[4]				
		Remittances or allowances	5 years	Any foreign resident	No limit	20(1)
		Compensation during training	12 consec. mos.	Lithuanian resident	$8,000	20(2)
		Compensation while gaining experience[2]	5 years	Other foreign or U.S. resident	$5,000 p.a.	20(1)
			12 consec. mos.	Lithuanian resident	$8,000	20(2)
		Compensation under U.S. Government program	1 year	U.S. Government or its contractor	$10,000	20(3)
Luxembourg	16	Independent personal services[7]	No limit	Any contractor	No limit	15
	17	Dependent personal services[12,17]	183 days	Any foreign resident	No limit	16
	42	Public entertainment	No limit	Any U.S. or foreign resident	$10,000 p.a.[25]	18
	18	Teaching or research[9]	2 years	Any U.S. or foreign resident	No limit	21(2)
	19	Studying and training:				
		Remittances or allowances[11]	2 years[45]	Any U.S. or foreign resident	No limit	21(1)
Malta	16	Independent personal services[53]	2 years[45]	Any U.S. or foreign resident	No limit	7
	17	Dependent personal services[12,17]	183 days	Any foreign resident	No limit	14
	42	Public entertainment	No limit	Any U.S. or foreign resident	$20,000 p.a.[25]	16
	19	Studying and training:				
		Remittances or allowances	1 year[45]	Any foreign resident	No limit	20(1)
		Compensation during study or training	No limit	Any U.S. or foreign resident	$9,000 p.a.	20(2)
		Compensation while gaining experience	No limit	Any U.S. or foreign resident	$9,000 p.a.	20
Mexico	16	Independent personal services[7]	182 days	Any foreign resident	No limit	14
	17	Dependent personal services[17,47]	183 days	Any U.S. or foreign resident	No limit	15
	42	Public entertainment	No limit	Any U.S. or foreign resident	$3,000 p.a.[30]	18
	19	Studying and training:				
		Remittances or allowances	No limit	Any foreign resident	No limit	21

¶1305

Country (1)	Code[1] (2)	Category of Personal Services — Purpose [22] (3)	Maximum Presence in U.S. (4)	Required Employer or Payer (5)	Maximum Amount of Compensation (6)	Treaty Article Citation (7)
Morocco	15	Scholarship or fellowship grant[15]	5 years	Any U.S. or foreign resident[6]	No limit	18
	16	Independent personal services[7]	182 days	Any contractor[13]	$5,000	14
	17	Dependent personal services[17]	182 days	Moroccan resident[13,16]	No limit	15
	19	Studying and training:[5]				
		Remittances or allowances	5 years	Any foreign resident	No limit	18
		Compensation during training	5 years	U.S. or any foreign resident	$2,000 p.a.	18
Netherlands	15	Scholarship or fellowship grant[15,33]	3 years	Any U.S. or foreign resident[6]	No limit	22(2)
	16	Independent personal services[7]	No limit	Any contractor	No limit	15
	17	Dependent personal services[17,47]	183 days	Any foreign resident	No limit	16
	42	Public entertainment	No limit	Any U.S. or foreign resident	$10,000 p.a.[25]	18
	18	Teaching[4,34]	2 years	U.S. educational institution	No limit	21(1)
	19	Studying and training:[33]				
		Remittances or allowances	Reasonable period	Any foreign resident	No limit	22(1)
		Compensation while gaining experience	Reasonable period	Any U.S. or foreign resident	$2,000 p.a.	22(1)
		Compensation while recipient of scholarship or fellowship grant	Reasonable period	Any U.S. or foreign resident	$2,000 p.a.[36]	22(2)
New Zealand	16	Independent personal services[53]	183 days	Any foreign resident	No limit	7
	17	Dependent personal services[17]	No limit	Any U.S. or foreign resident	$10,000[25]	15
	42	Public entertainment				17
	19	Studying and training: Remittances or allowances[11]	No limit	Any foreign resident	No limit	20
Norway	15	Scholarship or fellowship grant[15]	5 years	Any U.S. or foreign resident[6]	No limit	16(1)
	16	Independent personal services[7]	182 days	Any contractor	No limit	13
	42	Public entertainment	90 days	Any contractor	$10,000 p.a.[28]	13
	17	Dependent personal services[17,56]	182 days	Norwegian resident[18]	No limit	14
	18	Teaching[4]	2 years	U.S. educational institution	No limit	15
	19	Studying and training:				
		Remittances or allowances	5 years	Any foreign resident	No limit	16(1)
		Compensation during training	5 years	U.S. or any foreign resident	$2,000 p.a.	16(1)
		Compensation while gaining experience[2]	12 consec. mo.	Norwegian resident	$5,000	16(2)
		Compensation under U.S. Government program	1 year	U.S. Government or its contractor	$10,000	16(3)

¶1305

Country (1)	Code[1] (2)	Category of Personal Services Purpose[22] (3)	Maximum Presence in U.S. (4)	Required Employer or Payer (5)	Maximum Amount of Compensation (6)	Treaty Article Citation (7)
Pakistan	15	Scholarship or fellowship grant[15]	No limit	Pakistani nonprofit organization	No limit	XIII(1)
	16	Independent personal services[16]	183 days	Pakistani resident contractor	No limit	XI
	17	Dependent personal services[16]	183 days	Pakistani resident	No limit	XI
	18	Teaching	2 years	U.S. educational institution	No limit	XII
	19	Studying and training:				
		Remittances or allowances	No limit	Any foreign resident	No limit	XIII(1)
		Compensation during training	No limit	U.S. or any foreign resident	$5,000 p.a.	XIII(1)
		Compensation while gaining experience[2]	1 year	Pakistani resident	$6,000	XIII(2)
		Compensation while under U.S. Government program	No limit	U.S. Government, its contractor, or any foreign resident employer	$10,000	XIII(3)
Philippines	15	Scholarship or fellowship grant[15]	5 years	Any U.S. or foreign resident[5]	No limit	22(1)
	16	Independent personal services[7]	89 days	Any foreign contractor	No limit	15
			89 days	Any U.S. resident	$10,000 p.a.	15
	17	Dependent personal services[17]	89 days	Any Philippines resident[18]	No limit	16
	42	Public entertainment	No limit	Any U.S. or foreign resident	$100 per day or $3,000 p.a.[28,50]	17
	18	Teaching[4,38]	2 years	U.S. educational institution	No limit	21
	19	Studying and training:				
		Remittances or allowances	5 years	Any foreign resident	No limit	22(1)
		Compensation during study	5 years	Any U.S. or foreign resident	$3,000 p.a.	22(1)
		Compensation while gaining experience[2]	12 consec. mo.	Philippines resident	$7,500 p.a.	22(2)
		Compensation while under U.S. Government program	1 year	U.S. Government or its contractor	$10,000 p.a.	22(3)
Poland	15	Scholarship or fellowship grant[15]	5 years	Any U.S. or foreign resident[5]	No limit	18(1)
	16	Independent personal services	182 days	Any contractor	No limit	15
	17	Dependent personal services[17]	182 days	Any foreign resident	No limit	16
	18	Teaching[4,41]	2 years	U.S. educational institution	No limit	17
	19	Studying and training:				
		Remittances or allowances	5 years	Any foreign resident	No limit	18(1)
		Compensation during training	5 years	U.S. or any foreign resident	$2,000 p.a.	18(1)
		Compensation while gaining experience[2]	1 year	Polish resident	$5,000	18(2)
		Compensation while under U.S. Government program	1 year	U.S. Government or its contractor	$10,000	18(3)
Portugal	15	Scholarship or fellowship grant[15]	5 years	Any U.S. or foreign resident[5]	No limit	23(1)
	16	Independent personal services[7]	182 days	Any contractor	No limit	15
	17	Dependent personal services[6,17]	183 days	Any foreign resident	No limit	16
	42	Public entertainment	No limit	Any U.S. or foreign resident	$10,000 p.a.[30]	19
	18	Teaching[4,42]	2 years	U.S. educational institution	No limit	22
	19	Studying and training:				
		Remittances or allowances	5 years	Any foreign resident	No limit	23(1)
		Compensation during study or training	12 consec. mos.	Portuguese resident	$8,000	23(2)
			5 years	Other foreign or U.S. resident	$5,000 p.a.	23(1)
		Compensation while gaining experience[2]	12 consec. mos.	Portuguese resident	$8,000	23(2)

¶1305

Country (1)	Category of Personal Services		Maximum Presence in U.S. (4)	Required Employer or Payer (5)	Maximum Amount of Compensation (6)	Treaty Article Citation (7)
	Code[1] (2)	Purpose [22] (3)				
Romania	15	Scholarship or fellowship grant[15]	5 years	Any U.S. or foreign resident[5]	No limit	20(1)
	16	Independent personal services	182 days	Any contractor	No limit	14
	42	Public entertainment	90 days	Any contractor	$3,000 p.a.[28]	14
	17	Dependent personal services[17]	182 days	Romanian resident[18]	No limit	15
	42	Public entertainment	89 days	Any U.S. or foreign resident	$2,999.99 p.a.[28]	15
	18	Teaching[4]	2 years	U.S. educational institution	No limit	19
	19	Studying and training:				
		Remittances or allowances	5 years	Any foreign resident	No limit	20(1)
		Compensation during training	5 years	U.S. or any foreign resident	$2,000 p.a.	20(1)
		Compensation while gaining experience[2]	1 year	Romanian resident	$5,000	20(2)
		Compensation while under U.S. Government program	1 year	U.S. Government or its contractor	$10,000	20(3)
Russia	15	Scholarship or fellowship grant[4,15,41]	5 years[31]	Any U.S. or foreign resident[6]	No limit	18
	16	Independent personal services[7]	183 days	Any contractor	No limit	13
	17	Dependent personal services[6,17,32]	183 days	Any foreign resident	No limit	14
	19	Studying and training:[4] Remittances or allowances	5 years[31]	Any foreign resident	No limit	18
Slovak Republic	15	Scholarship or fellowship grant[4,15]	5 years	Any U.S. or foreign resident[6]	No limit	21(1)
	16	Independent personal services[7]	183 days	Any contractor	No limit	14
	17	Dependent personal services[12,17]	183 days	Any foreign resident	No limit	15
	42	Public entertainment	No limit	Any U.S. or foreign resident	$20,000 p.a.[30]	18
	18	Teaching[4,35]	2 years	U.S. educational or research institution	No limit	21(5)
	19	Studying and training:[4]				
		Remittances or allowances	5 years	Any foreign resident	No limit	21(1)
		Compensation during training	5 years	U.S. or any foreign resident	$5,000 p.a.	21(1)
		Compensation while gaining experience[2]	12 consec. mos.	Slovak resident	$8,000	21(2)
		Compensation while under U.S. Government program	1 year	U.S. Government	$10,000	21(3)
Slovenia	15	Scholarship or fellowship grant[4]	5 years[10]	Any U.S. or foreign resident[5]	No limit	20(1)
	16	Independent personal services[7]	No limit	Any contractor	No limit	14
	17	Dependent personal services[12,17]	183 days	Any foreign resident	No limit	15
	42	Public entertainment	No limit	Any U.S. or foreign resident	$15,000 p.a.[30]	17
	18	Teaching or research[4]	2 years[40]	Any U.S. or foreign resident	No limit	20(3)
	19	Studying and training:[4]				
		Remittances or allowances	5 years[10]	Any foreign resident	No limit	20(1)
		Compensation during training	12 mos.	Slovenian resident	$8,000	20(2)
		Compensation while gaining experience[2]	5 years[10]	Other foreign or U.S. resident	$5,000 p.a.	20(1)
			12 mos.	Slovenian resident	$8,000	20(2)

Country (1)	Code[1] (2)	Category of Personal Services — Purpose[22] (3)	Maximum Presence in U.S. (4)	Required Employer or Payer (5)	Maximum Amount of Compensation (6)	Treaty Article Citation (7)
South Africa	16	Independent personal services[7]	183 days	Any contractor	No limit	14
	17	Dependent personal services[12,17]	183 days	Any foreign resident	No limit	15
	42	Public entertainment	No limit	Any U.S. or foreign resident	$7,500 p.a.[30]	17
	19	Studying and training: Remittances or allowances[11]	1 year[45]	Any foreign resident	No limit	20
Spain	15	Scholarship or fellowship grant[4,16]	5 years	Any U.S. or foreign resident[6]	No limit	22(1)
	16	Independent personal services[7]	No limit	Any contractor	No limit	15
	17	Dependent personal services[17]	183 days	Any foreign resident	No limit	16
	42	Public entertainment	No limit	Any U.S. or foreign resident	$10,000 p.a.[30]	19
	19	Studying and training:[4]				
		Remittances or allowances	5 years	Any foreign resident	No limit	22(1)
		Compensation during training	5 years	Any U.S. or foreign resident	$5,000 p.a.	22(1)
		Compensation while gaining experience[2]	12 consec. mo.	Spanish resident	$8,000	22(2)
Sri Lanka	16	Independent personal services[7,12]	183 days	Any contractor	No limit	15
	17	Dependent personal services[12,17]	183 days	Any foreign resident	No limit	16
	42	Public entertainment	No limit	Any U.S. or foreign resident	$6,000 p.a.[30]	18
	19	Studying and training:				
		Remittances or allowances[11]	No limit	Any foreign resident	No limit	21(1)
		Compensation while gaining experience[2]	1 year	Sri Lankan resident[19]	$6,000	21(2)
Sweden	16	Independent personal services[7]	No limit	Any contractor	No limit	14
	17	Dependent personal services[12,17]	183 days	Any foreign resident	No limit	15
	42	Public entertainment	No limit	Any U.S. or foreign resident	$6,000[25]	18
	19	Studying and training: Remittances or allowances[11]	No limit	Any foreign resident	No limit	21
Switzerland	16	Independent personal services[7]	No limit	Any contractor	No limit	14
	17	Dependent personal services[8,17]	183 days	Any foreign resident	No limit	15
	42	Public entertainment	No limit	Any U.S. or foreign resident	$10,000 p.a.[25]	17
	19	Studying and training: Remittances or allowances[11]	No limit	Any foreign resident	No limit	20

¶1305

Country (1)	Code[1] (2)	Category of Personal Services — Purpose[22] (3)	Maximum Presence in U.S. (4)	Required Employer or Payer (5)	Maximum Amount of Compensation (6)	Treaty Article Citation (7)
Thailand	15	Scholarship or fellowship grant	5 years	Any U.S. or foreign resident[6]	No limit	22(1)
	16	Independent personal services[7]	89 days	Any U.S. resident or permanent establishment	$10,000 p.a.	15
			89 days	Any foreign contractor	No limit[49]	15
	17	Dependent personal services[17,47]	183 days	Any foreign resident	No limit	16
	42	Public entertainment	No limit	Any U.S. or foreign resident	$100 per day or $3,000 p.a.[48]	16
	18	Teaching or research[4,38]	2 years	Any U.S. or foreign resident	No limit	19
	19	Studying and training:				23
		Remittances or allowances	5 years	Any U.S. or foreign resident	No limit	22(1)
		Compensation during training	5 years	Any U.S. or foreign resident	$3,000 p.a.	22(1)
		Compensation while gaining experience	12 consec. mos.	Thai resident[2]	$7,500 p.a.	22(2)
		Compensation under U.S. Government program	1 year	U.S. Government	$10,000	22(3)
Trinidad and Tobago	15	Scholarship or fellowship grant[15]	5 years	Any U.S. or foreign resident[6]	No limit	19(1)
	16	Independent personal services[14]	183 days	Any foreign resident contractor	No limit	17
			183 days	Any U.S. contractor	$3,000[6]	17
	17	Dependent personal services[14]	183 days	Any foreign resident	No limit	17
			183 days	Any U.S. resident	$3,000[6]	17
	18	Teaching[4]	2 years	U.S. educational institution or U.S. Government	No limit	18
	19	Studying and training:				
		Remittances or allowances	5 years	Any foreign resident	No limit	19(1)
		Compensation during study or research	5 years	U.S. or any foreign resident	$2,000 p.a.[6]	19(1)
		Compensation during professional training	5 years	U.S. or any foreign resident	$5,000 p.a.[6]	19(1)
		Compensation while gaining experience	1 year	Trinidad–Tobago resident[2]	$5,000[6]	19(2)
		Compensation under U.S. Government program	1 year	U.S. Government or its contractor	$10,000[6]	19(3)
Tunisia	15	Scholarship and fellowship grant[11,15]	5 years	Any U.S. or foreign resident[6]	No limit	20
	16	Independent personal services[7]	183 days	U.S. resident contractor	$7,500 p.a.	14
	17	Dependent personal services[17]	183 days	Any foreign resident	No limit	15
	42	Public entertainment	No limit	Any U.S. or foreign resident	$7,500 p.a.[25]	17
	19	Studying and training:[11]				
		Remittances or allowances	5 years	Any foreign resident	No limit	20
		Compensation during training	5 years	Any U.S. or foreign resident	$4,000 p.a.	20
Turkey	16	Independent personal services[7]	183 days	Any contractor	No limit	14
	17	Dependent personal services[12,17]	183 days	Any foreign resident	No limit	15
	42	Public entertainment	No limit	Any U.S. or foreign resident	$3,000 p.a.[48]	17
	18	Teaching or research	2 years	Any foreign resident	No limit	20(2)
	19	Studying and training:				
		Remittances or allowances[11]	No limit	Any foreign resident	No limit	20(1)

¶1305

Country (1)	Code[1] (2)	Category of Personal Services / Purpose [22] (3)	Maximum Presence in U.S. (4)	Required Employer or Payer (5)	Maximum Amount of Compensation (6)	Treaty Article Citation (7)
Ukraine	15	Scholarship or fellowship grant[41]	5 years[31]	Any U.S. or foreign resident[5]	No limit	20
	16	Independent personal services[3,7]	No limit	Any contractor	No limit	14
	17	Dependent personal services[3,17]	183 days	Any foreign resident	No limit	15
	19	Studying and training: Remittances or allowances[4]	5 years[31]	Any foreign resident	No limit	20
United Kingdom	16	Independent personal services[53]				7
	17	Dependent personal services[12,17]	183 days	Any foreign resident	No limit	14
	42	Public entertainment	No limit	Any U.S. or foreign resident	$20,000 p.a.[25]	16
	18	Teaching or research[4]	2 years	Any U.S. educational institution	No limit	20A
	19	Studying and training: Remittances or allowances[11]	1 year[45]	Any foreign resident	No limit	20
Venezuela	15	Scholarship or fellowship grants[4]	5 years[10]	Any U.S. or foreign resident[5]	No limit	21(1)
	16	Independent personal services[7,12]	No limit	Any contractor	No limit	14
	17	Dependent personal services[12,17]	183 days	Any foreign resident	No limit	15
	42	Public entertainment	No limit	Any U.S. or foreign resident	$6,000 p.a. [30]	18
	18	Teaching[4]	2 years[40]	Any U.S. or foreign resident	No limit	21(3)
	19	Studying and training:[4] Remittances or allowances	5 years[10]	Any foreign resident	No limit	21(1)
		Compensation during training	12 mos.	Venezuelan resident	$8,000	21(2)
		Compensation while gaining experience	5 years[10]	Other foreign or U.S. resident	$5,000 p.a.	21(1)
			12 mos.	Venezuelan resident[2]	$8,000	21(2)

Publication 515 (2015)

¶1305

1 Refers to income code numbers under which the income is reported on Forms 1042-S. Personal services must be performed by a nonresident alien individual who is a resident of the specified treaty country.

2 Applies only if training or experience is received from a person other than alien's employer.

3 The exemption does not apply to income received for performing services in the United States as an entertainer or a sportsman. However, this income is exempt for U.S. income tax if the visit is (a) substantially supported by public funds of Ukraine, its political subdivisions, or local authorities, or (b) made under a specific arrangement agreed to by the governments of the treaty countries.

4 Does not apply to compensation for research work primarily for private benefit.

5 Grant must be from a nonprofit organization. In many cases, the exemption also applies to amounts from either the U.S. or foreign government. For Indonesia and the Netherlands, the exemption also applies if the amount is awarded under a technical assistance program entered into by the United States or the foreign government, or its political subdivisions or local authorities.

6 Reimbursed expenses are not taken into account in figuring any maximum compensation to which the exemption applies. For Japan and Trinidad and Tobago, only reimbursed travel expenses are disregarded in figuring the maximum compensation.

7 Exemption does not apply to the extent income is attributable to the recipient's fixed U.S. base. For residents of Korea and Norway, the fixed base must be maintained for more than 182 days (for Norway, 30 days in the case of the exploration or exploitation of the seabed and sub-soil and their natural resources); for residents of Morocco, the fixed base must be maintained for more than 89 days.

8 Does not apply to fees paid to a director of a U.S. corporation.

9 Does not apply to compensation for research work for other than the U.S. educational institution (or, for Italy, a medical facility that is primarily publicly funded) involved.

10 Applies to any additional period that a full-time student needs to complete the educational requirements as a candidate for a postgraduate or professional degree from a recognized educational institution.

11 Applies only to full-time student or trainee.

12 Fees paid to a resident of the treaty country for services performed in the United States as a director of a U.S. corporation are subject to U.S. tax.

13 Exemption does not apply if, during the immediately preceding period, such individual claimed the benefits of Article 23(1).

14 Does not apply to compensation paid to public entertainers that is more than $100 a day.

15 Does not apply to payments from the National Institutes of Health under its Visiting Associate Program and Visiting Scientist Program.

16 Exemption applies only if the compensation is subject to tax in the country of residence.

17 The exemption does not apply if the employee's compensation is borne by a permanent establishment (or in some cases a fixed base) that the employer has in the United States.

18 Exemption also applies if the employer is a permanent establishment in the treaty country but is not a resident of the treaty country.

19 Applies also to a participant in a program sponsored by the U.S. Government or an international organization.

20 The exemption is also extended to journalists and correspondents who are temporarily in the U.S. for periods not longer than 2 years and who receive compensation from abroad.

21 Also exempt are amounts of up to $10,000 received from U.S. sources to provide ordinary living expenses. For students, the amount will be less than $10,000, determined on a case by case basis.

22 Withholding may be required if the factors on which the treaty exemption is based may not be determinable until after the close of the tax year. Athletes and entertainers may be able to enter into a central withholding agreement with the IRS for reduced withholding provided certain requirements are met.

23 A student or trainee may choose to be treated as a U.S. resident for tax purposes. If the choice is made, it may not be changed without the consent of the U.S. competent authority.

24 Does not apply to amounts received in excess of reasonable fees payable to all directors of the company for attending meetings in the United States.

25 Exemption does not apply if gross receipts (including reimbursements) exceed this amount.

26 Exemption does not apply if net income exceeds this amount.

27 Exemption does not apply to payments borne by a permanent establishment in the United States or paid by a U.S. citizen or resident or the federal, state, or local government.

28 Exemption does not apply if compensation (or gross income for the Phillipines and Romania) exceeds this amount.

29 The exemption applies only to income from activities performed under special cultural exchange programs agreed to by the U.S. and Chinese governments.

30 Exemption does not apply if gross receipts (or compensation for Portugal and Venezuela), including reimbursements, exceed this amount. Income is fully exempt if visit to the United States is substantially supported by public funds of the treaty country or its political subdivisions or local authorities.

31 The 5-year limit pertains only to training or research.

32 Compensation from employment directly connected with a place of business that is not a permanent establishment is exempt if the alien is present in the United States for a period not exceeding 12 consecutive months. Compensation for technical services directly connected with the application of a right or property giving rise to a royalty is exempt if the services are provided as part of a contract granting the use of the right or property.

33 Exemption does not apply if, during the immediately preceding period, the individual claimed the benefits of Article 21.

34 Exemption does not apply if, during the immediately preceding period, the individual claimed the benefits of Article 22.

35 Exemption does not apply if the individual either (a) claimed the benefit of Article 21(5) during a previous visit, or (b) during the immediately preceding period, claimed the benefit of Article 21(1), (2), or (3).

36 Exemption applies only to compensation for personal services performed in connection with, or incidental to, the individual's study, research, or training.

37 If the compensation exceeds $400 per day, the entertainer may be taxed on the full amount. If the individual receives a fixed amount for more than one performance, the amount is prorated over the number of days the individual performs the services (including rehearsals).

38 Exemption does not apply if, during the immediately preceding period, the individual claimed the benefits of Article 22(1).

39 Exemption does not apply if, during the immediately preceding period, the individual claimed the benefits of Article 24(1).

40 The combined benefit for teaching cannot exceed 5 years.

41 Exemption does not apply if, during the immediately preceding period, the individual claimed the benefits of Article 18(1).

42 Exemption does not apply if the individual either (a) previously claimed the benefit of this Article, or (b) during the immediately preceding period, claimed the benefit of Article 23. The benefits under Articles 22 and 23 cannot be claimed at the same time.

43 The combined period of benefits under Articles 20 and 21(1) cannot exceed 5 years.

44 Exemption does not apply if the individual previously claimed the benefit of this Article.

45 The time limit pertains only to an apprentice or business trainee.

46 Exemption does not apply if gross receipts exceed this amount.

47 Fees paid to a resident of the treaty country for services as a director of a U.S. corporation are subject to U.S. tax, unless the services are performed in the country of residence.

48 Exemption does not apply if gross receipts exceed this amount. Income is fully exempt if visit to the United States is substantially supported by public funds of the treaty country or its political subdivisions or local authorities.

49 A $10,000 limit applies if the expense is borne by a permanent establishment or a fixed base in the United States. Exemption does not apply if the recipient maintains a permanent establishment in the U.S. with which the income is effectively connected.

50 This provision does not apply if these activities are substantially supported by a nonprofit organization or by public funds of the treaty country or its political subdivisions or local authorities. For Indonesia and the Phillipines, the competent authority of the sending state must certify that the visit qualifies.

51 Exemption does not apply if gross receipts, including reimbursements, exceed this amount during the year. Income is fully exempt if visit is wholly or mainly supported by public funds of one or both of the treaty countries or their political subdivisions or local authorities.

52 Exemption applies to a business apprentice (trainee) only for a period not exceeding 1 year (2 years for Belgium and Bulgaria) from the date of arrival in the United States.

53 Treated as business profits under Article 7 (VII) of the treaty.

54 Employment with a team which participates in a league with regularly scheduled games in both countries is covered under the provisions for dependent personal services.

55 Exemption does not apply if during the immediately preceding period, the individual claimed the benefit of Article 20(2), (3), or (4).

56 Labor or personal services performed in connection with the exploration or exploitation of the seabed and sub-soil and their natural resources is fully exempt for a period of 60 days in the tax year.

Table 3. **List of Tax Treaties** (Updated through November 30, 2014)

Country	Official Text Symbol[1]	General Effective Date[4]	Citation	Applicable Treasury Explanations or Treasury Decision (T.D.)
Australia	TIAS 10773	Dec. 1, 1983	1986-2 C.B. 220	1986-2 C.B. 246
Protocol	TIAS	Jan. 1, 2004		
Austria	TIAS	Jan. 1, 1999		
Bangladesh	TIAS	Jan. 1, 2007		
Barbados	TIAS 11090	Jan. 1, 1984	1991-2 C.B. 436	1991-2 C.B. 466
Protocol	TIAS	Jan. 1, 1994		
Protocol	TIAS	Jan. 1, 2005		
Belgium	TIAS	Jan. 1, 2008		
Bulgaria	TIAS	Jan. 1, 2009		
Canada[2]	TIAS 11087	Jan. 1, 1985	1986-2 C.B. 258	1987-2 C.B. 298
Protocol	TIAS	Jan. 1, 1996		
Protocol	TIAS	Dec. 16, 1997		
Protocol	TIAS	Jan. 1, 2009		
China, People's Republic of	TIAS 12065	Jan. 1, 1987	1988-1 C.B. 414	1988-1 C.B. 447
Commonwealth of Independent States[3]	TIAS 8225	Jan. 1, 1976	1976-2 C.B. 463	1976-2 C.B. 475
Cyprus	TIAS 10965	Jan. 1, 1986	1989-2 C.B. 280	1989-2 C.B. 314
Czech Republic	TIAS	Jan. 1, 1993		
Denmark	TIAS	Jan. 1, 2001		
Protocol	TIAS	Jan. 1, 2008		
Egypt	TIAS 10149	Jan. 1, 1982	1982-1 C.B. 219	1982-1 C.B. 243
Estonia	TIAS	Jan. 1, 2000		
Finland	TIAS 12101	Jan. 1, 1991		
Protocol	TIAS	Jan. 1, 2008		
France	TIAS	Jan. 1, 1996		
Protocol	TIAS	Jan. 1, 2007		
Protocol	TIAS	Jan. 1, 2009		
Germany	TIAS	Jan. 1, 1990		
Protocol	TIAS	Jan. 1, 2008		
Greece	TIAS 2902	Jan. 1, 1953	1958-2 C.B. 1054	T.D. 6109, 1954-2 C.B. 638
Hungary	TIAS 9560	Jan. 1, 1980	1980-1 C.B. 333	1980-1 C.B. 354
Iceland	TIAS	Jan. 1, 2009		
India	TIAS	Jan. 1, 1991		
Indonesia	TIAS 11593	Jan. 1, 1990		
Ireland	TIAS	Jan. 1, 1998		
Israel	TIAS	Jan. 1, 1995		
Italy	TIAS	Jan. 1, 2010		
Jamaica	TIAS 10207	Jan. 1, 1982	1982-1 C.B. 257	1982-1 C.B. 291
Japan	TIAS	Jan. 1, 2005		
Kazakhstan	TIAS	Jan. 1, 1996		
Korea, Republic of	TIAS 9506	Jan. 1, 1980	1979-2 C.B. 435	1979-2 C.B. 458
Latvia	TIAS	Jan. 1, 2000		
Lithuania	TIAS	Jan. 1, 2000		
Luxembourg	TIAS	Jan. 1, 2001		
Malta	TIAS	Jan. 1, 2011		
Mexico	TIAS	Jan. 1,1994		
Protocol	TIAS	Oct. 26, 1995		
Protocol	TIAS	Jan. 1, 2004		
Morocco	TIAS 10195	Jan. 1, 1981	1982-2 C.B. 405	1982-2 C.B. 427
Netherlands	TIAS	Jan. 1, 1994		
Protocol	TIAS	Jan. 1, 2005		
New Zealand	TIAS 10772	Nov. 2, 1983	1990-2 C.B. 274	1990-2 C.B. 303
Protocol	TIAS	Jan. 1, 2011		
Norway	TIAS 7474	Jan. 1, 1971	1973-1 C.B. 669	1973-1 C.B. 693
Protocol	TIAS 10205	Jan. 1, 1982	1982-2 C.B. 440	1982-2 C.B. 454

¶1305

Table 3. (continued)

Country	Official Text Symbol[1]	General Effective Date[4]	Citation	Applicable Treasury Explanations or Treasury Decision (T.D.)
Pakistan	TIAS 4232	Jan. 1, 1959	1960-2 C.B. 646	T.D. 6431, 1960-1 C.B. 755
Philippines	TIAS 10417	Jan. 1, 1983	1984-2 C.B. 384	1984-2 C.B. 412
Poland	TIAS 8486	Jan. 1, 1974	1977-1 C.B. 416	1977-1 C.B. 427
Portugal	TIAS	Jan. 1, 1996		
Romania	TIAS 8228	Jan. 1, 1974	1976-2 C.B. 492	1976-2 C.B. 504
Russia	TIAS	Jan. 1, 1994		
Slovak Republic	TIAS	Jan. 1, 1993		
Slovenia	TIAS	Jan. 1, 2002		
South Africa	TIAS	Jan. 1, 1998		
Spain	TIAS	Jan. 1, 1991		
Sri Lanka	TIAS	Jan. 1, 2004		
Sweden	TIAS	Jan. 1, 1996		
Protocol	TIAS	Jan. 1, 2007		
Switzerland	TIAS	Jan. 1, 1998		
Thailand	TIAS	Jan. 1, 1998		
Trinidad and Tobago	TIAS 7047	Jan. 1, 1970	1971-2 C.B. 479	
Tunisia	TIAS	Jan. 1, 1990		
Turkey	TIAS	Jan. 1, 1998		
Ukraine	TIAS	Jan. 1, 2001		
United Kingdom	TIAS	Jan. 1, 2004		
Venezuela	TIAS	Jan. 1, 2000		

[1] (TIAS) — Treaties and Other International Act Series.

[2] Information on the treaty can be found in Publication 597, *Information on the United States-Canada Income Tax Treaty*.

[3] The U.S.-U.S.S.R. income tax treaty applies to the countries of Armenia, Azerbaijan, Belarus, Georgia, Kyrgyzstan, Moldova, Tajikistan, Turkmenistan, and Uzbekistan.

[4] Date listed is the effective date for most income taxes. Check the treaty and/or protocol for other effective dates, including, for example, taxes withheld at source.

How To Get Tax Help

Do you need help with a tax issue or preparing your tax return, or do you need a free publication or form?

Preparing and filing your tax return. Find free options to prepare and file your return on IRS.gov or in your local community if you qualify.

- Go to IRS.gov and click on the Filing tab to see your options.
- Enter "Free File" in the search box to use brand name software to prepare and *e-file* your federal tax return for free.
- Enter "VITA" in the search box, download the free IRS2Go app, or call 1-800-906-9887 to find the nearest Volunteer Income Tax Assistance or Tax Counseling for the Elderly (TCE) location for free tax preparation.
- Enter "TCE" in the search box, download the free IRS2Go app, or call 1-888-227-7669 to find the nearest Tax Counseling for the Elderly location for free tax preparation.

The Volunteer Income Tax Assistance (VITA) program offers free tax help to people who generally make $53,000 or less, persons with disabilities, the elderly, and limited-English-speaking taxpayers who need help preparing their own tax returns. The Tax Counseling for the Elderly (TCE) program offers free tax help for all taxpayers, particularly those who are 60 years of age and older. TCE volunteers specialize in answering questions about pensions and retirement-related issues unique to seniors.

Getting answers to your tax law questions. IRS.gov and IRS2Go are ready when you are—24 hours a day, 7 days a week.

- Enter "ITA" in the search box on IRS.gov for the Interactive Tax Assistant, a tool that will ask you questions on a number of tax law topics and provide answers. You can print the entire interview and the final response.
- Enter "Tax Map" or "Tax Trails" in the search box for detailed information by tax topic.
- Enter "Pub 17" in the search box to get Pub. 17, Your Federal Income Tax for Individuals, which features details on tax-saving opportunities, 2014 tax changes, and thousands of interactive links to help you find answers to your questions.
- Call TeleTax at 1-800-829-4477 for recorded information on a variety of tax topics.
- Access tax law information in your electronic filing software.
- Go to IRS.gov and click on the Help & Resources tab for more information.

Tax forms and publications. You can download or print all of the forms and publications you may need on *IRS.gov/formspubs*. Otherwise, you can:

- Go to *IRS.gov/orderforms* to place an order and have forms mailed to you, or
- Call 1-800-829-3676 to order current-year forms, instructions, publications, and prior-year forms and instructions (limited to 5 years).

You should receive your order within 10 business days.

Where to file your tax return.

- There are many ways to file your return electronically. It's safe, quick and easy. See *Preparing and filing your tax return*, earlier, for more information.
- See your tax return instructions to determine where to mail your completed paper tax return.

Getting a transcript or copy of a return.

- Go to IRS.gov and click on "Get Transcript of Your Tax Records" under "Tools."
- Download the free IRS2Go app to your smart phone and use it to order transcripts of your tax returns or tax account.
- Call the transcript toll-free line at 1-800-908-9946.
- Mail Form 4506-T or Form 4506T-EZ (both available on IRS.gov).

Using online tools to help prepare your return. Go to IRS.gov and click on the Tools bar to use these and other self-service options.

- The *Earned Income Tax Credit Assistant* determines if you are eligible for the EIC.
- The *First Time Homebuyer Credit Account Look-up* tool provides information on your repayments and account balance.
- The *Alternative Minimum Tax (AMT) Assistant* determines whether you may be subject to AMT.
- The *Online EIN Application* helps you get an Employer Identification Number.
- The *IRS Withholding Calculator* estimates the amount you should have withheld from your paycheck for federal income tax purposes.
- The *Electronic Filing PIN Request* helps to verify your identity when you do not have

Chapter 14

Section 367—Outbound, Inbound and Foreign-to-Foreign Transfers of Property

¶ 1401 OUTBOUND TRANSFERS OF PROPERTY TO A FOREIGN CORPORATION

.01 Outbound Toll Charge

In response to changing business conditions, U.S. corporations routinely organize new subsidiaries and merge or liquidate existing subsidiaries. These routine corporate adjustments generally are tax-free transactions, based on the principle that the transactions involve a change in the form of the corporation's investment, not the shareholders' ultimate control of the investment. For example, in a wholly-domestic context, if a U.S. corporation transfers appreciated property to a newly-organized subsidiary in exchange for all of the shares of that U.S. subsidiary, the gain realized on that exchange is not recognized immediately, but is instead deferred by having the subsidiary take a carryover basis in the property received.[1] However, if the subsidiary is a foreign corporation, then the ultimate disposition of the appreciated property may occur outside the U.S. taxing jurisdiction. As a consequence, transfers of appreciated property to a foreign corporation may represent the U.S. Treasury's last opportunity for taxing the appreciation.

> **Example 14.1:** During the current year, USAco (a U.S. corporation) organizes EURco, a distribution subsidiary incorporated in a foreign country. USAco then transfers inventory, which has a basis of $1 million and a fair market value of $3 million, to EURco in exchange for all of EURco's shares.

---

[1] Code Secs. 351(a) and 362.

Immediately thereafter, EURco sells the inventory to local customers for $3 million. Ignoring Code Sec. 367, USAco's outbound transfer to EURco is not subject to U.S. tax because it is part of a tax-free incorporation. EURco's gain on the sale of the inventory also avoids U.S. taxation because the United States generally does not tax the foreign-source income of foreign corporations. In sum, the $2 million gain does not incur U.S. tax at either the foreign corporation or the U.S. shareholder level.

Code Sec. 367 closes this loophole by requiring a U.S. person to recognize gain when transferring appreciated property to a foreign corporation. This result is achieved by denying the foreign corporation corporate status[2] (and a tax-free incorporation)[3] so that the general rules for taxable exchanges apply.[4]

> **Example 14.2:** The facts are the same as in Example 14.1, except now take into account the effects of Code Sec. 367(a). USAco's transfer of inventory to EURco in exchange for all of EURco's shares is treated as a taxable exchange. As a result, USAco recognizes a $2 million gain, which represents the excess of the value of shares received ($3 million) over USAco's basis in the inventory ($1 million).

The outbound toll charge applies only for purposes of recognizing gains, which are determined on an item-by-item basis and without being offset by individual losses. Transfers of property that produce losses are still generally accorded nonrecognition treatment if the transaction satisfies the requirements of the applicable corporate nonrecognition provision.[5] The character and source of the gain produced by the outbound toll charge is determined as if the transferor had sold the property in a taxable transaction.[6] For example, if the outbound transfer involves inventory that the taxpayer purchased for resale, any resulting gain would be ordinary income sourced under the title passage rule applicable to inventory sales.[7] Finally, the U.S. transferor's basis in any shares received in an outbound

---

[2] Code Sec. 367(a)(1).
[3] Code Sec. 351.
[4] Code Sec. 1001.

[5] Temp. Reg. § 1.367(a)-IT(b)(3)(ii).
[6] Temp. Reg. § 1.367(a)-IT(b)(4)(i)(A).
[7] Reg. § 1.861-7(c).

transfer equals the U.S. transferor's basis in the property transferred, increased by the amount of the gain recognized on the transfer.[8]

The types of corporate transactions governed by the Code Sec. 367(a) outbound toll charge provisions include:

(i) *Incorporations*—A U.S. person's contribution of property to a foreign corporation in exchange for shares of the foreign corporation, where immediately after the exchange, the U.S. person controls the foreign corporation;[9]

(ii) *Contributions*—A U.S. person's contributions to the capital of a foreign corporation controlled by the transferors;[10]

(iii) *Reorganizations*—A U.S. person's transfer of shares, securities, or property to a foreign corporation as part of a corporate reorganization; and[11]

(iv) *Liquidations*—A U.S. corporation's transfer of assets to its foreign parent in exchange for the U.S. corporation's shares.[12]

However, there are numerous special rules that apply to the outbound toll charge, including:

(i) *Active foreign business use exception*—The outbound toll charge does not apply to certain types of property transferred to a foreign corporation for use by that corporation in the active conduct of a trade or business located outside the United States;[13]

(ii) *Branch loss recapture rule*—A U.S. person must recognize a gain on the incorporation of a foreign branch to the extent that the U.S. person has previously deducted branch losses against its other taxable income;[14]

(iii) *Deemed royalty regime for intangible property*—An outbound transfer of intangible property is treated as a sale in return for a series of payments that are both received annually over the useful life of the intangible and are contingent on the productivity, use, or disposition of the intangible;[15] and

(iv) *Transfers of stock or securities*—Outbound transfers of stock or securities are subject to special rules, which vary depending on whether the transfer involves stock or securities of a foreign versus a domestic corporation.[16]

These special rules are discussed in the following sections.

.02 Active Foreign Business Use Exception

The outbound toll charge does not apply to property transferred to a foreign corporation if the following requirements are satisfied:

---

[8] Temp. Reg. § 1.367(a)-IT(c)(3)(i)(B).

[9] Code Sec. 367(a)(1), which denies the nonrecognition treatment otherwise provided by Code Sec. 351.

[10] Code Sec. 367(c)(2).

[11] Code Sec. 367(a)(1) and (e)(1), which deny the nonrecognition treatment otherwise provided by Code Secs. 354, 355, 356, and 361.

[12] Code Sec. 367(e)(2) and Reg. § 1.367(e)-(2).

[13] Code Sec. 367(a)(3)(A).

[14] Code Sec. 367(a)(3)(C).

[15] Code Sec. 367(d). These payments are similar to a royalty.

[16] Code Sec. 367(a)(2) and Reg. § 1.367(a)-3.

(i)   the foreign corporation actively conducts a trade or business;

(ii)   the trade or business is conducted outside the United States; and

(iii)   the foreign corporation uses the property in that trade or business.[17]

In these situations, the policy of allowing companies to make routine corporate adjustments unaffected by taxes is considered more important than the policy of taxing all appreciated property being transferred out of the U.S. taxing jurisdiction.

Whether a particular transfer satisfies the requirements of the active foreign business use exception is a question of fact.[18] In general, the active conduct of a trade or business requirement is satisfied only if the officers and employees of the foreign corporation or the officers and employees of related entities, if supervised and paid by the foreign corporation, carry out substantial managerial and operational activities.[19] To satisfy the requirement that the business be conducted outside the United States, the foreign corporation must conduct abroad the primary managerial and operational activities of the trade or business and, immediately after the transfer, substantially all of the transferred assets must be located abroad.[20]

Example 14.3: During the current year, USAco (a U.S. corporation) organizes MEXco, a manufacturing subsidiary incorporated in Mexico. USAco then transfers some appreciated machinery used solely in USAco's factory to MEXco in exchange for all of MEXco's shares. At the time of the transfer, the basis and the fair market value of the transferred assets are as follows:

	Basis	Fair Market Value
Machinery	$10 million	$15 million

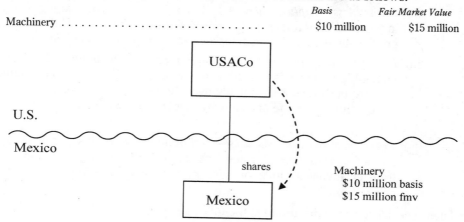

Assuming MEXco's foreign manufacturing operation satisfies the active foreign business requirements, the outbound transfer does not trigger U.S. taxation of the $5 million of built-in-gain [$15 million fair market value - $10 basis] on the machinery's appreciation.

---

[17] Code Sec. 367(a)(3)(A). To qualify for this exception, the transferor also must attach Form 926, Return by Transferor of Property to a Foreign Corporation, Foreign Estate or Trust, or Foreign Partnership, to its regular tax return for the year of the transfer. Temp. Reg. § 1.367(a)-2T(a)(2) and Reg. § 1.6038B-1.

[18] Temp. Reg. § 1.367(a)-2T(b)(1).

[19] Temp. Reg. § 1.367(a)-2T(b)(3).

[20] Temp. Reg. § 1.367(a)-2T(b)(4).

Special rules apply to property that the foreign corporation will lease,[21] property that is expected to be sold in the reasonably foreseeable future other than in the ordinary course of business,[22] working interests in oil and gas property,[23] and compulsory transfers.[24] In addition, certain assets are ineligible for the active foreign business use exception. These tainted assets include the following:

(i) inventories, including raw materials and supplies, work-in-process, and finished goods;[25]

(ii) installment obligations, accounts receivable, and similar property;[26]

(iii) foreign currency or other property denominated in foreign currency, such as an installment obligation, forward contract, or account receivable;[27]

(iv) intangible property; and[28]

(v) property that the transferor is leasing at the time of the transfer, with certain exceptions.[29]

Finally, the U.S. transferor still must recapture and recognize as ordinary income any depreciation deductions claimed on depreciable property that was used in the United States.[30]

Example **14.4:** During the current year, USAco (a U.S. corporation) organizes MEXco, a manufacturing subsidiary incorporated in Mexico. USAco then transfers inventory and some appreciated machinery used solely in USAco's factory to MEXco in exchange for all of MEXco's shares. At the time of the transfer, the basis and the fair market value of the transferred assets are as follows:

	Basis	Fair Market Value
Inventory	$5 million	$7 million
Machinery	$10 million	$15 million

---

[21] Temp. Reg. § 1.367(a)-4T(c).

[22] Temp. Reg. § 1.367(a)-4T(d).

[23] Temp. Reg. § 1.367(a)-4T(e).

[24] Temp. Reg. § 1.367(a)-4T(f).

[25] Code Sec. 367(a)(3)(B)(i) and Temp. Reg. §§ 1.367(a)-5T(b).

[26] Code Sec. 367(a)(3)(B)(ii).

[27] Code Sec. 367(a)(3)(B)(iii) and Temp. Reg. § 1.367(a)-5T(d). An exception applies to an obligation

that is denominated in the currency of the transferee's country of incorporation and that was acquired in the ordinary course of the business of the transferor that will be carried on by the transferee.

[28] Code Sec. 367(a)(3)(B)(iv).

[29] Code Sec. 367(a)(3)(B)(v) and Temp. Reg. §§ 1.367(a)-5T(f) and 1.367(a)-4T(c).

[30] Temp. Reg. § 1.367(a)-4T(b).

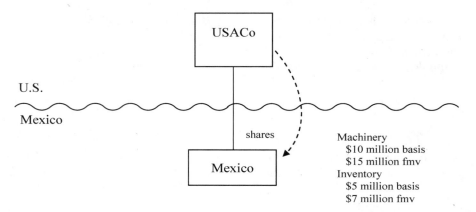

Again, assuming MEXco's foreign manufacturing operation satisfies the active foreign business requirements, the outbound transfer does not trigger U.S. taxation of the $5 million of built-in-gain [$15 million fair market value - $10 basis] on the machinery's appreciation. However, the inventory is a tainted asset and, therefore, USAco must recognize only the $2 million of gross income [$7 million market value - $5 million basis] on its transfer to incorporate MEXco.

Now assume that instead of the machinery appreciating in value, USAco bought the machinery for $15 million, which has retained its value, and deducted $4 million of depreciation on it prior to the transfer. Because USAco previously used the machinery and equipment in its U.S. factory, USAco must recognize $4 million of depreciation recapture income. The inventory is a tainted asset and USAco must recognize $2 million of gross income [$7 million market value - $5 million basis] on its transfer. In sum, USAco must recognize $6 million of income on the incorporation of MEXco, the $4 million of depreciation recapture and the $2 million for the outbound transfer of inventory.

The active foreign business use exception will not apply if, at the time the U.S. person transfers the property, it is reasonably believed that the transferee foreign corporation will soon dispose of the transferred property other than in the ordinary course of business. If the transferee foreign corporation transfers the property to another person as part of the same transaction, the active foreign business use exception will not apply to the initial transfer. Furthermore, any subsequent transfers to a third party in the next six months are presumed to be part of the initial transfer. A facts and circumstances test applies to subsequent transfers that occur more than six months after the original transfer.[31]

Example **14.5:** USAco, a U.S. corporation, organizes CANco, a manufacturing subsidiary incorporated in Canada. USAco transfers machinery purchased last month to CANco this month in exchange for all of CANco's shares. At the time of the transfer the machinery had a basis of $30 million and a fair market value of $32 million because the recently purchased machinery has

---

[31] Temp. Reg. § 1.367(a)-2T(c)(1).

jumped in value due to its suitability for use in the suddenly lucrative refracting process in the petroleum industry.

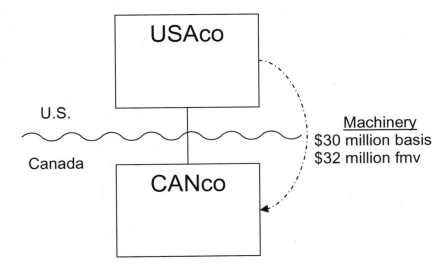

Assuming CANco's foreign manufacturing operations satisfy the active foreign business use exception, the outbound transfer does not trigger the U.S. taxation of the $2 million of appreciation in the value of the machinery [$32 million fair market value minus the $30 million basis]. However, if three months later CANco transfers the machinery to a third party, the subsequent transfer is presumed to be part of the initial transfer and USAco would recognize the $2 million gain. If such a subsequent transfer occurred seven months later, which is more than six months after the initial transfer, a facts and circumstances test would apply to determine whether the subsequent transfer was part of the initial transfer.

In the case of an outbound transfer of assets that is part of a reorganization transaction (e.g., a domestic corporation transferring its assets to a foreign corporation as part of a statutory merger), the active foreign business use exception[32] only applies if the U.S. transferor corporation is 80 percent or more owned by five or fewer U.S. corporations.[33]

.03 Branch Loss Recapture Rule

Under the branch loss recapture rule, a U.S. person must recognize gain on the incorporation of a foreign branch to the extent the U.S. person has previously deducted branch losses against its other taxable income. The recaptured income is treated as foreign-source income that has the same character as the related branch losses.[34] The policy behind the branch loss recapture rule is to prevent flowing

---

[32] Code Sec. 367(a)(3).
[33] Code Sec. 367(a)(5).

[34] Code Sec. 367(a)(3)(C).

through losses from a foreign branch before incorporating the foreign branch as a foreign corporation to defer U.S. taxation when profits are imminent.

   Example **14.6:** Two years ago, USAco (a U.S. corporation) established a foreign branch. During each its first two years of operations, the foreign branch lost $5 million, which USAco deducted against its other taxable income. If USAco were to incorporate the branch as FORco in year 3, USAco would have to recognize $10 million of branch loss recapture income.

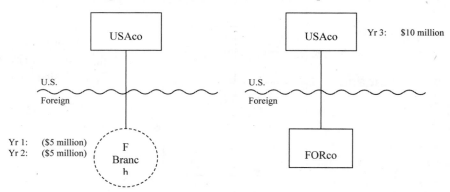

   It is not necessary to recapture pre-incorporation losses to the extent those losses are either offset by items of branch income or did not provide the taxpayer with a U.S. tax benefit. Therefore, the pre-incorporation losses are reduced by the following amounts:

   (i)   any taxable income of the branch recognized prior to incorporation;[35]

   (ii) any amount of any foreign-source income that the taxpayer had to recharacterize as U.S.-source in the current or a prior taxable year by reason of the overall foreign loss recapture provisions of the foreign tax credit limitation;[36]

   (iii) any gain recognized on the transfer of the branch's appreciated property to the newly organized foreign corporation;[37]

   (iv) any branch losses that were part of an expired net operating loss or capital loss carryforward;[38] and

   (v)   any taxable income equivalent amount for foreign tax credit carryforwards that expired by reason of the foreign tax credit limitation.[39]

   After accounting for these reductions, the remaining branch loss recapture income is further limited to the amount of gain that the taxpayer would have

---

[35] Temp. Reg. § 1.367(a)-6T(e)(2).

[36] Temp. Reg. § 1.367(a)-6T(e)(3) and (e)(5). *See* Code Sec. 904(f)(3) regarding the computation of the foreign loss recapture amount. *See also* the discussion of overall foreign losses in Chapter 4 (¶ 406).

[37] Temp. Reg. § 1.367(a)-6T(e)(4). Special rules apply for purposes of computing the creditable gain with respect to intangible property. Temp. Reg. § 1.367(d)-1T(g)(3).

[38] Temp. Reg. §§ 1.367(a)-6T(d)(2) and (d)(3).

[39] Temp. Reg. § 1.367(a)-6T(d)(4).

recognized on a taxable sale of the transferred property if each item was sold separately and without offsetting individual losses against individual gains.[40]

Example **14.7:** USAco (a U.S. corporation) established a foreign branch. During each its first two years of operations, the foreign branch lost $5 million, which USAco deducted against its other taxable income. In year 3, the foreign branch earned $1 million of taxable income for USAco. If USAco were to incorporate the branch as FORco in year 4, USAco would have to recognize $9 million of branch loss recapture income (the $10 million loss from the first two years less the $1 million of taxable income previously reported).

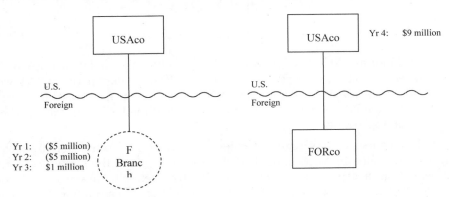

.04 Deemed Royalty Regime for Intangible Property

The market value of patents, trademarks, and other intangibles often is highly uncertain, due to the inherent uniqueness of these assets. This uncertainty significantly weakens the deterrent effect of a one-time toll charge imposed at the time of the transfer, since new technologies and products can turn out to be far more successful than originally anticipated. As a consequence, a special deemed royalty regime for intangibles treats an outbound transfer of an intangible as a sale in return for a series of payments that are received annually over the useful life of the intangible and that are contingent on the productivity, use, or disposition of the intangible (similar to a royalty) and are sourced by the location of the intangible's use.[41] This income is characterized as a royalty for purposes of the foreign tax credit limitation.[42]

Example **14.8:** USAco (a U.S. corporation) incorporates ASIAco, a manufacturing subsidiary incorporated in a foreign country by transferring a patent to ASIAco in exchange for all of ASIAco's shares. USAco had a zero basis in the patent because USAco had deducted the related research and development expenditures as these expenditures were incurred.[43]

---

[40] Temp. Reg. §§ 1.367(a)-6T(c)(2) and 1.367(a)-1T(b)(3)(i).

[41] Code Sec. 367(d).

[42] Code Sec. 367(d)(2)(C).

[43] Code Sec. 174.

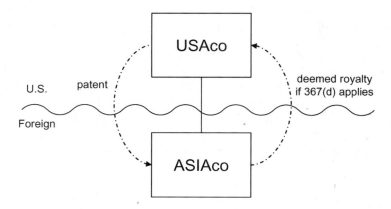

Ignoring Code Sec. 367(d), USAco's outbound transfer to ASIAco is not subject to U.S. tax because it is part of a tax-free incorporation.[44] However, Code Sec. 367(d) recharacterizes the incorporation as a sale in return for foreign-source payments received annually over the life of the patent, which is similar to a royalty.

The deemed royalty regime applies to a U.S. person's transfer of intangible property to a foreign corporation in exchange for shares of the foreign corporation as part of an incorporation or reorganization transaction.[45] However, the deemed royalty regime does not apply to a U.S. subsidiary's distribution of intangible property in complete liquidation to its foreign parent.[46] In addition, a limited exception to the deemed royalty regime is available for transfers of certain operating intangibles (e.g., supply contracts or customer lists) if the U.S. transferor elects to recognize, in the year of the transfer, U.S.-source ordinary income equal to the excess of the intangible's fair market value over its basis.[47]

For purposes of the deemed royalty regime, intangible property includes any patent, invention, formula, process, design, pattern, know-how, copyright, literary, musical, or artistic composition, trademark, trade name, brand name, franchise, license, contract, method, program, system, procedure, campaign, survey, study, forecast, estimate, customer list, technical data, or other similar item.[48] However, the deemed royalty requirement specifically exempts foreign goodwill and going concern value,[49] which a U.S. person can transfer tax-free to a foreign corporation that satisfies the active business use exception.

The deemed royalty must be an arm's-length amount consistent with the provisions of Code Sec. 482 and the regulations thereunder.[50] The deemed royalty

---

[44] Code Sec. 351(a).

[45] Code Sec. 367(d)(1).

[46] However, such transfers generally are subject to the outbound toll charge that governs tangible property. Temp. Reg. § 1.367(a)-5T(e).

[47] Temp. Reg. § 1.367(d)-1T(g)(2).

[48] Code Sec. 367(d)(1) and 936(h)(3)(B). This is the same definition used for transfer pricing.

[49] Temp. Reg. § 1.367(d)-1T(b). A copyright, literary, musical, or artistic composition transferred by the taxpayer whose personal efforts created the property also is exempted from the deemed royalty requirement, but is still subject to the outbound toll charge of Code Sec. 367(a)(1). Temp. Reg. §§ 1.367(d)-1T(b) and 1.367(a)-5T(b)(2).

[50] Temp. Reg. § 1.367(d)-1T(c)(1). *See* Chapter 12 (¶ 1202.03) for a discussion of transfer pricing methods for intangible property.

amount also must be "commensurate with the income attributable to the intangible."[51] In other words, the deemed royalty amounts must reflect the actual profit experience realized subsequent to the outbound transfer. To meet this requirement, the parties must annually adjust the royalty amount to reflect any unanticipated changes in the income actually generated by the intangible.[52] For example, if a new patent leads to a product that turns out to be far more successful than the parties expected at the time of the transfer, the U.S. person must increase the amount of the deemed royalty amount to reflect that unanticipated profitability. If, subsequent to the transfer, the foreign corporation disposes of the intangible to an unrelated person, the U.S. person must recognize a gain equal to the excess of the intangible's fair market value on the date of the subsequent disposition over its basis on the date of the initial transfer.[53]

To prevent double taxation of the foreign corporation's income, the foreign corporation reduces its earnings and profits by the amount of the deemed royalty amount included in the income of the U.S. person who transferred the intagible. In addition, the deemed royalty is treated as an expense properly allocable to the foreign corporation's Subpart F income.[54] The U.S. person can establish an account receivable for the deemed royalty amount, in which case any royalty actually paid by the foreign corporation with respect to the intangible is treated as a tax-free payment on account.[55]

In light of the deemed royalty regime, a taxpayer may find it advantageous to structure the transfer of intangible property to a foreign corporation as an actual license. One advantage of an actual license is that the foreign corporation ordinarily can deduct an actual royalty payment for foreign tax purposes, whereas the foreign corporation may generally not deduct the deemed royalty amount under foreign law. One potential disadvantage of an actual license is that the royalty payments may be subject to foreign withholding taxes, although tax treaties often reduce or exempt the withholding. Even under an actual license, the U.S. person still must adjust its royalty income annually to reflect any unanticipated changes in the income actually generated by the intangible for the foreign corporation.[56]

The deemed royalty regime extends to a U.S. partnership's transfer of intangible property to a foreign corporation. Accordingly, the transfer will be treated as a sale that generates deemed royalty payments from the foreign corporation to each partner based on the partner's percentage ownership of the U.S. partnership.[57] These payments must be established on an arm's-length basis and be commensurate with the annual income attributable to the intangible.

---

[51] Code Sec. 367(d)(2)(A).

[52] Reg. § 1.482-4(f)(2)(i).

[53] Temp. Reg. § 1.367(d)-1T(f). Special rules also apply if, subsequent to the initial transfer of the intangible, the U.S. transferor disposes of the shares of the foreign corporation before the intangible's useful life expires. Temp. Reg. § 1.367(d)-1T(d) and (e).

[54] Temp. Reg. § 1.367(d)-1T(c)(2)(ii).

[55] Temp. Reg. § 1.367(d)-1T(g)(1)(i). If no actual payments are made by the last day of the third taxable year following the year in which the account was established, the account receivable is recharacterized as a contribution to the capital of the foreign corporation, which increases the U.S. transferor's basis in the shares of that foreign corporation. Temp. Reg. § 1.367(d)-1T(g)(1)(ii).

[56] Reg. § 1.482-4(f)(2)(i).

[57] Temp. Reg. § 1.367(a)-IT(c)(3).

.05 Liquidation of a Domestic Subsidiary into Its Foreign Parent

Under U.S. tax principles, an 80 percent owned subsidiary corporation liquidates into its parent corporation tax-free to both parties.[58] This rule is based, in part, on the premise that any appreciated property not taxed at the time of the liquidation will still incur corporate-level U.S. tax when the surviving parent corporation subsequently disposes of the property. However, if a U.S. subsidiary liquidates into its foreign parent, the liquidating distribution may represent the U.S. Treasury's last opportunity for taxing appreciation that occurred within the United States. As a consequence, the U.S. subsidiary must recognize a gain equal to the excess of the distributed property's fair market value over its basis.[59]

Example 14.9: FParent, a corporation incorporated in a foreign country, owns all the shares of USSub, a U.S. corporation. USSub's assets have a basis of $5 million and a fair market value of $7 million. Despite the profitability of USSub, FParent desires to liquidate USSub to eliminate this business in a manner that is consistent with FParent's world-wide business plan. As a result, FParent liquidates USSub.

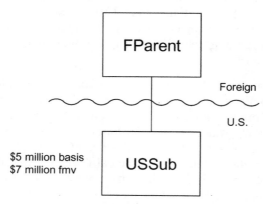

Because this is the last opportunity for the $2 million of appreciation of USSub's assets to be taxed, USSub must recognize $2 million of gain on its final return.

Three rules mitigate the effects of the outbound toll charge imposed on the complete liquidation of a U.S. subsidiary. First, unlike the regular outbound toll charge, to the extent the liquidating subsidiary must recognize gains on appreciated property, the liquidating subsidiary also may recognize offsetting losses on depreciated property.[60] Second, the basis of the property distributed to the foreign parent equals the basis of the property in the hands of the liquidating subsidiary, increased by the amount of net gain, if any, recognized by the liquidating subsidiary.[61] Third, an exception applies to property that remains for use within the United

---

[58] Code Secs. 332 and 337.

[59] Code Sec. 367(e)(2) and Reg. § 1.367(e)-2(b)(1)(i). Code Sec. 367(a)(1) does not apply to such a liquidation. Reg. § 1.367(e)-2(a)(2).

[60] Code Sec. 897(a); Reg. § 1.367(e)-2(b)(1)(ii). However, losses cannot be recognized on property that the distributing corporation acquired in a nontaxable exchange within five years before the date of liquidation.

[61] Reg. § 1.367(e)-2(b)(3).

States even though that property is now held by a foreign corporation. This U.S.-use exception to the outbound toll charge even covers U.S. real property interests, the transfer of which the U.S. taxes as effectively connected income.[62] This U.S-use exception also covers property used by the foreign corporation in the conduct of a U.S. trade or business, but only if the following requirements are satisfied:

(i) the foreign corporation is not a CFC;

(ii) the foreign corporation continues to use the property in the conduct of a U.S. trade or business for 10 years after the distribution (or, in the case of inventory, until the foreign corporation sells the property); and

(iii) the liquidating subsidiary and the foreign corporation file a gain recognition agreement whereby an amended tax return must be filed and back taxes plus interest paid, if requirement (ii) is not satisfied.[63]

.06 Information Reporting for Outbound Transfers

To help the IRS better police outbound transfers, a U.S. person who transfers property to a foreign corporation must attach Form 926, Return by Transferor of Property to a Foreign Corporation, to their regular tax return for the year of the transfer.[64] (A completed Form 926 is reproduced in the Appendix to this chapter.) This reporting requirement applies to outbound transfers of both tangible and intangible property. The penalty for a failure of a U.S. person to properly report a transfer to a foreign corporation equals 10% of the fair market value of the property transferred. However, the penalty does not apply if the U.S. person can show that the failure to comply was due to reasonable cause and not due to willful neglect. Moreover, the total penalty cannot exceed $100,000 unless the failure is due to an intentional disregard of the reporting requirements.[65]

.07 Transfers to Non-Corporate Foreign Entities

If a U.S. person contributes appreciated property to a foreign partnership, the U.S. person will be allocated any gain when the foreign partnership disposes of that appreciated property.[66]

> *Example* 14.10: During the current year, USAco (a U.S. C corporation) contributes appreciated property for a 50% interest in MEXpart, a Mexican partnership. At the time of the transfer, the basis and the fair market value of the transferred machinery is as follows:

	Basis	Fair Market Value
Machinery	$10 million	$15 million

---

[62] Reg. § 1.367(e)-2(b)(2)(ii). However, the U.S.-use exception does not apply to shares of a former U.S. real property holding corporation.

[63] Temp. Reg. § 1.367(e)-2(b)(2)(i)(B). This exception does not apply to intangible property described in Code Sec. 936(h)(3)(B).

[64] Reg. § 1.6038B-I(b)(1)(i).

[65] Code Sec. 6038B(c) and Reg. § 1.6038B-1(f).

[66] Code Sec. 704(c). Code Sec. 721(c) empowers the Treasury Department to write regulations dealing with an outbound transfer to a foreign partnership, and although the Treasury Department has not written regulations dealing with the technical merits of transfer to a foreign partnership, the Treasury Department has written regulations regarding the reporting of such a transfer. Reg. § 1.6038B-2.

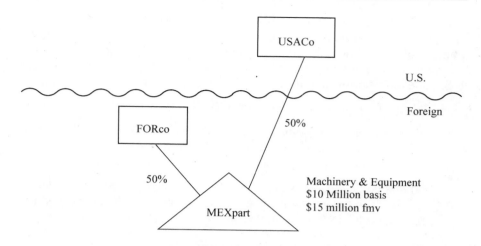

If MEXpart sold the machinery, MEXpart would allocate the $5 million of built-in-gain [$15 million fair market value - $10 basis]on the machinery's appreciation to USAco.

In the case of foreign trusts and estates, any transfer of property by a U.S. person to a foreign trust or estate is taxable as a sale or exchange of the property for its fair market value except to the extent provided by regulations.[67] The U.S. person must recognize gain equal to the excess of the property's fair market value over its basis. The gain recognition rule does not apply if the U.S. person is considered to be the owner of the trust under the grantor trust rules.[68]

¶ 1402 INBOUND TRANSFERS - LIQUIDATION OF A FOREIGN SUBSIDIARY INTO ITS U.S. PARENT

As aforementioned, an 80% owned U.S. subsidiary liquidates into its U.S. parent tax-free to both parties.[69] This is based, in part, on the premise that the United States has already taxed the distributed earnings as derived by the U.S. subsidiary. This assumption does not hold true, however, with respect to the foreign earnings of a foreign subsidiary. In contrast to an outbound liquidation, which could result in the loss of U.S. tax on appreciated assets, an inbound liquidation of a foreign subsidiary may represent the U.S. Treasury's only opportunity for subjecting those foreign earnings to the corporate-level U.S. tax.

Example **14.11:** Several years ago, USAco (a U.S. corporation) organized AFRIco, a wholly-owned subsidiary incorporated in a foreign country. Since its inception, AFRIco has derived $50 million of earnings and profits from foreign manufacturing activities. None of these foreign earnings have been taxed to USAco as a Subpart F inclusion, nor have any of AFRIco's earnings been distributed to USAco as a dividend. Therefore, AFRIco's earnings have not yet incurred U.S. taxation at either the foreign subsidiary or domestic

---

[67] Reg. § 1.864-3.
[68] Code Sec. 684(a).

[69] Code Secs. 332 and 337.

parent level. At the end of the current year, AFRIco distributes all of its assets to USAco in complete liquidation.

Ignoring Code Sec. 367(b), AFRIco's inbound repatriating liquidation is not subject to U.S. tax because the liquidation is part of a tax-free parent-subsidiary liquidation. As a consequence, the $50 million of earnings derived by AFRIco and then transferred to USAco would escape U.S. tax at both the foreign subsidiary and domestic parent levels.

To prevent this result, regulations under Code Sec. 367(b) provide that a domestic parent receiving a liquidating distribution from an 80% owned foreign subsidiary must include as a dividend all of the foreign subsidiary's earnings and profits.[70] Any gain in excess of the foreign subsidiary's earnings and profits is accorded tax-free treatment.[71] This dividend[72] allows a U.S. parent a deemed paid foreign tax credit for the foreign income taxes related to those earnings and profits.[73] However, the U.S. parent takes a carryover basis in the property received and does not receive a step-up in basis for the dividend income recognized on the liquidation.[74]

Example 14.12: Several years ago, USAco (a U.S. corporation) organized FORco, a wholly-owned subsidiary incorporated in a foreign country. At the end of the current year, FORco distributes all of its assets to USAco as part of a complete liquidation. On the date of the liquidation, FORco had $3 million of earnings and profits and $1 million of foreign income taxes that have not yet been deemed paid by USAco. The assets of FORco have an adjusted basis of $6 million and a fair market value of $7 million.

---

[70] Reg. § 1.367(b)-3(b)(3)(i). *See* Reg. § 1.367(b)-2(d) for a definition of earnings and profits for this purpose.

[71] Reg. § 1.367(b)-3(b)(3)(ii)(Exs. 1 and 2) and Code Sec. 332.

[72] Reg. § 1.367(b)-3(b)(3)(i).

[73] Reg. § 1.367(b)-2(e)(4)(Ex. 1) and Code Sec. 902(a). If the U.S. parent is an S corporation instead of a C corporation, the U.S. individuals that own the S corporation will treat the dividend at the lower qualified dividend rates if the foreign subsidiary is located in a country with which the United States has a tax treaty.

[74] Reg. § 1.367(b)-3(b)(3)(ii)(Ex. 2) and Code Sec. 334(b).

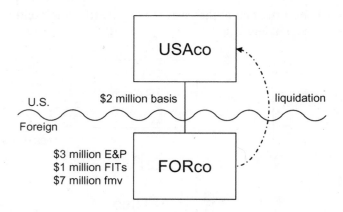

Pursuant to Code Sec. 367(b), USAco recognizes a dividend equal to FORco's earnings and profits of $3 million. Moreover, the $3 million dividend income will carry with it $1 million of deemed paid foreign taxes. Therefore, the pre-credit U.S. tax on the liquidation is $1.4 million [35% U.S. tax rate × ($3 million deemed dividend plus $1 million gross-up)], the deemed paid credit is $1 million, and will reduce USAco's pre-credit U.S. tax of $1.4 million to $400,000. USAco will take a carryover basis of $7 million in the assets distributed.

¶ 1403 ACQUISITIVE REORGANIZATIONS—BACKGROUND

The acquisition by one corporation of a controlling interest in the stock of another corporation is generally a taxable event. The shareholders of the target corporation recognize gain or loss on the stock sale[75] and the acquiring corporation takes a basis equal to the amount of cash, debt financing, or other consideration paid for the stock.[76] Likewise, the acquisition of a target corporation's assets is generally a taxable event, with the target recognizing corporate-level gains and losses on the asset sale and the acquiring corporation taking a basis in the assets equal to the fair market value price paid. If the acquiring corporation uses its own stock as consideration in the stock or asset acquisition, however, the acquisition may qualify as a nontaxable reorganization. The common types of acquisitive reorganizations include the following transactions:

(i) a statutory merger ("Type A") which may include foreign corporations;[77]

(ii) an exchange of the shares of the acquiring corporation for the shares of the target corporation ("share-for-share acquisitions," also known as "Type B");[78]

(iii) an exchange of the shares of the acquiring corporation for the assets of the target corporation ("share-for-asset acquisitions," also known as "Type C");[79]

---

[75] Code Sec. 1001.
[76] Code Sec. 1012.
[77] Code Sec. 368(a)(1)(A); Reg. §1.368-2(b)(1)(iii)(Ex. 13).
[78] Code Sec. 368(a)(1)(B).
[79] Code Sec. 368(a)(1)(C).

(iv) forward triangular mergers;[80] and

(v) reverse triangular mergers.[81]

Each transaction type must satisfy certain statutory requirements (which vary by transaction type) to qualify as a nontaxable reorganization. Furthermore, any reorganization must satisfy four non-statutory requirements: (1) a continuity of interest requirement; (2) a continuity of business enterprise requirement; (3) a business purpose requirement; and (4) a plan of reorganization requirement.

A transaction that fails to qualify as one of these acquisitive reorganization types is often referred to as a "failed reorganization" and results in a taxable transaction.

These acquisitive reorganizations will not result in U.S. tax to the target corporation's foreign shareholders[82] because any gain to the foreign shareholders would be foreign-source income (see ¶ 302.06) of a foreign person.

¶ 1404 OUTBOUND TRANSFERS IN AN ACQUISITIVE REORGANIZATION

This section provides a brief introduction to the U.S. taxation of outbound transfers to a foreign corporation that qualifies as a nontaxable acquisitive reorganization, including a Type A statutory merger, Type B share-for-share acquisition, Type C share-for-asset acquisition, forward triangular merger, or reverse triangular merger. In general, a transfer of stock or securities by a U.S. person to a foreign corporation in an otherwise tax-free reorganization is recast as a taxable exchange by the outbound toll charge rules.[83] A limited-interest exception applies, however, if certain requirements are met. The limited-interest exception is based on the premise that when the U.S. persons who own shares of the transferred U.S. target receive a minority stake in the acquiring foreign corporation, the outbound toll charge should not apply because there is little chance or motive to avoid U.S. tax. Accordingly, the limited-interest exception applies if the following five requirements are met:[84]

(i) The U.S. persons transferring the target receive 50% or less of the shares of the transferee foreign corporation in the exchange;

(ii) There is not a control group of U.S. persons with respect to the transferee foreign corporation immediately after the transfer. Under this control group test, U.S. officers, U.S. directors and 5% or greater shareholders of the domestic corporation may not, in the aggregate, own more than 50% of the voting power or value of the transferee foreign corporation immediately after the transfer;[85]

---

[80] Code Sec. 368(a)(2)(D).

[81] Code Sec. 368(a)(2)(E).

[82] An exception that would result in tax would occur if the target corporation were a U.S. real property holding corporation under the FIRPTA provisions (¶ 904.02).

[83] Code Sec. 367(a)(1); Reg. § 1.367(a)-3(a).

[84] Reg. § 1.367(a)-3(c). The exception for outbound transfers of stock of a foreign corporation is found in Reg. § 1.367(a)-3(b).

[85] This requirement differs from the requirement described in (i) as it includes both (a) U.S. persons who had previously owned shares of the transferee foreign corporation and (b) U.S. officers and directors who may not have previously owned shares of U.S. target.

(iii) The transaction satisfies the active trade or business test, which is comprised of two parts, both of which must be satisfied:

- The transferee foreign corporation has engaged in an active trade or business outside the United States for 36 months; and

- At the time of the exchange, neither the U.S. transferors nor the transferee foreign corporation intend to discontinue or dispose of the trade or business of the transferee foreign corporation.

(iv) A U.S. transferor who owns 5% or more of the transferee foreign corporation immediately after the exchange must enter into a five-year gain recognition agreement. Under the gain recognition agreement, the U.S. transferor must recognize any gain deferred on the initial transfer if the transferee foreign corporation disposes of the target's shares within five years; and

(v) The value of the transferee foreign corporation is, at the time of the exchange, equal to or greater than the value of the target.

Example **14.13:** Skipper, a U.S. citizen, wholly owns and is the only officer of USMinnow, a U.S. corporation in the cruise business. In what would otherwise constitute a nontaxable Type B share-for-share acquisition, Skipper exchanges 100% of his shares of USMinnow for 3% of the shares of CANwhale, a Canadian corporation, which has operated a cruise business specializing in three-hour tours for years and hopes to continue to do so.

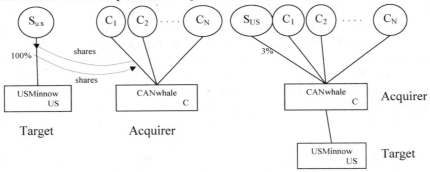

Skipper, who wants to stay in the cruise business, does not recognize gain as a result of satisfying the limited-interest exception as follows:

(i) Skipper receives 50% or less of CANwhale (only 3%);

(ii) As the only shareholder, officer or 5% shareholder of USMinnow, there is not a control group as Skipper does not own more than 50% of CANwhale, the transferee foreign corporation, immediately after the transfer (Skipper only owns 3%);

(iii) CANwhale has operated for more than 36 months and neither Skipper nor CANwhale intends to discontinue or dispose of CANwhale's trade or business;

(iv) By acquiring only 3% of CANwhale, Skipper does not have to enter a gain recognition agreement. However, if Skipper acquires between

5% and 50% of CANwhale, he would have to file a five-year gain recognition agreement; and

(v) Considering that CANwhale is a substantially larger company than USMinnow, the value of the transferee foreign corporation is, at the time of the exchange, greater than the value of the target.

.01 Outbound Type A Statutory Merger

To qualify as a nontaxable Type A merger, the merger must be pursuant to the corporate laws of the United States, a State, or the District of Columbia[86] and may occur with foreign corporations.[87]

Example 14.14: Assume that U.S. Target merges with and into Foreign Acquiror. Further assume that U.S. Target's shares are worth $1 million at the time of the merger and that U.S. Target's U.S. shareholders have $100,000 of basis in their U.S. Target shares and that the U.S. Target shareholders receive Foreign Acquiror shares with a fair market value of $1 million.

Although the merger occurs with a foreign corporation, the merger qualifies as a Type A merger. Pursuant to the Code Sec. 367(a) outbound toll charge, gain recognition would result by treating Foreign Acquiror as if it were not a corporation. Therefore, the U.S. persons who own shares of U.S. Target should recognize gain of $900,000 (the $1 million fair market value of Foreign Acquiror's shares less the $100,000 basis in their shares of U.S. Target), unless the limited-interest exception applies.

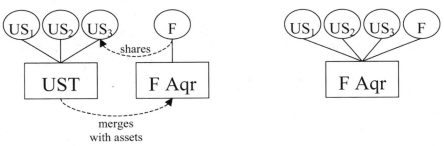

A merger that does not qualify as a Type A merger is a taxable transfer of the target corporation's assets and liabilities to the acquiring corporation in exchange for the merger consideration, followed by a liquidation of the target corporation.

.02 Outbound Type B Share-For-Share Acquisitions

A Type B share-for-share acquisition is nontaxable as long as there is no consideration other than the voting shares and the acquiring corporation has control of the target corporation immediately after the transaction. The outbound toll charge would apply to treat the foreign corporation as if it were not a corporation and, therefore, result in gain recognition, unless the limited-interest exception applies.

---

[86] Reg. § 1.368-2(d)(1).

[87] Reg. § 1.368-2(b)(1)(iii)(Ex. 13).

Example **14.15:** Assume that Foreign Acquiror wishes to acquire U.S. Target. Further assume that U.S. Target's single class of voting shares with a basis of $100,000 is worth $1 million. Finally, assume that Foreign Acquiror issues $1 million worth of Foreign Acquiror voting shares to U.S. Target's U.S. shareholders in exchange for their U.S. Target shares. The share exchange should qualify as a Type B acquisition. However, pursuant to the outbound toll charge, gain recognition would result by treating the Foreign Acquiror as if it were not a corporation. Therefore, the U.S. persons who own shares of U.S. Target should recognize gain in the amount of the fair market value of the Foreign Acquiror shares received over their basis in their U.S. Target shares, unless the limited-interest exception applies.

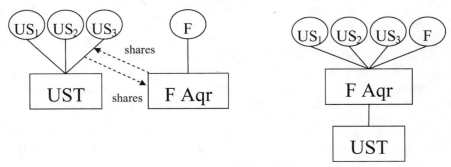

However, if Foreign Acquiror had used any cash as consideration (or assumed any debt), the solely for voting shares requirement would not be satisfied and the transaction would become a failed Type B reorganization. Consequently, U.S. Target's U.S. shareholders would still recognize capital gain in the amount of the $1 million fair market value of the Foreign Acquiror's shares received over their $100,000 basis in their U.S. target shares.

.03 Outbound Type C Share-For-Asset Acquisitions

A nontaxable Type C acquisition involves both the acquisition by a corporation for all or part of its voting shares of substantially all of the assets of the target and the subsequent liquidation of the target. In determining whether the exchange is solely for voting shares, unlike in a Type B acquisition, the acquiror's assumption of the target's liabilities may be disregarded.

Example **14.16:** Assume Foreign Acquiror acquires U.S. Target's assets for Foreign Acquiror voting shares. Further assume that U.S. Target subsequently distributes the Foreign Acquiror's shares to its shareholders in liquidation of U.S. Target. As a result, the transaction should qualify as a Type C acquisition. However, the Code Sec. 367 outbound toll charge requires U.S. Target's shareholders to recognize gain unless the limited-interest exception applies.

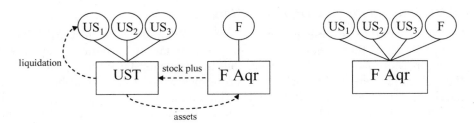

As described above, a Type C acquisition is subject to a solely for voting shares requirement, similar to Type B's solely for voting shares requirement. However, unlike the Type B acquisition rules, the Type C acquisition rules provide for a boot relaxation rule, which allows the acquisition of ordinary business liabilities. If the boot relaxation rule applies, liabilities assumed are no longer ignored, but are included in the calculation as boot.

.04 Outbound Forward Triangular Mergers

A nontaxable forward triangular merger occurs when an acquiring corporation uses stock of its parent as consideration in a merger in which the target corporation merges into the acquiror, resulting in the acquiror receiving substantially all of the target's assets.[88] The outbound toll charge would apply to treat the foreign corporation as if it were not a corporation and, therefore, result in gain recognition unless the limited-interest exception applies.

> **Example 14.17:** Assume that Foreign Parent, a publicly traded corporation, wishes to acquire U.S. Target's business, but does not want to incur the expense of obtaining its own shareholders' approval for a straight merger with U.S. Target. As a result, Foreign Parent forms a wholly-owned subsidiary, U.S. Acquiror, for the purpose of obtaining U.S. Target's business. Finally, assume that U.S. Target merges with and into U.S. Acquiror, with U.S. Target's shareholders receiving Foreign Parent's shares as the merger consideration and with U.S. Acquiror surviving the merger. This transaction should qualify as a forward triangular merger. However, the U.S. Target's U.S. shareholders should recognize gain unless the limited-interest exception applies.

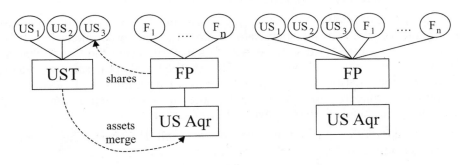

---

[88] Code Sec. 368(a)(2)(D).

.05 Outbound Reverse Triangular Mergers

A nontaxable reverse triangular merger is similar to a forward triangular merger, except that the surviving entity is the target corporation and not the acquiror. Moreover, after the transaction, the surviving target must hold substantially all of its own and the acquiror's properties while former shareholders of the surviving target exchange their shares for shares of the acquiror's parent. The outbound toll charge would apply to treat the foreign corporation as if it were not a corporation and, therefore, result in gain recognition unless the limited-interest exception applies.

> **Example 14.18:** Assume that Foreign Parent, a publicly-traded corporation, wishes to acquire U.S. Target's business, but does not want to incur the expense of obtaining its own shareholders' approval for a straight merger of Foreign Parent into U.S. Target (which must survive due to a non-transferrable contract). Further assume that Foreign Parent owns a wholly-owned subsidiary, U.S. Acquiror, as an acquisition vehicle. Finally, assume that U.S. Acquiror merges with and into U.S. Target, with U.S. Target's shareholders receiving Foreign Parent shares as the consideration and with U.S. Target surviving the merger. This merger should qualify as a reverse triangular reorganization.[89] However, the U.S. Target's U.S. shareholders should recognize gain unless the limited-interest exception applies.

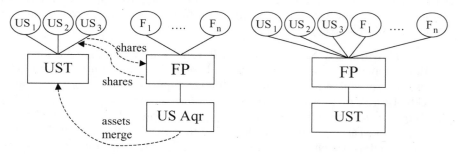

¶ 1405 THE ANTI-INVERSION PROVISIONS TO PREVENT OUTBOUND TRANSFERS

Congress enacted the outbound toll charge of Code Sec. 367(a), in part, to tax shareholders who transfer appreciated shares of U.S. corporations for shares of foreign corporations because these transfers may represent the United States' last opportunity for taxing the appreciation. Despite the fact that the rules provide for an outbound toll charge by treating the foreign corporation as if it were not a corporation, concern arose over whether the rules were detrimental enough to discourage so-called corporate "inversion" transactions.[90]

U.S. corporations invert because of the high U.S. corporate tax rate, the foreign tax credit system, and Subpart F's taxing jurisdiction.

---

[89] Temp. Reg. § 1.367(a)-3(d)(1)(ii); Reg. § 1.368-2(b)(1)(iii)(Ex. 13).

[90] IRS Notice 94-46, 1994-1 CB 356.

¶1404.05

The United States corporate tax rate is second only to Japan's. A high corporate tax rate encourages businesses to organize in other countries.

The deemed paid foreign tax credit system of the United States described in ¶ 409, ultimately results in a U.S. parent paying tax in both the foreign subsidiary's county and the United States at the top U.S. corporate rate of 35%. In contrast, most countries (e.g., Canada) exempt a foreign dividend from income, resulting in their foreign subsidiaries only incurring tax at the foreign country's presumably lower rate.

Suppose, for example, that USCo owns UKCo, a United Kingdom company that pays tax at a 21% rate. If UKCo earns $100 of income, UKCo will pay $21 of U.K. tax. When receiving a dividend distribution, USCo has income of $100, receives a foreign tax credit of $21, and pays $14 to the United States. As a result, the income earned by UKCo incurs the top U.S. corporate tax rate of 35%—21% to the United Kingdom and 14% to the United States.

In contrast, suppose that ForCo, a foreign company, owns UKSub, another United Kingdom company that similarly pays tax at a 21% rate. Country F uses an exemption system so that ForCo will not pay tax on foreign dividends received from UKSub. UKSub's income would incur tax of only $21 in the United Kingdom. There would not be any additional Country F tax on a dividend that ForCo receives. The only tax incurred is the U.K. tax at a 21% rate.

Pursuant to Subpart F, the United States can tax some of the income earned by foreign subsidiaries. If these foreign subsidiaries were owned by parents in other foreign corporations and not by U.S. corporations, Subpart F would not apply. Many inversion strategies separate foreign subsidiaries from their U.S. owners.

> **Example 14.19:** USAco, a publicly held U.S. C corporation, owns FSub, a controlled foreign corporation. HAVENco, a foreign corporation incorporated in a tax haven, is formed and in turn forms a U.S. acquisition corporation, USAcq. In a transaction designed to be a tax-free forward triangular reorganization,[91] USAco's shareholders receive 100 percent of the shares of HAVENco as USAco merges into USAcq. The resulting structure has the former USAco shareholders now owning all the shares of HAVENco. USAcq, which now operates the business of the former USAco, owns FSub and distributes FSub's shares to HAVENco. Although USAco will not report any income on the transaction, the former shareholders of USAco should recognize capital gain to the extent that the fair market value of the HAVENco shares received exceeds their basis in the USAco shares.[92] Gain on USAcq's transfer of FSub's shares to HAVENco should be eliminated via foreign tax credits.[93]

---

[91] Code Sec. 368(a)(2)(E).
[92] Code Sec. 367(a).

[93] Code Secs. 902 and 1248.

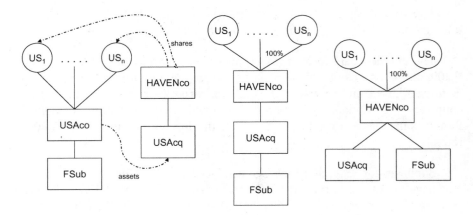

Despite the fact that the transaction results in an outbound toll charge to the former USAco shareholders, the many future tax benefits may be greater than the outbound toll charge, whose rate could be as low as 20 percent.

The USAco assets are now part of USAcq, which is still a U.S. corporation and subject to tax on its worldwide income. The former customers of USAco, who are now customers of USAcq, may not detect this change as the U.S. operations can continue to operate seamlessly. Moreover, USAcq does not own any foreign subsidiaries whose dividends will be subject to U.S. tax before repatriation to HAVENco.

More specifically, FSub is no longer a CFC. As a result, its income should never result in U.S. tax.

Finally, assuming that FSub and HAVENco are both incorporated in low-tax rate jurisdictions, there will be little corporate-level tax—United States or foreign—on the earnings of FSub.

This is classic inversion whereby the operations of a U.S. corporation become a subsidiary of a foreign parent. Other techniques by which inversions may be formed include tax-free reincorporations of U.S. corporations as foreign corporations,[94] asset inversions, and other types of share inversions.

The Anti-Inversion Rules of Code Sec. 7874. Congress enacted the Code Sec. 7874 anti-inversion rules to limit the U.S. tax benefits of corporate inversions by providing different methods of taxation depending on whether the former U.S. shareholders own at least 80 percent of the new foreign corporation or at least 60 percent (but less than 80 percent) of the shares of the new foreign corporation.

More specifically, the anti-inversion rules apply if (i) U.S. shareholders own 80 percent or more of the shares of the foreign corporation as a result of the inversion transaction, (ii) the U.S. corporation either becomes a subsidiary of a foreign corporation or transfers substantially all its properties to a foreign corporation, and (iii) the group does not have substantial business activities in the foreign corpora-

---

[94] Code Sec. 368(a)(1)(F).

tion's country of incorporation compared to the total worldwide business activities of the group.[95] In this type of inversion transaction, Code Sec. 7874 denies the intended tax benefits by deeming the top-tier foreign corporation to be a U.S. corporation for all U.S. tax purposes, including, of course, being subject to U.S. tax on its world-wide income. Moreover, deeming the top-tier foreign corporation to be a U.S. corporaton results in any foreign subsidiaries being controlled foreign corporations, whose Subpart F income and any upstream dividends will incur U.S. taxation.

> *Example* **14.20:** USAco, a publicly-held U.S. C corporation, owns FSub, a controlled foreign corporation. HAVENco, a foreign corporation incorporated in a tax haven, is formed and HAVENco forms a U.S. acquisition corporation, USAcq. In a transaction designed to be a tax-free forward triangular reorganization,[96] USAco's shareholders receive 100 percent of the shares of HAVENco as USAco merges into USAcq. The resulting structure has the former USAco shareholders now owning all the shares of HAVENco. USAcq, which now operates the business of the former USAco, now owns FSub and transfers FSub's shares to HAVENco. Gain on USAcq's sale of FSub's shares to HAVENco should be eliminated via foreign tax credits.[97]

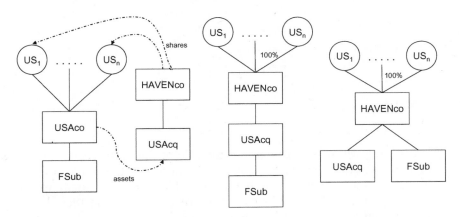

Under the anti-inversion rules, the former USAco shareholders own 80 percent or more of HAVENco and (1) USAco transfers substantially all of its property to HAVENco and (2) the group of HAVENco, USAcq, and FSub does not have substantial business activities in HAVENco's country of incorporation compared to the total worldwide business activities of the group. As a result, HAVENco is treated as if it were a U.S. corporation that will incur tax on its worldwide income (the U.S. shareholders will not have to recognize gain under the outbound toll charge). Finally, income of FSub may be Subpart F income of FSub, which was and remains a CFC.

---

[95] Substantial business activities result when the foreign corporation's country of incorporation encompasses 25% of the group's assets, income, and employee compensation. Reg. § 1.7874-3T(b).

[96] Code Sec. 368(a)(2)(D).
[97] Code Secs. 902 and 1248.

If U.S. shareholders own at least 60 percent (but less than 80 percent), by vote or value, of the foreign corporation, Code Sec. 7874 provides that the U.S. tax on any applicable gain may not be offset by any net operating losses or foreign tax credits for ten years following the inversion transaction.

Example **14.21:** USAco, a publicly held U.S. C corporation, owns FSub, a controlled foreign corporation. HAVENco, a foreign corporation incorporated in a tax haven, is formed and HAVENco owns a U.S. acquisition corporation, USAcq. In a transaction designed to be a tax-free forward triangular reorganization,[98] USAco's shareholders receive 60 percent of the shares of HAVENco as USAco merges into USAcq. The resulting structure has the former USAco shareholders now owning 60 percent of the shares of HAVENco. USAcq, which now operates the business of the former USAco, now owns FSub and transfers FSub's shares to HAVENco.

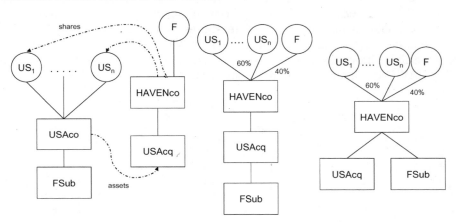

USAcq will recognize gain on the sale of the FSub shares to the extent their fair market value exceeds basis. Furthermore, the former USAco shareholders should incur the outbound toll charge to the extent that the fair market value of the HAVENco shares received exceeds their basis in the USAco shares.[99] Finally, because the former USAco shareholders own at least 60 percent (but less than 80 percent) of the shares of HAVENco, all gain recognized may not be reduced via any foreign tax credits or net operating losses over the next 10 years.

Further Anti-Inversion Rules for Corporations. Due to an increased number of inversions in recent years, the IRS issued Notice 2014-52[100] in an attempt to reduce planning designed to avoid the application of section 7874. These often involve avoiding the 80% or 60% test by either increasing the size of the foreign acquiror or decreasing the size of the U.S. target.

Some planning involved stuffing transactions, whereby the foreign corporation's size was inflated with passive assets (i.e., cash), such that the U.S. sharehold-

---

[98] Code Sec. 368(a)(2)(D).
[99] Code Sec. 367(a).

[100] IRB 2014-42.

ers would not acquire 80% of the foreign acquiror's shares in the reorganization. However, under the anti-stuffing rule of Notice 2014-52,[101] the ownership test ignores shares of the foreign acquiror attributable to passive assets when over 50% of the assets of the foreign acquiror's group are passive assets.

Other planning involved skinny down transactions, whereby the U.S. target made large distributions to reduce its size to avoid the ownership tests. The anti-skinny down rule of Notice 2014-52 applies by disregarding any distributions the U.S. corporation makes in the 36 months before the inversion.[102]

Notice 2014-52 also attempts to defeat inversions with rules preventing hop-scotch loans[103] (CFCs trying to avoid an investment in U.S. property[104] by loaning money to an upper tier foreign parent instead of a dividend distribution upstream through an intermediary U.S. corporation), de-controlling transactions to avoid CFC[105] status,[106] and other transactions designed to prevent a tax-free transfer of property from a CFC to a non-CFC.[107]

Application to U.S. partnerships. Code Sec. 7874's prohibition against using net operating losses or foreign tax credits also applies to inversions where U.S. partners exchange their partnership interests for at least 60 percent of the shares of a new foreign corporation.

> *Example* **14.22:** USLLC, a U.S.-organized limited liability company that is treated as a U.S. partnership for U.S. tax purposes, has U.S. citizens as all its members and does not own any valuable intangibles. USLLC owns FSub, a controlled foreign corporation. HAVENco is formed and HAVENco forms a foreign acquisition entity, FORco. USLLC's owners receive shares of HAVENco as USLLC merges its assets into FORco. The resulting structure has the former USLLC owners now owning 60 percent of the shares of HAVENco and HAVENco owning FORco. FORco now operates the business of the former USLLC and also owns FSub.
>
> Although USLLC will not report any income on the transaction, the former members of USLLC should recognize gain to the extent that the fair market value of the HAVENco shares received exceeds the basis in the USLLC membership interests relinquished. Because the former USLLC members own at least 60 percent of the shares of HAVENco, they may not reduce any gain recognized pursuant to the outbound toll charge by any foreign tax credits or net operating losses over the next 10 years.

---

[101] §2.01(b) of Notice 2014-52.
[102] §2.02(b) of Notice 2014-52.
[103] §3.01(b) of Notice 2014-52.
[104] Code Sec. 956. *See* §501.08.

[105] Code Sec. 957. *See* §501.03.
[106] §3.02(e) of Notice 2014-52.
[107] §3.03(b) of Notice 2014-52.

¶ 1406 INBOUND TRANSFERS IN AN ACQUISITIVE REORGANIZATION

This section provides an introduction to the U.S. taxation of inbound transfers from a foreign corporation that qualifies as a nontaxable acquisitive reorganization, including a Type A statutory merger, Type B share-for-share acquisition, Type C share-for-asset acquisition, forward triangular merger, or reverse triangular merger. The regulations under Code Sec. 367(b) are designed to prevent U.S. shareholders from using inbound reorganizations to avoid U.S. tax on the unrepatriated earnings and profits of a foreign corporation by requiring such shareholders to recognize a dividend equal to an allocable portion of a foreign corporation's earnings and profits.[108] This is similar to the dividend when a foreign subsidiary liquidates into its U.S. parent (see ¶ 1402).

More specifically, if a U.S. Shareholder (a U.S. person that owns 10%)[109] of a controlled foreign corporation (CFC)[110] loses his status as a U.S. shareholder of a CFC as a result of the inbound acquisition, she will recognize a dividend equal to her portion of the CFC's earnings and profits.[111] Other U.S. persons that owned target's shares must recognize the gain or elect to include their portion of the CFC's earnings and profits as a dividend.[112]

.01 Inbound Type A Statutory Merger

Pursuant to the Type A merger rules, a merger may include a foreign corporation.[113] To avoid the loss of the U.S. taxing jurisdiction over a foreign corporation's unrepatriated earnings and profits, the U.S. Shareholders of a foreign corporation merged out of existence must include their share of the foreign corporation's

---

[108] Reg. § 1.367(b)-3.

[109] A U.S. shareholder is defined under the Subpart F rules to be a U.S. person that owns 10% of a controlled foreign corporation. Code Sec. 951(b).

[110] A controlled foreign corporation is a foreign corporation that over 50% of its vote or value is owned by U.S. shareholders. Code Sec. 957(a).

[111] Reg. § 1.367(b)-3(b).

[112] Reg. § 1.367(b)-3(c).

[113] Reg. § 1.368-2(b)(1)(iii)(Ex. 13).

earnings and profits as a deemed dividend.[114] Other U.S. persons that owned target's shares must recognize the gain or elect to include their portion of the CFC's earnings and profits as a dividend.[115]

Example **14.23:** Assume that Foreign Target merges with and into U.S. Acquiror. Further assume that Foreign Target's shares are worth $1 million at the time of the merger and that the U.S. persons owning Foreign Target have a $100,000 tax basis in their Foreign Target shares. Finally, assume that the consideration received by the U.S. persons that own Foreign Target consists of U.S. Acquiror shares with a fair market value of $1 million. Although the merger involves a foreign corporation, it qualifies as a Type A merger.[116] The U.S. Shareholders of Foreign Target must include a dividend of the earnings and profits of Foreign Target.[117] Other U.S. persons that owned less than 10% of Foreign Target's shares must recognize the gain or elect to include their portion of the Foreign Target's earnings and profits.[118]

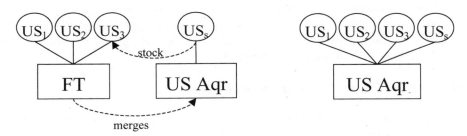

.02 Inbound Type B Share-For-Share Acquisitions

A nontaxable Type B share-for-share acquisition strictly limits the consideration to voting shares of the acquiring corporation and requires that the acquiring corporation has control of the target corporation immediately after the transaction.

Example **14.24:** Assume that U.S. Acquiror wishes to acquire Foreign Target. Further assume that Foreign Target's single class of shares is worth $1 million. Finally, assume that U.S. Acquiror issues $1 million worth of U.S. Acquiror's voting shares to the U.S. perons that own Foreign Target in exchange for their Foreign Target shares. The share-for-share exchange should qualify as a Type B acquisition. The U.S. persons that own Foreign Target should not recognize gain because both (1) they are acquiring property (the U.S. Acquiror's shares) within the U.S. taxing jurisdiction and (2) the earnings of Foreign Target could still come within the U.S. taxing jurisdiction. As a result, the regulations do not require any of the U.S. persons to include the earnings and profits of Foreign Target as a dividend.[119]

---

[114] Reg. § 1.367(b)-3(b)(3).
[115] Reg. § 1.367(b)-3(c).
[116] Reg. § 1.368-2(b)(1)(iii)(Ex. 13).

[117] Reg. § 1.367(b)-3(b)(3)(i).
[118] Reg. § 1.367(b)-3(c).
[119] Code Sec. 367(b).

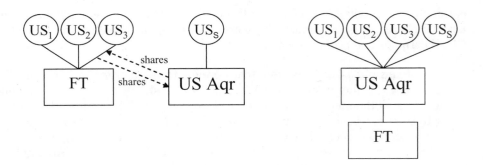

However, if U.S. Acquiror used just $1 of cash as consideration, the solely for voting shares requirement would not be satisfied and the transaction would become a failed reorganization. Consequently, Foreign Target's U.S. owners would recognize capital gain in the amount of the fair market value of the U.S. Acquiror's shares received over their basis in their Foreign Target shares. Practitioners should strive to ensure that inbound Type B acquisitions to not have boot in the form of debt assumed.

.03 Inbound Type C Share-For-Asset Acquisitions

A nontaxable Type C acquisition involves the acquisition of substantially all of the assets of the foreign target by a U.S. acquirer for its voting shares and the subsequent liquidation of the foreign target. To avoid the loss of the U.S. taxing jurisdiction, the U.S. Shareholders of a foreign corporation reorganized out of existence must include their share of the foreign corporation's earnings and profits as a dividend.[120] Other U.S. persons that owned target's shares must recognize the gain or elect to include their portion of the CFC's earnings and profits as a dividend.[121]

> **Example 14.25:** Assume that U.S. Acquiror acquires Foreign Target's assets for U.S. Acquiror's voting shares. Further assume that Foreign Target subsequently distributes the U.S. Acquiror's shares to its U.S. persons in liquidation. This transaction should qualify as a Type C acquisition. Depending on the circumstances, any U.S. Shareholders of Foreign Target should recognize a dividend to the extent of earnings and profits of the Foreign Target.[122] Other U.S. persons that owned less than 10% of Foreign Target's shares must recognize the gain or elect to include their portion of the target's earnings and profits as a dividend.[123] Even if Foreign Target had significant liabilities incurred in the ordinary course of business, the transaction would still be a good Type C acquisition.

---

[120] Reg. § 1.367(b)-3(b)(3)(ii)(Ex. 5).
[121] Reg. § 1.367(b)-3(c).

[122] Reg. § 1.367(b)-3(b)(3)(i) and (ii)(Ex. 6).
[123] Reg. § 1.367(b)-3(c).

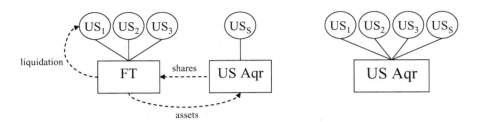

As previously described, a Type C acquisition is subject to a solely for voting shares requirement, similar to Type B's solely for voting shares requirement. However, unlike the Type B acquisition rules, the Type C acquisition rules provide for a boot relaxation rule, which allows the acquisition of some liabilities. If the boot relaxation rule applies, liabilities assumed are no longer ignored, but are included in the calculation as boot.

.04 Inbound Forward Triangular Mergers

A nontaxable forward triangular merger occurs when an acquiror uses the shares of its parent as the target merges into the acquiror, resulting in the acquiror receiving substantially all of the target's assets. To avoid the loss of the U.S. taxing jurisdiction, the U.S. shareholders of a foreign target merged out of existence must include their share of the foreign target's earnings and profits as a deemed dividend.[124]

> **Example 14.26:** Assume that U.S. Parent, a publicly-traded U.S. corporation, wishes to acquire Foreign Target's business, but does not want to incur the expense of obtaining its shareholders' approval for a straight merger of Foreign Target into U.S. Parent. Further assume that U.S. Parent forms a wholly-owned subsidiary, U.S. Acquiror, for the purpose of obtaining Foreign Target's business. Finally, assume that Foreign Target merges with and into U.S. Acquiror, with U.S. persons owning Foreign Target receiving U.S. Parent shares as consideration and U.S. Acquiror surviving the merger while obtaining Foreign Target's assets. If the various requirements are satisfied, the transaction would qualify as a forward triangular merger. Each U.S. Shareholder of Foreign Target must include the earnings and profits of Foreign Target as a dividend. Other U.S. persons that owned less than 10% of Foreign Target's shares must recognize the gain or elect to include their portion of the Foreign Target's earnings and profits as a dividend.[125]

---

[124] Reg. § 1.367(b)-3(b)(3)(i).   [125] Reg. § 1.367(b)-3(c).

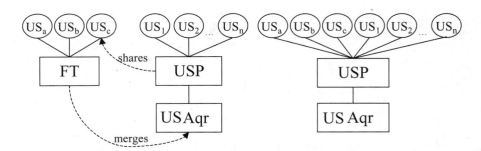

.05 Inbound Reverse Triangular Mergers

A reverse triangular merger is similar to a forward triangular merger, except that the surviving entity is the target and not the acquiror. More specifically, after the transaction, the surviving target holds substantially all of its own and the acquiror's assets and the former shareholders of the surviving target exchange their shares for shares of the acquiror's parent. Because the foreign target still exists, the rules focus on whether its U.S. Shareholders (its 10% U.S. owners) are still U.S. Shareholders of a CFC. If not, presumably the United States has lost some of its taxing jurisdiction and the former U.S. Shareholders must include a dividend of their share of the foreign target's earnings and profits.[126]

> **Example 14.27:** Assume that U.S. Parent, a publicly-traded corporation, wishes to acquire Foreign Target's business, but does not want to incur the expense of obtaining its shareholders' approval for a straight merger with Foreign Target (which must survive due to a non-transferable contract). Further assume that U.S. Parent forms a wholly-owned subsidiary, U.S. Acquiror, as an acquisition vehicle. Finally, assume that U.S. Acquiror merges with and into Foreign Target, with U.S. persons owning Foreign Target receiving U.S. Parent shares as the merger consideration. Foreign Target survives the merger. Because Foreign Target, with its earnings and profits, remains in existence, a dividend is unnecessary as long as the former U.S. Shareholders of Foreign Target are still U.S. Shareholders of a CFC.[127] If any former U.S. Shareholders of Foreign Target are no longer U.S. Shareholders of a CFC, they will include their portion of Foreign Target's earnings and profits as a dividend. Other U.S. persons that owned less than 10% of Foreign Target's shares must recognize the gain or elect to include their portion of the Foreign Target's earnings and profits as a dividend.[128]

---

[126] Reg. § 1.367(b)-3(b)(3)(i).

[127] Reg. § 1.367(b)-3(b)(3) only applies when assets of the foreign target are acquired.

[128] Reg. § 1.367(b)-3(c).

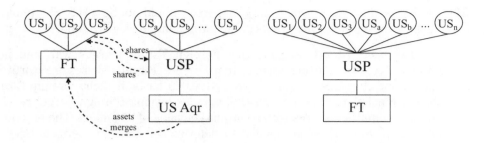

¶ 1407 FOREIGN-TO-FOREIGN TRANSFERS IN AN ACQUISITIVE REORGANIZATION

Provisions similar to those governing inbound and outbound transactions also govern a variety of other exchanges involving transfers of property from one foreign corporation to another foreign corporation.[129] The purpose of these provisions is to preserve the ability of the United States to tax both built-in gain on the shares of the foreign corporation tendered (similar to the outbound rules) and the earnings and profits of a foreign corporation attributable to shares owned by U.S. persons (similar to the inbound rules).

As a result, there is a two-prong analysis.[130] First, to the extent these transactions can be considered an outbound tax-free transaction, the outbound toll charge rules apply. If the outbound toll charge applies, the U.S. person recognizes gain and the analysis ends.[131] If the outbound toll charge does not apply, such as due to the limited-interest exception, the U.S. person must analyze the inbound rules to see if there is an income inclusion. Under the inbound rules, an income inclusion results if a U.S. Shareholder (a U.S. person that owns 10%)[132] of a controlled foreign corporation (CFC)[133] loses her status as a U.S. Shareholder of a CFC due to the transaction. If that status is lost, the U.S. Shareholder must include her share of the earnings and profits of the foreign target as a dividend.[134] Other U.S. persons that owned the foreign target's shares must recognize the gain or elect to include their portion of the CFC's earnings and profits as a dividend.[135]

.01 Foreign-To-Foreign Type A Statutory Merger

Because a merger may include foreign corporations,[136] the outbound toll charge rules must be analyzed. If the outbound toll charge applies, the analysis ends and the U.S. persons now owning shares of foreign target will recognize gain.[137] If the outbound toll charge does not apply, such as due to the limited-interest exception, then a U.S. Shareholder of a CFC who receives shares of a non-

---

[129] Code Sec. 367(b), and Reg. § 1.367(b)-4.

[130] Reg. § 1.367(a)-3(b)(2)(i).

[131] Reg. § 1.367(a)-3(b)(2)(i)(A).

[132] A U.S. shareholder is defined under the Subpart F rules to be a U.S. person that owns 10% of a controlled foreign corporation. Code Sec. 951(b).

[133] A controlled foreign corporation is a foreign corporation that over 50% of its vote or value is owned by U.S. shareholders. Code Sec. 957(a).

[134] Reg. § 1.367(a)-3(b)(2)(ii); Reg. § 1.367(b)-1(a).

[135] Reg. § 1.367(b)-4(b)(1)(i).

[136] Reg. § 1.368-2(b)(1)(iii)(Ex. 13).

[137] Reg. § 1.367(a)-3(b)(2).

CFC or shares of a CFC in which the U.S. person would not be a U.S. Shareholder must include the earnings and profits of the foreign target as a dividend.[138]

    Example **14.28:** Assume that Foreign Target merges with and into Foreign Acquiror. Further assume that Foreign Target's shares are worth $1 million and that U.S. persons have a $100,000 basis in their Foreign Target shares. Finally, assume that the U.S. persons owning Foreign Target receive Foreign Acquiror's shares with a fair market value of $1 million. The outbound toll charge rules must be applied to determine if the U.S. persons have to recognize built-in gain on their shares of Foreign Target. If there is gain, the analysis ends. If there is not any gain, such as due to the limited-interest exception, further analysis is required. More specifically, if the former Foreign Target would not be a CFC or any U.S. Shareholders would no longer be U.S. Shareholders (as that phrase is defined in Subpart F), the former U.S. Share-holders must include a dividend to the extent of their share of Foreign Target's earnings and profits. Other U.S. persons that owned Foreign Target's shares must recognize the gain or elect to include their portion of the CFC's earnings and profits as a dividend.[139]

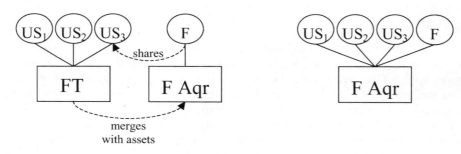

If it is not a valid Type A statutory merger, all the U.S. persons owning shares of Foreign Target must recognize gain from a sale of shares.

.02 Foreign-To-Foreign Type B Share-For-Share Acquisitions

    A Type B share-for-share acquisition is tax-free as long as the only considera-tion used is voting stock of the acquiring corporation and the acquiror has control of the target immediately after the transaction. Because this could be considered an outbound tax-free incorporation, the outbound toll charge rules must be analyzed. If the outbound toll charge applies, the analysis ends and the U.S. persons will recognize gain.[140] If the outbound toll charge does not apply, such as due to the limited-interest exception, then a U.S. Shareholder of a CFC (as those phrases are defined in the Subpart F rules) who receives shares of a non-CFC or shares of a CFC in which the U.S. person would not be a U.S. Shareholder must include the earnings and profits of the foreign target as a dividend.[141] Other U.S. persons that

---

[138] Reg. § 1.367(b)-4(b)(1)(i).
[139] Reg. § 1.367(b)-3(c).

[140] Reg. § 1.367(a)-3(b)(2).
[141] Reg. § 1.367(b)-4(b)(1)(i).

owned Foreign Target's shares must recognize the gain or elect to include their portion of the CFC's earnings and profits.[142]

> ***Example* 14.29:** Skipper, a U.S. citizen, wholly owns FMinnow, a foreign corporation engaged in the shipping business. In what would otherwise constitute a share-for-share acquisition, Skipper exchanges 100% of his shares of FMinnow for 3% of the shares of CANwhale, a publicly-held Canadian corporation on the Toronto Stock Exchange. This transaction satisfies the Type B rules and the limited-interest exception should apply to avoid the outbound toll charge. However, to prevent the loss of the U.S. taxing jurisdiction (Skipper is no longer a U.S. Shareholder of a CFC), Skipper must include a dividend to the extent of FMinnow's earnings and profits.

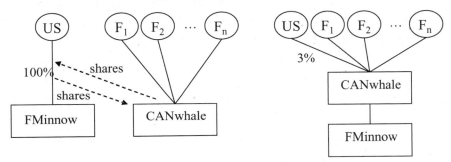

However, if CANwhile used just $1 of cash as consideration, the solely for voting shares requirement would not be satisfied and the transaction would become a failed Type B reorganization. Consequently, Skipper, the sole U.S. owner of FMinnow would recognize capital gain in the amount of the fair market value of CANwhile's shares received over his basis in FMinnow's shares. Practitioners should strive to ensure that foreign-to-foreign Type B acquisitions to not have boot in the form of debt assumed.

.03 Foreign-To-Foreign Type C Shares-For-Asset Acquisitions

As aforementioned, a nontaxable Type C acquisition allows an acquiror, for all or part of its voting shares, to acquire substantially all the assets of the target. Because this could be considered an outbound tax-free incorporation, the outbound toll charge rules must be analyzed. If the outbound toll charge applies, the analysis ends and the U.S. persons owning Foreign Target will recognize gain.[143] If the outbound toll charge does not apply, such as due to the limited-interest exception, then a U.S. Shareholder of a CFC (as those phrases are defined in the Subpart F rules) who receives shares of a non-CFC or shares of a CFC in which the U.S. person would not be a U.S. Shareholder must include the earnings and profits of the foreign target as a dividend.[144] Other U.S. persons that owned foreign target's shares must recognize the gain or elect to include their portion of the CFC's earnings and profits.[145]

---

[142] Reg. § 1.367(b)-3(c).

[143] Reg. § 1.367(a)-3(b)(2).

[144] Reg. § 1.367(b)-4(b)(1)(i).

[145] Reg. § 1.367(b)-3(c).

Example **14.30:** Skipper, a U.S. citizen, wholly owns FMinnow, a foreign corporation engaged in the shipping business. In what would otherwise constitute a tax-free shares-for-assets acquisition, CANwhale, a publicly-held Canadian corporation traded on the Toronto Stock Exchange, acquires all of FMinnow's assets for 3% of CANwhale's voting shares. Further assume that FMinnow subsequently distributes the CANwhale shares to Skipper in liquidation. As a result, the transaction should qualify as a Type C acquisition. The outbound toll charge rules must be applied to determine if Skipper has to recognize built-in gain on his shares of FMinnow. If there is gain, the analysis ends. If there is not any gain, such as due to the application of the limited-interest exception, further analysis is required. More specifically, because Skipper, who was formerly a U.S. shareholder in a CFC (FMinnow) now owns only 3% of the shares of a non-CFC (CANwhale), Skipper must include the earnings and profits of FMinnow as a dividend.

As previously described, a Type C acquisition is subject to a solely for voting shares requirement, similar to Type B's solely for voting shares requirement. However, unlike the Type B acquisition rules, the Type C acquisition rules provide for a boot relaxation rule, which allows the acquisition of some liabilities. If the boot relaxation rule applies, liabilities assumed are no longer ignored, but are included in the calculation as boot.

.04 Foreign-To-Foreign Forward Triangular Mergers

A nontaxable forward triangular merger occurs when an acquiror uses the shares of its parent as the target merges into the acquiror, resulting in the acquiror receiving substantially all of the target's assets. Because this could be considered an outbound tax-free incorporation, the outbound toll charge rules must be analyzed. If the outbound toll charge applies, the analysis ends and the U.S. persons who own the foreign target will recognize gain.[146] If the outbound toll charge does not apply, such as due to the limited-interest exception, then a U.S. Shareholder of a CFC who receives shares of a non-CFC or shares of a CFC in which the U.S. person would not be a U.S. Shareholder must include the earnings and profits of the target as a dividend.[147]

---

[146] Reg. § 1.367(a)-3(b)(2).   [147] Reg. § 1.367(b)-1(a).

Example **14.31:** Assume that Foreign Parent, a foreign corporation, wishes to acquire Foreign Target's business, but does not want to incur the expense of obtaining its shareholders' approval for a straight merger of Foreign Target into Foreign Parent. Further assume that Foreign Parent wholly owns a subsidiary, Foreign Acquiror, for the purpose of obtaining Foreign Target's business. Finally, assume that Foreign Target merges with and into Foreign Acquiror, with the U.S. persons who own Foreign Target receiving Foreign Parent shares as the merger consideration and Foreign Acquiror surviving the merger while obtaining the assets of Foreign Target. If the various requirements are satisfied, the merger qualifies as a forward triangular reorganization. If this transaction satisfies the limited-interest exception, the outbound toll charge should not apply. Because the transaction is also covered by the inbound rules, any U.S. Shareholders that are no longer U.S. Shareholders of a CFC (Foreign Target) must include a dividend to the extent of their share of the earnings and profits of Foreign Target.[148] Other U.S. persons that owned Foreign Target's shares must recognize the gain or elect to include their portion of the CFC's earnings and profits as a dividend.[149]

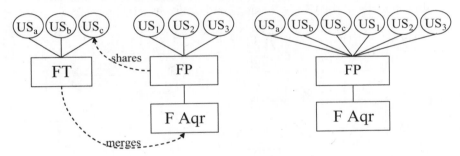

If this does not qualify as a forward triangular reorganization, U.S. persons owning Foreign Target will recognize gain to the extent that the fair market value of Foreign Parent's shares exceed their basis in Foreign Target's shares.

.05 *Foreign-To-Foreign Reverse Triangular Mergers*

A nontaxable reverse triangular merger is similar to a forward triangular merger, except that the surviving entity is the target and not the acquiror. More specifically, after the transaction, the surviving target holds substantially all of its own and the acquiror's assets and the former shareholders of the surviving target exchange their shares for shares of the acquiror's parent. Because this could be considered an outbound tax-free reorganization, the outbound toll charge rules must be analyzed. If the outbound toll charge applies, the analysis ends and the U.S. persons owning foreign target will recognize gain.[150] If the outbound toll charge does not apply, such as due to the limited-interest exception, then a U.S. Shareholder of a CFC who receives shares of a non-CFC or shares of a CFC in

---

[148] Reg. § 1.367(a)-3(d)(1)(i).
[149] Reg. § 1.367(b)-3(c).

[150] Reg. § 1.367(a)-3(b)(2).

which the U.S. person would not be a U.S. Shareholder must include the earnings and profits of the foreign target as a dividend.[151]

> *Example* **14.32:** Assume that Foreign Parent, a publicly-traded foreign corporation, wishes to acquire Foreign Target's business, but does not want to incur the expense of obtaining its shareholders' approval for a straight merger with Foreign Target (which must survive due to a non-transferable contract). Further assume that Foreign Parent forms a wholly-owned subsidiary, Foreign Acquiror, as an acquisition vehicle. Finally, assume that Foreign Acquiror merges with and into Foreign Target, with U.S. persons owning Foreign Target receiving Foreign Parent shares as the merger consideration. Foreign Target survives the merger. This transaction could be covered by the outbound rules,[152] but if the transaction satisfies the limited-interest exception, the outbound toll charge should not apply. Although Foreign Target, still exists, if its former U.S. shareholders are no longer U.S. shareholders of a CFC (Foreign Target or Foreign Parent), they must include a dividend to the extent of their share of the earnings and profits of Foreign Target.[153] Other U.S. persons that owned Foreign Target's shares must recognize the gain or elect to include their portion of the CFC's earnings and profits as a dividend.[154]

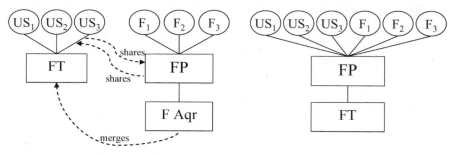

If this does not qualify as a forward triangular reorganization, U.S. persons owning Foreign Target will recognize gain to the extent of the fair market value of Foreign Parent's shares exceed their basis in Foreign Target's shares.

---

[151] Reg. § 1.367(b)-1(a).
[152] Reg. § 1.367(b)-4(b)(1)(i) and -4(b)(1)(iii)(Ex. 3).

[153] Reg. § 1.367(a)-3(d)(1)(i).
[154] Reg. § 1.367(b)-3(c).

¶1407.05

¶ 1408 APPENDIX

On January 1, 20X1, Mark Twain, a U.S. citizen, contributes $15 million to a newly formed German corporation called WallCo. Twain must prepare a Form 926 that indicates the $15 million contribution.

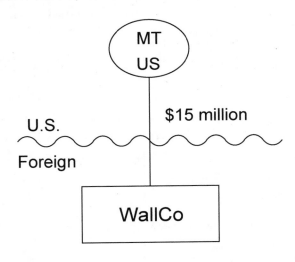

Form **926**	**Return by a U.S. Transferor of Property**	
(Rev. December 2013)	**to a Foreign Corporation**	OMB No. 1545-0026
Department of the Treasury Internal Revenue Service	▶ Information about Form 926 and its separate instructions is at *www.irs.gov/form926.* ▶ Attach to your income tax return for the year of the transfer or distribution.	Attachment Sequence No. **128**

Part I   U.S. Transferor Information (see instructions)

Name of transferor	Identifying number (see instructions)
Mark Twain	

1   If the transferor was a corporation, complete questions 1a through 1d.

a   If the transfer was a section 361(a) or (b) transfer, was the transferor controlled (under section 368(c)) by 5 or fewer domestic corporations? . . . . ☐ **Yes** ☐ **No**

b   Did the transferor remain in existence after the transfer? . . . . ☐ **Yes** ☐ **No**

If not, list the controlling shareholder(s) and their identifying number(s):

Controlling shareholder	Identifying number
Mark Twain	123-45-6789

c   If the transferor was a member of an affiliated group filing a consolidated return, was it the parent corporation? . . . . ☐ **Yes** ☐ **No**

If not, list the name and employer identification number (EIN) of the parent corporation:

Name of parent corporation	EIN of parent corporation

d   Have basis adjustments under section 367(a)(5) been made? . . . . ☐ **Yes** ☑ **No**

2   If the transferor was a partner in a partnership that was the actual transferor (but is not treated as such under section 367), complete questions 2a through 2d.

a   List the name and EIN of the transferor's partnership:

Name of partnership	EIN of partnership

b   Did the partner pick up its pro rata share of gain on the transfer of partnership assets? . . . . ☐ **Yes** ☐ **No**

c   Is the partner disposing of its **entire** interest in the partnership? . . . . ☐ **Yes** ☐ **No**

d   Is the partner disposing of an interest in a limited partnership that is regularly traded on an established securities market? . . . . ☐ **Yes** ☐ **No**

Part II   Transferee Foreign Corporation Information (see instructions)

3 Name of transferee (foreign corporation)	**4a Identifying number**, if any
WallCo	
5 Address (including country)	**4b** Reference ID number (see instructions)
Berlin, Germany	

6   Country code of country of incorporation or organization (see instructions)

GM

7   Foreign law characterization (see instructions)

Corporation

8   Is the transferee foreign corporation a controlled foreign corporation? . . . . ☑ **Yes** ☐ **No**

For Paperwork Reduction Act Notice, see separate instructions.	Cat. No. 16982D	Form **926** (Rev. 12-2013)

Form 926 (Rev. 12-2013)   Page **2**

Part III   **Information Regarding Transfer of Property** (see instructions)

Type of property	(a) Date of transfer	(b) Description of property	(c) Fair market value on date of transfer	(d) Cost or other basis	(e) Gain recognized on transfer
Cash	1/1//X1		15,000,000		
Stock and securities					
Installment obligations, account receivables or similar property					
Foreign currency or other property denominated in foreign currency					
Inventory					
Assets subject to depreciation recapture (see Temp. Regs. sec. 1.367(a)-4T(b))					
Tangible property used in trade or business not listed under another category					
Intangible property					
Property to be leased (as described in final and temp. Regs. sec. 1.367(a)-4(c))					
Property to be sold (as described in Temp. Regs. sec. 1.367(a)-4T(d))					
Transfers of oil and gas working interests (as described in Temp. Regs. sec. 1.367(a)-4T(e))					
Other property					

Supplemental Information Required To Be Reported (see instructions):

_____
_____
_____
_____
_____

Form **926** (Rev. 12-2013)

¶1408

Part IV   **Additional Information Regarding Transfer of Property** (see instructions)

9   Enter the transferor's interest in the foreign transferee corporation before and after the transfer:

     (a) Before   0 %   **(b)** After   100 %

10   Type of nonrecognition transaction (see instructions) ▶ --

11   Indicate whether any transfer reported in Part III is subject to any of the following:

		Yes	No
a	Gain recognition under section 904(f)(3)	☐ Yes	☑ No
b	Gain recognition under section 904(f)(5)(F)	☐ Yes	☑ No
c	Recapture under section 1503(d)	☐ Yes	☑ No
d	Exchange gain under section 987	☐ Yes	☑ No

12   Did this transfer result from a change in the classification of the transferee to that of a foreign corporation?   ☐ Yes ☑ No

13   Indicate whether the transferor was required to recognize income under final and Temporary Regulations sections 1.367(a)-4 through 1.367(a)-6 for any of the following:

		Yes	No
a	Tainted property	☐ Yes	☑ No
b	Depreciation recapture	☐ Yes	☑ No
c	Branch loss recapture	☐ Yes	☑ No
d	Any other income recognition provision contained in the above-referenced regulations	☐ Yes	☑ No

14   Did the transferor transfer assets which qualify for the trade or business exception under section 367(a)(3)?   ☐ Yes ☑ No

15a   Did the transferor transfer foreign goodwill or going concern value as defined in Temporary Regulations section 1.367(a)-1T(d)(5)(iii)?   ☐ Yes ☑ No

   b   If the answer to line 15a is "Yes," enter the amount of foreign goodwill or going concern value transferred ▶ $ -------------------------------

16   Was cash the only property transferred?   ☑ Yes ☐ No

17a   Was intangible property (within the meaning of section 936(h)(3)(B)) transferred as a result of the transaction?   ☐ Yes ☑ No

   b   If "Yes," describe the nature of the rights to the intangible property that was transferred as a result of the transaction:

_____

_____

_____

_____

Chapter 15
State Taxation of International Operations

¶ 1501 OVERVIEW OF STATE CORPORATE INCOME TAXES

Forty-five states and the District of Columbia impose some type of income-based tax on corporations. Nevada, Ohio, South Dakota, Washington, and Wyoming do not levy a corporate income tax. However, Ohio does impose a gross receipts tax called the *commercial activity tax*, and Washington imposes a gross receipts tax called the *business and occupation tax*. Texas imposes a tax on gross margin,called the *margin tax*.

Most states that impose a corporate income tax use either federal taxable income before the net operating loss and special deductions (federal Form 1120, line 28) or federal taxable income (federal Form 1120, line 30) as the starting place for computing state taxable income. The use of the federal tax base as the starting point eases the administrative burden of computing state taxable income. Despite the broad conformity, each state requires numerous addition and subtraction modifications to arrive at state taxable income. Examples of common addition modifications include interest income received on state and municipal debt obligations, state income taxes, royalties and interest expenses paid to related parties, federal bonus depreciation under Code Sec. 168(k), and the Code Sec. 199 domestic production activities deduction. Examples of common subtraction modifications include interest income received on federal debt obligations, state net operating loss deductions, state dividends-received deductions, and federal Subpart F and Code Sec. 78 gross-up income.

States employ a wide variety of consolidation rules for a group of commonly controlled corporations. A few states require each group member that is taxable in the state to file a return on a separate company basis. About 20 states permit or require a group of commonly controlled corporations to file a consolidated return if certain requirements are met. Roughly another 20 states require members of a unitary business group to compute their taxable income on a combined basis. A unitary business group consists of two or more commonly controlled corporations that are engaged in the same trade or business, as exhibited by such factors as functional integration, centralized management, and economies of scale.

To prevent double taxation, corporations that are engaged in business in two or more states may apportion their income among the taxing states. These multistate corporations use state-mandated apportionment formulas to compute an apportionment percentage for each state. These formulas generally reflect the principles embodied in the Uniform Division of Income for Tax Purposes Act (UDITPA), which is a model law for allocating and apportioning income that was promulgated by state tax officials in 1957. Under UDITPA, taxpayers apportion their business income among each taxing state. In contrast, an item of nonbusiness income is specifically allocated to a single state.

The UDITPA distinction between business and nonbusiness income is related to the U.S. constitutional restrictions on the ability of a state to tax an out-of-state corporation. Specifically, the Commerce Clause and Due Process clause limit the ability of states to tax an item of income that has no relationship to the business activity which the corporation conducts in the state. For example, in *Allied-Signal, Inc. v. Division of Taxation,*[1] a Delaware corporation that was taxable in New Jersey and was commercially domiciled in Michigan realized a $211.5 million capital gain from the sale of 20.6 percent of the stock of ASARCO. The U.S. Supreme Court held that New Jersey could not tax an apportioned percentage of the gain because the taxpayer and ASARCO were "unrelated business enterprises whose activities had nothing to do with the other," and because the taxpayer's ownership of the ASARCO stock did not serve an "operational rather than an investment function" in the taxpayer's business. As a consequence, the gain was nonbusiness income which was specifically allocable to the state of commercial domicile.

State formulas for apportioning business income are usually based on the relative amounts of property, payroll, and sales that the corporation has in each taxing state. Each apportionment factor equals the ratio of the corporation's property, payroll, or sales in the state to its property, payroll, or sales everywhere. About 10 states use a formula where the apportionment percentage equals the simple average of the property factor (in-state property ÷ total property), payroll factor (in-state payroll ÷ total payroll), and sales factor (in-state sales ÷ total sales). Most states use either a three-factor formula that assigns more weight to the sales factor than to the property or payroll factor, or a single-factor formula that includes only a sales factor.

¶ 1502 REVIEW OF FEDERAL TAXATION OF INCOME FROM FOREIGN SUBSIDIARIES

Federal tax law plays an important role in state taxation of a domestic corporation's foreign earnings because states generally use federal taxable income (federal Form 1120, line 28 or 30) as the starting point for computing state taxable income.

---

[1] 504 U.S. 768 (1992).

The federal government taxes the worldwide taxable income of a domestic corporation,[2] and allows a credit for the foreign income taxes imposed on foreign-source income.[3] On the other hand, the federal government generally does not tax the undistributed foreign-source income of a foreign corporation, even if the foreign corporation is a wholly-owned subsidiary of a domestic corporation.[4] Moreover, foreign corporations are not includible in a federal consolidated income tax return.[5] Consequently, if a domestic corporation operates abroad through foreign subsidiaries, the foreign earnings of those foreign corporations are generally not subject to U.S. taxation until the earnings are repatriated to the U.S. parent through a dividend distribution. This policy, which is known as *deferral*, is designed to allow U.S. companies to compete in foreign markets on a tax parity with foreign competitors.

A U.S. parent corporation's receipt of a dividend distribution from a foreign corporation generally represents the federal government's first opportunity to tax the underlying foreign earnings. Therefore, the domestic corporation generally includes any foreign dividends in its federal taxable income,[6] and is not allowed an offsetting dividends-received deduction.[7] A dividends-received deduction may be available, however, if a 10%-or-more-owned foreign corporation distributes a dividend out of earnings that are attributable to income derived from the conduct of a U.S. trade or business or dividends received from an 80%-or-more-owned domestic corporation.[8]

To mitigate double taxation of a foreign subsidiary's earnings, upon receiving a dividend from a foreign subsidiary, a U.S. parent corporation may claim a deemed paid foreign tax credit for the foreign income taxes that a 10%-or-more-owned foreign corporation pays on its earnings.[9] Because the amount of dividend income recognized by a U.S. parent corporation is net of any foreign income taxes paid by a foreign subsidiary, the domestic corporation is implicitly allowed a deduction for those foreign taxes. To prevent a double tax benefit, the domestic corporation must gross up its dividend income by the amount of the deemed paid foreign taxes, which offsets the implicit deduction[10] The domestic corporation reports its gross-up income as Dividends on Line 4 of Form 1120 (see Schedule C, Line 15).

A policy of unrestricted deferral would create an opportunity to avoid U.S. taxes on portable income, such as passive investment income or inventory trading profits, which is easily shifted to a foreign corporation located in a tax haven country. In 1962, Congress attempted to close this loophole by enacting Subpart F (Code Secs. 951–965), which denies deferral to certain types of tainted income earned through a foreign corporation. Code Section 951 requires a U.S. shareholder of a controlled foreign corporation (CFC) to include in gross income its share of the CFC's Subpart F income, as well as its share of the CFC's investment of earnings in U.S. property. A foreign corporation is a CFC if U.S. shareholders

---

[2] Code Sec. 61.
[3] Code Sec. 901.
[4] Code Sec. 881 and 882.
[5] Code Sec. 1504.
[6] Code Sec. 61.

[7] Code Sec. 243.
[8] Code Sec. 245.
[9] Code Sec. 902.
[10] Code Sec. 78.

own more than 50 percent of the stock of the foreign corporation, by vote or value.[11] Subpart F income is the sum of a CFC's foreign base company income and its insurance income.[12] Under Code Sec. 954, foreign base company income is the sum of foreign personal holding company income, foreign base company sales income, foreign base company services income, and foreign base company oil related income. A U.S. parent corporation reports a Subpart F inclusion as dividend income on Line 4 of Form 1120 (see Schedule C, Line 14).

¶ 1503 WORLDWIDE VERSUS WATER'S-EDGE COMBINED REPORTING

About 20 states require members of a commonly controlled group of corporations engaged in a unitary business to determine their taxable income on a combined basis. Generally, each group member that has nexus in the state apportions its business income by multiplying the combined business income of all the members of the unitary business group by an apportionment percentage that is based on factors, the denominators of which include the factors everywhere of all group members, and the numerators of which include the in-state factors of only the taxpayer member.

The states that require combined reporting generally take one of two approaches to dealing with unitary group members that are incorporated in a foreign country or conduct most of their business abroad. The first approach is a worldwide combination, under which the combined report includes all members of the unitary business group, regardless of the country in which the group member is incorporated or the country in which the group member conducts business. The second approach is a water's-edge combination, under which the combined report includes all members of the unitary business group, except for certain group members that are incorporated in a foreign country or conduct most of their business abroad. A common approach is to exclude so-called *80/20 corporations*, which are corporations whose business activity outside the United States, as measured by some combination of apportionment factors, is 80 percent or more of the corporation's total business activity.

Requiring the use of worldwide combined reporting is controversial for a number of reasons, including the difficulty of converting books and records maintained under foreign accounting principles and in a foreign currency into a form that is acceptable to the states, and the inability of states to readily access or audit books and records located in foreign countries.

Despite the practical difficulties of apportioning income on a worldwide basis, the constitutionality of requiring a corporation to compute its state taxable income based on the combined income of a worldwide unitary group has been firmly established. In *Container Corp. of America v. Franchise Tax Board*,[13] the Supreme Court ruled that California's worldwide combined reporting method was constitutional with respect to a U.S.-based parent corporation and its foreign country

---

[11] Code Sec. 957.
[12] Code Sec. 952.

[13] 463 U.S. 159 (1983).

subsidiaries. In *Barclays Bank plc v. Franchise Tax Board*,[14] the Supreme Court held that California's worldwide combined reporting method was also constitutional with respect to a foreign-based parent corporation and its U.S. subsidiaries. California repealed mandatory worldwide combined reporting in 1988, and permits a unitary group to make a water's-edge election.

Although a water's-edge combination generally reduces the compliance burden, it may also increase the taxpayer member's state tax liability if the unitary group's U.S. operations are more profitable than its foreign operations. The inclusion of a foreign member's profits increases the combined income of the group, whereas the inclusion of the foreign member's property, payroll, and/or sales in the denominators of the apportionment factors generally reduces the state's apportionment percentage. The net effect can be a reduction in state taxable income if the group's foreign operations are less profitable than its U.S. operations, and an increase in state taxable income if the group's foreign operations are more profitable than its U.S. operations.

California, Idaho, Montana and North Dakota generally require a worldwide combination, but give taxpayers the option to elect a water's-edge combination. Massachusetts, Utah and West Virginia generally require a water's-edge combination, but give taxpayers the option to elect a worldwide combination. Alaska requires a water's-edge combination, except for oil and gas companies, which must use worldwide combined reporting. The other mandatory combined reporting states, such as Illinois, Michigan, New York and Texas, require a water's-edge combination.

¶ 1504 DIVIDENDS FROM FOREIGN SUBSIDIARIES

Most states do not permit worldwide combined reporting, in which case the foreign income of a foreign subsidiary is not included in the U.S. parent corporation's state taxable income until those earnings are distributed as a dividend. Thus, consistent with the federal policy of deferral, a state's first opportunity to tax the foreign-source income of a foreign subsidiary is generally when those earnings are repatriated by the U.S. parent corporation as a dividend.

.01 Inclusion in Apportionable Income

Assuming either the activities of the foreign corporation or the stock of the foreign corporation is a unitary part of the business conducted by the U.S. parent corporation in the states in which the U.S. parent has nexus, the dividend is included in the U.S. parent's apportionable business income.[15] On the other hand, if the activities and the stock of the foreign corporation have nothing to do with the activities of the U.S. parent in the taxing state, then the dividend may be nonbusiness income that is allocable only to the U.S. parent's state of commercial domicile.

In *Mobil Oil Corp. v. Commissioner of Taxes*,[16] the Supreme Court addressed the issue of whether dividends from foreign corporations are includible in a U.S.

---

[14] 512 U.S. 298 (1994).

[15] *See*, for example, *MeadWestvaco Corporation v. Illinois Department of Revenue*, 553 U.S. 16 (2008); or *Allied-*

Signal, Inc. v. Director, Division of Taxation, 504 U.S. 768 (1992).

[16] 445 U.S. 425 (1980).

¶1504.01

parent corporation's apportionable business income. Mobil was a vertically integrated petroleum company that was commercially domiciled in New York. Mobil argued that Vermont could not constitutionally tax the dividends that Mobil received from its foreign subsidiaries because the activities of the foreign subsidiaries were unrelated to Mobil's activities in Vermont, which were limited to marketing petroleum products. Stating that "the linchpin of apportionability in the field of state income taxation is the unitary business principle," the Supreme Court ruled that Vermont could tax an apportioned percentage of the dividends because the foreign subsidiaries were part of the same integrated petroleum enterprise as the business operations conducted in Vermont. In other words, dividends received from unitary subsidiaries are business income. The Court also noted that if the business activities of the foreign subsidiaries had "nothing to do with the activities of the recipient in the taxing state, due process considerations might well preclude apportionability, because there would be no underlying unitary business."

.02 Dividends-Received Deductions

In sharp contrast with federal law, which generally limits its dividends-received deduction to dividends received from domestic corporations, most states provide a deduction for dividends received from both domestic and foreign corporations. For example, consistent with how they treat domestic dividends, many states provide a 100 percent deduction for dividends received from an 80-percent-or-more-owned foreign corporation.

In *Kraft General Foods, Inc. v. Department of Revenue*,[17] the U.S. Supreme Court ruled that an Iowa law that allowed taxpayers to claim a dividends-received deduction for dividends from domestic, but not foreign, subsidiary corporations was unconstitutional. During the tax years in question, Iowa conformed to the federal dividends-received deduction. As a consequence, Iowa did not tax dividends received from domestic corporations, but did tax dividends received from foreign corporations unless the dividend represented a distribution of U.S. earnings. The Court ruled that the Iowa provision which taxed only dividends paid by foreign corporations out of their foreign earnings facially discriminated against foreign commerce, in violation of the Commerce Clause.

Since the *Kraft* decision, a number of state courts have also struck down dividends-received deduction schemes that favored dividends received from domestic corporations over dividends received from foreign corporations.

In *Dart Industries, Inc. v. Clark*,[18] the Rhode Island Supreme Court ruled the Rhode Island provision which allowed a deduction for dividends from domestic but not foreign subsidiaries was discriminatory in violation of the Commerce Clause. Likewise, in *D.D.I Inc. v. North Dakota*,[19] the North Dakota Supreme Court declared unconstitutional a North Dakota statute that permitted a dividends-received deduction, but only to the extent the dividend payer's income was subject to North Dakota corporate income tax. In *Hutchinson Technology, Inc. v. Commissioner of Revenue*,[20] the Minnesota Supreme Court ruled that a state statute which excluded

---

[17] 505 U.S. 71 (1992).
[18] 657 A.2d 1062 (R.I. Sup. Ct., 1995).

[19] 657 N.W.2d 228 (N.D. Sup. Ct., 2003).
[20] 698 N.W.2d 1 (Minn. Sup. Ct., 2005).

dividends paid by certain foreign sales corporations from the state's dividends-received deduction was discriminatory in violation of the Commerce Clause. In *Emerson Electric Co. v. Tracy*,[21] the Ohio Supreme Court declared unconstitutional an Ohio statute that permitted a 100 percent deduction for dividends from domestic subsidiaries, but only an 85 percent deduction for dividends from foreign subsidiaries. In *Conoco Inc. v. Taxation and Revenue Department*,[22] the New Mexico Supreme Court ruled that the New Mexico scheme under which foreign but not domestic dividends were included in the tax base facially discriminated against foreign commerce, even through the state allowed a taxpayer to include a portion of the dividend-paying foreign subsidiaries' property, payroll, and sales in the denominators of its apportionment factors, thereby reducing the state apportionment percentage.

.03 Dividends-Received Deductions in a Water's-Edge Combined Report

In footnote 23 of its decision in *Kraft*, the Supreme Court stated that:

> "If one were to compare the aggregate tax imposed by Iowa on a unitary business which included a subsidiary doing business throughout the United States (including Iowa) with the aggregate tax imposed by Iowa on a unitary business which included a foreign subsidiary doing business abroad, it would be difficult to say that Iowa discriminates against the business with the foreign subsidiary. Iowa would tax an apportioned share of the domestic subsidiary's entire earnings, but would tax only the amount of the foreign subsidiary's earnings paid as a dividend to the parent."

In addition, the supreme courts in several water's-edge combined reporting states have ruled that it is constitutionally acceptable to include dividends paid by foreign subsidiaries in the tax base, while excluding dividends paid by domestic subsidiaries that are included in the water's-edge combined report.

In *Appeal of Morton Thiokol, Inc.*,[23] the Kansas Supreme Court noted that *Kraft* did not address the taxation of foreign dividends by water's-edge combined reporting states (because Iowa is an elective consolidation state), and that "the aggregate tax imposed by Kansas on a unitary business with a domestic subsidiary would not be less burdensome than that imposed by Kansas on a unitary business with a foreign subsidiary because the income of the domestic subsidiary would be combined, apportioned, and taxed while only the dividend of the foreign subsidiary would be taxed." Likewise, in *E.I. Du Pont de Nemours & Co. v. State Tax Assessor*,[24] the Maine Supreme Judicial Court held that Maine's water's-edge combined reporting method was distinguishable from the Iowa's single-entity reporting method because the income of a domestic subsidiary is included in the Maine combined report. Therefore, taxing dividends paid by foreign but not domestic subsidiaries did not constitute the kind of facial discrimination found in the Iowa system.

In *General Electric Company, Inc. v. Department of Revenue Administration*,[25] General Electric challenged the constitutionality of a New Hampshire statute that permits a U.S. parent corporation to claim a dividends-received deduction for

---

[21] 735 N.E.2d 445 (Ohio Sup. Ct., 2000).

[22] 122 N.M. 736 (N.M. Sup. Ct., 1996).

[23] 864 P.2d 1175 (Kan. Sup. Ct., 1993).

[24] 675 A.2d 82 (Maine Sup. Ct., 1996).

[25] 914 A.2d 246 (N.H. Sup. Ct., 2006).

dividends received from foreign subsidiaries only to the extent the foreign subsidiary has business activity and is subject to tax in New Hampshire. None of General Electric's unitary foreign subsidiaries had business activities in New Hampshire during the tax years in question. Thus, General Electric could not claim a dividends-received deduction for the dividends received from those foreign subsidiaries. The New Hampshire Supreme Court ruled that the New Hampshire tax scheme did not discriminate against foreign commerce because both a unitary business with foreign subsidiaries operating in New Hampshire and a unitary business with foreign subsidiaries not operating in New Hampshire are each taxed only one time. Thus, there was no differential treatment that benefits the former and burdens the latter.

In *Schlumberger Technology Corp. & Subsidiaries v. Department of Revenue*,[26] the Alaska Supreme Court held that Alaska tax law has not adopted by reference Code Sec. 882, because the federal sourcing rule is inconsistent with the state's formulary apportionment approach for determining the in-state business income of a taxpayer. Under Code Sec. 882, a foreign corporation must report only income "effectively connected with the conduct of a trade or business within the United States," and may exclude all of its foreign-source dividend income. In contrast, Alaska law provides only an 80 percent subtraction modification for the foreign dividend income of a member of the water's-edge group, regardless of whether the member is a foreign corporation or a domestic corporation. Consequently, the domestic subsidiary of a foreign multinational corporation that computes its Alaska taxable income using the water's-edge combined reporting method must include 20 percent of any foreign dividends in its apportionable income.

.04 Apportionment Factor Relief

The inclusion of dividends received from a foreign subsidiary in the apportionable income of a U.S. parent corporation raises the issue of whether the parent's apportionment factors should reflect the foreign subsidiary's property, payroll, and sales. In his dissent in *Mobil Oil Corp.*, Justice Stevens raised the issue of factor representation, noting that "[u]nless the sales, payroll, and property values connected with the production of income by the payor corporations are added to the denominator of the apportionment formula, the inclusion of earnings attributable to those corporations in the apportionable tax base will inevitably cause Mobil's Vermont income to be overstated."

In *NCR Corp. v. Taxation and Revenue Department*,[27] the New Mexico Court of Appeals rejected the taxpayer's argument that the taxation of dividends received by a U.S. parent corporation from its foreign subsidiaries without factor representation resulted in constitutionally impermissible double taxation. Similar arguments made by NCR were also rejected by state supreme courts in Minnesota and South Carolina.[28] Caterpillar, Inc. also litigated the issue of factor representation with respect to dividends received from foreign subsidiaries, and met with limited

---

[26] 331 P.3d 334 (Alaska Sup. Ct., 2014).

[27] 856 P.2d 982 (N.M. Ct. App. 1993), cert. denied, 512 U.S. 1245 (1994).

[28] *NCR Corp. v. Commissioner of Revenue*, 438 N.W.2d 86 (Minn. Sup. Ct., 1989), cert. denied, 493 U.S. 848 (1989); *NCR Corp. v. Tax Commission*, 439 S.E.2d 254 (S.C. Sup. Ct., 1993), cert. denied, 512 U.S. 1245 (1994).

success. See, for example, *Caterpillar, Inc. v. Commissioner of Revenue*,[29] and *Caterpillar, Inc. v. Department of Revenue Administration*.[30] Finally, in *Unisys Corp. v. Commonwealth of Pennsylvania*,[31] the Pennsylvania Supreme Court ruled that factor representation was not constitutionally required because the taxpayer failed to prove that the state was unfairly taxing income earned outside its jurisdiction.

.05 Subpart F Inclusions and Code Sec. 78 Gross-up Income

The rationale for including the Code Sec. 78 gross-up amount in federal taxable income does not apply for state tax purposes because no state allows a domestic corporation to claim a deemed paid credit for the foreign income taxes paid by a foreign subsidiary. As a consequence, nearly all states provide a subtraction modification or dividends-received deduction for Section 78 gross-up income, in effect, excluding the federal gross-up amount from state taxation.[32]

Consistent with the notion that a Subpart F inclusion is a deemed dividend from a controlled foreign corporation, most states provide a dividends received deduction or subtraction modification for income recognized under Subpart F. California does not provide a dividends-received deduction for Subpart F income, but instead requires that the Subpart F income and the related apportionment factors of a controlled foreign corporation be included in a water's-edge combined report to the extent of the controlled foreign corporation's Subpart F income.[33] In addition, some states provide only limited deductions for inclusions in gross income under Subpart F.

¶ 1505 CHECK-THE-BOX FOREIGN BRANCHES

A foreign business entity's status as a "corporation" for U.S. federal income tax purposes is determined under the check-the-box regulations.[34] Consequently, the classification of a foreign business entity as a corporation, partnership or a disregarded entity (branch) may differ for U.S. and foreign tax purposes. For U.S. federal income tax purposes, a so-called "per se" corporation must be treated as a corporation for U.S. tax purposes. A business entity that is not a per se corporation (i.e., an "eligible entity") that has two or more owners can elect to be classified as a corporation or a partnership, whereas an eligible entity that has one owner can elect to be classified as a corporation or a disregarded entity. If a domestic corporation organizes a wholly-owned foreign corporation and elects to treat the foreign corporation as a disregarded entity, the income of the check-the-box foreign branch is treated as income earned directly by the U.S. parent corporation.

States generally conform to the federal check-the-box rules for state income tax purposes. Thus, a foreign entity that is a corporation for foreign tax purposes

---

[29] 568 N.W.2d 695 (Minn. Sup. Ct., 1997), cert. denied, 522 U.S. 1112 (1998).

[30] 741 A.2d 56 (N.H. Sup. Ct., 1999), cert. denied, 120 S. Ct. 1424 (2000).

[31] 812 A.2d 448 (Pa. Sup. Ct., 2002).

[32] In *Amerada Hess Corp. v. North Dakota* [704 N.W.2d 8 (N.D. Sup. Ct., 2005)], the North Dakota Supreme

Court ruled that Section 78 gross-up amounts did not qualify as "foreign dividends" under the applicable North Dakota tax statute, and therefore did not qualify for the partial exclusion from income under North Dakota's water's-edge combined unitary reporting method of determining the state corporate income tax.

[33] Cal. Rev. and Tax Code § 25110.

[34] Reg. § 301.7701 to 3.

but is a branch or partnership for U.S. federal tax purposes is generally treated as a branch or partnership for state income tax purposes.

In *Manpower Inc. v. Commissioner of Revenue*,[35] a domestic corporation owned 99 percent of Manpower France S.A.R.L (MPF), a French entity analogous to a U.S. limited liability company. In 1999, MPF made a federal check-the-box election, which caused the liquidation of a foreign corporation (MPF's previous federal tax status) and a contribution of the distributed assets to a new partnership. For Minnesota tax purposes, income of "foreign corporations and other foreign entities" is not included in apportionable income. The Commissioner argued that when the French subsidiary elected to be classified as a partnership for federal tax purposes, a newly formed partnership was created under U.S. law. The taxpayer argued that, despite the federal check-the-box election, MPF still qualified as a "foreign entity" for Minnesota tax purposes, because it was created in France under French law and operated in France. The Minnesota Supreme Court agreed, ruling that the check-the-box election changed the French entity's legal nature but not its nationality. The subsidiary was still a foreign entity, and the only effect of its check-the-box election was to convert it from a foreign corporation to a foreign partnership for federal income tax purposes.

¶ 1506 TREATMENT OF FOREIGN INCOME TAX PAYMENTS

For federal tax purposes, a domestic corporation may claim either a deduction or a credit for foreign income tax payments, but not both.[36] If the taxpayer elects to claim a foreign tax credit, the credit is limited to the portion of the domestic corporation's pre-credit U.S. tax attributable to its foreign source taxable income.[37] A domestic corporation that receives a dividend from a 10 percent-or-more-owned foreign corporation may also claim a deemed paid foreign tax credit for the portion of the foreign corporation's foreign income taxes which are attributable to the dividend.[38] When a domestic corporation claims a deemed paid foreign tax credit, it must gross up its dividend income by the amount of the deemed paid foreign income taxes.[39]

In contrast to federal law, no state allows a corporation to claim a credit for foreign income taxes. However, some states allow a deduction for foreign income taxes, but generally only if a deduction is claimed for federal tax purposes. For federal tax purposes, taxpayers generally elect to claim a foreign tax credit under Code Sec. 901 rather than a deduction under Code Sec. 164, because a credit is usually more valuable than a deduction. A handful of states allow a deduction even if the taxpayer claims the credit for federal tax purposes. Many states, such as California, do not permit a deduction for foreign income taxes, regardless of whether a deduction or a credit is claimed for federal tax purposes.[40]

---

[35] 724 N.W.2d 526 (Minn. Sup. Ct., 2006).

[36] Code Secs. 164, 275 and 901.

[37] Code Sec. 904.

[38] Code Sec. 902.

[39] Code Sec. 78.

[40] Cal. Rev. and Tax Code § 24345.

¶ 1507 STATE VERSUS FEDERAL NEXUS STANDARDS FOR FOREIGN CORPORATIONS

.01 Federal Nexus Standards

U.S. trade or business. If the foreign corporation is "engaged in trade or business within the United States," the United States taxes the net amount of income effectively connected with that U.S. trade or business at the regular graduated rates.[41] Neither the Code nor the Regulations provide a comprehensive definition of the *term trade or business.* Code Sec. 864(b) provides that a U.S. trade or business includes "the performance of personal services within the United States," but does not include the trading of stocks, securities or commodities, if such trades are either made through an independent agent or are made for the taxpayer's own account (unless the taxpayer is a dealer). These exceptions do not apply if the foreign corporation has an office in the United States through which the trades are made. Case law suggests that a foreign corporation is engaged in a U.S. trade or business if its employees are engaged in considerable, continuous, and regular business activity within the United States.[42] The conduct of a U.S. trade or business by a domestic subsidiary corporation is not imputed to a foreign parent corporation.[43] However, if a partnership, estate, or trust is engaged in a U.S. trade or business, then each partner or beneficiary is considered to be engaged in a U.S. trade or business.[44]

Permanent establishment. The United States has entered into bilateral income tax treaties with approximately 60 foreign countries, including most of its major trading partners. The United States Model Income Tax Convention of November 15, 2006 (hereinafter the "U.S. Model Treaty") reflects the baseline negotiating position of the United States in establishing income tax treaties with other countries. Many treaties are patterned after, or have provisions similar to, the U.S. Model Treaty. Therefore, it is used as a reference point in the following discussion of treaty provisions.

A primary goal of income tax treaties is to mitigate international double taxation through tax reductions or exemptions on certain types of income derived by residents of one treaty country from sources within the other treaty country. These tax benefits are available only to a treaty country "resident," which is generally defined as any person who, under the country's internal laws, is subject to taxation by reason of domicile, residence, citizenship, place of management, place of incorporation, or other criterion of a similar nature.[45]

Treaties generally include a permanent establishment provision, which provides that the business profits of a foreign corporation that is a resident of the treaty country are exempt from U.S. taxation unless the foreign corporation carries on business in the United States through a permanent establishment situated therein. If a foreign corporation has a permanent establishment in the United States, the

---

[41] Code Sec. 882.

[42] *See*, for example, *Spermacet Whaling & Shipping Co. S/A v. Commissioner*, 30 T.C. 618 (1958); and *Inverworld, Inc. v. Commissioner*, 71 TCM 3231 (1996).

[43] *Eugene Higgins v. Commissioner*, 312 U.S. 212 (1941).

[44] Code Sec. 875.

[45] Article 4 (¶ 1304.04) of U.S. Model Treaty.

¶1507.01

United States may tax the foreign corporation business profits, but only to the extent those business profits are attributable to the permanent establishment.[46]

A *permanent establishment* generally includes a fixed place of business, such as a place of management, a branch, an office, a factory, a workshop, or a mine, well, quarry, or other place of natural resource extraction. There are numerous exceptions, however. In particular, a permanent establishment does not include the following:

1. The use of facilities solely for the purpose of storage, display or delivery of goods or merchandise belonging to the foreign corporation;

2. The maintenance of a stock of goods or merchandise belonging to the foreign corporation solely for the purpose of storage, display or delivery;

3. The maintenance of a stock of goods or merchandise belonging to the foreign corporation solely for the purpose of processing by another enterprise;

4. The maintenance of a fixed place of business solely for the purpose of purchasing goods or merchandise, or of collecting information, for the foreign corporation;

5. The maintenance of a fixed place of business solely for the purpose of carrying on, for the foreign corporation, any other activity of a preparatory or auxiliary character;

6. The maintenance of a fixed place of business solely for any combination of the activities mentioned above, provided that the overall activity of the fixed place of business resulting from this combination is of a preparatory or auxiliary character.

A permanent establishment also exists if employees or other dependent agents of the foreign corporation habitually exercise in the United States an authority to conclude sales contracts in the taxpayer's name. Employees who limit their activities to auxiliary or preparatory functions, such as collecting information about potential customers, with sales concluded in the home country, will not create a permanent establishment. Marketing products in the United States solely through independent brokers or distributors also does not create a permanent establishment. Finally, the mere presence of a U.S. subsidiary does not create a permanent establishment for a parent company incorporated in another country.[47]

Treaty permanent establishment provisions are not binding for state nexus purposes, however, because income tax treaties generally apply only to selected types of federal taxes.[48]

.02 State Nexus Standards

Overview. In contrast to the federal nexus standards of engaging in a trade or business within the United States or carrying on business in the United States through a permanent establishment situated therein, state income tax nexus stan-

---

[46] Article 7 (¶ 1304.07) of U.S. Model Treaty.
[47] Article 5 (¶ 1304.05) of U.S. Model Treaty.

[48] Article 2 (¶ 1304.02) of U.S. Model Treaty.

¶1507.02

dards generally require only a physical presence within the state of a type that is not protected by Public Law 86-272. In addition, some states have enacted economic nexus or factor presence nexus standards, under which an in-state physical presence is not an absolute prerequisite for income tax nexus. Instead, licensing intangibles or making substantial sales in the state can, by itself, be sufficient to create state income tax nexus.

As a consequence, it is possible for a foreign corporation to have nexus for state but not federal income tax purposes. For example, if a foreign corporation leases warehouse space in a state solely for the purpose of storing and delivering its merchandise to U.S. customers, the physical presence of company-owned inventory would generally create state income tax nexus, but not necessarily federal income tax nexus, because the mere storage of inventory does not constitute a permanent establishment.

Physical presence test. Historically, states have asserted that virtually any type of in-state business activity creates nexus for an out-of-state corporation. Such behavior reflects the reality that it is politically more appealing to tax out-of-state corporations than to raise taxes on in-state business interests. The desire of state lawmakers and tax officials to, in effect, export the local tax burden has been counterbalanced by the Due Process Clause and Commerce Clause of the U.S. Constitution. The U.S Constitution prohibits a state from taxing an out-of-state corporation unless the requirements of both the Due Process Clause and the Commerce Clause are satisfied. The Due Process Clause provides that no state shall "deprive any person of life, liberty or property, without due process of law," and the Commerce Clause gives Congress the exclusive authority to regulate interstate commerce.

In *National Bellas Hess, Inc. v. Department of Revenue*,[49] the Supreme Court established the principle that constitutional nexus requires an in-state physical presence, at least with respect to sales and use taxes. In this case, the Court ruled that Illinois could not require a Missouri-based mail-order vendor to collect use tax on sales to Illinois residents, because the Missouri corporation had no offices, property, employees or any other type of physical presence in Illinois. In 1992, the Supreme Court reaffirmed the physical presence requirement in Quill Corp. v. North Dakota[50], which was another case involving the collection of use tax by an out-of-state mail-order company. However, the Court did not specifically address the issue of whether the physical presence test also applied to income tax nexus.

Public Law 86-272. Another major federal restriction on state tax jurisdiction is Public Law 86-272,[51] which Congress enacted in 1959 to provide out-of-state corporations with a limited safe harbor from the imposition of state taxes on "net income." Specifically, Public Law 86-272 prohibits a state from taxing the income of an out-of-state corporation (i.e., a corporation that is not incorporated in the taxing state) if the corporation's only in-state activity is solicitation of orders by company representatives for sales of tangible personal property, which orders are sent

---

[49] 386 U.S. 753 (1967).
[50] 504 U.S. 298 (1992).

[51] 15 U.S.C. 381.

¶1507.02

outside the state for approval or rejection, and if approved, are filled by shipment or delivery from a point outside the state. By its terms, Public Law 86-272 applies only to "interstate commerce" and does not directly apply to foreign commerce. Individual states are free, however, to extend the protections of Public Law 86-272 to foreign commerce to ensure that foreign and interstate commerce are treated the same.

Although Public Law 86-272 can provide significant protections, it has several important limitations. First, it applies only to taxes imposed on net income, and therefore provides no protection against the imposition of a sales and use tax collection obligation, gross receipts taxes (e.g., Ohio commercial activity tax, or Washington business and occupation tax), or corporate franchise taxes imposed on net worth or capital. Second, the protection of Public Law 86-272 is available only to businesses that sell tangible personal property. It provides no protection to businesses that lease tangible personal property, sell services, sell or lease real estate, or sell or license intangibles. Third, for businesses that do sell tangible personal property, their employees must limit their in-state activities to the solicitation of orders that are sent outside the state for approval, and if approved, are filled by shipment or delivery from a point outside the state. Public Law 86-272 does not protect the presence of salespersons who perform nonsolicitation activities, such as repairs, customer training, or technical assistance, within a state.

Economic nexus. In *Quill*, the Supreme Court ruled that a corporation satisfies the Commerce Clause's "substantial nexus" requirement only if the taxpayer has a physical presence in the state. Yet, in *Geoffrey, Inc. v. South Carolina Tax Commissioner,*[52] the South Carolina Supreme Court held that a trademark holding company that licensed its intangibles for use in South Carolina had nexus for income tax purposes despite the lack of any tangible property or employees in South Carolina. Geoffrey was the trademark holding company of the toy retailer, Toys "R" Us. Geoffrey was incorporated and domiciled in Delaware and had a license agreement with South Carolina retailers allowing them to use its trademarks and trade names, including the Toys "R" Us trademark, in exchange for a percentage of net sales. The court rejected Geoffrey's claim that it had not purposefully directed its activities toward South Carolina and held that, by licensing intangibles for use in the state and receiving income in exchange for their use, Geoffrey had the minimum connection and substantial nexus with South Carolina required by the Due Process Clause and the Commerce Clause. The *Geoffrey* court did not follow the precedent established by *Quill* because it believed that ruling applied only to the issue of nexus for sales and use tax purposes.

Since the *Geoffrey* decision in 1993, there has been a significant amount of litigation regarding the issue of whether an in-state economic presence is, by itself, sufficient to satisfy the Commerce Clause's substantial nexus requirement. In addition, many states have adopted economic nexus standards. The highest courts in several states have ruled that an economic presence is sufficient to create income

---

[52] 437 S.E.2d 13 (S.C. 1993), cert. denied, 114 S. Ct. 550 (1993).

tax nexus in cases dealing with out-of-state intangible property holding companies,[53] as well as cases dealing with out-of-state credit card banks.[54]

Factor presence nexus. In addition to the theory of economic nexus, some states has adopted a "factor presence" nexus standard for income tax nexus. Under this approach, a corporation has substantial nexus in a state if the corporation's sales in the state exceed a specified threshold. For example, for purposes of the California corporate franchise tax, a corporation is considered to be doing business in the state if sales of the taxpayer in California, including sales by the taxpayer's agents and independent contractors, exceed the lesser of $529,562 (2014) or 25 percent of the taxpayer's total sales.[55] The protections of Public Law 86-272 still apply to a corporation selling tangible personal property.

---

[53] *Lanco, Inc. v. Division of Taxation*, 908 A.2d 176 (N.J. Sup. Ct., 2006), cert. denied, U.S. Sup. Ct., 06-1236, June 18, 2007; and *KFC Corporation v. Iowa Department of Revenue*, 792 N.W.2d 308 (Ia. Sup. Ct., 2010), cert. denied, U.S. No. 10-1340, Oct. 3, 2011.

[54] *Tax Commissioner v. MBNA America Bank, N.A.*, 640 S.E.2d 226 (W.Va. Sup. Ct., 2006), cert. denied, U.S.

Sup. Ct., 06-1228, June 18, 2007; and *Capital One Bank v. Commissioner of Revenue*, 899 N.E.2d 76 (Mass., Sup. Ct., 2009), cert. denied, U.S. Sup. Ct., No. 08-1169, June 22, 2009.

[55] Cal. Rev. and Tax Code § 23101.

Chapter 16
International Tax Practice and Procedure

¶ 1601   INTRODUCTION

As the major economies of the world have become global in nature, the frequency and complexity of cross-border transactions have increased significantly. The combination of expense allocation methods and the foreign tax credit limitation has generally resulted in U.S. companies having excess foreign tax credits.[1] Likewise, foreign-owned multinationals with U.S. subsidiaries are subject to a myriad of reporting requirements[2] and provisions with respect to transfer pricing, the deductibility of related party interest[3] and, in turn, the capital structure of their U.S. subsidiaries. While many of the same procedural issues present in Internal Revenue Service (IRS) audits of domestic businesses are germane, there are other unique problems facing U.S.-based multinationals (outbound activities) as well as U.S. subsidiaries of foreign parent companies (inbound activities). These issues often focus on the ability of the IRS to obtain information from abroad.

In addition to dealing with the IRS, multi-national companies must be concerned with foreign tax authorities. The world-wide audits of complex international tax structures and transactions is the impetus behind the Organization for Economic Cooperation and Development's (OECD) recent initiative on Base Erosion and Profits Shifting (BEPS), which provides guidance for dealing with harmful tax practices. Although the various guidance that the OECD provides is not binding on

---

[1] Code Secs. 901 through 904.
[2] Code Sec. 6038A and 6114.

[3] Code Sec. 163(j).

its thirty-four member countries, one of which is the United States, the OECD's guidance is influential.

¶ 1602 ORGANIZATION OF THE INTERNAL REVENUE SERVICE INTERNATIONAL OFFICES

The International Examiners are assigned to the industry groups within the Large Business and International (LB&I) Division,[4] which is one of the four Divisions of the IRS. LB&I further divides itself into five international functions: Assistant Deputy Commissioner, International; International Business Compliance; International Individual Compliance; International Strategy; and Transfer Pricing Operations.[5]

The Assistant Deputy Commissioner, International oversees tax treaty administration, including the Treaty Assistance and Interpretation Team. The office also interacts with other countries to exchange information while assisting the Treasury Department in negotiations of tax treaties and other international agreements.

International Business Compliance provides technical expertise on international tax issues to ensure that multi-national companies comply with their U.S. tax obligations.

International Individual Compliance develops strategies and conducts examinations with respect to the foreign activities of U.S. persons and U.S. activities of foreign persons. This function is also responsible for enforcing withholding under the Foreign Account Tax Compliance Act (FATCA)[6] and has assumed all the international functions regarding individuals that the Small Business/Self-Employed Division previously performed.[7]

International Strategy oversees the development and implementation of all aspects of the IRS's international strategic program, including risk assessment, data management, trend analysis, training, and knowledge management capabilities while assisting with developing and maintaining key contacts outside the IRS.

Transfer Pricing Operations includes two segments—the Advance Pricing and Mutual Agreement Program (APMA) and the Transfer Pricing Practice (TPP). By acting as the U.S. Competent Authority, APMA is responsible for negotiating advance pricing agreements with taxpayers and foreign tax administrations and for resolving double tax cases with foreign tax administrations. The Transfer Pricing Practice assists examination teams in transfer pricing case selection and case development to ensure optimal compliance impact and the efficient resolution of transfer pricing disputes.

¶ 1603 INTERNATIONAL EXAMINATIONS

Given the extraordinary complexity of the international provisions of the Internal Revenue Code, the importance and involvement of the International Examiner has increased in multinational corporation audits. Recognizing this, the IRS has

---

[4] IRM 4.60.4.

[5] Large Business and International (LB&I) Division Directory, April 17, 2014.

[6] *See* ¶ 903.

[7] IRM 4.1.9.

retrained many of its domestic agents as International Examiners. Whereas previously International Examiners were located only in large metropolitan areas, many audits of corporations in rural areas with international operations now have International Examiners assigned to their audits.

The International Examiners are crucial in any audit involving international issues. Involved in a complex and sophisticated tax administration, the International Examiners receive special training to deal with issues involving controlled foreign corporations, cross-border transfers and reorganizations, transfer pricing, foreign tax credit issues, export benefits, and withholding taxes.[8] Although the International Examiners are assigned to the LB&I Division, they may receive referrals from the Small Business/Self-Employed (SB/SE) Division when international issues arise.[9]

Due to the increased emphasis by the Internal Revenue Service on intercompany transfer pricing, the IRS has created the Transfer Pricing Team, a nationwide group of transfer pricing specialists who assist on transfer pricing issues at all stages of a controversy—examination, appeals, and litigation. The Transfer Pricing Team includes economists, who identify potential transfer pricing issues early in the examination process and assist in gathering factual information in support of the IRS's position.

.01 Coordinated Industry Case Examinations

The IRS established the Coordinated Industry Case Program to provide a team approach to the examination of very large corporate cases that meet specific criteria for size and complexity. This program brings together as one unit for audit purposes the primary taxpayer and all of the taxpayer's effectively controlled corporations and other entities. A Coordinated Industry Case, therefore, will usually involve a large group of closely affiliated, centrally controlled, widely dispersed, and highly diversified business entities. As a result, the coordinated audit group may include domestic and foreign corporations, partnerships, joint ventures, syndicates, unincorporated businesses, individual, trusts, estates, foundations, pension and profit sharing trusts and other exempt organizations.[10]

.02 Other Examinations

When the multinational taxpayer's examination is not classified as a Coordinated Industry Case, the taxpayer and the examination team may still hold a pre-examination conference. During this meeting, the taxpayer should meet with the team manager for purposes of providing basic data, establishing the scope and depth of the examination and arranging for computer assistance.[11] The taxpayer will also learn who the IRS has assigned to its audit and may want to begin its own investigation to better prepare for the audit. Also at this meeting, if not before, the

---

[8] IRM 4.60.4.7.

[9] IRM Exhibits 4.60.5-1 and 4.60.5-2.

[10] IRM 4.45.2.2.2.

[11] The IRS's goals for the pre-audit conference often include reaching an agreement with the taxpayer regarding (i) the lines of communication between the IRS and the taxpayer, (ii) the use of taxpayer resources, such as office space, (iii) the procedures for providing the IRS with returns of related parties, (iv) the procedures for the taxpayer to present documentation of items that may reduce its tax liability, (v) the procedures for resolving questions regarding the content of IDRs, (vi) the periods of time for submitting and responding to IDRs, and (vii) procedures and timing of the examination of off-site records and facilities.

taxpayer should agree, preferably in writing,[12] to procedures during the audit with respect to international issues.

.03 Taxpayer Resolution Options

Similar to domestic examinations, international taxpayers have many options to resolve international tax controversies, which are divided between pre-examination resolution techniques, examination resolution techniques, and post-examination resolution techniques.[13]

The goal of the pre-examination resolution techniques is to avoid any examination of an issue. These techniques include industry issue resolution[14], pre-filing agreements,[15] advance pricing agreements,[16] determination letters,[17] private letter rulings,[18] and the compliance assurance process.[19]

Examination resolution techniques try to streamline the resolution of the issue at the examination level. These techniques include technical advice memoranda,[20] fast track settlement,[21] delegated settlement authority from appeals,[22] accelerated issue resolution,[23] and early referral to appeals.[24]

Post-examination resolution techniques try to resolve a matter without going to litigation. These techniques include post-appeals mediation[25] and binding arbitration.[26]

.04 International Practice Units of LB&I

To coordinate its approach to examining international tax issues, LB&I created forty-six International Practice Units. These International Practice Units provide a knowledge resource to the International Examiners with a guide to the process of examining a particular issue that includes the process steps, ancillary issues, and training resources. Oddly, these resources do not contain sample Information Document Requests to use when auditing an issue. The Appendix to this Chapter contains a complete list of the forty-six International Practice Units, almost all of which are dealt with in this book in one form or another. Taxpayers facing an examination of any of these issues should review these materials on the IRS's website.[27]

Previously, LB&I used an Industry Issue Focus strategy, which tried to coordinate greater national control and consistency over important issues that range across industry lines.[28] Pursuant to this initiative, the International Examiners identified potential compliance issues through the normal course of an audit.

[12] In many IRS areas, there appears to be an objective to have a written audit agreement with every taxpayer under audit.

[13] Misey and Goller, *Federal Taxation: Practice and Procedure*, 11th ed. (2014), pp. 146-152.

[14] Rev. Proc. 2003-36, 2003-1 CB 859; IRM 4.45.5.7.

[15] Rev. Proc. 2009-14, 2009-1 CB 324; IRM 4.46.5.6.12.

[16] Rev. Proc. 2006-9, 2006-1 CB 78; Rev. Proc. 2008-31, 2008-1 CB 1133.

[17] IRM 7.25.1; Rev. Proc. 2015-6, 2015-1 IRB 200.

[18] IRM 32.3.2; Rev. Proc. 2015-1, 2015-1 IRB 1.

[19] Ann. 2005-87, 2005-2 CB 1144.

[20] IRM 33.2.1; Rev Proc. 2015-2, 2015-1 IRB 105.

[21] Rev. Proc. 2003-40, 2003-1 CB 1044; IRM 8.26.8.

[22] IRM 1.2.43.22; IRM 1.2.43.23.

[23] Rev. Proc. 94-67, 1994-2 CB 800; IRM 4.46.5.6.8.

[24] Rev. Proc. 99-28, 1999-2 CB 109; IRM 4.46.5.6.11.

[25] Rev. Proc. 2009-44, 2009-2 CB 462; IRM 8.26.5.

[26] Rev. Proc. 2006-44, 2006-2 800; IRM 8.26.6.

[27] *International Practice Units,* issued by the IRS on December 15, 2014.

[28] IRM 4.51.5.

Unfortunately, the focus resulted in the control of various audits by individuals that did not have contact with the taxpayer. Although the Industry Issue Focus no longer exists, a taxpayer subject to an audit of any of the Focus' issues should consult the program's materials to better prepare for audit.[29]

.05 Statute of Limitations

The statute of limitations for the IRS to make an assessment is normally three years,[30] but may extend to six years due to a 25% understatement of gross income.[31] Moreover, an extension to six years may also occur when amounts attributable to foreign financial assets[32] total more than $5,000 and are not reported on a return.

> **Example 16.1:** USCo, a U.S. company, wholly owns and, therefore, files a Form 5471 for ForSub, a foreign subsidiary. ForSub owes $35,000 of additional income tax attributable to $100,000 of interest that constituted Subpart F income. USCo failed to report this item of Subpart F income on the Form 5471 filed with its 20X1 return on September 15, 20X2. If this omission exceeds 25% of gross income, the statute of limitations on the $100,000 of Subpart F interest income is the 6-year statute of limitations, which expires on September 15, 20X8.

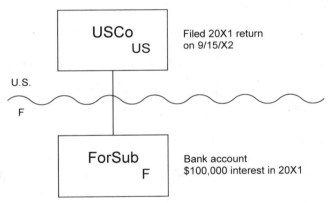

The statute of limitations for a return only begin to run when the taxpayer has reported to the IRS all the information that a number of Code sections[33] require.[34] In effect, the entire return is considered not filed, failing to trigger the running of the statute of limitations when a taxpayer has not attached a required information reporting schedule.

> **Example 16.2:** USCo is a U.S. corporation that wholly-owns ForCo, a foreign corporation. USCo files its Form 1120 for 20X1 on September 15, 20X2

---

[29] The internationally-oriented Industry Focus Issues included (i) section 936 exit strategies, (ii) domestic production deduction under Code Sec. 199, (iii) foreign earnings repatriation, (iv) foreign tax credit generators, (v) international hybrid instrument transactions, (vi) cost-sharing arrangements with buy-in payments, (vii) reporting and withholding on U.S.-source fixed, determinable, annual, or periodic income, (viii) cost-sharing stock-based compensation, and (ix) extraterritorial income exclusion effective date and transition rules.

[30] Code Sec. 6501(a).

[31] Code Sec. 6501(e).

[32] Code Sec. 6038(D).

[33] Code Secs. 1295(b), 1298(f), 6038, 6038(A), 6038(B), 6038(D), 6046, 6046(A) and 6048.

[34] Code Sec. 6501(c)(8).

¶1603.05

without filing a Form 5471. The 3-year statute of limitations with respect to any item on the return will not begin to run until USCo files a Form 5471.

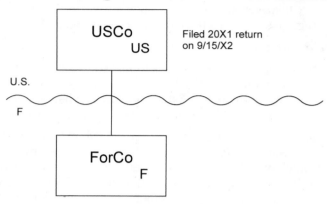

Although the next logical step is to treat this as a failure to file a return, the IRS has not stated whether it would assert the delinquency penalty in these situations.

¶ 1604 IRS PROCEDURAL TOOLS

The primary authority for recordkeeping requirements of an entity potentially liable for U.S. tax is Code Sec. 6001 of the Internal Revenue Code and the related Regulations.[35] Accordingly, the IRS has the specific authority to examine any books, papers, records, or other data that may be relevant or material to ascertain the correctness of any return, determining the tax liability of any person, or collecting any tax. Since most taxpayers and other individuals voluntarily produce records and answer questions when the IRS requests, this primary authority in itself is normally sufficient to obtain the necessary information.

An initial problem confronting U.S. taxpayers is that most of their foreign affiliates do not have records that are in a usable format, as the foreign affiliates often prepare records in foreign languages. Must a U.S. taxpayer spend a large amount of time and money translating the documents into English for the IRS?

This issue was confronted in the case of *Nissei Sangyo America, Ltd. v. United States*.[36] *Nissei* involved the audit of a U.S. subsidiary of a Japanese parent. In response to an IRS summons, the U.S. subsidiary had randomly selected documents relating to the issue under examination and provided full translations. The Japanese parent had also randomly selected and translated documents. In addition, the U.S. subsidiary translated the subject matter headings or titles of 1,441 pages of Japanese correspondence and prepared English translation keys for the travel

---

[35] The Regulations may require generally that any person subject to tax under subtitle A of the Code ". . . or any person required to file a return of information with respect to income, shall keep such permanent books or account or records . . . as are sufficient to establish the amount of gross income, deductions, credits, or other matters required to be shown by such person in any return of such tax or information." Reg. § 1.6001-1(a). Additionally, "[t]he director may require any person, by

notice served upon him, to make such returns, render such statements, or keep such specific records as will enable the director to determine whether or not such person is liable for tax under subtitle A of the Code." Reg. § 1.6001-1(d).

[36] DC Ill., 95-2 USTC ¶ 50,327. The internal procedures of the IRS require the IRS to request documents, review them and then specify the documents to be translated. Reg. § 1.6038A-3(b)(3).

expense authorization forms. The IRS demanded that all documents described in the summonses be translated to English, which the company estimated would cost from $850,000 to $1.5 million. The court held that the IRS could not compel the translation of documents that were not relevant to the tax liability or that the IRS already had in its possession.[37]

Most cases do not involve translation costs of $1 million, but just as there are subtle nuances of meaning in the definitions in the Internal Revenue Code, there are subtle nuances of meaning in the translation of languages. Considering the diverse army of employees that the IRS has to consult with for translations, a representative should encourage a taxpayer to engage a translator who will resolve any ambiguities in meaning in the taxpayer's favor. Although *Nissei* involved summons enforcement, this lesson is applicable to any type of information gathering tool the IRS may use.

.01 Information Document Requests

The IRS typically exercises its general authority under Code section 6001 in an Information Document Request (IDR). An IDR requests information or documents from taxpayers when there are voluminous records to examine. Requested on Form 4564 (a copy of which is reproduced in the Appendix to this Chapter), an IDR provides the IRS a convenient means to request information and simultaneously yields a permanent record of what was requested of or received from, and returned to the taxpayer.

An International Examiner in both Coordinated Industry Case and non-Coordinated Industry Case audits will often begin by issuing IDRs for information relevant to the scope of the review. For example, if intercompany purchases or sales of inventory exist, a typical IDR would request a copy of any intercompany pricing agreements as well as any contemporaneous documentation of transfer pricing methodology.[38] As a further example, if the examination involved a foreign tax credit, the International Examiner would generally request copies of the proof of foreign income taxes paid and the allocation and apportionment schedules for the sourcing of expenses.

After reviewing the information gathered from these initial IDRs, the International Examiner will focus on those areas with the largest potential for possible adjustments. As the examination progresses, IDRs generally become more narrow in scope and tend to focus on specific items or transactions.

In addition to this authority, an International Examiner can employ several procedural tools to obtain information beyond that obtained via IDRs. These include on site inspection, summons, designated summons, formal document requests, transfer pricing documentation, Code Secs. 6038A and 6038, and exchanges of information under treaties.

---

[37] *See* the general summons standard of *M. Powell*, SCt, 642 USTC ¶ 9858, 379 US 48, *infra*.

[38] Code Sec. 6662(e)(3)(B)(i)(III).

.02 On Site Inspections

In addition to IDRs, International Examiners appear to have taken an increased interest in foreign site visits and plant tours over the past few years.[39] While IRS budget constraints and internal administrative requirements may occasionally affect the number or duration of such visits, taxpayers should expect such requests and prepare to respond. The taxpayer should remember that the IRS is requesting, not ordering, and that any request may be negotiated in terms of choosing the facility to visit (the taxpayer may want to substitute a domestic plant for a foreign plant), the duration of the visit, the timing of the visit, and the number of IRS employees involved. Careful planning of any such trip may result in an opportunity to present, in effect, key facts supporting the taxpayer's position. The taxpayer should prepare the plant personnel for the visit. Two issues result in the most foreign plant site visits—transfer pricing and Subpart F. For transfer pricing, the International Examiners want to see the functions performed and risks assumed at the foreign plant (see ¶ 1202.01). For Subpart F, the International Examiners want to see if the activities at the foreign plant constitute manufacturing, an exception to foreign base company sales income (see ¶ 501.06).[40] The taxpayer may consider pre-screening the tour to determine if the plant's operations cover processes or procedures relevant to the audit cycle and pre-interviewing all involved personnel to sensitize them to the potential issues.

.03 The Summons Power

To give force and meaning to this general authority to examine, the IRS has the power to compel a taxpayer or any other person to produce records and to testify under oath, which the IRS executes by issuing a summons.[41] The IRS may summon any person to appear at a time and place named in the summons for the purpose of giving testimony under oath and producing books, papers, records, or other data. The IRS has delegated the authority to issue summonses to those agents and other personnel within the IRS who are responsible for the examination of returns, collection of taxes, and investigation of tax offenses.[42] Therefore, International Examiners, Revenue Agents, Tax Auditors, Revenue Officers and Special Agents may all issue a summons.

When a corporation is under examination, the IRS may direct the summons to either a specific corporate officer or the corporation itself.[43] The summons should indicate the officer's corporate position or title. When a corporation receives a summons, the IRS must serve an officer, director, managing agent or other person authorized to accept service of process on behalf of the corporation.

---

[39] I.R.M. 4.46.3.10.2 through 4.46.3.10.5.

[40] IRM Exhibit 4.61.3-1. International Examiners have the following instructions for plant tours: (i) Obtain information about departmental cost sheets or schedules; (ii) Learn the training requirements of each type of production employee; (iii) Obtain any records regarding sales to all customers; (iv) Ascertain the extent of product development performed at the plant; (v) Interview plant employees; (vi) If the company is a controlled foreign corporation, determine how and to whom it sells its products; (vii) Obtain all company manuals regarding the operations of the plant; (viii) Obtain all job descriptions prior to the plant tour; (ix) Obtain all annual evaluations of the employees to be interviewed; and (x) Obtain all company "programmer" manuals. This manual offers guidance to the programmer to construct the program, so that software can be readily translated and localized. *see also, IRS International Continuing Professional Education materials*, Chicago, Illinois, May 2013.

[41] Code Sec. 7602(a)(2).

[42] T.D. 6421, 1959-2 CB 433; Delegation Order No. 4.

[43] IRM 25.5.2.3.

¶1604.02

After service of the summons, the individual serving the summons prepares and signs a certificate of service on the reverse side of the Form 2039 retained by the IRS. The server enters the date, time, and manner of service on the certificate. The signed certificate of service is evidence in any proceeding to enforce the summons.[44] The date the summons requires for compliance cannot be less than ten days from the date the IRS serves the summons.[45]

Scope of the summons power. The IRS may only use the summons for the purposes set forth in Code Sec. 7602. These purposes are the verification, determination, and collection of the tax liability of any person. The IRS also has specific authorization to issue summonses for the purpose of investigating any criminal tax offense.[46]

Pursuant to the standards of *United States v. Powell*,[47] to enforce a summons, the IRS must show that:

- There is a legitimate purpose for the audit;
- The material sought is relevant to that purpose;
- The material sought is not already within the IRS's possession; and
- Those administrative steps that are required by the Internal Revenue Code are followed.

Use of summonses in Tax Court proceedings. The use of administrative summonses by the IRS during Tax Court proceedings has raised objections by taxpayers. The Tax Court discovery rules permitting both parties to obtain relevant information before trial are much more restricted in their scope than the summons power available to the IRS. In certain situations, the Tax Court has held that to allow the IRS in a pending case to use evidence obtained through issuing a summons would give the government an unfair advantage over the taxpayer. In effect, such use of the summons would permit the IRS to circumvent the limitations of the Tax Court's discovery rules. Therefore, the Tax Court will issue a protective order to preclude the IRS from using information obtained by such abusive use of a summons.[48] In *Ash v. Commissioner*,[49] the Tax Court set forth its guidelines to determine whether it should issue a protective order when the IRS tries to obtain information during a pending case by means of a summons.

Where Tax Court litigation has commenced and the IRS issues a summons for the same taxpayer and taxable year involved in the litigation, the Tax Court will issue a protective order to prevent the IRS from using any of the summoned evidence in the litigation.[50] However, the Tax Court will not issue a protective order if the IRS can show that it issued the summons for a sufficient reason that was independent of the pending litigation.

When the IRS issue the summons before the taxpayer commences litigation by filing a Tax Court petition, the Tax Court will not issue a protective order regarding

---

[44] Code Sec. 7603.

[45] Code Sec. 7605(a). A longer period is required for third-party recordkeeper summonses.

[46] Code Sec. 7602(b).

[47] SCt, 64-2 USTC ¶ 9858, 379 US 48, 85 SCt 248.

[48] Tax Court Rule 103.

[49] 96 TC 459, Dec. 47,221.

[50] The Tax Court issued such an order in *Universal Manufacturing Co.*, 93 TC 589, Dec. 46,154.

any information obtained as a result of the summons. The Tax Court, in *Ash*, explained that before a taxpayer files a petition, the Tax Court does not have jurisdiction and there is no basis for viewing the summons as an attempt to undermine the Tax Court's discovery rules.[51]

Finally, where litigation has commenced, and the IRS issues a summons with regard to a different taxpayer or a different taxable year, the Tax Court in *Ash* normally will not issue a protective order.[52] However, the Tax Court stated that it would issue a protective order if the taxpayer could show that the IRS lacked an independent and sufficient reason for the summons.

.04 Designated Summonses

If, after issuing a summons, the IRS does not obtain the desired information, the IRS may consider issuing a designated summons.[53]

A designated summons tolls the running of the statute of limitations for the duration of the judicial enforcement proceeding and for either 30 or 120 days thereafter, depending on whether or not the court orders compliance with the summons. The legislative history indicates Congress was concerned that taxpayers made a practice of responding slowly to IRS requests for information without extending the statute of limitations.[54] Congress did not intend to extend the statute of limitations in a large number of cases, but to encourage taxpayers to provide requested information on a timely basis by realizing that the IRS had this tool available. In addition to satisfying the aforementioned *Powell* standards, the internal procedures the IRS personnel have to follow to issue designated summonses impedes their issuance. Both the LB&I Division Commissioner and Division Counsel-LB&I[55] must approve a designated summons, which the IRS must issue at least 60 days before the expiration of the statute of limitations.[56]

> **Example 16.3:** A distributor of computers, USAco is a subsidiary of ASIAco. USAco buys computers from ASIAco and resells them in the United States. The IRS's International Examiner conducts a transfer pricing audit of USAco. After USAco fails to respond to the International Examiner's IDR requesting all agreements between USAco and ASIAco, just over 60 days remain on the statute of limitations. USAco will not sign a consent to extend the statute of limitations. Concerned about the possibility that the statute of limitations will expire, the International Examiner issues a designated summons for the agreements. The designated summons tolls the statute of limitations during enforcement proceedings and for a short time thereafter.[57]

---

[51] *Bennett*, ND Tex, 2000-2 USTC ¶ 50,717.

[52] In an earlier case involving this type of situation, the issuance of a protective order was justified by the "compelling facts." *Westreco, Inc.*, 60 TCM 824, Dec. 46,882(M), TC Memo. 1990-501.

[53] Code Sec. 6503(j).

[54] *Norwest Corp. v. United States*, 8th Cir., 97-2 USTC ¶ 50,510.

[55] Prop. Reg. § 301.6503(j)-1(c)(1)(i).

[56] Code Sec. 6503(j)(2)(A).

[57] *Derr*, CA-9, 92-2 USTC ¶ 50,369.

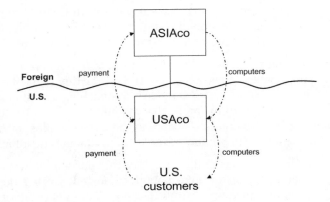

.05 Formal Document Requests

If, through IDRs, the IRS cannot gather the foreign information it considers necessary to conduct its examination, the IRS may issue a formal document request (FDR). Congress did not intend the IRS to use the FDR as a routine tool at the beginning of an examination, but instead as a mechanism for securing information that the IRS could not obtain through IDRs.[58] The IRS serves an FDR by sending via either certified or registered mail the Letter 2261 (see the Appendix), which states:

(i) The time and place for the production of the documentation;

(ii) A statement of the reason the documentation previously produced (if any) is not sufficient;

(iii) A description of the documentation; and

(iv) The consequences to the taxpayer of the failure to produce the documentation sought.[59]

If the taxpayer does not furnish the requested information within 90 days of the mailing of the FDR, the taxpayer cannot later introduce the requested documentation at trial.[60] Foreign-based documentation is "any documentation which is outside the United States and which may be relevant or material to the tax treatment of the examined item."[61] Therefore, the IRS has broad authority to request virtually any relevant information as long as the request satisfies the aforementioned *Powell* standards.[62] The purpose of the FDR procedure is to discourage taxpayers from delaying or refusing disclosure of certain foreign-based documentation.

To avoid the later exclusion of documents, the taxpayer must substantially comply with the FDR, which depends on all the facts and circumstances.[63] For example, if the taxpayer submits nine out of ten requested items and the court

---

[58] *See* Joint Committee on Taxation, General Explanation of the Tax Equity and Fiscal Responsibility Act of 1982, HR 4961, 97th Cong., 2d Sess. 246-247.

[59] Code Sec. 982(c)(1).

[60] *Flying Tigers Oil Co. v. Commissioner*, 92 T.C. 1261 (1989).

[61] Code Sec. 982(d).

[62] *Yujuico*, ND Cal, 93-1 USTC ¶ 50,097.

[63] *See Good Karma, LLC v. United States*, N.D. IL, 2008-2 USTC ¶ 50,646.

believes the missing item is the most substantial, the court may find that the taxpayer failed to substantially comply with the FDR. Accordingly, the court could later prevent the taxpayer from introducing the missing documentation.

Any taxpayer that receives an FDR has the right to begin proceedings to quash the request within ninety days after the IRS mails the FDR. The standard for quashing a FDR is the same *Powell* standard for quashing a summons.[64] Moreover, the taxpayer may contend, for example, that the information requested is irrelevant, that the requested information is available in the United States, or that reasonable cause exists for the failure to produce or delay in producing the information.[65]

In a proceeding to quash, the IRS has the burden of proof to show the relevance and materiality of the information requested. During the period that a proceeding to quash or any appeal from that proceeding is pending, the statute of limitations is suspended.[66]

The legislative history to Code Sec. 982 specifies that three factors should be considered in determining whether there is reasonable cause for failure to furnish the requested documentation. These factors are: (i) whether the request is reasonable in scope; (ii) whether the requested documents are available within the United States; and (iii) the reasonableness of the requested place of production within the United States.[67]

An example of an unreasonable scope may be a request "for all the books and records and all the supporting documents for all the entries made in such books or records" for a related foreign entity. However, a request for the general ledger, an analysis of an account, and supporting documents for a particular transaction of such a foreign entity would be reasonable in scope. Moreover, the place of production of records is generally at the taxpayer's place of business or the International Examiner's office. The key to reasonableness of the place for production is its mutual convenience to both the taxpayer and the International Examiner. More specifically, requesting the production of records in New York City by a taxpayer that resides in and is engaged in a trade or business in Los Angeles would be unreasonable.

.06 Transfer Pricing Documentation

As more fully described in Chapter 12 (¶ 1204), the IRS can assess a penalty for transfer pricing transgressions. If applicable, the taxpayer can only show reasonable cause to avoid the penalty by contemporaneously preparing transfer pricing documentation. The voluminous amount of information contained in transfer pricing documentation will aid an International Examiner when auditing any international issue, not merely transfer pricing. As a result, an International Examiner may request transfer pricing documentation even when she is not concerned with the taxpayer's transfer pricing.

---

[64] *Yujuico v. United States*, N.D. Cal, 93-1 USTC ¶ 50,097.

[65] Code Sec. 982(e). Reasonable cause does not exist where a foreign jurisdiction would impose a civil or criminal penalty on the taxpayer for disclosing the requested documentation.

[66] Code Sec. 982(e).

[67] Conference Committee Report on P.L. 97-248, The Tax Equity and Fiscal Responsibility Act of 1982.

¶1604.06

.07 Code Secs. 6038A and 6038

Congressional perception that foreign-owned U.S. subsidiaries were not paying their proper share of U.S. tax and the inability of the IRS to obtain foreign-based documentation caused Congress to expand greatly the application of Code Sec. 6038A. The section places the reporting burden on a U.S. subsidiary for its intercompany transactions with a foreign parent (a foreign corporation that owns at least 25 percent of the U.S. subsidiary). The U.S. subsidiary, the "reporting corporation," must furnish certain information annually and maintain records necessary to determine the correctness of the intercompany transactions. In addition, the U.S. subsidiary must furnish the required information by filing Form 5472 on an annual basis.

Reg. § 1.6038A-3(a)(1) specifies that a U.S. subsidiary "...must keep the permanent books of account or records as required by section 6001 that are sufficient to establish the correctness of the federal income tax return of the corporation, including information, documents, or records ('records') to the extent they may be relevant to determine the correct U.S. tax treatment of transactions..." with its foreign parent. These records may include, for example, cost data, if appropriate, to determine the profit or loss from the transfer pricing of intercompany transactions.

Failure to maintain or timely furnish the required information may result in a penalty of $10,000 for each taxable year that the failure occurs for each foreign party.[68] If any failure continues for more than ninety days after notice of the failure to the reporting corporation, the IRS can assess an additional penalty of $10,000 per thirty-day period while the failure continues. Further penalties apply if the taxpayer fails to maintain records after the ninety-day notification.[69]

More specifically, Code Sec. 6038A(e) allows the IRS to reduce the cost of goods sold when a taxpayer does not obtain its foreign parent's permission to be an agent for the request of certain documents. Within thirty days after an IRS request, a foreign parent must appoint its U.S. subsidiary as its limited agent for service of a summons. Failure to appoint such an agent can result in penalties for noncompliance.[70] In such a case, the LB&I Industry Director in his sole discretion shall determine the amount of the relevant deduction or the cost to the reporting corporation.

The IRS is prepared to adhere to Code Sec. 6038A(e) as shown in *Asat, Inc. v. Commissioner*.[71] In *Asat*, the Tax Court literally applied Code Sec. 6038A(e) against the taxpayer, upholding the IRS's reduction to the cost of goods sold. Following the legislative history, the Tax Court further found irrelevant that the foreign parent during the taxable year in issue was not the parent at the time of the audit.

> **Example 16.4:** A distributor of toy dolls, USAco is a subsidiary of ASIAco. USAco buys toy dolls from ASIAco and resells them in the United States. The IRS's International Examiner conducts a transfer pricing audit of USAco. Wanting to obtain documents from ASIAco, the International Exam-

---

[68] Reg. § 1.6038A-4(a)(1).
[69] *Id.* Reg. § 1.6038A-4(d)(1).

[70] *Id.* Reg. § 1.6038A-5.
[71] 108 TC 147, Dec. 51,966.

iner requests that ASIAco appoint USAco as its agent for service of a summons. If ASIAco does not either appoint USAco as its agent or provide the pricing data to the International Examiner, the IRS can reduce USAco's cost of goods sold to $0.

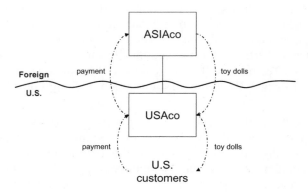

Although there is not the same perception that U.S. parents of foreign subsidiaries are not paying their proper share of U.S. tax, Code Sec. 6038 places a reporting burden for intercompany transactions on a U.S. parent of a controlled foreign corporation. The U.S. owner reports this information by filing Form 5471.

As with the Code Sec. 6038A penalty, the failure to maintain or timely furnish the Code Sec. 6038 information may result in a penalty of $10,000 for each taxable year that the failure occurs.[72] If any failure continues for more than 90 days after notice of the failure, the IRS can assess an additional penalty of $10,000 per 30-day period while the failure continues. If the U.S. owner fails to maintain records after receiving notification, the IRS can levy additional penalties, such as reducing any foreign tax credits taken by the U.S. parent by 10%[73]

> ***Example* 16.5:** Uncle Sam, a U.S. citizen, inherits all the shares of FSub, a controlled foreign corporation that is incorporated in Country F. During the taxable year, FSub pays a gross dividend of $100,000, which FSub reduces by the $10,000 withholding tax that Country F imposes. Although Uncle Sam takes a $10,000 direct foreign tax credit on his return, he never files a Form 5471 for FSub. The IRS can reduce Uncle Sam's foreign tax credit by $1,000.

---

[72] Code Sec. 6038(b).   [73] Code Sec. 6038(c).

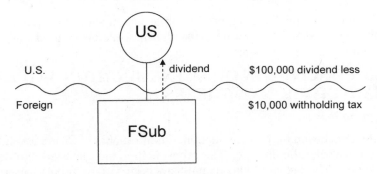

.08 Exchanges of Information Under Tax Treaties

Under the exchange of information provisions of a tax treaty, the IRS can generally request information from a foreign country that is either in the foreign country's possession or available under the respective tax laws of that foreign country. These provisions generally do not require the exchange of information that would disclose any trade or business secret.

The IRS exercises discretion and judgment when both requesting and furnishing information. In general, the IRS will not request information from another country unless the IRS believes: (i) that the information is necessary to determine the tax liability of a specific taxpayer; (ii) the information is not otherwise available; and (iii) the requested information is in the possession of, or available to, the foreign government from whom the information is being requested.[74]

> **Example 16.6:** A distributor of "Crazylegs" sports shoes, USAco is a subsidiary of ASIAco. USAco buys the sports shoes from ASIAco and resells them in the United States. The IRS's International Examiner conducts a transfer pricing audit of USAco. After USAco fails to respond to the International Examiner's IDR requesting all agreements between USAco and ASIAco, the International Examiner requests the information from ASIA country's tax authority pursuant to the exchange of information provision in the U.S.-ASIA tax treaty.

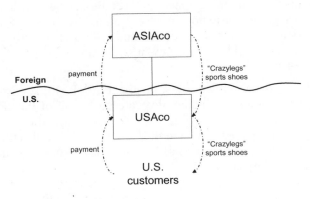

---

[74] *Stuart v. United States*, 109 S.Ct. 1183 (1989).

The IRS's internal guidelines require that information sought from another competent authority must specifically describe the information desired and the reason why the information is necessary.[75]

¶ 1605 CONCLUSION OF AN EXAMINATION AND THE APPEALS DIVISION OF THE IRS

.01 Settling Issues

At the conclusion of the examination, the International Examiner will prepare a report summarizing the findings. The report is then incorporated into the Revenue Agent's report. The taxpayer may dispute any issues in the report with the Appeals Office along with other domestic issues raised during the examination.

Under the authority of Code Sec. 7121, the team manager may settle certain issues over which there is disagreement by entering a closing agreement. This authority exists where the Appeals Office has previously approved a settlement agreement involving the same issue in a Coordinated Industry Case in a prior year involving the same taxpayer or a taxpayer directly involved in the transaction.[76]

.02 Protest Requirements

After completion of an examination, the examining office may issue the taxpayer a thirty-day letter proposing a deficiency. The taxpayer may object to any proposed tax adjustments and request a conference with the Appeals Office by filing a protest with the Appeals Office. The taxpayer must formally request the conference by means of a document known as a protest. The protest must be in writing and must include certain elements to meet the requirements of the Appeals Office.[77]

.03 Procedure at the Appeals Division

Proceedings before the Appeals Office are informal. Although testimony is not taken under oath, the Appeals Office may require submission of affidavits or declarations under the penalties of perjury. The taxpayer or the representative will meet with the Appeals Officer and informally discuss the pros and cons of the various positions taken by the taxpayer and the IRS. Appeals will follow the law and the recognized legal construction in determining the facts and applying the law. Appeals will determine the correct amount of the tax with strict impartiality between the taxpayer and the Government and without favoritism or discrimination between taxpayers.[78]

Although an Appeals Officer must be impartial, she must, nevertheless, protect the rights of the IRS and act as an advocate on behalf of the IRS. Therefore, an Appeals Officer can raise a new issue or propose a new theory in support of the examining agent's proposed adjustment. However, an Appeals Officer generally will not do so unless the grounds for raising such new issues are substantial and the effect on the tax liability is material.[79]

---

[75] IRM 4.60.1.2.4.2.
[76] IRM 4.45.15.2.1.
[77] Reg. § 601.106(a)(1)(iii).

[78] Reg. § 601.106(f)(1).
[79] IRM 8.6.1.4.

.04 Appeals Process for a Coordinated Industry Case

Unlike normal audit and appeal procedures, however, in a Coordinated Industry Case, members of the examination team from LB&I and Appeals personnel are authorized and, in some instances, required to hold a conference before Appeals Office personnel meet with the taxpayer.[80] The purpose of this unique pre-conference is to discuss the issues, the taxpayer's protest, and the written rebuttal by the LB&I team members to the protest. Such a conference also serves to identify the need for additional information and development of issues.

Although the pre-conference procedure encourages the examination team to share its views on the issues, including its assessment of litigating hazards, the parties may not use the pre-conference to secure a commitment from Appeals that any particular issue should be defended or settled.[81] The parties should not compromise the detached objectivity of Appeals at the pre-conference.

.05 Settlement Agreements

The IRS describes the "Appeals Mission" as one to resolve tax controversies without litigation, on a basis that is fair and impartial to both the government and the taxpayer and in a manner that will enhance voluntary compliance and public confidence in the integrity and efficiency of the IRS.[82] Therefore, the Appeals Officer can split or trade issues where there are substantial uncertainties as to the law, the facts, or both the law and the facts. In splitting a "legal issue," the Appeals Officer will ordinarily consider the hazards that would exist if the case were litigated. The Appeals Officer may not settle cases simply on nuisance value.[83] Moreover, the Appeals Officer will weigh the testimony of the potential witnesses, evaluate the trends that the courts have followed in similar cases, and generally try to predict the outcome of the matter if the case were actually tried.

When a case involves concessions by both the government and the taxpayer "for purposes of settlement" and where there is substantial uncertainty as to how the courts would interpret and apply the law or what facts the court would find, a settlement is classified as a mutual concession settlement. Pursuant to a mutual concession settlement, the parties will sign a Form 870–AD agreement.[84]

However, when a taxpayer and the Appeals Officer have reached an agreement as to some or all of the issues in controversy, the Appeals Officer will request the taxpayer to sign a Form 870, the same agreement used at the Examination level.

The special appeals Form 870-AD differs from the normal Form 870 in several ways. The Form 870-AD agreement contains pledges against reopening that the Form 870 does not contain. Furthermore, the Form 870 becomes effective as a Waiver of Restrictions on Assessment when received by the IRS, whereas the special 870-AD is effective only upon acceptance by or on behalf of the Commissioner of Internal Revenue. Finally, the running of interest is suspended thirty days

---

[80] IRM 8.6.1.2.7.

[81] *Id.*

[82] IRM 8.6.1.3.

[83] IRM 8.6.4.1.3.

[84] IRM 8.8.1.1.2.

¶1605.05

after the IRS receives a Form 870,[85] whereas with a Form 870-AD, interest is not suspended until thirty days after the IRS executes the Form 870-AD.

¶ 1606 COMPETENT AUTHORITY PROCEDURE

If the taxpayer is unable to agree with Appeals on an adjustment that results in double taxation, the taxpayer may seek relief through the Competent Authority Procedure. An integral part of all U.S. Income Tax Treaties is a mutual agreement procedure that provides a mechanism for relief from double taxation. The Director of the Advance Pricing and Mutual Agreement (APMA) program acts as the U.S. Competent Authority. The Competent Authority's primary objective is to make a reasonable effort to resolve double taxation matters when U.S. taxpayers were denied benefits provided for by a treaty.[86] The taxpayer may request the Competent Authority Procedure when the actions of the United States, the treaty country, or both will result in taxation that is contrary to provisions of an applicable tax treaty. Revenue Procedure 2006-54[87] explains how to request assistance of the U.S. Competent Authority in resolving conflicts between treaty partners. As soon as a treaty partner proposes an adjustment that appears inconsistent with a treaty provision or would result in double taxation, the taxpayer should seek assistance via the Competent Authority Procedure (the index to Revenue Procedure 2006-54, which details specific procedures, is reproduced in the Appendix to this Chapter).

The opportunities to resolve disputes via the Competent Authority Procedure have increased from the traditional Mutual Agreement Procedure to include the Simultaneous Appeals Procedure and the Accelerated Competent Authority Procedure. All these methods have the potential to resolve disputes of international tax issues in a manner that avoids litigation.

.01 Mutual Agreement Procedure

The Mutual Agreement Procedure (MAP) treaty articles generally apply when the actions of the U.S. or foreign income tax authorities result in taxation not in accordance with the provisions of the applicable treaty.[88] Distribution, apportionment, or allocation under transfer pricing rules may subject a taxpayer to U.S. federal income taxation on income that the taxpayer had attributed to a foreign related party. Without an offsetting decrease in income reported by the foreign related party, the U.S. person may be subject to double taxation of the same income.

> **Example 16.7:** A widget distributor, USAco is a subsidiary of ASIAco. USAco buys widgets from ASIAco for $100 and resells them in the United States at a mark-up. The IRS argues that the arm's length price from ASIAco to USAco should be $90 and makes an adjustment. Because $10 of income (the difference between the $100 ASIAco charged and the $90 the IRS believes is arm's length) is taxed by both the IRS and ASIA's tax administration, USAco and ASIAco can request relief from their respective competent authorities. The competent authorities will negotiate with each other to determine who will tax the $10.

---

[85] Code Sec. 6601(c). (Forms 870 and 870-AD are reproduced in the appendix to this chapter.)

[86] IRM 4.60.2.1.

[87] Rev. Proc. 2006-54, IRB 2006-49.

[88] *Id.* at § 4.01. A small case procedure also exists *Id.* at § 5.01.

Pursuant to the MAP, the U.S. Competent Authority and the foreign Competent Authority will exchange position papers. Under some treaties, if the two competent authorities cannot resolve the issue within a certain time period, they will mandatorily submit the issue to binding arbitration.[89]

.02 Simultaneous Appeals Procedure

Under the Simultaneous Appeals Procedure (SAP), taxpayers may seek simultaneous Appeals and Competent Authority consideration of an issue.[90] SAP allows taxpayers to obtain Appeals involvement in a manner consistent with the ensuing Competent Authority Procedure and should reduce the time required to resolve disputes by allowing taxpayers more proactive involvement in the process. SAP further opens the possibility of developing strategies to explore the view likely to be taken by the other country's tax authority.

Taxpayers may request SAP with the Competent Authority in three situations:

(i) After Examination has proposed an adjustment with respect to an issue that the taxpayer wishes to submit to the Competent Authority;[91]

(ii) After Examination has issued a 30-day letter, the taxpayer can file a protest, sever the issue, and seek Competent Authority assistance while other issues are referred to or remain at Appeals;[92] or

(iii) After the taxpayer is at Appeals, the taxpayer can request Competent Authority assistance on an issue.[93]

SAP is a two-part process. First, the Appeals Officer prepares an Appeals Case Memorandum (ACM) on the issue. The Appeals Officer shares the ACM with the U.S. Competent Authority representative, but not with the taxpayer. The ACM is a tentative resolution that the U.S. Competent Authority considers when preparing the U.S. position paper for presentation to the foreign Competent Authority. The

---

[89] See, for example, paragraphs 6 and 7 of Article 26 of the U.S.-Canadian Income Tax Treaty.

[90] Id. at § 8.01.

[91] Id. at § 8.02(1)(a).

[92] Id. at § 8.02(1)(b).

[93] Id. at § 8.02(1)(c).

U.S. Competent Authority then meets with the taxpayer to discuss the technical issue and they may ask the Appeals Officer to participate. Second, the U.S. Competent Authority prepares and presents the U.S. position paper to the foreign Competent Authority, as in the mutual agreement procedure. If either the Competent Authorities fail to agree or if the taxpayer does not accept the mutual agreement reached, the taxpayer can refer the issue to Appeals for further consideration.[94]

The taxpayer also can request SAP with Appeals after making a Competent Authority request.[95] However, the U.S. Competent Authority will deny the request if it has already sent its position paper to the foreign Competent Authority. The U.S. Competent Authority also can request the procedure.[96]

.03 Accelerated Competent Authority Procedure

The Accelerated Competent Authority Procedure (ACAP) shortens the time required to complete a case.[97] A taxpayer requesting ACAP assistance with respect to an issue raised by the IRS may request that the Competent Authority resolves the issue for subsequent tax years ending prior to the date of the request for the assistance.[98] In such a request, the taxpayer must agree that the inspection of books and/or records under the ACAP will not preclude or impede a later examination or inspection for any period covered in the request and the IRS need not comply with any procedural restrictions before beginning such an examination or inspection. The U.S. Competent Authority will contact the appropriate LB&I Director to determine whether it should resolve the issue for subsequent tax years. If the Director consents, the U.S. Competent Authority will present the request to the foreign Competent Authority.[99]

> **Example 16.8:** Beginning in 20X1, USAco buys widgets from its parent, ASIAco, for $100 and resells them in the United States at a mark-up. The IRS adjusts the arm's length price to $90. Because $10 of income (the difference between the $100 ASIAco charged and the $90 the IRS believes is arm's length) is taxed by both the IRS and ASIA's tax administration, in 20X4 USAco and ASIAco request competent authority relief over the $10. USAco and ASIAco have taken the same transfer pricing position on their 20X2 and 20X3 returns, which are filed, but are not under audit. USAco may request ACAP for 20X2 and 20X3.

---

[94] *Id.* at § 8.07.
[95] *Id.* at § 8.02(2).
[96] *Id.* at § 8.01.

[97] *Id.* at § 7.06.
[98] *Id.*
[99] *Id.*

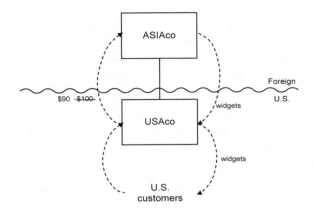

¶ 1607 LEGAL ACTIONS BY TAXPAYERS

A taxpayer may contest an adverse IRS determination in one of three tribunals. A taxpayer may file a petition with the U.S. Tax Court, which will stay assessment and collection of the deficiency until the Court's decision becomes final. Alternatively, the taxpayer may pay the deficiency including interest and penalties and sue for a refund in a U.S. District Court or the U.S. Court of Federal Claims.[100] A nonresident alien or a foreign corporation is not a resident of any U.S. district and may only file a refund suit in the U.S. Court of Federal Claims.

Filing a Petition in the U.S. Tax Court does not require payment of any tax, penalties or interest until final determination of the taxpayer's liability. If, on the other hand, the taxpayer sues for a refund in either a U.S. District Court or the U.S. Court of Federal Claims, the taxpayer must initially pay the tax, plus interest and penalties.

In a suit brought in a U.S. District Court the taxpayer may request that a jury determine factual issues.[101] A party cannot obtain a jury trial before the U.S. Tax Court or the U.S. Court of Federal Claims. Taxpayers must consider many factors in selecting the forum, including previous rulings on the particular issue by the particular court and whether the issue will affect tax liabilities for future years.

¶ 1608 UNCERTAIN TAX POSITIONS AND SCHEDULE UTP

In an effort to require large taxpayers to disclose uncertain tax positions, which often include international tax issues, the IRS has promulgated Schedule UTP. Schedule UTP aids the IRS in focusing its examination resources on returns containing specific uncertain tax positions that are of particular interest or of sufficient magnitude to warrant IRS inquiries. More specifically, the Schedule UTP requirements expand a taxpayer's obligation to self-report sensitive income tax matters on its tax returns beyond existing requirements for any tax shelters or listed transactions.

---

[100] Judicial Code Sec. 1346; Code Sec. 7422.

[101] 28 U.S.C. Sec. 2402.

Corporations who must file Schedule UTP include the following:[102]

(i) Corporations that file Forms 1120, 1120F, and other corporate forms;

(ii) Corporations whose assets have a book value of at least $10 million;

(iii) Corporations who receive an audited financial statement that covers all or a portion of the corporation's operations during the taxable year; and

(iv) Corporations with one or more uncertain tax positions.

Uncertain Tax Positions are either: (i) positions for which FIN 48 or other accounting standards (e.g., IFRS) require establishing a tax reserve in the taxpayer's financial statements or (ii) any position for which the corporation has not recorded a tax reserve because the taxpayer expects to prevail on the position, if litigated. For example, the taxpayer may determine that, if the IRS had full knowledge of the position, there would be a less than 50% chance of settlement and, if litigated, that the taxpayer has a greater than 50% chance of prevailing.[103]

> **Example 16.9:** USCo has a branch in foreign country F and pays foreign country F taxes. An old Revenue Ruling by the IRS incorrectly states that country F's taxes are not creditable for foreign income tax purposes because, in determining the country F tax, country F does not allow deductions and, therefore, country F's tax fails the net income requirement. USCo's tax director knows that this Revenue Ruling is inapplicable because foreign country F's tax regime now allows deductions and, as a result, USCo does not take a tax reserve on its 20X1 financial statements with respect to the foreign tax credit position in country F. USCo's tax director realizes that if the IRS knows of USCo taking a foreign tax credit for country F taxes, USCo will be audited on this issue with less than a 50% chance of settlement (due to the old Revenue Ruling), but if litigated, the Tax Court would agree with USCo. As a result, USCo does not have to report the foreign tax credit position in country F on a Schedule UTP.

> **Example 16.10:** USCo sells $10 million of widgets to ForCo, resulting in operating income to USCo of $500,000 with a return on sales of 5%. USCo's tax director does not conduct a transfer pricing study, but believes that an appro-

---

[102] Reg. § 1.6012-2(a)(4).

[103] Announcement 2010-75, 2010-2 CB 428; Instructions for Schedule UTP (Form 1120).

priate return on sales for a company that performs the functions and assumes the risks of USCo would be 6%, resulting in operating income of $600,000. As a result, USCo's tax director books a reserve with respect to transfer pricing of $35,000 (35% of a potential $100,000 adjustment). USCo's tax director has an uncertain tax position and, therefore, USCo must file a Schedule UTP.

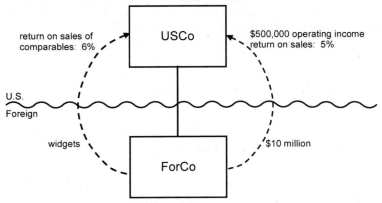

The Schedule UTP requires the corporation to rank all the tax return positions based on the U.S. federal income tax reserve recorded for the position on the return and state whether a particular UTP results in at least 10% of the total potential tax liability of all UTPs. Tax return positions includes transfer pricing and valuation positions.

The concise description of each UTP must provide "sufficient detail" so that the IRS can identify the tax position and the nature of the issue. A completed Schedule UTP is attached to the Appendix for this Chapter.

¶ 1609 OFFSHORE INITIATIVE

In LB&I, the International Individual Compliance function is responsible for offshore initiatives with respect to individuals.[104] More specifically, the International Individual Compliance function has jurisdiction for the Report of Foreign Bank and Financial Accounts on FinCEN 114 (FBAR), a completed sample of which is reproduced in the Appendix to this chapter. As a result of the Bank Secrecy Act, the Treasury Department has authority to seek information with respect to U.S. persons that control foreign bank accounts.[105] The Treasury Department has delegated this authority for enforcement of these FBAR filings to the IRS. Taxpayers may also have to file Form 8938 if they have specified foreign financial assets.

.01 Potential FBAR Filers

Any U.S. person with financial interest in or signatory authority over a foreign bank account aggregating more than $10,000 at any time during the year must report that account on an FBAR. A foreign bank account does not include an account with a U.S. branch of a foreign bank or a foreign branch of a U.S. bank.[106]

---

[104] IRM 4.1.9.
[105] 31 C.F.R. § 103.56(g).

[106] 31 C.F.R. § 103(o). C.F.R. § 103.24.

The definition of a U.S. person includes a U.S. citizen, U.S. resident, U.S. partnership, U.S. corporation, U.S. estate, and U.S. trust.[107]

Example **16.11:** Bob, a U.S. citizen, is on special assignment during the winter at his condominium in Mexico. For his convenience, Bob opens an account at the Last National Bank of Mexico. At its peak, the account balance is $15,000, but on December 31 the balance is only $8,000. Because its highest balance is above $10,000, Bob must file an FBAR.

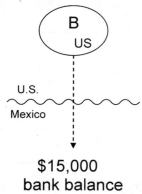

$15,000
bank balance

Multiple accounts are aggregated to determine whether the account holder meets the $10,000 threshold.

Example **16.12:** Bob, a U.S. citizen, is on special assignment during the winter at his condominium in Mexico. Bob has two bank accounts in Mexico. The first, at the Hacienda Local Bank, has a peak balance of $2,500 and a year-end balance of $55. The second, at the Last National Bank of Mexico, has a peak balance of $8,000 and a year-end balance of $3,000. Because the aggregate of the peak balances exceed $10,000 ($2,500 plus $8,000 is $10,500), Bob must file an FBAR for the two accounts.

---

[107] 31 C.F.R. §103.11(z) and (n)(n); IRS Announcement 2010-16, 2010-11 I.R.B. 450.

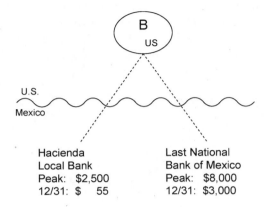

A U.S. person also has to file an FBAR if he owns more than 50% of a foreign corporation that has a foreign bank account in excess of $10,000.[108]

Example 16.13: Betsy Ross wholly owns a European subsidiary called Flag Europa. Flag Europa has a bank account with a dollar equivalence of $25,000 at the Brinker Bank of the Netherlands. Betsy Ross must file an FBAR with respect to Flag Europa's account with the Brinker Bank of the Netherlands.

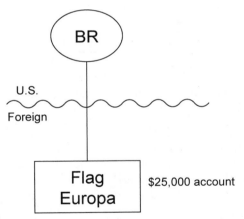

In addition to U.S. individuals having to file FBARs, flow-through[109] entities, such as U.S. partnerships and U.S. S corporations, may also result in a U.S. individual having to file an FBAR. More specifically, a U.S. individual must file an FBAR when indirectly owning more than 50% of a foreign corporation.

Example 16.14: Uncle Sam, a U.S. citizen, is the only U.S. person owning a share (60%) of a U.S. limited partnership. The U.S. limited partnership owns 90% of a foreign corporation (ForCo). Because Uncle Sam's indirect

---

[108] *FBAR Questions and Answers* issued by the IRS on March 19, 2014.

[109] *FBAR Questions and Answers* issued by the IRS on March 19, 2014.

ownership (his 60% interest in the U.S. limited partnership times the U.S. limited partnership's 90% interest in ForCo) is 54%, Uncle Sam's ownership exceeds 50%. Both Uncle Sam and the U.S. limited partnership must file an FBAR for any foreign bank accounts of ForCo in excess of $10,000.

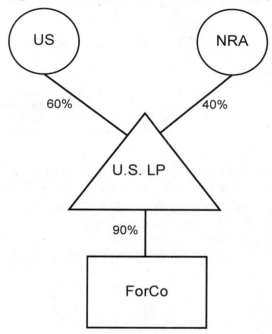

A financial account is more than just a bank account. More specifically, the definition includes securities, securities derivatives, mutual funds, deficit cards and prepaid credit accounts.[110]

A U.S. person files the FBAR electronically by June 30 (no extensions are allowed) for accounts held the prior taxable year.[111] Also, unlike a federal tax return, the U.S. person electronically files the FBAR with the Financial Crimes Enforcement Network, not an IRS Service Center. The various due dates for filing and the different locations may cause confusion for some taxpayers.

Example 16.15: Johnny, a U.S. citizen, has $20,000 in a bank account with the First Bank of Italy. Each year, Johnny files his Form 1040 and his FBAR by April 15. This year, due to some late information from various partnerships in which Johnny owns interests, Johnny extends his income tax return and electronically files both his Form 1040 and his FBAR on October 15. Although Johnny has timely filed his income tax return, the FBAR, which Johnny should have electronically filed by the June 30 due date and for which extension is not allowed, is late.

---

[110] IRS News Release 2007-15.

[111] Timely mailing is not timely filing as Code Sec. 7502(a)(1), which permits timely mailing as timely filing, only applies to filings related to Title 26 of the U.S. Code (the Internal Revenue Code) and the FBAR filing is a Title 31 requirement.

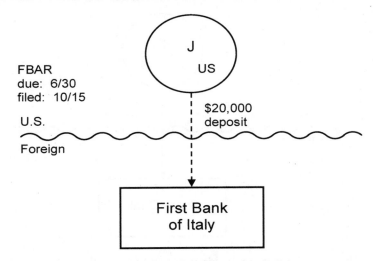

Failure to file FBARs may result in either civil or criminal penalties.

Civil penalties depend on whether the failure to file was non-willful or willful. A non-willful failure to file results in a penalty that may not exceed $10,000.[112] A willful failure to file can result in a penalty of the greater of $100,000 or half of the balance that the FBAR should have reported.[113]

The normal three-year statute of limitations for income tax cases do not apply to FBAR matters. Instead, the statute of limitations on assessment of civil penalties is six years from the June 30 date that the FBAR was due.[114]

> ***Example* 16.16:** Boss Hogg, a U.S. person, deposits his unreported moonshine income of $20,000 in a Swiss Bank account in 20X1. Boss Hogg should electronically file an FBAR that details the account by June 30, 20X2. If he fails to file the FBAR, the statute of limitations remain open until June 30, 20X8, six years after its due date.

---

[112] 31 USC section 5321(a)(5)(B). Reasonable cause may be difficult to obtain if the taxpayer files a Form 1040 that inquires about foreign bank accounts and directs the taxpayer to an instruction describing the FBAR.

[113] 31 USC section 5321(a)(5)(C).
[114] 31 USC section 5321(b)(1); ¶ 1603.05.

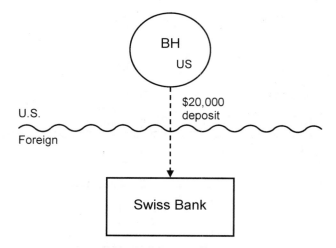

The IRS may also pursue criminal penalties for willful failure to file an FBAR. Those criminal penalties can result in a fine of up to $250,000 and five years of imprisonment.[115]

.02 Statement of Specified Foreign Financial Assets

In order to encourage compliance with the FATCA withholding regime on investment-type income (see ¶ 903), specified persons must provide a Statement of Specified Foreign Financial Assets on Form 8938.[116] These specified persons must have an interest in specified foreign financial assets whose value exceeds the applicable threshold, which begins at $50,000 for the aggregate value of all specified foreign financial assets on December 31 or $100,000 at any time during the year.[117]

Form 8938 has resulted in new terminology. Specified persons primarily includes individuals who are either U.S. citizens or U.S. residents for any part of the taxable year. An interest in specified foreign financial assets includes financial accounts maintained by a foreign financial institution and foreign financial assets that result in either ongoing income or whose sale results in a gain.[118] More specifically, financial accounts maintained by foreign financial institutions include deposit accounts and custodial accounts, while foreign financial assets include assets held for investment, such as shares in a foreign entity.

Example 16.17: Betsy Ross wholly owns a European subsidiary called Flag Europa. Flag Europa has a bank account with a dollar equivalence of $100,000 at the Brinker Bank of the Netherlands. Betsy Ross must file an FBAR with respect to Flag Europa's account at the Brinker bank of the Netherlands and a Form 8938 with respect to her shares in Flag Europa, which is a foreign entity. However, she does not have to file a Form 8938 with respect to Flag Europa's $100,000 at the Brinker Bank.

---

[115] 31 USC section 5322(a).
[116] Code Sec. 6038D.

[117] Code Sec. 6030D(a).
[118] Code Sec. 6038D(b).

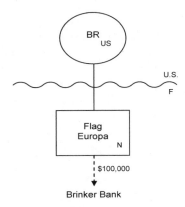

There is a $10,000 penalty for failure to file the Form 8938 by the return's due date, which can increase to a maximum of $50,000 for continual failure to file.[119] The IRS may also assess an accuracy-related penalty of 40% of any underpayment of tax due that is attributable to a specified foreign financial asset that the taxpayer did not disclose. The IRS may abate the penalty if a taxpayer shows reasonable cause.[120]

.03 Penalties for Underpayment Attributable to Undisclosed Foreign Financial Assets

The accuracy related penalty on underpayments[121] was amended to include a penalty for an "undisclosed foreign financial asset understatement." An undisclosed foreign financial asset understatement includes the portion of an underpayment attributable to any transaction involving an undisclosed foreign financial asset. The penalty is 40% of the underpayment due to the lack of disclosure on a relevant form.[122]

More specifically, undisclosed foreign financial assets are those assets with respect to required information, which the taxpayer failed to disclose to the IRS pursuant to the following information reporting requirements:

    (i) Code Sec. 6038 reporting for foreign corporations and partnerships (Forms 5471, 5472 and 8865);

    (ii) Code Sec. 6038B reporting for transfers to foreign persons (Forms 926, 5471 and 8865);

    (iii) Code Sec. 6038D reporting for foreign financial assets held by individuals (Forms 5471 and 8865);

    (iv) Code Sec. 6046A reporting for foreign partnership interests (Form 8865);

    (v) Code Sec. 6048 reporting for foreign trusts (Form 3520-A).

    ***Example* 16.18:** USCo, a U.S. company, wholly owns and, therefore, files a Form 5471 for ForSub, a foreign subsidiary. An IRS audit results in $350,000 of additional income tax attributable to $100,000 of interest earned on

---

[119] Code Sec. 6038D (d).
[120] Code Sec. 6038D (g).

[121] Code Sec. 6662.
[122] Code Sec. 6662 (j).

an unreported bank deposit by ForSub that constituted Subpart F income. USCo is subject to the Code Sec. 6662 accuracy related penalty on underpayments with respect to an undisclosed foreign financial asset understatement.

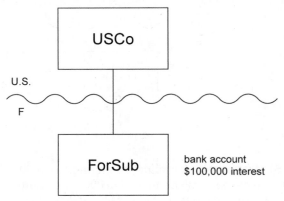

Reasonable cause is a defense to the penalty for the understatement of financial assets.[123]

.04 Voluntary Offshore Disclosure Procedures

U.S. persons who have failed to comply with the reporting of foreign assets or foreign income include U.S.-born citizens and U.S. immigrants. The IRS has found that well-intentioned taxpayers continually fail to comply for fear of revealing potential criminal liability for earlier years.[124] As a result, the IRS created an offshore voluntary disclosure program to incentivize these taxpayers to comply.[125]

If the IRS accepts in to its program a taxpayer, who abides by its terms, the taxpayer will not incur any criminal penalties. However, a taxpayer will pay, in addition to back taxes and interest, a one-time 27.5% offshore penalty on the highest year's aggregate balance of undisclosed foreign accounts. Moreover, if the failure to report foreign assets on income is not willful, the taxpayer may be eligible for the streamlined program, which reduces the one-time offshore penalty from 27.5% to 5%.[126]

---

[123] Code Sec. 6662(b)(6); IRM 20.1.1.3.2.
[124] Code Secs 7201 and 7206(1).

[125] *Offshore Voluntary Disclosure Program: Frequently Asked Questions and Answers,* Issued by the IRS on September 10, 2014.
[126] *Streamlined Filing Compliance Procedures,* Updated by the IRS on October 9, 2014.

¶ 1610 APPENDIX

International Practice Units

As part of LB&I International's knowledge management efforts, Practice Units are developed through internal collaboration and serve as both job aids and training materials on international tax issues. For example, Practice Units provide IRS staff with explanations of general international tax concepts as well as information about a specific type of transaction. Practice Units will continue to evolve as the compliance environment changes and new insights and experiences are contributed. Please visit this site periodically for new and updated Practice Units which are shared below.

To provide feedback on a specific Practice Unit, please send an email to LBI Practice Unit Public Feedback and specify the Practice Unit's name and Document Control Number (DCN), which are both listed on the Practice Unit's cover page. Please do not reference a specific individual or entity in your email as comments may be subject to future release. The IRS does not commit to respond to suggestions or comments.

Practice Units are available in Adobe PDF and must be viewed with the Acrobat Reader.

NOTE: Practice Units are not an official pronouncement of law, and cannot be used, cited or relied upon as such. Further, Practice Units may not contain a comprehensive discussion of all pertinent issues or law or the IRS's interpretation of current law. These Practice Units and any non-precedential material that may be referenced in a Unit, such as written determinations (a ruling, determination letter, technical advice memorandum or Chief Counsel advice), may not be used or cited as precedent by taxpayers or the IRS.

2014

12-15-2014	Interest Income Derived by CFC or QBU Engaged in Banking Financing or Similar Business	(PDF, 548 KB)
12-15-2014	Computing Foreign Base Company Income	(PDF, 287 KB)
12-15-2014	Subpart F Overview	(PDF, 279 KB)
12-15-2014	Disposition of a Portion of an Integrated Hedge	(PDF, 430 KB)
12-15-2014	Asset Valuation using the FMV Method for Interest Expense Allocation to Calculate FTC Limitation	(PDF, 350 KB)
12-15-2014	Overview of Interest Expense Allocation and Apportionment in Calculation of the FTC Limitation	(PDF, 217 KB)
12-15-2014	French Foreign Tax Credits	(PDF, 196 KB)
12-15-2014	Exhaustion of Remedies	(PDF, 566 KB)
12-15-2014	Exhaustion of Remedies and Transfer Pricing	(PDF, 611 KB)
12-15-2014	Exhaustion of Remedies in Non Transfer Pricing Situations	(PDF, 632 KB)
12-15-2014	How to Allocate and Apportion Research and Experimental Expenses	(PDF, 216 KB)
12-15-2014	Interest Expense Limitation Computation under IRC 163j	(PDF, 345 KB)
12-15-2014	Issuing a Formal Document Request when a US Taxpayer is Unresponsive to an IDR	(PDF, 503 KB)
12-15-2014	Section 861 Home Office and Stewardship Expenses	(PDF, 374 KB)
12-15-2014	License of Foreign Owned Intangible Property by US Entity	(PDF, 334 KB)
12-15-2014	Management Fees	(PDF, 331 KB)
12-15-2014	Purchase of Tangible Goods from a Foreign Parent CUP	(PDF, 711 KB)

	Method	
12-15-2014	CPM Simple Distributor Inbound	(PDF, 354 KB)
12-15-2014	Foreign Shareholder Activities and Duplicative Services	(PDF, 511 KB)
12-15-2014	Best Method Determination for an Inbound Distributor	(PDF, 567 KB)
12-15-2014	Services Cost Method Inbound Services	(PDF, 293 KB)
12-15-2014	Arms Length Standard	(PDF, 600 KB)
12-15-2014	Outbound Liquidation of US Corp to Foreign Parent IRC Section 367 e 2 Overview	(PDF, 1,038 KB)
12-15-2014	Comparability Analysis for Tangible Goods Transactions Inbound	(PDF, 541 KB)
12-15-2014	Review of Transfer Pricing Documentation by Inbound Taxpayers	(PDF, 454 KB)
12-15-2014	Pricing of Platform Contribution Transaction in Cost Sharing Arrangements Initial Transaction	(PDF, 478 KB)
12-15-2014	Cost Sharing Arrangements vs Licensing Alternative	(PDF, 442 KB)
12-15-2014	License of Intangible Property from US Parent to a Foreign Subsidiary	(PDF, 248 KB)
12-15-2014	Distinguishing Between Sale License and other Transfers of Intangibles to CFCs by US Transferors	(PDF, 509 KB)
12-15-2014	Sale of Tangible Goods from a CFC to a USP CUP Method	(PDF, 360 KB)
12-15-2014	CPM Simple Distributor Outbound	(PDF, 534 KB)
12-15-2014	Rev Proc 99 32 Outbound Guidance	(PDF, 707 KB)
12-15-2014	Outbound Transfers of Property to Foreign Corporation - IRC Section 367 Overview	(PDF, 788 KB)
12-15-2014	Dual Consolidated Losses Overview	(PDF, 838 KB)
12-15-2014	Comparability Analysis for Tangible Goods Transactions Outbound	(PDF, 435 KB)
12-15-2014	Determining Tax Residency Status of Lawful Permanent Residents	(PDF, 450 KB)
12-15-2014	Substantial Presence Test	(PDF, 498 KB)
12-15-2014	Election under Section 6013g	(PDF, 348 KB)
12-15-2014	Election under Section 6013h	(PDF, 434 KB)
12-15-2014	First Year Election under 7701b4	(PDF, 471 KB)
12-15-2014	IRC 911 Election and Revocation	(PDF, 100 KB)
12-15-2014	Tax Home for Purposes of IRC Section 911	(PDF, 86 KB)
12-15-2014	Branch Profits Tax Concepts	(PDF, 543 KB)
12-15-2014	Qualification for Treaty Benefits under the Publicly Traded Test	(PDF, 608 KB)
12-15-2014	Creation of a Permanent Establishment through the Activities of Seconded Employees in the United States	(PDF, 702 KB)
12-15-2014	Overview of FDAP	(PDF, 306 KB)

Page Last Reviewed or Updated: 15-Dec-2014

Form **870** (Rev. March 1992)	Department of the Treasury — Internal Revenue Service **Waiver of Restrictions on Assessment and Collection of Deficiency in Tax and Acceptance of Overassessment**	Date received by Internal Revenue Service

Names and address of taxpayers *(Number, street, city or town, State, ZIP code)*	Social security or employer identification number

	Increase (Decrease) in Tax and Penalties			
Tax year ended	Tax	Penalties		
	$	$	$	$	$
	$	$	$	$	$
	$	$	$	$	$
	$	$	$	$	$
	$	$	$	$	$
	$	$	$	$	$
	$	$	$	$	$

(For instructions, see back of form)

Consent to Assessment and Collection

I consent to the immediate assessment and collection of any deficiencies *(increase in tax and penalties)* and accept any overassessment *(decrease in tax and penalties)* shown above, plus any interest provided by law. I understand that by signing this waiver, I will not be able to contest these years in the United States Tax Court, unless additional deficiencies are determined for these years.

YOUR SIGNATURE——▶ HERE		Date
SPOUSE'S SIGNATURE——▶		Date
TAXPAYER'S REPRESENTATIVE HERE ——▶		Date
CORPORATE NAME ——▶		
CORPORATE OFFICER(S) SIGN HERE		Title	Date
		Title	Date

Catalog Number 16894U   Form **870** (Rev. 3-92)

¶1610

Form **870-AD** (Rev. April 1992)	Department of the Treasury—Internal Revenue Service **Offer to Waive Restrictions on Assessment and Collection of Tax** **Deficiency and to Accept Overassessment**	
Symbols	Name of Taxpayer	SSN or EIN

Under the provisions of section 6213(d) of the Internal Revenue Code of 1986 (the Code), or corresponding provisions of prior internal revenue laws, the undersigned offers to waive the restrictions provided in section 6213(a) of the Code or corresponding provisions of prior internal revenue laws, and to consent to the assessment and collection of the following deficiencies and additions to tax, if any, with interest as provided by law. The undersigned offers also to accept the following overassessments, if any, as correct. Any waiver or acceptance of an overassessment is subject to any terms and conditions stated below and on the reverse side of this form.

Deficiencies (Overassessments)
and Additions to Tax

Year Ended	Kind of Tax	Tax				
		$	$	$		
		$	$	$		
		$	$	$		
		$	$	$		
		$	$	$		
		$	$	$		

Signature of Taxpayer	Date
Signature of Taxpayer	Date
Signature of Taxpayer's Representative	Date
Corporate Name	Date
By Corporate Officer Title	Date

For Internal Revenue Use Only	Date Accepted for Commissioner	Signature
	Office	Title

Cat. No. 16896Q   **(See Reverse Side)**   Form **870-AD** (Rev. 4-92)

This offer must be accepted for the Commissioner of Internal Revenue and will take effect on the date it is accepted. Unless and until it is accepted, it will have no force or effect.

If this offer is accepted, the case will not be reopened by the Commissioner unless there was:

- fraud, malfeasance, concealment or misrepresentation of a material fact
- an important mistake in mathematical calculation
- a deficiency or overassessment resulting from adjustments made under Subchapters C and D of Chapter 63 concerning the tax treatment of partnership and subchapter S items determined at the partnership and corporate level
- an excessive tentative allowance of a carryback provided by law

No claim for refund or credit will be filed or prosecuted by the taxpayer for the years stated on this form, other than for amounts attributed to carrybacks provided by law.

The proper filing of this offer, when accepted, will expedite assessment and billing (or overassessment, credit or refund) by adjusting the tax liability. This offer, when executed and timely submitted, will be considered a claim for refund for the above overassessment(s), if any.

This offer may be executed by the taxpayer's attorney, certified public accountant, or agent provided this is specifically authorized by a power of attorney which, if not previously filed, must accompany this form. If this offer is signed by a person acting in a fiduciary capacity (for example: an executor, administrator, or a trustee) Form 56, Notice Concerning Fiduciary Relationship, must accompany this form, unless previously filed.

If this offer is executed for a year for which a joint return was filed, it must be signed by both spouses unless one spouse, acting under a power of attorney, signs as agent for the other.

If this offer is executed by a corporation, it must be signed with the corporate name followed by the signature and title of the officer(s) authorized to sign. If the offer is accepted, as a condition of acceptance, any signature by or for a corporate officer will be considered a representation by that person and the corporation, to induce reliance, that such signature is binding under law for the corporation to be assessed the deficiencies or receive credit or refund under this agreement. If the corporation later contests the signature as being unauthorized on its behalf, the person who signed may be subject to criminal penalties for representing that he or she had authority to sign this agreement on behalf of the corporation.

*U.S. GPO: 1992-617-016/49236

Form **870-AD** (Rev. 4-92)

¶1610

Summons

In the matter of _____

Internal Revenue Service (Division): _____

Industry/Area (name or number): _____

Periods: _____

The Commissioner of Internal Revenue

To: _____

At: _____

You are hereby summoned and required to appear before _____
an officer of the Internal Revenue Service, to give testimony and to bring with you and to produce for examination the following books, records, papers, and other data relating to the tax liability or the collection of the tax liability or for the purpose of inquiring into any offense connected with the administration or enforcement of the internal revenue laws concerning the person identified above for the periods shown.

Do not write in this space

Business address and telephone number of IRS officer before whom you are to appear:

_____

Place and time for appearance at _____

IRS

on the _____ day of _____, _____ at _____ o'clock _____ m.
(year)
Issued under authority of the Internal Revenue Code this _____ day of _____, _____ .
(year)

Department of the Treasury
Internal Revenue Service

www.irs.gov

Form 2039 (Rev. 12-2001)
Catalog Number 21405J

_____
Signature of issuing officer   Title

_____
Signature of approving officer *(if applicable)*   Title

Original — to be kept by IRS

Service of Summons, Notice and Recordkeeper Certificates

(Pursuant to section 7603, Internal Revenue Code)

I certify that I served the summons shown on the front of this form on:

Date	Time

How Summons Was Served

1. ❑ I certify that I handed a copy of the summons, which contained the attestation required by § 7603, to the person to whom it was directed.

2. ❑ I certify that I left a copy of the summons, which contained the attestation required by § 7603, at the last and usual place of abode of the person to whom it was directed. I left the copy with the following person (if any): _____

3. ❑ I certify that I sent a copy of the summons, which contained the attestation required by § 7603, by certified or registered mail to the last known address of the person to whom it was directed, that person being a third-party recordkeeper within the meaning of § 7603(b). I sent the summons to the following address: _____

Signature	Title

4. This certificate is made to show compliance with IRC Section 7609. This certificate does not apply to summonses served on any officer or employee of the person to whose liability the summons relates nor to summonses in aid of collection, to determine the identity of a person having a numbered account or similar arrangement, or to determine whether or not records of the business transactions or affairs of an identified person have been made or kept.

I certify that, within 3 days of serving the summons, I gave notice (Part D of Form 2039) to the person named below on the date and in the manner indicated.

Date of giving Notice: _____   Time: _____

Name of Noticee: _____

Address of Noticee (if mailed): _____

How Notice Was Given

❑ I gave notice by certified or registered mail to the last known address of the noticee.

❑ I left the notice at the last and usual place of abode of the noticee. I left the copy with the following person (if any).

❑ I gave notice by handing it to the noticee.

❑ In the absence of a last known address of the noticee, I left the notice with the person summoned.

❑ No notice is required.

Signature	Title

I certify that the period prescribed for beginning a proceeding to quash this summons has expired and that no such proceeding was instituted or that the noticee consents to the examination.

Signature	Title

Form **2039** (Rev. 12-2001)

¶1610

Form **4564** (Rev, September 2006)	Department of the Treasury - Internal Revenue Service **Information Document Request**	Request Number 0001

To: *(Name of Taxpayer and Company Division or Branch)* Taxpayer *Please return Part 2 with listed documents to requester identified below*	Subject December 31, 20X1
	SAIN number	Submitted to:
	Dates of Previous Requests (mmddyyyy)

Description of documents requested

Tax Period(s):   20X1

1- Written History of Business Activities (including business location, phone #, fax #, extraordinary events, etc.)

2- Written explanation of Partner's duties

3- Bank Statements and Bank Reconciliations for all accounts from January to December 20X1

4- Brief explanation of Accounting & Bookkeeping (software, who does, etc.)

5- Copy of Chart of Accounts

6- Explanation of the following transactions (Start through finish, who approves, who does, how often, etc.)

       -Sales/Receipt of Income
       -Disbursement/Expenses

7- Major Customers and Major Supplies

Information due by 02/25/20X4   At next appointment ☐   Mail in ☒

From:	Name and Title of Requester Internal Revenue Agent	Employee ID number	Date (mmddyyyy) 01/31/20X4
	Office Location:		Phone: Fax:

Catalog Number 23145K   www.irs.gov   Part 2 - To be Returned by Taxpayer with Reply   Form **4564** (Rev. 9-2006)

14784537

¶1610

Delivered by
Certified/Registered Mail

Taxpayer's name
Taxpayer's last known address

FORMAL DOCUMENT REQUEST

(Salutation)

This letter, including the attachment(s), constitutes a FORMAL DOCUMENT REQUEST under Internal Revenue Code section 982, and relates to documentation necessary to determine your United States tax liability for year(s)_____. We are providing you with the following information, as required by section 982:

(1) **Time and place for production of documentation:**_____AM; PM,
_____19__,at (physical address); or by mail postmarked before this date and
sent to: (mailing address).

(2) **Why previously submitted documentation is not sufficient:** You did not provide the requested information described on Form 4564, Information Document Request, which was mailed to you at your above address on _____. _____. (State other reason if applicable.)

(3) **Description of documents requested:** The documents are those shown on Form 4564, Information Document Request, which is attached and made a part of this request. You are required to provide a certified translation into English for requested documents that are in any language other than English.

(4) **Consequences of failure to comply:** Code section 982(a) states that if a taxpayer "fails to substantially comply with any formal document request arising out of the examination of the tax treatment of any item (hereafter in this section referred to as the 'examined item') **before the 90th day after the date of the mailing of such request on** motion by the Secretary, any court having jurisdiction over a civil proceeding in which the tax treatment of the examined item in an issue **shall prohibit the introduction by the taxpayer of any foreign-based documentation covered by such request**" (Emphasis added).

Further, if the requested items are not received before the 90th day after the date of the mailing of this Formal Document Request (insert tax adjustments to be made). Thus, under the provisions of section 982, you will lose your opportunity to present any of the requested documents to any court having jurisdiction to adjudicate your case in a civil proceeding.

We further advise you that Code section 982(c)(2) allows you to bring a proceeding to quash a Formal Document Request not later than the 90th day after the day such request was mailed. You may institute such a proceeding in the United States District Court for the district in which you reside or are found. Under Code section 7701(a)(39), any citizen or resident of the United States who does not reside in (and is not found in) any United States judicial district shall be treated as residing in the District of Columbia for purposes of any provision of the Internal Revenue laws relating to jurisdiction of courts or enforcement of summons. Should you institute a proceeding to quash, the running of the 90-day period for complying with this Formal Document Request shall be suspended while the proceeding is pending. In a proceeding to quash, section 982 also allows the Secretary of the Treasury to seek to compel compliance with the Formal Document Request.

We urge you to promptly comply with this Formal Document Request.

Sincerely,

(Signature)
(Title)

Attachment:
As Stated

Letter 2261(P)(3–87)

15230388

¶1610

Rev. Proc. 2006-54

SECTION 1. PURPOSE AND BACKGROUND

.01 Purpose

.02 Background

.03 Changes

SECTION 2. SCOPE

.01 In General

.02 Requests for Assistance

.03 General Process

.04 Failure to Request Assistance

SECTION 3. GENERAL CONDITIONS UNDER WHICH THIS PROCEDURE APPLIES

.01 General

.02 Requirements of a Treaty

.03 Applicable Standards in Allocation Cases

.04 Who Can File Requests for Assistance

.05 Closed Cases

.06 Foreign Initiated Competent Authority Request

.07 Requests Relating to Residence Issues

.08 Determinations Regarding Limitation on Benefits

SECTION 4. PROCEDURES FOR REQUESTING COMPETENT AUTHORITY ASSISTANCE

.01 Time for Filing

.02 Place of Filing

.03 Additional Filing

.04 Form of Request

.05 Information Required

.06 Other Dispute Resolution Programs

.07 Other Documentation

.08 Updates

.09 Conferences

SECTION 5. SMALL CASE PROCEDURE FOR REQUESTING COMPETENT AUTHORITY ASSISTANCE

.01 General

.02 Small Case Standards

.03 Small Case Filing Procedure

¶1610

SECTION 6. RELIEF REQUESTED FOR FOREIGN INITIATED ADJUSTMENT WITHOUT COMPETENT AUTHORITY INVOLVEMENT

SECTION 7. COORDINATION WITH OTHER ADMINISTRATIVE OR JUDICIAL PROCEEDINGS

SECTION 8. SIMULTANEOUS APPEALS PROCEDURE

SECTION 9. PROTECTIVE MEASURES

¶1610

(d) No Consultation between Competent Authorities until Formal Request is Filed

.04 Effect of a Protective Claim

.05 Treaty Provisions Waiving Procedural Barriers

SECTION 10. APPLICATION OF REV. PROC. 99-32

SECTION 11. DETERMINATION OF CREDITABLE FOREIGN TAXES

SECTION 12. ACTION BY U.S. COMPETENT AUTHORITY

.01 Notification of Taxpayer

.02 Denial of Assistance

.03 Extending Period of Limitations for Assessment

.04 No Review of Denial of Request for Assistance

.05 Notification

.06 Closing Agreement

.07 Unilateral Withdrawal or Reduction of U.S. Initiated Adjustments

SECTION 13. REQUESTS FOR RULINGS

.01 General

.02 Foreign Tax Rulings

SECTION 14. FEES

.01 Requests to Which a User Fee Does Not Apply

.02 Requests to Which a User Fee Applies

.03 Acceptance of Requests

.04 Address to Send Payment

.05 Refunds of User Fee

SECTION 15. EFFECT ON OTHER DOCUMENTS

SECTION 16. EFFECTIVE DATE

SECTION 17. PAPERWORK REDUCTION ACT

SECTION 18. DRAFTING INFORMATION

¶1610

USCo, a U.S. C corporation, wholly-owns ForCo, a foreign corporation. ForCo has $800,000 of accumulated e&p and accumulated foreign taxes paid of $200,000. During the taxable year, ForCo distributes a dividend of $800,000, which is subject to foreign country F's withholding tax, which is based not on the gross amount of the dividend, but on the amount of the annual income of ForCo at a 10% rate for $30,000. Because of the question over the creditability of the withholding tax as a Section 903 credit for a tax in lieu of an income tax, USCo's tax director books a $30,000 reserve. Accordingly, USco must file a Schedule UTP with its Form 1120.

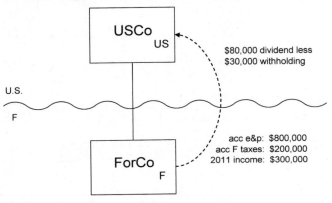

¶1610

SCHEDULE UTP (Form 1120)	Uncertain Tax Position Statement	OMB No. 1545-0123
Department of the Treasury Internal Revenue Service	▶ File with Form 1120, 1120-F, 1120-L, or 1120-PC. ▶ Information about Schedule UTP (Form 1120) and its separate instructions is at *www.irs.gov/scheduleutp*.	2014

Name of entity as shown on page 1 of tax return	EIN of entity
USCo	65-8794321

This Part I, Schedule UTP (Form 1120) is page __1__ of __1__ Part I pages.

Part I   **Uncertain Tax Positions for the Current Tax Year.** See instructions for how to complete columns (a) through (g). Enter, in Part III, a description for each uncertain tax position (UTP).

Check this box if the corporation was unable to obtain information from related parties sufficient to determine whether a tax position is a UTP (see instructions) ▶ ☐

(a) UTP No.	(b) Primary IRC Sections (e.g., "61", "108", "263A", etc.) / Primary IRC Subsections (e.g. (f)(2)(A)(ii))	(c) Timing Codes (check if Permanent, Temporary, or both)		(d) Pass-Through Entity EIN	(e) Major Tax Position	(f) Ranking of Tax Position	(g) Reserved for Future Use
C 1	903 ( )( )( ))( )( )( ))( )( )( )	✔	T	-	☐		
C	( )( )( ))( )( )( ))( )( )( )	P	T	-	☐		
C	( )( )( ))( )( )( ))( )( )( )	P	T	-	☐		
C	( )( )( ))( )( )( ))( )( )( )	P	T	-	☐		
C	( )( )( ))( )( )( ))( )( )( )	P	T	-	☐		
C	( )( )( ))( )( )( ))( )( )( )	P	T	-	☐		
C	( )( )( ))( )( )( ))( )( )( )	P	T	-	☐		
C	( )( )( ))( )( )( ))( )( )( )	P	T	-	☐		
C	( )( )( ))( )( )( ))( )( )( )	P	T	-	☐		
C	( )( )( ))( )( )( ))( )( )( )	P	T	-	☐		
C	( )( )( ))( )( )( ))( )( )( )	P	T	-	☐		
C	( )( )( ))( )( )( ))( )( )( )	P	T	-	☐		
C	( )( )( ))( )( )( ))( )( )( )	P	T	-	☐		
C	( )( )( ))( )( )( ))( )( )( )	P	T	-	☐		
C	( )( )( ))( )( )( ))( )( )( )	P	T	-	☐		
C	( )( )( ))( )( )( ))( )( )( )	P	T	-	☐		
C	( )( )( ))( )( )( ))( )( )( )	P	T	-	☐		
C	( )( )( ))( )( )( ))( )( )( )	P	T	-	☐		
C	( )( )( ))( )( )( ))( )( )( )	P	T	-	☐		
C	( )( )( ))( )( )( ))( )( )( )	P	T	-	☐		

For Paperwork Reduction Act Notice, see the Instructions for Form 1120.   Cat. No. 54658Q   Schedule UTP (Form 1120) 2014

Schedule UTP (Form 1120) 2014   Page **2**

Name of entity as shown on page 1 of tax return	EIN of entity
USCo	65-8794321

This Part II, Schedule UTP (Form 1120) is page   **1**   of   **1**   Part II pages.

Part II   **Uncertain Tax Positions for Prior Tax Years.**
See instructions for how to complete columns (a) through (h). Enter, in Part III, a description for each uncertain tax position (UTP).

Check this box if the corporation was unable to obtain information from related parties sufficient to determine whether a tax position is a UTP (see instructions) ► ☐

(a) UTP No.	(b) Primary IRC Sections (e.g., "61", "108", "263A", etc.) / Primary IRC Subsections (e.g. (f)(2)(A)(ii))	(c) Timing Codes (check if Permanent, Temporary, or both)	(d) Pass-Through Entity EIN	(e) Major Tax Position	(f) Ranking of Tax Position	(g) Reserved for Future Use	(h) Year of Tax Position
P	( )( )( ) ( )( )( )( ) ( )( )( )( )	P T	-	☐			
P	( )( )( ) ( )( )( )( ) ( )( )( )( )	P T	-	☐			
P	( )( )( ) ( )( )( )( ) ( )( )( )( )	P T	-	☐			
P	( )( )( ) ( )( )( )( ) ( )( )( )( )	P T	-	☐			
P	( )( )( ) ( )( )( )( ) ( )( )( )( )	P T	-	☐			
P	( )( )( ) ( )( )( )( ) ( )( )( )( )	P T	-	☐			
P	( )( )( ) ( )( )( )( ) ( )( )( )( )	P T	-	☐			
P	( )( )( ) ( )( )( )( ) ( )( )( )( )	P T	-	☐			
P	( )( )( ) ( )( )( )( ) ( )( )( )( )	P T	-	☐			
P	( )( )( ) ( )( )( )( ) ( )( )( )( )	P T	-	☐			
P	( )( )( ) ( )( )( )( ) ( )( )( )( )	P T	-	☐			
P	( )( )( ) ( )( )( )( ) ( )( )( )( )	P T	-	☐			
P	( )( )( ) ( )( )( )( ) ( )( )( )( )	P T	-	☐			
P	( )( )( ) ( )( )( )( ) ( )( )( )( )	P T	-	☐			
P	( )( )( ) ( )( )( )( ) ( )( )( )( )	P T	-	☐			
P	( )( )( ) ( )( )( )( ) ( )( )( )( )	P T	-	☐			
P	( )( )( ) ( )( )( )( ) ( )( )( )( )	P T	-	☐			
P	( )( )( ) ( )( )( )( ) ( )( )( )( )	P T	-	☐			
P	( )( )( ) ( )( )( )( ) ( )( )( )( )	P T	-	☐			
P	( )( )( ) ( )( )( )( ) ( )( )( )( )	P T	-	☐			

Schedule UTP (Form 1120) 2014

Name of entity as shown on page 1 of tax return	EIN of entity
USCo	65-8794321

This Part III, Schedule UTP (Form 1120) is page   1   of   1   Part III pages.

Part III   **Concise Descriptions of UTPs.** Indicate the corresponding UTP number from Part I, column (a) (e.g. C1) or Part II column (a) (e.g. P2). Use as many Part III pages as necessary (see instructions).

UTP No.	Concise Description of Uncertain Tax Position
1	During the taxable year, ForCo distributed a dividend that was subject to withholding tax for which the taxpayer took a credit pursuant to Code sec. 903. The issue is whether the withholding tax constitutes a creditable tax.

¶1610

Bob, a U.S. citizen, is on special assignment during the winter at his condominium in Mexico. For his convenience, Bob opens an account at the Last National Bank of Mexico. At its peak, the account balance is $150,000, but on December 31 the balance is only $8,000. Because its highest balance is above $100,000, Bob must file both a Form 8938 (with his federal income tax return) and an FBAR (electronically by June 30).

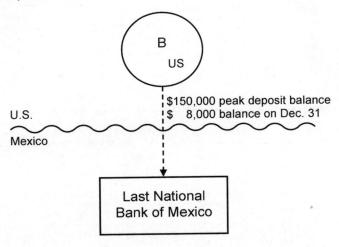

Form **8938** (Rev. December 2014) Department of the Treasury Internal Revenue Service	**Statement of Specified Foreign Financial Assets** ► Information about Form 8938 and its separate instructions is at *www.irs.gov/form8938.* ► Attach to your tax return. For calendar year 20 ____ or tax year beginning ____ , 20 ____ and ending ____ , 20 ____	OMB No. 1545-2195 Attachment Sequence No. **175**

If you have attached continuation statements, check here ☐ **Number of continuation statements** _____

Name(s) shown on return	TIN
Bob	123-45-6789

Part I   **Foreign Deposit and Custodial Accounts Summary**

1	Number of Deposit Accounts (reported on Form 8938) . . . . ►		1
2	Maximum Value of All Deposit Accounts	$	150,000
3	Number of Custodial Accounts (reported on Form 8938) . . . . ►		
4	Maximum Value of All Custodial Accounts	$	
5	Were any foreign deposit or custodial accounts closed during the tax year?	☐ Yes ☑ No	

Part II   **Other Foreign Assets Summary**

1	Number of Foreign Assets (reported on Form 8938) . . . . ►		
2	Maximum Value of All Assets	$	
3	Were any foreign assets acquired or sold during the tax year?	☐ Yes ☐ No	

Part III   **Summary of Tax Items Attributable to Specified Foreign Financial Assets** (see instructions)

(a) Asset Category	(b) Tax item	(c) Amount reported on form or schedule	Where reported	
			(d) Form and line	(e) Schedule and line
1 Foreign Deposit and Custodial Accounts	1a Interest	$ 1,500	1040,8a	B, 1
	1b Dividends	$		
	1c Royalties	$		
	1d Other income	$		
	1e Gains (losses)	$		
	1f Deductions	$		
	1g Credits	$		
2 Other Foreign Assets	2a Interest	$		
	2b Dividends	$		
	2c Royalties	$		
	2d Other income	$		
	2e Gains (losses)	$		
	2f Deductions	$		
	2g Credits	$		

Part IV   **Excepted Specified Foreign Financial Assets** (see instructions)

If you reported specified foreign financial assets on one or more of the following forms, enter the number of such forms filed. You do not need to include these assets on Form 8938 for the tax year.

1. Number of Forms 3520 _____   2. Number of Forms 3520-A _____   3. Number of Forms 5471 _____

4. Number of Forms 8621 _____   5. Number of Forms 8865 _____   6. Number of Forms 8891 _____

Part V   **Detailed Information for Each Foreign Deposit and Custodial Account Included in the Part I Summary** (see instructions)

If you have more than one account to report, attach a continuation statement for each additional account (see instructions).

1	Type of account ☑ Deposit ☐ Custodial	2	Account number or other designation 98-7654321
3	Check all that apply a ☑ Account opened during tax year b ☐ Account closed during tax year c ☐ Account jointly owned with spouse d ☐ No tax item reported in Part III with respect to this asset		
4	Maximum value of account during tax year . . . . $ 150,000		
5	Did you use a foreign currency exchange rate to convert the value of the account into U.S. dollars? . . ☐ Yes ☑ No		
6	If you answered "Yes" to line 5, complete all that apply.		

(a) Foreign currency in which account is maintained	(b) Foreign currency exchange rate used to convert to U.S. dollars	(c) Source of exchange rate used if not from U.S. Treasury Financial Management Service

For Paperwork Reduction Act Notice, see the separate instructions.   Cat. No. 37753A   Form **8938** (Rev. 12-2014)

Form 8938 (Rev. 12-2014) Page **2**

Part V Detailed Information for Each Foreign Deposit and Custodial Account Included in the Part I Summary (see instructions) (continued)

7a Name of financial institution in which account is maintained **b** Reserved

Last National Bank of Mexico

8 Mailing address of financial institution in which account is maintained. Number, street, and room or suite no.

1234 Poquito Way

9 City or town, state or province, and country (including postal code)

Monterey, Mexico

Part VI Detailed Information for Each "Other Foreign Asset" Included in the Part II Summary (see instructions)

Note. *If you reported specified foreign financial assets on Forms 3520, 3520-A, 5471, 8621, 8865, or 8891, you do not have to include the assets on Form 8938. You must complete Part IV. See instructions.*

If you have more than one asset to report, attach a continuation statement for each additional asset (see instructions).

1 Description of asset **2** Identifying number or other designation

3 Complete all that apply. See instructions for reporting of multiple acquisition or disposition dates.

a Date asset acquired during tax year, if applicable . . . .

b Date asset disposed of during tax year, if applicable . . . .

c ☐ Check if asset jointly owned with spouse **d** ☐ Check if no tax item reported in Part III with respect to this asset

4 Maximum value of asset during tax year (check box that applies)

a ☐ $0 - $50,000 **b** ☐ $50,001 - $100,000 **c** ☐ $100,001 - $150,000 **d** ☐ $150,001 - $200,000

e If more than $200,000, list value . . . . $

5 Did you use a foreign currency exchange rate to convert the value of the asset into U.S. dollars? . . . ☐ Yes ☐ No

6 If you answered "Yes" to line 5, complete all that apply.

(a) Foreign currency in which asset is denominated	**(b)** Foreign currency exchange rate used to convert to U.S. dollars	**(c)** Source of exchange rate used if not from U.S. Treasury Financial Management Service

7 If asset reported on line 1 is stock of a foreign entity or an interest in a foreign entity, enter the following information for the asset.

a Name of foreign entity _____ **b** Reserved

c Type of foreign entity **(1)** ☐ Partnership **(2)** ☐ Corporation **(3)** ☐ Trust **(4)** ☐ Estate

d Mailing address of foreign entity. Number, street, and room or suite no.

e City or town, state or province, and country (including postal code)

8 If asset reported on line 1 is not stock of a foreign entity or an interest in a foreign entity, enter the following information for the asset.

Note. *If this asset has more than one issuer or counterparty, attach a continuation statement with the same information for each additional issuer or counterparty (see instructions).*

a Name of issuer or counterparty _____

Check if information is for ☐ Issuer ☐ Counterparty

b Type of issuer or counterparty

(1) ☐ Individual **(2)** ☐ Partnership **(3)** ☐ Corporation **(4)** ☐ Trust **(5)** ☐ Estate

c Check if issuer or counterparty is a ☐ U.S. person ☐ Foreign person

d Mailing address of issuer or counterparty. Number, street, and room or suite no.

e City or town, state or province, and country (including postal code)

Form **8938** (Rev. 12-2014)

Form 8938 (Rev. 12-2014)   Page _____

(Continuation Statement)

Name(s) shown on return	Identifying number

Part V **Detailed Information for Each Foreign Deposit and Custodial Account Included in the Part I Summary**
(see instructions)

1 Type of account   ☐ Deposit   ☐ Custodial   **2** Account number or other designation

3 Check all that apply   **a** ☐ Account opened during tax year   **b** ☐ Account closed during tax year
c ☐ Account jointly owned with spouse   **d** ☐ No tax item reported in Part III with respect to this asset

4 Maximum value of account during tax year . . . . $

5 Did you use a foreign currency exchange rate to convert the value of the account into U.S. dollars? . . ☐ Yes   ☐ No

6 If you answered "Yes" to line 5, complete all that apply.

(a) Foreign currency in which account is maintained	**(b)** Foreign currency exchange rate used to convert to U.S. dollars	**(c)** Source of exchange rate used if not from U.S. Treasury Financial Management Service

7a Name of financial institution in which account is maintained   **b** Reserved

8 Mailing address of financial institution in which account is maintained. Number, street, and room or suite no.

9 City or town, state or province, and country (including postal code)

Part VI **Detailed Information for Each "Other Foreign Asset" Included in the Part II Summary** (see instructions)

1 Description of asset   **2** Identifying number or other designation

3 Complete all that apply. See instructions for reporting of multiple acquisition or disposition dates.
a Date asset acquired during tax year, if applicable . . . . _____
b Date asset disposed of during tax year, if applicable . . . . _____
c ☐ Check if asset jointly owned with spouse   **d** ☐ Check if no tax item reported in Part III with respect to this asset

4 Maximum value of asset during tax year (check box that applies)
a ☐ $0 - $50,000   **b** ☐ $50,001 - $100,000   **c** ☐ $100,001 - $150,000   **d** ☐ $150,001 - $200,000
e If more than $200,000, list value . . . . $

5 Did you use a foreign currency exchange rate to convert the value of the asset into U.S. dollars? . . . ☐ Yes   ☐ No

6 If you answered "Yes" to line 5, complete all that apply.

(a) Foreign currency in which asset is denominated	**(b)** Foreign currency exchange rate used to convert to U.S. dollars	**(c)** Source of exchange rate used if not from U.S. Treasury Financial Management Service

7 If asset reported on line 1 is stock of a foreign entity or an interest in a foreign entity, enter the following information for the asset.
a Name of foreign entity _____   **b** Reserved
c Type of foreign entity   **(1)** ☐ Partnership   **(2)** ☐ Corporation   **(3)** ☐ Trust   **(4)** ☐ Estate
d Mailing address of foreign entity. Number, street, and room or suite no.

e City or town, state or province, and country (including postal code)

8 If asset reported on line 1 is not stock of a foreign entity or an interest in a foreign entity, enter the following information for the asset.
a Name of issuer or counterparty
Check if information is for   ☐ Issuer   ☐ Counterparty

b Type of issuer or counterparty
(1) ☐ Individual   **(2)** ☐ Partnership   **(3)** ☐ Corporation   **(4)** ☐ Trust   **(5)** ☐ Estate

c Check if issuer or counterparty is a   ☐ U.S. person   ☐ Foreign person
d Mailing address of issuer or counterparty. Number, street, and room or suite no.

e City or town, state or province, and country (including postal code)

Form **8938** (Rev. 12-2014)

¶1610

Report of Foreign Bank and Financial Accounts   Version Number: 1.0

FinCEN Form 114 OMB No. 1506-0009   Effective October 1, 2013

The FBAR must be received by the Department of Treasury on or before June 30th of the year
immediately following the calendar year being reported. The June 30th filing date may not be extended.

IMPORTANT : After you have completed this FBAR, you must **Sign the Form** and **Save** in order to activate
the **Ready to File** button, which will direct you to a page where you can attach and submit your report. Click
Validate to identify missing or incorrectly formatted data at any time during preparation of this report. Click
Print to print a copy of this report for record keeping purposes.

Filing name (e.g. SMITH FBAR 2013)   **Bob**

Sign the Form	Save	Validate	Print	Ready To File

**If this report is being filed late,
select the reason for filing late**

¶1610

1 This report is for calendar year ended 12/31 [   ]   Amended ☐   Prior Report BSA Identifier [   ]

Part I   Filer Information

2 Type of filer | Individual |

3 U.S. Taxpayer Identification Number | 123-45-6789 |

3a TIN type | |

4 Foreign identification

　　　a Type | |

　　　b Number | |

　　　c Country/Region of issue | |

5 Individual's date of birth | August 5, 19XX |

6 Last name or organization's name | |

7 First name | Bob |

8 Middle name | |

8a Suffix | |

9 Address | |

10 City | Milwaukee |

11 State | Wisconsin |

12 ZIP/postal code | 53217 |

13 Country/Region | United States of America |

14a Does the filer have a financial interest in 25 or more financial accounts?

☐ Yes   Enter number of accounts [   ]   **If "Yes" is checked do not complete Part II or Part III, but retain**
☒ No   records of this information

14b Does the filer have signature authority over but no financial interest in 25 or more financial accounts?

☐ Yes   Enter number of accounts [   ]   **If "Yes" is checked Complete Part IV items 34 through 43 for each person on**
☒ No   whose behalf the filer has signature authority.

¶1610

Part II   **Information on Financial Account(s) Owned Separately 1   of   1**

15 Maximum account value	$150,000.00	15a Maximum account value unknown ☐
16 Type of account	Bank	
17 Financial institution name	Last National Bank of Mexico	
18 Account number or other designation	CW2 3AB	
19 Address	1234 Hacienda Lane	
20 City		21 State
22 Foreign postal code		23 Country/ Region Mexico

¶1610

Part III   Information on Financial Account(s) Owned Jointly   1   of   1

Account Information

15 Maximum account value	15a Maximum account value unknown ☐
16 Type of account	
17 Financial institution name	
18 Account number or other designation	
19 Address	
20 City	21 State
22 Foreign postal code	23 Country/Region
24 Number of joint owners	

Principal Joint Owner Information

25 Taxpayer Identification Number (TIN)	25 a TIN type
26 Last name or organization name	
27 First name	
28 Middle name	
28a Suffix	
29 Address	
30 City	31 State
32 ZIP/postal code	33 Country/Region

¶1610

Part IV   Information on Financial Account(s) Where Filer has Signature or Other Authority but No financial Interest in the Account(s)   1   of   1

Account Information

15 Maximum account value   [   ]   15a Maximum account value unknown   ☐

16 Type of account   [   ]

17 Financial institution name   [   ]

18 Account number or other designation   [   ]

19 Address   [   ]

20 City   [   ]   21 State   [   ]

22 Foreign postal code   [   ]   23 Country/ Region   [   ]

Owner Information

34 Last name or organization name   [   ]

35 Taxpayer Identification Number (TIN)   [   ]   35 a TIN type   [   ]

36 First name   [   ]

37 Middle name   [   ]

37a Suffix   [   ]

38 Address   [   ]

39 City   [   ]

40 State/territory/province   [   ]

41 ZIP/postal code   [   ]

42 Country/Region   [   ]

43 Filer's title with this owner   [   ]

¶1610

Part V   Information on Financial Account(s) Where Filer is Filing a Consolidated Report 1   of 1

Account Information

15 Maximum account value   [_____]   15a Maximum account value unknown   ☐

16 Type of account   [_____]   [▓▓▓▓▓▓▓▓▓▓▓▓▓▓]

17 Financial institution name   [_____]

18 Account number or other designation   [_____]

19 Address   [_____]

20 City   [_____]   21 State   [_____]

22 Foreign postal code   [_____]   23 Country/ Region   [_____]

Owner Information

34 Organization name   [_____]

35 Taxpayer Identification Number (TIN)   [_____]   35 a TIN type   [_____]

38 Address   [_____]

39 City   [_____]

40 State/territory/province   [_____]

41 ZIP/postal code   [_____]

42 Country/Region   [_____]

¶1610

Signature 44a Click here ☐ if this report is completed by a third party preparer, complete the third party preparer section.

44 Filer signature
> Please return to the Home tab to sign the report.

45 Filer title

46 Date of signature   (Date of signature will be auto-populated when the report is signed.)

Third Party Preparer Use Only

47 Preparer's last name

48 First name

49 Middle name/Initial

50 Check ☐ if self employed

51 Preparer's TIN   51a TIN type

52 Contact phone number   52a Extension

53 Firm's name

54 Firm's TIN   54a TIN type

55 Address

56 City

57 State

58 ZIP/postal code

59 Country/Region

¶1610

Index

GRACE IKEGAMI
ikegami.grace@gmail.com